KT-403-501

INTERNATIONAL
CIVIL PROCEDURES

INTERNATIONAL CIVIL PROCEDURES

Editor
CHRISTIAN T. CAMPBELL
LL.B., LL.M.
Member, New York State Bar

PUBLISHED UNDER THE AUSPICES
OF THE
CENTER FOR INTERNATIONAL LEGAL STUDIES
Salzburg, Austria

LONDON   NEW YORK   HAMBURG   HONG KONG
LLOYD'S OF LONDON PRESS LTD.
1995

Lloyd's of London Press Ltd.
Legal and Business Publishing Division
27 Swinton Street, London WC1X 9NW

USA AND CANADA
Lloyd's of London Press Inc.
Suite 308, 611 Broadway
New York, NY 10012 USA

GERMANY
Lloyd's of London Press GmbH
59 Ehrenbergstrasse
2000 Hamburg 50, Germany

SOUTH EAST ASIA
Lloyd's of London Press (Far East) Ltd.
Room 1101, Hollywood Centre
233 Hollywood Road
Hong Kong

©
Dennis Campbell and contributors
1995

First Published 1995
All rights reserved. No part of this publication may be reproduced,
stored in a retrieval system, or transmitted, in any form or by any
means, electronic, mechanical, photocopying, recording or otherwise,
without the prior written permission of Lloyd's of London Press Ltd.

British Library Cataloguing in Publication Data
A catalogue record for this book is available from the British Library

ISBN 1-85044-863-9

Text set in Sabon by
The Center for International Legal Studies
Salzburg, Austria
Printed in Great Britain by
The Headway Press
Reading, Berkshire

Preface

To indulge in a platitude, the continuing growth of international trade, finance, business travel and personal travel have increased the prospects for international disputes and litigation involving at least one party that is not resident in or a national of the forum State. That heightened litigiousness, a greater preference for adjudication over commercial settlement, an opening of domestic legal systems — supported by international State-to-State arrangements — to resolution of international dispute, for example, by facilitating jurisdiction, service of process, the securing of evidence or the enforcement of awards, and counsel's greater skill and inclination to pursue such recourse have contributed to the volume of international litigation can also be assumed.

The purpose of *International Civil Procedures* is not to enable the reader to conduct civil litigation in one of the foreign jurisdictions treated in its chapters. Practically, it would be impossible to achieve this in a work of this size. Rights of audience and legal representation are restrictively regulated in these jurisdictions making such an undertaking legally difficult. Rather, this book is intended to bridge the linguistic and conceptual gaps that may divide local counsel from her foreign client or referring agent, and to help them to explain and to monitor the course of civil proceedings before foreign courts.

The authors of the various chapters have made great efforts to present their civil procedure systems to the English language reader in a clear, uniform format. This task is not made easy by the divergent, underlying legal philosophies and the absence of adequate English language/law equivalents to foreign legal concepts. However, their achievements will become apparent in the following pages. The chapters summarise the law as it stood at the end of 1994. Given their summary, general nature, these should not be understood as legal advice or relied on in particular disputes. In such cases appropriate legal counsel should be sought.

At least a few — inadequate — words of acknowledgement should go to the authors for the expertise, effort and time they have invested, not to mention their patience with my own shortcomings, a characteristic also demonstrated by the administrative and production staff of the Center for International Legal Studies and by the people at Lloyd's of London Press. If this book is received as well as it was intended, then I am sure that they will all feel justly rewarded.

Christian Campbell

Center for International Legal Studies
Salzburg, Austria
March 1995

v

CONTENTS

CONTENTS

CHAPTER 2   CANADA

CONTENTS

CHAPTER 3   DENMARK

CONTENTS

CHAPTER 4   ENGLAND

CONTENTS

CONTENTS

CHAPTER 6   FRANCE

CONTENTS

CHAPTER 7   GERMANY

CONTENTS

CHAPTER 8   GREECE

CONTENTS

CHAPTER 9   INDIA

CONTENTS

CHAPTER 11   ITALY

CONTENTS

CHAPTER 12 MEXICO

CHAPTER 13   SPAIN

CHAPTER 14 SWEDEN

CONTENTS

CHAPTER 15 SWITZERLAND

CHAPTER 16   UNITED STATES

CONTENTS

CONTENTS

CHAPTER 17   INSTITUTIONS OF THE EUROPEAN UNION

CONTENTS

The Contributors

Mario Beltramo is the senior partner in the Rome firm Studio Legale Beltramo. He graduated as a Doctor of Jurisprudence from Rome University and has been a member of the Rome Bar since 1947.

Johan Boström is a partner with the Helsinki firm Bardy & Boström. A graduate of the University of Helsinki, he was admitted to the Finnish Bar in 1982 and has since continuously practised litigation in commercial matters in several Courts of Law in Finland.

René Bösch is an associate of the Zürich law firm Homburger Rechtsanwälte. He holds degrees from the University of Zürich (Dr.iur.) and the University of Chicago (LL.M.). He specialises in commercial, securities and banking law.

Frants Dalgaard-Knudsen is a senior associate with the Copenhagen law firm Koch-Nielsen & Grønborg. He graduated from the University of Århus in 1984 and he also holds the degree of Doctor of Laws of the European University Institute.

Philip Van Doorn is an associate at the Brussels Office of the Paris based firm Thieffry & Associés.

Peter Fogh is a partner with the Copenhagen based law firm Koch-Nielsen & Grønborg. He has been admitted to the Supreme Court of Denmark since 1990. Peter Fogh is a graduate from the University of Copenhagen and has obtained a master degree from the London School of Economics and Political Science.

Nikos Frangakis, born in Athens 1945, is Director of the Greek Centre for European Studies and Research (EKEME). Since 1971, he has been a member of the Athens Bar and partner of the law firm Souriadakis, Frangakis & Associates. Between 1986 and 1989, he was head of the Legal Service of the Permanent Representation of Greece to the EC in Brussels. He is Editor-in-Chief of the Nomiko Vima law journal, published by the Athens Bar, and member of the editorial board of the European Communities Review.

Franz Hoffet is a partner with the Zürich law firm Homburger Rechtsanwälte. He holds degrees from the University of Zürich (Dr.iur.) and the University of Chicago (LL.M.). He specialises in commercial litigation and arbitration and in antitrust law.

Lothar Hofmann is a partner with the firm Rustler, Frotz & Partner in Vienna, Austria. Holding law degrees from the Universities of Vienna and Chicago, he specialises in international business transactions and has been admitted to practise in Austria and New York.

Bill Holohan is a partner in the Irish firm of GJ Moloney & Company, working from its Dublin office. He is a graduate of University College, Cork and is also an associate of the Chartered Institute of Arbitrators of London. Mr. Holohan is also a registered trade mark agent and has been a Council Member of the Irish Maritime Law Association for some ten years. He is co-author of Bankruptcy Law and Practice in Ireland (1991).

Ueli Huber is a partner with the Zürich law firm Homburger Rechtsanwälte. He hold degrees from the University of Zürich (lic.iur.) and the University of California, Los Angeles (LL.M.). He specialises in corporate and bankruptcy law.

Nassia Kazantzi has studied in the University of Athens Law School (Ptychion in Law) and the London School of Economics of the University of London (LL.M. in European law). She is a practising lawyer before the Athens Bar and an associate of Souriadakis, Frangakis & Associates law firm.

Christine Lécuyer-Thieffry, a member of the Paris Bar, is a partner of the French international business law firm Thieffry & Associés whose Paris, Brussels, New York, Hong Kong, and Shanghai offices handle matters over a broad spectrum. She lived five years in the United States where she gained experience as a Foreign Legal Consultant in New York. Ms. Lécuyer-Thieffry is a member of the panel of arbitrators of the American Arbitration Association and has been highly involved with arbitration as both a lawyer and an arbitrator. She holds a *Diplôme d'Etudes Approfondies* from Paris University in International Law. She has co-authored a book on civil and commercial litigation between France and the United States and has written numerous articles on international commercial arbitration and business relations, both in French and in English.

Thomas Müller is a partner with the Zürich law firm Homburger Rechstanwälte. He holds degrees from the University of Zürich (Dr.iur.) and the University of California, Los Angeles (LL.M). He specialises in commercial litigation and arbitration and commercial law. Thomas Müller also serves as an alternate the Zürich District Court.

Bo G. H. Nilsson is a partner with the Stockholm firm Rydin & Carlsten Advokatbyrå AB and specializes in commercial litigation. He is a graduate as well as a lecturer of the University of Uppsala and has served as a Junior Judge in the District Court and Court of Appeal.

CONTRIBUTORS

Kimmo Rekola is an associate of the Bardy & Boström in Helsinki. He graduated from the University of Helsinki in 1983 and served as General Legal Counsel in Finnish Corporate Finance Ltd. 1983–1989 and in Oy Unisys Ab 1989–1994. He joined the Law Office Bardy & Boström in 1994.

Hemant Sahai, is an advocate, practising law in India with a focus on direct foreign investments, commerical and business laws including banking, finance, intellectual property, taxation, petroleum laws and arbitration and litigation. He studied law at the Faculty of Law, Delhi University, India and completed his legal education in 1988. Currently, he is a senior Associate with, J. Sagar Associates, a firm of lawyers based in Neh Delhi.

Hara Saounatsou has studied in the University of Athens Law School (Ptychion in Law) and the University College, University of London (LL.M. in Commercial law). She is a practicing lawyer before of the Athens Bar.

Ralf Stucken, a partner with the Hamburg firm Huth Dietrich Hahn, is graduate of the University of Hamburg and specialises in corporate and commercial law, litigation and real estate matters. He speaks German and English.

Patrick Thieffry is a partner with the Paris based firm Thieffry & Associés, with offices in New York, Brussels, Hong Kong and Shanghai where he is in charge of the firm's United States matters. A graduate from the University of Paris I, Paris II and a former visiting student at Emory University, he is admitted to practice in Paris, New York and Georgia.

Max Thum is a former partner, now a consultant, in the London based law firm of Ashurst Morris Crisp. He is former head of the litigation department and specializes in intellectual property, arbitration and general commercial litigation, defamation and trade libel, product liability, professional negligence, judicial review, and foreign disputes. He was appointed as a Deputy Taxing Master in May 1993. He is a Fellow of the Chartered Institute of Arbitrators, and a member of the International Association of Defense Counsel, American Bar Association, and International Bar Association, and an Honorary Member of the Association of Fellows and Legal Solicitors of the Center for International Legal Studies.

Juan Francisco Torres-Landa R. is a partner with the law firm of Barrera, Siqueiros y Torres-Landa in Mexico City. He has practised law in the areas of corporate, foreign investment, environmental, real estate, foreign trade, immigration and general contract law. Mr. Torres-Landa obtained his basic Mexican law degree from the National Autonomous University of Mexico in 1988, and received an LL.M. degree from Harvard Law School in 1990. He teaches corporate law at both the National Autonomous University of

Mexico and the Universidad Iberoamericana, Mr. Torres-Landa is currently the Vice-Chair of the Mexican Law Committee of the ABA.

Frank S. Towner, Jr. is a partner in the San Francisco regional office of Robins, Kaplan, Miller & Ciresi, where he specializes in domestic and international litigation, insurance law and commercial law. A graduate of Loyola Law School, he has served Chairman of the American Bar Association's International Tort and Insurance Law Committee. He speaks English and French.

Edward Veitch teaches in the Faculty of Law, University of New Brunswick and is a member of the law firm of Gilbert, McGloan, Gillis in Saint John, New Brunswick. He is currently the editor of the Canadian Bar Review.

Antonio Viñal received his Bachelor of Laws Degree from the Universidad Santiago de Compostela and his Master of Laws from Columbia University in New York. He holds the office of Minister Plenipotentiary and speaks Spanish, English, French and Italian. His practice specialises in international contracts, intellectual property litigation and arbitration.

Sara Watson is an assistant solicitor with the London firm Ashurst Morris Crisp and specialises in general commercial litigation. A graduate of the University of Leeds, she was admitted as a solicitor of the Supreme Court of England and Wales in 1991.

Jonas H. Westerberg, an associate of the Stockholm firm Rydin & Carlsten Advokatbyrå AB, holds degrees from the University of Uppsala and was also educated at the University of Minnesota Law School.

Markus Wirth is a partner with the Zürich law firm Homburger Rechstanwälte. He holds degrees from the University of Zürich (Dr.iur.) and the University of Toronto (LL.M). He specialises in commercial litigation and arbitration and serves as Chairman of the Arbitral Tribunal of the Zürich Chamber of Commerce.

Georg A. Wittuhn is a partner with the Hamburg firm Huth Dietrich Hahn. A graduate of the University of Hamburg and McGill University, he specialises in corporate and commercial law, banking law, trusts and estates. He speaks English, French, Spanish and German.

Humberto Zacarías F. an associate with the law firm of Barrera, Siqueiros y Torres-Landa in Mexico City, practises law in the areas civil and commercial litigation and general contract law. Mr. Zacarías received his basic Mexican law degree from the National Autonomous University of Mexico in 1991.

Contributors' Contact List

Austria
Lothar Hofmann
Rustler, Frotz & Partner
Mariahilfer Straße 196
1150 Vienna
Austria
Tel: (222) 891 29–0
Fax: (222) 894 26 96

Canada
Edward Veitch
Gilbert, McGloan, Gillis
P.O. Box 7174, Station "A"
Saint John, New Brunswick
Canada E2L 4S6
Tel: (506) 634 3600
Fax: (506) 634 3612

Denmark
Peter Fogh and Frants Dalgaard-Knudsen
Koch-Nielsen & Grønborg
Applebys Plads 1
Postboks 19
1001 Copenhagen K
Denmark
Tel: (45) 3296 0808
Fax: (45) 3296 0707

England
Max Thum and Sara Watson
Ashurst Morris Crisp
Broadwalk House
5 Appold Street
London EC2A 2HA
.England
Tel: (0171) 638 1111
Fax: (0171) 972 7990

Finland
Johan Boström and Kimmo Rekola
Bardy & Boström
Eteläesplanadi 22 A
00130 Helsinki
Finland
Tel: (358–0) 607 211
Fax: (358–0) 601 048

France
Christine Lécuyer-Thieffry
Thieffry & Associés
23, Avenue Hoche
75008 Paris
France
Tel: (1) 4562 4554
Fax: (1) 4225 8007

Germany
Georg A. Wittuhn and Ralf Stucken
Huth Dietrich Hahn
Postfach 30 24 29
20308 Hamburg
Germany
Tel: (0–40) 4152 50
Fax: (0–40) 4152 5111

Greece
Nikos Frangakis, Nassia Kazantzi
and Hara Saounatsou
Souriadakis, Frangakis & Associates
6, Kriezotou St.
106 71 Athens
Greece
Tel: (01) 36 26 888
Fax: (01) 36 31 631

India
Hemant Sahai
J. Sagar Associates
16, Aradhana, Ring Road
R.K. Puram-XIII
New Delhi-110066
India
Tel: (011) 688–5655/1170/8944
Fax: (011) 688–6070/1733

Institutions of the European Union
Patrick Thieffry and Philip Van Doorn
Thieffry & Associés
23, Avenue Hoche
75008 Paris
France
Tel: (1) 4562 4554
Fax: (1) 4225 8007

Ireland
Bill Holohan
GJ Moloney & Company
Courthouse Chambers
27–29 Washington Street
Cork, Ireland
Tel: (353–21) 27 52 61
Fax: (353–21) 27 15 86

Italy
Mario Beltramo
Studio Legale Beltramo
Via Lazio, 20/C
00187 Rome
Italy
Tel: (06) 481 7747
Fax: (06) 482 0281

Mexico
Juan Francisco Torres-Landa R.
and Humberto Zacarías F.
Barrera, Siqueiros y Torres-Landa, S.C.
Montes Urales #470, Piso 1
Col. Lomas Dechapultepec
Delegacion Miguel Hidalgo
11000 Mexico, D.F.
Tel: (525) 540 8000
Fax: (525) 520 5115

Spain
Antonio Viñal
Antonio Viñal & Co.
Moreto 15
28014 Madrid
Spain
Tel: (341) 420 2427
Fax: (341) 420 1233

Sweden
Bo G. H. Nilsson and Jonas H. Westerberg
Rydin & Carlsten Advokatbyrå AB
Norrmalmstorg 1
P.O. Box 1766
111 87 Stockholm
Sweden
Tel: (468) 679 5170
Fax: (468) 611 4850

Switzerland
René Bösch, Franz Hoffet, Ueli Huber,
Thomas Müller and Markus Wirth
Homburger Rechtsanwälte
Postfach 326
8035 Zürich
Switzerland
Tel: (01) 265 3535
Fax: (01) 265 3511

CONTRIBUTORS' CONTACT LIST

U.S.A.
Frank S. Towner, Jr.
Robins, Kaplan, Miller & Ciresi
Suite 2700
444 Market Street
San Francisco, California
U.S.A. 94111–5332
Tel: (415) 391 9799
Fax: (415) 391 1968

TABLE OF CASES

TABLE OF LEGISLATION, CODES AND CONVENTIONS

CANADA
Federal

Provincial/Territorial
British Columbia

New Brunswick

Newfoundland

Ontario

GERMANY

SWEDEN

SWITZERLAND

Federal

EUROPEAN AND INTERNATIONAL INSTITUTIONS/ CONVENTIONS

CHAPTER 1

AUSTRIA

LOTHAR HOFMANN
Rustler, Frotz & Partner
Vienna, Austria

INTRODUCTION

The Viennese Arbitral Center of the Federal Chamber of Commerce has gained major importance in international arbitration. Proceedings are conducted in compliance with its Rules of Arbitration and Conciliation (Vienna Rules), as opposed to the Federal law of civil procedure,[1] which is the topic of this chapter.

According to the Austrian Constitution, civil law and civil procedure are exclusively Federal law (published in the *Bundesgesetzblatt* — BGBl). As a consequence, the *Jurisdiktionsnorm* governs civil litigation all over Austria. The *Zivilprozeßordnung* — Federal law, as well — concentrates on litigation; "non-contentious" proceedings are regulated in the *Außerstreitgesetz*. All Austrian courts are Federal courts.

TYPES OF JURISDICTION

The *Jurisdiktionsnorm* does not list types of cases falling within the jurisdiction of Austrian courts. As a rule, Austrian courts have jurisdiction whenever a case is covered by a statutory venue provision. Moreover, Austrian jurisdiction is assumed whenever there is some kind of link between the case and Austria. In the absence of statutory venue, in cases where Austria is obligated to grant jurisdiction as a consequence of international treaties or when looking for relief outside Austria would be impossible or undue, the Supreme Court has to determine a specific place inside Austria to be venue.[2]

1. Useful German language reference works on civil procedure in Austria are: Fasching, *Lehrbuch des österreichischen Zivilprozeßrechts*, Vienna, 1990. Rechberger-Simotta, *Grundriß des österreichischen Zivilprozeßrechts (Erkenntnisverfahren)*, Vienna, 1994; Rechberger-Simotta, *Exekutionsverfahren*, Vienna, 1989.

2. *Jurisdiktionsnorm*, Section 28, Norm (1).

Jurisdiction over the parties of the action

Personal jurisdiction involves the ability of the court having subject matter jurisdiction (i.e., jurisdiction over the type of case) to exercise power over a particular defendant or item of property. Reference is made mainly to venue provisions in the *Jurisdiktionsnorm*.

Natural persons

Natural persons may be sued at their domicile or usual place of physical presence. A domicile is defined as a place where a person maintains a home, the intention to stay being evident.[3] Persons who do not have a domicile or usual place of presence — neither in Austria, nor anywhere else — can be sued wherever they are staying.[4]

Corporations

Austrian corporations may be sued at the place of their registered domicile,[5] foreign corporations at the location of their permanent representation inside Austria.[6]

Subject matter jurisdiction

There are numerous situations in which Austrian jurisdiction is based not on personal circumstances of the defendant but on the subject matter of the case.

A registered businessperson may sue his trade debtors at his place of business if order and conveyance of goods have been documented.[7] A party to a contract may sue with regard to that contract where it has been or should have been executed; in general documentary proof is required,[8] whereas among merchants acceptance of a receipt stating where payment has to be made and naming that place as forum is sufficient.[9] The place

3. *Jurisdiktionsnorm*, Section 66.
4. *Jurisdiktionsnorm*, Section 67.
5. *Jurisdiktionsnorm*, Section 75(1).
6. *Jurisdiktionsnorm*, Section 99(3).
7. *Jurisdiktionsnorm*, Section 87(a).
8. *Jurisdiktionsnorm*, Section 88(1).
9. *Jurisdiktionsnorm*, Section 88(2).

of payment of a bill of exchange is also a proper venue.[10] Other important categories are property claims and damage or violation of rights.

Property claims

Under Austrian law actions concerning real property are exclusively assigned to the court at the location of the property.[11]

Against both natural persons and legal entities who do not have another venue inside Austria, pecuniary claims may be filed at any court where property owned by them is found or where a debtor of them is located provided the defendants' property inside Austria is not disproportionately lower than the amount in dispute.[12]

Damage or violation of rights

Compensation claims as a result of death or injury or damage of goods may be filed where the underlying event took place.[13]

Article 3 of the Treaty of Lugano

Although Austria has become a member of the European Union, and party to the Brussels Convention.[14] It has now also signed the Treaty of Lugano.[15] Article 3(1) of the Lugano Treaty states that a defendant domiciled in a member country may be sued only according to the rules of the Treaty. National (extraordinary) venue provisions listed in Article 3(2) do not apply against such a defendant.

Venue

General principles

Venue provisions allocate litigation among the various branches of the judicial organisation. Some important provisions have been mentioned above for their additional function of establishing Austrian jurisdiction.

10. *Jurisdiktionsnorm*, Section 89.
11. *Jurisdiktionsnorm*, Sections 81 and 83.
12. *Jurisdiktionsnorm*, Section 99.
13. *Jurisdiktionsnorm*, Section 92(a).
14. January 1995.
15. Having stood aside during the negotiations.

Transfer of venue

If the competent court has been successfully challenged, the superior court names another court of the same subject matter jurisdiction.[16] Moreover, the Higher Regional Court may grant a transfer of venue for practical reasons.[17] If all parties unanimously move for transfer of venue prior to the in-case hearing, the court has to transfer the case.[18] The court may transfer the case to another court, even absent a motion by one of the parties if a similar claim out of the same casualty is pending there.[19]

Service of summons or writs

By post

Service inside Austria is processed in general by mail, under specific circumstances by court clerk or municipal clerk. These special servers may only proceed within one and the same court circuit or municipal district.[20]

If service cannot be perfected but there is reason to believe that the addressee is present on a regular basis, the writ has to be deposited at the post station or a municipal authority.[21] The server has to leave a written notice. The writ has to be kept for at least two weeks. Then, it goes back to the addresser.

Personal service

According to Austrian law, there is no personal service made by a party or its attorney.

Consular or diplomatic channels

With regard to service outside Austria reference is made to treaties, or the law of the country where service has to be executed, or international practice.[22] In the absence of a law enforcement treaty, service is perfected by post in foreign countries according to Austrian court order.[23] Service

16. *Jurisdiktionsnorm*, Section 30.
17. *Jurisdiktionsnorm*, Section 31.
18. *Jurisdiktionsnorm*, Section 31(a)(1).
19. *Jurisdiktionsnorm*, Section 31(a)(2).
20. *Zivilprozeßordnung*, Section 88(1).
21. Service of Legal Documents Law — *Zustellgesetz* (ZustG), Section 17(1).
22. Service of Legal Documents Law (ZustG), Section 11(1).
23. RHE. Ziv. 1986 JABl 53, Section 121(1) *Zivilprozeßordnung*.

to privileged foreigners and international organisations is proceeded through the Austrian Ministry of Foreign Affairs.[24]

Unless specific rules are stated in a convention, service of foreign documents inside Austria is realised according to the provisions of the *Zustellgesetz* (ZustG). A request for a different procedure can be granted if there is no *ordre public* objection.[25] Foreign documents lacking a duly authorised translation into German can only be served to a consenting addressee. Consent is presumed if the addressee does not oppose within three days after service.[26]

Publication

If the authorities do not know a place where service could be carried out, service in non-criminal proceedings can be executed by publication at the authority's notice-board. In that case service is deemed perfect after two weeks.[27] In civil procedure service by publication is permissible only if service does not cause the addressee's duty to respond. Service of summons by publication is not sufficient;[28] a representative has to be nominated.[29]

Methods provided by the Hague Convention

Austria is party to the Hague Convention (BGBl 1957/91), providing for service via consular (Austrian court — Austrian consul — foreign court) instead of diplomatic channels (Austrian court — Austrian Ministry of Foreign Affairs — foreign central authority — foreign court).

Bilateral treaties frequently prescribe direct contacts between Austrian and foreign courts.

ASCERTAINING THE APPLICABLE LAW

Regional law

The Austrian Constitution states that all civil law and civil procedure is national law. A regional law of civil procedure does not exist in Austria.

24. Service of Legal Documents Law (ZustG), Section 11(2).
25. Service of Legal Documents Law (ZustG), Section 12(1).
26. Service of Legal Documents Law (ZustG), Section 12(2).
27. Service of Legal Documents Law (ZustG), Section 25.
28. *Zivilprozeßordnung*, Section 106.
29. *Zivilprozeßordnung*, Section 116; Civil Code(ABGB), Section 276.

Substantive law is also national. Provincial and municipal ordinances may affect certain aspects of legal relationships locally, but their scope is limited.

National law

There is no Austrian statute determining the applicable law of civil procedure. The statute concerning substantive international private law (IPRG) is in conformity with international standards such as *lexi loci delicti (commissi)* and *lex contractus (solutionis)*. With regard to civil procedure Austrian courts apply the common principle of *lex fori*.

In many respects, Austria's participation in the European Union and in the Brussels and Lugano Conventions can be expected to increase the harmonisation of its civil procedure private international law rules with those of the other Member States, both through the interpretations of the European Union and European Economic Area courts and the legislative measures of the former's institutions.

COURT PROCEDURE — PLEADINGS

Complaint

The complaint must state the underlying facts, the evidence to be presented, and a prayer for relief (*petitio*).[30]

The *petitio* may state an order to pay and/or to perform, an injunction or a declaratory judgment.

The *petitio* may state a declaration concerning legal relations provided the plaintiff is able to show legally sufficient interest in such a judgment.[31] In case a *petitio* for performance would be justified the plaintiff may not move for a declaration.

A commission agent, for example, may combine an action for account with a *petitio* to pay, although the amount in dispute is not yet known.

Answer

At the formal first hearing[32] or — if the court expects the defendant to deny — immediately without a formal first hearing,[33] the court issues a

30. *Zivilprozeßordnung*, Section 226.
31. *Zivilprozeßordnung*, Section 228.
32. *Zivilprozeßordnung*, Section 230(1).
33. *Zivilprozeßordnung*, Section 243(4).

demand for answer to the complaint to be filed within a period determined by the court not exceeding four weeks.[34] The defendant has to state a request, facts and evidence.

The answer may contain a specific or general denial, affirmative defences, and counterclaims.

Substantive and fundamental procedural defences can be pleaded later on. However, the court may refuse protracting pleadings.

Before the in-case hearing, the plaintiff may file a reply to the answer.[35]

Amendments to pleadings

Prior to service of the complaint amendments to pleadings are allowed without restrictions provided the competency of the trial court is not exceeded. Later on, amendments altering the complaint are only allowed if either the adversary agrees or the court has jurisdiction also over the amended complaint and does not believe that there will be a relevant complication or delay.[36]

Supplemental pleadings

The adversaries are allowed to allege additional facts and present additional evidence as long as there is no alteration of the claim. The court may refuse to take pleadings into consideration if they obviously have not been brought in earlier in order to protract the litigation.[37]

Joinder of claims and parties

A plaintiff may join claims against a defendant if all claims fall within the jurisdiction of the same court and the same type of procedure is applicable.[38]

A joinder of plaintiffs or defendants may take place if parties form a unity of interests or claims refer to the same legal or factual context.[39] Provided the court has jurisdiction over all defendants, claims referring to a similar legal or factual context may be joined as well.[40] Joinder of parties is mandatory if one judgment necessarily has consequences for several persons.[41]

---

34. *Zivilprozeßordnung*, Section 243(1).
35. *Zivilprozeßordnung*, Section 258.
36. *Zivilprozeßordnung*, Section 235.
37. *Zivilprozeßordnung*, Section 179(1).
38. *Zivilprozeßordnung*, Section 227.
39. *Zivilprozeßordnung*, Section 11, No. 1.
40. *Zivilprozeßordnung*, Section 11, No. 2.
41. *Zivilprozeßordnung*, Section 14.

Separate proceedings before one court may be combined for trial if they are between the same adversaries or if different parties have the same opponent provided the proceedings will be accelerated or the expenses will be diminished.[42] On the other hand, the court may separate trial with regard to various claims stated in the same complaint.[43]

Counterclaim

If a defendant has a claim from the same transaction or occurrence as the plaintiff, or if it might offset the plaintiff's claim, or with regard to precedents of the plaintiff's claim, she may file her claim at the same court.[44]

Cross-claims

Co-parties may assert claims against each other that arise out of the same transaction or occurrence as the main action by filing cross-claims. There are no specific rules for cross-claims under the Austrian law of civil procedure.

Third-party claims

A third party claiming rights that are under dispute may file a claim against both adversaries at the very same court, as long as the first litigation is pending there.[45]

Impleader

A defendant holding a property or a property interest may claim that he is holding the property for another person. Immediately after service of the summons such a defendant has to demand from that other person a statement as to her relationship to the object of dispute. The named third party may take the defendant's position. If she does not respond the defendant is entitled to leave the property to the plaintiff.[46]

42. *Zivilprozeßordnung*, Section 187.
43. *Zivilprozeßordnung*, Section 188.
44. *Jurisdiktionsnorm*, Section 96(1).
45. *Zivilprozeßordnung*, Section 16; *Jurisdiktionsnorm*, Section 94(1).
46. *Zivilprozeßordnung*, Sections 22 *et seq.*

Interpleader and intervention

A litigator who for legal reasons has to notify the dispute to a third party may ask her for help.[47]

According to the Austrian law of civil procedure, intervention has to be granted as of right whenever the applicant has a legal interest that one of the parties in a dispute will win.

OBTAINING INFORMATION PRIOR TO TRIAL

Pre-trial discovery is not provided for under Austrian civil procedure. However, there are special proceedings for the preservation and perpetuation of evidence.[48] If there is reason to believe that otherwise a piece of evidence would be lost or could become difficult to use, judicial inspection, witness or expert testimony are admissible at any stage of the litigation and even prior to trial. The moving party has to name facts to be proved, means of evidence and a justification for preservation and perpetuation of the evidence.

INTERIM PROTECTION OF ASSETS PENDING TRIAL

A party may move for an interlocutory injunction to protect her claim. Such a motion is available if otherwise execution would hardly be feasible, with regard to non-pecuniary claims in addition to that if it is meant to protect against violence or irrecoverable damage.[49]

SUMMARY JUDGMENTS

Adjudication without trial or by special proceeding

Mahnverfahren

The *Mahnverfahren* is a special procedure with regard to claims for payment of not more than ATS 100,000. The court issues an order to pay without hearing or participation of the defendant.[50] The order is subject to objection by the defendant, which has to be filed within 14 days

47. *Zivilprozeßordnung*, Section 21.
48. *Zivilprozeßordnung*, Sections 384 *et seq.*
49. *Exekutionsordnung*, Sections 379 and 381.
50. *Zivilprozeßordnung*, Sections 448 *et seq.*

after service. The order form has to contain the inscription *Zahlungsbefehl* (which means order for payment) and the order to pay the amount in dispute (plus interest plus cost) or file an objection (called *Einspruch*) within fifteen days after service, otherwise the sum would be collected by way of execution; upon objection, ordinary proceedings will be opened.[51]

Even if the amount in dispute is more than ATS 30,000, the defendant does not need an attorney for the first step of objecting.[52]

Automated data processing has been introduced to speed up the proceedings.[53]

Mandatsverfahren

The *Mandatsverfahren*[54] may be used with regard to claims for money or fungible goods. The plaintiff may move for an order to pay or perform provided all essential facts are documented by papers of unobjectionable appearance. These papers must be either public documents drawn up in Austria, or private documents with a duly authenticated signature of the issuer, or other documents that have been the basis of an undisputed tabulation of rights in an Austrian register. No hearing or interrogation of the defendant is required.[55]

The court issues an order to fulfil or to file an objection (named *Einwendungen*).[56] There is no appeal against such an order except with regard to the cost decision.[57] An objection having been filed within due time, the court schedules a hearing.[58]

With regard to actions on bills, the plaintiff may move for an order to pay if she is able to produce the original bill and the original record of protest.[59]

Summary judgments

If the court determines that there is no genuine issue of material fact to be tried, it may enter a summary judgment.

51. *Zivilprozeßordnung*, Section 449.
52. *Zivilprozeßordnung*, Section 451(1).
53. *Zivilprozeßordnung*, Section 453.
54. *Zivilprozeßordnung*, Sections 548 *et seq.*
55. *Zivilprozeßordnung*, Section 550(1).
56. *Zivilprozeßordnung*, Section 550(2).
57. *Zivilprozeßordnung*, Section 552(1).
58. *Zivilprozeßordnung*, Section 552(3).
59. *Zivilprozeßordnung*, Section 557(1).

Default judgments

If a party misses the first formal hearing, the pleadings of the person appearing are deemed to be true unless they have been disproved by evidence presented to the court. The party present may move for default judgment.[60] Against this judgment the other party may file an objection called *Widerspruch* within 14 days of service of the judgment. If filed by the defendant, this objection has to contain an answer to the complaint.[61] The party seeking relief from default need not show excuse.

Moreover, the plaintiff may seek a default judgment if the defendant fails to file an answer to the complaint within due time.[62] Only if the then defaulting defendant has not been represented at the first formal hearing by an attorney, may she file a *Widerspruch*.[63]

Other termination without plenary trial

If the plaintiff abandons the claim defendant may move for dismissal.[64] Dismissal for failure to prosecute is dealt with as another form of default. The modalities are as discussed above. The court may try to settle the dispute at any stage of the trial.[65]

TRIAL

Setting the case for trial

It can take some time before a case is set for trial. Some cases need several hearings and sometimes are pending for several years before the court is ready to make a decision.

The scope of the trial is determined by the facts and evidence brought in by the parties. The court may refuse to take evidence considered to be irrelevant[66] or if it is convinced that such evidence has been offered for the sole purpose of protracting litigation.[67]

60. *Zivilprozeßordnung*, Section 396.
61. *Zivilprozeßordnung*, Section 397(a).
62. *Zivilprozeßordnung*, Section 398.
63. *Zivilprozeßordnung*, Section 398.
64. *Zivilprozeßordnung*, Section 394.
65. *Zivilprozeßordnung*, Section 204(2).
66. *Zivilprozeßordnung*, Section 275(1).
67. *Zivilprozeßordnung*, Section 275(2).

A special court order states the facts in dispute and what evidence will be taken.[68] During the course of the trial the court is not bound by its prior order.[69]

Submission of evidence

The parties have to submit evidence to prove the facts alleged. Evidence is submitted by the parties and taken by the judging court.[70] Apart from that the court is, to a certain extent, free to hear evidence even if not submitted by a party to the trial. The court serves witnesses with a writ to appear. The presiding judge may disallow improper questions to the witnesses asked by the parties or their attorneys.[71]

Evidence is introduced to prove alleged facts or to let them seem probable. If a fact is admitted by the adversary, no presentation of evidence is necessary.[72] The court takes such facts as given.

Kinds of evidence

Evidence may be submitted in various forms and subject to certain restriction and probative value.

Documents

Official documents give full proof of what the authority decrees or declares or attests; nevertheless rebuttal is admissible.[73] The same evidential weight is ascribed to documents that have been declared official,[74] and documents executed outside the area of application of the *Zivilprozeßordnung* as official documents if duly authenticated.[75]

Documents seeming to be official with regard to form and content are presumed genuine.[76] It is within the court's discretion to take pieces of evidence that look like foreign authorities' documents as genuine without further proof.[77]

68. *Zivilprozeßordnung*, Section 277(1).
69. *Zivilprozeßordnung*, Section 277(2).
70. *Zivilprozeßordnung*, Section 276(1).
71. *Zivilprozeßordnung*, Section 289(1).
72. *Zivilprozeßordnung*, Section 266(1).
73. *Zivilprozeßordnung*, Section 292.
74. *Zivilprozeßordnung*, Section 293(1).
75. *Zivilprozeßordnung*, Section 293(2).
76. *Zivilprozeßordnung*, Section 310.
77. *Zivilprozeßordnung*, Section 311(1).

A signed private document gives full evidence that the content originates from the issuer.[78] The undersigned is deemed to be the issuer if the adversary does not oppose.[79]

The adversary must not refuse to produce documents if:

(1) She herself has referred to the document in her presentation of the case;
(2) She has to produce the document according to substantive law; or
(3) The document with regard to its content is common to both parties, i.e., created in the interest of both parties, governing the mutual relations or consists of correspondence between the parties or between them and a common intermediary with regard to a business transaction.[80] The adversary may refuse to produce documents for important reasons, but not only in order to protract the other's presentation of the case.[81]

Privilege

The following persons must not testify:

(1) Individuals unable to perceive or to communicate their perceptions;
(2) Ministers with regard to the seal of confession and other professional secrets; and
(3) Public servants with regard to official secrets unless dispensed by a superior.[82]

In the following situations a witness may refuse to answer specific questions:

(1) Direct property disadvantage;
(2) Publicly approved duty to secrecy;
(3) Attorney-client privilege;
(4) Art or business secrets; and
(5) Secrecy of vote.[83]

78. *Zivilprozeßordnung*, Section 294.
79. *Zivilprozeßordnung*, Section 312.
80. *Zivilprozeßordnung*, Section 304.
81. *Zivilprozeßordnung*, Section 305.
82. *Zivilprozeßordnung*, Section 320.
83. *Zivilprozeßordnung*, Section 321.

Party testimony

The exclusions listed in Section 320 of the *Zivilprozeßordnung* concerning witnesses also apply for party testimony.[84]

JUDGMENT AND KINDS OF RELIEF

Final judgment

The final judgment has to be rendered by the trial court, by judges who have sat out the hearings.[85]

The written judgment has to contain the:

(1) Name of court;
(2) Names of the deciding judges;
(3) Names and addresses of the parties and their representatives (in personal status matters in addition to the parties' date and location of birth);
(4) Award or verdict; and
(5) Grounds of decision.[86]

Entry of judgment

The *Zivilprozeßordnung* prescribes that if possible the judgment has to be rendered and pronounced together with the reasons directly after the last hearing.[87] Practically, the vast majority of judgments is delivered in writing.[88]

The judgment is valid after notification to the parties; the court is already bound as soon as the judgment has been pronounced or handed over to the court clerk for notification.[89]

POST-TRIAL MOTIONS

Attacks on judgments

Where important reasons exist, a judgment may be contested by nullity action or motion for a new trial. A nullity action may be filed only against a judgment subject to no further appeal. Grounds for nullity action are:

84. *Zivilprozeßordnung*, Section 372.
85. *Zivilprozeßordnung*, Section 412.
86. *Zivilprozeßordnung*, Section 417.
87. *Zivilprozeßordnung*, Section 414.
88. *Zivilprozeßordnung*, Section 415.
89. *Zivilprozeßordnung*, Section 416.

(1) Judge rendering judgment was precluded from deciding the case; and
(2) Party was not heard but only if the party did not have a chance to raise these questions earlier, for example, by an appeal.[90]

Grounds for a motion for a new trial are:

(1) Forged documents;
(2) False testimony by a party under oath, by witness or expert witness;
(3) Certain specific crimes;
(4) Criminal conduct by the judge;
(5) Underlying criminal verdict unappealably rescinded;
(6) *Res judicata*; and
(7) New facts or evidence.

The last two reasons can be pleaded only if the moving party did not have an opportunity to raise that topic earlier.[91]

ENFORCEMENT AND EXECUTION OF JUDGMENTS

Remedies

According to the Austrian *Exekutionsordnung,* money can be collected by:

(1) Execution by seizure of real property;
(2) As a result of sequestration;
(3) Attachment of salary; and
(4) Levying of movable property.

Other means of execution are:

(1) *Räumung* — execution by writ of possession;
(2) *Wegnahme* — execution or enforcement by writ of delivery; and
(3) *Ersatzvornahme* — substitute performance.

Fines and arrest to make a debtor perform acts or conduct himself that cannot be substituted.

90. *Zivilprozeßordnung,* Section 529.
91. *Zivilprozeßordnung,* Section 530.

Enforcement of foreign judgments

As a prerequisite for recognition in Austria, a judgment has to be a proper title for execution according to the rules in the country where it was generated.[92]

Concerning the enforcement of arbitral awards, Austria is a party to the Geneva Convention of 1927[93] and the New York Convention of 1958;[94] bilateral treaties covering arbitral awards and/or court decisions are in force with:

(1) Belgium;[95]
(2) France;[96]
(3) Germany;[97]
(4) Great Britain, North Ireland and Hong Kong;[98]
(5) Israel;[99]
(6) Italy;[100]
(7) Liechtenstein;[101]
(8) Luxembourg;[102]
(9) The Netherlands;[103]
(10) Sweden;[104]
(11) Switzerland;[105]
(12) Spain;[106]
(13) Tunisia;[107] and
(14) The successor countries of the former Yugoslavia.[108]

In connection with its upcoming membership to the European Union, Austria will become a party to the Brussels Convention.

92. *Exekutionsordnung* (EO), Section 79.
93. BGBl 1930/343.
94. BGBl 1961/200.
95. BGBl 1961/287.
96. BGBl 1967/288.
97. BGBl 1960/105.
98. BGBl 1962/224, 1971/453 and 1978/90.
99. BGBl 1968/349.
100. BGBl 1974/521.
101. BGBl 1975/114.
102. BGBl 1975/610.
103. BGBl 1966/37.
104. BGBl 1983/556.
105. BGBl 1962/125.
106. BGBl 1985/373.
107. BGBl 1980/305.
108. BGBl 1961/115 for arbitral awards and settlements in commercial matters and BGBl 1962/310 concerning maintenance rights.

If no treaty is applicable, reciprocity must be guaranteed by government statement, published in the *Bundesgesetzblatt*. In order to achieve enforceability in Austria, decisions of or settlements in front of foreign authorities must be issued by a body having jurisdiction according to the Austrian rules of competency (i.e., the Austrian Formula of Jurisdiction). In case the party liable did not appear, he must have been served personally. The party filing for execution has to present a certificate of enforceability by the foreign authority having issued the title.

Regardless of compliance with the prerequisites stated above, execution must not be granted if the liable party has not been heard, a conduct unenforceable under Austrian law is requested, or the title does not comply with Austrian *ordre public*.

APPEAL

Issues subject to review

Generally, only final judgments and orders are reviewable. However, certain interlocutory orders are also subject to review. The appealing party may raise questions of law, questions of fact, and procedural issues (especially nullity, if fundamental procedural principles have been violated).

Scope of review of facts

Usually, the court's factual finding is appealable. This is not true with regard to certain special proceedings where the appellate procedure takes place without hearing, and all cases where the amount in dispute is less than ATS 15,000.

Review as of right

The unsuccessful party — with regard to a certain point of dispute — is entitled to appeal the judgment of the first instance within four weeks.[109] The adversary is entitled to file an answer to the appeal.[110]

In some special proceedings, where there is no judgment but a final order, the time limit for the appeal is fourteen days.

If the sum in dispute exceeds ATS 50,000 and in cases concerning some specific topics of family law and the law of tenancy, there is a right of

109. *Zivilprozeßordnung,* Section 464(1).
110. *Zivilprozeßordnung,* Section 468(2).

appeal with regard to the appellate court's judgment to the Highest Court. In this procedure, the appellant may raise only remarkably important questions of substantive law or civil procedure.[111] In general, the Highest Court decides the case without hearing.[112]

Under the Austrian rules of civil procedure a court is not bound by court decisions in prior cases between different parties. Austria does not have a system of *stare decisis*, and so one could argue that its Supreme Court decisions are not so important for the development of the legal system. Nevertheless, practically, the lower courts do follow the "guidelines" issued by higher courts. A reason might be that when a judgment has been vacated on appeal, the case frequently goes back to the lower instance, which is further bound by the appeal decision.

Discretionary review

In certain cases important questions of law can be raised in an appeal procedure by permission comparable to the United States *certiorari* procedure.

CONCLUSIVENESS OF JUDGMENT

Res judicata

The parties to a lawsuit are barred from trying the same cause of action once again. *Res judicata* applies only to the parties of the dispute and their legal successors. On the other hand — at least theoretically — there are no precedents for similar cases arising later on.

Law of the case

A court is bound by its own decision once issued.[113] The appellate court's determination on a legal issue is binding for both the trial court on remand and the appellate court on a subsequent appeal.

---

111. *Zivilprozeßordnung*, Section 502.
112. *Zivilprozeßordnung*, Section 509(1).
113. *Zivilprozeßordnung*, Section 416(2).

CHAPTER 2

CANADA

EDWARD VEITCH
Gilbert, McGloan, Gillis
Saint John, New Brunswick, Canada

CANADIAN JUDICIAL STRUCTURE

A federal state like Canada is made up of a number of units each possessing its own legal judicial system. There are some 13 jurisdictions which comprise — Federal Canada, ten provinces and two territories. "Thus, each province or territory is a legal unit except as to matters governed by federal law, and Canada is a legal unit except as to matters governed by provincial or territorial law."[1] In such a constitutional arrangement there are of necessity limitations on the specific jurisdictions of each court within the judicial hierarchical system. That system must be understood not only in terms of hierarchy, both among federal systems and provincial systems, but also in terms of the division of responsibility between federal and provincial courts. Within this federal structure two of the world's great legal systems exist: the Civil Law in the province of Quebec and the Common Law in the other provinces and territories.

Within the federal system we can identify the courts as federal courts, superior provincial courts and inferior provincial courts:

Federal courts

The Federal Courts are constituted under federal laws and whose judges are federally appointed. Thus, at the apex there is the Supreme Court of Canada made up of the Chief Justice and eight Justices, and thereunder the Federal Court of Canada, appellate and trial divisions, and the Tax Court of Canada.

Superior provincial courts

The superior provincial courts are constituted under provisional laws but the judges are federally appointed, and similarly with the Territories. The

---

1. Castel, *Canadian Conflict of Laws*, 2nd ed. (Butterworths 1986) p. 4.

structure here, identified as that of the superior courts, takes the form of an appellate court and a trial division although there are individual provincial variations such as divisional, county, district or surrogate courts falling within this heading. In addition, many provinces have adopted a unified family court system in which all matters relating to the family, including divorce, are heard by federally appointed judges.

Inferior provincial courts

The inferior provincial courts are made up of those courts set up under provincial statutes but whose judicial officers are provincially appointed. These comprise, within the civil jurisdiction, the Family Courts, where the unified system has not been adopted, and the Small Claims Courts.

It would be tedious to describe the jurisdiction of each and every provincial court in Canada. However, since the courts do share similar functions in the various provinces and territory, the jurisdiction of the courts may be described in general terms. The federally constituted courts exercise the same functions uniformly throughout all of the provinces. There are several texts of recent vintage covering in detail the practice and procedure before most of the various courts.[2]

LEGISLATED CIVIL JURISDICTION

Supreme Court of Canada

The law governing the Supreme Court of Canada is An Act Respecting the Supreme Court of Canada RSC 1985, c. S–26.[3] Appeals to the Court are possible only with leave on any matter of public importance or on an important issue of law or of mixed law and fact. The Court

2. Crane & Brown, *Supreme Court of Canada Practice* (Carswell 1991–2); Sgayias et al., *Federal Court Practice* (Carswell 1993); McMechan & Bourgard, *Tax Court Practice* (Carswell 1993); Watson & McGowan, *Ontario Civil Practice* (Carswell 1993); *Nova Scotia Annotated Rules of Practice* (Ehrlich ed., Carswell 1984); Reid, *Code de Procedure Civile du Quebec* (5th ed., Wilson & Lafleur 1989); Brierly, *Quebec Civil Law* (Emond Montgomery, 1993); *Manitoba Queen's Bench Rules Annotated* (ed. Busby. Carswell 1993); *Western Practice Digest* (Carswell 1992); *British Columbia Practice* (McLachlin & Taylor eds., 1990); Meagher & Meagher, *Parties to An Action* (Butterworths 1988); Muldoon, *The Law of Intervention* (Canada Law Book 1989); Ross-Hendriks, *Court Motions Handbook* (Carswell 1991); Mew, *The Law of Limitations* (Butterworths 1991); Zuker, *Ontario Small Claims Court Practice* (Carswell 1993); and *Annotations to the New Brunswick Rules of Court* (Chiasson ed., Carswell 1989).

3. Am. RSC 1985, c. 34 (3rd Supp.); SC 1990, c. 8.

can also give opinions, through the reference mechanism, on matters such as the interpretation of the Constitution, the powers of the Parliament of Canada or the Legislatures of the Provinces and Territories or any referred matter involving federal, provincial or territorial legislation.

Federal Court of Canada

The principle laws affecting the Federal Court of Canada include An Act Respecting the Federal Court of Canada RSC 1985, c. F–7.[4]

The Appellate Division hears appeals from the Trial Division of the Federal Court; it reviews decisions of federal boards, commissions and other tribunals, and adjudicates appeals under specific federal legislation such as the Income Tax Act and the Canadian Citizenship Act.

Prior to 1992, the Trial Division enjoyed exclusive jurisdiction in certain areas, such as suits against the federal Crown, however, as a consequence of changes to its jurisdiction, the rule today is one of concurrence with those provincial courts that are staffed by federally appointed judicial officers. This leaves the exclusivity of the Trial Division's jurisdiction only where a federal statute expressly so determines.[5] As a consequence of these very recent changes, a plaintiff can commence an action against the federal Crown in the court of their choice. The jurisdictional alterations were designed to obviate multiplicity of proceedings where the Crown was a co-defendant with others but the efficacy of this has already been doubted by some.[6] This court retains a residual jurisdiction where no other Canadian court has jurisdiction and is likely to enjoy principal jurisdiction in such areas of law as aeronautics, intellectual property, admiralty and citizenship appeals.

Tax Court of Canada

The controlling legislation comprises the Tax Court of Canada Act RSC 1985, c. T–2; An Act to Amend the Tax Court of Canada and other Acts in Consequence thereof RSC 1985, c. 51 (4th Supp.). This court's jurisdiction extends to appeals from assessments made under the Income Tax Act and under the Canada Pension Plan Act.

4. Am. RSC 1985, c. 41 (1st Supp.); RSC 1985, c. 30 (2nd Supp.); RSC 1985, c. 16 (3rd Supp.); RSC 1985, c. 51 (4th Supp.); SC 1990, c. 8.
5. For example, Expropriation Act, RSC 1985, c. E–21.
6. See Sgayias et al., Federal Court Practice p. 21.

Superior provincial courts

The most recent reform of the legislation which determines the jurisdiction of this level of courts has been enacted in the Province of
Ontario.[7]

The appellate divisions hear appeals from the trial divisions and
decisions of such variants as the District, County or Surrogate courts. The
trial divisions — sometimes called courts of Queen's Bench, Trial Divisions or Supreme Court — enjoy a broad scope. Their original, first
instance jurisdiction encompasses all matters involving "property and
civil rights" along with such issues as domestic relations and including
judicial review of the administrative acts of provincial boards and
tribunals. Where county courts or district courts remain, their jurisdiction gathers all civil matters within a given monetary range while
the surrogate courts have jurisdiction over matters of wills and probate.[8]

Inferior provincial courts

The Family Courts have been retained by the minority of provinces and
territories that have not adopted the unified family court system. These
courts have jurisdiction over maintenance and custody under provincial
statutes along with matters of adoption and guardianship. The Small
Claims Courts set up by some provinces enjoy jurisdiction determined by
monetary limits such as Can. $4,000 in the Province of Alberta or Can.
$1,000 in the Province of Quebec. More recently, the trend has been to
increase the jurisdiction of the Small Claims Court and to have cases
heard by superior court judges as in the Provinces of New Brunswick and
Ontario.[9]

Province of Quebec

The court structure of Quebec, as with its substantive and procedural
laws, is individual and different from that of the other provinces and
territories.

7. See Courts of Justice Act, RSO 1990, c. C43 (am. SO 1991, c. 46).

8. These statements are applicable to all provinces and territories other than that
of Quebec, which is dealt with individually below.

9. See, for example, An Act to Revise and Consolidate the Law Respecting the
Organization, Operation and Proceedings of Courts of Justice in Ontario, RSO 1990,
c. C43 (am. SO 1990, c. 46).

Court of Appeal

The Court of Appeal is a provincial court established under provincial law but whose judges are federally appointed. It hears both civil and criminal appeals.

Superior Court

The Superior Court is also a court established by the laws of Quebec and whose judges are federally appointed. It enjoys both civil and criminal jurisdiction.

Court of Quebec

The Court of Quebec is roughly the equivalent of the provincial courts of the other provinces but is in fact a court which encompasses the jurisdictions of the former Provincial Court, Court of Sessions of the Peace, Small Claims Court and Youth Court. The judges are provincially appointed. The court is divided into regions within which there are three units: a civil division, a criminal and penal division and a youth division. The civil division can hear disputes of less than Can. $15,000 while the small claims sub-division of this division deals with claims of Can. $1,000 or less.

Municipal Courts

The Municipal Courts are provincial courts set up under the law of Quebec and staffed by provincially appointed judges. Their jurisdiction is restricted to offences under provincial laws and municipal by-laws.

ESTABLISHING JURISDICTION

Types of jurisdiction

Jurisdiction over the parties of the action

In general, Canada conforms to the usual practices of federal states by determining jurisdiction over natural persons by use of such ideas of domicile or residence. Jurisdiction over corporations is asserted on the basis of incorporation or the carrying on business within the jurisdiction. However, difficult questions have arisen when a group of natural persons who are plaintiffs reside in various jurisdictions, and the several corporate defendants to the action are incorporated and do business in a variety of jurisdictions. Here, the problem is how to determine what courts of a particular country or state should, or should not, go into action and what weight, if any, is to be given to the claims or judgments of other courts or states.

The Supreme Court of Canada in *Amchem Products Inc. et al.* v. *Workers' Compensation Board* (BC)[10] has attacked this question directly. In that case, 194 persons who had worked in industries in British Columbia using asbestos products sued several asbestos manufacturers in the State of Texas in the United States of America on the premise that their present injuries were caused by exposure to the products whose dangers were known to the manufacturers. When the action was commenced, a number of the plaintiffs were resident in other Canadian provinces and in the State of Washington in the United States. The manufacturing companies were incorporated in various states of the United States and carried on business in the State of Texas but were not incorporated there. None had any connection with the province of British Columbia.

The Texas court affirmed its jurisdiction over the matter. However, the company-defendants applied to the court in British Columbia for an injunction to prevent continuation of the plaintiffs' claims in Texas. The British Columbia Supreme Court granted the companies' application for the anti-suit injunction which decision was upheld by the Court of Appeal. The Supreme Court of Canada allowed the further appeal and set down the policy that where a foreign court has assumed jurisdiction on bases which conform to Canadian jurisprudence then the overriding principle is that of comity. The burden lies on the applicant to show that the assumption of jurisdiction by the foreign court would be inequitable, for example, by depriving the applicant of some legitimate judicial advantage.

The Court noted that this decision was of special importance in a global economy and in light of a trend by courts to expand their jurisdictions over events and persons outside of their territory. The Court noted in addition that an "anti-anti-suit" injunction had been issued in Texas aimed at preventing further applications to the courts of British Columbia in the matter.

The Supreme Court of Canada recognised the fact that where multiple defendants carrying on business in many jurisdictions are sued by plaintiffs resident in a variety of jurisdictions, it is difficult to pinpoint the location of the occurrence giving rise to the litigation. In such situations, the Court urged that a parochial approach should be eschewed and that proper respect should be paid to the foreign court having the closest connection with the matter all the while ensuring that "forum shopping" for some illicit advantage is to be discouraged.

10. (1993) 150 NR 321 (SCC). See Walsh, Comment (1994) 13 CBR 394.

The Court reviewed the means by which the determination of jurisdiction can be made: Firstly, by the stay of the proceeding which enables the court utilised by the plaintiff to determine at the defendant's behest that another court should be recognised to have jurisdiction; secondly, the "anti-suit" injunction through which the plaintiff moves to restrain the defendant from proceeding in the courts of another jurisdiction. This latter device was recognised as being an *in personam* order and not directed to the foreign court itself. Nevertheless the impact on that other court raised serious issues of comity. Both the stay and the injunction have as their goal the selection of the correct jurisdiction for the particular matter. Yet the stay is a decision of a court as to its own jurisdiction while the injunction is an intrusive direction as to the jurisdiction, or lack thereof, of another court. The policy of the Court on comity had been expressed earlier in *Morguard Investments Ltd. et al.* v. *De Savoye*[11] by Justice La Forest as follows:

"'Comity' in the legal sense is neither a matter of absolute obligation on the one hand, nor of mere courtesy and good will on the other. However, it is the recognition which one nation allows within its territory to the legislative, executive or judicial acts of another nation, having due regard both to international duty and convenience, and to the rights of its own citizens or of other persons who are under the protection to its laws . . .".

In *Amchem*, the Court then observed that, in a world of perfect comity, where a case did not clearly adhere to a particular jurisdiction then should the parties not settle on one there could be parallel proceedings in two jurisdictions with the first judgment given resolving the matter. The Court then reviewed the relevant law of England as expressed in *Société Nationale Industrielle Aerospatiale* v. *Lee Kui Jak*[12] that of the United States as in *Laker Airways* v. *Sabena, Belgian World Airlines*[13] and that of Australia in *National Mutual Holdings Pty. Ltd.* v. *Sentry Corp.*[14]

The Court advised as a matter of policy that "anti-suit" injunctions must be used with the greatest caution and with the sole purpose of preventing abuse of courts' systems by vexatious actions. After reviewing a number of relevant decisions of Canadian provincial superior courts, the Court enunciated a test comprising the principles laid out by the Privy Council in *Société Nationale Industrielle Aerospatiale* allied to the Court's own policies outlined in *Morguard Investment Inc.*

Thus, the court hearing such an application must determine, using the closest connection test with respect to the action and the parties, whether or not it is the court having jurisdiction. If it arrives at a determination

11. (1990) 3 SCR 1077, 1096.
12. [1987] AC 871 (PC).
13. (1984) 731 F2d 909 (DCFCA).
14. (1989) 87 ALR 539 (FC).

that another court should retain jurisdiction then the application should be dismissed. On the other hand if the court hearing the application concludes that the other court assumed jurisdiction on principles alien to the hearing court then the question is — would the granting of the application deprive the plaintiff of advantages in that other court of which it would be unjust to deprive them? The response to that question must take account of any disadvantage to be suffered by the defendant. Ultimately, if a foreign court assumes jurisdiction on a basis which conforms to Canadian jurisprudence that decision will be respected by Canadian courts and will not be second-guessed by the court hearing the application; or at its simplest, courts recognising comity, will be accorded comity.

Jurisdiction over the subject matter of the action

Canada conforms to the generally accepted rules with respect to jurisdiction over real property, the law of the situation of the land, and over moveable property, the law of their location subject to the realities of portability. In issues involving damage or violation of rights the plaintiff, however, the court hearing the claim will resort to the criteria of real and substantial connection along with the balance of convenience in order to determine the amenability of jurisdiction.[15]

More difficult questions arise where obligations are undertaken in one jurisdiction and when disputes arise one or more of the parties have moved to another jurisdiction. In such circumstances, the decision as to where to bring the action is inextricably tied up with the question of enforceability of foreign judgments. For example, if a citizen and resident of the province of Saskatchewan, Canada sues in Saskatchewan persons who are residents and citizens of Nebraska in the United States and who then wish to transfer the Saskatchewan judgment to the province of New Brunswick, Canada, where the Nebraskans have property, how should the New Brunswick court determine the issue of enforceability of that judgment?

The Supreme Court of Canada has recently addressed the question of recognition of judgments by Canadian courts and sought to lay out clear policies for application in a federal state such as Canada in *Morguard Investments Ltd. v. De Savoye*.[16] In a confederation, it is necessary to have rules in place to determine in which of the provinces' superior or the federal courts a civil suit may be brought. It has been left to the provinces to determine for themselves the scope of litigation they will receive.

15. See *Monahan v. Trahan* (1993) 13 CPC (3d) 52 (NS TD).
16. (1990) 3 SCR 1077.

In *Morguard*, the appellant had obligated himself to the respondents through land owned in the province of Alberta. He moved to the province of British Columbia, on default of the mortgages, while the respondents proceeded before the courts of Alberta. The appellant was duly served in British Columbia but neither appeared nor contested the proceeding so that a default judgment was rendered. The respondents then sued in British Columbia to enforce the Alberta judgment. The trial and appellate courts of British Columbia resisted the appellant's attempts to defend the action. The Supreme Court of Canada then determined to resolve a question crucial to a federation — in what circumstances should the judgment in a personal action in one province be recognised by a sister-province?

The Court took the position that the 19th century rules expressed in the English case of *Emanuel* v. *Symon*,[17] which had been long followed in Canada now had little relevance to the modern world. The notion that jurisdiction was territorial, meaning that a state's law had no binding effect outside of its jurisdiction, must give way to the fact of the interchange between modern states. It was argued that jurisdictional reciprocity and comity should be called in aid of the free flow of wealth, skills and persons across state boundaries. Equally, it was deemed inappropriate to permit persons to evade legal responsibilities merely by moving jurisdictions. On the other hand, it was recognised that a duty of fairness to defendants was owed so that courts should not assume jurisdiction unless there was a real and substantial connection between the damage suffered and the jurisdiction. The concepts therefore in play in any analysis comprise reciprocity, comity, full faith and credit and real and substantial connection.

Thus, in *Morguard* the plaintiff's British Columbia action to enforce the Alberta judgment was upheld on the basis that British Columbia courts should enforce judgments from other Canadian courts exercising a jurisdiction which British Columbia courts would exercise.

With respect to subject matter jurisdiction the Supreme Court of Canada in *Ste. Anne Nackawic Pulp & Paper Co.* v. *CPU Local 219*[18] considered whether courts had jurisdiction over matters between employees and employers whether the consequences of strike activity or even of negligent acts where the matters are governed by a collective agreement in force between the parties. In *Ste. Anne*, the Supreme Court of Canada determined that a court has no jurisdiction to consider a claim by an employer for damages flowing from a strike that was both illegal and a breach of the applicable collective agreement. Justice Estey stated:[19]

---

17. (1908) 1 KB 302 (CA).

18. (1986) 1 SCR 704; *Galea* v. *GM (Canada) Ltd.* (1994) 5 WDCP (2d) 20 (Ont. Gen. Div.).

19. (1986) 1 SCR 704, 720.

"The courts have no jurisdiction to consider claims arising out of rights created by a collective agreement. Nor can the courts properly decide questions which might have arisen under the common law of master and servant in the absence of a collective bargaining regime if the collective agreement by which the parties to the action are bound makes provision for the matters in issue, whether or not it explicitly provides a procedure and forum for enforcement."

It seems that an employer may sue an employee for damage caused by negligence in cases where the collective agreement is silent on the matter and the claim does not arise under the collective agreement or involve its interpretation, application or administration.[20]

Venue

General principles

Generally, the plaintiff has the right to determine the place of trial in the statement of claim. In choosing the location, the plaintiff must act on rational bases which are usually laid out in the procedural rules so to avoid capricious choices of locations having no connection with the matter.[21] In addition, there are provincial legislative provisions which direct where an action shall be tried.[22]

Transfer of venue

An application may be made to change the place of trial. There, the applicant is required to show that it would be more convenient or in the best interests of justice if the action is heard at the location proposed. The procedural rules provide sample criteria to be taken into account by the presiding judge and which include:

(1) Will a transfer expedite or delay the trial;
(2) Will a transfer reduce the costs to all parties;

20. See *Irving Oil Ltd.* v. *Energy Workers Union Local 691* (1983), 45 NBR (2d) 115 (QB).

21. See, as examples, RFB v. TLB (1990), Alta R 67 (Fam. Div.); *Wahler* v. *Assn. of Professional Engineers* (Sask.) (1992), 95 Sask. R 281 (QB).

22. See, for example, Defamation Act Ch. D–5, RSNB 1973, Section 15, which mandates the locale of the head office of the media defendant or the county of residence of the plaintiff in a libel suit; also *McCain* v. *Agric. Pub. Co. Ltd.* (1978), 22 NBR (2d) 30 (QB) and *McCain* v. *Agric. Pub. Co. Ltd.* (1980), 103 DLR (3d) 724 (Ont. HC).

(3) Will a transfer facilitate the convenience of the witnesses, including experts;

(4) Will a transfer provide access of the judge to visit the subject matter of the dispute; and

(5) Will it be possible to empanel a fair jury in the place selected by the plaintiff?[23]

Service of summons or writs

By post and personal service

The procedural rules for the service of originating documents within the jurisdiction of the provincial courts have moved very far from the day when "personal service" meant exactly personal service on the individual. Thus, for example, service by certified mail is treated as equal to personal service or service of a document at the party's residence followed up with a copy sent by mail will meet the requirements of service. What has been developed are rules of service varying with the legal capacity of the party to be served. Service is effected on:

(1) Natural persons by leaving a copy with the individual;

(2) Municipal corporations by leaving a copy with an officer such as the mayor or solicitor;

(3) Corporations by leaving a copy with an officer, director, agent or person in control of any office of the corporation;

(4) Unincorporated associations by leaving a copy with an officer or with a person in control of an office of the association;

(5) A board or commission by serving the secretary, an officer or member of the board or commission;

(6) Companies doing business in the jurisdiction by service on a representative of the party who is *ex juris*;

(7) Incompetent persons by personal service on the committee charged with managing the affairs of the affected party;

(8) Minors by service made effectively on a parent or guardian in control of the party;[24]

(9) Partnerships by service on any partner or on a person in control of an office; and

(10) Sole proprietorships by service on the proprietor or any person seemingly in control of an office.

23. See *Doucett v. Crowther* (1992), 123 NBR (2d) 5 (QB).

24. However, minors over 16 years of age must also be served themselves.

Service on the Crown in Right of New Brunswick (or other provinces), the Crown in Right of Canada, insane persons and estates is governed by the express provisions of relevant legislation.[25]

The rules of procedure have set up equivalencies to personal service such as certified mail or deposit of a copy at a location followed up by a postal delivery. In addition to these modes of service, there are also the possibilities of service on the solicitor of the party.[26] In the case of corporations whose head office is unknown or are extra-provincial operations, it is possible to serve the last address filed with the appropriate government regulatory authority.

Material other than the originating documents may be served personally or by mail. However, following receipt of the originating documents, the party will usually be represented by counsel so that service is effected for such as pleadings or affidavits by service on the solicitor for the party.

Publication

It may not be possible in certain situations to effect personal service of the originating documents either because the party is evading service or cannot be otherwise found. In such cases, it is appropriate to apply to the court for an order authorising substituted service in the form of advertising in the major newspapers of the various jurisdictions. To persuade a court to grant such an order, it is necessary to explain why service cannot be effected and the likelihood of substituted service being brought to the knowledge of the defendant in addition to pleading the problems of time, trouble and expense. Service is effected as of the date of publication of the advertisement.

Service outside of the jurisdiction

Leave of the court by *ex parte* application, supported by affidavit showing where the party may be found and the grounds in support of the application, is required in some provinces to serve an originating summons outside of the jurisdiction. Such is typical when the subject matter of the action is land situated within the jurisdiction or with respect to a tort committed within the jurisdiction. The procedural rules also make provision to ensure that a party is not subjected to the forum without just cause. Accordingly, the party so served is permitted to apply to the court

25. For example, Proceedings Against the Crown Act; Crown Liability Act; Mental Health Act; Presumption of Death Acts of the various jurisdictions.

26. See 841656 *NWT Ltd.* v. *Jodphur Holdings Ltd.* (1992), 7 CPC (3d) 165 (NWT CA).

to set aside, stay or dismiss the proceeding on the ground that service
was not authorised by the local rules or on the argument that the court
was without jurisdiction or that the local court was not the *convenient
forum*. Due to the diversity of the provincial rules these are best illus-
trated in diagrammatic form.

SERVICE EX JURIS IN CANADA

SERVICE		*APPLICATION TO SET ASIDE*
Newfoundland	**Rule 6.07** With leave enumerated heads.	**Rule 10.05** Before filing defence or appearing. *Grounds*: Not duly served application not deemed to be submission to the jurisdiction.
Nova Scotia	**Rule 10** Without leave *re* Canada or the USA; with leave elsewhere.	**Rule 11** Before filing defence or appearing. No grounds expressed. Application not deemed to be submission to the jurisdiction.
Prince Edward Island	**Rule 10** Without leave *re* Canada or the USA; with leave elsewhere.	**Rule 11** Before filing defence or appearing. No grounds expressed. Application not deemed to be submission to the jurisdiction.
New Brunswick	**Rule 19** Without leave. Enumerated heads (18) with leave where one or more party resides in N.B and necessary to secure just deteration.	**Rule 19** Within time for filing response. *Grounds*: Not authorized by Rules. No jurisdiction *forum conveniens*. Application not deemed to be submission to the jurisdiction.
Quebec	CPC 137 with leave in Canada.	
Ontario	**Rule 17** Without leave, Enumerated heads otherwise with leave.	**Rule 17** Before delivering defence. *Grounds*: Not authorized by Rules. Order granting leave should be set aside. *Forum conveniens*.

SERVICE		APPLICATION TO SET ASIDE
Manitoba	**Rules 28–30** Without leave enumerated heads. Otherwise with leave where on contract, judgment or alimony and defendant has assets worth in Manitoba.	
Saskatchewan	**Rule 31** Without leave enumerated heads. Otherwise with leave.	**Rule 33** Before delivery of defence. *Grounds*: Service should not have been made. Court should decline jurisdiction. Failure to deliver supporting statement of grounds.
Alberta	**Rule 30** Enumerated heads with leave.	**Rule 27** Before delivery of defence. *Grounds*: Irregular process. Application not deemed to be submission to the jurisdiction.
British Columbia	**Rule 13(1)(3)** Without leave enumerated heads otherwise with leave.	**Rule 13(10)** Without entering appearance. Service should not have been made.
		Rule 14(6) Not entered an appearance. *Grounds*: Process invalid or expired or service invalid. Whether appearance or not. *Ground*: Court no jurisdiction or should decline jurisdiction. Application to deemed submisseion to the jurisdiction.

ASCERTAINING THE APPLICABLE LAW

Regional law and national law

The problems for Canada in identifying the applicable law derive from the fact that:

(1) There are a multiplicity of courts and different systems of laws in the world;

(2) Canada has within its boundaries two major legal systems, the Civil Law and the Common Law; and

(3) Its constitutional structure as a federal system comprises 13 jurisdictions, which permits the development of discrete bodies of provincial and federal laws.

The Constitution Act (1867) grants each province legislative authority to enact statutes but limits the legislative competence of each to certain classes of matters.

In addition to the statutory body of law there are the decisions of the judges both in the Civilian and Common Law systems. The legal system of Quebec is based on the French and Roman traditions of codification as regards its private law but has derived its public law from the Common Law tradition. This "mixed" jurisdiction, having similarities with the State of Louisiana and the countries of South Africa and Scotland, derives from the colonial history of North America. The province of Quebec is also subject to the laws passed by the Parliament of Canada within its sphere of competence. Accordingly, the laws of Quebec have been much affected by the judgments of the Supreme Court of Canada and by the Charter of Rights and Freedoms contained within the Constitution Act of 1982.[27]

The rest of Canada is identified as being a member of the Common Law family. However, this major source of law develops at a provincial level with some "nationalising" influence from judgments rendered on appeals reaching the Supreme Court of Canada. However, even such "nationalising" influences can be deflected by a provincial jurisdiction exercising its legislative power to abrogate the effect of any judgment of the highest court.[28]

Regional law takes the form of provincial or territorial legislation and case law, while national law takes the form of legislation passed by the Federal Parliament and its interpretations by all of the judges of all of the courts having jurisdiction to determine cases under any particular federal enactment. The issue of the development of federal Common Law has been debated but at this time there is no agreement that such a body of law exists.[29]

Accordingly, the courts of Canada may decide a civil case by the law of the province of the court's location, by the law of another province, by the federal law of Canada or by the law of another state. Frequently, in Canada the issue of the applicable law, provincial or federal, is

27. See Wheat, "The Disposition of Civil Law Appeals by the Supreme Court of Canada" (1980), 1 Sup. Ct. LR 425, 427.

28. See Veitch, "Language, Culture and Freedom of Expression in Canada" (1990), 39 ICLQ 101, 115.

29. See Evans and Slattery, "Federal Jurisdiction" (1989), 68 CBR 817.

bound up with the question of the appropriate forum. Thus, in *Monahan*
v. *Trahan*,[30] which involved a hydro-plane accident in the province of
Quebec in which the plaintiffs were residents of the province of Nova
Scotia and the directors of the corporate defendant were resident in the
provinces of Ontario and Quebec and which corporation did business
throughout Canada, the applicable law was determined to be the federal law — the Canada Shipping Act, RSC 1985, c. S–9. Using the test of
"real and substantial connection", the proper forum was found to be
Nova Scotia.

Conflict of laws

The rules which inform a court when it is appropriate to employ "foreign" law, that is the law of a sister-province or that of another state,
constitute Canada's law of conflict of laws. The courts frequently
employ "foreign" law in order to do fairness to parties and to ensure
that their disputes are not determined according to a body of law which
was utterly beyond their contemplation at the time when they entered
the transaction from which their dispute derives. As might be expected,
since the judiciary are not juridically omniscient, the foreign law is
required to be pleaded and proved, often by the employment of expert
witnesses.

In light of the range of possibilities in Canada, it is standard practice
to determine by express clauses the law of the transaction although this
must be done with care. For example, the International Paper Agreement (the IPA) designates the substantive law of the agreement along with
the forum for its determination, but this has given rise to disputes as to the
applicable remedial and procedural law to be used in resolving any
dispute arising under the IPA. Thus, it is desirable that the applicable law
provisions be exhaustive in their coverage.[31]

Foreign judgments

Under what conditions will courts recognise foreign judgments where
jurisdictions have not bound each other by treaties or by the adoption of
laws that guarantee the enforcement of their civil judgments? In Canada
the response is that there are four regimes:

---

30. (1993), 13 CPC (3d) 52 (NS TD).
31. See *Ash* v. *Corp. of Lloyd's* (1992), 7 CPC (3d) 343 (Ont. Gen. Div.).

(1) The reciprocal enforcement of judgments legislation;
(2) The Common Law rules established by the courts in provinces other than Quebec;
(3) The Civil Law rules of Quebec; and
(4) Foreign judgments legislation.

RECIPROCAL ENFORCEMENT LEGISLATION

The reciprocal enforcement legislation[32] permits *ex parte* orders to be made directing that judgments obtained elsewhere in Canada be registered by the receiving court. The affidavits in support of such an application are required to show either that the defendant was personally served or that the defendant had submitted to the jurisdiction of the court. The *ex parte* order will issue whether the personal service was made within the jurisdiction of the original court or was made *ex juris*.[33] The policy therein is that the courts of one province should recognise the judgments of another so long as the first court properly exercised jurisdiction.

The reciprocal enforcement legislation is also applicable to judgments obtained outside of Canada but only where the judgments were obtained in a reciprocating state. Thus, if the Lieutenant Governor in Council of a province has declared a state of the United States to be a reciprocating jurisdiction for the purposes of the provincial legislation then proceedings are taken under that provincial act. Where that is not the case it is to be determined by consideration of the Common Law principles regarding jurisdiction and recognition of foreign judgments.

COMMON LAW RULES

The principle decision on the Common Law rules is that of the Supreme Court of Canada in *Morguard Investments Ltd.* v. *De Savoye*.[34] That decision sought to deal with the problem in which a dispute occurred wholly within one jurisdiction, but when the litigation took place the defendant had moved to another jurisdiction. This left the plaintiffs with the sole option of suing the defendant in the new location. On the bases of the policies of reciprocity, comity, and full faith and credit the Court recognised that the tests for recognition

32. See, for example, Reciprocal Enforcement of Judgments Act CR–3 RSNB 1973.
33. See *First City Capital Ltd.* v. *Winchester Computer Corporation* (1987) 6 WWR 212 (Sask. CA).
34. (1990) 3 SCR 1077.

should be threefold — presence, submission or a real and substantial connection to the judgment forum.

Since that decision on intra-Canada judgments, lower courts have adopted the *Morguard* principle to recognise both *in personam* and *in rem* judgments outside of Canada.[35] In the later cases, the judges have recognised the judgment of a foreign court where the defendant:

(1) Was not resident in the foreign state when the action was commenced;

(2) Did not submit to the jurisdiction of the foreign state; and

(3) Did not appear in the action but because the court was satisfied that there was a real and substantial connection between the original action with the foreign state such that the receiving court would have exercised jurisdiction in like circumstances.

The policies outlined in *Morguard* with respect to inter-provincial recognition have been re-iterated by the Supreme Court of Canada in *Amchem Products Inc. et al.* v. *Workers' Compensation Board* (BC)[36] with regard to the recognition of foreign judgments.

CIVIL LAW RULES

The ready acceptance of the *Morguard* principles in Common Law Canada has been extended to the recognition of judgments from the civilian province of Quebec.[37] However, it is important to appreciate that the *Morguard* principle collides with the policies implicit in the provisions of the Code of Civil Procedure of Quebec.[38] The Quebec conflict rules must be seen to be what they are — an independent set of principles native to that province. In essence the policy is for the Quebec court to exercise some degree of control over foreign judgments, the degree of control varying with the origin of the judgment — whether of a sister-province or of a foreign state. It is that degree of control or willingness to review the substance of a matter which separates the Quebec practice from that of the rest of Canada. Thus, for a judge in Quebec to recognise a foreign judgment the following criteria must be met:

35. See *Clarke* v. *Lo Bianco* (1991), 59 BCLR (2d) 334 (BC SC) and *Moses* v. *Shore Boat Builders Ltd.* (1992), 68 BCLR (2d) 394 (BC SC).

36. (1993), 150 NR 321 (SCC).

37. See 87313 *Canada Inc.* v. *Neeshat Oriental Carpet Ltd.* (1993), 11 CPC (3d) 7 (Ont. Gen. Div.) and *Amopharm Inc.* v. *Harris Computer Corp.* (1992) 57 OAC 1984.

38. CPC, Articles 17 8–180.

(1) The judgment was rendered by a competent authority according to the Quebec conflict rules;
(2) The defendant was domiciled within the jurisdiction;
(3) The action took place within that jurisdiction and the defendant was personally served;
(4) The defendant has assets within that jurisdiction, or the parties have expressly adopted that jurisdiction;
(5) The judgment is final as opposed to interlocutory;
(6) The judgment is not contrary to public policy or tainted by fraud; and
(7) The foreign court applied a law which the Quebec court would have applied by its conflict rules in the same circumstances.[39]

Whether or not these criteria are met, the Quebec court may choose to reconsider the foreign judgment since Section 1220(1) of the Civil Code of Quebec states that a foreign judgment merely creates a presumption that a right has been acquired which presumption may be contested on the merits. What this means is that where a defendant is subject to a judgment in another sister-province but was not personally served nor appeared then he can plead in Quebec any defence which might have been set up in the original action.

The difference between the Quebec practice and the *Morguard* principle is crystal clear and is exemplified in Article 3164 of the new Civil Code of Quebec. That new law will also introduce into the law of the province the notion of "sufficient connection" with Quebec[40] and something approaching the comity policy[41] expressed by the Supreme Court of Canada in *AmChem*.[42]

FOREIGN JUDGMENTS LEGISLATION

Two Common Law provinces, New Brunswick and Saskatchewan, have enacted foreign judgments acts.[43] These enactments, applicable to both intra- and extra-Canada judgments, provide that where an action is brought

39. However, see CPC, Article 3157.
40. CPC, Article 3136.
41. CPC, Article 3137.
42. For a proper treatment of the difficult issues, see Glenn, "Foreign Judgments, the Common Law and the Constitution: De Savoye v. Morguard Investments Ltd." (1992), McGill LJ 537; Blom, "Morguard Investments Ltd. v. De Savoye, Case Comment" (1991), 70 Can. BR 733.
43. Foreign Judgments Act c. F–19 RSNB 1973 and Foreign Judgments Act CF–18 RSS 1978.

on a foreign judgment, it is a sufficient defence that the defendant was not duly served with the process of the original court and did not appear. The courts have held that these tests are to be read conjunctively that the provisions are conclusive of the law of the provinces and have not been superseded nor impinged on by the *Morguard* decision,[44] as, for example, in *Cardinal Couriers Ltd. v. Noyes.*[45]

The Province of British Columbia has enacted the Enforcement of Canadian Judgments Act[46] and the question is whether or not other provinces will follow that lead. It can be said that while the Supreme Court of Canada in *Morguard* lowered the Common Law barriers to enforcement of judgments between sister-provinces, the statutory provisions in the two provinces place higher obstacles to enforcement. On the other hand, the new post-*Morguard* British Columbia statute lists only four defences to oppose the enforcement of an extra-provincial judgment:

(1) There is an order staying the judgment in the original jurisdiction;
(2) The defendant intends to bring a proceeding to set aside the judgment in the original jurisdiction;
(3) Some limiting order is permitted under the statutes of the original jurisdiction restricting the remedies available; or
(4) The original judgment is contrary to the public policy of the recipient jurisdiction.

This simple statute would appear to embrace, without express statement, the policies of *Morguard* and to hone in on fairness to defendants. It may not, however, be perfect.[47]

COMMENCING THE ACTION

Court procedure — pleadings

Complaint, types of answer and reply

By Canadian practice, the purpose of pleadings, the written statements exchanged between the parties following the service of the originating

44. *Ontario Ltd. v. Vander Pluijm* (1992), 12 CPC (3d) 71 (NB QB).
45. (1993), 13 CPC (3d) 144 (Sask. CA); see also Walsh, "Canadian International Law After De Savoye v. Morguard Investments" (1992) 8 NB Sol.J 1.
46. C. 37 SBC 1992.
47. See Black, "Uniform Enforcement of Canadian Judgments Act" (1992), 71 Can. BR 721.

process, is to define and inform the parties and the court of the following: the issues and causes of action, the materials facts, and the relief sought. These written documents, usually in the form of a statement of claim, a statement of defence and a reply statement, form the essence of the action and determine such other matters as: any interlocutory proceedings with respect to the modes of discovery or preliminary determinations of law or fact; the range of evidence which will be admissible and the nature of the relief; these will form the basis of any judgment or appeal thereafter; and lie as a record as to the matter litigated for future litigants.

The procedural rules provide forms for all pleadings and require in the drafting that numbered paragraphs be used with each allegation of fact being contained in a separate paragraph.

The rules of pleading can be reduced as follows:

(1) A pleading will include material facts but not evidence in support of the cause of action;

(2) A point of law may be pleaded so long as all of the material facts in support of that conclusion are pleaded;

(3) A party need not plead a fact which is presumed by law, for example, those under the Bills of Exchange Act RSC 1985 c. B–5;

(4) The performance of a condition precedent need not be pleaded unless it has been denied by the other party;

(5) Alternative allegations of fact are permissible. However, where allegations are made in a reply statement these must conform with the earlier statement of claim;

(6) It is sufficient to allege an implied agreement as a fact without pleading the events from which the implication is drawn;

(7) The effect of a document is to be pleaded concisely, but where the exact words are material, they may be pleaded. In exceptional circumstances such as presented by an especially complex document that may be annexed to the statement of claim;

(8) Fraud, misrepresentation and breach of trust must be pleaded with full particulars;

(9) Any relief claimed must be specified with particulars of damages given if known; otherwise further particulars of damages are to be filed as soon as these are known and no later than entry for trial;

(10) General damages need not be quantified;

(11) A declaratory order may be pleaded as a form of relief alone;

(12) Facts occurring after the delivery of the pleading can be pled by amendment by leave of the court; and

(13) The specific Section of a statute must be pleaded.

The procedural rules also speak to the pleading of the statements of defence and the reply statement. Thus:

(1) Every allegation of fact shall be denied, or if not then it shall be deemed so admitted;

(2) A party may plead a different version of the facts rather than merely deny the version of the other side;

(3) Every matter in defence shall be pleaded which might otherwise take the other party by surprise or raise a new issue;

(4) The mere denial of an agreement is no more than the denial of the making of the agreement or the facts from which it is implied;

(5) The denial of the legality of a contract must be specifically pleaded; and

(6) The amount of damages is always in issue unless specifically admitted.

Amendment to pleadings

Most of the Canadian jurisdictions have undertaken revisions of the rules of procedure during the last 20 years with the goal of ensuring that the rules are liberally construed to secure the just, most expeditious and least expensive determination of every civil proceeding on its merits.[48] This has resulted in a more relaxed approach to the pleading process and while there can still be questions as to the mode of commencement,[49] the courts are prepared to overlook deficiencies in the drafting of pleadings if they disclose a reasonable cause of action.[50] Thus, the plea to strike the pleadings on the grounds that they disclose no cause of action or are frivolous and vexatious has become more difficult to sustain.[51]

Also, while pleading in the alternative is readily accepted, one may also plead inconsistent causes of action, for example, pleading both a void contract and a valid obligation.[52] At the same time, the courts have also adopted an increasingly lenient approach to amendments even where these have added new causes of action[53] under the policy of ensuring that

48. See R 1.04 (1) Rules of Civil Procedure of Ontario.

49. By petition or by writ of proceeding: *Snyder v. Snyder* (1992), 9 CPC (3d) 193 (BC SC).

50. See *Jane Doe v. Bd. of Police Commrs.* (1990), 40 OAC 161.

51. See *Hunt v. Carey Canada Inc.* (1990) 2 SCR 959.

52. See *Bratsch Ltd. v. LeBrooy* (1992), 3 CPC (3d) 192 (BC SC).

53. Cp. *Cardinal v. Canada* (1992), 47 FTR 203 and *Francoeur v. MNR* (1992), FC 389 (CA).

all issues in dispute are before the court. Even negligent or reprehensible delay will not necessarily be fatal to a plea to amend.[54] Such delays may mean on occasion that the plea to amend is made after the expiry of some relevant limitation period, however, the courts have adopted a common sense and compassionate approach particularly where the pleading error has been that of misnomer, for example, proceeding against a deceased rather than the personal representative.[55] The Saskatchewan Court of Appeal in *G& R Trucking Ltd.* v. *Walbaum*[56] has attempted to identify nine occasions when a court should exercise its discretion to permit amendments after the expiry of limitation periods.[57]

In light of this relaxed form of practice, what protections are afforded to defendants with respect to applications for extensive and late amendments? In *Seaway Trust Co.* v. *Markle*,[58] an Ontario court set out three clear tests to be observed in this regard:

(1) Would the amendment cause injustice to a responding party that cannot be compensated in costs;
(2) Would the amendment, if pleaded *ab origo*, have offended the rules of procedure; and
(3) Does the amendment clearly disclose a reasonable cause of action or defence?

Supplementary pleadings

By Canadian practice, provision is made for the supplementing of pleadings by such as:

(1) Particulars furnished in response to a demand from the other party;
(2) Amendments to the pleadings themselves;
(3) Interrogatories;
(4) Admissions; or
(5) Interlocutory applications to the court on preliminary matters.

Following these pleading steps, the parties should have a clear picture of the facts and issues in dispute. It is then appropriate to proceed to file and notice trial with the appropriate court officer with copies to all of the

54. See *Gauvin Enter. Ltd.* v. *Canada* (1992), FTR 306.
55. See *Frank* v. *King Estate* (1989), 25 CPC (2d) 291 (Alta. CA).
56. (1983), 2 WWR 622 (Sask. CA).
57. Compare *Med. Finance Co. SA* v. *Bank of Montreal* (1993), 79 BCLR (2d) 222 (CA).
58. (1988), 25 CPC (2d) 64 (Ont. HC).

parties. Also, while in most cases the issues and material facts are now finalised, it is nevertheless still possible that amendments may be made to the pleadings.

Joinder of claims and parties

The present Canadian rules regulating joinder in both actions and applications are liberal with a presumption in favour of joinder unless such a choice will unduly complicate or delay the action or cause undue prejudice to a party in which case the court will grant relief against joinder. Joinder may even be granted outside of the expiry of pertinent limitations legislation in aid of the plaintiff's action.[59] This liberal attitude has meant that there are greater numbers of cases involving multiple plaintiffs and multiple defendants.

Thus, there is no limit to the numbers of claims which can be joined in a proceeding against an opposite party. The rules speak in the singular and while they do not prohibit claims by several parties against several defendants there is no doubt the more complex the proceeding then the more likely there will be a motion to sever the claims or strike the parties.[60] However, it is agreed that the modern joinder of claims rules are intended to broaden the possibilities for plaintiffs to have matters heard that are "compatible" and so the term "claims" is to be read as being wider in meaning than "cause of action". This means that a plaintiff can join any number of claims against a number of respondents none of whom are responsible individually for all of the relief claimed in the suit.

Basically joinder of plaintiffs or defendants is done without leave of the court where:

(1) There is some common question of fact or law which must arise in all of the proceedings; and
(2) All of the relief claimed derives from the same transaction or series of transactions.

Conversely, an opposing party, by interlocutory application, may apply for an order to:

(1) Remove any party;
(2) Add any other person as a party; or
(3) Move to sever the matters due to prejudice of some kind.

---

59. See *Gracey* v. *Thompson Newspapers Co.* (1991), 4 OR (3d) 180 (Gen. Div.).

60. See *Someplace Else Restaurant Ltd.* v. *Calendar Magazine Ltd.* (1979), 107 DLR (3d) 636 (Ont. HC).

In practice, this means that plaintiffs can sue in various capacities: For example, in personal injury or death cases, the plaintiff may appear personally, as a beneficiary, as an executrix or as a litigation guardian.

The rules require that certain persons be joined as parties. Also, while in most cases party-plaintiffs will join without external encouragement, where they are reluctant to join in there is no rule which will force them to do so. In such situations, the reluctant party is joined as a defendant. The policy is that everyone whose presence is required to permit the court to make a decision on all of the issues before the court must be joined.

With regard to party-defendants there are two additional categories which pertain to them. Where there is doubt as to the party from whom the applicant is entitled to relief or where the plaintiff has suffered damage at the hands of several parties albeit in different claims then joinder is permissible.[61] As with joinder of claims, the jurisprudence on relief from joinder of parties utilises the criteria of undue complication or delay of the trial or prejudice to the applicant. Current practice in complex actions tends to be to deny such applications where it would have the affect of dismissing some part of the action and to order the matter to proceed even though there is the possibility that it may be established that there has been an improper joinder of plaintiffs or defendants.[62]

Counterclaim

A defendant may assert by counterclaim any right or claim against a plaintiff, even though the subject matter of the counterclaim does not relate to the subject matter of the claim, and may join as defendant to the counterclaim any other person who is a necessary party thereto. At the same time, the court has a discretion to determine that the counterclaim should be tried separately although Canadian procedural rules presume that a counterclaim is to be tried with the main action.[63]

There is a requirement, however, that the counterclaim be filed with the statement of defence unless it would be manifestly unjust to permit the plaintiff to proceed without its addition.[64] Where both the claim and the counterclaim are successful then the court may give judgment for the balance.[65]

61. See *Moncton (City)* v. *Aprile Contracting Ltd.* (1980), 29 N BR (2d) 631 (CA); *Becker* v. *Cleland's Estate* (1981), 35 NBR (2d) 542 (CA).

62. See, for example, *Fundy Formwork Ltd. et al.* v. *Basic Management et al.* (1993), NBJ Number 322 (QB).

63. See *Renegade Capital Corp.* v. *Hees International Bankcorp Inc.* (1991), 3 OR (3d) 251 (Gen. Div.).

64. See *Rio Alto Exploration Ltd.* v. *White* (1990), 104 AR 84 (QB).

65. See *Brosseau & Assocs.* v. *Edmonton* (City) (1990), 105 AR 13 (QB); *Purdy* v. *Fulton Ins. Agencies Ltd.* (1991), 1 CPC (3d) 241 (NS CA).

Cross-claims

A defendant can cross-claim against a co-defendant where the latter is liable for any part of the plaintiff's claim or for any relief relating to the subject matter of the dispute. The present procedural rules, by permitting co-defendants to so cross-claim, dispense with the need for third party proceedings. Where a defendant claims contribution against a co-defendant under the contributory negligence legislation, then this must be done by cross-claim. The co-defendants so named need not respond by way of defence if they have already entered a statement of defence to the main action. A defendant who asserts contribution on the part of the plaintiff must do so by counter-claim.

The parties to a cross-claim who are adverse in interest may conduct discovery against each other, which is usual prior to the trial of the cross-claim along with the main action.[66]

Third party claims

When a defendant is sued she may have a separate claim against a co-defendant or a third person with regard to the plaintiff's claim. For example, where employees of a company-employer are injured by exposure to a product sold to the employer by one corporation which product is manufactured under licence by another corporation according to a process owned by yet another licensor-corporation then: the employees may sue their employer who in turn will sue the seller as a third party who in turn will sue the manufacturer as a fourth party who will sue the licensor as a fifth party. All of these claims will be heard in the one action. This procedure will be called into action particularly where the plaintiffs have declined to name one or more of the other parties as defendants. Of course, since it is the rights of the plaintiff which may be affected by third party claims our procedural rules provide the plaintiff with an express right to challenge any such third party activity among defendants.

Once such a third party claim has been issued, then the third party is to be served with all documents relating to the main action and parties to a third party claim who are adverse in interest may discover each other. The jurisprudence on the timing of the decision to employ the third party proceeding is particularly murky.[67]

66. See *Mahoney* v. *Kent Ins.* Co. (1992), 7 CPC (3d) 338 (NBCA).

67. See, for example: *Allied Signal Inc.* v. *Dome Petrol Ltd.* (1992), 131 AR 134 (CA); *Peace Hills trust Co.* v. *Prof. Management Ltd.* (1992), 1 CPC (3d) 185 (Alta. QB); *Brampton HydroElec. Comm.* v. *BC Polygrinders Ltd.* (1992), 6 CPC (3d) 275 (Ont. Gen. Div.).

Interpleader

This form of joinder is utilised by persons who hold personal property which is not their own and who wish to hand it over to the rightful party when faced by two competing claims. Some jurisdictions have extended their rules to include real property.[68] The classic bill of interpleader was used in situations where two persons deposited a deed with a third party who agreed to redeliver it; thereafter one of the persons brought an action against the holder in detinue at which time the third party would issue a notice calling on the other persons to become a defendant in the action.[69] Modern rules distinguish between two kinds of interpleader: that brought by a person as stakeholder and that brought by a sheriff. A request for interpleader relief may take one of two forms:

(1) Notice of motion where an action has already been commenced; or
(2) Notice of application as an originating process where an action has not been commenced.

The affidavits in support of such requests should include allegations as follows:

(1) That two or more persons are making claims as to the same subject matter;
(2) Details of the actions which the applicant faces or expects to face;
(3) That the applicant is not colluding with either or any of the other parties; and
(4) That the applicant is willing to deliver the property to the court or to dispose of it as directed by the court.

Where a sheriff has taken property under execution; that officer may have recourse to the interpleader application where any person other than the judgment debtor claims it. In this situation, the sequence of events usually commences with a notice of claim to the sheriff by the person claiming an interest whereupon the sheriff gives notice of that claim to each execution creditor. If those served admit the claim then the sheriff may release the property, failing which the sheriff may apply for interpleader relief. The jurisprudence in this field is not extensive.[70]

68. See Rules of Court of New Brunswick R 43.02.

69. See *Cababe on Interpleader* (2nd ed. London 1988).

70. See *Danbrie Agri-Products Manufacturing Ltd.* v. *Martens Pipe Products Inc.* (1987), 16 CPC (2d) 175 (Ont. Dist. Ct.) and *Hudson's Bay Co.* v. *ICC Euroleasing Co.* (1986), 13 CPC (2d) 304 (Ont HC).

Where a party appeals an interpleader order that petition should be allied to a stay of proceeding application pending the hearing of the appeal. The permissible bases for an appeal have been recently litigated.[71]

Intervention

Canadian procedural rules permit the courts to grant leave in a proceeding to a non-party to intervene:

(1) As a party who has some interest in the proceeding or its outcome;[72]
(2) As a friend of the court (*amicus curiae*); or
(3) As a court-appointed expert.

As jurisprudence on Canada's Charter of Rights and Freedoms has developed since 1982, the term party now includes, *inter alia*, private or public interest intervenors unless there is some barrier posed by the terms of some statute which is at the heart of the dispute.[73]

Where intervenors join as added parties, they have the right to plead, introduce evidence, examine and cross-examine witnesses, present arguments and render appeals as any other party. To achieve that status, intervenors must by notice of motion satisfy the court that they have an interest in the subject matter of the suit or that any judgment in the matter will adversely affect the intervenors. On the other hand, where the intervenors join as friends of the court, and not as parties, their presence is to assist the court by the presentation of written or oral argument. Since the degree of intrusion of the friend of the court is discretionary, on occasions, the distinction between the two types of intervenors may become blurred. One can say generally that the added party has greater involvement than the amicus curiae. One crucial difference between the two types of intervenors is in the matter of costs: The added party bears their own costs while those of the friend of the court are borne by the parties.

While it was anticipated at the time of the reform of procedural rules in Canada that interventions would be rarely authorised, the fact is that many lawsuits in Canada are developing beyond the narrow adjudication of disputes between two parties. Thus, there are frequent applications by

71. See *Van's Nurseries Inc.* v. *Leung* (1992), 29 WAC 161 (BCCA).

72. See *United Parcel Service Can. Ltd.* v. *Ontario (Highway Transport Board)* (1989), 44 CPC (2d) 213 (Ont. Div. Ct.).

73. See *Metropolitan Toronto Housing Authority* v. *Arsenault* (1990), 44 CPC (2d) 152 (Ont. Dist. Ct.).

private or public interest groups who wish to be added to make heard some point of view with respect to a judicial decision which will have some impact on the public at large.[74]

This is particularly true of issues affecting women or minorities or such as the labour movement or the environment. The judges are therefore faced with difficult choices between accommodating the public interest proponents yet at the same time protecting interests of the original disputants from being lost in the policy quagmire. The court appointed expert may be added at the request of a party or on the initiative of the court. The difference between the expert and the *amicus curiae* lie in the restriction of the former to assisting the court with factual or highly technical matters such as engineering principles in construction disputes.[75]

Allied to this heading are the rules with respect to class actions which are defined as:

"Where there are numerous persons having the same interest in one cause or matter, one or more of them may sue or be sued, or may be authorised by the court to defend, on behalf or for the benefit of all persons so interested."[76]

While the rules read simply, the decisions of courts have in the past severely limited their impact.[77] Thus, the tests imposed have usually been too stringent for all but a few groups to meet:[78]

(1) The class must be properly defined;
(2) Members must have a common interest;
(3) There must be a wrong common to all;
(4) Damage must be the same to all other than in amount;
(5) The relief sought must be beneficial to all; and
(6) None of the members of the class must be adverse in interest.

The result has been that it has only been employed with success by small groups of persons identically situated, for example, condominium owners.[79]

The province of Ontario has been the first to attempt reform by two pieces of legislation — the Class Proceedings Act, SO 1992, c. 6 and the Law Society Amendment Act (Class Proceedings Funding), SO 1992,

74. See Reference Re Electoral Divisions Statutes Amendment Act, 1993 (1993), 6 WWR 148 (Alta. CA).

75. See *John Maryon International* v. *NB Tel* (1981), 33 NBR (2d) 543 (QB).

76. Rules of Court of New Brunswick, Rule 14.

77. See *General Motors of Can. Ltd.* v. *Naken* (1983), 32 CPC 138 (SCC).

78. See *Butler* v. *Regional Assessment Commr. Assessment Region Number 9* (1982), 39 OR (2d) 365 (Ont. H Ct.).

79. See *Lucyk* v. *Shipp Corp.* (1991), 4 OR (3d) 684 (Gen. Div.).

c. 7 effective 1 January 1993. Their policies are aptly described by Mr. Justice Montgomery as follows:[80]

". . . this provision [Section 25] poignantly characterises this Act's greatest strength: its wise and judicious balance of the rights of the individual to state his/her case, to participate personally in the judicial process, while at the same time allowing the victims of mass wrongs a degree of participation and representation they would not otherwise have had, in a manner which reduced administrative expenses and thereby increases the resources available for compensation."

The legislation's crucial provisions comprise those determining the retaining of the class counsel, the means of certification of the class, the opting procedure, the mode of trial of common issues, damage assessment and distribution, the arrangements for settlement of class actions and the establishing of a class action fund to assist parties in such proceedings.[81] Other provinces are likely to await developments in Ontario before acting although some others have already issued studies of their own in response to discrete problems.[82]

OBTAINING INFORMATION PRIOR TO TRIAL

Types of discovery

The purposes of discovery are to:

(1) Ascertain evidence in support of a claim and that adduced by the other side;
(2) To obtain admissions in support or prejudicial to the other side;
(3) To establish the truth of any fact or the authenticity of any document;
(4) To more closely define the issues; and
(5) To obtain an order dismissing a claim or granting a judgment.

The Canadian procedural rules organise the various types of discovery in the following order:

(1) Discovery of documents;
(2) Examination for discovery;
(3) Inspection of property; and
(4) Medical examination of parties.

80. LSUC Conference, "Ontario's New Class Proceedings Act: Are You Prepared?" Toronto, 14 April 1992.

81. See Cochrane, *Class Actions* (Canada Law Book, 1993). But see *Sutherland* v. *Canadian Red Cross Society* (1994) 5 WDCP (2d) 50 (Ont. Gen. Div.).

82. For example, Alberta Corporate and Consumer Affairs, A Blueprint for Fairness: The Report of the Committee on Fair Dealing in Consumer Savings and Investments, Edmonton 1989.

These are followed by the rules governing the conduct of the examination for discovery whether by oral examination or by written questions.

Examination for discovery

There is a right to the oral examination of any party who is adverse in interest and, with leave, non-parties who are believed to have information relevant to the action. There are individual sub-rules governing the examination of certain parties, for example, corporations where an officer, director or manager may be selected; a person under disability where the litigation guardian or committee may be examined; or a bankrupt and trustee in bankruptcy, both of whom may be examined.

Procedural reforms over the years have enlarged the scope of the discovery so that evidence is discoverable and permit cross-examination relating to an issue other than the credibility of the witness and cross-examination on the affidavit of documents of the examinee. In this process, the person examined is required to answer to the best of her knowledge, information and belief any proper questions relating to the issue in the action. A party who thereafter realises that an answer given is in error, incomplete or has been overtaken by events is under a duty to provide fresh information in writing to every other party.

The refusal to answer a proper question or a refusal based on privilege carries with it the risk that the answer cannot be introduced at trial, except with leave. Counsel may respond on behalf of the party at the examination and this binds the party unless the party repudiates prior to the close of the examination. In addition, the expanded rules now render the findings, opinions and conclusions of experts discoverable as is the existence and contents of any pertinent insurance policy.

The practice is that counsel should pose all questions in the examination for discovery so that a court-ordered second examination is available only where a party has refused to answer.[83]

In a further attempt to advance full disclosure on discovery and so shorten trials, the rules permit the examination of "any person who has, or is likely to have, information relevant to a material issue in the action".[84] This allows for the discovery of a range of parties including employees, agents, partners, spouse of a party; officers, directors or auditors of corporations; officers of subsidiaries of a corporation; expert witnesses, unless these will not be called at trial; and persons under disabilities. These parties may be asked questions to obtain information relating to a material issue in the action. That is, simple relevancy is not

83. See *Mann* v. *Ulrich* (1992), 5 CPC (3d) 284 (Alta. QB) and *Muslija* v. *Pilot Insurance Co.* (1991), 3 OR (3d) 378 (Gen. Div.).

84. Rules of Court of New Brunswick R 32.10.

the test so that fishing expeditions directed at any potential witness is not permissible.[85] The courts retain overall control of this process and may limit the number of persons to be examined so to prevent abuses, delays or expense.[86]

While the rules provide that no party may serve a notice of examination until he or she has served an affidavit of documents, this has generated a race to complete the pleadings, serve the affidavit of documents with the notice for examination attached. While the courts have adhered to a "first past the post" practice, recent case law shows that in the interests of justice on the case, the judges will vary that practice to defeat tactical gameplaying.[87]

Interrogatories to parties

Most Canadian procedural regimes do not permit both oral and written examination without leave of the court, and in fact, examination by written questions is relatively rare in Canada. The leave requirement has been imposed to avoid falling into the American practice of double examination, that is, written questions followed up by oral examination. However, there is no doubt that these are proper when dealing with very technical matters, with a party who cannot communicate or where the party is in another jurisdiction.[88]

The rules determine that where a party objects to any question they must do so in the affidavit and with reasons; where the answers are unsatisfactory, then a new set of questions may be submitted; and that where the answers are evasive or unresponsive, then a court-ordered oral examination may be held.[89]

Discovery and production of property

In order to take account of modern technology, the word "document" has been broadly defined so to include not only films, video tapes and sound recordings but also information stored by any device. Further, any insurance policy which may indemnify a party to an action is discoverable. As

85. See *Famous Player Dev. Corp.* v. *Central Capital Corp.* (1992), 3 CPC (3d) 286 (Ont. Div. Ct.).

86. See *Sorrel 1985 Ltd. Partnership* v. *Sorrel Resources Ltd.* (1992), 7 CPC (3d) 129 (Alta. QB).

87. See *Crysdale* v. *Carter-Baron* (1985), 37 CPC (2d) 222 (Ont. H Ct.); *Reichmann* v. *Toronto Life* (1989), 42 CPC (2d) 170 (Ont. H Ct.) and *Ceci* v. *Bonk* (1992), 6 CPC (3d) 304 (Ont. CA).

88. See *A-Dec Inc.* v. *Dentech Prods. Ltd.* (1989), 32 CPC (2d) 290 (BC SC).

89. See *Sanford* v. *Halifax Insur. Co.* (1992), 5 CPC (3d) 53 (NS CA).

with oral examination, it is permissible to discover documents in the possession of non-parties such as a subsidiary or affiliated corporation or by any company controlled directly or indirectly by a party to the action.

The freedom to so discover a non-party is limited to documents pertaining to material issues in the action. Such documents should not, in fairness, be denied the applicant in pursuit of their claim. The significance of this expanded mode of discovery is to facilitate settlement by providing an investigative procedure pre-trial which should uncover crucial materials or key witnesses and so obviate the necessity of a trial.

There have, however, been problems posed by the editing of documents such as tape recordings as well as the leaking of video-taped materials to the media prior to trial, which have required judicial rulings as to their admissibility.[90]

Affidavit of documents

The policy here is of disclosure of all documents relating to any matter in issue that is or, has been in the possession, control or power of a party whether or not privilege is claimed in respect of any particular document. After the close of pleadings every party is required to serve an affidavit of documents as a pre-condition of the right to examination for discovery. The affidavit comprises several lists:

(1) Documents to be produced;
(2) Documents no longer in possession; and
(3) Documents for which privilege is claimed.

Where a claim of privilege is made, then the grounds in support must be given but at the same time sufficient detail must be given so as to identify the document(s).[91] The disclosure obligation is on-going with the result that there is a requirement that errors in the original affidavit be corrected and that admissions be made as to after-acquired documents.

The production and inspection of documents may be postponed or denied by court order where there is the possibility of serious prejudice to a party by production or according to some notion of public policy, for example, the secrecy of minutes of confidential meetings.[92]

Where privilege is claimed then the document may not be used at trial other than to impeach a witness or otherwise by leave of the court.

90. See, respectively, *Roy v. Saulnier* (1993), 102 DLR (4th) 234 (Que. CA) and *Walker v. York Finch Hotel* (1993), 15 CPC (3d) 23 (Ont. Gen. Div.).

91. See *Visa Int. Service Assn. v. Block Brothers Realty Ltd.* (1993), 4 CPC (3d) 147 (BC CA).

92. See *Goud v. Cavanagh* (1992), 5 CPC (3d) 105 (Alta. QB).

Where a party has inadvertently omitted to claim privilege that may be asserted by a supplementary affidavit.[93]

The most contentious issue in this area has been the claim of privilege and the determination of the bases on which such a claim can be made. The dual tests have been: was the document prepared for the "dominant" purpose of litigation or merely the "substantial" purpose of anticipated litigation?[94] This question has resulted in considerable differences of judicial opinion with respect to, *inter alia*, insurance adjusters' reports (which are routinely prepared) and surveillance reports (which are sometimes prepared).[95]

Canada's courts are in the process of seeking a middle way between privilege granted to documents prepared in the face of certain litigation and giving privileged status to documents put together on the mere chance of litigation. Will a compromise in which documents are accorded privilege when prepared in response to a reasonable prospect of litigation be reached?

The ready availability of photocopies and their transmission by facsimile machine have created problems. Where copies have been made of non-private documents by counsel and included in a brief, the courts have so far held that privilege can be claimed.[96] There is concern as to this outcome since it suggests that public documents can acquire the status of privileged documents merely by passing through the hands of counsel. This matter has been addressed by the English Court of Appeal in *Ventouris* v. *Mountain*,[97] in which the judges spoke to their uneasiness with such a practice. Nevertheless, later English decisions have taken the Canadian position.[98]

The question of privilege has exercised the courts of all of the provinces in recent years. The one exception recognised by the Supreme Court of Canada is that a solicitor should speak to a will which she or he has prepared.[99] Some of the most recent judgments have been concerned with the waiver of privilege — whether the decision must be that of the client alone, express or implied, or whether privilege can be lost unintentionally.[100]

93. See *Waxman* v. *Waxman* (1991), 49 CPC (2d) 113 (Ont. Div.).

94. See *Keuhl* v. *McConnell* (1991), 2 WDCP (2d) 549 (Ont. Gen. Div.).

95. See Samworth, "Practical Approach to the Use of Surveillance from Affidavit of Documents to Trial" (1993), 15 Ad. Q 113.

96. See *Hodgkinson* v. *Simms* (1988), 36 CPC (2d) 24 (BC SC) and *Ottawa-Carleton* v. *Consumers Gas Co.* (1990), 74 OR (2d) 637 (Div. Ct.).

97. (1991) 1 WLR 619 (CA).

98. See *Dubai Bank Ltd.* v. *Galadari* (No. 7) (1992) 1 WLR 106 (Ch. D).

99. *Goodman Estate* v. *Geffen* (1991), 80 Alta. LR (2d) 293 (SCC).

100. See *Lloyd's Bank of Canada* v. *Canada Life Assurance Co.* (1991), 47 CPC (2d) 157 (Ont. Ge. Div.); Newbold, "Inadvertent Disclosure in Civil Proceedings" (1991) 107 LQR 99; and *Re Markovina* (1991), 57 BCLR (2d) 73 (SC).

While it has always been the practice that a court can impose an express confidentiality order restraining the use of information such as corporate operational details obtained in the discovery process and indeed on rare occasions to ban publication of the pleadings themselves,[101] the question has arisen whether or not there is an implied obligation not to abuse the discovery process.[102]

Appellate decisions both on the issue of implied undertakings and on the balance to be struck between the public's interests in knowing and the private interest in privacy are pending.[103]

Use of discovery at trial

The use of the discovery process at trial gives rise to very considerable differences of opinion among both judges and counsel. In essence, a party may read into evidence any portion of the discovery of an adverse party which otherwise would be admissible as evidence. The evidence obtained under examination may be used to impeach the deponent's inconsistent statements.[104] The court retains the authority to ensure that all of the examination is read where only a portion is selected that requires qualification.[105] Where an examined party is not available for trial then, with leave, the examination of that party may be used as evidence.[106]

INTERIM PROTECTION OF ASSETS PENDING TRIAL

Provisional attachment

Attachment orders are necessarily allied to the inspection and preservation of property or are aimed at property which is necessary to the determination of an issue in the proceeding. The latter are wider in their impact since the concept of property is not limited to that which is subject matter of the dispute but extends to such as the inspection and preservation

---

101. See *McCain* v. *McCain Foods Group Inc.* (1993), NBJ Number 375 (QB).

102. See *Reichman* v. *Toronto Life Publishing Co.* (1990), 44 CPC (2d) 206 (Ont. HC) and *Rocca Enterprises Ltd.* v. *University Press of New Brunswick Ltd.* (1989), 103 NBR (2d) 224 (QB).

103. See Morrison, "Protective Order, Plaintiff, Defendants and the Public Interest in Disclosure: Where does the Balance Lie?" (1990) 24 U Rich. LR 109.

104. However, see the particular provisions of the Evidence Act, RSO 1990, c. E23, Sections 20 and 21.

105. See *Int. Corona Resources Ltd.* v. *LAC Minerals Ltd.* (1986), 8 CPC (2d) 39 (Ont. HC).

106. See *Calandra* v. *BA Cleaners Ltd.* (1990), 73 OR (2d) 449 (Dist. Ct.).

of exhibits and other related materials. There is also provision made for
compensation for any damage caused by such inspection: For example,
where trees are cut or removed in the course of a survey of property then
a compensation order can be invoked.

In addition to inspection, a court may also grant an attachment order
for the detention, preservation or custody of property as well as an order
for the sale of perishable goods. This attachment order is particularly
appropriate where there is a justified fear that a non-resident may flee the
jurisdiction or there is some apprehension that there may be some fraudulent dealing in property by a party. Where property is held under a lien
for security, it may be recovered subject to monies being paid into court.
The interim recovery of personal property before trial may be obtained
by use of the replevin or recovery order. It has been suggested that the
courts, through the inherent discretion of a superior court, have wider
powers than those expressly described in the procedural rules with regard
to injunctive protections.[107]

Interlocutory injunction

The most important change in the rules has been the making available
of injunctive relief prior to the commencement of proceedings. An
injunction so granted will be *ex parte* and enjoys a ten-day currency.
The party applying for such an order is deemed to have given an
undertaking to indemnify the other party in the event that the order
was granted in error.[108] There has been some controversy as to the
appropriate tests for the granting of an interlocutory injunction (the
so-called *Mareva* injunction) which has resulted in a codification of
the tests in some jurisdictions[109] and differing judicial formulations in
others.[110]

Under present practice, the applicant is required to make full and frank
disclosure as to all material matters; to offer clear statements of the
strengths and weakness of their case; and a statement as to the risks
anticipated as to the property in question; along with an undertaking as
to possible damages. Allied to the interlocutory proceedings there is also

107. See *First Farm Inc.* v. *Henderson Surveys Ltd.* (1993), NBJ Numbers 209 and
248 (QB).
108. See *Sask. Co-op Fin. Services* v. *Tarel Hotel Ltd.* (1992), 5 CPC (3d) 112 (Sask.
QB).
109. For example, Rules of Court of New Brunswick R 40.03.
110. See *Di Menza* v. *Richardson Greenshields of Canada Ltd.* (1989), 43 CPC
(2d) 87 (Ont. Div. Ct.); *Kuehne & Nagel Ltd.* v. *Redirack Ltd.* (1991) 3 WDCP (2d)
14 (Ont. Gen. Div.); *Barnes* v. *Harbour Grace* (1991), 7 CP C (3d) 92 (N'fld. SC); and
CBC v. *CKPG TV Ltd.* (1992), 4 CPC (3d) 134 (BC CA).

available the certificate of pending litigation which may be issued whenever the title to or an interest in land is in issue.[111]

SUMMARY JUDGMENTS

Adjudication without trial or by special proceeding

An action or proceedings may be brought to a close by:

(1) A discontinuance;
(2) A withdrawal;
(3) A dismissal; or
(4) By a stay of proceeding.

Items (1) and (2) have the effect of terminating the proceeding and lie within the initiative of the moving party; whereas (3) and (4) will occur either as a result of an agreement between the parties or by leave of the court. The stay of proceeding means that the matter may be reactivated later with leave of the court. The discontinuance of the whole action may be done without leave but the other party is free to apply to the court for costs. The withdrawal is usually restricted to some claim made by one of the parties whereas the dismissal reflects the ending of the dispute usually in the form of a settlement. The stay, on the other hand, may represent the desire of the parties to "freeze" the proceeding pending the working out of the details of a proposed settlement.

There are three other proceedings by which a matter may be brought to an end without the requirement of a trial:

(1) The determination of questions before trial;[112]
(2) The determination of questions of law by stated case — where the parties have agreed on the facts, questions of law and the relief, then the court may move to judgment accordingly;[113]
(3) A motion to strike the pleadings as disclosing no reasonable cause of action;[114] and
(4) Because the court lacks jurisdiction.[115]

111. For full treatment, see Ellyn and Goodman, "Certificates of Pending Litigation" (1992), 5 CPC (3d) 65.

112. See, for example, with respect to bars presented by workers' compensation legislation or limitations of actions acts: *Rostland Corp.* v. *Toronto* (City) (1991), 2 OR (3d) 421 (Gen. Div.).

113. *Patterson* v. *Guptill* (1993), NBJ Number 331 (QB).

114. See *Hunt* v. *T & N plc* (1990), 43 CPC (2d) 105 (SCC) and *Doe* v. *Metro Toronto Commrs. of Police* (1992), 50 CPC (2d) 92 (Div. Ct.).

115. See *Buchar* v. *Weber* (1990), 46 CPC (2d) 60 (Ont. HC).

Summary judgments

Former procedural practice granted the motion for summary judgment to plaintiffs alone and only in restricted circumstances. The present rules have extended this mode of disposition without trial to defendants, with a resulting high volume of such motions in all jurisdictions. The moving party is required to submit affidavit materials or other evidence and to respond to cross-examination.[116]

The test to be applied by the court is whether or not there is a genuine issue trial with respect to the claim or defence.[117] In light of the materials brought before the court, the judges have determined that they should adopt a "robust application" of the rules and take a "hard look" at the merits, limiting their powers to award judgment only where there are questions of credibility which would best be tested at a trial of all of the issues.[118]

Default judgments

The plaintiff may take default proceedings if:

(1) The defendant fails to deliver a statement of defence; or
(2) Where the defence has been struck out.

When this occurs, the plaintiffs may request the officer of the court to note the defendant in default thereby determining that the defendant has admitted the truth of all of the allegations in the statement of claim. With leave, the defendant may have that noting in default set aside. After this proceeding, the plaintiff may move to either obtain judgment by means of the court officer signing judgment (where the dispute involves a debt, a liquidated damages claim or claims respecting land or chattels), or (where the dispute involves none of the items listed immediately above) the plaintiff may move for judgment before a judge with affidavit evidence in support. At that latter hearing, the judge may grant judgment or set the matter down for trial. The court has authority to set aside or vary a default judgment on such terms as are just.

116. See *Principal Savings & Trust Co.* v. *Bowlen* (1992), 1 CPC (3d) 206 (Alta. QB).

117. See *Ron Miller Realty Ltd.* v. *Honeywell, Wotherspoon* (1992), 1 CPC (3d) 134 (Ont. Gen. Div.); *MF Schurman Co.* v. *Westland Homes Ltd.* (1992), 2 CPC (3d) 49 (PEI SC); *Ingram-Ellis* v. *Edwards* (1992), 2 CPC (3d) 43 (BC SC); and *Lloyd's Bank of Canada* v. *Sherwood* (1990), 64 Man. R (2d) 288 (QB).

118. See *Irving Ungerman Ltd.* v. *Galanis* (1992), 1 CPC (3d) 248 (Ont. CA).

It is in these setting aside proceedings that differences have developed between provinces ostensibly using similar procedural rules. These differences centre on whether the tests for setting aside the noting in default and the default judgment should be the same or whether that for the setting aside of the noting in default should be less stringent.[119]

The criteria for setting aside the default judgments are more settled and comprise:

(1) The application must be made as soon as possible after the defendant has knowledge;

(2) The defendant must show by affidavit the excuse for the default judgment and the circumstances in which it occurred; and

(3) The defendant must support the affidavit by disclosing the facts in which he or she relies on to show that the claimed defence has merit.[120]

Other means of termination without plenary trial

Voluntary dismissal

Where a plaintiff wishes to discontinue after the close of pleadings then this may be done only with leave. The purpose of the rule is to ensure that the discontinuance is a defence to any subsequent action brought on the same cause of action. Where the plaintiff moves to discontinue against a defendant who has a counter-claim, the onus rests on the defendant to give notice of the continuation of the claim, which failing it, is dismissed with costs.[121]

Also, where a plaintiff discontinues against a defendant who has cross-claimed or made a third party claim, these are deemed to have been dismissed with costs unless the court orders otherwise. The policy within the relevant rules is to determine all of the issues in one proceeding which relate to the same events or series of events hence the requirement that defendants, against whom proceedings are discontinued, move affirmatively to preserve any claim they may have asserted.

119. Compare *Metro Toronto Condominium Corp. Number 706* v. *Bardmore Developments Ltd.* (1991), 3 OR (3d) 278 (Ont. CA) with *First Farm Inc.* v. *Henderson Surveys Ltd.* (1993), NBJ Numbers 209 and 248 (QB).

120. See *Beaubear Credit Union Ltd.* v. *Ahern* (1993), 132 NBR (2d) 223 (QB) and *Marissink* v. *Kold-Pac Inc.* (1993) NSJ Number 202 (CA).

121. See *Provincial Crane Inc.* v. *AMCA International Ltd.* (1990), 44 CPC (2d) 46 (Ont. HC).

Dismissal for failure to prosecute

A defendant that is not in default may move to have an action dismissed for delay where the plaintiff has failed:

(1) To serve a statement of claim in time;
(2) To note in default a defendant who has failed to file a statement of defence; or
(3) To set the action down for trial within six months after the close of pleadings.

The dismissal is the punishment meted out to a plaintiff who has not moved ahead with the proceeding and so has fallen foul of the goals of the procedural rules — greater efficiency in litigation and quicker results for all parties to a dispute.[122] To this end, court officers are empowered to maintain case-lists and to require parties to attend status-hearings at which time the court will determine, on all of the information provided, which is the most expeditious mode of proceeding for the particular dispute. In the exercise of this discretion, the court may hand down a calendar of dates setting out all of the steps to be taken through to the opening of the trial hearing itself.

Judicially assisted settlement

The policy of judicial assistance to settlement of disputes is contained in express provisions governing the pre-trial conference. These are held by judges, or other court officer with the aims of:

(1) Simplifying issues;
(2) Obtaining admissions of facts and documents;
(3) Concretising the quantum of damages claimed;
(4) Securing the amendments to pleadings or other documents;
(5) Gaining agreement as to the number of witnesses to be called; or
(6) Separating out some issue, such as a constitutional question, which should be tried prior to the main action.

At these conferences the presiding judges' aims are:

(1) To obtain a settlement; or
(2) To facilitate a quicker and less expensive trial.

122. See *Family Housing Assn. (Ltd.)* v. *Michael Hyde and Partner* (1993) 1 WLR 354 (CA).

The judge holding the pre-trial conference does not preside at the trial.[123] At the close of the conference the parties may sign a document listing the items of damages agreed on and their respective admissions along with the issues left to be determined and which document is binding on them. In addition to the above, on occasion, the parties will draft a settlement agreement which mandates that any default thereunder will trigger a motion for judgment invoking the inherent discretion of the court to so order.[124]

TRIAL

Setting the case for trial

While the jurisdictions do have rules for trial by judge with jury, the fact is that the civil jury is almost extinct in some provinces, rare in others and only sparingly used in the remainder. That reality is explained because in a number of provinces civil juries are permitted only in cases of defamation, wrongful arrest, false imprisonment and malicious prosecution. Where juries are used on a wider scale,[125] the plaintiff is required to proceed by way of notice of trial with jury to all other parties at the close of pleadings or by application to the court immediately following the issuance of a notice of trial. As the decision to grant a jury trial is discretionary, the applicant is required to set out the grounds on which the judge will be asked to exercise his or her powers.[126]

The steps for setting down or listing for trial are to be taken by the party who wishes to set a date for trial in a defended action and who at that time is required to furnish all other parties with a trial record. The purpose here is to provide a screening mechanism so that documents, such as "without prejudice" letters, relating to possible settlement do not accidentally appear in the record presented to the court. Once the case has been set down, then the appropriate court official will place the trial on a trial list leaving the parties to attend at the regular "motions day" to arrange for other, more convenient dates. The completion of these steps triggers the status hearing procedures through which the efficiency of litigation is controlled by the courts. Any settlement concluded after the setting down for trial must be communicated to the court officials.

123. See Rules of Court of Ontario R 50.04.

124. See *Marlin Watson Home Corp.* v. *Taylor* (1992), 3 CPC (3d) 82 (Ont. Gen. Div.); *Smith* v. *Robinson* (1992), 4 CPC (3d) 262 (Ont. Gen. Div.).

125. See Rules of the Supreme Court of Newfoundland R 40.05 (1) and the Jury Act c. 76 SNfld. 1991, Section 32 (3).

126. See *Harding* v. *Peddle* (1993) NJ Number 95 (SC); *Pipher* v. *Shelburne Dist. Hosp.* (1985), 5 CPC (2d) 110 (Ont. HC).

Scope and order of the trial

A number of jurisdictions[127] have introduced the concept of the "split trial" which allows for the trial of an issue as soon as it is ready. Thus, in personal injury actions, where the medical questions may take years to finalise, the liability issue can be resolved with some interim payment of advance compensation made to the successful plaintiff.[128] It is hoped that this restricted type of trial will benefit parties who have suffered financially or who have need for funds for specialised medical care in the period between the incident and the final assessment of their damage.

The conduct and order of trials is governed in part by the rules of procedure and in part by judicially inspired practice. The usual order is as follows:

(1) If the parties fail to make an appearance then the judge may simply dismiss the claims and any counterclaim allowing for the possibility for their later restoration by leave of the court;

(2) If there is an application for adjournment on the day of the hearing the presiding judge will discontinue if all parties consent or where there are compelling reasons supporting the request;

(3) If all of the parties are present then counsel for the plaintiff opens the trial with a concise opening speech encompassing the events leading to the action, giving a summary of the evidence and a statement of the issues and law, an introduction of documents, the setting-out of admissions and agreements and a description of the relief claimed; and

(4) Counsel for the defendant may make a brief statement referring to defences, such as contributory negligence, but more often will elect to speak at length at the close of the plaintiff's case.

Thereafter the counsel for the plaintiff will call and examine each witness, and after cross examination by the other party, will re-examine on any matter raised in the cross-examination. Plaintiff's counsel may cross-examine any witness brought by the opposing party, adduce any evidence in rebuttal and at the end of the defendant's counsel's speech make a speech in response.

Submission of evidence

One noteworthy alteration to the procedural rules is the granting to a judge the power to appoint an independent expert to inquire into and

127. See Rules of Court of New Brunswick R 47.03.

128. See *Stamper v. Finnigan* (1988), 85 NBR (2d) 355 (SCC).

report on a question of fact or opinion relevant to an issue in the action.[129] Such experts are not to be confused with the judicial advisors or assessors on technical matters since the appointed expert will usually be chosen from a list agreed on by the parties. Such expert may make inquiries, tests or experiments and render a report to the court, where it is entered as an exhibit prepared by an impartial person.

This is a valuable device in complex litigation where rafts of conflicting materials have been prepared by the experts engaged by the opposing parties. The exhibit rules are simple albeit extensive. The court reporters are required to make lists or exhibits describing each and stating which party placed them in evidence. The clerk of the court is charged with retaining custody of the exhibits, forwarding these to the appellate division if necessary and ultimately returning them to the solicitors of record for the redistribution to the parties.

Role of the trial judge in the presentation of evidence

The rules of most jurisdictions permit the trial judge to inspect any place or thing mentioned at trial. This practice is increasing in claims arising from motor vehicle and manufacturing accidents. The judge may act on impressions formed at any such inspection even if these differ from the evidence led at trial. The modern rules have retained the court's power to exclude witnesses to avoid tailoring of testimony until they are called to give evidence. The exceptions are:

(1) Any party who is to instruct counsel may not be excluded but is required to testify before all of the other witnesses;
(2) The parties themselves; and
(3) Expert witnesses.

The rules permit an application by a defendant at the close of the plaintiff's case for a non-suit on the premise that the evidence presented does not disclose a *prima facie* case.[130] The court may admit evidence obtained after the opening of the hearing by the plaintiffs but which must be presented before final argument and only if the evidence was non-discoverable at an earlier date.[131]

Usually, the courts have refused to give advisory opinions on the admissibility prior to the hearing preferring to determine such issues at

129. See Rules of Court of Ontario R 52.03 (1).
130. See *Petit (Lou) Trucking Co.* v. *Petit* (1990), 64 Man. R (2d) 139 (QB).
131. See *McGinn* v. *Bain Insul. and Supply Ltd.* (1992), 6 CPC (3d) 8 (Alta. QB).

the trial of all of the matters.[132] The related rules generally permit a party to re-open their case to prove a fact or document omitted through inadvertence such as the proving of the incorporation of a party.[133] The courts will not permit photographs of locations which exposures have been taken some time following the occurrence and where alterations have been made which fact is desired to be used to prove a line of argument.[134]

Evidence

Nature and purpose of evidence

The purpose of evidence is to obtain support for a party's action and its nature includes:

(1) Obtaining statements from the party or any witnesses;
(2) Inspecting documentary evidence and the site central to the claim;
(3) Legal research; and
(4) The employment of experts, consultants or special counsel.

The evidence of witnesses is taken by oral examination, cross-examination and re-examination at trial with witness attendance compellable by summons. The rule against leading questions has been relaxed to permit a party calling an evasive witness to so approach the matters relevant to the issue. Where a witness speaks neither of Canada's two official languages, then the witness is to be provided with the services of a competent and independent interpreter.

Where a witness is to be called merely to prove a document or a signature then this may now be taken by affidavit and so avoid the cost and inconvenience of a personal appearance. Conversely, a witness required to bring documents to the hearing can also be required to deliver over everything in their possession or control relating to the action whatever these items may be. Witnesses who fail to attend may be apprehended by a sheriff and brought to the court.

Most of the modern rules have eliminated the risk involved in calling an adverse party as a witness by allowing the party calling that adverse party to cross-examine the party who may then be re-examined by their own counsel.

132. See *Ed Miller Sales & Rentals Ltd.* v. *Caterpillar Tractor Co.* (1992), 7 CPC (3d) 223 (Alta. QB).

133. See *Russell* v. *Searle* (1957), 6 DLR (2d) 356 (NB QB).

134. See *McMahon* v. *Harvey* (Township) (1991), 2 CPC (3d) 154 (Ont. Gen. Div.).

Kinds of evidence

The kinds of evidence consist of party-witnesses, inspections of property and the site of the occurrence giving rise to the action, expert-witness reports, documents and commission evidence from those unable to attend whether by age, illness or infirmity.

Documents

The term "document" now includes films, photographs, video tapes, charts, graphs, maps, plans, surveys, accounts, sound recordings and information stored by any manner of device. In essence, the courts have held that any material capable or open to interpretation or amenable to providing information is a discoverable document.

Privilege

The volume of litigation under this sub-head in Canada has been such as to justify the publication of a monograph: Manes and Silver, *Solicitor-Client Privilege in Canadian Law* (Butterworths 1993). The authors preface their volume with two opposed aphorisms — "Justice is better served by candor than by suppression" and "Without the sanctity of solicitor-client privilege, there is no justice". These two competing notions explain the large volume of reported cases. By our practice, a claim of privilege is to be clearly stated in the affidavit of documents which must give an adequate description of the document together with the basis of the claim for privilege.[135] The grounds for claiming privilege are usually listed as including:

(1) Solicitor-client communications;[136]
(2) Documents prepared for the action;[137]
(3) Documents privileged in another action;[138]
(4) Physician-patient communications;[139]
(5) Hospital records;
(6) Expert opinions;

135. For example, "This document, of the stated date, is a communication between solicitor and client".

136. See Vaver, "Keeping Secrets, Civilly Speaking" (1992), 13 Ad. Q 334.

137. See *Keuhl v. McConnell* (1991), 2 WDCP (2d) 549 (Ont. Gen. Div.).

138. See *Pioneer Insul. Ltd. v. Nfld. Processing Ltd.* (1992), 6 CPC (3d) 346 (Nfld. TD).

139. See *Desmarais v. Morrissette* (1992), 3 CPC (3d) 297 (Ont. Gen. Div.).

(7) "Without prejudice" correspondence;[140]

(8) Tax returns; and

(9) Trade secrets.

However, the litigation shows that there are fine decisions to be made with respect to materials to be found in these classes of documents listed above.[141]

Party testimony

The practice is for counsel to interview all parties and witnesses prior to trial and to ensure:

(1) That the witnesses have read and reviewed any exhibits;

(2) That they have understood the substance of the evidence to be presented;

(3) To raise possible questions which may be raised on cross-examination; and

(4) To prepare the expert witnesses whose technical language may require simplifying.

The basic rules of oral examination by direct, cross and re-examination is tempered by the court's powers to control the proceeding so as to protect witnesses from harassment or embarrassment and to require the re-call of a witness for further examination.

JUDGMENT AND KINDS OF RELIEF

Final judgment

Historically, the decisions of the courts of Canada have taken the form of judgments, orders, decrees and rulings, however, more recent usage hasincluded all of the above in the term "order".[142] Nevertheless, the words "judgment" and "order" still carry recognisably different meanings:

140. See *Family Housing Assn. Ltd.* v. *Michael Hyde and Partners* (1993) 1 WLR 354 (CA).

141. In order to appreciate the subtlety of the judicial decisions in this area, it is necessary to consult Manes and Silver, *Solicitor-Client Privilege in Canadian Law* (Butterworths 1993).

142. See Rules of Court of Ontario R 59.01.

(1) A judgment is a final determination of all questions in an action; and

(2) An order determines some preliminary question relating to some procedural or subsidiary issue within the main action.

Despite this, it is still necessary for an appellate court to determine just what a particular judicial determination has been so to work out to which court an appeal should lie.[143]

Orders are frequently drawn by the successful party in co-operation with the other side, then approved by the judge and filed thereafter. Where the spirit of co-operation fails then the court will finalise the wording of the order following submissions from the parties. Where the final determination is in the form of a judgment then there is a two-step process:

(1) The giving of the decision by the court; and

(2) The entry of the judgment in the registry by a court official.

Entry of judgment

The rules require that a judge deliver a "decision directing judgment" which is a decision directed toward the parties to the action. On receiving that decision, the successful party must then register an entry of judgment following which a formal judgment may be obtained. Execution may only follow the entering of the judgment. The court official sends the parties a copy of the decision and states the date of its effectiveness and the successful party moves for entry to gain the judgment on which execution is based. This final judgment is in skeletal form containing the style of the cause of action; the effective date; the name of the judicial officer; the date of the judgment; the operative portions of the judgment; and the signature of the judge. The reasons for judgment are usually provided at a later date.

Kinds of relief

Specific performance

Traditionally, the petition for a decree of specific performance has been granted only where the subject matter in dispute is land or some other item categorised as unique or at least scarce. However, there is evidence

---

143. See *Hughes* v. *Eglinton Market Inc.* (1992), 2 CPC (3d) 313 (Ont. Gen. Div.); *Laurentian Plaza Corp.* v. *Martin* (1992), 6 CPC (3d) 381 (Ont. CA); and *Iron* v. *Saskatchewan* (1993), 6 WWR 1 (Sask. CA).

that this form of relief may becoming more readily available although it has not yet achieved the status of the plaintiff's remedy of choice being granted only at the discretion of the court.[144]

Substitution relief

Damages are perceived to be the primary remedy for parties suffering injury.[145] The Supreme Court of Canada has set out to establish both policy and principles in several damage fields in relatively recent time. In the area of personal injury and death, the justices, since the so-called "trilogy" in 1978,[146] have continued to this time[147] to establish clear rules of assessment so to facilitate settlements and diminish the volume of litigation. In wrongful dismissal actions, the court has acted to restrain such claims by limiting damages to pecuniary claims and so arresting the development of awards for intangible harm arising from termination of employment.[148] Also, lastly in recent cases the court has sought to lay down guidelines as to compensation for negligently inflicted pure economic loss.[149]

Rectification recission

The action for rectification arises where due to a common mistake of the parties the written document does not contain their agreement so that the court "revises" the contract. On the other hand, the claim for rescission of a contract is an equitable right whose granting results in the contract being set aside. The grounds for rescission usually range from fraudulent misrepresentation to mutual mistake or concealment of information relevant to contracts of utter good faith, such as contracts of insurance.[150]

144. See Clark, "Rethinking the Role of Specific Relief in the Contractual Setting" in *Remedies: Issues and Perspectives* (Berryman ed., Carswell 1991). A complete statement of the law is to be found in Sharpe, *Injunctions and Specific Performance* (2nd. ed. Canada Law Book 1992).

145. See Waddams, "The Principles of Damages" in *Essays on Damages* (Finn ed., The Law Book Company 1992).

146. See, for example, *Andrews v. Grand & Toy (Alta.) Ltd.* (1978) 2 SCR 229.

147. See *Ratych v. Bloomer* (1990), 69 DLR (4th) 25 (SCC) and *Laferriere v. Lawson* (1991), 78 DLR (4th) 609 (SCC).

148. See *Vorvis v. ICBC* (1989) 1 SCR 1085.

149. See *Sunrise Co. Ltd. v. The Ship "Lake Winnipeg"* (1991), 77 DLR (4th) 701 (SCC) and *The "Norsk"* (1992) 1 SCR 1021.

150. Current Canadian practice with respect to these two claims is described in Waddams, *The Law of Contract* (3rd. ed. Canada Law Book 1993).

Declarations concerning legal relations

When a declaratory judgment is sought then the statement of claim should set out the material facts in support even though a court may make such a declaration of rights of its own initiative.[151] This form of relief is claimed either on its own or alongside other claims. It is therefore not ordinarily a summary process but rather runs as any other action.[152] The use of declarations has increased in recent time[153] and particularly in cases which involve governments or their agents.[154]

POST-TRIAL MOTIONS

Attacks on judgments

The rules anticipate that from time to time judicial officers will make slips in the calculation of the relief claimed or by the misreading of a statute and its erroneous application to the dispute. Thus, a motion for variance of the judgment must be made to the judge who presided over the action, and this is required to be done before entry of the judgment where the error is other than a mere clerical error or omission. Failing this, the only avenue is an appeal to a higher court.[155] Where the error falls into the class of mere clerical slip then a motion can be made after the entry of judgment to any other judge of the court for amendment. These provisions also apply to judgments of the appeal courts which require variance.

Grounds for a new trial

Mistake and excusable neglect

The grounds of attack on a judgment comprise:

(1) Misdirection of the jury;[156] and
(2) Judicial self-misdirection characterised as gross and palpable error either in principle[157] or in the drawing of erroneous inferences from the evidence,[158] or lack of jurisdiction.

---

151. See Supreme Court Act, c. S–10 RSPEI 1988, Section 30.

152. See *Fisher* v. *Albert* (1921), 50 OLR 68 (HC); *Re Bell* (1955), 3 DLR 521 (Man. CA).

153. See Sarna, *The Law of Declaratory Judgments* (2nd ed. Carswell 1988).

154. See *Rusche* v. *ICBC* (1992), 4 CPC (3d) 12 (BC SC); *Horton Bay Holdings Ltd.* v. *Wilks* (1992), 3 CPC (3d) 112 (BC CA).

155. See *Strelchuk* v. *Vella* (1991), 44 CPC (2d) 172 (Ont. Gen. Div.); *Freuhauf Trailer Co.* v. *McCrea* (1955), 38 MPR 151 (NB CA); *Vicckies* v. *Vicckies* (1990), 45 CPC (2d) 200 (Ont. HC).

156. See Smith & Bouck, *Civil Jury Instructions 1989 to Date*, CLE BC.

157. See *Santerre* v. *Mazerolle* (1993), 130 NBR (2d) 141 (CA); *Donnelly* v. *Belanger* (1992), 122 NBR (2d) 48 (CA).

158. See *Kelly* v. *Chase* (1990), 97 NBR (2d) 244 (CA).

Current appellate policy renders such attacks on judgments difficult, with many appellate decisions taking the form of dismissals on the grounds of no "gross and palpable" error by the trial judge. Equally the courts of appeal have made it clear that they are not amenable to quantum appeals and are quite unwilling to substitute their assessment of an award for that of the trier of fact even where it would have differed. The attack by way of lack of jurisdiction is seen in disputes arising between employer and employee where the policy enunciated by the Supreme Court of Canada[159] precludes judges trying disputes which fall within a collective bargaining regime.

Newly discovered evidence

A trial judge who remains seized of a matter can re-open a trial to hear new evidence,[160] but the jurisprudence is uneven as to whether in other circumstances it is appropriate to apply to a judge of co-ordinate jurisdiction with the original judge or to an appellate court.[161] Where new evidence is discovered between the entering of the trial judgment and the opening of the appellate hearing, it is possible for that new evidence to be heard so to alter the result.[162]

Fraud

The basis of a motion to set aside a judgment for fraud has been exhaustively laid out in a relatively recent judgment, *Int. Corona Resources Ltd.* v. *LAC Minerals Ltd.*,[163] in which the principal criteria were said to be:

(1) Fraud must be proven on the balance of reasonable probability;
(2) The fraud must be vital to the case;
(3) The fraud must have been discovered after the trial;
(4) The moving party must act with celerity;

159. See *Ste. Anne Pulp & Paper Co.* v. *CPU Local 219* (1986) 1 SCR 704.
160. See *Castlerigg Invests. Inc.* v. *Lamb* (1991), 2 OR (3d) 216 (Gen. Div.).
161. See *AH Al-Sagar & Bros. Engineering Project Co.* v. *Al-Jabouri* (1990), 46 CPC (2d) 69 (Ont. HC); *Stancroft Trust Ltd.* v. *Asiamerica Capital Ltd.* (1993), 11 CPC (3d) 19 (BC CA); *Sengmueller* v. *Sengmueller* (1994) 5 WDCP (2d) 52 (Ont. CA).
162. See *Rayner* v. *Knickle* (1990), 64 DLR (4th) 158 (PEI CA).
163. (1988) 54 DLR (4th) at 647 and 666 (Ont. HC).

(5) Fraud by a non-party is tested more stringently than that of a party; and

(6) The new facts must provide a reason to set aside the judgment.

ENFORCEMENT AND EXECUTION OF JUDGMENTS

Remedies

The methods of enforcement of judgments and order are fourfold:

(1) Order for seizure and sale;
(2) Order for possession of land;
(3) Order for delivery of chattels; and
(4) Order of contempt.

Seizure and sale

Seizure and sale is an order to a sheriff to seize goods and sell them whether by private sale, tender or by auction to satisfy the judgment where the judgment-debtor has failed to respond to a demand for payment. Delays by judgment creditors in enforcing their judgments may impede their right to issue this order as may a change of circumstances such as the death of the other party. The initial order is valid for a two-year period and the renewal process is simple. There are provisions for judgment-debtors to apply for relief and to pay the judgment so to avoid the seizure and sale of rare or unique items.

Possession of land

Possession of land orders are more closely regulated. They are obtainable only if:

(1) Specifically provided for in the judgment; or
(2) Where the order is subsequently granted by leave of the court and only where it is shown by affidavit evidence that every party having an interest in the land has been notified of the proceeding.

Personal property

The order for delivery of personal property is designed to aid the recovery of specific property after judgment. If the particular property has been disposed of or has been hidden away then the judgment-creditor may apply to have other property taken in lieu. Such property will be held by the court to encourage the judgment-debtor to comply with the original judgment. If there is no compliance then the court will determine the manner of disposition of the substitute property and the amount of monies to be given to the judgment-creditor.

Order of contempt

The order of contempt is used only where the original order required the doing of some act or the abstaining from some action and is operative where a party disobeys a court order issued *in personam*. In recent years the courts have determined that parties in contempt proceedings should be accorded the protections available in criminal proceedings.[164] Where a party is found to be in contempt then they become subject to various penalties such as:

(1) Sequestration. This is the seizure of real or personal property to be held so as to deprive the owner of any benefits such as rents or profits; and

(2) Committal. This order is made to a court to ask that the delinquent party be contemned as the judge thinks fit — by fine, committal to jail or by an order to provide security for compliance to the order. The uncodified nature of the law of contempt and the criminal sanctions attached to it[165] have more recently raised concerns as to the constitutionality of this area of the law and particularly its relationship with the protections granted by the Charter of Rights and Freedoms within the Constitution Act (1982).

APPEAL

Prior to launching an appeal, it is necessary to apply for a stay of the trial judgment pending appeal.[166] The stay is put by motion to a single judge of the court of appeal, at which time it is necessary to satisfy the court

---

164. See Kearney, *Non-Compliance with Court Orders* (Carswell 1986).

165. See *Poge v. A-G (BC)* (1953) 1 SCR 516. A civil sanction may include a stay of proceedings where the plaintiff is in contempt: *R v. Innovation and Development Partners Inc.* (1994) 5 WDCP (2d) 123 (FCA).

166. See *Bannan Estate v. Wisotzki* (1990), 44 CPC (2d) 39 (Ont. CA); *Peper v. Peper* (1990), 1 OR (3d) 145 (CA); *Fulton Ins. Agencies Ltd. v. Purdy* (1992), 112 NSR (2d) 86 (CA); *Kelly v. PEI Agric. Dev. Bd.* (1993), PEIJ Number 41 (PEI CA).

that there is some exceptional or unusual circumstance to justify the invoking of the jurisdiction.[167] The case law teaches that the filing of an appeal does not of itself act as a stay unless ordered by the court. The grounds for stay are that:

(1) There would be undue prejudice to the appellant if no stay were granted;
(2) There has been a significant change of circumstances subsequent to the order appealed from;
(3) It appears that the appeal is based on *prima facie* strong grounds; and
(4) The appellant has discharged the burden imposed by the grounds above.

The right to appeal from a superior provincial court staffed by a single judge to an appellate body made up of three or more judges is governed both by the legislation applicable to the particular appeal court as well as by the procedural rules. Thus, the grounds of appeal may vary by jurisdiction although the mode of proceeding is the same:

(1) By notice of appeal;
(2) By preparation of an appeal book;
(2) The composition of factums; and
(4) The hearing itself.

The notice of appeal gives details of the court and of the order appealed from; the grounds of appeal; the relief desired; and a draft form of the order sought. The appeal book contains the pleadings, transcripts of evidence, exhibits and notice of appeal and the decision and judgment appealed from. The factums or submissions summarise the relevant facts; state the errors in the decision and judgment; state the law relied on in the form of judicial decisions and statutory provisions, a description of the relief claimed and a request for costs of the matter. At the hearing, counsel for the appellant addresse's the court on the issues, followed by the respondent's counsel and concluding with a final reply by the appellant. At the close of the hearing the court may issue a decision but usually will reserve judgment. The court may:

(1) Set aside, affirm or vary the order appealed from;
(2) Allow any amendment;

167. See *Mullin* v. *Mullin* (1992), 2 PEIR B20; *Clow* v. *MacNevin* (1986), 60 Nfld. & PEIR 360 (PEI CA).

(3) Allow a new trial; or

(4) Make a determination *de novo*.

CONCLUSIVENESS OF JUDGMENT

Res judicata

The plea *res judicata* is predicated usually on the existence of a prior action between the same parties in which a final decision was rendered and which dealt with the same matter as that in the impugned action.[168] The courts, however, distinguish the dispute as to the recognition of a foreign judgment and the action in the foreign court which dealt with the merits of the case. Thus, the plea does not bar the action to recognise.[169]

The courts have distinguished between a restitution order, under Section 725 of the Criminal Code of Canada, made in a criminal fraud trial and a subsequent damage claim made in a later civil suit based on the fraudulent conduct.[170] Otherwise, the plea of res judicata will be effective where there has been an earlier judicial decision by a tribunal properly seized of jurisdiction whose decision was final and which spoke to the same questions involving the same parties now appearing before the court.[171]

Law of the case

The final judgment of the court of appeal may be appealed to the final appellate court, which is the Supreme Court of Canada.[172] Leave to appeal must be obtained from the court appealed from or from the final court itself. Since the Supreme Court of Canada hears only approximately 100 cases annually, the decisions of the provincial courts of appeal provide the law of the case for most civil disputes. The final court will only hear cases which raise a matter of public importance or

168. See *Sharma* v. *Ouellette* (1991), 2 CPC (3d) 289 (Ont. Gen. Div.).

169. See *Bridal Fair Inc.* v. *AD and D Promotions Ltd.* (1992), 6 CPC (3d) 152 (Alta. QB).

170. See *London Life Ins. Co.* v. *Zavitz* (1992), 5 CPC (3d) 14 (BC CA).

171. See *Ottawa Mut. Invest. Corp.* v. *Edmunds* (1992), 7 CPC (3d) 71 (Ont. Gen. Div.).

172. As to what is or is not a "final judgment", see *Vanderlaan* v. *Edinburgh Developments Ltd.* (1976) 1 SCR 294 and *National Capital Commission* v. *Pugliese* (1979) 2 SCR 104.

where the issue of law is worthy of resolution from a national perspective. Thus, the "final and conclusive" judgment of a matter is that of the intermediate appellate body.[173]

173. Cf. An Act Respecting the Supreme Court of Canada RSC 1985, c. S–26 Section 52.

CHAPTER 3

DENMARK

PETER FOGH AND FRANTS DALGAARD-KNUDSEN
Koch-Nielsen & Grønborg
Copenhagen, Denmark

ESTABLISHING JURISDICTION

Introduction

In Denmark, the judicial system is separated in ordinary and special courts. The ordinary courts treat all disputes that for lack of special character have not been referred to other courts or authorities. The ordinary courts are the Lower Courts (*Byretten*), of which there are 82 in Denmark, the High Courts (*Landsretten*) of which there are two covering the eastern and western part of Denmark respectively, and finally the Supreme Court (*Højesteret*). Further, there is a special type of ordinary court, located in Copenhagen, namely the Maritime and Commercial Court (*Sø-og Handelsretten*), which deals with maritime and commercial matters.

The most important special courts are probate courts and courts dealing with the relationship between land-owners and tenants. These courts rank next to the Lower Courts in the hierarchy of the Danish courts.

In general, a decision of a court may be appealed once, i.e., first instance Lower Court decisions to a High Court and first instance High Court decisions to the Supreme Court. Under very special circumstances, the Ministry of Justice may grant special leave to appeal whereby a judgment originally handed down by the Lower Court may finally be decided by the Supreme Court. Whether or not a case should be commenced before the Lower Court or the High Court is basically a question of the financial importance of the dispute. A dispute over an amount in excess of DKK 500,000 (approximately US $80,000) may be commenced before the High Court without a prior decision of the Lower Court. That has the advantage that the decision can automatically be appealed to the Supreme Court. Further, a High Court case is heard by three judges where only one judge is deciding a Lower Court case.

The organisation of the courts and the procedural rules applicable are all found in the Act on Civil Procedure (*Lov om Rettens Pleje* — the Civil Procedure Act), which contains more than 1,000 paragraphs.

Jurisdiction

Domicile

PHYSICAL PERSON

The main rule, which can be found in Section 235, Sub-sections 1 and 2 of the Civil Procedure Act, is that cases must be commenced at the domicile of the defendant. Domicile in Denmark is defined as the defendant's place of residence.

If the defendant has neither a known residence in Denmark nor abroad a case may be commenced in the circuit where he is temporarily present, even though he has not taken up residence. If the defendant has neither residence nor temporary presence, the case may be commenced in the circuit where he is known to have been residing last or was last seen.

CORPORATIONS AND OTHER JURIDICAL PERSONS

The government of Denmark is domiciled in the circuit where the authority being sued on behalf of the Danish state has its principal office.

Legal corporations, partnerships and the like are domiciled in the circuit where their principal office is located. If the corporation has no principal office or relevant information cannot be obtained, the corporation is deemed to be domiciled in the circuit where a member of the board of directors or the management is domiciled. In limited companies (*aktieselskaber/anpartsselskaber*) the domicile must appear from the articles of association of the company. The articles of association are publicly available, and consequently, the domicile of a limited company for jurisdictional purposes can always be established.

Additional basis for jurisdiction

In certain circumstances, a plaintiff may commence legal proceedings before courts other than the court of the domicile of the defendant. The more important of these possibilities are the following.

COMMERCIAL PEOPLE

With respect to claims arising out of commercial activities, the plaintiff may commence litigation in any circuit where the activity in dispute has been carried out. This is true even in cases where the domicile of the defendant is elsewhere.

IMMOVABLE PROPERTY

With respect to immovable property, cases may be commenced in the circuit where the immovable property is situated.

CONTRACTUAL CLAIMS

In matters relating to a contract, a defendant may be sued in the courts of the place of performance of the obligation in question. It should, however, be noted that this very important additional rule of jurisdiction is not applicable in respect of claims for payment of money. The reason for this is that according to Danish law the place of performance with respect to a money claim is always the domicile of the creditor. Consequently the Danish creditor would always be entitled under the place of performance rule to commence legal proceedings before a Danish court. That position was not deemed acceptable by the Danish Parliament.

International jurisdiction

As a member of the European Community (EC), Denmark has ratified the Brussels Convention[1] from 1968 as subsequently amended. This Convention provides protection to persons domiciled in the European Community (EC) in a way that they may only be sued in Denmark when the conditions of the Convention have been met.

Similar protection is now to be granted through the Lugano Convention to persons domiciled in those European Free Trade Association (EFTA) countries that are not already members of the EC (Norway and Switzerland).

For persons domiciled outside the EC and EFTA, jurisdiction in Denmark may be established based on temporary presence or based on property belonging to the defendant. Consumers domiciled in Denmark are granted a right to sue vendors or producers domiciled outside Denmark if the product has been advertised or offered for sale in Denmark prior to the purchase being made.

1. The Convention on Jurisdiction and the Enforcement of Judgments in Civil and Commercial Matters.

Choice of jurisdiction

Finally, jurisdiction may be established as per agreement. The Danish courts have a tradition for accepting jurisdiction clauses provided that the agreement is clear.

The only exception is that Danish courts will not accept jurisdiction over disputes that have no relation to Denmark whatsoever. The Danish courts are consequently not available for general international dispute resolution.

Service of summons or writs

Legal action in Denmark is commenced at the time when the writ is received by the court. The court will arrange for service on the defendant, and the defendant will at the same time receive guidelines as to how to behave in order to protect his interests. A judgment by default will not be given unless proper service has been made.

Domestic service

Domestic service may be made by postal means, and personal delivery.

BY POST

For postal service, the writ is posted directly to the defendant.

BY PERSONAL SERVICE

An employee of the court will deliver the writ by hand to the defendant either at his place of domicile, his temporary residence or his place of work. If the defendant personally cannot be found, service may be made on other members of the family or the employer.

The court decides whether service should be made by letter or by personal service. If neither are successful, the court may, at the request of the plaintiff, decide to make service by publication in the *Official Gazette* (*Statstidende*).

Service abroad

If the defendant has a known domicile or place of residence abroad, service should as far as possible be carried out abroad, and by the foreign authorities. Denmark has ratified the Hague Convention of 15 November 1965 on service abroad, which sets out very detailed regulations for service abroad.

ASCERTAINING THE APPLICABLE LAW

Regional law

Except for certain legislation applicable on the Faroe Islands (*Færøerne*) and Greenland (*Grønland*) which are part of the Danish Kingdom, Denmark does not have regional law.

The Faroe Islands and Greenland are in general covered by the law of the Kingdom of Denmark, but some legislation has been drafted specifically with respect to the Faroe Islands and Greenland, and some legislation has been passed by the local parliament. Certain provisions of the Civil Procedure Act, the corporate legislation and the bankruptcy legislation are not applicable on the Faroe Islands or Greenland.[2]

International conflicts of law

Danish courts do not at their own motion apply foreign law. Neither do Danish courts have an obligation to be familiar with foreign law nor at their own initiative to produce information in this respect. It is left to the parties of the litigation to inform the courts, firstly, whether foreign law is applicable and, secondly, the content of the foreign law system that should be applied. A choice of law clause will, however, be accepted by Danish courts and would not be contrary to any Danish statutes except in certain cases relating to consumers.

Denmark has ratified a number of Conventions which among other things deal with choice of law. One of the most important Conventions is the EC Convention on choice of law on contractual obligations (the Rome Convention).

The principles of all the Conventions, which are consistent with the principles applicable under Danish international conflicts of law rules, are that the parties' choice will be accepted, if such a choice has been made. Where no choice has been made, the law of the country to which the matter has its closest connection will be applicable. There are certain rules of presumption in Danish law and the above-mentioned Convention as to what factors are decisive in this question.

---

2. It would be beyond the scope of this chapter to go into detail with the differences, even more so as they are constantly being changed.

As a rule, the law of the country where the party who performs the characteristic obligation is domiciled will be applicable. In the case of immovable property, there is a presumption that the law of the country where the property is situated will be applicable (*lex rei sitae*). In disputes relating to transport, there is a presumption that the law of country where the transporter has his place of business is applicable.

Even though the Danish courts accept the parties' free will to choose the applicable law, this rule is subjected to certain restrictions in dealings with consumers. A consumer cannot, by accepting foreign law, lose the protection that he otherwise would have had under national mandatory legislation. The same will apply with respect to employment agreements, agency agreements and sole distributorship agreements.

COMMENCING THE ACTION

Written pleadings exchanged

Statement of claim

According to Paragraph 348 of the Civil Procedure Act, an action is commenced when a writ is submitted to the court. The writ must contain certain minimum information that is defined in the Civil Procedure Act. The information required is name and address of the parties, the name of the relevant court, the claim of the plaintiff, the evidence that will be submitted and a brief statement of the facts. In more complicated matters, the statement of facts and the statement of legal arguments will of course be more extensive.

The court has been seized of the matter when the writ is received by the court, even though it may take some time until the writ has been served on the defendant.

The plaintiff may ask for either payment of a certain amount of money plus interest and costs or request the defendant to recognise a right of the plaintiff. The latter will normally be asked for when the financial value of the plaintiff's claim cannot be ascertained or no financial value is present.

Further, the plaintiff may submit several claims, either cumulative, alternative or with different ranking. The fact that a plaintiff principally requests payment of x, and secondly requests payment of a lesser amount will neither in law nor in practice prejudice his legal position. The court will not take the fact that a subsidiary claim has been presented as a sign of weakness or a sign that the plaintiff accepts that his principal claim is not legally justified.

The court will not take claims or legal arguments into consideration if they have not been presented to the court in writing. The court has a right — and to a certain extent an obligation — to request the parties to clarify their legal documentation if the court does not find it sufficiently clear. The court may also direct the attention of the parties to a certain legal angle that has not yet been touched on by the parties. The court will, however, be reluctant to do so, if the parties are represented by counsel.

Statement of defence

When the writ has been served on the defendant, the court calls for the first meeting in the court, when the defendant is required to submit his statement of defence.

If the defendant does not appear or does not submit a statement of defence, the court may render judgment in default. If the defendant does appear, either personally or by counsel, the court will normally without exception grant a limited extension in order for the defendant to prepare his statement of defence, if he has not had sufficient time. During the preparation of the case, the parties will be called to appear before the court in preparatory meetings. These preparatory meetings are only meant for the purpose of exchanging pleadings, and no decisions are reached. They are very brief (often less than one minute). If the parties have retained counsel, counsel will normally be represented by a junior clerk or his secretary. The presence of clients during these preparatory meetings is not necessary and extremely rare.

Defendants domiciled abroad should be aware that any objections to the Danish jurisdiction must be made in the first preparatory meeting, and that the defendant otherwise will be held to have submitted to the jurisdiction of the Danish court. This basic principle is only deviated from under very special circumstances, and the exception should not be relied on.

Even though a defendant does not appear, and the court consequently finds in favour of the plaintiff by a judgment in default, the defendant may subsequently request the case to be reassumed within certain time limits. The court will generally allow such a request, but it will often be made conditional on the defendant providing security for the additional costs of the plaintiff related to the case being reheard.

Reply and rejoinder

Normally, either party is entitled to exchange one further written pleading (*replik* and *duplik*). There are no formal requirements as to the contents of these pleadings, and they often concentrate on a few items that have not been dealt with in sufficient detail in the statement of claim and the statement of defence.

When the final written pleading has been exchanged, the preparation is considered closed and a date for the final hearing is fixed. In theory, neither party may introduce new documents or legal arguments subsequent to the finalisation of the preparation, but in practice, the situation is somewhat different, provided that the opponent is given sufficient time to consider the new documents or arguments. Documents and arguments submitted shortly before the final hearing will consequently not be acceptable.

Joinder of claims by plaintiff

The plaintiff is entitled to submit a variety of claims against the same defendant in the same legal action, but he is also at liberty to commence separate legal actions, each dealing with a separate and independent claim.

This right of the plaintiff is, however, restricted to claims where a Danish court has jurisdiction. A claim against a defendant domiciled outside Denmark for which the Danish courts have jurisdiction does not give the plaintiff the right to join a totally independent claim against the same defendant for which the Danish courts do not have jurisdiction.

Joinder of claims by defendant

The defendant is entitled not only to request the claim of the plaintiff to be set aside, but also to introduce a counterclaim, even though not directly related to the claim of the plaintiff. Also, this counterclaim is subjected to the jurisdictional limitation that the counterclaim must be under Danish jurisdiction.

Joinder of parties

A plaintiff may commence the same legal action against a number of defendants, but the court will only accept the plaintiff's request to join the actions if the court has jurisdiction with respect to all the claims, or the claims are so closely related that in the view of the court, they ought to be dealt with in the same legal action. With respect to defendant's domicile abroad, it should be noted that Article 6 of the Brussels Convention gives the right to join a foreign defendant to a case commenced before the Danish courts.

Third party claims

Both the plaintiff and the defendant may join third parties under the action, provided that the claims are linked in a way that they ought to decided during the same action. The request to join a third party should be made at the earliest possible time in order not to unduly delay the principal action between the original plaintiff and defendant.

A third party may at his own motion decide to step into a pending action. This intervention may either be in the capacity as an actual party to the action, or merely in support of either of the original parties.

OBTAINING INFORMATION PRIOR TO TRIAL

Discovery of information prior to filing a writ

Introduction

With respect to physical evidence it can be necessary to ascertain the existence of such prior to submission of a writ to the court.

In order to secure the value of the evidence as such, it is important that the evidence is discovered by the parties in common.

Testimonies and statements from expert witnesses retrieved by one of the parties alone has only limited value as evidence in case the other party in a lawsuit causes doubt about the quality of the evidence retrieved on behalf of one of the parties alone.

Out-of-court expert witness statements

The parties to a dispute can establish an agreement to the effect that the disputed object is inspected and considered by an expert person without prior submission of the matter before a court.

If the parties have agreed to obtain an out-of-court expert statement, this agreement is usually interpreted so that a statement obtained in common prior to trial can be used as evidence during a subsequent lawsuit.

If the out-of-court inspection has been conducted reasonably, and if there is no reasonable doubt about the neutrality and the knowledge of the expert, the statement issued by the expert will be regarded as having similar evidentiary value as an expert statement obtained from an expert appointed in-court.

In-court expert witness statements without filing a writ

It is possible to advance a petition to the court concerning the appointment of an expert without filing a lawsuit at the same time. The appointment and the inspection are carried out in accordance with the rules concerning expert witness statements obtained in connection with a pending trial according to Section 196 and subsequent of the Civil Procedure Act. The court appoints the expert and fixes the salary to be paid to the expert.

The party that has submitted the petition concerning appointment of an expert carries all costs related to the inspection and the expert statement, including fees to the expert and to the court. The party invoking this procedure need not reimburse the costs of the opposite party to fees to lawyers and other expertise. However, the other party might advance claims for compensation of costs in connection with a subsequent trial.

Independent retrieval of evidence

It is possible to establish the existence of evidence, even if this does not take place for the purpose of a pending trial. This follows from Section 343 of the Civil Procedure Act.

A petition concerning independent establishment of evidence must be submitted to the court of the place where, for instance, the witness in question lives. With respect to inspection of physical evidence, the petition is submitted to the court at the place where this physical evidence can be found.

Where the evidence must be discovered in a foreign country, the petition must be submitted to the court to which any subsequent writ will be filed.

According to Section 343 of the Civil Procedure Act, the court can order the party invoking this procedure to compensate any costs incurred by the other party.

Discovery of information during a pending trial prior to oral pleadings

Introduction

After a writ has been filed with the court and until a date has been fixed for oral pleadings, the parties are free to obtain new information and to submit new documents and new evidence.

Obligation to produce evidence

Both parties to a civil court case have an obligation to produce any documents that the party has in his possession, and that the party intends to call on to support his claim. The plaintiff will list the necessary documents and evidence in his writ, and the plaintiff will submit copies of the documents to the court together with the writ, insofar as the plaintiff is in possession of the documents.

A similar rule applies to the defendant. The defendant will submit any documents that he wants to call on, together with his written reply to the writ. This follows from Section 351 of the Civil Procedure Act. However, these rules do not prevent the parties from subsequent submission of additional documents.

Prior to the oral pleadings, the parties can call on each other to submit documents and other physical evidence. If the parties omit to submit documents, which are necessary to support their claims, this may result in the case being dismissed, or the defendant being found liable in accordance with the claim advanced in the writ.[3]

If a party omits to fulfil a request from the other party to submit any documents in pleadings of the first party, the result is the same as if the party fails to provide an explanation during the oral pleadings. When the court judges on the evidence, the court may let the failure have effect to the benefit of the other party according to Section 298 of the Civil Procedure Act.

Third parties are also obliged to submit any relevant documents according to Section 299 of the Civil Procedure Act. Against third parties, this obligation can be enforced by the same means as used against witnesses, who unlawfully fail to provide their testimony. The rules concerning testimonies from witnesses are discussed briefly below.

Before the court orders the other party or a third party to submit documents, the party in question will have the opportunity to advance any objections against the order.[4]

According to Section 339 of the Civil Procedure Act, the court has a possibility to request a party to produce evidence. The court can do this at its own motion (*ex officio*). If the party in question does not comply with this request, the court can choose to let the failure have effect to the benefit of the other party in accordance with Section 344 of the Civil Procedure Act.

Expert witness statements during trial

The rules of the Civil Procedure Act concerning the competencies of the court in connection with in-court expert witness statements connote that the court has great influence on the carrying out of any inspections of physical evidence, and thereby the court has influence on the discovery of evidence.

3. Civil Procedure Act, Section 354.
4. Civil Procedure Act, Section 300.

The court has the possibility of rejecting a petition for appointment of an expert witness. The court may do so if the court finds that the questions to the expert include issues without relevance to the matter. The court can also reject a petition if the questions are beyond the expected competence and knowledge of the expert in question.

Statements from professional organisations

In certain types of cases, the parties usually request organisations or associations in the profession in question to submit a statement in general terms concerning the issues at stake. Often these statements are used instead of traditional statements from expert witnesses.

Explanations and testimony prior to oral pleadings

It is a basic rule that all evidence will be given directly during the oral pleadings before the court, which will decide the matter. Under particular circumstances, however, it is possible to interrogate parties, witnesses and expert witnesses prior to the oral pleadings. This might occur before another court. Typically, this might take place, if a witness lives distant from the court where the trial is pending, or if a witness or a party is seriously ill.

The court that decides the entire matter also decides if and where any interrogations prior to the oral pleadings will take place.

Use of discovery during oral pleadings

During the oral pleadings, the entire matter is presented to the court, and the relevant parts of the documents are extracted.

Subsequently, the parties, the witnesses and any expert witnesses are questioned, unless the interrogation has taken place during the preparation of the case for the oral pleadings.

The parties are not obliged to explain themselves orally during the proceedings. However, the court can let failure to provide an oral explanation cause procedural disadvantage to the party in question, whereby the failure is interpreted to the benefit of the other party according to Section 344 of the Civil Procedure Act. The same applies in the situation where the party does provide an oral explanation, but fails to reply to specific questions.

As witnesses, expert witnesses are obliged to provide supplementary explanation during the oral pleadings, if one or both of the parties so desire. The rules concerning witnesses are found in Chapter 18 of the Civil Procedure Act. This chapter contains rules, which grant relatives and other persons close to any of the parties the right to be exempted from the duty to testify in court.

INTERIM PROTECTION OF ASSETS PENDING TRIAL

Introduction

Within the sphere of civil procedure, Danish law offers two types of interim legal actions. One type is provisional attachment or injunction, used to freeze specific assets of a debtor. The other type is the interlocutory injunction or prohibition, which is used to make the other party abstain from carrying out any specified activity.

The interim actions are characterised in particular by the fact that the plaintiff has not established his right by means of a court judgment. Therefore, it is usually a condition for using the interim measures that the plaintiff puts forward certain security, usually a bank guarantee, for any liability for damages that might occur in the event of a wrongful interim legal action. The costs of financing a bank guarantee are not reimbursable in the subsequent calculation of a claim against the debtor.

It would be against the purposes of interim legal actions, if it was allowed to put forward extensive documentation before the Probate Court.

The limitation of the documentation is redeemed by the requirement for financial security for any claims for damages. After the issuance of a provisional attachment or an interlocutory injunction, the plaintiff must follow up by filing a writ to the ordinary courts in a so-called justification-case. The justification-case is needed to establish through an ordinary court procedure whether the plaintiff has the claimed rights, and whether it was correct to enforce the interim legal measures.

Despite any agreements concerning arbitration or foreign venue, the latter question will always be decided by a Danish court according to Danish law. However, the justification-case can be postponed until after the delivery of a court judgment in a pending trial before a foreign court or an arbitration tribunal.

The majority of the rules concerning attachment and prohibition are to be found in Sections 627–640 and 641–653, respectively. The conditions for using the interim measures were considerably tightened in 1989. To achieve a provisional attachment, it is now necessary to refer to specific circumstances that indicate that it is likely that the debtor is going to reduce the possibilities of the plaintiff to enforce any claims at a later point in time.

Provisional attachment

Attachment is an interim procedure that can only be used to secure claims for money. The purpose of attachment is to maintain the existence of assets, which at a later point in time can be sold to cover the claims of the plaintiff. However, the provisional attachment does not hinder other creditors to seek coverage in the attached assets. Therefore, provisional attachment in reality is to the benefit of all creditors, because the priority of the attachment in the asset in question, for instance, real estate, can be used by any other creditor, which obtains an order for levy of execution. In other words, the provisional attachment only establishes a protection against the debtors own dispositions.

A petition for effecting a provisional attachment will be submitted in writing to the Probate Court of the circuit where the assets are situated. The petition describes the specific circumstances that threaten the possibilities of the plaintiff to obtain his money later. The petition should also list any documents, which the plaintiff calls on. If these basic needs of documentation are not fulfilled, the Probate Court will dismiss the petition.

It is a condition that the plaintiff's claim concerns money. The outstanding amount need not be overdue, however. It is also a condition that the plaintiff does not possess a final judgment or other grounds, which otherwise would make the plaintiff in a position, where he would be able to enforce the claim directly.

Furthermore, the plaintiff must establish a likelihood of the fact that later it will be more difficult to obtain coverage of the claim. The plaintiff must refer to specific circumstances concerning the personal or financial situation of the debtor. The establishment of a probable cause can be done by means of documents or witnesses.

The plaintiff need not submit substantive documentation in order to establish the existence of a claim against the debtor. Attachment is excluded only if it is immediately quite clear that the claim does not exist. The plaintiff must substantiate the existence of the claim during the subsequent justification case.

The Probate Court will almost always require the putting forward of security, for instance, by means of an irrevocable on-demand bank guarantee, prior to the execution of an attachment. The sum of the guarantee can be subject to changes until the moment where the injunction has been executed. As a main rule, it will be required to put forward a guarantee of a sum equivalent to the creditors claim with addition of costs of the case.

In cases where the fulfilment of the conditions is absolutely clear, the court might refrain from demanding security. In cases where the creditor is not domiciled in Denmark, the courts have a tendency to demand security for a higher sum than the amount claimed by the creditor. With respect to ships, one should expect that the security will be equivalent to the charter cost for a limited period of time, often three to five days.

The court procedure itself can take place within the locality of the Probate Court, but often the execution takes place without prior notice at the domicile or the place of business of the debtor.

The debtor is allowed to avoid the attachment by means of putting forward security for the creditors claim with addition of interest and costs of the case, including the costs of the subsequent trial.

In case of execution in cash amounts, the assets are taken into custody by the Probate Court. An attachment with respect to negotiable bonds or shares, or with respect to warehouse stock means that the assets will be taken into custody by the creditor in order to constitute security against any third parties obtaining rights in good faith. With respect to attachment in relation to real estate, the creditor must register the attachment with the official land registry in order to obtain security against rights obtained by agreement in good faith.

If the debtor after the execution of the attachment still denies the existence of the claim, the creditor is obliged to file a writ with the ordinary courts within a week after the execution of the attachment. In this writ the claimant must claim the amount due, and must claim that the execution of the attachment was justifiable. If the court case concerning the existence of the claim must be filed with a foreign court, the time limit for filing the writ is extended to two weeks. If the writ is not filed in time, the consequence is that the attachment is null and void.

If, at the end of the court trial, it is found that the execution of the attachment was not justified or if the attachment was executed for a too large an amount of money, or if the grounds for the execution of the attachment subsequently have changed, the court will decide to repeal the attachment partially or in whole. In this connection the creditor can be obliged to pay compensation for damages to the debtor. There is strict liability if the claim did not exist. In other respects the liability is based on negligence. A preliminary attachment is automatically null and void if the debtor is declared bankrupt or if the estate of a deceased debtor is insolvent. If the debtor has registered a suspension of all payments, attachments cannot be executed.

Prohibition

By the issuance of a prohibition, the Probate Court can order persons and companies to omit actions that are in violation of the rights of the claimant.

The purpose of a prohibition is to secure the respect of a duty to an omission, and by means of a prohibition it is possible in an expedient manner to prohibit specific actions, which are violating or threatening to violate the rights of the claimant.

The conditions for execution of a prohibition are firstly, that the claimant establish and substantiate that the acts which he wants to be prohibited are in contradiction to his rights; secondly, that the defendant will carry out the actions; and thirdly, that the purpose of the right is lost if the claimant is required to establish his right through ordinary trial.

The Probate Court can refuse to execute a prohibition, if the court finds that ordinary rules concerning punishment and compensation for damages according to law, or possibly any economic security offered by the defendant, establish sufficient security of the right of the claimant. However, normally, the defendant cannot avoid a prohibition by means of setting up financial security.

Also, principles of proportionality apply, i.e., the Probate Court is not entitled to execute a prohibition, if the prohibition would impose damage or inconvenience to the defendant to an extent that is quite out of proportion with the interests of the plaintiff in the execution of the prohibition.

Accordingly, the Probate Court carries out a comprehensive investigation of the request from the claimant. If the claimant is not in a position to justify the execution of the prohibition immediately, the Probate Court can demand the setting up of economic security, normally by means of an on demand bank guarantee, for any liability for damages in case of an unjust prohibition. The size of the guarantee will depend on the character of the matter involved. Normally, the Probate Court notifies the parties about the execution of the prohibition after the claimant has put forward the security demanded.

A request for execution of a prohibition must be submitted in writing to the Probate Court in the district where the defendant has his venue. The procedural rules are similar to the rules applying in an ordinary civil trial in the first instance. However, the Probate Court can cut off evidence in cases, where the extent of the evidence is in conflict with the need for a quick execution of the prohibition, for instance, in connection with violation of intellectual property rights.

It follows from the ordinary rules of civil procedure that the defendant is not obliged to be present in the meeting in the Probate Court and is not obliged to submit any statements. The prohibition can be executed if the request has been served properly. A prohibition can also be executed without prior notice to the defendant, if this is of importance to the purpose of the prohibition. However, if the defendant is not encountered during the procedures of an execution of a prohibition without prior notice, the execution of the prohibition only takes place if the claimant is capable to substantiate that the conditions of the execution of the prohibition are fulfilled.

When a prohibition has been executed, the Probate Court, and if need be the police force, is required to assist the claimant to enforce the prohibition. The Probate Court is entitled to confiscate any movables, which have been used in connection with violation of the prohibition, or if there are certain grounds to expect that certain movables will be used for such purposes. The storage of such movables is at the cost of the claimant. In the event of an intentional violation of a prohibition, the Act entitles the claimant to initiate a penal court case with the purpose of imposing a penalty of fines or simple detention on the defendant. Furthermore, the defendant can be obliged to pay compensation for damages.

Within two weeks after the execution of the prohibition, the claimant is obliged to file a writ for an ordinary trial to justify the execution of the prohibition. The rules applying with respect to cases concerning justification of injunctions apply in the same manner.

Special rules concerning injunctions and prohibitions

Apart from the Civil Procedure Act, there a number of legislative provisions concerning injunctions and prohibitions.

Act Number 387 of 1938 includes certain provisions concerning exemption from injunctions and prohibition with respect to aircraft belonging to national states or which are used in public route traffic. Furthermore, Act Number 198 of 1950 contains rules concerning the possibilities of injunctions or prohibitions with respect to vessels belonging to foreign sovereign states.

Cases concerning injunctions in sea-going ships with a prohibition against the ship leaving the port in order to secure a maritime claim are dealt with in accordance with rules contained in Chapter 12A of the Maritime Act. Rules concerning prohibitions may also be found in Section 14 and Section 16 of the Marketing Practices Act. The latter provisions provide the consumer ombudsman with the right to execute a preliminary prohibition against actions in contradiction to certain provisions in the Act on Marketing Practices.

Finally, it should be mentioned that Section 653 of the Civil Procedure Act includes a provision whereby the Probate Courts are competent authorities in cases comprised by EEC Regulation Number 3842/86 of 1 December 1986, concerning protective measures to the effect of prohibition against the access of counterfeit products to the market.

SUMMARY JUDGMENTS

Generally, decisions of a court are handed down as judgments, orders or rulings.

Adjudication without trial or by special proceeding

As a starting point, the rules of procedure are not definitively binding since the rules of procedure can be amended by the parties by means of agreement. However, certain types of agreements are not valid, for instance, arrangements that create interference with the ordinary organisation of the courts or which deviate from principles of due process.

The parties can limit or clarify the case by means of explicit agreement or unilateral declaration that certain requirements or facts will not be disputed or will not be called on, or by writing off certain allegations.

Summary judgments

Summary judgments do not exist as such in the Danish system of procedure. However, it should be mentioned that the courts, if desired, can deliver a ruling distinctively concerning formalities, for instance, concerning dismissal of the case in the event of improper venue or mistaken identity of the defendant.

Default judgments

A court may deliver a default judgment if the defendant does not appear in court or if the defendant by other means does not represent himself properly. It is a condition for handing down a default judgment that the writ has been served correctly according to Danish law giving the defendant the proper possibility of appearing in court.

The defendant's failure to appear in court is usually caused by a positive decision of non-appearance, for instance, if the defendant acknowledges the claims or if the defendant simply gives up the matter. The failure to appear in court can also be caused by mistake or an accident.

Default judgments are handed down when the defendant does not appear in court; omits to submit a written reply or if he does not put forward any documents, which the defendant might call on. Failure in appearance is by far the most common ground for default judgments.

After the point in time where a date has been fixed for the oral proceedings in the trial, the defendant's failure in appearance does not cause the handing down of a default judgment. If the defendant has appeared in court or has been represented by a Danish attorney, the courts will be reluctant to deliver a default judgment without prior notification to the defendant.

As a main rule, default judgments are handed down in accordance with the claim of the plaintiff. The court's examination of the claim is limited to control whether the claims are consistent with the facts put forward in the writ. The facts presented by the plaintiff are accepted as a basis for the judgment.

If the claims are not consistent with the facts put forward in the writ, the verdict of the court will be in favour of the defendant. If the facts put forward only provide basis for a part of the claims of the plaintiff, the verdict will be in favour of the plaintiff to a corresponding extent. If the facts put forward are insufficient, the court might choose either to dismiss the case or to rule in favour of the defendant. However, the plaintiff can ask for a postponement of the ruling in order to supplement or correct the facts put forward.

However, even if the defendant has failed to appear in court, the court can choose to omit to hand down a default judgment, and instead postpone the case for a new meeting. In this connection the court will consider whether the failure has been caused by justifiable reasons or whether there are other excusable circumstances, as well as consider the points of view of the plaintiff with respect to a postponement of the case.

Other means of termination without plenary trial

Voluntary dismissal

A court case is regarded as voluntarily revoked by the plaintiff if the case is closed without the court having delivered any judgment or ruling.

According to Section 354, the court will close the case as voluntary revoked by the parties if both parties fail to appear in court. The plaintiff can file a new writ concerning the same issue, and if this takes place within three months, the plaintiff need not pay a new court fee.

Furthermore, if the parties agree, a court case can be revoked until the very moment where the court is adjourned in order to consider its ruling in the matter. Usually, the courts are willing to accept a revocation of the case until the very moment, where the court is going to deliver its judgment, if both parties agree on the revocation.

The plaintiff can revoke the case unilaterally until the moment that he advances his claims orally during the final oral proceedings of the trial. This follows from Section 359 and Section 366. After this point in time, revocation requires the consent of the defendant, because the defendant might wish to obtain a judgment in his own favour. Furthermore, the defendant might have counterclaims or might wish to protect himself against new writs in the same matter.

In cases of appeal, the plaintiff is not allowed to revoke the appeal writ without the consent of the defendant in the appeal case.

Dismissal for failure to prosecute

According to Section 354, Sub-section 1, the court will dismiss a case *ex officio* if the plaintiff fails to appear in court in the first formal court meeting. Notice concerning the order of dismissal is conveyed to the parties. In the case of dismissal the defendant is granted an amount to cover parts of his costs in connection with the case. Any rulings concerning costs to be paid from the plaintiff to the defendant remain in force even if the plaintiff in a subsequent court case obtains a judgment in its favour.

The court will also dismiss the case if the plaintiff appears in court, but omits to put forward any documents called on in the writ, or if the claim of the plaintiff is unclear.

Judicially assisted settlement

In all civil court cases, at first instance, the courts are obliged to try to settle the dispute between the parties, unless the court considers it impossible to reach a voluntary settlement of the matter.[5] Also, higher court instances are entitled to try to settle a court dispute.

An in-court settlement of a dispute can be reached by the parties themselves or the parties can acknowledge a proposal for a settlement put forward by the court. Frequently, a settlement is reached when the court informally has explained its immediate view of the case after the oral proceedings of the trial. In this way, the parties obtain a decision instantly. For the court, it is an advantage not to need to draft a judgment, which would take time and could be subject to an appeal. An in-court settlement of a court case is written down in the protocols of the courts. In connection with the settlement, the parties can agree on the distribution of the cost of the case, or the parties can decide to let the court rule on the cost issue alone.

An in-court settlement of a case is seen as an agreement between the parties and the validity of the settlement is based on the law of contract, and not on the rules of procedural law. As a starting point, violation of the settlement will be seen as a violation of the terms of a contract. However, an in-court settlement written down in the protocols of the court does benefit from the rules of execution. If the settlement concerns payment of a sum of money, the plaintiff typically has the right to invoke assistance from the Probate Courts after a fortnight, if the defendant has not fulfilled the agreement.

With respect to substantive law it should be mentioned that a new court case concerning the same issue as the court settlement does not result in dismissal, but will result in ruling in favour of the defendant according to the principle of *ne bis in idem*.

TRIAL

Trial stages

Setting the case for trial

A civil court case is ready for setting a date for the oral court proceedings when the parties have exchanged copies of the procedural documents; the

5. Civil Procedure Act, Section 268, Sub-section 1.

writ, the statement of defence, the plaintiffs reply (*replik*) and the defendants rejoinder (*duplik*) and any possible additional written statements, as well as after the filing of any written statements from expert witnesses. During the preparation, the case may have been clarified with respect to judicial and factual disputes. This often takes place in a special in-court preparatory meeting according to Section 355.

At the last preparatory court meeting before the oral proceedings, the parties must notify the court about which parties, witnesses and expert witnesses are going to be heard during the oral proceedings. Furthermore, the parties will estimate how many hours or days the court should reserve for the oral proceedings.

Depending on the general work load of the court in question, the date for the oral proceedings will be set for some three to twelve months ahead. When the date has been fixed the plaintiff must pay an additional court fee amounting to 0.2 per cent of the value of the case.

Not later than a fortnight before the oral proceedings are to take place, the attorney of the plaintiff must submit a booklet with copies of all documents or an extract of these to the court, if the case is pending before one of the High Courts or before the Supreme Court. In reasonable time before the oral proceedings, each of the parties will also notify its witnesses in order to attend the proceedings at specific points in time. If any of the witnesses are reluctant to appear in court, these witnesses can be ordered to do so by the court.

The scope and order of trial

The members of the court have, generally speaking, not been acquainted with the documents and the particular details of the case before the oral proceedings. The reason is that the Danish law of procedure is based on a principle of direct evaluation according to Section 148. In principle, it should be possible to judge on a court case on the basis of everything presented orally during the oral proceedings. The purpose of the oral proceeding is to establish a basis for the court to judge in the matter.

Due to the principle of direct evaluation, anything of particular importance in the matter will be dealt with in detail during the oral proceedings. At the beginning of the oral proceedings, the attorneys of each of the parties will read up the claims advanced by his client. The attorneys might put forward informal documents containing outlines of the claims and possibly also the allegations. Sometimes, the courts will ask the attorneys to provide an overview of the main grounds of the parties at the beginning of the oral proceedings in order to enable the court to see the purpose of the evidence put forward during the oral proceedings.

According to Section 663, either of the parties may object if the other party at this late point in time advances new claims, allegations or evidence. The court may disregard the objection where delayed advancement is excusable or it will cause a disproportionate loss to the other party if the objection is admitted. The court might also by itself reject new claims, allegations or evidence, even if the other party has not made objections. After the claims have been presented by the attorneys, the attorney of the plaintiff will explain the factual events of the case. Any circumstance of relevance to the case included in the information presented during the written preparation of the case or included in the documents will be described. Central issues can be brought forward directly in a natural context in the presentation. The presentation must be made in a bona fide manner so that factual disputes between the parties are described in a way whereby the attorney has not advocated solely the points of view of the plaintiff.

After the presentation of the entire case, the parties and witnesses are heard. After all evidence has been presented, including witness statements, the attorneys must advocate the points of view of the parties. The attorneys will highlight the factual circumstances supporting the points of view of their respective clients. In connection with the factual circumstances the attorneys will make the necessary legal references. The legal references will include explanations of the relevant legislative norms as well as court practice in the field in question.

Following the pleadings of the attorneys, the court frequently will offer to explain its preliminary and immediate view of the case. If the court consists of several judges, the points of view of the court will be expressed after a short break, during which the judges will consider the judgment. After the judges have delivered their manifestation, the parties can choose to settle the case on the basis of the guidelines expressed by the court.

If the parties do not want the court to express its preliminary view of the case or if the parties do not accept the result of the preliminary manifestation, the court will take the matter under consideration. The judgment is delivered in writing in a short court meeting, typically some one to three months after the oral proceedings.

Submission of evidence

All relevant written evidence is numbered and put forward during the preceding preparation of the oral procedure. To the extent necessary, this written evidence will be described and possibly read into the record during the presentation of the case at the beginning of the oral proceedings made by the attorney of the plaintiff. During the hearing of the parties and the witnesses they can be asked about their comments to parts of the written evidence. During the final pleadings made by the the parties' attorneys, these will set out and possibly repeat the content of central themes of the written evidence.

The points of view of the parties and the witnesses will to some extent become apparent from the documents of process exchanged between the parties during the preparation of the case. The documents of process are not pieces of evidence, however. The explanations given by the parties and the witnesses during the oral court hearing are therefore of central importance.

If expert witnesses have been called in during the preparation of the case, these expert witnesses will typically have delivered an expert statement, which has been filed during the preparation of the case. Such statements of expert witnesses are pieces of evidence. The oral statements made by the expert witnesses during the oral court hearing frequently are supplementary explanations to questions arising from the formulation of the written expert witness statements.

It is not uncommon to show pictures or samples of disputed physical evidence during the oral proceedings. Typically, pictures and descriptions of physical evidence have been put forward during the preparation of the case.

Presentation of evidence and the trial judge

Depending on the capability of the attorneys to describe the case and to examine factually and legally relevant issues, and depending on the comprehension of the members of the court, the court will to some extent during the oral proceedings direct questions to the attorneys of the parties and directly to persons being heard. Any questions from the members of the court are typically posed when the attorneys have finished their interrogation of the persons in question. However, often the Chairperson of the court will interfere in interrogations, if the interrogations are meaningless, irrelevant or biased. Interference by the Chairperson of the court might be caused by an objection from the attorney of the other party.

The members of the court normally do not interfere in the initial presentation of the case made by the attorney of the plaintiff, unless specific points need to be clarified. The court does not interfere in the final pleadings of the attorneys.

Evidence

Nature and purpose of evidence

A piece of evidence is always evidence of a relative value and the purpose of producing evidence always is to establish prevailing likelihood of one or another claimed fact. No pieces of evidence are of an absolute nature and this implies that any relevant piece of evidence should be included in the entire context of evidence.

It is an important task for the attorneys to create context and continuity in the many pieces of evidence produced. It is also an important task to filter unnecessary evidence concerning factual circumstances, which are not disputed.

Any piece of evidence can be taken into consideration, but the value of each piece of evidence is in the specific situation clearly dependent on the credibility of each piece of evidence.

Types of evidence

Evidence can be produced in almost any form. The pieces of evidence should be produced as original and immediate as possible. Because of this basic principle, any important explanations and statements from parties, witnesses and expert witnesses should be made or repeated orally during the hearing in court. The courts will attach importance to statements made directly in court because the presence in court gives the other party and the members of the court the access to interrogate the person in question and because statements made in court are made under the obligation to tell the truth. Violation of the latter obligation is sanctioned with fines, simple detention or imprisonment of up to four years.

JUDGMENT AND REMEDIES

Final judgment

During the in-court preparation of the case several decisions may have been made as orders or decisions. A decision, which finalises the pending of the trial before the court usually is made as a judgment.

Before a case is decided by means of delivery of a judgment, the court may have delivered a partial judgment concerning a part of the case. This partial judgment is delivered after in-court oral pleadings concerning that part of the dispute.

If the parties do not accept a settlement proposed by the court it will deliver a judgment. The result of the judgment will almost with certainty be identical to the result of the preliminary opinion stated by the court.

Entry of judgment

The final and full text of the judgment will include a summary of the claims and the factual circumstances of the case, as well as a summary of the allegations of the parties. Furthermore, the judgment must include reference to the factual and legal circumstances of importance to the final decision. The court is limited by the claims filed by the parties, whereby the court is not in a position enabling it to grant a party a higher amount of money than claimed by the party.[6] Similarly, the court may only take into consideration the allegations, which the party has advanced or which cannot be left out of consideration according to law.

The court is entitled to grant a party less than claimed by the party, even if the party in question has not advanced a secondary claim, if the lesser claim can be regarded as included in the major claim advanced by the party.

Under very particular circumstances, the court has a possibility to act *ex officio* and take into consideration allegations that have not been advanced by the party. In a dispositive case, for instance, concerning rights of parenthood, the court will also take into account circumstances and allegations not advanced.

In cases before the Supreme Court and before the High Courts the judgment or ruling will contain information about the different opinions expressed in connection with the vote casting of the judges concerning the result as well as concerning the grounds of a verdict. The names of the judges will also be revealed according to Section 218, Sub-section 1 of the Civil Procedure Act.

Types of remedy

Specific performance

The purpose of verdicts concerning specific performance typically is to establish the legal situation in cases where the opposing party is willing and able to honour the result of the verdict. A lawsuit concerning specific performance is of relevance in a situation, for instance, where the verdict will provide the plaintiff with the right to access via a specific road, or where the plaintiff will become owner of a specific object.

Substitution remedy

A judgment concerning substitution remedy is a judgment, by which the plaintiff obtains the legal basis for execution, typically for an economic claim.

A judgment, which constitutes a basis for action via the Probate Courts by means of execution is referred to as an enforceable judgment.

6. Civil Procedure Act, Section 338.

In order to obtain a substitution remedy, it is necessary that the claim is due for payment. A party can only obtain a judgment concerning a conditional obligation if it would not be reasonable that the party be required to fulfil the condition before the opposing party fulfilled its obligations.

Constitution, transformation or rescission

A constitutive judgment is a judgment that constitutes a new right between the parties. By the verdict, the court decides how the legal situation will be in a specific situation. The legal rights and implications exist at the moment when the constitutive judgment is handed down.

All court cases must, as a precondition, concern a specific situation. Danish courts will dismiss any cases that only have the purpose of clarifying a theoretical legal problem or situation.

POST-TRIAL MOTIONS

As a starting point, a judgment is final, and if a party has objections to a judgment, the judgment must be subject to appeal. The possibilities under appeal are dealt with in the section concerning appeal. If the courses of appeal have been exhausted or are not of actual relevance, there are a few other possibilities.

Attacks on judgments

A judgment, which cannot be changed by appeal or by reassumption without special permission has legal validity. This also applies even if the court subsequently should come to the conclusion that the judgment was, wrong. There exist no possibilities of alteration of a judgment once handed down.

However, the court is entitled to correct obvious errors of writing and calculation. Likewise, the court may also correct wrongful summaries of the allegations and circumstances referred to by the parties. Corrections can take place on the request of one of the parties, however, only after the opposing party has had the possibility to make a statement.

Grounds for new trial

Before a judgment has been delivered, the court may reassume the proceedings of a case, if the court finds it unreasonable to deliver a judgment on the basis of the documentation put forward. This follows from Section 346 of the Civil Procedure Act. Reassumption can take place *ex officio* or on request of one of the parties. However, it is a discretionary right of the courts.

The courts may accept the presentation of *nova* as new evidence or new allegations, if the reason for the delay is excusable errors or excusable negligence, according to Section 663 and Section 346 of the Civil Procedure Act. Even if the parties agree on filing of *nova* after the oral pleadings, the court may reject this.

New evidence can only be advanced if the court considers this evidence of importance to the case according to Section 339 of the Civil Procedure Act. After a judgment has been delivered, a new case concerning the same claims between the same parties will, generally be dismissed from the courts.

If a party is basing a new case concerning the same issues on new allegations, the new case is only admissible if the party did not or ought not to have known of the allegations, when the previous case was pending. Permission to file a claim concerning the same issues can be obtained if the allegations are of considerable importance to the matter and if it would cause considerable damage to the party in question if the first verdict was upheld.

If a party is basing a new case concerning the same issues on new evidence the party can obtain permission to carry out appeal, possibly to the third instance according to Section 399 of the Civil Procedure Act if the court considers the new evidence of importance to the case.

In the rare cases of procedural fraud, the first verdict is not cancelled, but according to Section 399 of the Civil Procedure Act, the Supreme Court can grant permission to extraordinary reassumption or appeal of the case.

Reassumption

Reassumption of a case entails an entirely new procedure within the same court, which has already delivered a judgment in the case. This is the major difference from appeal. Normally reassumption is only possible in case of default judgments, and thereby reassumption normally is a possibility for the defendant only.

Reassumption can take place without any particular permission if the defendant has filed a request for reassumption within four weeks after the delivery of the judgment.[7] The filing of a request for reassumption has suspensive effects on the judgment first delivered.

---

7. Civil Procedure Act, Section 367.

After the four week period has lapsed, reassumption may only take place with particular permission, which for instance, can be granted if the defendant did not obtain knowledge about the verdict until a later point in time.

EXECUTION OF JUDGMENTS

Remedies

Executive judgments, i.e., judgments that require certain actions from the judgment debtor are enforceable unless the judgment debtor voluntarily honours the claim of the judgment creditor.

The judgment debtor is awarded a time limit of fourteen days to honour the judgment unless the judgment specifies otherwise. It may be ruled in the judgment that enforceability can take place even if the judgment debtor has appealed the decision. Enforcement may be carried out in two ways, either through individual enforcement or general enforcement. Individual enforcement is the customary way of enforcing judgments.

Individual enforcement

Basis for enforceability

It is stipulated in Section 478 of the Civil Procedure Act which documents may serve as a basis for enforcement. A reference is made to judgments and decisions handed down by Danish courts or other authorities, whose decisions are enforceable. It is a precondition that the time limit for enforceability, i.e., 14 days has expired.

The Ministry of Justice is further authorised to give rules whereby judgments and other decisions handed down by courts and authorities in other countries are enforceable in Denmark. This has lead to Nordic judgments and EC judgments being enforceable under separate conventions, and will in future lead to EFTA judgments also becoming enforceable.

It is further stipulated in Section 478 of the Civil Procedure Act that enforceability may be carried out on the basis of a settlement provided that the settlement is in writing, that the settlement relates to a debt which has already fallen due, and provided that the settlement specifically states that it may be used as the basis for enforcement.

Similarly, enforcement may be made on the basis of an instrument of debt provided the instrument of debt so specifies. Finally, bank cheques and promissory notes may form the basis for enforcement.

Order for levy of execution

A request for an order for levy of execution must be in writing and a copy of the judgment or a settlement made in court must be submitted along with the request. If the request is made on the basis of other documents, such as an out of court settlement or an instrument of debt, the original document must be shown during the hearing in the Bailiff Court. When a request for enforcement of a money claim is made, the request must also contain a computation of the claim including interest and costs awarded. It is stipulated in Section 487 of the Civil Procedure Act that the request may be submitted to the Bailiff Court in the circuit where either the debtor has a domicile, conducts business or security may be found. If it is a request to be granted possession of a certain object the request should be submitted to the Bailiff Court in the circuit where the object is located.

If no circuit is competent based on the above principles, the request may be submitted to the circuit where the debtor can be found, even though he has no domicile in that circuit. The Bailiff Court serves the judgment debtor with the time and the place for the hearing, and further notifies the creditor or the creditor's counsel.

If the debtor does not appear even though having been notified properly, the hearing cannot be continued, but the court may decide that the debtor should be taken into custody by the police, after which the hearing will be continued.

During the hearing the debtor is obligated — under threat of criminal liability — to provide the information that the Bailiff Court finds necessary in order to carry out the enforcement. The debtor is consequently obligated to give information on his and his family's financial position.

If the debtor declares during the hearing that he cannot honour the request for payment, and that he is not able to grant any security for the claim and such declarations are given under oath, the creditor is barred from requesting a new order of levy of execution until six months after the declaration was given. The same applies if the Bailiff Court has knowledge that the debtor has given such a declaration of insolvency within the last six months. The purpose of this rule is that a debtor should not be forced to appear in Bailiff Court if it has no practical purpose.

Object of levy of execution order

Generally speaking an order can be made against all the assets of the debtor, of course provided that he can be identified as the owner of the asset.

There are, however, certain exceptions from this rule. The most important exception is that orders cannot be made as toward assets that are deemed necessary to maintain a modest home and a modest livelihood for the debtor and his family. An order may, however, always be made against real estate owned by the debtor. The relevant provisions may be found in Section 509, Sub-section 1 of the Civil Procedure Act.

A similar exception is set out in Section 515 of the Civil Procedure Act, according to which an order may not be made against assets which have special personal attachment for the debtor and his family, for instance, a wedding ring. The debtor may point to specific assets in which the order should be made. The creditor may consequently not choose freely between several assets if one is sufficient. An order may, however, always be made against cash and any security that was granted by the debtor.

The debtor may retain possession of the object provided that he enters into and fulfils an agreement of payment by instalments. Such an agreement will be made in the Bailiff Court, and the creditor is obligated to accept such an agreement provided that the full amount is repaid in less than 10 months.

Security against other creditors' rights

Execution levied against real estate and cars must be registered with the local court subsequent to attachment. Execution levied against assets other than real estate, cars, ships and aircraft become null and void after one year, unless the creditor before that time has requested an enforced sale of the object.

Realising the asset

The asset must be realised by public auction, and the creditor receives the revenue after deduction of costs. Real estate is often the most interesting object of orders for levy of execution, and the procedure governing an enforced sale of real estate may shortly be described as follows.

When the request for auction has been received, the Bailiff Court fixes a date for a meeting where the debtor will be advised as to his rights and obligations, provided that the real estate is the home of the debtor or his family.

If disputes between the creditors are expected or there are any other special circumstances, the Bailiff Court may call all registered creditors to a preparatory meeting.

Subsequently, the time for the auction is set, and the Bailiff Court notifies the debtor and all registered mortgagors. The auction will be published in newspapers and the *Official Gazette*. The auction is carried out by the Bailiff Court in the circuit where the property is located.

Enforceability of non-money claims

Claims not related to money may be enforced, under certain circumstances, without a proper basis for enforceability. The proceedings in the Bailiff Court are then referred to as immediate procedures (*umiddelbar fogedforretning*).

The rules for such procedures are found in Chapter 55 of the Civil Procedure Act. They are commonly used in disputes between divorced parents regarding their children and in disputes regarding repossession of assets bought on credit.

The request must be submitted to the Bailiff Court and contain the information necessary and proper documentation for the claim. Where the requesting party has shown to have a claim, but have not proved it in such a way that the Bailiff Court is entirely satisfied, the Bailiff Court may decide that the request should be enforced provided that the requesting party establishes security for the harm which may be caused to the other party.

General enforcement

Bankruptcy

The purpose of bankruptcy is to distribute the assets of the debtor equally between the creditors at the time of bankruptcy. Bankruptcy may be requested by a creditor or by the debtor himself by submitting a request to the Probate Court in the circuit where the debtor is domiciled.

The requesting party must be able to substantiate the basis of his claim toward the Probate Court and further to establish that the claim has fallen due or to show that the debtor will not be able to pay when the claim falls due.

The condition for bankruptcy is that the debtor is not able to pay his debts as they fall due. One may consequently be declared bankrupt based on bad liquidity. Mere insolvency is not sufficient.

Unless the debtor clearly has sufficient assets to cover the costs related to the bankruptcy proceedings, the requesting party will be asked to give security for costs. The security is presently set at DKK 15,000 (approximately US $2,500). The security will be released if it is established that sufficient assets are available. The obligation of the requesting party is limited to the security, and one will therefore not become liable to cover all the costs of the bankruptcy proceedings if they exceed the security established.

As of the date of bankruptcy no order for levy of execution may be given, no forced sale may be carried out, and no seizure of the assets are acceptable. Seizures and orders of levy of execution carried out less than three months prior to the date of bankruptcy become null and void without further action of the estate. Forced sale may only be carried out on behalf of the estate.

In certain circumstances, it is possible to have transactions set aside, even though they have been carried out prior to the date of the bankruptcy. A payment may for instance, be set aside if the creditor knew that the debtor was in severe financial difficulties when he received the payment. The assets of the debtor are distributed equally between the creditors. Some creditors have, however, preferential claims which must be settled before any dividend is paid to simple creditors. The preferential claims are costs related to the bankruptcy proceeding, certain claims of employees and certain taxes and dues.

The handling of bankruptcy estates is traditionally undertaken by lawyers.

Suspension of payments and composition

Under Danish law, it is possible to seek the assistance of the Probate Court in order to establish a composition of debt by reducing the claim of all creditors to a certain percentage. A request for such assistance and a request for suspension of payment may only be made by the debtor and cannot be initiated by any creditors.

A forced composition is conditional on a dividend to the simple creditors of no less than 25 per cent of the claims. A request for suspension of payment will be accepted by the Probate Court provided that the debtor shows that he will no longer be able to pay his debts as they fall due. The purpose of a suspension of payment is typically to obtain a period during which the debtor and his advisors may consider whether a forced composition is possible or if a request for bankruptcy should be filed.

Forced reduction of debt by court order

Private individuals may under certain circumstances request the court to grant them a reduction of their debts. The legal Danish term is *Gældssanering*. The rules can be found in the Danish Act on Bankruptcy.

The reasoning behind the institution of *Gældssanering* is that a creditor is generally better off receiving a small amount of his money instead of maintaining a huge claim that the debtor will be never be able to pay in full or in part. A debtor would have no initiative to earn a living and try to repay his debts if from the outset, it was evident that he would never be able to pay all his debts.

Consequently, the Danish Parliament has found that a private individual debtor with huge debts should be given a possibility of starting over. The remedy for this is *Gældssanering*.

Liquidation

Liquidation proceedings are only relevant with respect to solvent companies. If the liabilities exceed the assets the dissolution of a company must be done in accordance with the rules set out in the Act on Bankruptcy.

Recognition and enforcement of judgments under the Brussels Convention

The Brussels Convention is a double convention in the sense that it not only sets out certain rules with respect to recognition and enforcement of foreign judgments, but also contains separate jurisdictional rules which are binding on all courts within the EC. The jurisdictional rules are basically incorporated into Danish law as they stand, but with respect to the rules on recognition and enforcement the contracting states must to a certain extent be allowed to take their national legislation into consideration with respect to the procedure that must be followed.

In Denmark, the procedure has been set out in Act Number 325 of 4 June 1986 (Act on the EEC Convention).

The Brussels Convention will be extended to cover also the EFTA-countries as per the Lugano Convention.

Recognition of judgments

According to Section 3 of said Act a judgment[8] that has been handed down by a court in another contracting state (the judgment state) must as a main rule be recognised in Denmark. If the question of recognition is raised during a pending case in Denmark, the court will decide whether recognition must be accepted or whether the limited exceptions in Articles 27 and 28 of the Brussels Convention are applicable. Further, the court may stay the Danish case if the decision from the judgment state has been appealed or reassumed in that state.

If, for instance, a Danish plaintiff instigates legal proceedings against a German defendant before a Danish court, and proceedings involving the same parties and the same cause of action has already been finalised

8. As defined in Article 25 of the Brussels Convention.

in one of the other contracting states, for instance, Germany, the Danish court must recognise the result of the German court. If the German judgment has been appealed by the plaintiff in the Danish case, the Danish court may stay its proceedings until the German appeal case has been finally decided.

Enforcement of judgment

A request for enforcement of a judgment handed down by the courts of a contracting state is submitted to the Bailiff (*fogedretten*) in the area where the judgment debtor is domiciled. The request must be accompanied by:

(1) A transcript of the judgment, confirmed by the relevant court;
(2) Proof that the judgment is enforceable in the contracting state which handed down the judgment;
(3) Proof that the judgment has been served on the judgment debtor; and
(4) In the case of a judgment by default, proof that the writ or a similar document has been served on or made known to the defaulting party.

The Bailiff may request an authorised translation of any of the above documents.

If the party who requests enforcement is domiciled outside Denmark, the request must specify a person in Denmark to whom procedural messages may be dispatched. Normally that will be a Danish lawyer retained by the foreign party.

The Bailiff will on receipt of the request decide whether the request is acceptable. That decision will be made without the judgment debtor being notified and consequently without the debtor having any possibility of putting up a defence. The Bailiff may only refuse enforcement for the very limited reasons set out in Articles 27 and 28 of the Brussels Convention.

If the Bailiff decides that the request should not be admitted, the judgment creditor may appeal that decision to the High Court. The appeal must be lodged no more than one month after the decision has been made known to the judgment creditor, or two months if the judgment creditor is domiciled outside Denmark.

If the Bailiff finds that enforcement should be allowed, this decision will be served on the judgment debtor. He may appeal this decision within the above-mentioned time limits. Until the appeal case has been finally decided, the judgment creditor may request the Bailiff Court to freeze assets as security for future enforcement.

The appeal court may at the request of the judgment debtor stay the case if the judgment forming the basis of the request for enforcement has been made subject to appeal or the time for appeal has not yet expired. The court may under these circumstances also decide that enforcement is conditional on that the judgment creditor establishes security in case the judgment forming the basis for the request of enforcement is subsequently reversed by an appeal decision in the judgment state.

Possible defence

The general trend with respect to recognition and enforcement is that Danish courts are extremely reluctant not to accept a judgment from the courts of another contracting state, provided that the formal requirements have been met. A judgment debtor may of course refer to the ground for defence set out in Articles 27 and 28.

The defence of public policy set out in Article 27(1) is often discussed in theory, but in practice one should not expect to have a valid defence based on that rule. Danish courts have always had, and still have, a very restrictive view on the defence of public policy, even where not governed by a convention, and in matters covered by the Brussels Convention that view will be even more restrictive.

Convention with Nordic countries

Finally, it should be noted that Denmark has entered into a convention with some of the other Nordic countries (Sweden, Norway and Finland but not Iceland), in which it has been agreed not to enforce a judgment based on long-arm statutes. It follows from Article 59 of the Brussels Convention that an international obligation of the Danish state is acceptable to the other states that are party to the Brussels Convention. This means that a Dutch judgment against a defendant domiciled or habitually resident in Sweden cannot be enforced against assets in Denmark if the jurisdiction of the Dutch court has solely been based on a Dutch long-arm statute contrary to the Nordic Convention.

APPEAL (ANKE)

Attack on judgments

In general, one is entitled to appeal a decision and have the case tried by a higher court. If the High Court (*Landsretten*) is deciding a matter in its capacity as appeal court, further appeals will, as stated above require a leave to appeal from the Ministry of Justice. Lower court decisions are appealed to the High Court, and High Court decisions are appealed to the Supreme Court, provided that the case is not thereby tried for the third time. The permission from the Ministry of Justice is only given if the case is of a principle nature or other specific grounds can be found.

Where the claim is less than DKK 10,000 even first appeals are generally not permitted. The rules on appeal cases can be found in Chapter 36 of the Civil Procedure Act. The rules are more or less similar when comparing appeals to the High Court with appeals to the Supreme Court.

The Court of Appeal is freely entitled to decide the matter both with respect to facts and law. The only boundaries are those imposed by the parties when preparing the case.

Apart from the plaintiff and the defendant, parties who have been joined in the action are also entitled to appeal. If a party has died or been placed in bankruptcy, the estate will step into the position of the party including the right to appeal.

In a joint case where several individual parties appear on either side, each of these may appeal the decision for their own account and similarly a party may appeal a decision or parts of a decision that have affected the internal relationship between several defendants. Where the parties have been joined as necessary parties, appeal must be accepted by all the necessary parties.

It is illegal under Danish law to waive the right to appeal until the judgment has been rendered. If the parties wish to make sure that a decision is not made subject to appeal, the parties must agree on arbitration which under Danish law only under very rare circumstances may be challenged by legal actions before the ordinary courts.

The right to appeal may be waived subsequent to the judgment having been handed down. No form is prescribed for such waiver, and it may be given both directly and implied. In practice a waiver is given if a party has honoured the decision of the court without at the same time reserving his right to appeal.

An appeal to the High Court must be lodged four weeks after the original decision was rendered, and an appeal to the Supreme Court must be lodged eight weeks after the decision of the High Court. If the time limit is not met, the Ministry of Justice may as an exception grant a right to appeal as late as one year after the judgment was handed down.

In general, the appeal case must concern the original dispute. If the parties agree, the appeal case may, however, be limited to only part of the original dispute or certain specific questions.

It is also possible to extend the object of the appeal case provided that circumstances have incurred after the original judgment was handed down. New claims are normally not taken under consideration. It is not specifically prohibited in the Civil Procedure Act, but the court has it within its powers to refuse such new claims even if the parties have agreed that the new claims should be accepted for consideration.

New documents and new evidence are admissible provided that the court is notified thereof at the latest two weeks before the scheduled date for hearing. Even if that time limit is not met, new evidence may be accepted by the court if the delay was excusable.[9]

New claims and new statements as to factual matters are admissible either with the acceptance of the other party or the acceptance of the court. Even if the other party does not accept the new claims or new statement of facts the court may grant permission provided that there is reason to believe that a refusal will inflict an unreasonable loss on one of the parties, or it is excusable that the submission has not been made earlier.

The new claims and statements with respect to factual matters must be presented during the preparation of the appeal case and not in the period after the preparation has been finalised but the hearing has not yet taken place.

The appeal is lodged when a request for appeal is delivered to the office of the Court of Appeal. As set out in Section 373 of the Civil Procedure Act, the request must contain:

(1) Identification of the decision made subject to appeal;
(2) Statement of the address of the defendant;
(3) The claim of the appellant;
(4) Statement of the facts, documents and other evidence which the appellant will refer to and which was not referred to in the Lower Court; and
(5) A postal address in Denmark where notifications to the appellant with respect to the matter may be transmitted and where service may be made.

A transcript of the decision subjected to appeal must be exhibited to the request for appeal.

The appellant may request the Lower Court's decision to be changed, annulled or referred for renewed consideration at the Lower Court. As prescribed in Section 376 of the Civil Procedure Act, the defendant's statement of defence in appeal must contain:

(1) The claim of the defendant;
(2) A reference of the statements, documents and other evidence which the defendant will rely on and which was not relied on in the Lower Court; and
(3) A postal address in Denmark whereto notifications to the defendant with respect to the matter may be transmitted and where service may be made. Any documents referred to, must be submitted along with the statement of defence.

9. Civil Procedure Act, Sections 380 and 381.

If the defendant only wishes the Lower Court's decision to be upheld, and does not wish to refer to any new statement of facts, documents, evidence or the like, a formal statement of defence is not necessary. The parties may exchange further written statements and preparatory meetings may be held in the court.

Generally speaking, the actual handling of the case in the Court of Appeal is corresponding to the way the case was dealt with in the Lower Court, as an appeal is a completely renewed trial. The Court of Appeal is restricted by the claims and submissions of the party, and the decision of the Court of Appeal will typically be either confirmation or amendment of the judgment subjected to appeal. The appeal may, however, be thrown out if the time limits have not been met or the request for appeal does not meet the requirements set out above.

Interlocutory appeal (kære)

Interlocutory decisions may be subjected to separate appeal *kære*. Alternatively, the judgment itself, which will be handed down at a later stage, may at that time be appealed. That later appeal will then incorporate an appeal on interlocutory decisions and decisions handed down during the preparation of the case.

Such decisions may be appealed by anyone to whom the decisions have implications or effects. It is not uncommon that other than the actual parties of the case have such a right to appeal. One example could be a third party having been ordered to submit certain documents to the court or give evidence, even though the person claims a right of privilege.

Such decisions may be appealed once, but further appeals will require leave to appeal from the Ministry of Justice. Also, unanimous decisions of the High Court may not be appealed without the decision of the Ministry of Justice.

The right to appeal also includes decisions from the Bailiff Court and the Probate Court. The request for appeal must be lodged within two weeks after the decision was handed down. The same time limit applies where the appeal is made to the High Court and to the Supreme Court.[10] Request for appeal of a decision of the Bailiff Court must, however, be made within four weeks. If the time limit has not been met, the Ministry of Justice may grant the right to appeal for as long as six months after the decision was made.

The appeal of an interlocutory decision is considered to be directed toward the court that made the decision. A request for appeal should be lodged with the court whose decision is made subject to appeal. The court

10. Civil Procedure Act, Section 294 .

will thereafter pass on the request for appeal to the Appeal Court, along with the files of the Lower Court and a statement of the court where the arguments for revision put forward by the appellant is countered.

Appeals of interlocutory judgments are normally dealt with in writing in a way that no oral hearing will be held. The Appeal Court may, however, allow oral hearing where special circumstances prevail.

CONCLUSIVENESS OF JUDGMENT

Introduction

In Danish law on procedure, a distinction is made between two types of conclusiveness — the formal conclusiveness and the substantive conclusiveness respectively. Both are, however, based on the concept that a winning party should be able to rely on the conclusiveness of the judgment when an appeal has not been lodged within the time prescribed.

The formal conclusiveness means that the judgment cannot be reversed, annulled or amended through an appeal or reassumption without special permission, whereas substantive conclusiveness has the effect that the decision will be binding between the parties, also in a possible future dispute.

Judgments rendered in Denmark are conclusive and enforceable in Denmark. The same applies with respect to foreign judgments if they have been handed down in one of the Nordic countries (Sweden, Norway and Finland) or in a contracting state to the Brussels Convention. Also, judgments from contracting states to the Lugano Convention will in the near future be directly enforceable in Denmark.

Decisions and orders are generally not conclusive if they are only interim procedural decisions. If the decision or order contains a ruling on a more factual issue (*materiel afgørelse*), such a decision or order will be conclusive and enforceable.

Substantive conclusiveness

The substantive conclusiveness has a positive consequence as well as a negative consequence. The positive consequence is that the findings in a judgement may be considered an established fact in other matters where it has prejudicial effect. Danish courts are, however, not bound by earlier decisions in the way that courts in Common Law countries would be.

The negative effect has as a consequence that a new proceeding, identical with a case that has already been decided, must be dismissed from the court. The dismissal may take place already while the first case is pending before the courts (*lis alibi pendens*). Subsequent dismissals are of course also a possibility under Danish law (*ne bis in idem*).

In practice it may be difficult to decide whether two causes of action are completely identical, but if new claims are made, identification is generally not considered to be present. If the new claim is, however, only a rephrasing of the old claim or only deviates from the old claim with respect to quantum, identification will be established. New legal arguments will not give the party the right to commence a new action, if the same cause of action has already been dealt with in an earlier decision between the same parties. The same will apply with respect to new evidence.

Formal conclusiveness

A decision is said to have formal conclusiveness when the customary time for appeal has expired, i.e., when four weeks have elapsed and an appeal has not yet been lodged with the High Court, or eight weeks have elapsed and an appeal has not yet been lodged with the Supreme Court. After the expiry of time the decision is conclusive in the sense that it is binding for the parties.

Generally, it will only be binding with respect to the parties of the case or the successors of the parties. There are, however, certain types of decisions or judgments that are also binding on third parties, but they are of an extremely limited nature and primarily related to family law and amortisation of promissory notes.

COSTS

In order to commence proceedings before a Danish court, the plaintiff must pay a court fee, which becomes due and payable when the writ is delivered to the court. The court fee is intended to cover the overall costs relating to the courts.

For money claims the initial court fee is 1 per cent of the claim. A further 0.2 per cent becomes due and payable when the preparation of the case is finalised and a date for the final hearing has been fixed.

If the claim is not for money, or it cannot be converted into money, the court fee is DKK 500, which approximately corresponds to US $75. The fees payable to technical experts and the parties' lawyers are paid by the parties themselves, but with a possibility of full or partial reimbursement from the losing party.

When the case is decided the court also decides whether a party will be awarded costs. It is not necessary for a party to submit a formal claim for costs, as it will be decided by the court at its own motion.

The main rule as stipulated in Section 312 of the Civil Procedure Act is that the losing party must reimburse the winning party the costs and expenses which the case has inflicted on him, unless the parties have made other separate agreement or the court under special circumstances finds it prudent to deviate from the principal rule.

If neither party can be said to have won the case, neither party is awarded costs, which means that the parties must bear their own costs. Where the court applies the main rule, and orders the losing party to reimburse the winning party the costs and expenses, these costs are fixed at a round figure. Expenses to technical experts are normally reimbursed "Kroner for Kroner" provided that the use of technical experts has not been excessive. The costs of counsel are, however, reimbursed on the basis of fixed percentages of the claim. The percentage used decreases as the claim increases. In general it can be said that the costs awarded in very large cases are sufficient, but in cases where the disputed amounts are less significant, the costs awarded will normally not cover the actual costs.

Generally speaking, a foreign national is awarded the same procedural position in Denmark as a Danish national. On the other hand, there are a few exceptions. One exception is that a foreign plaintiff may be asked to submit security for costs if the defendant so requests, and if the request of the defendant is accepted by the court. Such a security may not be requested by people domiciled in states that are contracting states to the Hague Civil Procedure Convention of 1954 or where bilateral agreements between Denmark and the country in question have been made on this issue. At present, this is the case with respect to Germany, France and the United States of America.

CHAPTER 4

ENGLAND

MAX THUM AND SARA WATSON
Ashurst Morris Crisp
London, England

ESTABLISHING JURISDICTION

Types of jurisdiction

Traditionally, the English courts have jurisdiction over England and Wales, but not over Scotland, the Channel Islands, the Isle of Man, or anywhere beyond the territorial waters. It should be noted that any subsequent reference in this chapter to England includes Wales.

The Civil Jurisdiction and Judgments Act 1982 (CJJA 1982) brought into force, for the purposes of United Kingdom law, the Brussels Convention on Jurisdiction and the Recognition of Enforcement of Judgments in Civil and Commercial Matters of 1968 (the Convention). The Convention to a large extent unifies among the Member States of the European Community the law applicable in determining the jurisdiction of civil proceedings. It applies when any dispute involves a foreign element. The CJJA 1982 was amended by the Civil Jurisdiction and Judgments Act 1991 to give effect to the Lugano Convention, which enables European Free Trade Association countries to join the Brussels Convention system. The Lugano Convention, although adopting the fundamental principles of the Brussels Convention, is not identical.

The Brussels Convention does not, however, cover all cases concerning EEC Member States. Proceedings outside the scope of the Convention include the status or legal capacity of natural persons, bankruptcy or winding up of insolvent companies, judicial arrangements or compositions, social security, arbitration, matrimonial property rights, revenue and customs, wills and succession.

It is, therefore, necessary when considering whether English courts have jurisdiction over cases concerning non-EEC defendants[1] or cases outside the scope of the Convention to apply the traditional English rules of jurisdiction.

---

1. Exception Convention, Articles 16 and 17; see below.

Jurisdiction over the parties to the action

NATURAL PERSONS

CJJA 1982 cases

The guiding principle in determining jurisdiction under the Convention is that the person domiciled in a contracting state should be sued there, and may be sued in another contracting state only in cases where the special rules of jurisdiction contained in the 1968 Convention apply.[2] Article 3 provides situations when persons domiciled in the contracting state may be sued in the courts of another contracting state.[3]

The Convention does not define the concept of domicile and states are required to refer to their own internal law for the definition. To bring English law into line with other contracting states, Sections 41–46 of the CJJA 1982 provide the definition of domicile for the purposes of jurisdiction. Section 41 provides that an individual is domiciled:

(1) In the United Kingdom, if he is resident in the United Kingdom and the nature and circumstances of his residence indicate that he has a substantial connection with the United Kingdom;

(2) In a particular part of the United Kingdom, if he is a resident in that part and the nature and circumstances of his residence indicate that he has a substantial connection with that part. If the individual satisfies the test as to domicile within the United Kingdom, but fails to satisfy the test as to domicile in a particular part, he will be treated as domiciled in the part in which he is resident;

(3) In a particular place in the United Kingdom, if he is domiciled in the part of the United Kingdom in which the place is situated and he is resident in that place; and

(4) In a state other than a contracting state, if he is resident in that state and the nature of circumstances of his residence indicate that he has a substantial connection with that state.

Residency is not defined, but would appear to mean purely the fact of living in a place. Similarly, substantial connection is not defined, but it will be presumed when an individual is resident for at least three months.[4] If an English court has jurisdiction by virtue of the CJJA 1982, a High Court writ may be served without leave outside the jurisdiction provided it is indorsed under the Rules of the Supreme Court (RSC) Order 6, Rule 7.

2. Article 2.
3. See below for more detail.
4. CJJA 1982, Section 41 (6).

Traditional rules

At Common Law, due service of process is sufficient to establish jurisdiction. As a general rule, service of process within the jurisdiction may be effected as of right, and service of process outside the jurisdiction (if not governed by the Convention) will only be permitted with leave of the court and will be subject to the court's discretion.

English courts claim jurisdiction over persons present in England and Wales even if their presence is only temporary. Persons who are members of a partnership firm can be served in accordance with the above rule. In addition, service can be effected at the firm's principal place of business (within the jurisdiction) on any person having at the time of service the control or management of the partnership business there or by sending a copy of the writ by ordinary first-class post to the firm at the principal place of business of the partnership, within the jurisdiction, whether or not any member of the partnership is out of the jurisdiction.[5]

The court does, however, have an inherent discretion to set aside proceedings because they are an abuse of the court process or to stay proceedings on the basis that the English Courts are not the most appropriate forum.

If the defendant is not resident in England or Wales, the courts have jurisdiction when a specific statute grants jurisdiction or if the defendant voluntarily submits to the jurisdiction. Where an overseas plaintiff commences proceedings in England and Wales, the court has jurisdiction to hear any counterclaim against him.

The High Court may also assume jurisdiction in an action on the grounds set out in RSC, Order 11.[6] Service of a writ on a defendant out of the jurisdiction is permissible with the leave of court in cases where:

(1) Relief is sought against a person domiciled in England (the definition of domicile is as stated in the CJJA 1982);[7]

(2) An injunction is sought ordering the defendant to do or refrain from doing anything in England (whether or not damages are also claimed);[8]

(3) A person is a necessary or proper party to a claim brought against a person duly served within or out of the jurisdiction;[9]

(4) The claim is brought to enforce, rescind, dissolve, annul, or otherwise effect a contract to recover damages or obtain other relief in respect of the breach of a contract if the contract:

5. RSC, Order 81.
6. This is connected with permission to serve process outside the court's jurisdiction.
7. RSC, Order 11, Rule 1 (1) (a).
8. RSC, Order 11, Rule 1 (1) (b).
9. RSC, Order 11, Rule 1 (1) (c).

(a) Was made within England;

(b) Was made by or through an agent trading or residing in England on behalf of a principal trading or residing out of England;

(c) Was by its terms or by its implication governed by English law; or

(d) Contains a term to the effect that the High Court shall have jurisdiction to hear and determine any action in respect of the contract.[10]

(5) The claim is brought in respect of a breach committed in England of a contract made in or out of England. This is irrespective of the fact that the breach was preceded or accompanied by a breach committed out of England that made performance within the jurisdiction impossible;[11]

(6) The claim is founded on a tort and the damage was sustained or resulted from an act committed within England;[12]

(7) The whole subject matter of the action is land situated in England or the perpetuation of testimony relating to land situated in England;[13]

(8) The claim is brought to construe, rectify, certify or enforce an act, deed, will, contract, obligation or liability effecting land situated in England;[14]

(9) The claim is made for a debt secured on immovable property or is made to assert, declare, or determine proprietary or possessory rights or rights of security, in or over movable property, or to obtain authority to dispose of the movable property situated in England;[15]

(10) The claim is brought to execute the trusts of the written instrument, being trusts that ought to be executed according to English law, and of which the person to be served with the writ is a trustee, or for any relief or remedy which might be obtained in any such action;[16]

(11) The claim is made for the administration of the estate of a person who died domiciled in England or for any relief or remedy that might be obtained in any such action;[17]

(12) The claim is brought in a probate action within the meaning of RSC, Order 76;[18]

---

10. RSC, Order 11, Rule 1 (1) (d).
11. RSC, Order 11, Rule 1 (1) (e).
12. RSC, Order 11, Rule 1 (f).
13. RSC, Order 11, Rule 1 (1) (g).
14. RSC, Order 11, Rule 1 (1) (h).
15. RSC, Order 11, Rule 1 (1) (i).
16. RSC, Order 11, Rule 1 (1) (j).
17. RSC, Order 11, Rule 1 (1) (k).
18. RSC, Order 11, Rule 1 (1) (l).

(13) The claim is brought to enforce any judgment or arbitral award;[19]

(14) The claim is brought against a defendant not domiciled in Scotland or Northern Ireland, in respect of a claim by the Commissioners of the Inland Revenue for or in relation to any of the duties or taxes which have been or are for the time being, placed under their care and management;[20]

(15) The claim is brought under the Nuclear Installations Act 1965 or in respect of contributions under the Social Security Act 1975;[21]

(16) The claim is made for a sum to which the Directive of the Council of the European Communities dated 15 March 1976 Number 76/308/EEC applies, and service is to be effected in a country that is a Member State of the European Economic Community;[22]

(17) The claim is made under the Drug Trafficking Offences Act 1986;[23]

(18) The claim is made under the Financial Services Act 1986 or the Banking Act 1987;[24]

(19) The claim is made under Part VI of the Criminal Justice Act 1988;[25]

(20) The claim is brought for money had and received or for an account or other relief against the defendant as constructive trustee and the defendant's alleged liability arises out of acts committed, whether by him or otherwise, within the jurisdiction;[26]

(21) The claim is made under the Immigration (carriers) Liability Act 1987.[27]

A plaintiff applying for leave under RSC, Order 11 must, as well as showing one of the grounds set out above, show that he has a good arguable case on the merits.[28] Leave to serve out of the jurisdiction is, however, subject to the discretion of the court, and in exercising its discretion the court's primary consideration should be whether the interests of justice are best served by proceedings in England or abroad.

19. RSC, Order 11, Rule 1 (1) (m).
20. RSC, Order 11, Rule 1 (1) (n).
21. RSC, Order 11, Rule 1 (1) (o).
22. RSC, Order 11, Rule 1 (1) (p).
23. RSC, Order 11, Rule 1 (1) (q).
24. RSC, Order 11, Rule 1 (1) (r).
25. RSC, Order 11, Rule 1 (1) (s).
26. RSC, Order 11, Rule 1 (1) (t).
27. RSC, Order 11, Rule 1 (1) (u).
28. *Spiliada Maritime Corporation v. Consulex Limited*, [1987] 1 AC 460.

CORPORATIONS

Civil Jurisdiction and Judgments Act 1982

The guiding principal of domicile, being the primary basis of jurisdiction under the Convention, applies to corporations as well as individuals. Article 53 of the Convention provides that the seat of a company or other legal person or association of natural or legal persons will be its domicile. "Seat" is not defined in the Convention. However, contracting states should refer to their national law for the definition.

Sections 42 and 43 of the CJJA provide that a corporation will have its seat in:

(1) The United Kingdom — if it was incorporated or formed under the law of a part of the United Kingdom and has its registered office or some other official address in the United Kingdom or its central management and control is exercised in the United Kingdom;

(2) A particular part of the United Kingdom — if it has its seat in the United Kingdom and either it has its registered office or some other official address in that part or its central management, and control is exercised in that part or it has a place of business in that part;

(3) A particular place in the United Kingdom — if it has its seat in a part of the United Kingdom in which place it is situated, and it has its registered office or some other official address, or its central management and control or its place of business in that place; and

(4) A state other than the United Kingdom — if it was incorporated or formed under the law of that state, and has its registered office or some other official address there or its central management, and control is exercised in that state, unless the court of that state would not regard it as having its seat there.

Official address means an address that it is required by law to register, and receive notices at. A corporation may under these laws have a seat in two or more places and, therefore, any jurisdictional conflicts should be settled in accordance with the provisions of Articles 21–23. Article 16 (2) provides that in proceedings concerned with the validity of the constitution, the nullity or the dissolution of companies or other legal persons or associations of natural or legal persons or the decisions of their organs, the courts of the contracting state in which the company, legal person or association has its seat will have exclusive jurisdiction. For a definition of "seat" in this case, see Section 43 of the CJJA 1982.

Traditional rules

As stated above, due service is, at Common Law, sufficient to establish jurisdiction. If a company is registered in England, then a writ may be served by leaving it at or sending it by post to its registered office and the English court will have jurisdiction.[29]

If a company is incorporated abroad, but.it has a place of business in Great Britain, it must in accordance with Section 691 (1) (b) (ii) of the Companies Act 1985 file with the Registrar of Companies the name and address of a person resident in Great Britain who is authorised to accept service of process on behalf of the company. Service is effected if such a person accepts service even if the company is no longer carrying on business in Great Britain.[30]

In *Rome v. Punjab National Bank* (No. 2),[31] it was held that it is not necessary for the person, whose name has been delivered to the Registrar of Companies to accept service. It is sufficient if the writ is left at the address for service. If the named person is no longer in Great Britain, or will not accept service or if for any other reason service cannot be effected in this manner, service can be effected by leaving the writ at, or posting to, any place of business established by the company in Great Britain.[32] Service may also be effected, if the corporation submits to the jurisdiction or the court assumes jurisdiction, as set out in the Rules of the Supreme Court.[33]

Article 3 of Brussels Convention

Article 3 of the Convention provides that persons domiciled in a contracting state may be sued in the court of another contracting state only by virtue of the Rules set out in Articles 5–18. As a result of this provision, English courts will have jurisdiction in the cases set out below.[34]

Where the parties, one of which is domiciled in a contracting state have agreed to submit to the English court, and if the agreement is in writing, or evidenced in writing, or is in a form which accords with practices which the parties have established between themselves, or in the case of international trade or commerce, if it is in a form that accords with usage of which the parties are or ought to have been aware and is widely known

29. Companies Act 1985, Section 725 (1).
30. *Sabatier v. The Trading Company* (1927) 1 Ch. 495.
31. [1989] 1 WLR 1211.
32. Companies Act 1985, Section 695 (2).
33. See above under "Natural Persons".
34. In Convention cases, jurisdiction can no longer be founded on presence of the defendant in the forum.

and regularly observed by parties to contracts of that type, the English courts will have jurisdiction by virtue of Article 17.

In the case of consumer and insurance contracts, the parties must comply with Articles 12–15 before they can rely on Article 17. Article 17 will have no effect where a court has exclusive jurisdiction under Article 16.

By virtue of Article 16, the English court will have exclusive jurisdiction regardless of domicile, jurisdiction agreement or submission to jurisdiction in the following cases:

(1) Proceedings which have as their objects rights *in rem* in immovable property or tenancies of immovable property where the property is in England;

(2) Proceedings that have as their object the validity of the constitution of a company;[35]

(3) Proceedings which have as their object the validity of entries in a public register if the register is kept in England;

(4) Proceedings concerned with the registration of or validity of patents, trademarks, designs or other similar rights required to be deposited or registered, if the deposit or registration has been applied for or has taken place in England or is under the terms of an international convention deemed to have taken place in England; and

(5) Proceedings concerned with the enforcement of a judgment if judgment has been or is to be enforced in England.

By virtue of Article 18, English courts shall have jurisdiction where the defendant submits to English jurisdiction by appearance, except where the appearance was entered solely to contest the jurisdiction or the court of another contracting state has exclusive jurisdiction pursuant to the terms of the 1968 Convention.[36]

By virtue of Articles 5 and 6, the plaintiff may choose to bring proceedings in the English court even if it is not the country of domicile of the defendant in the following cases:

(1) Where England is the place of performance of the obligations of the contract, the contracting state must determine, in accordance with its own conflict of law rules, what is the law applicable to the legal relationship in question, and define in accordance with that law the place of performance of the obligation. In relation to matters relating to individual contracts of employment, the

35. See above under "Corporations".

36. Under English law, the relevant rules of procedure relating to what would be regarded as an appearance in the High Court are contained in RSC, Order 12 Rules 7, 8 and 10.

place of performance of the obligation in question is "where the employee habitually carries out his work";[37]

(2) Certain matters relating to maintenance;[38]

(3) In matters relating to tort, delict or quasi-delict if the damage occurred or the event leading to the damages occurred in England;[39]

(4) Where a civil claim for damages or restitution is made in criminal proceedings against the Defendant domiciled in another contracting state or in Scotland or Northern Ireland to the extent that the court has jurisdiction under English law to entertain civil proceedings;[40]

(5) In the case of a dispute arising out of the operations of a branch, agency or other establishment, if the branch, agency or other establishment is situated in England;[41]

(6) Where the claim is made against a settlor, trustee or beneficiary of a trust,[42] if the trust is domiciled in England;[43]

(7) With regard to a dispute concerning the payment of remuneration claimed in respect of the salvage of a cargo or freight under the authority of the English court if the cargo or freight has been arrested to secure payment or could have been so arrested had bail or other security not been given. The defendant must have an interest in the cargo or freight or must have had an interest at the time of salvage;[44]

(8) Where the English court has jurisdiction in an action relating to the liability from the use or operation of a ship, the English court has jurisdiction over claims for limitation of such liability;[45]

(9) Where there are a number of defendants, one of which is domiciled in England;[46]

(10) To determine a third party claim brought by the defendant against the person domiciled in another contracting state or in another part of the United Kingdom in cases where the defendant is sued in proceedings in England, unless proceedings were instituted to deprive the third party of jurisdiction of the

---

37. Article 5 (1).
38. Article 5 (2).
39. Article 5 (3).
40. Article 5 (4).
41. Article 5 (5).
42. Article 5 (6).
43. See CJJA 1982, Section 45 to determine where trust is domiciled.
44. Article 5 (7).
45. Article 6 (A).
46. Article 6 (1).

court of the country which would otherwise be competent to determine the claim against him;[47]

(11) Where a plaintiff domiciled in another contracting state or in Scotland or Northern Ireland sues in English law, the English Court has jurisdiction to determine a counterclaim arising from the same contract or facts on which the original claim was based;[48] and

(12) In matters relating to contract, if the action may be combined with an action against the same defendant in matters relating to rights *in rem* in immovable property in England.[49]

The Convention also provides special jurisdiction provisions for insurance and consumer contracts.[50]

Defendant domiciled in Scotland or Northern Ireland

Section 16 of the CJJA provides that the Modified Convention in Schedule 4 of the CJJA shall have effect for allocating jurisdiction between the various legal systems in the United Kingdom in relation to matters within the scope of the 1968 Convention. The rules follow the 1968 Convention, but are not identical. These rules apply where the subject matter of the proceedings is within the scope of the 1968 Convention (whether or not the Convention has effect in relation to the proceedings) and the defendant is domiciled in the United Kingdom or the proceedings fall within Article 16 of the 1968 Convention (exclusive jurisdiction regardless of domicile).[51]

Resort must be had to Schedule 4 to determine allocation of jurisdiction within the United Kingdom, where under the 1968 Convention the courts of the United Kingdom would have jurisdiction. Schedule 4 determines jurisdiction for the most part by the domicile of the defendant. To determine whether an individual or company is domiciled in a particular part of the United Kingdom refer to Sections 41 (3) and 42 (4) of the CJJA. Differences from the 1968 Convention include the following:

(1) Article 5A provides that proceedings which have as their object a decision of an organ of a company or other legal person or of an association of natural or legal persons may be brought in the part of the United Kingdom where the company, etc. has its seat;[52]

47. Article 6 (2).
48. Article 6 (3).
49. Article 6 (4).
50. Articles 7 to 15.
51. CJJA 1982, Section 16 (1).
52. See CJJA 1982, Section 43 (3) for meaning of "seat".

(2) Article 5 (3) includes threatened wrongs and gives jurisdiction to the court in the part of the United Kingdom where the threatened wrong is likely to occur;

(3) Article 5 (8) provides that the courts of the part of the United Kingdom in which the property is situated shall have jurisdiction in proceedings concerning a debt secured on immovable property or which are brought in connection with proprietary or possessory rights or security rights in relation to movable property;

(4) Article 17 of the Convention is altered in three ways by the CJJA in respect of the allocation of jurisdiction between the English, Scottish and Northern Irish courts. First, the CJJA provides that if the parties have chosen the courts of a part of the United Kingdom as the forum for the trial, those courts will have jurisdiction. However, such an agreement does not give exclusive jurisdiction and a plaintiff can use the other bases of jurisdiction set out in the CJJA to sue in another part of the United Kingdom. Secondly, there is no requirement in respect of the form of the agreement, although there must be real agreement. Thirdly, the agreement must be effective to confer jurisdiction under the law of the part of the United Kingdom that the parties have elected to be the forum; and

(5) The provisions of the 1968 Convention relating to insurance and exclusive jurisdiction in relation to patents do not apply in relation to allocation of jurisdiction between United Kingdom legal systems.[53]

Venue

General principles

Most civil cases in England and Wales are heard at first instance either in the High Court by a High Court Judge or in the County Court by Registrars or Circuit Judges. Interlocutory hearings in a civil action are usually heard in Chambers before a Master (junior judge) in the High Court or a district judge in the County Court.

The High Court comprises of three divisions:

(1) The Chancery Division (which includes the Companies Court and the Patents Court);

53. For more detailed information regarding jurisdiction, refer to Dicey & Morris, The Conflict of Laws (12th edition) and Cheshire & North, Private International Law (12th edition).

(2) The Queen's Bench Division (which includes the Admiralty Court and the Commercial Court); and

(3) The Family Division.

Business between the three divisions is allocated primarily in accordance with the Supreme Court Act 1981, Section 61. However, all the three divisions have equal jurisdiction and each has wide powers to transfer any case to any other division or to hear a case even if it was started in the wrong division.

High Court actions are commenced either in London (Royal Courts of Justice) or in local District Registries. The High Court's jurisdiction is unlimited subject to a few exceptional cases. The High Court essentially deals with cases that involve complex law or facts or where a large amount of money is involved. The procedure in the High Court is regulated by the Rules of the Supreme Court 1981, which are divided into Orders.

County Courts have a jurisdiction that is limited to their locality. The general rule as to where a County Court action should be commenced is stated in the County Court Rules Order 4, Rule 2. An action may be commenced in the court for the district in which the defendant or one of the defendants resides or carries on business or in the court for the district in which the cause of action wholly or in part arose, or in the case of a default action in any County Court.

If a case is commenced in the wrong court that court may decide to continue it there or may transfer it to the proper court or may order it to be struck out.[54] In proceedings relating to land, the action must be commenced in the court for the district in which the land or any part thereof is situated.[55] The County Court's jurisdiction is set out in the County Courts Act 1984 Part II as amended by the High Court and County Courts Jurisdiction Order 1991. Although very wide, its jurisdiction is not unlimited.

Transfer of venue

BETWEEN DISTRICT REGISTRIES OR A DISTRICT REGISTRY
AND ROYAL COURTS OF JUSTICE IN LONDON

Transfer orders in the above case can be made on the application of any party or by a District Judge/Master without application.[56] Further, a defendant can by his acknowledgement of service apply for a transfer if the defendant's residence, or place of business or registered office (if a limited company) is not within the district of the issuing District Registry

54. CCR, Order 16, Rule 2.
55. CCR, Order 4, Rule 3.
56. RSC, Order 4, Rule 5.

and if there is no endorsement on the writ that the plaintiff's cause of action arose wholly or in part within the district.

TRANSFER BETWEEN DIVISIONS OF THE HIGH COURT

An action can be transferred between divisions on application under RSC, Order 4, Rule 3. The court has a discretion whether to grant the transfer. However, requesting a transfer in order to obtain an earlier trial date is generally not permissible.

TRANSFER FROM THE HIGH COURT TO COUNTY COURT

Under the County Court Act 1984, Section 40, the High Court has power to transfer the whole or any part of any High Court proceedings to the County Court. A party can apply by summons to a district judge/Master for an order of transfer and the court may also transfer the matter of its own motion.

RSC, Order 107, Rule 2 provides that no transfer will be ordered by the Court, unless the parties have either consented or have had the opportunity of being heard on the issue. The court shall take into account financial substance, importance, complexity and speed of trial when deciding whether to grant a transfer.[57] The High Court and County Courts Jurisdiction Order also sets out certain presumptions relating to value.

The criteria stated above apply in cases where no presumption operates, and are also relevant where a party is seeking to rebut a presumption. If the value of the claim is less than £25,000, the proceedings are presumed suitable for a trial in the County Court. If the value is greater than £50,000, the proceedings are presumed suitable for trial in the High Court. For actions involving sums between these two amounts, there is no presumption and the court will apply the criteria set out above.

TRANSFER FROM COUNTY COURT TO HIGH COURT

The County Court Act 1984, Section 41 provides that an application can be made in the High Court under RSC, Order 107 for the transfer to the High Court of the whole or part of any proceedings in a County Court. In addition, County Court Act 1984, Section 42 provides that the County Court may on the application of any party, order the transfer of the whole or part of any proceedings to the High Court if it thinks fit. Cases that

57. High Court and County Courts Jurisdiction Order 1991, Article 7.

should not have been commenced in a County Court must be transferred to the High Court or be struck out if the plaintiff(s) knew or should have known of the need to commence in the High Court.

In the case of matters that could have been tried in either Court, the court will apply the same criteria and presumptions as set out above. However, where the value of claim is over £50,000 the court will not apply the presumption that it is unsuitable for the County Court if it has been commenced there.

Service of writ of summons

Personal and postal service

RSC, Order 10, Rule 1 (1) provides that a writ must be served personally on each defendant by the plaintiff or his agent. RSC, Order 65, Rule 2 provides that personal service is effected by leaving a copy of the document with the person to be served. However, RSC, Order 10, Rule 1 (2) provides postal service as an alternative where the defendant is within the jurisdiction.

The proper place for service for individuals is their usual or last known address, while for partnerships, it is the principal place of business of the firm, and for limited companies, it is the registered office of the body. The date of service of a writ which is served by post or inserted through the letter box for the address of the defendant (other than a defendant company served under Section 725 of the Companies Act 1985) will, unless the contrary is shown, be deemed to be the seventh day after the date on which the copy writ was sent or inserted through the letter box.

A writ must not be served by registered post nor by recorded delivery as these means would afford the defendant an opportunity to refuse to take the letter. Service by post on companies under the Companies Act 1985 need not be sent by first-class post and is presumed to be delivered in the "ordinary course of post". In the case of limited companies, unless the contrary is shown, the date of service will be presumed to be, if posted by first-class mail, the second working day after posting and if posted by second-class mail the fourth working day after posting.

RSC, Order 11, Rule 5 provides that a writ served out of the jurisdiction need not be personally served as long as it is served in accordance with the law of the country in which service is effected, and need not be served by the plaintiff or his agent, but can be served by a British consular authority or by the government or judicial authorities of that country or by any other authority designated in respect of that country under The Hague Convention.[58]

58. RSC, Order 11, Rule 5 (5).

Publication

RSC, Order 65, Rule 4 provides that the court may make an order for substituted service of documents that must be served personally or a document to which RSC, Order 10, Rule 1 applies if it appears impracticable for any reason to serve the document in the prescribed manner. Substituted service is effected by taking such steps as the court may direct to bring the document to the notice of the person to be served. It may take the form of service by letter, advertisement or otherwise as may seem just. Substituted service should not be ordered where the defendant is out of the jurisdiction, but it may be ordered if the defendant is out of the jurisdiction with the aim of evading service.

Service of foreign process in England and Wales

Unlike many countries, the United Kingdom does not impose any substantial restrictions on the service of foreign process in the country. Plaintiffs are free to use whatever means of service available to them under the procedural rules of the relevant foreign court. It is for the foreign court to decide whether the mode of service employed has satisfied that court's "due process" requirements.

All that is required by English domestic law is that plaintiffs should have due regard to the substantive laws of England and Wales governing the acts of individuals, for example, service must not be effected in a way that would amount to an act of trespass or assault. Therefore, any attempt to effect service of foreign process in England must begin with a detailed consideration of the rules of the Court in which the action is pending.

However, it is necessary to consider treaty obligations between the United Kingdom and the relevant foreign country that provide for methods of service of process between the two countries. Such conventions may be permissive (in that they establish mechanisms for effecting service which exist as optional alternatives to any other method allowed by the laws of each country) or they may be mandatory (in that any attempt to effect service between the two countries must be conducted in accordance with the procedures established by the Convention).

The Hague Convention of 15 November 1965

"The Hague Convention on the Service Abroad of Judicial and Extra Judicial Documents in Civil or Commercial Matters" is a multilateral treaty governing the service within the territory of one Convention state of documents emanating from another Convention state. The United Kingdom is a party to the Convention. The treaty is stated in Article 1 to be of mandatory application.

The prevailing view at present is that if The Hague Service Convention is available, then it must be used. The basic mechanism it establishes for extra territorial service of process involves the transmission of documents between the central authorities of the two countries concerned. Each convention country is required to designate a central authority to whom formal request for service must be addressed.

Within England and Wales, the central authority is the Secretary of State for Foreign Affairs or alternatively, the Senior Master of the Supreme Court. In practice, all requests for service are dealt with by the Senior Master. The request sent to the Senior Master must comply, in form and content, with the requirements of The Hague Convention and of the Rules of the Supreme Court. The Senior Master is required to arrange for service to be effected in accordance with the provisions of RSC, Order 69.

Once service has been effected, the Senior Master will send to the person from whom the request was received a certificate, sealed with the Court Seal, stating when and how service has been effected. In addition to creating the basic central authority procedure for service, The Hague Convention also recognises and permits the use of the following methods of service.

CONSULAR AUTHORITIES

In accordance with Article 8, the United Kingdom permits the diplomatic or consular staff of other Convention countries to effect service of documents directly on a defendant resident within it's jurisdiction.

POST

In accordance with Article 10 (a) of The Hague Convention, the United Kingdom permits overseas plaintiffs to serve documents on defendants resident in it's jurisdiction simply by sending those documents to the defendant by post.

SERVICE BY JUDICIAL OFFICERS, OFFICIALS OR OTHER COMPETENT PERSONS OF THE STATE OF DESTINATION

This method is probably the most frequently used in practice. It allows for foreign process to be served in England directly by any person designated by English law as a "judicial officer, official or other competent person" of the United Kingdom. The United Kingdom has confirmed in writing to the Permanent Bureaux of The Hague Conference on Private International Law that Articles 10 (b) and (c) of The Hague Convention are interpreted as permitting any person in another Convention State who is interested in proceedings in that state (including lawyers) to effect service in the United Kingdom directly through an English solicitor retained for that purpose.

The solicitor will effect service in accordance with ordinary principles of English law and will swear an affidavit to that effect. It will be for lawyers of the foreign country to advise whether an affidavit of service sworn by an English solicitor will satisfy the procedural requirements of the courts of that country.

The use of any of the above methods is subject to the rights of each Convention state to object to any or all of those methods being used to effect service within its territory.

Brussels Convention

Article IV of the 1968 Protocol to the Convention creates a procedure somewhat akin to service through "central authorities" under The Hague Convention. Documents may be transmitted:

". . . by the appropriate public officers of the State in which the document has been drawn up directly to the appropriate public officers of the State in which the addressee is to be found".

The receiving "public officers" shall effect service and issue a certificate confirming that they have done so.

ASCERTAINING THE APPLICABLE LAW

Conflict of laws principles

In cases containing a foreign element, it is necessary to ask:

> (1) Does the English court have jurisdiction to entertain the case; and
> (2) If so, the law of which legal system will apply?[59]

Application of foreign law

The English court will initially apply the English choice of law rules in assessing whether the matter will be governed by English law. Having decided that a foreign law applies, the English courts must decide whether to apply the domestic law of the foreign country, or whether to apply the whole of the law of the foreign country, including its rules as to the conflict of laws.[60] If the latter option is adopted, the foreign legal system's

59. The general principles of jurisdiction are discussed above under "Establishing Jurisdiction".

60. *Halsbury's Laws of England*, Volume 8, para 413.

rules on conflict of laws may make a reference back to English law. This is called "renvoi". If this happens, the English court must then decide again which legal system will apply and whether it will accept the *renvoi*.

Domicile and residence

Many questions concerning the personal status of an individual are governed by his personal law. Domicile is the legal relationship between an individual and a territory with a distinctive legal system, which invokes that system as his personal law.[61]

An English Court will determine the question as to whether or not a domicile has been acquired for the purposes of English choice of law rules solely by reference to the principles of English law.[62]

Any person not legally dependent on another may at any time change his existing domicile and acquire a domicile of choice by the fact of residing in a country other than that of his domicile of origin with the intention of continuing to reside there indefinitely.[63]

Contracts

General

The "proper law" of a contract is the law that governs the contract and the parties' obligations under it; the law that determines (normally) its validity and legality, its construction and effect and the conditions of its discharge. The proper law according to English Common Law may be determined in three ways:

> (1) Express choice: parties to a contract may expressly stipulate that a contract should be governed by a particular law. The English courts will generally recognise that choice, provided that the choice is *bona fide* and legal and that there is no reason for avoiding the choice on the grounds of public policy;[64]
>
> (2) Implied choice: if there is no express choice of the proper law, the court will consider whether it can ascertain that there was

---

61. *Henderson* v. *Henderson* [1965] 1 All ER 179.

62. *Annesley, Davidson* v. *Annesley* [1926] Ch. 692. English law attributes to everyone at birth a domicile of origin. This is determined by the domicile, at the time of the child's birth, of the person on whom he is legally dependent.

63. See *Halsburys' Laws of England*, Volume 8, para 320.

64. *Vita Food Products Inc.* v. *Unus Shipping Company Limited* [1939] AC 277.

an inferred or implied choice of law by the parties. If the parties agree that the courts of a particular country shall have jurisdiction over the contract, there is a strong inference that the law of that country is to be the proper law; and

(3) Closest and most real connection: if the intention of parties cannot be expressed or inferred, the contract is governed by the system of law with which the transaction has its closest and most real connection. The principal factors that are taken into consideration are the place of contracting, the place of performance, the places of residence or business of the parties and the nature and subject matter of the contract.

Contract (Applicable Law) Law Act 1990

This Statute gives effect to the EEC Convention on the proper law applicable to contractual obligations. It applies to contracts entered into after 1 April 1991. Article 2 of the Rome Convention provides that any law specified in the Convention is to be applied whether or not it is the law of the other contracting state. Thus, English courts must apply its rules if, for example, the contract is between English law and New York law.

The basic principle under this Act is that the contract is to be governed by the law chosen by the parties. Article 4 provides that in the absence of choice, the contract is to be governed by the law of the contract to which it is most closely connected. A severable part of the contract that has a close connection with any other country may, by way of exception, be governed by the law of that country. Article 4 (2) sets out a number of presumptions, which are intended to identify the country with which the contract is most closely connected.

In general, it is to be presumed that the contract is most closely connected with the country where the party who is to effect the performance that is characteristic of the contract has at the time of completion of the contract, his habitual residence or, in the case of a body corporate or unincorporate, its central administration. However, if a contract is entered into in the course of that party's trade or profession that country shall be the country in which the principal place of business is situated or, where under the terms of the contract the performance is to be effected through a place of business other than the principal place of business, the country in which that other place of business is situated.

Article 4 (2) does not apply if the characteristic performance cannot be determined and the presumptions are to be disregarded if it appears from the circumstances as a whole that the contract is more closely connected with another country. This Statute also sets out rules for determining the applicable law concerning questions of existence or validity of the contract or in limited cases the capacity of the parties.

Torts

Where a tort takes place in England, the English court will apply English law to determine the rights and liabilities of the parties, even if the parties are aliens having only a temporary connection with England.[65]

There are no special rules as to jurisdiction applying generally to actions in respect of torts that took place in a foreign country. Accordingly, the English court has jurisdiction in respect of foreign torts whenever it has jurisdiction *in personam* over the defendant. A person claiming in the English court in respect of an act done in a foreign country must generally establish:

(1) That had it been done in England, the act would have been actionable as a tort according to English law; or
(2) That it is actionable, but not necessarily as a tort, under the law of the foreign country.

It is necessary to identify the place in which the tort is to be treated as having occurred. The primary consideration in jurisdictional cases would seem to be the place in which the defendant acted or failed to act.

Property

According to English law, property is classified as either movable or immovable stock. The law of the place where the property is situated determines whether that property is movable or immovable. In general, the English court has no jurisdiction to determine title to or the right to the possession of immovable property situated outside England. The English court therefore will not entertain any action for a declaration as to title to foreign immovables, or for possession of such immovables, or for injunctions having a similar effect.[66]

COMMENCING THE ACTION

Originating process

In the High Court, proceedings may be commenced by the following originating processes:

65. *Szalatnay-Stacho* v. *Fink* [1947] KB 1.

66. For further information, see Dicey & Morris, *Conflict of Laws* or *Halsbury's Laws of England*, Volume 8.

(1) Writ;[67]

(2) Originating Summons — this is applicable in cases where the principal question at issue is the construction of a statute or of any instrument made under an Act, or of any deed, will, contract or other document or some other question of law, or in cases where there is unlikely to be any substantial dispute of fact;[68]

(3) Originating Notice of Motion — this is applicable in non-contentious probate applications and judicial review;[69] and

(4) Petition — this is applicable in divorce cases and winding up petitions.[70]

The procedure in each case depends directly on the form of originating process used. Actions in the High Court are most frequently commenced by writ. What is set out in the remainder of this chapter is the court procedure specifically relating to writ actions, unless stated otherwise.

In the County Court, there are also four types of originating summons, namely:

(1) Summons (default or fixed date actions);[71]

(2) Originating Applications;[72]

(3) Petition (divorce and bankruptcy cases); and[73]

(4) Request for entry of appeal (for example, against demolition orders or closing orders made by local authority).[74]

The summons procedure is the most common process in the County Court, which is roughly equivalent to the High Court writ procedure.

Writ

A writ can be issued out of the Central Office of the High Court in London or out of any District Registry. In addition to the parties' names

67. RSC, Order 5, Rule 2.
68. RSC, Order 5, Rule 4.
69. RSC, Order 5, Rule 5.
70. RSC, Order 5, Rule 5.
71. CCR, Order 3, Rule 3.
72. CCR, Order 3, Rule 4.
73. CCR, Order 3, Rule 5.
74. CCR, Order 3, Rule 6.

and the names and addresses of the solicitor issuing the writ, each writ must contain one of the following indorsements:

(1) A concise statement of the nature of the claim made and the relief or remedy required (general indorsement); and

(2) An indorsement of the statement of claim, thus avoiding the need for a separate statement of claim to be served later ("specially indorsed writ"). This is only used in simple cases, for example, debt cases.[75]

The general indorsement forms the blue print of what the statement of claim may contain and, although it does not need to be a precis of the statement of claim, it must give sufficient details to enable the defendant to identify the occasion when the breach of contract or other wrong relied on is alleged to have occurred.[76]

Where the claim made by the writ is one which the Court has power to hear and determine by virtue of the Civil Jurisdiction and Judgments Act 1982,[77] the writ must be indorsed with a statement that the court has power under that Act to hear the claim and that no proceedings involving the same cause of action are pending between parties in Scotland, Northern Ireland or another Convention territory. This indorsement removes the need to seek leave to issue a writ for service outside England and Wales.[78]

RSC, Order 6 Rules 2 to 5 and RSC, Order 15, Rule 10A (1) also provide for indorsements in particular cases.

Drafting pleadings

Pleadings contain the statements of each parties' case. When drafting pleadings generally, the following points should be considered:

(1) Generally, facts not law or evidence should be pleaded;[79]

(2) Material facts only are to be pleaded, and anything immaterial will be struck out;[80]

(3) All material facts must be pleaded that is, every fact that a party needs to prove in order to establish its case. If a party omits to plead a matter, he will not be entitled to give any evidence of it at trial;

75. RSC, Order 6, Rule 2.
76. *The Jangmi* [1988] 2 Lloyd's Rep. 462 and [1989] 2 Lloyd's Rep 1 CA.
77. See above under "Establishing Jurisdiction".
78. RSC, Order 6, Rule 7.
79. RSC, Order 18, Rule 7.
80. *Davy* v. *Garrett* [1878] 7 Ch.D 473.

(4) The party need not plead any fact that the law presumes in his favour or the burden of disproving it lies on the other party, unless the other party has specifically denied it in his pleading. The party need not plead performance of a condition precedent since due performance is implied in every pleading;[81] and

(5) Points of law may be pleaded.[82]

Complaint — statement of claim

STATING THE ESSENTIAL ELEMENTS

When drafting a statement of claim, the general principles relating to pleadings as stated above should be adhered to, and the statement of claim should therefore include all material facts of the claim. In an action for negligence, the claim should always cover four issues, namely, the incident complained of, that the incident was caused by the defendant's negligence, the loss or damage the plaintiff has suffered thereby, and a claim for interest. In an action for a breach of a term of a contract, the claim should set out the following facts, namely, the agreement and consideration, term alleged to have been broken, breach of that term, consequences of breach, loss plaintiff has suffered thereby and claim for interest.

General damages, that is damages which the law will presume to be the natural or probable consequence of the defendant's action, need not be pleaded. In a claim for aggravated damages, the facts relied on to support the claim should be pleaded. A claim for exemplary damages or for provisional damages must be specifically pleaded together with the facts on which the party pleading relies.[83] Special damages, that is loss which depends on special circumstances of the case, must be specifically pleaded and particularised to be recovered. At trial, it must be proved by evidence that the loss was incurred and that it was the direct result of the defendant's conduct.

A statement of claim must not contain any allegation or claim in respect of a cause of an action, unless that cause of action is mentioned in the writ or arises from facts which are the same as, or include or form part of, facts giving rise to a cause of action mentioned in the writ, but subject to that, a plaintiff may in his statement of claim, alter, modify or extend any claim made by him in the indorsement of the writ without amending the indorsement.[84]

81. RSC, Order 18, Rule 7 (3) and (4).
82. RSC, Order 18, Rule 11.
83. RSC, Order 18, Rule 8 (3).
84. RSC, Order 18, Rule 15.

STATING THE RELIEF SOUGHT

A statement of claim must state specifically the relief or remedy which the plaintiff claims, but costs need not be specifically claimed.[85] It is normal practice for the prayer for the relief or remedy to come at the end of the statements of facts and to start. "The Plaintiff claims . . .", and then to set out separately and distinctly in numbered paragraphs the items of relief or remedy which are claimed.

The plaintiff should always claim in the one action every kind of relief to which he is entitled as he will be prevented from bringing a second action against the same defendant on the same cause of action in order to obtain relief that he might have obtained in the first action.

Where the damages claimed are unliquidated the plaintiff need not insert a specific figure, but may claim damages generally. Where the claim is for an injunction, the full terms of the injunction should be set out. The prayer should not be used to plead any material facts or to particularise any allegation of loss. The court has power to award interest under Section 35A of the Supreme Court Act 1981 and Section 69 of the County Court Act 1984, but it must be specifically pleaded in the prayer of the statement of claim.[86]

Types of answer — defence

In High Court proceedings, the defence must be served before the expiration of fourteen days after service of the statement of claim or after the time limited for acknowledging service of the writ, whichever is the latest.[87]

When drafting a defence, the general principles relating to pleadings, as stated above, should be adhered to. Every allegation of fact made in a statement of claim must be specifically traversed by the defendant in his defence otherwise it is deemed to be admitted. The defendant, when dealing with each fact, has the following options; namely:

(1) Admit — "plain and acknowledged facts which it is neither to his [defendant's] interest nor in his power to disprove".[88] The plaintiff will then not need to adduce evidence as to it at trial;

(2) Non-admission — facts where the defendant has insufficient information to allow him to deny or admit the matter and so will require the plaintiff to prove this part of his case; and

85. RSC, Order 18, Rule 15 (1).
86. RSC, Order 18, Rule 8 (4).
87. RSC, Order 18, Rule 2.
88. *Lee Conservancy Board* v. *Button* [1879] 12 Ch. 383.

(3) Denial — facts that the defendant intends to contest. The defendant should put forward a positive case, which he intends to advance. It is a usual practice when drafting a defence to include a "general traverse" at the end of the defence, such as: "Save as hereinbefore admitted the defendant denies each and every allegation contained in the statement of claim as if the same were herein set out and traversed each in turn."[89]

RSC, Order 18, Rule 8 provides that whenever a party has a special ground of defence or raises an affirmative case to destroy a claim, he must specifically plead the matter he relies on for such purpose. A list of examples of such "special defences" is set out below:

(1) In contract cases: discharge, release, variation or agency;
(2) In debt cases: defendant tendered the debt before the action was commenced;
(3) In damages actions: mitigation, quantum;
(4) In negligence actions: contributory negligence or negligence of third party;
(5) In assault and battery cases: self defence; and
(6) In any action: undue influence or mistake, fraud, the Limitation Acts, set-off, mitigation or damages.

Reply

A plaintiff must reply to the defendant's defence within 14 days after the service of the defence. RSC, Order 18, Rule 14 provides that if there is no reply to a defence, then there is an implied joinder of issue on that defence.

Replies therefore are unnecessary where the plaintiff just intends to deny the defences raised and it will only be needed where the plaintiff intends to give new facts to defeat the defendant's case to comply with RSC, Order 18, Rule 8 or to make any admission. The plaintiff must not in its reply make any allegations of fact or raise any new grounds of claims inconsistent with the statement of claim.[90]

Amendments to pleadings

The plaintiff only requires leave of the court to amend its writ if the writ has been served and if the amendments consist of altering the parties or

89. *Warner v. Sampson* [1959] 1 QB 297.
90. RSC, Order 18, Rule 10.

causes of action. Subject to such amendments, the plaintiff may prior to the close of pleadings[91] amend the writ once without leave of the court.

Prior to the close of pleadings, a party may amend any pleadings once without leave of the court.[92] The party served with the amended pleading may make, to his pleading, any consequential amendments. A party may amend its pleadings at any stage of the proceedings with the written consent of the other party[93] or with leave of court.[94] If the application is before trial, it should be made by summons to a Master, and if it is at or after trial leave can only be granted by the judge who tries the action.

The basic principle is that all amendments ought to be made "for the purpose of determining the real question in controversy between the parties to any proceedings or of correcting any defect or error in any proceedings".[95] In the case of *Clarapede* v. *Commercial Union Association*[96] Brett MR stated:

". . . however negligent or careless may have been the first omission, and, however, late the proposed amendment, the amendment should be allowed if it can be made without injustice to the other side. There is no injustice if the other side can be compensated by costs".

Amendments should be in the following sequential colours, namely, red, green, violet and yellow.

Supplemental pleadings

No pleading subsequent to a reply or a defence to counterclaim may be served except with the leave of court.[97] It is very rare that further pleadings, namely rejoinder (defendant), surrejoinder (plaintiff), rebutter (defendant), surrebutter (plaintiff), are ordered and leave will not be granted, unless it is really required so as to raise matters that must be specifically pleaded.

If a party's pleading omits to give any particulars that ought to be given or if the particulars given are insufficient or inadequate, the other party may apply for an order for particulars or for further and better particulars.[98]

91. Four days after the last pleading was served: RSC, Order 18, Rule 20.
92. RSC, Order 20, Rule 3.
93. RSC, Order 20, Rule 12.
94. RSC, Order 20, Rule 5.
95. Per Jenkins LJ in *GL Baker Ltd* v. *Medway Building & Supplies Limited* (1958) 1 WLR 1216.
96. (1883) 32 WR 262.
97. RSC, Order 18, Rule 4.
98. RSC, Order 18, Rule 12.

It is a normal practice to first make a written request for the required particulars and then it is only if the other party refuses to give such particulars that he can apply by summons to a Master. The court has power to order particulars on such terms as it thinks just which means it may order that if proper particulars are not served within a certain time the action shall stand dismissed or the defence be struck out.

Joinder of claims and parties

Joinder by plaintiff

The plaintiff may, in an action, join in more than one cause of action against the same defendant in the following cases:

(1) If he claims, and the defendant is alleged to be liable in the same capacity in respect of all the causes of action; or

(2) If he claims, and the defendant is alleged to be liable in the capacity of executor or administrator of an estate in respect of one or more of the causes of action and in his personal capacity, but with reference to the same estate in respect of all the others; or

(3) With leave of the court.[99]

Applications for leave are made *ex parte* by affidavit before the issue of the writ, and the affidavit must state the grounds of the application.[100] Unless the proposed joinder of causes of action is glaringly improper or obviously embarrassing or likely to cause delay or inconvenience, leave to join several causes of action will generally be allowed, leaving the defendant to object under Order 15, Rule 5 that they cannot be conveniently tried together or that joinder may embarrass or delay the trial.

Two or more persons may be joined together in one action as plaintiff or defendant with the leave of the court, or where the separate actions were brought by or against each of them, and some common question of law or fact would arise in all the actions and all rights to relief claimed in the action (whether they are joint, several or alternative) are in respect of or arise out of the same transaction or series of transactions.[101]

No person may, however, be added as a plaintiff without his consent in writing or any other manner as may be authorised.[102] All persons entitled to any relief or remedy jointly and not severally must join as plaintiffs, and if any one of them refuses he must be joined as a defendant.

99. Order 15, Rule 1 (1).
100. RSC, Order 15, Rule 1 (2).
101. RSC, Order 15, Rule 4 (1).
102. RSC, Order 15, Rule 6 (4).

Where it appears that the joinder of parties may embarrass or delay the trial or is otherwise inconvenient, the court may well order separate trials or make such other order as may be expedient.[103]

Joinder by defendant

The defendant can join causes of action by bringing a counterclaim. The defendant can add a co-defendant to the counterclaim without leave of court if the plaintiff is a defendant to the counterclaim and provided that the other person is liable to the defendant along with the plaintiff in respect of the subject matter of the counterclaim or the counterclaim is for relief or remedies related to or connected with the original subject matter of the action.[104]

Counterclaim

Where a defendant in an action alleges that he has any claim against a plaintiff or is entitled to any relief or remedy against the plaintiff in the action, in respect of any matter whatsoever, he may instead of bringing a separate action make a counterclaim.[105] The counterclaim does not need to arise out of the same transaction as the plaintiff's claim or be in any way connected with the main action. The court does, however, have power under RSC, Order 15, Rule 5 to exclude a counterclaim if satisfied that the defendant's claim should be brought as an independent action.

For virtually all purposes, the claim and counterclaim are treated as two independent actions and the counterclaim is governed by the same rules for pleadings as the statement of claim. A counterclaim stands as a cross action against the plaintiff. The plaintiff against whom a counterclaim is pleaded can in certain cases counterclaim against the defendant's counterclaim and the plaintiff may also bring third party proceedings. For Limitation Act purposes the counterclaim is deemed to be brought on the date that the writ was issued and not the date the counterclaim was served. The counterclaim must be served at the same time as the defence.

Cross actions

Where two or more actions are pending in the same division of the court and the same (common) question of law or fact arises in both or all of

103. RSC, Order 15, Rule 5 (1).
104. RSC, Order 15, Rule 3.
105. RSC, Order 15, Rule 2.

them, or the right to relief claimed arose in respect or arose out of the same transaction or a series of transactions or for some other reason where it is desirable to do so, the court may order the consolidation of two or more actions or order that they be tried at the same time or one immediately after the other or stay one of the actions until the other is determined.[106]

Third party claims

RSC, Order 16, Rule 1 provides that a defendant who has given notice of intention to defend may bring third party proceedings where:

(1) He claims against a person not already a party to the action for a contribution or indemnity; or

(2) He claims against a person who is not already a party for relief or any remedy relating to or connected with the original subject matter of the action and substantially for the same relief or remedy claimed by the plaintiff; or

(3) He requires that any question or issue relating to or connected with the original subject-matter of the action should be determined not only as between the plaintiff and the defendant, but also as between either or both of them and a third person not already a party.

Third party proceedings are possible only in cases commenced by writ or originating summons. No leave is necessary if the action was begun by writ and the defendant issues the notice before he serves the defence.[107] The defendant commences third party proceedings by issuing a third party notice and serving it on the third party with copies of the writ and any pleadings already served in the action.

The notice must state the nature and grounds of the claim or the nature of the questions to be determined and the relief sought. The third party is put in the position of the defendant in relation to the defendant who brings him in, and so may give notice of intention to defend or defend and counterclaim against the defendant. Immediately after the third party gives notice of intention to defend, the defendant must take out and serve a summons for third party directions on the third party and all parties to the action.[108]

On the defendant's summons for third party directions, any objections by the plaintiff must be considered and in giving or refusing directions,

106. RSC, Order 4, Rule 9.
107. RSC, Order 16, Rule 1 (2).
108. See RSC, Order 16, Rule 4 for orders the court may make.

care should be taken so that the plaintiff is not duly embarrassed or put into additional expense, delay or difficulty. The plaintiff may wish to seek leave to amend the writ to add the third party as second defendant. If the plaintiff does not, there is no direct procedural relationship between him and the third party and therefore if the third party is found liable the plaintiff's claim will fail.

Interpleader

Interpleader[109] is a proceeding initiated by a person, from whom two or more persons claim the same money, goods or chattels, and who does not himself claim the goods or chattels or dispute the debt. It is initiated in order to protect the person from legal proceedings by calling on the two or more persons to interplead that is, claim against one another, so that the title to the property or debt may be decided.

There are two types of interpleader, namely, cases where a sheriff seizes or intends to seize goods by way of execution and a person other than a judgment debtor claims them ("sheriff's interpleader") and all other cases ("stakeholder interpleader").

An application is made by originating summons, unless it is made in a pending action, in which case the application may be made by interlocutory summons. The court will then stay all proceedings other than the interpleading proceedings. The applicant (in the case of the sheriff only if ordered by the court) must produce affidavit evidence stating that he claims no interest in the money, goods or chattels (other than for charges or costs), does not collude with any claimant and is willing to dispose of the property as the court may direct.

On the hearing of the summons, the Master may dismiss the application, decide the merits of the claim summarily, refer the matter to a judge, transfer the proceedings to the County Court, refer the dispute to arbitration, order that a claimant be made defendant in an action already commenced or order that the issue be stated and tried.

Intervention

The general rule is that a plaintiff is entitled to choose the person against whom to proceed and to leave out any person against whom he does not desire to proceed. However, RSC, Order 15, Rule 6 (2) (b) permits a person who is not a party to be added as a party against the wishes of the plaintiff either on the application of the defendant or on his own intervention or in rare cases by the court, by its own motion.

109. RSC, Order 17.

The jurisdiction of the court under this rule is entirely discretionary. The purpose of this rule is to prevent the multiplicity of actions and to enable the court to determine disputes between all the parties in one, action and prevent the same or substantially the same questions being tried twice, with possibly different results.

An application by a person, who is not a party to an action, to intervene and to be joined as a party must be supported by an affidavit showing his interest in the matters in dispute or in the cause or matter, or showing the question or issue to be determined as between him and any party to the cause or matter. Generally speaking, intervention can only be insisted on in a representative action where the intervener is one of a class whom the plaintiff claims to represent, or where proprietary or pecuniary rights of the intervener are directly affected by the proceedings or where the intervener may be rendered liable to satisfy any judgment either directly or indirectly.

OBTAINING INFORMATION PRIOR TO TRIAL

The process of obtaining information prior to trial is generally known as discovery.

Types of discovery

Depositions

A deposition is a written record of the oral evidence of a witness on oath that is given before trial. Unlike the United States, depositions are rarely used in English proceedings and will only be ordered by the court in unusual circumstances.

RSC, Order 39 gives the court power in any cause or matter to make an order for the examination of a person on oath before a judge, an officer or examiner of the court where it appears necessary for the purposes of justice. The exercise of the power is discretionary, but the usual grounds on which such an order is made are where the witness is too old or too ill to attend a trial or might die or intends to leave the country before the trial.

The appointed examiner usually fixes a convenient time and place for the examination, when advocates of both sides can attend and evidence is taken in the usual way.[110] The application for such an order is made by summons before a Master, and if it is not made by consent, it must be

110. See Trial below.

supported by an affidavit setting out the circumstances in full detail and including the names of witnesses to be examined.

If the witness to be examined is outside England and Wales, the High Court can issue a letter of request to the judicial authorities of the country concerned for them to carry out the examination, or an order can be made for examination by a British consular authority (usually in the case of countries with whom a convention is made, for example, The Hague Convention of 1970 on the Taking of Evidence Abroad in Civil or Commercial Matters. The exercise of the court's power is as aforesaid discretionary and because the cost of obtaining evidence abroad is high, it will usually only be exercised where it is not possible to obtain evidence in other ways.

Interrogatories to parties

Interrogatories concern the discovery of facts and are a useful method by which to extract admissions or information from the other party by way of cross-examination. RSC, Order 26 allows any party to administer, without the leave of the court, interrogatories relating to any matter in question between the applicant and the other party in the cause or matter, which are necessary either for disposing fairly of the cause or matter or for saving costs.

Fishing expeditions will not be allowed and the rules specifically state that questions which relate solely to credit or to evidence of the party interrogated will similarly be disallowed.

Interrogatories may only be served twice without the leave of the court. The parties seeking the interrogatories must specify a period of time (not less than 28 days from the date of service) within which interrogatories are to be answered. If a party fails to answer interrogatories sufficiently or at all, the court may order that the action be dismissed or the defence be struck out.[111]

A party served with interrogatories may within fourteen days of service apply to the court for the interrogatories to be varied or withdrawn and on any such application the court may make such order as it thinks fit. The interrogatories must first be answered by affidavit, unless the court orders otherwise. The principles of privilege for discovery of documents apply equally to interrogatories.

Discovery of documents

Discovery in its narrower sense is the disclosure by one party to another of the existence of documents relevant to the action, which are or have

---

111. RSC, Order 26, Rule 6.

been in the parties' possession, custody or power.[112] The basic principle was formulated in *Compagnie Financiere du Pacifique* v. *Peruvian Guano Co.*[113] — any document must be disclosed which:

". . . it is reasonable to suppose contains information which may enable the party [applying for discovery] either to advance his own case or to damage that of his adversary or which may fairly lead him to a train of inquiry which may have either of these two consequences".

Discovery is, thus, not necessarily limited to documents which would be admissible in evidence. Discovery cannot, however, be used for "fishing expeditions" in order to find some claim/defence to raise. Discovery is an equitable remedy and, as such, the court has a discretion whether to grant it and can make such orders as are appropriate to prevent the remedy being used oppressively.

Disclosure of documents includes any record of information, for example, tapes and videos, photographs and computer records. There is a continuing obligation to make discovery, but documents that are disclosed can only be used in the action in respect of which they have been disclosed.

In most actions begun by writs, general discovery occurs automatically. RSC, Order 24, Rule 2 provides that fourteen days after close of pleadings, the parties must exchange lists in the prescribed form of all relevant documents that are or have been in their possession, custody or power. The documents must be made available for inspection within seven days and the inspecting party is entitled to take copies of documents. In practice, the parties normally agree to extend the time for discovery to take place. A foreign party to proceedings before the English courts is subject to the same discovery obligations as a resident party.

To attack another party's discovery, the parties may obtain an order that the opponent serve an affidavit verifying the list;[114] serve a further and better list; serve an affidavit stating whether the particular documents are or were in his possession, custody or power and if the latter when it ceased to be in his possession.[115] If a party fails to give discovery, a court can order that unless discovery is done within a set time the action should be dismissed or the defence struck out.[116]

The remedy of discovery is only *prima facie* obtainable against the persons properly joined as parties to an action and between whom some general question and action must be decided (that is, it is not usually ordered between third parties and the plaintiff). It is improper to join a

112. RSC, Order 24.
113. [1882] 11 QB 55 at 63.
114. RSC, Order 24, Rule 3.
115. RSC, Order 24, Rule 7.
116. RSC, Order 24, Rule 16.

stranger as a party merely for the purposes of obtaining discovery.[117] Exceptions to this rule are: (1) personal injury actions;[118] and (2) under the rule laid down in the case of *Norwich Pharmacal Co. and Others v. Customs & Excise Commissioners*,[119] where a non party has:

". . . got mixed up in the tortious acts of others so as to facilitate their wrong doing, he may incur no personal liability, but he comes under a duty to assist a person who has been wronged by giving him full information and disclosing the identity of the wrong-doers".[120]

Discovery of real evidence

Under RSC, Order 29, Rule 2, the court may make an order for the detention, custody, preservation of any property, which is the subject matter of the cause or matter or as to which any question may arise or the inspection of any such property in the possession of a party to the proceedings.

The court has the power to authorise any person to enter on any land or building in the possession of any party for this purpose. The court also has power to order as well as authorise a sample to be taken, observation made or experiment tried,[121] the delivery up of any goods under Section 4 of the Torts (Interference with Goods) Act 1977, which are the subject matter of the cause or matter or as to which any question may arise therein,[122] the recovery of personal property subject to a lien which may be on terms that the value of the lien be paid into court to abide the event of the action.[123]

The court also has similar powers prior to the commencement of proceedings under Section 33 (1) of the Supreme Court Act 1981 and in personal injury cases in respect of property that is not the property of or in the possession of a party to the action.[124]

In addition to the court's powers set out in the Rules, it also has power to grant an "Anton Piller Orde" permitting a plaintiff or potential plaintiff to enter the defendant or potential defendant's premises, inspect and remove specified documents or articles. The application may be made in any type of action (most common in patent and copyright actions) and is usually made *ex parte*.

117. *Elder* v. *Carter* [1890] 25 QB 194.

118. RSC, Order 24, Rule 7A.

119. 1974 AC 133.

120. See *Bankers Trust Company* v. *Shapira* [1980] 3 All ER 353 CA and *Arab Monetary Fund* v. *Hashim* (No. 5) [1992] 2 ALL ER 911.

121. RSC, Order 29, Rule 3.

122. RSC, Order 29, Rule 2A.

123. RSC, Order 29, Rule 6.

124. Supreme Court Act 1981, Section 34.

The Court of Appeal first approved such orders in the case of *Anton Piller KG* v. *Manufacturing Processes Limited* [1976] Ch. 55 and such an order is available where the court is satisfied that the applicant has an extremely strong *prima facie* case, the potential or actual damage to the applicant is very serious and the defendant has incriminating documents or things in his possession and there is a real possibility that he may destroy such material before an application *inter partes* can be made.

On granting *Anton Piller* orders, the court will require that the plaintiff gives undertakings including the following:

(1) The order and supporting evidence will be served on the defendant by a solicitor and the solicitor will explain the terms of the order to the defendant and advise him to seek immediate legal advice;

(2) Any documents obtained will be used solely for the purpose of the pending action;

(3) A writ will be issued if an order is made before time to issue a writ; and

(4) Cross-undertakings as to damages (the court will want to be satisfied that the plaintiff can comply with any undertaking). It is essential for an *Anton Piller* order to be granted that the defendant be subject to the court's jurisdiction and jurisdiction over a foreign party should not be assumed on an *ex parte* application nor before the foreign party has had an opportunity to contest it. In the case of *Cook Industries Incorporate* v. *Galliher*[125] it was held that the English court had jurisdiction to order a foreign defendant over whom it had jurisdiction to disclose the contents of a flat, in the defendant's name, situate out of the jurisdiction. Whether such jurisdiction should be exercised, however, is subject to the court's discretion.

It should be noted that there has been increasing judicial concern over the granting of *Anton Piller* orders due to their intrusive nature, particularly as they are made *ex parte* and often enforced at a stage where the defendant may not be in a position to obtain legal advice. *Anton Piller* orders are not therefore granted as readily as they once were and the courts have restricted the circumstances under which it will make such orders.[126]

125. [1979] Ch. 439.

126. See *Columbia Picture Industries Inc.* v. *Robinson* [1987] 1 Ch. 38, *Bhimji* v. *Chatwani* [1991] 1 ALL ER 705 and *Universal Thermosensors Limited* v. *Hibben* [1992] 1 WLR 840.

Use of discovery at trial

Depositions

A deposition will not be receivable as evidence in trial unless it was made pursuant to an order of the court and either the person against whom the evidence is offered consents or it is proved to the satisfaction of the court that the deponent is dead or beyond the jurisdiction of the court or unable from sickness or infirmity to attend the trial.[127] A party intending to use any deposition evidence at the trial must notify the other party of his intent within a reasonable time before trial.

Interrogatories

A party may put in evidence at trial only some of the answers to interrogatories or any part of an answer without putting in evidence of the other answers or the whole of the answer. The court may, however, look at the whole of the answers and if it is of the opinion that any answer or any other part of an answer is so connected with the answer or part used in evidence that the one ought not to be used without the other, the court may direct that the other answer or part be put in evidence.[128] The party who puts the interrogatories in as evidence is not bound to accept their truthfulness but may call other evidence which contradicts them.

Documentary evidence

A party who produces a document as evidence must prove to the court that it is authentic. Where a party is served with a list of documents under RSC, Order 24 that party is, as a general rule, deemed to accept the authenticity of every document contained in the list.[129] In other cases, a party who wishes to provide a document as evidence can serve within 21 days after the action is set down for trial a notice to admit.

If a notice of non-admission is not served by the opposing party within 21 days, the document is deemed to be admitted.[130] If a party unreasonably refuses to admit a document it may have a costs order awarded against it. To avoid the expense of proving every fact contained in a document a party should serve on the other not later than 21 days after setting down for trial a notice to admit facts under RSC, Order 27, Rule 2.

127. RSC, Order 38, Rule 9.
128. RSC, Order 26, Rule 7.
129. RSC, Order 27, Rule 4.
130. RSC, Order 27, Rule 5.

Generally, if any party wishes to put in a document as evidence at trial, he must produce the original document and if the original is not produced its loss or destruction must be proved. Where the original document is in the possession of the other party that party should be served with a notice to produce documents specified in the notice.[131] Where a party has served a list of documents that party is deemed to have been served with a notice to produce those documents at trial.

In practice, where a list of documents has been served, the usual procedure is for the parties' solicitors to get together to agree to a bundle of documents for use at trial. It should be noted that as generally the only documents disclosed to opposing parties are those documents that are in the possession, custody or power of the other party, documents in the possession of witnesses may only be revealed at trial for the first time.

The court can, however, order under RSC, Order 38, Rule 13 that any person attend any proceeding (interlocutory hearings and/or trial) and produce any documents necessary for the purposes of the proceedings. This Rule does not, however, confer any additional right of discovery against non-parties and in most cases will not enable documents to be produced sufficiently prior to trial to enable them to be considered. To overcome this problem, a practice has developed by which an application is made to the court supported by affidavit evidence requesting that the date of trial be brought forward for the purpose of a witness on whom a subpoena has been served to provide the required document. The trial will then be adjourned to the original set date.

INTERIM PROTECTION OF ASSETS PENDING TRIAL

Mareva injunction

In cases where a plaintiff is concerned that the defendant may dissipate or conceal its assets so as to make a judgment against him worthless or difficult to enforce, the plaintiff may apply to the court for a *Mareva* injunction, which will in effect freeze the defendant's assets. This form of relief was first approved by the Court of Appeal in the case of *Mareva Compania Naviera SA v. International Bulk Carriers SA the Mareva*.[132] This procedure is now embodied in Section 37 (3) of the Supreme Court Act 1981 (SCA 1981):

"... (3) the power of the High Court ... to grant an interlocutory injunction restraining a party to any proceedings from removing from the jurisdiction of the High Court or otherwise dealing with assets located within that jurisdiction shall be exercisable in cases where that party is, as well as in cases where he is not, domiciled, resident or present within that jurisdiction."

131. RSC, Order 27, Rule 5.
132. [1980] 1 All ER 213.

Generally, before a *Mareva* injunction is granted, the plaintiff must satisfy the court that the court has jurisdiction over the underlying claim of the action, he has a good arguable case, there are assets of the defendant within the jurisdiction, there is a real risk of removal or disposal of the assets, and that he is able to satisfy its undertaking as to damages. It should, however, be noted that the court will balance these requirements against hardship or prejudice that may be caused to the defendant or the third party as a result of the order.

An initial application for a *Mareva* injunction is made *ex parte* and an applicant must produce to the court a writ (or draft writ), affidavit and draft injunction. The plaintiff is under a duty to make full and frank disclosure and so the affidavit must give proper particulars of the claim, stating any arguments expected to be advanced by the defendant. The plaintiff should inform the defendant forthwith of the terms of the order, writ and affidavit and inform third parties affected by the court of their right to apply to the court for the order to be varied.

A *Mareva* injunction should also allow the defendant to draw reasonable living, business and legal expenses, which should take into account any special circumstances. The defendant may be required to make discovery as to his assets or administer interrogatories to ensure the injunction is effective.

The court may in rare cases consider it appropriate to grant a *Mareva* injunction that extends to assets outside the jurisdiction. A world-wide *Mareva* may be justified where there are foreign assets that are at a high risk of being disposed of and where there are insufficient English assets to satisfy a judgment. The court will want to be satisfied, however that the defendant is not oppressed and is protected by an undertaking or otherwise against misuse of information gained from orders for disclosure and that the position of third parties is protected. The court has granted world-wide *Marevas* in *inter alia* the following cases: *Babanaft International* SA v. *Bassatne*,[133] *Derby* v. *Weldon* (Nos. 3 and 4)[134] and *Derby & Co. Limited* v. *Weldon* (No. 6).[135]

SUMMARY JUDGMENTS

Adjudication without trial or by special proceeding

Striking out pleadings and indorsements of writs

By virtue of RSC, Order 18, Rule 19, the court may at any stage of the proceedings order that any pleading or the indorsement of any writ be

133. [1990] Ch. 13.
134. [1990] Ch. 65.
135. [1990] 3 All ER 263.

struck out or amended on the ground that it discloses no reasonable cause of action or defence, as the case may be; or is scandalous, frivolous or vexatious; or may prejudice, embarrass or delay the fair trial of the action; or is otherwise an abuse of the process of the court.

Not every pleading that offends the Rules will be struck out. The applicant must establish that he has been prejudiced in some way by the irregularity. The application should specify exactly what order is being sought and the grounds relied on. No evidence is admissible if the ground on which the application is made is that the pleading discloses no reasonable cause of action or defence,[136] but in all other cases the application should be supported by affidavit evidence.

Trial without pleadings

In most writ actions, where a defendant has given notice of intention to defend, either party may apply to the court under RSC, Order 18, Rule 21 for an order that the action may be tried without further pleadings. The court may make such an order if it is satisfied that the action can be properly tried without such further pleadings, and may instead make provisions for a statement of the issues in dispute to be prepared. The court may also give any further directions as to the conduct of the action as may be appropriate in the circumstances.

Disposal of a case on point of law

RSC, Order 14A provides that a court may on the application of a party or of its own motion determine any question of law or construction of any document at any stage of the proceedings where it appears that such a question is suitable for determination without a full trial and that such determination will finally determine the entire cause or matter or any claim or issue.

The court may not, however, decide any such question unless both parties have either had an opportunity of making representations on the issue or have consented to such an order being made. The court has the power not only to consider "plain and obvious" cases, but also to determine more complex questions of law, which might require more lengthy argument. However, it is essential that there be no dispute as to fact. This order strengthens the powers of the court when dealing with an application for summary judgment under RSC, Order 14,[137] since the court may in an appropriate case be able instead of granting leave to defend on the basis

136. RSC, Order 18, Rule 19 (6).
137. See below.

that the defendant has raised an arguable defence on a question of law proceed directly to determine that question and give summary judgment.

Judgment on admissions

Under RSC, Order 27, Rule 3, where a defendant has made a clear admission, a plaintiff may apply under this Order for judgment on that admission.

Summary judgments

Rules of the Supreme Court, Order 14

The procedure contained in RSC, Order 14 enables a plaintiff in most writ actions to obtain summary judgment (or a defendant in the case of a counterclaim) on his claim or part of his claim without the delay and expense of a full trial in cases where he can satisfy the court that the claim is unanswerable. The plaintiff can only apply for summary judgment once the writ and statement of claim have been served and the defendant has given notice of intention to defend.

An application under RSC, Order 14 is commenced by summons returnable before a Master or Registrar, unless the claim can only be granted by a judge (for example, an injunction). The application should be supported by an affidavit, which must verify the facts on which the claim or part of the claim to which the application relates is based and must state the deponent's belief that there is no defence to the claim or no defence except as to the amount of damages claimed. If a defence has been served or if there is some other delay between notice of intention to defend and issue of the summons, the reason for the delay should be explained.

The defendant may swear an affidavit in reply, which must show that there is an issue or question in dispute that ought to be tried or that there ought for some other reason to be a trial. The defendant does not need to show a complete defence, but all he must show is that there is a triable issue. The defendant can oppose the application by showing either that there is a preliminary or technical objection, for example, the case is not within RSC, Order 14 or the statement of claim or affidavit in support is defective, or by showing cause on the merits, for example, the defendant has a good defence to the claim, or a difficult point of law is involved or there is a dispute as to the facts that ought to be tried.

Unless the defendant satisfies the court that there is an issue or question that ought to be tried or that there ought for some other reason to be a trial of the plaintiff's claim, the court may give such judgment on the claim as may be just. Judgment can be confined to the whole or part of the claim. Usually in a successful claim for unliquidated damages, interlocutory judgment with damages to be assessed will be given. If the defendant satisfies the court that there is a triable defence or for some other reason there ought to be a trial, the court must grant the defendant leave to defend.

The court has power to grant conditional leave to defend (for example, leave can be granted subject to providing security for costs or payment into court of the whole or part of the sum claimed), where there are grounds for believing that the defence set up is a sham defence, or where there is something suspicious about the defendant's presentation of his case or where the court is left with "real doubt" about the defendant's good faith. If the defendant fails to comply with the condition, the plaintiff will be given leave to enter final judgment.

Rules of the Supreme Court, Order 86

The provisions of RSC, Order 86, which specifically relate to summary judgment in actions for specific performance, are very similar to those of the more widely applicable Order 14. In any action in the Chancery Division indorsed with a claim for either specific performance of an agreement for sale, purchase, exchange, mortgage or charge of a property; or grant or assignment of a lease; or rescission of such an agreement; or for forfeiture or return of any deposits made under such an agreement, a plaintiff may apply to the court for judgment on the ground that the defendant has no defence to the action.[138] An application may be made under this, Rule regardless of whether or not the defendant has acknowledged service of the writ. The procedure is the same as under RSC, Order 14 above.

Rules of the Supreme Court, Order 113

RSC, Order 113 provides for summary proceedings for possession of land that is occupied by trespassers, whose identity may or may not be known ("squatters procedure"). The application is brought by originating summons supported by an affidavit stating the applicant's interest in the land, circumstances in which the land has been occupied without licence or consent and in which the claim to possession arises and that the applicant does not know the name of any person occupying the land who is not named in the summons.

138. RSC, Order 86, Rule 1.

Default judgments

Judgment in default of notice of intention to defend

The defendant is generally given 14 days after service of the writ in which to acknowledge service.[139] In the case of countries that are party to the European Community Convention on Civil Jurisdiction and the Enforcement of Judgments, the period has been fixed at 21 days by Civil Jurisdiction and Judgments Act 1982. In the case of other countries, the time limit is specified by the Extra Jurisdiction Tables set out in Practice Direction (QB) 15, Paragraph 727.

RSC, Order 13 provides that if a defendant fails to give notice of intention to defend, the plaintiff may in writ actions indorsed with a claim for a liquidated or unliquidated demand (Rules 1 and 2) or for detention of goods (Rule 3) or for possession of land (Rule 4), after the prescribed time limit has expired enter judgment in default. Default judgments generally cannot be obtained in any case where a claim includes an equitable remedy (except default for service of defence), claim for provisional damages, admiralty actions *in rem*, where the defendant is a person under a disability (until guardian *ad litem* is appointed).

Where the claim indorsed on the writ does not come within the scope of Order 13 Rules 1–4, a plaintiff must proceed with the action as if the defendant had given notice of intention to proceed. In cases where the writ is indorsed for a liquidated demand or for the recovery of land only, then the plaintiff may enter final judgment. In cases where the writ is indorsed for an unliquidated demand or for detention of goods, the plaintiff is only entitled to enter interlocutory judgment (for example, in case of unliquidated demand, judgment for liability with damages to be assessed at a later date, while in a case of default judgment against one of several defendants, damages will be dealt with by a judge at full trial).

Generally, judgment under RSC, Order 13 can be entered without leave by lodging at the court office the writ, two copies of the form of judgment and proof that the writ has been served. Default judgments generally cannot be entered without leave of the court in crown proceedings,[140] tort actions between husband and wife,[141] re-opening of consumer credit agreements[142] and proceedings for the possession of a dwelling house.[143]

139. RSC, Order 12, Rule 5.
140. RSC, Order 77, Rule 9.
141. RSC, Order 89.
142. RSC, Order 83, Rule 3.
143. RSC, Order 19, Rule 5 and Order 13, Rule 4.

Leave is also required for entering judgment in default of intention to defend where the writ is served out of the jurisdiction under the Civil Jurisdiction and Judgments Act 1982[144] and where the defendant is a State.[145]

Judgment in default of service of statement of claim

In cases where the plaintiff fails to serve a statement of claim within the prescribed period, the defendant may apply to the court under RSC, Order 19, Rule 1 for an order dismissing the action. An application under this Order is made by summons to a Master, but the defendant cannot sign judgment as above and no affidavit is necessary. The court has a discretion under this Order to dismiss the action or make such order as it thinks fit. The court will always allow an extension of time where the default is due to an honest mistake by the plaintiff personally or by his solicitors, provided that the defendant is not prejudiced.

Judgment in default of service of defence

Where the defendant has failed to serve his defence within the prescribed time limit, the plaintiff may under Order 19, Rules 2–5 enter judgment against the defendant in the case of the same claims as under RSC, Order 13.[146] Similarly, a defendant who counterclaims can enter judgment when the plaintiff fails to serve a defence to counterclaim. If a defence is served out of time but before the plaintiff's application for judgment, judgment in default cannot be entered.

Judgment may be entered by depositing at the court office the original copy of the writ and two copies of the judgment with one copy certified by the plaintiff's solicitors to the effect that time for service has expired and the defendant has defaulted. The procedure is similar to the one under RSC, Order 13 and so judgment entered may be final or interlocutory, depending on the nature of the claim. In cases where the claim is not covered by Order 19, Rules 2–5, and the defendant fails to serve a defence, the plaintiff can apply to the court for judgment, and on the hearing of such an application, the court shall give such judgment as the plaintiff appears entitled to on the statement of claim. The application is by summons or motion.

144. RSC, Order 13, Rule 7B.
145. RSC, Order 13, Rule 7A.
146. See above.

Other means of termination without plenary trial

Voluntary dismissal

WITHDRAWAL OF ACKNOWLEDGEMENT OF SERVICE

By virtue of RSC, Order 21, Rule 1, a party who has acknowledged service may withdraw that acknowledgement at any time with the leave of the court. The application for leave is made *ex parte* to the Practice Master on production of the consent of the plaintiff's solicitor. If the plaintiff does not consent, the application must be made by summons to a Master. The leave of court will be indorsed on a sealed copy of the acknowledgement of service and the plaintiff will be entitled to proceed for judgment.

DISCONTINUANCE OF ACTION WITHOUT LEAVE

RSC, Order 21, Rule 2 (2) provides that a defendant to a writ action may without leave withdraw his defence or any part of it at any time by serving a written notice on the plaintiff. On such a withdrawal, the plaintiff will be at liberty to proceed either on the basis of a default of defence under RSC, Order 19 or on the basis of admissions in the defence under RSC, Order 27, Rule 3.

A plaintiff may under Order 21, Rule 2 (1) discontinue an action begun by writ or withdraw any particular claim without leave provided that discontinuance or withdrawal is effective within fourteen days of service of the defence, the notice of discontinuance or notice of withdrawal of a particular claim is served on each defendant concerned and an order for interim payment under RSC, Order 29, Rule 11 has not been made in the plaintiff's favour.

Where the plaintiff discontinues the action or withdraws a claim without leave, the defendant is entitled under RSC, Order 62, Rule 5 (3) to tax his costs against the plaintiff without an order of the court. If the costs are not paid within four days after taxation, judgment may be signed for them. The position of the defendant who wishes to withdraw or discontinue his counterclaim is similar in all material respects to that of the plaintiff.

DISCONTINUANCE OF ACTION WITH LEAVE

Leave of the court is required for discontinuance of an action or counterclaim or withdrawal of any particular claim or question where the action was begun otherwise than by writ or originating summons or if notice of discontinuance or withdrawal has not been served or effected in due time or in cases where an order for interim payment has been made.

mons for directions under RSC, Order 25, Rule 7.[147] The court will
normally grant the plaintiff leave to discontinue provided no injustice
will be caused to the defendant and the defendant will not be deprived
of any advantage that has already been gained in the litigation.

The court has a wide discretion as to the terms on which it may grant
leave to a plaintiff or defendant to discontinue or withdraw the whole or
part of the action or counterclaim, including imposing terms as to costs.
It should be noted that the fact that a party has discontinued any action
or withdrawn a particular claim shall not, by that fact alone, prevent that
party from bringing another action on the same subject matter.

Dismissal for failure to prosecute

The court has been given express power to dismiss an action for want of
prosecution where certain procedural requirements have not been complied with. These procedural requirements include: default in service of
the statement of claim;[148] default in the giving of discovery;[149] default in
the answering of interrogatories;[150] default in the issuing of summons for
directions;[151] and default in setting down.[152] The court also has power to
strike out an action where a party has failed to comply with a pre-emptory
or final order made pursuant to RSC, Order 42, Rule 2.

In addition to the express provisions in the Rules of the Supreme
Court, the court may also strike out an action under its inherent jurisdiction.
The principles that the court will apply when asked to dismiss an action
are the same whether the court is acting under its express powers or under
its inherent jurisdiction. In the absence of deliberate fault by the plaintiff, a
defendant must first establish that the plaintiff has been guilty of inordi-
nate and inexcusable delay. In addition, the defendant must establish that
there is a substantial risk either that it will not be possible to have a fair
trial or the delay is likely to have or has caused prejudice to the defendant.

Judicially assisted settlement

If the parties conclude a settlement, any rights of action they had will be
replaced by rights under the contract of compromise or settlement. After

147. RSC, Order 21, Rule 3 (2).
148. RSC, Order 19, Rule 1.
149. RSC, Order 24, Rule 16.
150. RSC, Order 26, Rule 6.
151. RSC, Order 25, Rule 1 (4).
152. RSC, Order 34, Rule 2 (2).

a settlement has been reached, the parties can end the proceedings by discontinuing the action[153] or by obtaining a consent judgment.

By virtue of RSC, Order 42, Rule 5A, the parties can, in certain cases in the Queens Bench Division of the High Court, obtain judgment and certain forms of order by consent without the need for a hearing before a judge or Master. This procedure applies to judgments or orders for the payment of money, delivery of goods or possession of land other than dwelling houses. This Rule includes judgments or orders for the dismissal, discontinuance or withdrawal of any proceedings wholly or in part; the stay of proceedings, either conditionally or on conditions as to the payment of money; the stay of proceedings on terms which have scheduled to it but which are not otherwise part of it; the stay of enforcement of a judgment, either conditionally or unconditionally or on condition that money due under a judgment is paid by instalments specified in the order; the setting aside of a judgment in default; the transfer of proceedings to the county court; the payment out of money in court; the discharge from liability of any party and the payment, taxation or waiver of costs.

In Queens Bench cases not falling within RSC, Order 42, Rule 5A or Chancery Division cases, the parties must apply by summons to a Master for judgment by consent. Often, in cases where the settlement reached does not just include a simple payment of money, the parties will agree to stay the proceedings on terms set out in the schedule to the order with liberty to restore, if necessary, for the purposes of carrying such terms into effect. This is known as a "Tomlin Order". In the event of default by the party, the enforcement is by way of an application for specific performance.

Where in any proceedings money is claimed by or on behalf of a person under a disability, that is minors or mental patients, no settlement, compromise or payment and no acceptance of money paid into court shall be valid unless it is approved by the court.[154] Application should be made by originating summons if settlement is before proceedings have begun or by summons once proceedings have been commenced.

TRIAL

Trial stages

Place and mode of trial

The place and mode of trial is determined by the court at the directions stage of the proceedings. The Order will normally contain an estimate of the length of the trial. Any such Order may be varied by a subsequent

153. See above.
154. RSC, Order 80, Rule 10.

order of the court. Most civil cases in the High Court are presided over by a judge sitting alone. A matter may also be tried before a judge with a jury, a judge with the assistance of assessors, a Master or a special or official referee.[155]

Generally, jury trials are limited to defamation cases and occasionally matters concerning fraud.[156] The court has power under RSC, Order 33 Rules 3 and 4 to order that any issue or question be tried separately from the main action. Usually, such orders are made in relation to the trial of a preliminary point of law, the determination of other preliminary issues or questions, and the separate determination of liability and damages. Under RSC, Order 33, Rule 7 if the resolution of any question or issue which has been tried separately substantially disposes of the whole cause or matter or renders the trial of it unnecessary, then the court may dismiss that cause or matter or make any other such order as may be just.

SETTING THE CASE DOWN FOR TRIAL

Usually at the directions stage of the proceedings, the court will in writ actions fix a period within which the plaintiff is to set down the action for trial. Should the plaintiff fail to do so within the fixed period, the defendant may then either set the action down for trial himself or may apply to the court for the action to be dismissed for want of prosecution.

Subject to any order of the court to the contrary, RSC, Order 34, Rule 3 provides that a party setting an action down for trial must deliver to the proper officer a request that the action be set down for trial at the place determined by the court and lodge with the court the appropriate setting down fee and two identical bundles consisting of the writ, any pleadings, further and better particulars, interrogatories, all orders made in the action, occasionally a statement of the value of the action, an estimate of the length of the trial, the list in which the action is to be included and if relevant any legal aid documents and third party notices.

Under RSC, Order 34, Rule 8, a party setting down an action for trial must notify the other parties to the action that he has done so within 24 hours. Later, the case appears in a warned list, which indicates the week during which it is expected to be heard. It is possible, however, once the action has been set down to apply for a fixed date for trial.

Fixing a date usually delays rather than accelerates the time of trial, but it is often necessary when calling expert witnesses. Two further bundles must be lodged at court by the plaintiff at least two but not more than seven clear days before the date fixed for trial.[157] At least 14 days

155. RSC, Order 33, Rule 2.
156. Supreme Court Act 1981, Section 69.
157. RSC, Order 34, Rule 10.

before the date fixed for trial, the defendant should identify to the plaintiff those documents that he wishes to be included in the bundle. The bundle should contain all witness statements and expert's reports, those documents that the defendant wishes to have included in the bundle and those central to the plaintiff's case.

The bundle should also include, when ordered by the court, a summary of the issues involved, a summary of any propositions of law to be advanced together with a list of the authorities to be cited, and a chronology of relevant events. The purpose of this rule is to allow the judge to obtain a grasp of the general nature of the case prior to the action being heard.

Scope and order of trial

The trial takes place in open court, unless for some special reason, for example, national security, the judge orders trial in camera. The judge may give directions as to the way in which the trial is to proceed and in cases where the judge has read witness statements and documents in advance, the judge may deal with the proceedings very quickly by questioning each advocate himself and then immediately asking for the witnesses to be called.

In the absence of any such directions, the rules of the Supreme Court establish the order in which the parties are to be heard.[158] RSC, Order 35, Rule 8, grants the judge power to inspect any place or thing with respect to which any question arises and this extends to land outside the jurisdiction.

In the majority of civil cases, the procedure will be as follows. The plaintiff's advocate has the right to begin, unless the burden of proof of all the issues lies with the defendant. The plaintiff's advocate begins by making an opening speech, which briefly outlines the facts on which the plaintiff relies, and further indicates areas of dispute, the legal principles involved and the areas where a ruling must be made. The plaintiff's advocate will then call the first witness who will take the oath or make a solemn affirmation.

The court may allow all or part of a witness statement to stand as evidence of a witness and the defendant's advocate should confirm whether he is content to accept all or any passage as evidence of that witness or whether he requires the witness to be examined. Unless the witness statement is allowed to stand, the plaintiff will examine-in-chief the witness during which leading questions may not generally be asked, although the court has a discretion to relax this rule when it is in the interests of justice to do so. The witness will then be cross-examined by

158. RSC, Order 35, Rule 7.

the defendant's advocate. During cross-examination leading questions may be asked, although irrelevant or vexatious questions may be disallowed by the judge.

The defendant's advocate must put his client's version of events to the witness because if he omits to cross-examine on any point, the witness statement is assumed to be accepted. If necessary, the witness will be re-examined by the plaintiff's advocate to restore the witnesses credibility or give the witness an opportunity to explain the points made in cross-examination.

Once all the plaintiff's witnesses are called, including expert witnesses, the defendant's advocate will open the case and call the witnesses in the same manner as the defendant. The judge may ask a witness to clarify some points in his testimony or clear up any obscure points. If there is a witness who is not called by either party but who the judge believes may provide useful evidence then that witness may be called by the judge and may be examined by the judge himself.

In certain cases, the plaintiff may be allowed to adduce further evidence after the closure of his case in order to rebut evidence adduced by the defendant, for example, if he has been taken by surprise by the defendant's evidence or in order to answer evidence adduced by the defendant to support an issue, the proof of which lay on him. Documents or objects may be produced by witnesses or put in by agreement of the defendant and will be marked by the court as exhibits. Once all the evidence has been heard the defendant's advocate and the plaintiff's advocate will make closing speeches.

Evidence

In general, the party alleging any given fact will have the burden of proving that fact. In civil cases, such facts must be proven on the balance of probability. There are a number of different matters by which evidence to establish such facts may be adduced by the parties at trial. In order to save costs, the parties should always endeavour to agree on evidence in advance whenever possible.

Kinds of evidence

ORAL EVIDENCE BY WITNESSES

The general rule[159] is that witnesses must attend the trial and give oral evidence on oath.[160] The court will normally, by virtue of RSC, Order 38,

159. See above for procedure at trial.
160. RSC, Order 38, Rule 1.

Rule 2A require parties to serve on each other prior to trial written statements of the oral evidence of issues of fact that each party intends to adduce at trial. Such an order is normally given by the court at the directions stage of the proceedings. A party who does not comply with such an order will not be entitled to adduce any evidence to which the order relates, unless the court gives leave.

In cases where a witness is unwilling to attend court to give evidence, a writ of subpoena should be issued under RSC, Order 38, Rule 14 to ensure the witness' attendance and if necessary bring documents. The subpoena should be personally served on the witness and conduct money should be tendered to cover travelling expenses and any other reasonable expenses incurred.

In cases where a witness is unable to attend trial to give evidence, for example, if he is in hospital or abroad, his evidence can be put in as a hearsay statement[161] or with the agreement of the other side. Other possibilities are to obtain leave from the court to put in evidence by affidavit,[162] which may carry more weight than a hearsay statement. The court will not make such an order where the evidence will be strongly contested and its credibility depends on the court's view of the witness. An alternative would be to take a deposition under RSC, Order 39.[163]

Another method of getting evidence from abroad would be to request that the court directs that at trial the evidence of the overseas witness be given through a live television link.[164] RSC, Order 38, Rule 36 generally precludes a party from producing expert evidence except with leave of court or where all the parties agree or where the evidence is given by affidavit.

HEARSAY STATEMENTS

Hearsay evidence is evidence of a statement made out of court that is being adduced to establish the truth of the substance of that statement. At Common Law, hearsay evidence was generally inadmissible. However, the Civil Evidence Act 1968 (CEA 1968) enables hearsay evidence to be adduced in specific circumstances. The procedure in the High Court is set out in Part III of RSC, Order 38. A party wishing to adduce hearsay evidence must serve a notice on the other party which must state the time, place and circumstances at or in which the statement was made, person by whom and to whom the statement was made, substance of statement and reason as to why the maker of the statement cannot be called as a witness at trial.

161. See below.
162. RSC, Order 38, Rule 2.
163. See above.
164. RSC, Order 38, Rule 3.

There are five permissible reasons, set out in Section 8 of the CEA 1968, why a maker of a statement cannot attend trial, namely that the witness is dead or, the witness is abroad or, the witness is unfit by reason of bodily or mental condition to attend the trial, or cannot with reasonable diligence be identified or found, or cannot reasonably be expected to have any recollection of matters relevant to the accuracy of the statement.

A party on whom a notice is served may within 21 days serve a counter notice stating that the maker of the hearsay statement should be called as a witness. If a reason is not given in the original notice, the counter notice will prevent the party from adducing evidence. If the notice does contain a reason, the counter notice will challenge that reason and the court will rule whether the reason is made out. If the reason is made out, the statement will be admissible as of right. The court also has a discretion to admit the statement even if the reason is not made out or if the procedural requirements are not complied with.

Section 4 of the CEA 1968 makes special provision for admissibility of records compiled by a person acting under a duty.

DOCUMENTARY EVIDENCE

Where possible, documentary evidence should be agreed by the parties to an action, so that it may automatically be put in evidence. In general, the original documents must be produced.[165]

REAL EVIDENCE

A party wishing to produce to the court an object not in its possession can get an order for its detention,[166] although normally the production of real objects is dealt with by consent. A party wishing to produce an object at trial must call a witness to identify the object, which will become an exhibit (leading questions may be asked).

JUDICIAL NOTICE

Notwithstanding the usual rule that the court may only take account of facts that have been proved by evidence, a court may take into account matters of law, custom and common knowledge without evidence of such facts being adduced. The court is also able to make certain presumptions and inferences of fact that will obviate the need for proof. Such facts may still be rebutted by producing appropriate evidence to the contrary.

165. See "Obtaining Information Prior to Trial" above.
166. See "Real Evidence under Obtaining Information Prior to Trial" above.

PRIVILEGE

There are a number of different types of evidence that a party is protected by privilege from producing to the court. The protection provided by the principle of privilege is designed to ensure a fair trial of an action, and to enable the parties to conduct pre-trial negotiations more easily. If a party makes an admission in an attempt to settle a dispute, and if that admission was made (either expressly or impliedly) without prejudice, then evidence of that admission may not be given by either side during the trial itself. Such evidence could only be admissible for the purpose of proving settlement that had already been reached between the parties.

All communications between the client and his legal adviser are privileged. Where there is evidence of communications between a third party and a litigant or his legal adviser, then these will be privileged provided that such communications were made in contemplation of pending or anticipated litigation and the purpose or dominant purpose was to prepare for the litigation.

English law also recognises privilege against incrimination, and by virtue of Section 14 (1) of the Civil Evidence Act 1968 a witness may refuse to disclose facts which would tend to expose the party producing them, or his spouse, to proceedings for a criminal offence or for the recovery of a penalty under the law of any part of the United Kingdom. Documents that would be injurious to the public interest are also privileged under RSC, Order 24, Rule 15.

JUDGMENT AND KINDS OF RELIEF

Final judgment

In cases where the matter proceeds to trial, the judge will deliver his judgment after counsel's closing speeches. In some proceedings, the judge will adjourn to the following day to give judgment and in particularly complex cases, a judge may expressly reserve the judgment in which event, the parties will be told at a later date when to attend the court to hear judgment delivered. The successful advocate will ask for final judgment to be entered.

In the High Court, successful claims for money judgments is payable forthwith and in the County Court within fourteen days. Payments should be made direct to the creditor and not into court. The judge may award interest and costs. The general principle being that "costs follow the event". The judge will also make a ruling in respect of costs of any interlocutory applications that were reserved. Judgments may be final or interlocutory or final and interlocutory as to part.

Where split trials have been ordered under RSC, Order 33, Rule 4 (2) (for example, the issue of liability and quantum to be heard separately), the issue of liability will be decided first, and if found in the plaintiff's favour, interlocutory judgment will be granted for damages to be assessed. The effect of such a judgment is final as to the right to recover damages, but interlocutory as to quantum.

Unless the parties agree to a settlement the assessment of damages will be undertaken by a Master or District Judge under RSC, Order 37. Similarly, in cases where unliquidated damages are claimed and the plaintiff succeeds in obtaining default judgment,[167] interlocutory judgment will be entered with damages to be assessed under RSC, Order 37. Once the damages are assessed, the interlocutory judgment becomes final.

In Chancery Division cases, which tend to be more complicated, the judge will often give an oral judgment, which indicates the general sense in which he will decide the action, but will not immediately order that judgment be entered. Instead the judge will give counsel on each side the opportunity to agree on the minutes of the judgment, which with the judge's approval will form the basis of the final judgment. As often in the Chancery Division parties will be seeking equitable relief, it is usual for a Chancery judgment to direct an account or inquiry or include the settlement of some document or sale of property. In such a case the matter will be referred to a Master in chambers to do whatever is necessary in order to make the order effective.

Entry of judgment

Once judgment is given, it must be drawn up. Until this has occurred, it cannot be enforced, costs cannot be taxed and money in court cannot be removed. At the end of the trial in the Queens Bench Division, the Court Associate will draw up a certificate certifying the time taken up by the trial, any order made allowing admission of plans, photographs or models under RSC, Order 38, Rule 5 or whether under RSC, Order 38, Rule 6 an order was made varying or removing certain orders as to evidence, every finding of fact by the jury (trial by jury), the judgment given by the judge, any order made as to costs.

The successful party should draw up the judgment and take it to the court office along with the writ and Associate's certificate for it to be sealed.[168] In the County Court and Chancery Division of the High Court, judgment will be automatically drawn up. The judgment will then be entered in the cause book. With consent judgments,[169] the order must be drawn up in the terms agreed and expressed as being by consent. The judgment, indorsed by each party's solicitor, should be presented to the court office where it will be entered and sealed like any other judgment.[170]

167. See "Default Judgments" above.
168. RSC, Order 42, Rule 5.
169. See "Judicially assisted settlement" above.
170. See generally "Summary Judgments" above.

Kinds of relief

Specific performance

Specific performance is an equitable remedy whereby one party to a contract is ordered to perform his obligations under the contract. The remedy of specific performance is only available where the remedy for breach of contract at law, namely damages, is inadequate, for example, where the contract deals with unique subject matters, such as land.

As specific performance is an equitable remedy, it is not available as a right, but at the court's discretion. Hence, it will not be granted in cases where damages form an entirely adequate remedy, the contract is voluntary, the performance of the contract would require continuous supervision by the court, performance of the contract could not be enforced or even if enforced would prove useless, the performance of the contract would involve ordering the defendant to perform an act he is not legally competent to perform or where the contract is one for personal work or services.

A plaintiff will also, as a general rule, be prevented from bringing an action for specific performance where he fails to issue a writ promptly and the delay may prejudice the defendant. Specific performance may be granted in relation to a contract for the sale of land outside the jurisdiction if the defendant is within it.

An action for specific performance in the High Court is begun by writ and the procedure is the same as in any other writ action. RSC, Order 86 provides a special procedure for obtaining summary judgment.[171] If judgment for specific performance is granted the court may grant consequential relief, which will depend on the type of contract to be performed.

In cases involving sale of land, an inquiry as to the vendor's title may be ordered if the plaintiff has not accepted title and the court will give directions for ascertaining any outstanding sum, for example, rent or costs, and for completion of the contract. The court may award damages in addition to or in lieu of specific performance (equitable damages awarded in circumstances where damages cannot be received at Common Law) and in cases where specific performance is refused, the court may award damages for breach of contract instead.

Substitution relief

RSC, Order 18, Rule 15 provides that a statement of claim must specifically state the relief or remedy which the plaintiff claims. The court, however, is not confined to granting the particular forms of relief set out in the statement of claim and has jurisdiction to grant any relief that it

171. See RSC, Order 86 above.

thinks appropriate to the facts as proved. If, in the course of a trial, the party seeks to raise a new claim that he has not adumbrated in his pleading, the court should not give relief without first offering the opposite party, if taken by surprise, the opportunity for an adjournment.

Rectification

Claims for rectification of a written document can be brought where, as a result of common mistake of the parties to the agreement, the written document does not contain the common intention of the parties. The mistake must be as to fact, not law, and the mistake must effect the essence of the contract or dealing.

As in all equitable remedies, the relief is discretionary and the courts will exercise its discretion with caution and only on the clearest of evidence. Oral evidence is admissible when making a claim for rectification of a written document, but the court is generally reluctant on oral evidence to vary deeds of settlement where it would defeat vested rights, unless there is clear uncontradicted oral evidence. The burden of proof lies with the plaintiff and it should be noted that any denial by any of the parties to a deed of settlement is likely to be conclusive, unless supported by clear documentary evidence. The court will not make any rectification order where it cannot restore the parties to their original position or where there has been a delay in bringing the proceedings or where the contract is incapable of performance. Generally, claims for rectification should be brought only by writ and in the Chancery Division.[172] Where the court orders the deed to be rectified, the court's judgment should be endorsed on the deed. An order for rectification is retrospective in that it should be read as if originally executed in its rectified form.

Rescission

The court may award the equitable remedy of rescission in cases of duress, mutual mistake, innocent or fraudulent misrepresentation, where a contract is entered into in ignorance of material facts, constructive fraud or undue influence. Rescission may also be granted where a defendant has failed to comply with an order for specific performance.

The court has a discretionary power to rescind an agreement and as in claims for rectification, it will not rescind a deed or agreement because of a mistake as to the law effecting the transaction. Actions to set aside or cancel deeds or written instruments are assigned to the Chancery Division of the High Court although a counterclaim may sometimes be brought in

---

172. Supreme Court Act 1981, Section 61 (1), Schedule 1, Paragraph 1.

the Queen's Bench Division. Actions for rescission will normally involve disputes of fact and so should be brought by writ. It is quite usual for rectification and rescission claims to be brought as alternative remedies.

Declaration concerning legal relations

There is no limit on the High Court's power to make a declaratory judgment. RSC, Order 15, Rule 16 provides that no action or other proceedings shall be open to objection on the ground that a merely declaratory judgment or order is sought thereby and the court may make binding declarations of right whether or not any consequential relief is or could be claimed.

The power of the court to make a binding declaration of right is, however, discretionary and will only be used sparingly. It is not the practice of the court to make a declaration of right in default of defence or on admissions or by consent of the party that is without trial or evidence. Limitations have been laid down by authorities as to the type of case where declarations unaccompanied by any other remedy should be made and it seems unlikely that the court would make a declaration where there is a specific alternative remedy available or where the court is asked to decide purely abstract or hypothetical questions.

As a general rule, the court will be prepared to make a declaration, although no other relief is sought, in cases involving status, construction of a deed or document or Act of Parliament or where a declaration would settle conclusively the rights of the parties. Where the principal relief sought is the declaration as to the construction of a deed, contract or Act of Parliament, proceedings should be commenced by originating summons. Where there is likely to be a substantial dispute of fact, it may be more appropriate to bring an action for a declaration by writ, and where the court considers it just and convenient to do so, a declaration may be made by way of application for judicial review.[173]

POST-TRIAL MOTIONS

Attack on judgments

Prima facie, once a judgment has been entered, it is conclusive between the parties and except by way of an appeal,[174] no court, judge or Master has power to rehear, review, alter or vary the judgment. The purpose of this general rule is to bring litigation to a finality, but it is subject to a number of exceptions.

173. RSC, Order 53 (1) and (2).
174. See "Appeal" below.

The court does have an inherent jurisdiction to alter the record of its order so as to make it conform with the actual order granted. RSC, Order 20, Rule 11 provides that clerical mistakes in judgments or orders or errors arising therein from any accidental slip or omission may, at any time, be corrected by the court on motion or summons without an appeal. This is generally known as the "slip rule" and may be used to correct judgments even when it is due to the solicitor's error in drafting the judgment. It does not, however, permit a judge to change his mind about a decision made; the proper remedy is to appeal the decision. A judgment may be amended or set aside in the following circumstances:

(1) Where the judgment is entered against a person who is in fact dead or non-existent;[175]
(2) Where there has been a breakdown in procedure or other irregularities in the proceedings that are so serious that the judgment or order ought to be treated as a nullity;[176]
(3) Where there has been a failure to comply with the Rules of Court, judgment may, at the court's discretion, be amended or set aside either wholly or in part under RSC, Order 2;
(4) Where a plaintiff obtains judgment against the Defendant for failure to give notice of intention to defend the court may, on such terms as it thinks just, set aside or vary a default judgment;[177]
(5) Where under RSC, Order 14 the plaintiff obtains summary judgment against the defendant on the grounds that there is no defence to the claim or the defendant obtains summary judgment against the plaintiff for its counterclaim, any such judgment given against a party who does not appear at the hearing may be set aside or varied by the court on such terms as it thinks just;[178]
(6) Where judgment has been entered against the third party for failure to give notice of intention to defend or serve a defence then the court has power to set aside or vary the judgment entered under RSC, Order 16, Rule 5 (3);
(7) Where judgment has been entered under RSC, Order 19 for default of service of a pleading, the court has power to set aside or vary the judgment under RSC, Order 19, Rule 9;
(8) RSC, Order 35, Rule 2 provides that any judgment, order or verdict obtained when one party does not appear at the trial may be set aside by the court on the application of that party,

---

175. See *Burr v. Anglo-French Banking Corporation Ltd.* (1933) 49 LT 405.
176. See *Woolfenden v. Woolfenden* [1947] 2 All ER 653.
177. RSC, Order 13, Rule 9.
178. RSC, Order 14, Rule 11.

on such terms as it thinks just. An application should be made within seven days after the trial and if possible to the judge who tried the action;

(9) A judgment that has been obtained by fraud may be impeached by means of an action which may be brought without leave. The court requires a strong case to be established before it will set aside the judgment and the action will be stayed or dismissed as vexatious unless the allegation of fraud has a reasonable prospect of success; and

(10) Unless all the parties agree, a consent order can generally only be set aside by a fresh action brought for the purpose, on any ground that would invalidate the compromise contained in the judgment, for example, fraud, misrepresentation on duress.

Grounds for new trial

The Court of Appeal has a discretionary power under RSC, Order 59, Rules 2 and 11 to order a new trial on a matter. The main grounds on which an application for a new trial may be founded are as follows:

(1) The judge misdirected the jury or the judge wrongly received or wrongly rejected evidence. The Court of Appeal is not, however, bound to order a new trial on these grounds unless some substantial wrong or miscarriage has been occasioned;[179]

(2) There was no evidence to go to the jury;

(3) Verdict was against the weight of the evidence. The court will be reluctant to order a new trial in the absence of any misdirection, unless the verdict was one that no reasonable person could have found;

(4) Newly discovered evidence — It must be shown that the evidence could not have been obtained with reasonable diligence before trial that the further evidence is such that if given, it would have an important influence on the result of the trial and that the evidence is such as is presumably to be believed;

(5) Surprise — This covers cases where a party has been prevented from having a fair trial, and which was not due to any fault on his part, for example, where action comes on for hearing unexpectedly when the defendant's material witnesses are absent;

(6) Misconduct of jury generally; and

(7) Fraud.

179. RSC, Order 59, Rule 11 (2).

In cases where a judgment has been obtained by fraud, the normal procedure is to set it aside. However, the Court of Appeal may in special cases allow a new trial if the charge of fraud is made out with a high degree of particularity.

ENFORCEMENT AND EXECUTION OF JUDGMENTS

Remedies

If a plaintiff obtains judgment against a defendant, neither the High Court nor the County Court will automatically enforce the judgment until the plaintiff puts into operation one or other of the procedures for enforcement of the judgment. Set out below is a brief summary of the methods open to the plaintiff to enforce judgment:

Oral examination of the judgment debtor

The judgment creditor can obtain an order bringing the debtor before the court in order to examine him on oath as to his means.[180] If the judgment debtor is a body corporate, the order can be made against an officer of the company. If the judgment debtor refuses to attend, it is possible to obtain an order for his committal to prison. An order for an examination is not a method of enforcement in itself and is merely a method of obtaining information to lead to means of enforcement.

Writ of fieri facias

This process[181] enables the sheriff's officer to seize and sell such of the debtors goods and chattels in his county or district as may be sufficient to realise the judgment debt and costs and the cost of enforcement. Leave to issue a writ of warrant is not usually required. The sheriff's officer must not effect forceful entry to any premises.

Garnishee proceedings

In garnishee proceedings,[182] if the judgment debtor is himself the creditor of another, it is possible to obtain an order that the judgment debtor's debtor

180. RSC, Order 48.
181. RSC, Order 47.
182. RSC, Order 49.

should pay the judgment creditor. Enforcement proceedings may be taken against the garnishee if he does not pay.

Charging order

Where the judgment debtor owns real estate, a charging order[183] may be obtained over the land. The charging order is not, as such, a method of enforcing the debt immediately; it is merely a matter of obtaining security for it. The creditor will stand in the position of mortgagee of the land and if no payments are made under the debt, may apply, in separate proceedings, to the court to enforce the charging order by ordering the sale of the land.

Attachment of earnings order

An order may be made compelling an employer to pay regular deductions from an individual judgment debtor's earnings and pay them into court.[184] If an order is made it specifies a normal deduction rate and a protected earnings rate below which the defendant's earnings may not fall.

Writ of sequestration

Where the defendant is in contempt of court by failing to comply with a judgment or order within the specified time limit laid down in the judgment or order, or where a defendant disobeys an order requiring him to abstain from doing an act, a writ of sequestration may be issued against the property of the individual or, in the case of a defendant company, against the property of any director or officer.[185] Leave of court must be obtained by motion to a judge.

Generally, prior to the enforcement of a judgment by writ of sequestration, a copy of the judgment indorsed with the penal notice must be served personally on the defendant before any time for compliance expires. A writ of sequestration authorises commissioners to enter the land of persons in contempt and take possession of all the real and personal property of that person.

---

183. RSC, Order 50.
184. Attachment of Earnings Act 1971 and CCR, Order 27.
185. RSC, Order 45, Rule 5.

Bankruptcy or liquidation

In cases where the defendant fails to pay a judgment debt exceeding £750, the plaintiff may apply for the bankruptcy (if individual) or winding up (if company) of a defendant. The plaintiff must first serve a statutory demand in the prescribed form on the defendant giving details of the debt and informing the defendant that if the demand is not dealt with within 21 days insolvency proceedings may follow. If the judgment debtor fails to comply with the demand after the expiry of 21 days, the plaintiff may issue a bankruptcy or winding up petition.

If the plaintiff has issued enforcement proceedings which have been returned unsatisfied, the plaintiff can issue winding up/bankruptcy proceedings without issuing a statutory demand. Proceedings are commenced by issuing a winding up/bankruptcy petition and filing an affidavit in support. On issue of the petition, a hearing date will be fixed. The petition and affidavit must be served on the defendant and an affidavit of service must be filed.

In the case of winding up proceedings, the hearing of the winding up petition must be advertised in the prescribed form. The bankruptcy petition is heard by a Bankruptcy Registrar (High Court) or District Judge (County Court). If the bankruptcy order is granted, the Official Receiver will immediately take control of the individual's estate and the bankrupt's property will be collected and the proceeds distributed among the creditors. A trustee of the bankruptcy may be appointed by a creditor's meeting, to distribute the estate.

The hearing of a winding up petition will take place in open court before the Registrar of the Companies Court. If a winding up order is made, the official receiver will conduct the litigation until a liquidator is appointed by the creditors.[186]

Arrest

The court has a general power to punish for contempt by imprisoning the offender. As a general rule, under Section 4 of the Debtors Act 1869 no person can be arrested or imprisoned for defaulting in payment of a sum of money. However, limited powers to imprison do remain, for example, in cases of penalties other than under a contract and in sums recoverable summarily before justices. Committal may be ordered for refusal or neglect to obey a judgment or order when the type of performance is specified or for disobedience to a prohibitive order.

186. See part IX and part IV of the Insolvency Act 1986 for details of bankruptcy and winding up proceedings.

An application for committal must be made by motion to a judge supported by affidavit. The procedure for committal is laid down in RSC, Order 52. The judgment indorsed with a penal notice must first have been served on the defendant personally, and the notice of motion and supporting affidavit must also be served personally, unless the court dispenses with service.

Brussels Convention recognition and enforcement

Under the Brussels Convention 1968 — Articles 25, 27, 28, 29, 32, 37, 40, 46 and 47 — the judgment given in a contracting state must be recognised in another contracting state without any special procedure. There are, however, certain matters that are outside the scope of the Convention.[187]

Judgment is defined in Article 25 as meaning any judgment given by a court or tribunal of a contracting state whatever it is called including, any decree, order, decision or writ of execution as well as the determination of costs or expenses by an officer of the court. It would according to this definition appear to recognise an injunction or decree of specific performance. To bring English law into line with the 1968 Convention "judgment" is defined for purposes relating to recognition and enforcement under the Convention as that in Article 25.[188] The duty under the Convention to recognise a judgment under the Convention applies, unless one of the following defences is available:

(1) Recognition is contrary to public policy;[189]
(2) Where judgment was given in default of appearance, if the defendant was not duly served with the document instituting the proceedings or with an equivalent document, in time to arrange a defence.[190] Reference must be made to the internal laws of the contracting state and conventions on service abroad to determine what constitutes due service;
(3) If a judgment is irreconcilable with a judgment given in a dispute between the same parties in the state in which recognition is sought;[191]
(4) If a court in arriving at its judgment has decided a preliminary question concerning the status or legal capacity of natural persons, rights in property arising out of a matrimonial relationship,

187. See "Establishing Jurisdiction" above.
188. CJJA 1982, Section 15 (1).
189. Article 27 (1).
190. Article 27 (2).
191. Article 27 (3).

wills or succession, in a way that conflicts with a rule of the private international law of the state in which the recognition is sought (unless the same result would have been reached by the application of the rules of private international law of that state);[192]

(5) If a judgment is irreconcilable with an earlier judgment given in a non-contracting state involving the same cause of action and between the same parties provided that the latter judgment fulfils the conditions necessary for its recognition in the state addressed;[193]

(6) If a judgment conflicts with jurisdictional provisions of Section 3 (insurance matters), Section 4 (consumer contracts) or Section 5 (exclusive jurisdiction) of Title II to the Convention or where under Article 59 the contracting state has agreed with a non-contracting state that it will not in certain circumstances recognise judgments, based on exorbitant jurisdiction, given in other contracting states against a defendant that is domiciled in that non-contracting state. Exorbitant jurisdiction in the United Kingdom includes rules where jurisdiction is founded on serving the defendant during his temporary presence in the United Kingdom, or presence of property of the defendant within the United Kingdom, or seizure by plaintiff of property situated in the United Kingdom. In examining the grounds of jurisdiction under this heading the court would be bound by findings of fact on which the court of the state in which the judgment was given based its jurisdiction; and

(7) Section 32 of the CJJA 1982 sets out an additional defence to enforcing foreign judgments in cases where proceedings are brought contrary to an agreement under which the dispute was to be settled otherwise than by proceedings in the courts of that country. This provision is applicable to all foreign judgments whether granted by contracting or non-contracting states, but in cases of contracting states, it is subject to the provisions of the Convention.

Subject to paragraph (6) above, the jurisdiction of the court of the state in which judgment was given may not be reviewed.[194] Article 29 also provides that under no circumstances may a foreign judgment be reviewed as to its substance. Article 32 provides that the application for enforcement of a judgment under the Convention should be made in

192. Article 27 (4).
193. Article 27 (5).
194. Article 28.

England and Wales to the High Court of Justice, and in the case of maintenance judgments to the Magistrates' Court on transmission by the Secretary of State.

Under Article 33, the procedure for making an application is governed by the law of the state in which enforcement is sought. The procedure for making an application for enforcement under English law is set out in RSC, Order 71 and Section 4 of the CJJA 1982. A judgment subject to an application under Article 31 for its enforcement in the United Kingdom should be registered in the High Court, Queen's Bench Division.[195]

Application for registration is made *ex parte* to a Master and must be supported by an affidavit exhibiting the judgment, or a verified or certified or otherwise duly authenticated copy of the judgment together with such other documents as may be requisite to show that, according to the law of the state in which it has been given, judgment is enforceable and has been served.

In the case of default judgments, a document showing that the party in default was served with the document instituting the proceedings or with an equivalent document must be attached as an exhibit. If appropriate, a document showing that a party is in receipt of legal aid and a translation of the judgment into English should also be attached as exhibits.

Section 11 of the CJJA 1982 provides that a document duly authenticated which purports to be a copy of a judgment given by a contracting state will be deemed to be a true copy without further proof, unless the contrary is shown. The document is duly authenticated if it bears the seal of the court, or is certified by any person in his capacity as a judge or officer of the court to be a true copy of the judgment given by that court. An original or certified copy of supporting documents will be evidence of any matter to which it relates.

The affidavit should state whether the judgment provides for payment of a sum of money, whether interest is recoverable in the state where judgment was given (if so, rate of interest and period in which it accrues), an address within the jurisdiction for service on the party making the application and the name and the usual or last known address or place of business of the person against whom judgment was given. The affidavit should state to the best of the information or belief of the deponent the grounds on which the right to enforce a judgment is vested in the party making the application and either that at the date of the application the judgment has not been satisfied or the part or amount in respect of which remains unsatisfied.[196]

Notwithstanding RSC, Order 23 a party making an application will not be required to give security of costs solely on the grounds that he is not domiciled within the jurisdiction. An order giving leave to register will state a time limit for the appeal and will stay execution of the

195. CJJA, Section 4.
196. RSC, Order 71, Rule 28.

judgment until the time expires. Registration of the judgment is effected by presentation of the order and a copy of the judgment at the court office.

The notice of registration must be served on the defendant informing him of his right to appeal and specifying the time limit imposed. The effect of registration under the CJJA 1982 is that the judgment may now be enforced in the same way as if it were a judgment of the High Court.[197] In the case of non-money judgments made in the United Kingdom, but outside England and Wales, the procedure outlined above applies save that in the case of challenges to registration, an application is made to set aside the order and is made to a District Judge not a High Court Judge. The procedure for enforcing money judgments made elsewhere in the United Kingdom is much simpler. The applicant must lodge at the High Court a certificate of judgment issued by the original court not more than six months prior, and the judgment creditor must produce a certified copy of the certificate, which the court clerk will seal and return to him. No application for leave is necessary.

Article 37 of the Convention provides that an appeal against decisions authorising enforcement must be lodged in accordance with the rules governing the procedure in contracting states. In the United Kingdom, the appeal is usually lodged with the High Court and must be made by summons to a judge. RSC, Order 71, Rule 33 (2) (a) provides that the summons must be served within one month of service of the notice of registration of the judgment or two months of service of such notice where the notice was served on a party not domiciled within the jurisdiction.

The court has power to extend further the period of appeal on the application of a party, not domiciled in a contracting state, made within two months of service of notice of registration. If an appeal is made under Order 71, Rule 33, execution of the judgment cannot be issued until after the appeal is determined. Article 40 of the Convention provides for an appeal by an applicant if the application for enforcement is refused. An English appeal is by summons to a judge of the High Court. The summons must be served within one month of determination of the application for registration.[198]

APPEAL

Appeals from County Courts and High Courts generally lie to the Court of Appeal, and from the Court of Appeal to the House of Lords. The Judicial Committee of the Privy Council hears appeals from a few countries that were formerly British Colonies or Protectorates. The ultimate

---

197. See "Remedies" above for enforcement methods; also CJJA 1982, Section 4.
198. RSC, Order 71, Rule 33 (2) b.

appeal court in the United Kingdom is the European Court of Justice for cases that fall within the ambit of the Treaty of Rome. It should be noted that there are strict time limits to be complied with when deciding whether or not to appeal against a decision of the English courts.

Appeal as of right

There is an appeal as of right from any order of a Master (or District Judge) to a judge in chambers,[199] and in the case of decisions made by a Master or District Judge, and cases referred to a Master under RSC, Order 36, Rule 11 (trial by Master/District Judge) or an assessment of damages made by a Master under RSC, Order 37 an appeal lies to the Court of Appeal.[200]

In the County Court, there is an appeal as a right from any decision of a District Judge to a Circuit Judge. RSC, Order 58, Rule 6 provides that subject to the exceptions, there is an appeal from any order of a judge in chambers to the Court of Appeal. Section 16 of the Supreme Court Act 1981 and the County Courts Act 1984, Section 77 provide that subject to certain exceptions[201] an appeal may be made to the Court of Appeal from any decisions of the High Court and County Court.

Discretionary appeal

Cases where appeal from the decision of the High Court to the Court of Appeal may only be made if leave is granted include the following:

(1) From an order of any court or tribunal made with the consent of the parties.[202] Leave may be given by the court or tribunal which made the order or by the Court of Appeal;

(2) Order of any court or tribunal as to costs only which are by law left to the discretion of that court or tribunal.[203] Leave may be given by the court or tribunal that made the order or by the Court of Appeal itself in certain circumstances;

(3) From an interlocutory order or judgment given by any court or tribunal (with certain exceptions). Leave may be given by the court or tribunal in question or Court of Appeal;[204] and

199. RSC, Order 58, Rule 1.
200. RSC, Order 58, Rule 2.
201. See below.
202. RSC, Order 59, Rule 1B (b).
203. RSC, Order 59, Rule 1B (b).
204. RSC, Order 59, Rule 1B (f).

(4) From the summary decision of a judge against the claimant in an interpleader matter.[205] Leave may be given by the judge or Court of Appeal.

Where leave may be given either by the court below or by the Court of Appeal, an application for leave must be made in the first instance to the lower court. If the lower court refuses the appeal, further application must be made to the Court of Appeal. Such an application is determined by a single judge and there is no appeal from his decision. The requirement of leave is intended to check unnecessary or frivolous appeals.

There will be no appeal to the Court of Appeal in the following cases:

(1) Generally, any judgment of the High Court in any criminal cause or matter;[206]

(2) An order extending time for appeal;[207]

(3) Any decision of the High Court where statute provides that decision is to be final;[208]

(4) The refusal of a High Court Judge to grant leave to institute or continue any legal proceedings made by a person who is subject to a vexatious litigant order;[209]

(5) For an order arising from an appeal to the High Court under the Arbitration Act 1979, except as provided by that Act;[210]

(6) A judgment or order of the High Court when acting as a Prize Court;[211]

(7) The parties have entered into an agreement not to appeal which is embodied in an order;

(8) Where a party takes the benefit of a judgment;

(9) Where the appeal concerns a matter which is no longer a contentious issue between the parties;

(10) Appeal against a decree absolute of divorce or nullity of marriage by a party who having had time and opportunity to appeal from the decree nisi on which that decree was founded, has not appealed from the decree nisi;[212]

(11) Where the question the Court of Appeal is asked to decide does not arise because the facts are hypothetical; and

(12) Where decision is not given in a judicial capacity.

205. RSC, Order 58, Rule 7.
206. SCA 1981, Section 18 (1) (a).
207. SCA 1981, Section 18 (1) (b).
208. SCA 1981, Section 18 (1) (c).
209. SCA 1981, Section 42 (4).
210. SCA 1981, Section 18 (1) (g).
211. SCA 1981, Section 16 (2).
212. SCA 1981, Section 18 (1) (d).

Appeals to the House of Lords from the Court of Appeal will only be allowed with leave of the Court of Appeal or leave of the House of Lords. When deciding whether leave should be granted, the general importance of the case, the likelihood of its success, and the degree of dissension the case may have previously caused is taken into account. If the Court of Appeal refuses to grant leave, a petition for leave to appeal may be presented to the House of Lords. Section 4 of the Administration of Justice Act 1876 (as extended by the Administration of Justice Act 1969) created a "leap frog procedure" whereby an appeal may be made direct to the House of Lords from the High Court.

Issues subject to review

In the case of appeals against decisions of a judge in chambers from an order of a Master or District Judge, there is a complete re-hearing and the judge treats the matter as though it came before him for the first time. The judge in chambers is in no way fettered by the previous exercise of the Master's discretion and on appeal from a decision of a judge in chambers, the Court of Appeal will treat the substantial discretion as that of the judge and not of the Master. The judge in chambers may admit further (additional) evidence by affidavit to that which was before the Master.

RSC, Order 59, Rule 3 provides that in most cases an appeal to the Court of Appeal is to be by way of a re-hearing. A re-hearing in this sense does not mean that witnesses are heard afresh, but indicates that the court considers the whole of the evidence given in the court below it and the whole course of the trial. Generally, it is a re-hearing of documents and the court is not confined to making an order which should have been made by the court below, but may consider facts that have occurred since the trial, any changes in law and receive fresh evidence, either orally or by affidavit or by deposition. Where there has been a hearing on the merits, no further evidence except as to matters that have occurred since the hearing may be admitted, save on special grounds.[213]

The Court of Appeal may make the following orders:

(1) Affirm, vary or discharge the order of the court or tribunal below it and may make an order that that court or tribunal could have made;[214]

(2) Order a new trial;[215]

213. RSC, Order 59, Rule 10 (2).
214. SCA 1981, Section 15 (3) and RSC, Order 59, Rule 10 (1).
215. SCA 1981, Section 17 and RSC, Order 59, Rules 2 and 11.

(3) Draw any inferences of fact and give any judgment or make any order that ought to have been made and make such further or other order as the case may require;[216] and

(4) Make any order, on such terms as the court thinks just, to ensure the determination, on the merits, of the real question in controversy between the parties (notwithstanding that no notice of appeal or respondent's notice has been given in respect of any particular part of the decision of the court or tribunal below, or that any ground for allowing the appeal or affirming that decision is not specified in the notice of appeal or respondent's notice).[217]

Appeals may be on a question of law or fact. The court usually confines itself to points of law raised in the notice of appeal and, generally, the party cannot appeal on a point that he did not raise in the court below, unless it would result in an abuse of the court process.

An appeal against an exercise of discretion is the hardest ground to succeed on as the appellant must show that the exercise of discretion was unjust or clearly wrong in principle and not just that members of the appellant court would have exercised the discretion differently. The appeal will be allowed if the appellant can show that the judge exercised his discretion under mistake of law, in disregard of principle or under a misapprehension as to the facts, or that he took into account irrelevant matters, or failed to exercise his discretion, or the conclusion which the judge reached in the exercise of his discretion "exceeded the generous ambit within which a reasonable disagreement is possible".[218]

An appeal on a point of law has a greater chance of success than an appeal on a question of fact. The court does, however, have power to substitute its own finding of fact on the basis of the evidence. Generally, the court will confine itself to issues of fact raised in the notice of appeal and will only look again at facts in dispute.

The Court of Appeal is reluctant to interfere with a finding of fact of a judge or jury as it has not had the opportunity of hearing witnesses and judging their demeanour and would, therefore, only upset findings of a judge if the appellant can satisfy them that the judge was plainly wrong. If the matter is in doubt, the Court of Appeal will not alter it.

Where the action was tried by a judge with a jury, it will be even more difficult to persuade an appeal court to allow an appeal on the finding of facts. It should be noted that in certain cases appeal is confined to questions of law (appeals by way of case stated such as tax appeals and

---

216. RSC, Order 59, Rule 10 (3).
217. RSC, Order 59, Rule 10 (4).
218. *G v. G* [1985] 2 All ER 225 HL.

appeals of the lands tribunals), appeals from decisions of the Employment Appeal Tribunal and certain County Court possession cases.[219]

CONCLUSIVENESS OF JUDGMENT

Res judicata

The doctrine of *res judicata* is a fundamental doctrine in English law based on the premise that it is in the public interest that there should be an end to litigation and no one should be jeopardised twice on the same grounds. The effect of the doctrine is that a party cannot bring an allegation that has previously been decided against it by a court of competent jurisdiction.

Res judicata operates as a defence as well as a ground for a stay of proceedings. The defence of *res judicata* must be specifically pleaded and the defendant must show that the cause of action was the same in both actions, the action was brought against the same defendants and the plaintiff had an opportunity of recovering in the first action that which it seeks to recover in the second action. To decide which questions of law or fact were determined in the earlier judgment, the court is entitled to look at the judge's reasons for his decision and is not confined to the court records.

The law of the case

English law has developed a doctrine of binding precedent. In general terms, this means that as a result of the hierarchical system of the English courts, the decision of one court binds those inferior and of an equivalent standing to it. One exception to this is where the decision is made *per incuriam* that is that a court has acted in ignorance of a particular statute or decision because it was not brought to its attention.

The House of Lords decisions bind all courts in England and in the case of *London Street Tramways Co. v. London County Council*,[220] it was held that the House of Lords was bound by its own decisions. However, in 1966, the House of Lords made a statement that their Lordships were free to depart from their own earlier decisions "when it appeared right to do so",[221] for example, where the reasoning had been based on outdated circumstances.

219. See County Courts Act 1984, Section 77 (6).
220. [1898] AC 375.
221. Practice Statement Judicial Precedent [1966] 3 ALL ER 77 HL (E).

The House of Lords decision may lose its authority by being overruled by statute or by a decision of the European Court of Justice, by being distinguished or if, in unlikely circumstances, the decision is given *per incuriam*. The decisions of the Court of Appeal are binding on High Court Judges, County Court, Crown Court, Divisional Courts (where appeal from Divisional Court lies to Court of Appeal) and on the court itself. Divisional Courts are bound by the decisions of the House of Lords and Court of Appeal and decisions of High Court Judges are binding on County Court Judges, but not binding on other High Court Judges, although they will be of persuasive authority.

Each decision in a case can be divided up into:

(1) Finding the material facts;
(2) Statements of principle of law applicable to legal problems disclosed by facts; and
(3) Reasons for judgment based on (1) and (2) above.

The only part of the decision that is binding as a precedent is (3) above, which is known as the *ratio decidendi* of the case. Other statements which go beyond the points raised in the pleadings that is, when a judge states that even if the facts had been different, the case would have been decided in the same way or the statement which, although based on the facts does not form the basis of the decision are not strictly binding on a later court. These statements are known as *obiter dicta* and although not binding, are of persuasive authority, particularly if made by a higher court. Decisions of the Scottish, Irish, Commonwealth and foreign courts are also of persuasive authority.

Findings on matters of fact are binding between parties and their privies, but are not binding on any other court. The court can "distinguish" precedents on their particular facts and not follow a cited precedent if it considers this inconsistent with the case before it. In some cases, the distinctions drawn are very fine. A precedent is good authority until it is overruled. Higher courts may overrule decisions of lower courts, but this is not deemed a change in law, but a correction of a wrong statement. Judicial overruling operates retrospectively unlike overruling by statute, which only operates after becoming law in the absence of express provision.

However, judgments in old cases where the time for appeal has lapsed will not be resurrected and reviewed only by reason of a subsequent change in precedent. The principle *rei publicae ut finis sit litium* applies.[222]

---

222. See, for example, *Lockyer* v. *Ferryman* 2 App. Cas. 519; *Brown* v. *Dean* (1910) AC 373.

CHAPTER 5

FINLAND

JOHAN BOSTRÖM AND KIMMO REKOLA
Bardy & Boström
Helsinki, Finland

ESTABLISHING JURISDICTION

Types of jurisdiction

Jurisdiction in Finland is vested according to the Constitution in independent and permanent courts of law. The ordinary courts, in which most civil disputes are handled, are hierarchically set up with three instances, with District Lower Courts at the low end, Appellate Courts as a general Court of Appeal and the Supreme Court, as the final resort of appeal.

One or a few towns or communities form a Court District territory, each with its own Local District Court. The District Court has sole jurisdiction over its territory in general court matters. All civil suits commence in the District Courts regardless of the importance of the dispute.

As ordinary courts of appeal, there are six Appellate Courts, each having jurisdiction over the decisions of the District Courts within its judicial territory.

The Supreme Court is the highest judicial instance. It has jurisdiction over the decisions of the Appellate Courts. In civil proceedings, the Supreme Court only deals with matters that are deemed to be of precedential or otherwise substantial importance.

Apart from the ordinary courts, there are special courts having jurisdiction over specific matters:

(1) Land Court — disputes related to the general reparceling of the land;
(2) Water Rights Court — disputes related to water rights;
(3) Assurance Tribunal — social security issues;
(4) Labour Court — disputes arising from collective labour agreements;
(5) Market Court — disputes relating to consumer protection, improper marketing and unfair competition.

As the ordinary courts have jurisdiction over all cases that do not explicitly fall under the jurisdiction of one of the special courts, most disputes in Finland start with litigation in the District Courts. In arbitration matters, the parties may also agree to resolve their dispute before an arbitral tribunal, which in such cases excludes the jurisdiction of the ordinary courts.

Jurisdiction over the parties

Jurisdiction over the parties of the action can be established by any ordinary court of first instance if the defendant so chooses by responding to the plaintiff's suit, without first objecting to the court's jurisdiction. Only when the dispute is to be handled by a court that has subject matter jurisdiction does venue become absolute and need it be considered *ex officio*. If the defendant wishes to object to the jurisdiction of the court, the court must have jurisdiction over the defendant according to certain rules of venue before jurisdiction can be established.

If the plaintiff has sued the defendant in a court that is not the legal venue of the defendant, the suit may be dismissed. The rules for the establishing of jurisdiction over the parties are essential for the success of the desired action.

The rules on jurisdiction over the parties of the action are usually discretionary, which means that the courts do not *ex officio* ensure their observance. However, if the defendant does not appear in the court, they become incontestable.

Natural persons

Natural persons must be sued in the District Court at the defendant's habitual domicile.[1] The Code of Judicial Procedure defines the defendant's place of general jurisdiction in Finland (*forum domicilii*). If a person does not have any habitual domicile in Finland, he may be sued in the court that has jurisdiction over the temporary place of stay of the defendant (*forum deprehensionis*) or where the defendant owns property.

Corporations

Legal venue of corporations[2] is the District Court at the corporation's domicile. The domicile of a corporation is the place, where the corporation's registered domicile is located.

Corporations that are run from several locations underlying different District Courts may be sued in the court within whose jurisdictional territory the dispute arose.

1. Code of Judicial Procedure, Chapter 10, Section 1.
2. Code of Judicial Procedure, Chapter 10, Section 6.

A partner of a partnership company has his legal venue in lawsuits concerning his personal liability either at the court at his or at the company's domicile. Members of the board of limited companies may be sued for their personal liability towards the company or the share holders in the District Court at the company's domicile.

Jurisdiction over the subject matter

When a court has jurisdiction over the subject matter, the venue generally becomes absolute. This means that the court at any stage of the proceedings is under the obligation to consider its jurisdiction. At any stage of the proceedings, the parties of the action may successfully invoke the jurisdiction of the court. The court may not by itself assume the power to hear the parties, nor does the consent of the parties permit the court to determine the controversy. If the court fails to have jurisdiction over the subject matter, the case must be dismissed.

The most common examples of jurisdiction over the subject matter in ordinary courts in Finland relate to property claims and claims based on inheritances. Maritime disputes are also usually concentrated in certain District Courts. The special courts mentioned at the beginning of this chapter also have sole jurisdiction over those matters that they have been established to deal with.

Property claims

According to Sections 14 and 19 of Chapter 10 of the Code of Judicial Procedure, property claims are to be handled before the court within which district the real estate is located (*forum rei sitae*). Not all claims related to real property will be litigated in the *forum rei sitae*. Only claims that are directly connected with the real estate fall within this jurisdiction. Examples of such claims are:

(1) Claims regarding title to real property;
(2) Claims regarding lease and possession of real property;
(3) Claims regarding certain legal rights of severance;
(4) Claims regarding rights of redemption; and
(5) Claims for compensation of damage caused to real property.

Damage or violation of rights

In Finland, matters concerning damage are not considered to be based on jurisdiction over the subject matter. Legal action concerning compensation of damage may be taken at the defendant's court of General

Jurisdiction, normally at his *forum domicilii*. Alternatively, such action may also be brought before the court, where the damage occurred (*forum delicti*). Neither of these forums are absolute.

Violations of rights to patents, trademarks, registered designs and other immaterial rights are to be handled by the City Court of Helsinki. This venue is absolute.

Lugano Convention, Article 3

Finland has ratified the Lugano convention on jurisdiction and the enforcement of judgments in civil and commercial matters. The said convention complies in all essential parts with the Brussels's Convention of 27 September 1968. According to Article 3 of the Lugano Convention persons domiciled in one State may be sued in the courts of another State only by virtue of the rules set out in Sections 2–6 of the said convention. The said sections set up rules of special jurisdiction relating *inter alia* to contracts, maintenance, tort, civil claims for damages, different claims relating to insurance, consumer contract and real estate. The ratification of the Lugano Convention has thus significantly enlarged the jurisdiction of the Finnish courts in respect of the citizens of the contracting states.

In Subsection 2 of Article 3 of said convention, Finland has accepted the following exemptions from our domestic law in favour of persons from the contracting states, namely the second, third and fourth sentences of Section 1 of Chapter 10 of the Code of the Judicial Procedure. The second sentence of the said Section establishes jurisdiction over a person without any habitual residence within the country to the temporary place of stay (*forum deprehensionis*) or ownership of property. The third sentence gives a court jurisdiction over Finnish citizens, who have moved abroad and the fourth sentence with regard to foreigners, who temporarily stay in Finland. Jurisdiction over these groups of people are thus being established according to the main rules of the Lugano Convention.

Venue

General principles

The District Court at the defendant's domicile is, according to the Finnish rules on venue, the place of general jurisdiction over both physical persons and corporations (*forum generale*). This court has jurisdiction over any law suit against the defendant, unless explicitly excluded by special rules of venue (*fora specialia*). Finnish law recognises exclusive as well as alternative *fora*. Some rules of venue are absolute and other discretionary. The classification of venue as being exclusive or supplementary is based on different aspects than the classification in absolute and discretionary *fora*.

The rules of venue in the Finnish Code of Judicial Procedure are rather complicated and partially obsolete. A detailed explanation of the rules of venue within the scope of this chapter is not possible. With reference to the above types of jurisdiction, the most important ones in civil proceedings are:

(1) Place of general jurisdiction (*forum domicilii*);
(2) Marriage law case jurisdiction (usually *forum domicilii* or the court, where the spouses had their last mutual habitual residence);
(3) Probate jurisdiction (*forum hereditatis*);
(4) *Forum* for real actions (*forum rei sitae*);
(5) *Forum* on the ground of the factual connection (*forum connexitatis*);

Forum rei sitae and *forum hereditatis* are absolute.

Transfer of venue

In Finland, all civil matters are brought to court by the initiative of the plaintiff and therefore the court has no *ex officio* right to transfer venue to another court. If the court according to the rules on jurisdiction or venue decides that it is not competent to handle the case at issue, the case must be dismissed. The court does not have any means to transfer the venue to another court, which would be competent to handle the case.

The right of contracting parties to agree on which court has jurisdiction over the contract is largely recognised in Finnish civil procedure. Jurisdiction agreements are, however, only valid in respect of discretionary *fora*, i.e., *fora* that are not absolute. Thus, venue cannot be changed in respect of real property claims or inheritance claims. Jurisdiction agreements cannot either affect the exclusive jurisdiction of special courts. To be effective jurisdiction agreements should be made in writing.

Service of summonses or notices

The rules for the service of summonses and notices are contained in Chapter 11 of the Code of Judicial Procedure. According to the new provisions entered into force on 1 December 1993 the court will see *ex officio* to the service of summonses and other notices. The court may also appoint a court official or a bailiff to the task. At the request of the party the court may also leave the service of a notice to be performed by the party, if it deems that there are justified grounds for this.

The service of a notice to a company, co-operative or association or to another corporation or consortium will be made on a person who is competent to represent the recipient of the notice.

If the order or decision to be served has been announced to the recipient in the court office or in a hearing, he will be deemed to have received service of the notice at that time.

If the addressee of the notice is in a pending case represented by an attorney, the notice may be served to the attorney. A summons (*haaste*) may be served to an attorney only if the attorney has been especially empowered by the defendant to receive service of summonses. However, a document ordering a person to appear in court in person or to otherwise undertake something personally must always be served to the said person.

By post

When the court undertakes the service of a notice, the main rule is that the service must be performed by sending the document by post against a receipt. The court will notify the postal authorities of the date when the service of the notice, at the latest, has to take place.

The service may also be performed by sending the document by an official letter if it may be presumed that the addressee will receive notice of the letter and will return within the fixed period a certificate of the service.

Procedural address

When the court undertakes the service of a notice, the most common method of serving notices other than summonses to the parties is the use of the procedural address of the recipient. In the application for a summons, the plaintiff must include the procedural address to which notices may be sent to him. The summons exhorts the defendant to include his procedural address in the response. The service of a notice is deemed to have taken place seven days after the notice has been given to be delivered by post.

Instead of using the posting address, the notice may also be sent as an electronic message (fax message, electronic mail, data transmission) if so declared by the party.

The procedural address of a party may also be the address of his attorney or legal representative.

Bailiff

A bailiff (*haastemies*) must be used to serve the notice personally to the recipient, if the service of a notice by post has failed or it may be deemed probable that the notice cannot be served by post or another special reason for this exists. A bailiff must also be used whenever the service of a notice has been left to be performed by a party.

The court will notify the bailiff of the date when the service, at the latest, has to take place. If the service of a notice has been left to be performed by the party, he will be notified of the date when the service, at the latest, has to take place and also when the receipt of the service must, at the latest, be delivered to the court. In the case of the service of a summons, the plaintiff will be notified that the receipt must be delivered within the determined time under threat that otherwise the case may be struck out.

If the bailiff has looked for a Finnish resident but has not found him or his legal representative and the circumstances indicate that the recipient is evading the service of the notice, the bailiff may perform the service by delivering the documents:

(1) To a household member, who has reached the age of 15 years; or
(2) If the recipient pursues a business, to a person employed in this business; or
(3) If none of the above can be found, to a local police authority.

In these cases, the bailiff will notify the recipient of his action by a letter to the recipient's home address and the service of the notice will be deemed to have taken place when the notification has been given to be delivered by post. This method may also be applied to companies that have no persons authorised to sign for the firm entered in the Trade Register.

Methods provided by the Hague Convention

If the recipient of a notice resides abroad and his address is known, the court will arrange that the documents are sent to the foreign authority as separately provided or as agreed with the foreign State in question. According to the Copenhagen Convention applied between the Nordic countries (Finland, Denmark, Iceland, Norway and Sweden), the request for service is sent directly to the Government authority responsible for performing service of notices in the country in question.

Finland has also adopted the Hague Convention on the Service Abroad of Judicial and Extrajudicial Documents in Civil and Commercial Matters. If the recipient resides in a country (other than the Nordic countries) that has adopted the Hague Convention, the request for service will be sent via the Ministry of Justice, otherwise it will be sent via the Ministry for Foreign Affairs, unless otherwise not provided or agreed.

Publication

If the whereabouts of the recipient or a person empowered by him to receive services cannot be discovered, the court will perform the service of the notice by announcement. The announcement is performed by keeping the document and its enclosures available in the court office and by publishing an overview of its contents and the place where it is kept in the *Official Gazette* of Finland. The announcement must also be posted on the court bulletin board. If a notice has already been served to the recipient by announcement, the service of a notice in the same case to the same recipient needs not to be published in the *Official Gazette* but it will be made available in the court office.

If the case relates jointly to two or several parties, the document must be served to each party separately. However, if the document is to be served to so many persons that it is difficult to serve it to each of them separately, the court may decide that the service is performed by serving the notice to one of the parties and by publishing an announcement of this in the *Official Gazette*.

Failure in the service of a notice

If the service of a notice is performed by the court and a party enters a plea in the response or statement that the service has not been performed within the fixed period or that it has been erroneously performed, the consideration of the case will be suspended or a new fixed period will be set for the presentation of a written response or statement, unless the court deems that this is unnecessary due to the insignificance of the error in the service.

Correspondingly, if the party fails to deliver the requested written response or fails to appear in court and the service of a notice has not been performed within the fixed period or it has been erroneously performed, the service must be performed again, unless the court deems that a new service is unnecessary due to the insignificance of the error.

If the service of a summons has been left to be performed by the plaintiff and he does not deliver a certificate that the service has been performed correctly in the determined time, the case will be struck out` unless the defendant responds without entering a plea or the court grants an extension to the fixed period, sets a new period or decides to see to the service itself. If a party does not present a certificate of the service of a document other than a summons, the court will see to the service.

ASCERTAINING THE APPLICABLE LAW

National law

Finnish National Law is generally applicable throughout the country on all disputes or other judicial matters, which they are set to regulate. Apart form the Parliament, the only regime in Finland that has the right to pass original laws is the self-government of the Åland Islands. The self-government of the Åland Islands is mainly set up to guarantee the right of the population of the islands to use the Swedish language.

Conflicts of laws

Finnish law does not contain any general act that would outline the principles for handling matters concerning conflicts of law. Most rules covering law conflicts between national and foreign parties are established by jurisprudence. Finland has historically had a close relationship with the other Nordic countries, Sweden, Denmark, Norway and Iceland. These countries have co-operated extensively in the legislative field to achieve conformity of most Civil Laws. Because of this, practical conflicts of law rarely result from relationships between citizens of the Nordic countries.

Apart from the large legislative co-operation with the Nordic countries, Finland has passed some material laws that deal with law conflicts in different fields of civil matters. The most important laws in this respect are as follows:

(1) Act on Certain International Relationships in Respect of Family Rights (5 December 1989/379);
(2) Act on Enforcement of the General Agreement on International Trade, entered into in Vienna on 19 April 1980 (6 November 1988/796);
(3) The Bills of Exchange Act also contain some provisions concerning law conflicts.

Finnish courts are at liberty to apply foreign material law in a dispute, if such law is applicable, but only if it is deemed not to be in conflict with the principles of *ordre public*. Mandatory domestic law cannot be overcome foreign law. If foreign law is applicable, the parties usually are urged by the court to present its contents for the court as evidence.

COMMENCING THE ACTION

Court procedure — pleadings

As of 1 December 1993, the processing of civil cases in the District Courts has been divided into two stages: the preliminary preparation (*valmistelu*) and the main hearing (*pääkäsittely*). The preliminary preparation is conducted by the court and the purpose of it is to determine the claims of the parties, the issues under dispute and the evidence to be presented so that the case can be considered in an oral, concentrated and continuous main hearing.

Certain uncomplicated cases may be resolved at the preparation stage in a summary procedure. The possibilities for a settlement will also be determined by the court in the preliminary preparation.

Application for a summons

A civil case is initiated by a written application for a summons (*haaste-hakemus*) delivered to the office of a District Court. Only one application is needed to commence the action against several defendants.

An application for a summons, like any other written statement or document, may be delivered to a District Court by post or by courier. As of 1 December 1993, a document that can be delivered to a District Court by post may also be delivered as an electronic message (i.e., fax message, electronic mail and, with authorisation by the Ministry of Justice, data transmission to the information system used by the court). If electronic mail or data transmission is used and if the document has to be presented in original, the court must reserve an opportunity to remedy the failure. The sender of an electronic message carries the risk of the transmission.

Before 1 December 1993, the case became pending only after the summons had been served to the defendant. Under the new regulations, the case becomes pending upon the arrival of the application to the office of the District Court. However, certain periods of limitation, such as the general 10 years' period for debts and the special periods for bills of exchange and cheques, are calculated from the service of summons and not from the filing of the application for the summons.

The preliminary preparation begins upon the arrival of the application to the court. The application lays the foundation for the preliminary preparation stage, and therefore the revised Code of Judicial Procedure contains detailed requirements for the contents of the application.

The following information must be included in the application:

(1) The name of the court;
(2) The names, occupations and residences of the parties as well as the telephone numbers and the posting addresses of the parties or their legal representatives or attorneys;
(3) The basis for the competence of the court, unless the competence can be inferred on the basis of the application for the summons or the documents enclosed with it;
(4) The plaintiff's specified prayers for relief;
(5) A detailed list of the circumstances (facts) on which the claim is based;
(6) As far as possible, the evidence the plaintiff intends to present and what he intends to prove with each piece of evidence, subject to varying stringency between summary and ordinary procedure;
(7) A claim for the compensation of legal costs, if the plaintiff deems this necessary.

It is also recommendable to initially state the nature of the claim (for example, claim for payment of money). In view of this and (4) above, if the claim is for payment of money, for example, the application must include if not the specific amount then at least the specified base for the calculation of the claim. The main principle is that civil action may not be changed during the proceedings, the allowed exceptions being listed in the Code and in some cases also the possibility to present subsidiary or new claims is not possible. Therefore the application should also contain secondary or alternative claims.

As it is the obligation of the court to know the law, the stating of applicable sections of law is not strictly speaking required. However, in cases of issues of law, the plaintiff should state his view on the application of applicable sections of law. The presentation of new circumstances at a later stage is allowed only in as far as it is deemed that the case at hand is not altered. If the defendant has not presented a written response or has failed to appear in court, the presentation of new circumstances is deemed a change of action if the defendant has not received a notice of the same. In addition the possibility to refer during the main hearing to a circumstance that has not been referred to in the preliminary preparation is even more restricted.

With regard to the evidence to be introduced, the names, telephone numbers and posting addresses of the witnesses and other persons to be heard must be included. The plaintiff may, during the preliminary preparation, refer without limitations to new evidence, even evidence already known to him at the time of filing the application for the summons. In the main hearing the possibility to refer to new evidence is restricted.

The contract, letter of commitment or other written evidence that the plaintiff refers to must be enclosed with the application unless the dispute will be dealt with in summary proceedings.

When the actual certificate of the claim is presented to the court the stamp duty (1.5 per cent) becomes payable. If the claim is based on a negotiable promissory note, a bill of exchange or a cheque, the document must be enclosed with the application in the original.

Certain cases can be resolved without continuation of the preliminary preparation in a summary procedure, for example, as a consequence of the passivity of the defendant. Therefore the specified claim for the compensation of legal costs is always advisable and often necessary because the compensation of legal costs is not adjudged *ex officio* and the action may be sustained by default even if the plaintiff has not so requested. A general statement claiming for the compensation of legal costs is not sufficient. The amount of the claim for the compensation of legal costs has to be specified. If the proceedings are continued, the claim for the compensation of legal costs can be presented at a later stage. Naturally, the claim for the compensation of legal costs can also be altered during the proceedings to reflect additional costs exceeding the original amount claimed.

The application must be signed by the plaintiff or, if he has not written the application, by the person who has written it, in which case also his occupation and residence must be included. The power of attorney must also be included. However, if the attorney is a member of the Finnish Bar Association or a public trial counsel, the power of attorney must be presented only if so especially requested by the court.

If the defendant is a registered company or association, an extract from the trade or association register must also be enclosed.

The plaintiff must enclose with the application for a summons the copies of the application and all documents necessary for the serving of the summons to the defendant (one copy for each defendant). If the plaintiff fails to do so, the court will arrange the copying at the expense of the plaintiff.

After the filing of an application for a summons, the court will verify that the application fulfils the requirements. If the application is inadequate, the court will exhort the plaintiff to remedy the inadequacy within a fixed period, if this is necessary in order to continue the preliminary preparation. The plaintiff will be informed as to how the application is inadequate and that the action may be dismissed or rejected, unless the plaintiff heeds the exhortation within the time period given.

The plaintiff's failure to remedy the inadequacy does not automatically result in a dismissal. The court will dismiss the action only if the plaintiff fails to remedy the inadequacy of the application and the application is so inadequate that the court deems it not fit to be basis for proceedings. The court will also dismiss the action if it for another reason cannot take the case upon consideration, for example, court is not competent to consider the action.

Summary procedure

Uncontested cases can be handled in summary proceedings. In these cases, the application for the summons can be simpler in content.

Only the circumstances on which the claim is directly based need to be included in the application if the plaintiff states that to his knowledge the matter is not under dispute, and the case relates to:

(1) A debt of a specific sum;
(2) Restoration of possession or a disrupted circumstance; or
(3) Eviction.

This means that neither a detailed list of circumstances nor the information on evidence are required. Likewise, the contract, letter of commitment or other written evidence that the plaintiff refers to need not be enclosed, but the document has to be specified precisely in the application for the summons. Because no written documents need to be enclosed, stamp duty does not become payable.

These cases may be resolved at the preparation stage in a summary procedure. If the defendant, however, denies the action and the action may not be sustained by default, the preparation is continued and the plaintiff has to present the document on which the claim is based and all other documents he refers to in connection with the continued preparation and list the evidence.

Summons and response

Unless the action has been dismissed or rejected, the court will issue a summons in which the defendant is exhorted to respond to the action in writing. The court will refrain from issuing a summons and reject the action by judgment at once, if the claim of the plaintiff is manifestly without a basis.

A separate summons must be issued for each defendant. If it appears that an oral response will advance the consideration of the case or that the defendant will not respond in writing, he may be exhorted to respond orally in a preliminary hearing. In these exceptional cases, the plaintiff will be invited to the hearing. At the request of the defendant and for special reasons, the court may also allow that the defendant who has been exhorted to respond in writing, respond instead orally.

However, if the claim is based on a negotiable promissory note, a bill of exchange or a cheque and the plaintiff has not requested that the defendant be exhorted to respond orally in a hearing, the defendant will always be exhorted to respond in writing. The purpose of this is to emphasise the need of the plaintiff to a quick resolution without an oral hearing.

The documents enclosed with the application for the summons must also be served to the defendant. If the case is to be handled in a summary procedure, the documents enclosed with the application for the summons need not to be served to the defendant and in the summons the defendant is notified that the documents are available to him at the office of the District Court and will be sent to him on request by post.

The summons must include the notification that the written response is to be delivered to the court office within the court-determined period from receipt of service. This period is largely dependent on the nature and scope of the case. An extension to the court-determined period may be granted for a special reason, if the request has been submitted to the court before the end of the period.

The summons must also include a notification of the consequences for failure to deliver a written response or, in case of an oral hearing, for failure to appear. In cases amenable to out-of-court settlement this means that the case can be resolved by default against the defendant. In a civil case not amenable to out-of-court settlement no real threat may be ordered for failure to deliver a written response. The preparation simply continues. If the defendant is ordered to appear in the court in person, this is always done under threat of a fine.

The main principle is that the response of the defendant should be similarly detailed as the application for the summons. Therefore, in the summons, the defendant is exhorted to:

(1) State whether he admits or denies the action;
(2) Present the grounds for denial that may be relevant in view of the resolution of the case, if he denies the action;
(3) List, as far as possible, the evidence he intends to introduce, what he intends to prove with each piece of evidence and state the posting addresses and telephone numbers of witnesses and other persons to be heard;
(4) Present prayer for payment of legal costs, if he deems this necessary;
(5) Enclose with the response the document on which the denial is based, in the original or as a copy, and the written evidence referred to in the response;
(6) Enter his pleas against the competence of the court.

If the defendant presents only irrelevant grounds for his denial, or in case of a negotiable promissory note, less than plausible reasons for the denial, the preliminary preparation may not be continued and the action will be sustained by default.

The defendant is also exhorted to include in the response the procedural address to which invitations and notices may be sent. The summons must include the notification that the service of a document to the defendant may be performed by sending the document to the posting address included in the response or as an electronic message if so declared by the defendant.

The response must be signed by the defendant or, if he has not written the response, by the person who has written it. The person who has written the response must include his occupation and residence in it.

Amendments to pleadings

The main rule is that a civil action may not be changed during the proceedings and the allowed exceptions are mentioned in Chapter 14 of the Code of Judicial Procedure. The presentation of new circumstances in support of the action will not be deemed a change of action, unless it alters the case at hand.[3]

3. The provisions regarding cumulation of several actions brought by the plaintiff against the defendant are described below.

The plaintiff has the right to the following changes:

(1) To claim a performance that has not been referred to in the action, if the new claim is based on a change in the conditions during the proceedings or on a circumstance that the plaintiff has only then become aware of;

(2) To claim the confirmation of a legal relationship under dispute in the proceedings between the parties, when the clarity of the relationship is a prerequisite for the resolution of the other parts of the case; and

(3) To claim interest or present another subsidiary claim or even a new claim, if it is based on essentially the same grounds.

The main purpose of the lower court reform was to concentrate the main hearing in one continuous hearing. Therefore, under the new provisions, the party may lose his right to present new claims or to refer to new circumstances or evidence or to present new evidence because of his passivity. Therefore, claims referred to in (2) or (3) will be dismissed if they are not presented by the main hearing and if their consideration delays the consideration of the case as a whole.

In cases amenable to out-of-court settlement, the possibility to refer to a new claim or circumstance or to refer to or to present new evidence is even further restricted. In the preliminary preparation the court may exhort a party to present within a fixed period his claims and the grounds for them, list all the evidence he intends to present and also present all the written evidence he refers to under the threat that after the fixed period has elapsed he may not refer to a new claim or circumstance or present new evidence, unless he establishes a probability that he had a valid reason for not doing so. Consequently in the main hearing the party may not refer to a circumstance or evidence that he has not referred to in the preliminary preparation, unless he establishes a probability that he had a valid reason for not doing so.

Cumulation in a civil case

The general prerequisites for a cumulation, i.e., consideration of actions in the same proceedings are that the actions have been brought in the same court, the court is competent to consider the actions to be joined and the actions may be considered according to the same procedure.

In the following situations, the cumulation is compulsory if the prerequisites are fulfilled:

(1) Several actions brought by a plaintiff against the same defendant at the same time, if the actions are based on essentially the same grounds (joinder of claims);

(2) Actions brought by a plaintiff against several defendants or by several plaintiffs against one or several defendants at the same time, if the actions are based on essentially the same grounds (joinder of parties);

(3) An action brought by a defendant against the plaintiff on a same or connected matter or on a debt that is admissible for set-off (counteraction — *vastakanne*);

(4) A person not party to the proceedings brings suit against one party or several parties on the subject of the dispute and requests cumulation (*pääväliintulo*);

(5) A party presents a claim for recourse or for damages or a comparable claim against a third party, if he loses the present case (indemnity); or

(6) A person brings an action against one party or several on a claim referred to in point (5) above, on the basis of the eventual outcome of the present case.

It is especially provided that actions brought against different defendants, i.e., actions referred to in (2), may all be considered in the court where one of the defendants is liable to respond if the actions are brought at the same time and if they are based on essentially the same grounds. An exception to this is *forum prorogatum*: A person not bound by such an agreement is not liable to respond in the court referred to.

It is also especially provided that a counteraction (3) as well as an action of the types referred to in (4), (5) and (6) will be considered in the court where the original action is pending.

If an action referred to in (3), (4), (5) or (6) is brought only after the preliminary preparation has been concluded, the court may, however, consider the actions separately, if their consideration in the same proceedings is not possible without undue inconvenience. The court may do the same when a party brings an action referred to in (3) or (5) after the period set by the court in the preliminary preparation for presenting the claims has elapsed.

Cases between the same or different parties may also otherwise be considered in the same proceedings, if the court deems that this furthers the clarification of the cases. In these situations the court may later detach the cases to be considered as separate cases.

Notwithstanding a cumulation, the separate parts of the case may be prepared separately, a main hearing may be ordered for the consideration of a matter that may be resolved separately and the court may also give partial judgments.

Counterclaim

If the case relates to a debt, the defendant may claim for set-off without bringing an actual counteraction against the plaintiff. The general prerequisites for set-off are that the claim of the defendant has fallen due and it is directly on the plaintiff. However, it does not have to be undisputed.

The claim for set-off should be presented as early as possible. The defendant may not refer to a new counterclaim after the period set by the court in the preliminary preparation for presenting the claims has elapsed or after the preliminary preparation has been concluded, unless he establishes a probability that he had a valid reason for not doing so.

If the original action is dismissed or rejected for reasons other than the counterclaim, there will be no judgment on the counterclaim. Also, there will be no judgment for the part the counterclaim exceeds the original claim. If the defendant wishes to get a judgment for his (total) claim he has to bring a counteraction against the plaintiff.[4]

Counteraction

A counteraction will be considered in the court where the original action is pending. If a counteraction is brought only after the period set by the court in the preliminary preparation for presenting the claims has elapsed or after the preliminary preparation has been concluded, the court may consider the actions separately, if their consideration in the same proceedings is not possible without undue inconvenience.

Intervention in a civil case

If a person wishes to participate in the proceedings by the side of either party as an intervenor without bringing his own action he must submit an application on the same to the court. The prerequisite for an intervention is that the intervenor presents plausible reasons for his statement that the case is about his rights. The application may be written or oral if submitted in an oral hearing. The parties will be reserved an opportunity to be heard on the application.

If the intervention is not rejected, the intervenor has the right to act in the proceedings as a party, for example, present evidence, but he may not change, admit or cancel the action or undertake other measures contrary to actions undertaken by a party. An intervenor has no right to appeal against a judgment or decision unless this is done together with a party. However, if the judgment is enforceable for or against the intervenor as

---

4. As to the possibility of a partial judgment, see "Partial and intermediate judgments" below.

if he were a party to the proceedings, the intervenor will have the status of a party to the proceedings and also a right to appeal.

OBTAINING INFORMATION PRIOR TO TRIAL

The law does not provide possibilities in civil cases to obtain information through discovery prior to initiating an action. The pre-trial possibilities to actions related to evidence are measures the purpose of which is to secure evidence and the presentation thereof.

If the rights of a person depend on the reception of the evidence and there is a danger that the evidence will be lost or that it will be difficult to present it later, the District Court will grant permission to present evidence in advance for a case that is not yet pending. If the rights of another person depend on the presentation of the evidence, he may be invited at the cost of the applicant.

It may also be possible to resort to general precautionary measures[5] to secure evidence for forthcoming presentation.

It should be also noted that even though a party who is in the preliminary hearing at the request of the opposing party is obliged to state whether he has in his possession a written piece of evidence referred to by the opposing party, there is no sanction for neglecting this obligation.

INTERIM PROTECTION OF ASSETS PENDING TRIAL

Precautionary measures

As a part of the lower court reform entered into force on 1 December 1993 the consideration of applications for precautionary measures (*turvaamistoimi*) was transferred to ordinary courts. The new provisions for the consideration of precautionary measures are contained in the new Chapter 7 of the Code of Judicial Procedure whilst the rules for enforcement of decisions on precautionary measures are contained in Chapter 7 of the Execution Act (*ulosottolaki*). The precautionary measures available to a party are defined in Sections 1–3 of Chapter 7 of the Code of Judicial Procedure.

On the application of a party the court may order an attachment (*takavarikko*) of:

(1) The real and/or movable property of the opposing party to secure the payment of a debt; or

5. See "Interim protection of assets pending trial" below.

(2) A specific object or other given property in the possession of the opposing party to which the applicant claims to have a better right.

The precautionary measures available to secure rights other than the payment of a debt or a better right to a specific object or other given property are listed in Section 3 of Chapter 7 of the Code of Judicial Procedure ("general precautionary measures"). According to this Section the court may:

(1) Prohibit the deed or action of the opposing party or order the opposing party to do something, both under threat of a fine;
(2) Empower the applicant to do something or to have something done;
(3) Order that property of the opposing party be placed under the administration and care of a trustee; or
(4) Order other measures necessary for the security of the right of the applicant to be undertaken.

The application for precautionary measures will not be granted without reserving the opposing party an opportunity to be heard. The court may, however, at the request of the applicant give a provisional decision on precautionary measures (*väliaikainen turvaamistoimi*) without reserving the said opportunity if the purpose of the precautionary measures may otherwise be compromised.

The effectiveness of the precautionary measures requires that they are considered urgently in a summary process and an interim conservative order may be issued, even without reserving the opposing party an opportunity to be heard. To offset this the applicant is liable to compensate the opposing party for the damage and the expenses caused by unnecessary precautionary measures and, before the precautionary measures are enforced, to deposit a security to cover the possible damage and the expenses.

Attachment

The general prerequisites for attachment of real and/or movable property are that:

(1) The applicant can establish a probability that he holds a debt that may be rendered payable; and
(2) There is a danger that the opposing party hides, destroys or conveys his property or takes other action endangering the payment of the debt.

The purpose of the attachment is to prevent the opposing party from disposing of his property. It does not give the applicant a preference in the attached property if the opposing party is declared bankrupt or if reorganisation proceedings are commenced or if the attached property is distrained.

Correspondingly, the prerequisites for attachment of a specific object or other property are that:

(1) The applicant can establish a probability that he has a better right to the object or property in question; and
(2) There is a danger that the opposing party will hide, destroy or convey the object or property in question or take other action endangering the rights of the applicant.

"Property" also includes accounts receivable, immaterial rights and other intangible assets.

Claims on money or rights to an object or other property to be secured must be enforceable by a court decision or by some other resolution enforceable in accordance with Chapter 3, Section 1, Paragraph 1 of the Execution Act: in a civil case, a court resolution that has gained legal force, settlement affirmed by a court, an arbitral award or a foreign judgment or arbitral award enforceable in Finland.

General precautionary measures

A decision on general precautionary measures requires that:

(1) The applicant can establish a probability that he has some other right than a claim on money or a right to an object or other property enforceable against the opposing party by a similar resolution as is required for obtaining attachment; and
(2) There is a danger that the opposing party by deed, action or negligence or in some other manner hinders or undermines the realisation of the right of the applicant or lessens essentially its value or significance.

When deciding general precautionary measures the court is obliged to consider that the opposing party does not suffer undue inconvenience in comparison with the benefit to be secured.

Competent court

The issue of precautionary measures is considered by ordinary courts. Normally, it is the court where the main action is pending. If the consideration of the main issue has been concluded, but the decision is still appealable or the time provided for response to the appeal has not yet elapsed, the competent court is the court that last considered the main action.

If the proceedings on the main action falling within the competence of an ordinary court are not (yet) pending, the competent court to consider the precautionary measures is determined by the general jurisdiction rules of Chapter 10 of the Code of Judicial Procedure.

If the parties have agreed that the main issue will be settled by arbitration or for some other reason no ordinary court is competent to consider the main issue, the applicant for precautionary measures has three alternatives to choose from:

(1) The District Court of the locality where the opposing party resides;
(2) The District Court where the property in question or a considerable part thereof is located; or
(3) The District Court where the purpose of the precautionary measures may otherwise be realised.

Proceedings for precautionary measures

The application for precautionary measures must be submitted in writing and may be included in the application for the summons of the main issue. If the main issue is already pending in an ordinary court, the application may also be submitted orally in the hearing of the main action.

The application for precautionary measures will be considered urgently, and under the aforementioned conditions, the court may give a provisional decision on precautionary measures without reserving the opposing party an opportunity to be heard (*ex parte* order).

If precautionary measures are applied for before an action on the main issue is commenced, the applicant must initiate an action on the main issue within one month of issue of the decision on the precautionary measures. If the precautionary measures have been directed to real property in order to secure payment of a debt not (yet) due, for which the real property is security, the one-month period will not begin until the due date of the debt.

It is also possible to apply for precautionary measures and to obtain a decision on them before the debt is matured. However, the debt has to be mature when initiating an action on it, and the time limit for initiating the main action is one month.

The commencement of proceedings in accordance with the law on the reorganisation of an enterprise usually prevents the possibility of seeking precautionary measures.

If a party has unnecessarily resorted to precautionary measures, he is liable to compensate the opposing party for the damage caused by these measures and their enforcement, and also to cover the expenses incurred. The enforcement of a decision on precautionary measures requires that the applicant deposit a pledge or a guarantee, usually a bank guarantee, to cover the possible damages caused by the enforcement of unnecessary precautionary measures. The court may, at the request of the applicant, release him from giving the security if the applicant is found unable to give the security and if the court considers that the right of the applicant is manifestly justified.

The liability to cover the expenses incurred by the application and enforcement of the precautionary measures is resolved, at the request of a party, in connection with the consideration of the main issue.

The decision on precautionary measures is subject to separate appeal. However, a resolution on provisional precautionary measures is not subject to appeal.

Enforcement of precautionary measures

A decision on precautionary measures is usually enforced by the distraint officer (*ulosottomies*). The enforcement of some of the general precautionary measures requires the order of the executor-in-chief (*ulosotonhaltija*). The distraint officer may require that the applicant makes an advance payment to cover the costs caused by the enforcement.

If the decision on precautionary measures is still appealable, the distraint officer must inform the opposing party in advance of the enforcement unless there is a reason to believe that the opposing party is evading the enforcement. However, a provisional decision on precautionary measures may be enforced without prior notice.

Within two weeks after the one-month period to initiate an action in the main issue has elapsed, the applicant must demonstrate to the distraint officer that the main action has been initiated. Otherwise, the distraint officer will cancel the enforcement if the opposing party so requests.

Instead of an attachment of the movable property, the distraint officer may place the property under an interdiction against dispersion if the applicant agrees to that or if the risk of dispersion is insignificant.

An attachment of the real or movable property to secure a debt will not be enforced if the opposing party deposits a bond. If the enforcement has already taken place, it will be retracted. The enforcement of precautionary measures to secure a right to a specific object or property or other right of the applicant can be prevented or retracted by depositing a bond only if the applicant approves the offered security or if the security properly and sufficiently corresponds to the need for protection sought by the applicant.

Cancellation of precautionary measures

The precautionary measures will be cancelled, at the request of either party applicant, by the court if the reason for which the precautionary measures have been undertaken no longer exists. If the main issue is abandoned, the court will cancel the precautionary measures *ex officio*.

When the court resolves the main issue, it will determine how long the precautionary measures will remain in force. If the main action is rejected or dismissed, the court may at the same time order that the precautionary measures remain in force until the main resolution becomes final.

The enforcement of the precautionary measures will be retracted, at the request of the opposing party, by a decision of the distraint officer if:

(1) The main action has not been initiated within the above mentioned one-month period; or
(2) The main action has been struck out, dismissed or rejected; or
(3) The opposing party presents a written statement from the applicant or other clear and reliable evidence that the debt has been paid.

SUMMARY JUDGMENTS

Pre-emptive dismissal or rejection

The court may dismiss the action without issuing a summons if the plaintiff fails to remedy the inadequacy of the application for the summons and the application is so inadequate that the court deems it not fit to be a basis for proceedings. The court will also dismiss the action if it for another reason cannot take the case upon consideration, for example, the court is not competent to consider the action. The dismissal does not have a *res judicata* effect.

The court will also refrain from issuing a summons and reject the action by judgment at once, if the claim of the plaintiff is manifestly without a basis.

Dismissal

The case must be dismissed if there is an impediment to an action. A dilatory plea must be entered when the defendant first answers in the case. If a dilatory plea is entered later, it will be dismissed unless it refers to a procedural requirement that the court will consider *ex officio*.

Withdrawal of an action

The plaintiff may withdraw the action in which case the action will be struck out and can be initiated again later on. However, if the plaintiff wishes to withdraw his action in a case amenable to out-of-court settlement after the defendant has responded to the action, the case will nevertheless be resolved by judgment if the defendant so requests.

Summary and default judgments

Resolution by default in a summary procedure

Usually, the preliminary preparation continues with an oral hearing, but some cases can be resolved during the preliminary preparation by a summary judgment.

If in a case amenable to out-of-court settlement the defendant has not delivered the required response within the fixed period or he has not presented grounds for his denial or has referred only to grounds that are manifestly irrelevant the case will be resolved without continuation of the preliminary preparation.

If the claim of the plaintiff is based on a negotiable promissory note, a bill of exchange or a cheque, the possibilities to a summary judgment are more extensive. The case will be resolved without continuation if the defendant has not delivered the required response or has not presented plausible reasons for his denial or has not presented a final judgment, a negotiable promissory note, a bill of exchange or a cheque that is admissible for set-off.

In both above mentioned cases the action is sustained by default (*yksipuolinen tuomio*) even if the plaintiff has not so requested. The action will, however, be rejected by judgment, partly because the plaintiff has abandoned his action and also partly because the action is manifestly without a basis.

Passivity of a party

If both parties are absent from a court hearing — whether a preliminary or main hearing — the case will be struck out.

A case amenable to out-of-court settlement can be resolved by default already in the preliminary preparation because of the passivity of a party. If a party has failed to appear in a hearing or has not presented a requested written statement indicating his opinion on issues listed in the request, the other party has the right to get the case resolved by default. If he does not request a resolution by default, the case is struck out.

If the case is resolved by default against the defendant, the action will be sustained. However, the case will be rejected by a judgment partly because the plaintiff has abandoned the action or it is manifestly without basis. Correspondingly, if the case is resolved by default against the plaintiff, the action will be rejected by a judgment except for the parts of the action that the defendant has admitted or which are manifestly justified and which will be sustained.

After the defendant has responded to the action, the party who has the right to have the case resolved by default,[6] has also the right, but only in the main hearing, to get the case resolved by a judgment and present the evidence necessary for this purpose thus avoiding the possibility of petition.

Petition

The party on whose request the case is resolved by default must ensure that notice of resolution is served to the opposing party. This naturally applies to the plaintiff if the case is sustained by default in the summary procedure. The party against whom the case has been resolved by default has the right to petition (*takaisinsaanti*) against the resolution in the court that gave the resolution but has no right to appeal against the resolution in a court of appeal. The petition must be submitted to the court within 30 days from the date when the petitioning party received verifiable notice of the resolution by default. The service of the notice may be performed, for example, in connection with execution proceedings.

If the petitioning party exceeds the above mentioned time limit, the petition will be dismissed. The petition must include a reason to amend the resolution that might have been relevant when the case was resolved. If the resolution by default has been based on the failure of the party to present a written statement indicating his opinion on the issues listed in the request, his opinion must be indicated in the petition. If the petition is inadequate on the aforementioned basis and the petitioning party does not remedy the failure, the petition will be dismissed.

Judicially assisted settlement

In the preliminary preparation, the possibilities for a settlement will be determined. It is expressly stated in the Code that in a case amenable to out-of-court settlement, the court will endeavour to persuade the parties

6. According to the above-stated conditions.

to settle the case. In this role, the court may in order to further the settlement also present its own suggestion to settle the case taking into consideration the wishes of the parties, the nature of the case and other circumstances.

A settlement affirmed by the court is enforceable.

TRIAL

The case becomes pending upon the arrival of the application for the summons to the office of the court. "Trial" in this chapter refers to measures which are taken if the action has not been sustained by default in a summary procedure and the preliminary preparation is continued.

Setting the case for trial

A civil case is handled in two stages, the preliminary preparation and the main hearing. Unless the case has been resolved in a summary procedure, the preliminary preparation is continued in an oral hearing. Before this the court may exhort a party to deliver a written statement on the issue determined by the court if the court deems this necessary.

It is especially emphasised that a party must prepare himself well enough so that the consideration of the case need not be suspended because of his neglect.

Scope and order of trial

The scope and order of trial will to a large extent be fixed by the claims filed by the plaintiff. The possibilities to change the action or to refer to a new claim or circumstance or to present new evidence during the proceedings have been discussed above.

Continuation of the preliminary preparation

The preliminary preparation is composed of oral and written preparation. The oral preliminary preparation must be concluded without delay and in one hearing, if possible, where the parties have been invited by the court. The court may exhort a party to deliver a written statement also between preliminary hearings, if it deems this necessary.

The following issues will be determined in the preliminary preparation:

(1) The claims of the parties and grounds for the claims;
(2) The issues under dispute;

(3) The evidence that will be presented and what is intended to be proved with each peace of evidence; and

(4) Whether a settlement is possible.

Separate parts of the case or procedural issues may be prepared separately by the court.

In a preliminary hearing, the case will be considered orally and the parties are not allowed to read or hand over briefs or other written statements. It is, however, naturally allowed to resort to written notes to support one's memory. A party may also read aloud his claims, direct references to judicial practice and textbooks and to documents containing technical and mathematical data.

In the preliminary preparation a party must present his claims and the grounds for them and also express his opinion on what the opposing party has presented. It is the obligation of the court to ensure that already in the preliminary preparation the parties state all the circumstances they intend to refer to.

In a case amenable to out-of-court settlement the court may exhort a party to present his claims and grounds for them, list all the evidence he intends to present and present all written evidence he refers to under the threat that he may not later refer to a new claim or circumstance or present new evidence, unless he can establish a probability that he had a valid reason for not doing so.

When the issues discussed at the preliminary preparation have been determined or when it is otherwise no longer expedient to continue the preliminary preparation the court will conclude the preparation and transfer the case to the main hearing. A separate main hearing may be ordered for a matter that may be resolved separately even if the preliminary preparation of the case otherwise is not concluded.

Main hearing and preliminary preparation

To avoid the consequences of a complete main hearing (postponement, additional costs, etc.), it is possible that the main hearing is conducted immediately in connection with the preliminary hearing. This requires that the parties agree to it or that the case is clear. As everything that was presented in the last preliminary hearing trial material will be considered, unless the court orders otherwise. The hearing of a witness or a party, under oath or otherwise, must always happen in a main hearing.

Main hearing

The main principles of a main hearing are that it must be immediate, concentrated and oral. Therefore it is provided that the judge presiding over the preliminary preparation will in the main hearing act as the chairperson or a member of the court and only the trial material that has been presented in the main hearing will be taken into account in the judgment. All the evidence must be received in the main hearing and a statement given by a party in the preliminary preparation will not be read in the main hearing.

The purpose of the preliminary preparation is that the case can be considered in a continuous main hearing. When commencing a main hearing the court will determine whether a case may be taken up for a final resolution. The court may order that the case or a part thereof is prepared again for the main hearing, in which the case the main hearing will be suspended or cancelled. Even after the conclusion of the main hearing, the court may supplement the consideration of the main hearing if the court finds this necessary. If the issue in question is a simple or minor one, the court may request a written statement on the issue from the parties. Otherwise the consideration is supplemented by continuing the main hearing or by conducting a new main hearing.

Normally a main hearing consists of an opening discussion in which the plaintiff presents his claims and the grounds for them, the defendant states whether he admits or denies the action and the parties elaborate on their statements and express their opinions regarding the statements of the opposing party. Thereafter the evidence is presented and finally in the closing discussion the parties present their closing arguments. This is also the order in which the main hearing will take place unless the court for a special reason decides to deviate from it.

If a main hearing cannot be conducted within one day, it may be interrupted in which case the hearing will be conducted, if possible, on consecutive days and during at least three weekdays a week. In extensive and complicated cases the main hearing may be interrupted for a maximum of three weekdays in order to allow for the parties to prepare for the presentation of the closing arguments.

The main hearing may not be commenced if a party, who is required to appear in person, or another person, whose personal presence is required, has failed to appear or if there is another impediment for the matter to be taken up for a final resolution. In these cases a new date will be announced for the main hearing. Oral evidence may, however, be received in certain cases despite the cancellation of the main hearing. In these cases the case may also be considered for other parts, if this is especially important in order to receive the evidence.

The main hearing may, however, be commenced and need not to be cancelled, if there is cause to presume that the consideration of the case need not be suspended regardless of an above mentioned impediment, for example, the impediment is expected to cease to exist during the commenced hearing. Also, even if the consideration of the case is to be suspended because of the impediment, the main hearing may be commenced, if the suspension does not cause undue difficulty in the consideration of the case and if there is cause to presume that total time of the suspension does not exceed the time limits described below.

The main hearing may be suspended only in accordance with the provisions of Section 10 of Chapter 6 of the Code of Judicial Procedure. According to the said Section the main hearing may be suspended only if new and important evidence has come to the knowledge of the court and the evidence may be received only later (note, however, the restriction to refer to new evidence in a case amenable to out-of-court settlement) or if the suspension is inevitable because of an unforeseeable circumstance or another important reason, (for example, an allowed change of action). Naturally, if the main hearing has been commenced regardless of an impediment, it may be suspended also later.

A new main hearing will be conducted if the main hearing has been suspended once or several times and the suspension has lasted longer than a total of 14 days. However, as long as the suspension has not lasted longer than a total of 45 days, a new main hearing need not to be conducted if this for a special reason is deemed unnecessary due to the nature of the case and if the continuity of the main hearing may be deemed to remain intact regardless of the suspension and interruption.

If a new main hearing is conducted, the case will be considered again in whole, and evidence will be received again for the part it has significance to in the case provided there is no impediment for the reception.

As to the principle of oral proceedings, corresponding provisions that are applied to the oral preparation apply also to the main hearing. If the main hearing is conducted even though a party is not present, the court will resort to the documents and explain what the absent party has stated.

In a case amenable to out-of-court settlement, a party may not in the main hearing refer to a circumstance or evidence that he has not referred to in the preliminary preparation, unless he establishes a probability that he has had a valid reason for not doing so.

Submission of evidence

All the evidence must be presented in the main hearing unless otherwise especially provided by the law. The purpose of the preliminary preparation is to ensure the court and parties are familiar with the pieces of evidence and themes of proof before the main hearing where the evidence is presented. Therefore in the preliminary hearing a party must list all the evidence he intends to present and what he intends to prove with each piece of evidence. All the written evidence referred to must also be presented already during the preliminary presentation.

Furthermore, in the preliminary preparation a party must at the request of the opposing party state whether he has in his position a written piece of evidence or an object, referred to by the opposing party that may be relevant in the case.

Possible decisions to obtain expert opinions, present written evidence, arrange inspections and undertake other preparatory measures will be made in the preliminary preparation, if such measures are necessary in order to ensure that the evidence is at hand at the same time in the main hearing. Requests for such measures must be presented by the parties during the preliminary preparation.

If a party wishes to present evidence in the main hearing that he has not listed in the preliminary preparation, he must without delay present it to the court and state what he intends to prove with the evidence as well as state a valid reason for not having presented the evidence in the preliminary preparation.

If a party to the proceedings is to be heard personally in order to take evidence this will take place before other oral evidence on the same issue is heard.

When a person to be heard has appeared in a main hearing, oral evidence may be received even though the main hearing is cancelled, if there is cause to presume that the evidence need not or cannot be presented again in a main hearing or the arrival of the person to be heard to a (new) main hearing causes undue costs or undue difficulty in comparison to the significance of the evidence.

The court may for a special reason decide that a document is received or a witness, an expert or a party is heard or an inspection arranged outside the main hearing in which case the court will invite the parties to that hearing. Evidence received outside a main hearing must be received again in the main hearing, unless there is an impediment for the reception. The same applies to evidence received when a party has not been present and evidence has been received. If evidence is received outside a main hearing, the evidence may be received also in another lower court.

Presentation of evidence

The main rule is that the parties must obtain the evidence necessary in the case. The court may, however, decide that evidence will be obtained if it deems this necessary. If the case is amenable to out-of-court settlement the court will not, against the consensus of the parties, decide that a new witness be heard or a document presented. The court may prevent the presentation of irrelevant evidence.

The hearing of a witness, an expert or a party will be performed by the chairperson of the court. The court may, however, leave the hearing to be performed by the parties if appropriate. It is expected that this will become more common after the lower court reform and the introduction of the preliminary preparation. The chairperson must *ex officio* deny apparently irrelevant, misleading and other inappropriate questions. Leading questions are allowed only if special reasons exist.

Evidence

Nature and purpose of evidence

In a civil case the plaintiff must prove the circumstances in support of the claim. If the defendant brings out a circumstance in favour of himself he must correspondingly substantiate it. The consideration of evidence is based on the principles of free evaluation of evidence and free production of evidence.

Evidence on notorious matters need not be presented. If foreign law is to be applied and the court is not familiar with it, the court will request the parties to present evidence on it, if not especially otherwise provided by the law. If the parties cannot present the requested evidence, the law of Finland will be applied.

If the party in a case amenable to out-of-court settlement acknowledges a circumstance, the circumstance becomes indisputable and presentation of evidence is not required. If the party later withdraws his acknowledgement, the court will consider, on the basis of grounds presented for the withdrawal and other circumstances, the importance of the acknowledgement as evidence.

Kinds of evidence

The forms of evidence recognised by Chapter 17 of the Code of Judicial Procedure are written evidence, witnesses, experts, inspections and hearing of parties.

DOCUMENTS

A document presented as evidence must be delivered in original, unless the court deems it sufficient that it be presented as a copy. If the document contains privileged information or information that otherwise may not be disclosed, the document will be presented as an excerpt from which the said information has been deleted.

A report of a private nature that someone has written for a commenced trial or a trial to be commenced will not be accepted as evidence in a District Court unless this is especially provided by the law, for example, to deny the action based on a promissory note, or the court for special reasons grants permission.

A person who has in his possession a document that may have significance as evidence is under obligation to deliver it to the court. The court may obligate him to present it under threat of fine or order that it be delivered to the court by a distraint officer.

PRIVILEGE

A close relative of a party is not obliged to witness against one's will. Correspondingly a party or a close relative of him is not obliged to present a document that contains communication between them or between other close relatives.

An official or a person carrying out a public duty may not testify as to a matter he must keep in secrecy because of his post. An attorney may not testify as to what his client has confined to him unless the client gives his consent to this. Specific provisions of the obligation of secrecy apply also to doctors and other medical personnel, priests and to anyone in matters of State security. These provisions apply also to a party heard under oath.

A person who has an obligation of secrecy may not present a document if it may be presumed that the document contains information of which they may not witness. Nor is a party in whose favour the privilege has been enacted obliged to present such a document.

A witness or a party heard under oath may refuse to answer a question or reveal a circumstance that would tend to incriminate him or a close relative of him. The same applies to the presentation of a document or bringing an object for inspection.

A person may also refuse to witness, present a document or bring an object for inspection if this would disclose a trade or professional secret, unless a matter of great importance so requires. The same applies to a party heard under oath and to an expert.

There are also specific provisions to protect the sources of press and other media.

HEARING OF A PARTY

A party may be heard for the purpose of obtaining evidence. A party may also be heard under oath on circumstances especially relevant to the resolution of the case. The same applies to his legal representative.

EXPERT

An expert is appointed by the court either on its own initiative or on the initiative of a party to give a statement in a matter the consideration of which requires special expertise. If a party without a court appointment leans on a person as an expert the said person will be treated as a witness. Before an expert is appointed, the court will reserve the parties an opportunity to express their opinions and if the parties agree on a person as an expert, he will be appointed unless there is an impediment. The court may appoint an additional expert.

No person may be appointed as an expert against his will unless he is obliged to act as an expert because of his post or a special provision of law.

INSPECTION

Corresponding provisions apply to the obligation to present an object for inspection as apply to the presentation of a document.

JUDGMENT AND KINDS OF RELIEF

The consequences of the absence of a party in a case admissible to out-of-court settlement have been discussed above. If in a case not admissible to out-of-court settlement the plaintiff is absent, the case will be struck out. If in such a case the defendant fails to appear in the main hearing or if the defendant ordered to be brought to the main hearing cannot be brought, the case may still be resolved, if the plaintiff requests a resolution and the court finds that there is sufficient evidence regardless of the absence of the defendant. If the plaintiff does not request a resolution, the case is struck out.

Partial and intermediate judgments

The case can be already resolved in the preliminary preparation by a judgment for the part that the action has been admitted or abandoned. Accordingly the court may resolve an independent issue in a case where several claims have been presented or the part of the claim that has been admitted by a partial judgment (*osatuomio*).

If the defendant has presented a claim for set-off by way of a counter-claim or counteraction, a partial judgment is not possible as the original claim and the claim for set-off will be resolved together at the same time unless the claim of the plaintiff is resolved by default in a summary procedure.

If the resolution of an action depends on the resolution of another action considered in the same proceedings, the court may resolve separately the latter action by an intermediate judgment (*välituomio*). If it is important for the resolution of a case that an issue at hand in another trial or other proceedings be resolved first, the court may correspondingly order that the consideration of the case be continued only after this impediment no longer exists.

At the request of a party the court may also resolve by an intermediate judgment an issue pertaining to one claim, if the resolution of the other parts of the claim depends on the resolution of this issue. In this situation an intermediate judgment may be passed against the will of the other party only for a special reason and the intermediate judgment may have a *res judicata* effect outside the case in question only if further consideration of the case is unnecessary due to the intermediate judgment, i.e., the action is rejected.

Final judgment

The main resolution in a civil case is judgment (*tuomio*). The judgment must be justified by indicating the circumstances and judicial reasoning on which the resolution is based and on what grounds an issue under dispute has been proven or left unproven.

If the case is resolved in the preliminary preparation everything presented may be taken into account. Otherwise it is expressly provided that only the trial material that has been presented in the main hearing and in the possible supplementation of the main hearing will be taken into account. If the main hearing has been conducted in connection with the preliminary preparation, what took place in the last preliminary hearing will, however, also be taken into account, unless the court has ordered that it will not be taken into account in the main hearing.

The court may not judge for more than that claimed by a party. Furthermore, in a case amenable to out-of-court settlement the judgment may not be based on a circumstance to which a party has not referred to in support of his claim or denial.

The deliberation takes place immediately after the main hearing and the judgment must be passed immediately after the consideration of the case has ended. When the case is resolved without conducting a main hearing or a preliminary preparation, the judgment is issued without delay in the court office.

In an extensive or complicated case the judgment may be issued in the court office within 14 days from the conclusion of the main hearing or for a special reason even later.

Entry of judgment

The judgment must contain:

(1) The name of the court, the names of the parties and the date of issue of the judgment;
(2) A report of the claims and responses of the parties and of the circumstances on which they are based; and
(3) The judicial decree, the justification of the judgment and the legal provisions and guidelines applied.

As to the statements of a party, only the claims or denials and the circumstances on which they are directly based are entered in the records of the District Court. The principal rule is that the hearing of a witness or another person, heard for the purpose of obtaining evidence, must be taped and only evaluated in the judgment. This is important to note if the judgment is appealed.

The judgment must also contain the names of the members taking part in the resolution and a notification as to whether a vote has been taken, in which case the dissenting opinions will also be entered.

The report may be replaced in part or in full by enclosing a copy of a document presented to the court. The judgment is signed by the chairperson.

A judgment modifying rights has a constitutive effect in itself and therefore a separate execution is not required.

Specific performance

In a judgment granting affirmative relief, the defendant is ordered to perform something specific and, if the defendant does not voluntarily comply with the judgment, the judgment may be enforced. Secondary and alternative claims should be included in the application for a summons. If during the proceedings the original performance claimed becomes impossible due to a change in the conditions, the plaintiff may have the right to change the action and claim another, substitutive performance.

Declaration concerning legal relations

The declaratory judgment may be a positive or a negative one. It cannot be executed and it does not have an effect in altering legal relationships. If the plaintiff wishes a certain legal relationship under dispute in the proceedings between the parties to be confirmed and resolved by a declaratory intermediate judgment with *res judicata* effect, he has the right to make a separate claim on this. If the defendant wishes the same, he may bring a counteraction seeking a negative declaratory judgment.

POST-TRIAL MOTIONS

The normal method of appealing a judgment is to appeal to the next court instance, however there are other extra-ordinary means of modifying the effects of a judgment.

Rectification of the judgment

If there is a typographical or arithmetical error or other comparable manifest error in the judgment, the court having issued the judgment will correct the errors and an appeal is not required. The parties will, if necessary, be reserved the opportunity be heard. A party has the right to petition for the review of the correction of an error within 30 days from receipt of notice of the rectification.

Supplementation of the judgment

If the judgment does not contain a resolution of a claim by the party, the court may, at the request of a party, supplement the judgment. The judgment may also be supplemented *ex officio*, if it does not contain a resolution of a claim in a case not amenable to out-of-court settlement.

The supplementation is possible only for a short period after the judgment has been passed. If a party wishes the judgment to be supplemented, he must request the supplementation within 14 days from the passing or issue of the judgment. The judgment may be supplemented *ex officio*, if within 14 days of the passing or issue of the judgment the party has been invited to a hearing concerning the supplementation or a written statement of the supplementation has been requested of him.

Extraordinary rights of appeal

The provisions on extraordinary rights to appeal are contained in Chapter 31 of the Code of Judicial Procedure. A non-appealable judgment may be stricken on grounds of grave procedural error (*kantelu*).[7] Annulment of a non-appealable judgment (*tuomion purkaminen*) is respectively possible under certain circumstances.[8] The third extraordinary appeal is appeal for the restoration of lapsed time (*menetetyn määräajan palauttaminen*).[9]

Procedural error

A non-appealable judgment may be stricken on the basis of an extraordinary appeal if:

7. Code of Judicial Procedure, Chapter 31, Section 1.
8. Set out in Code of Judicial Procedure, Chapter 31, Section 7.
9. Code of Judicial Procedure, Chapter 31, Section 17.

(1) The court has not been competent or the court should have dismissed the case *ex officio*;
(2) A judgment has been passed against a person absent and not summoned or if a person not heard is otherwise hindered by the judgment;
(3) The judgment is so confusing and incomplete that it does not become evident what the judgment is; or
(4) Another procedural error has occured and it may be presumed that the error has essentially affected the judgment.

The time period to file the extraordinary appeal in situations (1) and (4) is six months after the judgment gained legal force and in situation (2) six months after the appellant became aware of the judgment. The *forum* to consider the extraordinary appeal is the same that would consider an ordinary appeal.

The court considering the extraordinary appeal will obtain further clarification if necessary. If it is established that a grave procedural error has taken place, the whole judgment or the necessary parts of the judgment will be stricken and, if the case will be considered again, the case must be assigned to a re-trial.

Annulment of a non-appealable judgment

The Supreme Court has the power to annul on request a non-appealable judgment in the following situations:

(1) A member or an official of court or an attorney or other representative or assistant of a party has in connection with the proceedings made himself guilty of criminal procedure and it may be presumed that this has affected the judgment;
(2) A document used as evidence has been false or the person who has presented the document has been aware that the document is untruthful or a party heard under oath or a witness or an expert has wilfully given a malicious testimony and it may be presumed that the document or testimony has affected the judgment; or
(3) A party refers to a circumstance or evidence that has not been presented earlier and the presentation of the same would probably have caused a different conclusion. The appellant must, however, establish a probability that he could not refer to that circumstance or evidence during the original proceedings or that he otherwise had a valid reason for not doing so.

The time period to appeal for annulment on the aforementioned grounds is one year after the appellant became aware of the circumstance on which the appeal is based, or if the appeal is based on the criminal procedure of a person, one year after legally final conviction of that person.

Annulment of a judgment is also possible if the judgment is based on manifestly incorrect application of the law, in which case the appeal must be submitted within one year after the judgment gained legal force.

Without weighty reason, an annulment is not possible if five years has elapsed since the judgment gained legal force. If the Supreme Court considers that a re-trial is necessary it will order how and where the case will be brought to re-trial. The Supreme Court may, however, alter the judgment if it considers that the case is clear. If the appellant neglects to commence the re-trial or remains absent, the annulment becomes void.

Restoration of lapsed time

If a party had a legal excuse not to undertake measures in legal proceedings within the prescribed time or he otherwise presents weighty reasons for his application, the Supreme Court may restore lapsed time. The application must be submitted within 30 days after the termination of the excuse and at the latest one year after the expiry of the time period.

ENFORCEMENT AND EXECUTION OF JUDGMENTS

The execution authorities are the executor-in-chief as the district administration authority and the distraint officer as the local authority. The executor-in-chiefs are the county administrative boards (*lääninhallitus*) and the distraint officers are in old towns the city bailiffs (*kaupunginvouti*) and in other municipalities the rural police chiefs-bailiffs (*nimismies*). In practice the actual measures are conducted by the assistant distraint officers (*avustava ulosottomies*).

Remedies

Writ of execution

Enforcement and execution of a judgment are usually requested directly from the distraint officer and the request may be presented orally or in writing, for example, by post. In exceptional cases the request will be presented to the executor-in-chief.

The main rule is that execution is sought from the execution authority of the domicile of the debtor. If the object of the execution is a certain property, the competent execution authority is that of the location of the property. If the request has been presented to a wrong distraint officer he must *ex officio* transfer the case to the competent distraint officer.

If the debtor has funds in different locations or if the judgment will be enforced against debtors in different locations, the distraint officer must request for executive assistance from the distraint officers of those locations i.e., the applicant must also in these cases present the request to only one distraint officer.

The applicant may expedite and increase the efficiency of the enforcement by providing accurate information on the debtor and the property and funds of the debtor or other object of the enforcement, for example, the identity number of the debtor is required to enable the distrainment of possible tax refunds.

The judgment or other grounds for enforcement must be enclosed in original with the application and, if applicable, the certificate of claim (for example, cheque, bill of exchange or promissory note) must also be enclosed in original. Judgment of a District Court may also be enforced using a copy of the judgment certified by the District Court.

The main principle as to court resolutions in civil cases is that enforcement requires that the judgment has gained legal force. Enforcement may, however, be requested even if the judgment has been appealed. The following provisions apply to the execution if the judgment has been appealed and has not gained legal force:

(1) A judgment with a liability to pay may be enforced by the distraint officer unless the debtor gives a pledge or a guarantee. The distrained property may not be converted into money before the judgment has gained legal force. However, a judgment based on a cheque or a bill of exchange is enforced as if the judgment had gained legal force;

(2) The distraint officer may enforce a judgment in which the losing party has been ordered to surrender the possession of a movable object if the winning party gives a security in case the judgment is changed. If the winning party does not give a security, the object will nevertheless be attached on his application;

(3) An eviction must be enforced if the winning party gives a security, to cover possible damages; and

(4) In other cases the executor-in-chief may order the enforcement if the winning party gives a security to cover possible damages and the enforcement does not make the appeal useless.

The higher court instance may prohibit or interrupt the enforcement of an appealed judgment with or without an obligation for the losing party to give a security. If distraint has already been levied, the court may also order that the distraint be cancelled. The petition does not prevent the enforcement unless the court otherwise orders.

If the judgment is changed the execution will be cancelled and the applicant is responsible to compensate the damage caused by the enforcement.

Execution must be levied on chattels before the real estate may be foreclosed. For social reasons certain objects may not be distrained and the distrainment can be directed at only a part of a person's wages, usually at one third of the net wage.

The distraint officer may draw up an execution report (*ulosotto-selvitys*) to acquire necessary information for the enforcement. In the execution report the debtor must give information of his funds, debts, incomes and employment. He must also give information of the transactions taken by him in order to find out whether possibilities of recovery exist. Recovery of transactions taken by the debtor is possible under the same conditions as applies to the recovery of a bankruptcy estate. The proceedings must be commenced not later than six months after the creditor was informed of the unsuccessful execution attempt.

The distrained property is converted into money usually by a compulsory auction.[10]

If a real estate is foreclosed or the object of distraint is other mortgageable property a meeting of creditors must be held before the auction. In this meeting the mortgage creditors and persons with rights of use to the property may present their claims and express their opinions of the claims of other creditors. Finally, a list of creditors in which the priorities of the claims are established will be prepared. The invitation to the meeting of creditors and the auction are published in the *Official Gazette* of Finland and also sent to the known mortgage creditors.

Precautionary measures

The precautionary measures available to a party before a final enforceable judgment is obtained have been discussed above. An appeal against the judgment does not prevent the enforcement of the judgment in many cases. Therefore, if the party has won the case, it may not be necessary at this stage to restore to precautionary measures even though the opposing party has appealed to the judgment and the judgment has therefore not yet gained legal force.

According to Section 11a of Chapter 7 of the Execution Act the distraint officer may, if the applicant so requests, make a decision on temporary precautionary measures if the applicant has an enforceable judgment that has gained legal force but his request for the enforcement cannot immediately be approved. The material requirements are the same as for precautionary measures ordered by a court.

10. The priority of the claims, is indicated below.

Bakruptcy or liquidation

Principally the bankruptcy proceedings fall under the jurisdiction of the District Court of the place of the domicile of the debtor. However, as to companies and associations the competent court is the court in which district the administration of the company or association is mainly conducted, i.e., not necessarily the formal (registered) domicile of the company or association. If there is no competent court by virtue of this, the competent court is also the court in which district the activities of the debtor have been mainly conducted; or the court in which district the debtor has assets; or the court in which it is considering the circumstances otherwise expedient to consider the case.

Special provisions apply to the bankruptcy court of group-member companies.

A written application by the debtor or a creditor is required. If the application is submitted by the debtor, no reason is required. An application submitted by a creditor must contain a clarification of his claim and the ground(s) for the opening of the bankruptcy proceedings.

The grounds for the opening of the bankruptcy proceedings by an application submitted by a creditor are listed in Sections 5 and 6 of the Bankruptcy Act (*konkurssisääntö*) and require that the claim of the creditor is clear and undisputed. The most common ground is that a debtor who is a merchant has not paid an undisputed and outstanding debt within eight days after having been verifiably notified of the debt. Other grounds are:

(1) The creditor has a clear and outstanding claim and the debtor is hiding;
(2) There is a risk of over-indebtedness of the debtor in the execution;
(3) The debtor hides or loses his assets;
(4) The debtor has been found insolvent in the execution;
(5) The debtor has not paid within eight days after demand a debt which the creditor is entitled to collect immediately in accordance with the Enterprise Mortgage Act (*yrityskiinnityslaki*); or
(6) The debtor is otherwise than temporarily only not able to pay his debts when they fall due.

The debtor may avoid the bankruptcy by giving to the creditor an acceptable security.

If the application is submitted by a creditor, the court will reserve the debtor a possibility to be heard before the court declares the debtor bankrupt and appoints a temporary administrator (*väliaikainen pesänhoitaja*). If the debtor opposes the application, the court will make its decisions after having considered the matter.

The main duties and authorities of the court in bankruptcy proceedings are:

(1) To make the decision of the adjudication of bankruptcy;
(2) To appoint the temporary administrator(s) and after the hearing of the creditors (*velkojainkuulustelu*) to appoint the trustee(s) (*uskottu mies*);
(3) To set the dates for the hearing of the creditors, for the filing of the claims (*valvonta*) and for the contesting of the filed claims (*riitautus*); and
(4) To pass the judgment in bankruptcy (*konkurssituomio*) in which the claims that are paid from the funds of the bankruptcy estate are confirmed and in which also the mutual order of priority of the claims is confirmed.

When the court declares the debtor bankrupt the court will appoint one or more temporary administrators to administer the bankruptcy estate until the hearing of the creditors. The main duties of the temporary administrator are to take over the management and administration of the bankruptcy estate and to draw up an estate inventory, which the debtor must confirm by oath in the hearing of the creditors.

If the proceedings are continued (the bankruptcy proceedings are not cancelled due to payment and the funds are sufficient to cover the costs of the proceedings) the court will appoint one or more trustees to replace the temporary administrators. Normally the trustees are appointed on the proposal of the creditors. The main duties of the trustees (who after the fixed date for filing the claims are called *toimitsijamies*) are to manage and administer the bankruptcy estate and to take care of the realisation of the bankruptcy estate and the distribution of the funds to the creditors.

Nowadays, the court usually orders that the filing of the claims must be submitted to the trustee(s) and that he or they must draw up the list of the filed claims. The trustee(s) must investigate the filed claims and contest groundless claims.

The creditors use their right to decision making in the creditors' meetings (*velkojainkokous*), for example, realisation of assets, lawsuits etc. and principally the creditors' meeting is competent to consider every issue of the bankruptcy estate. In practice, however, the authority is usually largely delegated by the decisions of the creditors' meetings to the trustees.

The bankruptcy estate consists of the assets the debtor owned on the day he was declared bankrupt, the assets the debtor gets or earns before passing the judgment in bankruptcy and the assets that can be recovered to the bankruptcy estate.

A specific act regulates the possibilities of recovery to a bankrupt's estate (*laki takaisinsaannista konkurssipesään*). The time periods to recover assets to the estate are calculated from the date the application to declare the debtor bankrupt was submitted to the court. The possibilities to cancel actions with persons or entities having a close relationship with the debtor are wider.

The main rule is that an action may become subject of recovery if either the debtor was insolvent when the action was performed or the action contributed to the insolvency of the debtor and:

(1) A creditor has been improperly favoured by the action; or
(2) Funds have been transferred out of reach; or
(3) Debts have been expanded to the loss of the creditors.

Furthermore, it is required that the other party was *mala fide*. If he is in a close relationship with the debtor he has to prove that he acted in good faith. If the action was performed more than five years before the insolvency proceedings became pending ("critical day"), the action may be cancelled only if it was performed with a person or entity having a close relationship with the debtor. Specific provisions apply to the recovery of presents.

A payment made during the last three months before the critical day may also become subject of recovery if:

(1) The payment has been made with extraordinary means of payment; or
(2) The payment relates to a debt that was undue; or
(3) The amount of payment is considerable compared to the funds of the estate, and the payment considering the circumstances was not customary.

If such a payment has been made to a person or entity having a close relationship with the debtor, the time limit is two years. These provisions apply also to the cancelling of a set-off if the creditor had not been entitled to set-off in the bankruptcy proceedings.

A deposit of guarantee may also be cancelled if the guarantee was deposited less than three months before the critical day and there was no agreement of the guarantee when the debt came into being or the necessary actions to complete the giving of the security were not performed without unnecessary delay after the debt came into being. The time limit with regard to a person or entity having a close relationship with the debtor is two years if it is not proven that the debtor was not and did not become insolvent because of the guarantee arrangement.

A creditor who wishes to get a payment for his claim from the funds of the bankruptcy estate has to file his claim in accordance with the provisions in the Bankruptcy Act. The court sets the date for the filing of the claims and the creditors are exhorted in a public summons published at least one month before the fixed date in the *Official Gazette* of Finland to send a written notice of their claims (*valvontakirjelmä*) by the fixed date for the filing of the claims. The trustee will also send a notice of the summons to the creditors, normally by post or telefax. However, the trustee is not obliged to send a notice to creditors who obviously will remain without distribution of the funds of the bankruptcy estate.

The creditor must state in his letter the amount and the ground of his claim and also, if interest is demanded, the amount or basis of interest and also the time period for which interest is claimed. If the creditor demands preference for his claim he must state the ground of the privilege. As to continuous obligations, the part of the claim that refers to the time before the commencing date of the bankruptcy must be indicated. A copy of the document on which the claim is based must be enclosed. If the notice of the claim is not in Finnish or Swedish, the trustee will see that the necessary parts of the letter are translated into Finnish or Swedish. The costs of translation may be deducted from the distribution payment to the creditor.

The filing of a claim by a creditor may be contested by the debtor and other creditors. The trustee has an obligation to contest groundless claims.

The new act on the order of payments (*laki velkojien maksunsaantijärjestyksestä*) entered into force on 1 January 1993 and the earlier privileges of, for example, wages (which are a to certain extent remunerated to employees by the State) and taxes were set aside, however, certain transition period provisions exist. If the opening of the bankruptcy proceedings has happened before 1 January 1993 the old provisions of preferences are applied.

The main rule is nowadays the equal right of the creditors to receive payment in bankruptcy. A pledge claim except for enterprise mortgage must, however, be satisfied to the full extent of the value of the pledged object.

A child's maintenance claim has retained its special privilege. If the insolvency proceedings are commenced before 1 January 1995, the wages from the present year and the previous year have the same privilege as a child's maintenance fees. Certain other transition period provisions also exist, for example, pension trust's claims based on voluntary supplementary benefits.

Thereafter, and before the "normal" claims, an enterprise mortgage has a privilege of up to 50 per cent (60 per cent if the proceedings become pending before 1 January 1995) of the value of the mortgaged property plus interest for three years.

Subordinated loans and certain governmental claims of sanctions similar to punishment in nature have a lower priority than other claims.

Under the old provisions (proceedings pending before 1 December 1993) a creditor may also use the judgment of bankruptcy as a ground for enforcement if the debtor (a private person) later earns an income or funds. Under the new provisions a new judgment must be obtained if enforcement is later sought. If the debtor is a legal entity and there is no surplus to account to the debtor after all creditors have been fully satisfied in the bankruptcy proceedings, a legal entity will cease to exist when the trustee has given the final account.

The Companies Act (*osakeyhtiölaki*) regulating companies limited by shares (*osakeyhtiö*) contains regulations of the obligation to place the company into liquidation and, if the funds of the company are not sufficient to pay the debts, to surrender the company into bankruptcy. A creditor may have a limited company placed in liquidation by a court order if the company does not have a board of directors or a managing director required by the Companies Act or the articles of the association.

Reorganisation of an enterprise

A special Act (*laki yrityksen saneerauksesta*) entered into force in February 1993 regulates the proceedings concerning the reorganisation of companies and enterprises. The model for this law was to a great extent Chapter 11 of the United States Bankruptcy Code. The purpose of the act is to provide possibilities to reorganise enterprises in financial difficulties but with potentiality to survive by confirming a reorganisation programme (*saneerausohjelma*).

Proceedings concerning the reorganisation of an enterprise have been concentrated to certain District Courts. The application to commence the reorganisation proceedings may be submitted by the debtor, a creditor or a probable creditor. The court will reserve to the major creditors and, if the application has been submitted by a creditor, to the debtor a possibility to give a written statement on the application.

If the court considers that the requirements set by the law to commence the reorganisation proceedings exist the court will appoint one or more administrators (*selvittäjät*) and usually also a committee of creditors (*velkojatoimikunta*). The proceedings may be commenced if, for example, the debtor and at least two creditors who represent at least a fifth of the known debts have requested for the proceedings and there are no reasons listed in the law not to commence the proceedings. The beginning of the reorganisation also means freezing of the payments, except for wages for three months, and prohibition of collection and enforcement against the debtor.

The main duties of the administrator are to prepare a report of the financial status of the debtor, to follow and supervise the actions of the debtor, to audit actions taken by the debtor before the beginning of the proceedings, to demand recovery to the estate of the debtor and to prepare in collaboration with the debtor and the creditors' committee a proposal for the reorganisation programme.

The creditors' committee will assist the administrator(s) as an advisory organ and supervise the activities of the administrator(s).

When deciding upon the commencement of the proceedings the court will set the fixed dates for the preparing of the report of the financial status of the debtor and the proposal for the reorganisation programme. Also, the court will set a fixed date for the filing of such claims of creditors that deviate from the statement of the debtor.

The creditors have a possibility to express their views on the proposal and they will vote on the approval or rejection of the proposal for the reorganisation programme. The confirmation of the programme by the court requires that a majority of the creditors determined in the law are in favour of the programme.

If the reorganisation proceedings are commenced the possibilities to recovery are the same as if the debtor were in bankruptcy.

All debts originated before the beginning of the reorganisation proceedings are subject of the proceedings. The debts arisen after the beginning of the proceedings are not subject to the proceedings and must be paid normally.

In the programme, the payment terms of the debts are rearranged which usually means also reduction of the amounts of the unsecured debts. Specific provisions apply to debts for the payment of which the creditor has a security.

During the proceedings the debtor retains in principle his ability to dispose over his property but his rights to act without the approval of the administrator are restricted. On the application of the administrator or a creditor, the court may furthermore issue prohibitions to the debtor not to undertake specific actions.

If the enterprise or company is not able to fulfil the obligations set in the programme, the reorganisation proceedings may be interrupted and the enterprise declared bankrupt.

If an application to commence the reorganisation proceedings is pending at the same time as an application to open bankruptcy proceedings is pending, the consideration of the latter is suspended until the decision whether to commence reorganisation proceedings or not is done. If the reorganisation proceedings are commenced, the application to open bankruptcy proceedings is dismissed. On the other hand an application to commence reorganisation proceedings submitted only after the debtor has been declared bankrupt will be dismissed.

The rearrangement of a private person's debts

An insolvent private person may on the basis of a special act (*laki yksityishenkilön velkajärjestelystä*) entered into force in February 1993 seek for the rearrangement of his/her debts. The purpose is to provide a remedy to the economic situation of the debtor by confirming a scheme of payment (*maksuohjelma*) that corresponds with the debtor's ability to pay. All the incomes and funds not necessary to the cost of living and maintenance liability of the debtor will be used to pay his/her debts. Specific provisions apply, for example, to the owner-occupied flat and the household effects of the debtor.

In the first phase the District Court of the domicile of the debtor decides the beginning of the rearrangement. All debts originated before the beginning of the rearrangement are subject of the rearrangement. The beginning of the rearrangement means also freezing of the payments and prohibition of collection and enforcement against the debtor.

In the second phase the court confirms the scheme of payment for a fixed time period, usually for five years. In the scheme the payment terms of the debts are rearranged which usually means also reduction of the amounts of the unsecured debts. Specific provisions apply to debts for the payment of which the creditor has a security.

The court may appoint an administrator to be in charge of the realisation of the rearrangement process.

The rearrangement may be granted only once and may be denied if the debtor has acted deliberately to the detriment of his/her creditors. If the debtor fails to fulfil the confirmed scheme of payment the court may, on the application of a creditor, declare the arrangement annulled.

If the debtor fulfils the confirmed scheme of payment he/she is released from the residual amounts of the debts subject to the scheme of payment.

Recognition and enforcement of foreign judgments

Finland has as from 1 July 1993 joined the Lugano Convention (Convention on Jurisdiction and the Enforcement of Judgments in Civil and Commercial Matters done at Lugano on 16 September 1968) the provisions of which correspond to the provisions in the Brussels Convention of 27 September 1968.

Before the Lugano Convention, Finland and the other Nordic countries (Denmark, Iceland, Norway and Sweden) signed in 1977 an agreement (replacing an agreement signed in 1932) on the recognition and enforcement of judgments in civil matters. Furthermore, Finland and Austria had in 1986 signed a bilateral agreement on the same subject. These agreements were replaced by the Lugano Convention.

The application on the basis of the Lugano Convention for the enforcement of a judgment given in a Contracting State must be submitted to the District Court of the place of domicile of the party against whom enforcement is sought. The application may also be delivered to the Ministry of Justice from where the application will be sent to the appropriate District Court.

APPEAL

A District Court judgment is appealed to a Court of Appeal (*hovioikeus*) and a Court of Appeal judgment, if a leave to appeal is granted, to the Supreme Court (*korkein oikeus*). However, the party against whom the case has been resolved by default in a District Court has no right to appeal to a court of appeal but he may instead get a re-trial by way of petition.

Appeal to the Court of Appeal

The judgment of a District Court, its decision to dismiss a case an its other connected resolutions are subject to appeal, unless appeal has been separately prohibited. No general restrictions, for example, as to the amount of interest exist. A decision of a District Court made during the proceedings is separately appealable only if especially provided for.

Notice of appeal

When passing an appealable resolution the District Court will at the same time notify of the right to appeal and of the actions a party must take to retain his right of action.

In order to retain his right of action and thus appeal to the Court of Appeal the party must at the latest on the seventh day from the passing or issue of the resolution register his intention to appeal by giving a notice of appeal (*tyytymättömyyden ilmoitus*). The notice can be made either orally or in writing and may be restricted to a certain part of the resolution. After the notice of appeal has been approved, the court will give detailed appeal instructions (*valitusosoitus*).

If a party fails to give a notice of appeal, the resolution gains legal force for his part. If his opposing party appeals to the Court of Appeal, he can only respond to the appeal of the opposing party but not claim for any amendments.

Letter of appeal and response

The letter of appeal must be delivered to the office of the District Court at the latest 30 days from the passing or issue of the resolution. Otherwise the appeal will be dismissed. The right to appeal is, however, not forfeited if the letter of appeal is delivered within the time prescribed erroneously to the office of the Court of Appeal.

The opposing party may respond to the appeal by delivering to the office of the District Court a written response at the latest on the 14 day from the expiry of the time limit for the appeal. On request he will be provided with a copy of the letter of appeal and the documents enclosed with it. As a party is not *ex officio* informed of an appeal a party must on his own initiative inquire whether or not the opposing party has appealed to a resolution.

The District Court may for special reasons set a new time limit for the appeal and/or the response if applied for before the expiry of the original time limit.

The information of the appellant and/or his attorney must be included in the letter of appeal and the letter of appeal must be signed by the appellant or by the person who has written it. The documents referred to in the letter of appeal must be enclosed. Corresponding provisions apply to the response.

Issues subject to review

Generally an appellate court may consider a case only to the extent it has been considered by the lower instance. Moreover, if the notice of appeal has been restricted to only a certain part of the resolution, the subject of the appeal is correspondingly restricted.

In the appeal the appellant must state which parts of the District Court resolution are appealed, the amendments claimed and the grounds thereof. He must also state for which parts, in his opinion, the justification of the resolution of the District Court is erroneous. Correspondingly the respondent must state in his response whether he denies or admits the claim for the amendments, his opinion of the grounds of the claims as well as the circumstances he refers to.

If the appeal is inadequate the Court of Appeal will exhort the appellant to remedy the inadequacy within a fixed time under the threat that unless the appellant heeds the exhortation the appeal may be dismissed.

The Court of Appeal may not judge for more than that claimed in the appeal and without a special reason the Court of Appeal may not consider the correctness of the resolution of the District Court for grounds and circumstances other than those stated in the appeal or response. This means that a party will not just refer to what has been presented in the District Court. It is important to note that not everything presented by a party is entered in the records of a District Court and that orally presented evidence is not usually entered in the records.

Therefore a party must expressly list in his brief to the Court of Appeal all the evidence, also what has been presented in the District Court, he refers to. If a party, for example, disagrees with the resolution of the District Court as to the evaluation of oral evidence presented, the taped statements must be written out, if the Court of Appeal deems this necessary, or the Court of Appeal may arrange a hearing.

In a Court of Appeal a party may not refer to circumstances or evidence other than what has been presented in the District Court, unless he can establish a probability that he has not been able to refer to the circumstance or evidence in the District Court or that he has otherwise had a valid reason for not doing so. If the party wishes to present new evidence in support of his appeal, he must list the evidence and state what he intends to prove with it and why the evidence has not been presented before. claim for a set-off presented only in the Court of Appeal may be dismissed, unless it can be considered without undue inconvenience.

Appeal to the Supreme Court

An appeal to a judgment given by a Court of Appeal as the second instance requires that a leave to appeal is first granted by the Supreme Court.

According to Section 3 of Chapter 30 of the Code of Judicial Procedure a leave to appeal may be granted only:

> (1) If it is important to bring the case to the Supreme Court because of the application of law in similar cases or the consistency of jurisdiction;
>
> (2) If there is a special reason for this due to such a procedural or other error that would lead to the removal or annulment of the judgment; or
>
> (3) If there is another weighty reason to grant a leave to appeal.

A leave of appeal may be granted to concern only a part of the resolution of the Court of Appeal.

The petition of appeal including both the application for leave and the appeal will be delivered to the office of the Court of Appeal at the latest 60 days from the issue of the resolution of the Court of Appeal.

The application for leave must state the above-mentioned grounds on which the leave is applied for and the reasons why the petitioner considers that there is an above-mentioned ground to grant the leave to appeal. The appeal must state which parts of the resolution of the Court of Appeal are appealed, the amendments claimed and the grounds thereof.

The Supreme Court will if necessary request a written response from the opposing party to the petition of appeal. If a leave to appeal is granted, a response will always be requested unless it has already been requested in connection with the consideration of the petition of appeal.

A party may not refer to circumstances or evidence other than what has been presented in the District Court or in the Court of Appeal, unless he can establish a probability that he has not been able to refer to the circumstance or evidence earlier or that he has otherwise had a valid reason for not doing so. The Supreme Court may also arrange a hearing.

CONCLUSIVENESS OF JUDGMENT

Res judicata

The Code of Judicial Procedure contains only a few rules on the effects of a judgment.

The negative extent of *res judicata* means that a case decided by a judgment that has become non-appealable may not be brought to the consideration of a court again.

If a matter decided in legal proceedings has gained legal force and this matter is a preliminary question later in other legal proceedings, it will be accepted as a basis of the judgment in the latter legal proceedings (the positive extent of *res judicata*).

The objective scope of *res judicata* extends to the legal relationship subject to the legal proceedings only in as far as the relationship was brought to the consideration and decision of a court.

The principal rule is that the subjective scope of *res judicata* extends usually only to the parties. However, it extends to persons who after the judgment has gained legal force have entered the legal relationship subject to the proceedings as the successors of a party. If a private universal succession has taken place during the proceedings the successor is automatically bound by the judgment, actually the successor has become thereafter a party in the case.

The evidentiary effect of a judgment that is to be separated from the *res judicata* is, mainly because of the principle of free evaluation of evidence, considered very convincing.

Law of the case

According to Finnish law, judgments (precedents) of the Supreme Court do not unconditionally bind lower courts despite Section 2 of Chapter 31 of the Code of Judicial Procedure, which expressly states that one of the grounds to grant the leave to appeal to the Supreme Court is the ground of the precedent.

However, because of the authoritative status of the judgments of the Supreme Court they have a strong guiding influence and generally a legal rule included in a Supreme Court judgment is followed in future legal decision making.

CHAPTER 6

FRANCE

CHRISTINE LÉCUYER-THIEFFRY
Thieffry & Associés
Paris, France

INTRODUCTION

Procedure in the French courts is adversarial, although the judge's role has been growing over the last few decades, especially since the adoption of the New Code of Civil Procedure (*Nouveau Code de Procédure Civile* — NCPC), which was adopted by Decree Number 75–1123 of 5 December 1975.

Although the time required to obtain a final judgment is generally felt to be rather long due to the courts' caseload as well as the necessities of the adversarial system, not unlike in Common Law countries, French litigation is significantly less time-consuming and less expensive by comparison. One of the major differences that make French litigation less burdensome is that there is no pre-trial discovery and, therefore, parties submit only those documents that they intend to rely on.[1]

The absence of a jury[2] accelerates the process at the hearing. Furthermore, evidence is mostly presented in written form and the limited amount of testimony offered is normally presented through written affidavits. Hearings themselves, even in complex matters, take no more than a few hours of oral argument presented by the *avocats*. In smaller matters, hearings only last a few minutes, which makes the pleadings and files prepared by counsel of critical importance.

ESTABLISHING JURISDICTION

While this chapter will deal solely with litigation in civil or commercial matters, it should be noted that as a result of the unique French concept of the separation of powers between the executive and judicial authorities, an administrative judiciary system, headed by the *Conseil d'Etat* — the

---

1. Mandatory production of documents may legally be ordered by the judge, however, this occurs rarely.

2. In civil and commercial matters there is no jury; there is a jury for the more severely punished criminal offences.

Supreme Court for all administrative matters — exists independently from the civil judiciary. The latter deals with all civil, commercial and criminal matters placed under the supervision of the *Cour de Cassation*.

Disputes as to jurisdiction between these two independent systems are decided by the *Tribunal des Conflits*. In addition, direct challenges to newly adopted laws based on constitutional grounds are submitted to the *Conseil Constitutionnel*.

In the French civil justice system, initial jurisdiction is distributed among various courts depending on the subject matter of the dispute, even though decisions rendered by these courts are all appealable to the same Court of Appeal. Decisions of the Court of Appeal may be reviewed on questions of law only by the *Cour de Cassation*.

There are three types of rules of jurisdiction in France:

(1) Some of the rules are based on the subject matter of the dispute, and are known as rules of jurisdiction *rationae materiae*;
(2) Other rules relate to the assignment of matters among courts of a certain category, according to their respective territorial jurisdiction; and
(3) Finally, the international jurisdiction of French courts is also asserted under specific rules.

Subject-matter jurisdiction

Depending on the subject matter of the dispute, a matter may fall within the jurisdiction of any one of the following courts, the most important of which are the *Tribunaux de Grande Instance* and the *Tribunaux de Commerce*.

Tribunal de Grande Instance

The *Tribunal de Grande Instance* has jurisdiction over all matters except those for which jurisdiction has been exclusively reserved by statute for another court.[3]

The *Cour de Cassation* (the highest court for civil matters), has long held that the *Tribunal de Grande Instance* has jurisdiction over the entire case even if it involves distinct civil and commercial claims, provided they cannot be resolved separately,[4] or when the action is brought against

3. Cass. Com. 25 June 1958, Bull. II, p. 303.
4. Cass. Civ. 21 January 1903, DP 1903, 1.1., 177; Paris, 2 May 1983, DI 1984, 347.

several defendants, some of whom would otherwise need to be sued before the commercial courts and others before the civil courts.[5]

In addition, the *Tribunal de Grande Instance* has exclusive jurisdiction[6] in certain types of matters, including actions involving the personal status of individuals, marriage, divorce,[7] property litigation and litigation involving major industrial or intellectual property rights. In the area of unfair competition, designs and models, however, the *Tribunal de Commerce* may, and in fact often does, have jurisdiction, unless the question is related to a trademark[8] or patent.[9]

With respect to the execution of judgments and other enforceable orders, a recent statute[10] gave jurisdiction to the *Président* — the chief judge — of the *Tribunal de Grande Instance* to settle "difficulties relating to the execution of enforceable rights and controversy which occur with respect to forced execution".[11]

Courts having jurisdiction over specific types of cases

Certain specialised courts have exclusive jurisdiction over specific kinds of matters according to areas of practice, for example, business disputes, social security, employment, and rent.[12]

TRIBUNAL DE COMMERCE

The *Tribunal de Commerce* has exclusive jurisdiction over bankruptcy proceedings.[13] It also resolves disputes between merchants — with respect to their business, disputes in relation to commercial paper, disputes between the shareholders or stockholders of a commercial company, and disputes relating to commercial transactions between any and all parties.[14]

5. Cass. Civ. 5 February 1907, DP 1907, 1.429.

6. See Vincent and Guinchard, *Procédure Civile,* Dalloz 1991, Number 115 to 126, 1.

7. Article 247 of the NCPC.

8. Law Number 91–7 of 4 January 1991, Article 34.

9. Law Number 68–1 of 2 January 1968, Article 68.

10. Law Number 91–650 of 9 July 1991.

11. *Code de l'Organisation Judiciaire,* Article L 311–12–1, as added by Law Number 91–650 of 9 July 1991; See Taormina, *Le nouveau droit des procédures d'exécution et de distribution,* Ed. du JNA 1993.

12. Only those courts most likely to be of interest to a foreign party are discussed below.

13. Law Number 85–96 of 25 January 1985, Article 7.

14. *Code de Commerce,* Article 631. The notion of "merchant" and "commercial transactions" have been the subject of extensive case law, see *Traité élémentaire de droit commercial,* Ripert, 14th ed., LGDJ 1991, Number 135, p. 105.

Transactions that occur between a merchant and a non-merchant or when one party is a consumer are called "mixed transactions". The wishes of the non-merchant party or the consumer are given preference in relation to jurisdiction in disputes over mixed transactions. Such a party may, if he is the defendant, object to the commercial court having jurisdiction; while, if he is the plaintiff, he can choose to bring his action before either the civil or the commercial court.[15] However, the *Tribunal de Commerce* has exclusive jurisdiction with respect to a non-merchant's commercial obligations.[16]

TRIBUNAL D'INSTANCE

The jurisdiction of the *Tribunal d'Instance* is limited to small claims relating to personal or property rights:

(1) In first and last resort — that is without the right of appeal — in disputes with claims not exceeding 13,000 FF; and
(2) Where there is the possibility of an appeal in disputes where the amount at stake does not exceed 30,000 FF.[17]

CONSEIL DE PRUD'HOMMES

The *Conseil de Prud'hommes* has exclusive jurisdiction over disputes arising out of employment contracts and other employment law matters.[18]

Territorial jurisdiction

Although the French rules of territorial jurisdiction traditionally differ to a significant extent from Anglo-American principles, such as those rules governing "venue" or those of "jurisdiction over the particular case", a parallel can be drawn between the two systems as to their practical results.

The single most striking difference is that in France, as a general rule, jurisdiction is given to the court where the defendant is domiciled.[19] If the defendant is a company, the court with jurisdiction is the one where

15. Vincent and Guinchard, *Procédure Civile*, Dalloz 1991, p. 169 and 170.
16. Cass. Com. 22 January 1991, Bull. IV, p. 25.
17. *Code de l'Organisation Judiciaire*, Article R 321–1.
18. *Code du Travail*, Article L 511–1, see Vincent and Guinchard, *Procédure civile*, Dalloz 1991, Number 182–198.
19. NCPC, Article 42.

the company's registered office is located.[20] Nevertheless,[21] it is also possible to bring an action where the defendant company has any establishment, provided a representative with the power to commit on behalf of the company can be found there, and on condition that the litigation is related to that establishment.[22] Where there are multiple defendants, the plaintiff has the option of choosing the court of the domicile of any one of them.[23]

In addition to the general rule of the domicile of the defendant, there are also alternative bases of jurisdiction, which vary according to the subject matter of the claim.

With respect to tort actions, the plaintiff may, at his option, bring an action in the court in the place where the tort occurred or where the damage was suffered.[24] French law makes a sharp distinction between contractual liability and tortious liability; generally there is no option of pleading either one or the other and, in principle, one cannot plead both.[25]

Where an action is brought in contract, it may be filed with the court in the place where the goods were actually delivered or where the services were carried out.[26]

Choice-of-court provisions are valid in business transactions provided that both parties reached the agreement in the capacity of merchants, and that the relevant clause is unambiguous and contained in a document in which the party against whom it is used obliged itself,[27] such as a signed written agreement or that party's own general sales conditions.

There are certain exceptions to these general rules: For example, in real property actions, the court where the property is located has exclusive jurisdiction,[28] while disputes over inheritance matters are within the exclusive jurisdiction of the court where the dispute arises.[29]

In addition, urgent or provisional measures can be ordered by the *juge des référés* — that is the chief judge of various courts, such as the *Tribunal de Grande Instance* or the *Tribunal de Commerce* — who has jurisdiction

---

20. NCPC, Article 43.

21. See Solus and Perrot, *Droit judiciaire privé, Tome II, La compétence*, Sirey 1973, Number 254 to 260.

22. Cass. Com. 12 January 1988, Bull. IV, p. 9.

23. NCPC, Article 42, Section 2.

24. NCPC, Article 46.

25. Cornu, *Le problème du cumul de la responsabilité contractuelle et de la responsabilité délictuelle, Rapport du VIème congrès de droit comparé, Études de droit contemporain*, 1962, pp. 239 *et seq.*

26. NCPC, Article 46.

27. NCPC, Article 48.

28. NCPC, Article 43.

29. NCPC, Article 45.

over the place where the measures sought must be taken.[30] Likewise, difficulties encountered in the execution of a judgment or order may be brought before the court in the place where the debtor resides or where the execution is to be carried out.[31]

Perhaps the strongest evidence that rules of territorial jurisdiction in France and in Common Law countries are based on very different concepts is that service of a summons is not a factor in establishing jurisdiction under French law, irrespective of whether there are sufficient contacts or not. Moreover, improper service can lead to the nullity of the service and of the procedure that follows, while having no consequence on the jurisdictional issue.

International jurisdiction of French courts

As a matter of principle, French rules of international jurisdiction are based on the above-described rules, which are applicable in domestic cases. This principle was set down in 1955 by the *Cour de Cassation*: It "extends the French rules of territorial jurisdiction internationally".[32]

Accordingly, as a general rule, the French courts will have jurisdiction if the defendant resides in France. Alternatively, in the absence of a valid choice of forum clause in the contract, a claim arising out of a contract with respect to goods delivered or services performed in France may, at the plaintiff's option, also be brought before the French courts. Tortious claims may likewise be filed with the French courts if the tort occurred or the injury was suffered in France.

However, jurisdiction over disputes in international matters may be resolved otherwise, mainly in the following circumstances:

(1) Where an international treaty applies;
(2) Where a choice of forum provision establishes the jurisdiction of the French courts; or
(3) Where a French citizen is a party to the dispute.

International conventions

France is a party to many bilateral treaties on judicial co-operation and enforcement of judgments, which frequently contain rules on international

30. Cass. Civ. 4 May 1910, S 1912, 1, 580; Cass. Civ. 2ème, 16 May 1957: JCP, 1957 Ed. G, IV, 94, Cass. Civ. 2ème, 9 December 1976, Gaz. Pal. 1977, 1, par. 82.

31. Law Number 91–650 of 9 July 1991.

32. That is mainly the above described rules provided for by NCPC, Articles 42 to 48; Civ. I, 30 October 1962, Scheffel, D 1963.109, note Holleaux, Rev. Crit. Dr. Int. Privé 1963.387, note Francescakis; see also Batiffol et Lagarde, *Droit international privé*, VIIème Ed., Tome 2, LGDJ 1983, Numbers 673 *et seq.*

jurisdiction. In addition, certain multilateral Conventions grant jurisdiction to, or take it away from the French courts.[33]

The most important Convention in this area is the European Community's Brussels Convention of 27 September 1968 on Jurisdiction and the Enforcement of Judgments in Civil and Commercial Matters.[34]

Another Treaty, the Lugano Convention of 16 September 1988 extends the principles of the Brussels Convention to the members of the European Free Trade Association (EFTA): Austria, Finland, Iceland, Liechtenstein, Norway, Sweden and Switzerland. The Lugano Convention came into force between the Netherlands, France and Switzerland on 1 January 1992 and on 1 February 1992 with Luxembourg.

The drafters of the Brussels Convention wished to allow the free circulation of judgments[35] within the European Community, to facilitate enforcement of judgments and legal certainty between Member States.

The Lugano Convention is in the process of extending this to EFTA. These treaties only apply in civil and commercial matters, and therefore do not extend to revenue, customs or administrative matters, legal capacity, matrimonial matters, succession, bankruptcy, social security and arbitration.[36]

The Brussels and Lugano Conventions provide rules of international jurisdiction that are substituted for the national rules when a defendant is domiciled in a Member State or one of the EFTA countries.

As a general rule, with the exception of certain instances discussed below, jurisdiction lies with the courts of the Contracting State in which the defendant is domiciled.[37] However, according to Article 5 of the Brussels and Lugano Conventions, a defendant domiciled in a Contracting State may also be sued, at the plaintiff's option:

> (1) In a contractual matter, before the court "for the place of performance of the obligation in question";[38]

33. Cass. Civ. 16 April 1985, Bull. I, p. 104.

34. The Brussels Convention initially came into force on 1 February 1973, among the first six Member States of the European Community. However, the scope of application of this Convention has been widened with the entry of new members to the Common Market. Since then, its application has progressively been extended to all twelve Member States.

35. Remarkably, the Brussels Convention intended that it receive a uniform interpretation by the European Court of Justice so that differences of interpretation between the courts of the Contracting States can be resolved.

36. See Brussels and Lugano Conventions, Articles 1, respectively.

37. Brussels and Lugano Conventions, Articles 2, respectively. This rule is similar to that provided for by the NCPC, Article 42.

38. Brussels and Lugano Conventions, Articles 5(1); the 1989 Accession Convention also provides for specific rules in relation to employment contracts.

(2) In the case of a claim based on a tort, before the court for the place where the harmful event occurred.[39] Note that, according to the European Court of Justice, when an act causing damage is carried out in one Contracting State but the injury occurs in another, the plaintiff may bring his action before the courts of either country.[40]

Choice of forum provisions

The Brussels and Lugano Conventions give effect to clauses through which the parties to a contract agree to give jurisdiction to a court of their choice. Where there is such an agreement, Articles 17 of both Conventions provide, firstly that the courts of the Contracting State selected by the parties have jurisdiction (without any discretionary power to refuse jurisdiction) and, secondly that such jurisdiction is exclusive (that is other Contracting States are deprived of jurisdiction).

For an agreement to come within the scope of Article 17, two requirements must be satisfied:

(1) The parties must have agreed that the courts of a Contracting State are to have jurisdiction to settle any disputes which have arisen or which may arise between them in connection with a particular legal relationship; and

(2) The agreement must satisfy certain requirements by either being:
(a) In writing or evidenced by writing; or
(b) In a form which accords with practices which the parties have established between themselves; or
(c) In the case of international trade or commerce, in a form which accords with custom or use of which the parties are or ought to have been aware of and which is widely known to, and regularly observed by, parties to contracts of the type involved in the particular trade or commerce concerned.

Jurisdiction based on French nationality

A party to litigation who is of French nationality enjoys a jurisdictional privilege granted by Articles 14 and 15 of the Civil Code by which he may:

39. Brussels and Lugano Conventions, Articles 5(3).

40. *Mines de Potasse d'Alsace*; ECJ 30 November 1976, D 1977.613, Note Droz; Cass. Civ. 8 January 1991, Bull. I, p. 4.

(1) Bring a suit before a French court, whatever nationality the defendant may be;[41] and
(2) Demand to be sued before a French court, whatever the circumstances.[42]

The jurisdiction of a French court based on these provisions can be invoked with respect to any type of legal action, even though Articles 14 and 15 of the Civil Code only expressly refer to "contractual obligations".[43] However, these jurisdictional bases are available when a French court already has jurisdiction under another criterion.[44] Furthermore, International Conventions such as those referred to above often provide for the exclusion of such jurisdictional privileges. Thus, Articles 3 of the Brussels and Lugano Conventions specifically set aside Articles 14 and 15 of the Civil Code.

Case law shows a broad notion of renunciation by French defendants of their privileged position relating to jurisdiction, and Article 15 of the Civil Code is subject to waiver, either express or implied. Generally, it is sufficient that a French defendant has not raised as a preliminary issue the lack of jurisdiction of the foreign court. In addition, a choice of jurisdiction agreement is deemed to be a waiver. However, the appearance of a French defendant in the foreign court for the sole purpose of challenging jurisdiction, without arguing the merits of the case, does not imply a waiver of Article 15.

ASCERTAINING THE APPLICABLE LAW

Regional law (European Community law)

As the European Community progresses toward a single market, European Community law has become increasingly important. European Community legislation, by way of regulations, directives, decisions and conventions, prevails over the domestic laws of the Member States even if they are enacted subsequent to European Community legislation. The European Court of Justice has clearly stated that every national court must apply European Community law in its entirety, and set aside any provision of national law conflicting therewith.[45]

41. Article 14 of the Civil Code.
42. Article 15 of the Civil Code.
43. Cass. Civ. April 22 and 17 November 1981, JCP 82, II–19920.
44. Cass. Civ. 19 November 1985, JCP 1987, II–20810, Note Courbe.
45. Case 106/77, *Administrazione delle Finanze dello Stato* v. *Simmenthal* (1978) European Community Reports 629.

The *Cour de Cassation* rapidly complied with the Doctrine of Supremacy of European Community law,[46] while the *Conseil d'Etat* has only more recently followed the European Court of Justice case law[47] after a long period of resistance.[48]

The efficacy of European Community law is strengthened by the so called "direct effect doctrine" under which citizens may invoke its provisions in the courts of Member States.[49]

The combination of these two doctrines is of great importance for companies doing business in the European Community, since the prime responsibility for applying Community legislation rests with the Member States, which must not only enact the necessary transposition measures but also ensure compliance. Businesses and individuals, suffering from obstacles — such as trade barriers — resulting from national legislation, and protectionist practices or behaviour from competitors may either complain to the European Commission, or start proceedings before French courts.

However, private persons cannot directly invoke those provisions of European Community law that leave certain discretion to Member States. This restriction is important for European Community directives, the European Community's most popular legal instrument.[50]

To achieve a single market in areas not subject to a Community policy, several hundreds of directives have been passed in order to harmonise the different national laws concerning a certain product or problem.[51]

A directive is only binding on the member state as to the result to be achieved. It leaves to the national authorities the choice of form and methods.[52] It is not directly applicable, except against the Member State and authorities emanating from it in certain circumstances.

---

46. *Administration de Douanes* v. *Société Café Jacques Vabre* (1975) *Common Market Law Reports*, 367.

47. See *Alitalia* case, 3 February 1989, RJF 3/89 No. 299, *Nicolo* case 20 October 1989, RJF 11/89 No. 1266; Louis, *L'ordre juridique communautaire*, 6ème édition, *Perspectives européennes*, Luxembourg 1993, p. 188.

48. See, for example, *Syndicat Général de Fabricants des Semoules de France* (1970) *Common Market Law Reports*, 395.

49. For the first time in case 26/62 *Van Gend en Loos* v. *Nederlandse Administratie der Belastingen* (1963) European Community Reports 1, which concerned the possibility for a company to invoke a provision of the European Community Treaty. In its subsequent case law, the European Court of Justice has extended its direct effect doctrine to secondary Community law.

50. For example, the vast majority of the legislative acts of the 1992 Single Market programme are directives.

51. As for the impact of one of these directives, see Thieffry, Van Doorn and Lowe, "Strict Product Liability in the EEC: Implementation, Practice and Impact on United States Manufacturers of Directive 85/374", *Tort and Insurance Law Journal*, Volume 25, No. 1, Fall 1989, p. 65.

52. EEC Treaty, Article 189.

Conflict of laws

Except for scattered substantive statutes, which include directive as to the scope of their application in international matters, French rules relating to the conflict of laws are found in several international conventions and in case law.

When dealing with international situations, French courts are now required to consider the issue of applicable law.[53] Nevertheless, parties may generally ignore the problem of the conflict of laws and instead accept the application of French law.[54]

The law applicable to a contract

With respect to an international contract for the sale of goods, a French court will rely on the rules provided for by The Hague Convention on the Law Applicable to Contracts for the International Sale of Goods of 15 June 1955, which was ratified by nine countries including France.[55]

A more recent Convention on the Law Applicable to Contracts for the International Sale of Goods was concluded at The Hague on 22 December 1986.[56] This is irrespective of whether the other party involved is from a country which is a signatory to the Convention, as no reciprocity is required for the Convention to apply. In the absence of a choice of law provision in the contract, the law of the country where the seller is domiciled applies as a result of the Convention.[57]

The Rome Convention on the Law Applicable to Contractual Obligations of 19 June 1980 has a broader scope of application. A European Community Convention,[58] it does not require reciprocity for its provisions to apply.

Therefore, all courts of European Community Member States may enforce its rules irrespective of the nationality of the other parties involved.

---

53. See two recent decisions of the *Cour de Cassation* of October 11 and 18, 1988 Rev. Crit. Dr. Int. Privé 1989, 368, Clunet, 1989, 349, Note Alexandre, JCP, 1989, II–21327, Note Courbe.

54. Civ. 4 December 1990, Rev. Crit. Dr. Int. Privé 1991, 558, Note Niboyet-Hoegy.

55. The others being Belgium, Switzerland, Italy, Sweden, Norway, Denmark, Finland and Nigeria.

56. As of the fall of 1993, The Hague Convention of 1986 had only been ratified by Argentina and has not yet come into force.

57. On the exceptions to and examples of the practical application of The Hague Convention of 15 June 1955, see Jean Thieffry and Chantal Granier, *La Vente Internationale*, Full Cite p. 196.

58. The Convention entered into force on 1 April 1991, following the ratification on 22 January 1991 by the United Kingdom, which followed that of France, Italy, Denmark, Luxembourg, West Germany and Belgium.

Two protocols, neither of which will come into force until the ratification of the second protocol by all 12 Member States of the European Community, grant special jurisdiction to the European Court of Justice for the interpretation of the Rome Convention. This is the same jurisdiction that it enjoys with respect to the Brussels and Lugano Conventions on Jurisdiction and the Enforcement of Judgments.

The Rome Convention does not apply to a number of matters, for example, questions involving the status or legal capacity of natural persons, contractual obligations relating to wills and succession, rights in property arising out of a matrimonial relationship, obligations arising under commercial paper that derive from their negotiable character, arbitration and choice of court agreements and questions of company law.

The main principle of the Rome Convention gives effect to the parties' choice as to the law applicable to their contract, whether or not the law chosen is that of a Contracting State,[59] on the condition that this choice is either expressed in the contract or appears as a clear result of the terms of the contract or the circumstances of the case.

Should the parties fail to choose the law applicable, "the contract shall be governed by the law of the country with which it is most closely connected". This is "presumed" to be "the country where the party who is to effect the performance that is characteristic of the contract has its main establishment" at the time of the conclusion of the contract.

However, this presumption is disregarded in several situations provided for by paragraphs (3), (4) and (5) of Article 4 of the Convention with respect to contracts the subject matter of which is immovable property or the transportation of goods, or when the characteristic performance of the contract cannot be determined. Specific rules on the application of the principle for various types of contracts are also given, notably for those contracts entered into with consumers or individual employment contracts.[60]

This Convention expressly provides that European Community law has priority over its provisions, and allows for the application of earlier international Conventions, so that, for example, The Hague Convention referred to above will continue to be applied by French courts to transactions within its scope.[61]

The Rome Convention also reserves the possibility of applying the "mandatory rules of the law of another country" that is those rules that apply regardless of the law applicable to the contract.[62]

59. Rome Convention, Articles 2 and 3.

60. Rome Convention, Articles 5 and 6.

61. See Lagarde "Le nouveau droit international privé des contrats après l'entrée en vigueur de la Convention de Rome". Rev. Crit. Dr. Int. Privé, June 1991.

62. Rome Convention, Article 7; these laws apply to specific disputes, for example, employment and social security law, regardless of the law chosen by the parties, or applicable under the various rules.

Rules of conflict of laws in tort actions

French courts determine tortious liability according to the law of the place where the tort was committed. This is either the law of the place where the act itself was committed or where the damage was suffered.[63]

French courts are bound by two Hague Conventions that deal specifically with tortious liability and which incorporate the principle of applying the *lex loci delicti commissi*:

(1) The Hague Convention on the Law Applicable in Traffic Accidents of 4 May 1971; and
(2) The Hague Convention on the Law Applicable to Strict Product Liability of 2 October 1973.

The Hague Convention on the Law Applicable in Traffic Accidents maintains that the applicable law is that of the country where the accident occurred. Nonetheless, in order to account for unforeseeable consequences of the accident, some exceptions favour the law of the country in which the vehicle involved is registered.

The Hague Convention on the Law Applicable to Strict Product Liability also provides for the application of the law of the place where the harmful act occurred, but only insofar as it does not conflict with the law of the country where the victim resides, or where the product was acquired. The law of the country where the victim resides will prevail if the defendant also resides or the product was acquired in that same country. In the absence of these factors, the Convention provides that the law of the defendant's principal place of business should apply, however, it does allow the victim to opt for the law of the place where the harmful event occurred.

Other conflict of laws rules

Aside from the principal conflicts of laws rule already discussed, there are a great many others. For example, property rights are governed by the law of the place where the goods are located, and corporate matters are to be settled according to the laws of the country where the corporation has its headquarters. Intellectual and industrial property rights are territorial, hence French courts apply French law to such rights if they are acquired in France.

63. Battifol and Lagarde, Number 561.

COMMENCING THE ACTION

Legal standing to sue

Certain preventative or anticipated claims, such as those for a declaratory judgment, are rejected, because the court is asked to give an immediate decision on the existence, the validity or the contents of a legal situation, independent from any actual damage caused.

A plaintiff must justify an interest in the litigation and this interest must be legitimate.[64] In addition, the plaintiff's interest must be positive and concrete, existing and current,[65] personal and direct.[66]

These requirements have generated an abundance of case law and scholarly arguments regarding the admissibility of actions brought, for example, by unions and associations to defend interests that are collective in nature.[67]

Statutes recognise the right of professional unions to defend the common interests of a particular profession, and the right of certain associations to seek enforcement of the class interests which they represent, An example of this is Article 8 of Law No. 92–60 of 18 January 1992,[68] augmenting consumer protection by providing that where several consumers have suffered individual harm from a single business, an approved and nationally recognised consumer organisation can bring an action for damages on their behalf, provided it is authorised in writing by at least two of the consumers concerned, and such authorisation is not obtained by public announcements of any kind.

Recent decisions have declared that actions brought, for example, by religious groupings or by the "League against Highway Violence" (*Ligue contre la violence routière*) are admissible[69] although it is doubtful whether the *Cour de Cassation* would share this liberal approach.[70]

---

64. NCPC, Article 31 states "The right to claim in court is open to all those who have a legitimate interest in the success or failure of a claim, with the exception of those cases for which the law only grants to a certain group of people the right to raise or defend a claim, or the right to defend a certain interest."

65. Solus and Perrot, *Tome I*, Number 223.

66. Vincent and Guinchard, *Procédure Civile*, Précis Dalloz, 1991, Number 28.

67. For a comparison with "class actions" allowed under American law, see P. Thieffry "Quelques aspects comparés de la procédure civile en France et aux Etats-Unis". Rev. Int. Drt. Comp. 1984, p. 783.

68. JO 21–01–92, p. 968.

69. Order of the *Président du Tribunal de Grande Instance* of Paris, 9 October 1984, Gaz. pal. 1985, I, Som. 91.

70. *Chronique J. Normand*, Rev. trim. dr. civ. 85, p. 767 *et seq.*

Complaint

A lawsuit is commenced by notifying the other party of the claim through the service of a writ of summons, generally referred to as an *assignation*.

Nevertheless, certain types of proceedings as well as actions in certain specialised courts, for example, the *Conseil de Prud'hommes*, the *Tribunal Paritaire des Baux Ruraux* or the *Tribunal d'Instance* are introduced by a simple request (*Requête*).

Whether an *assignation* or a *requête*, the initial pleading has a broader purpose than the simple initial pleadings used in the United States. Generally, it is an initial statement of the case, both in fact and in law, and contains the plaintiff's arguments at this initial stage. Indeed, it must be sufficiently complete to enable the defendant to respond.

Service is effected by an authorised process-server who has the status of a sworn court office, an *huissier*.[71] If the defendant is to be served abroad, it is addressed to the public prosecutor's office and done through diplomatic channels,[72] unless service is governed by an international convention which allows a process-server to serve the writ directly on the party concerned. International treaties, such as The Hague Convention on the Service of Process, provide for alternative methods of service.

The writ of summons must be written in French and must contain the details of the plaintiff, the process server who served the writ, the defendant, the court in which the claim is brought, the subject matter of the claim, a summary of the legal arguments and a warning as to the consequences of failing to appear at the hearing. If this information does not appear, the writ may be deemed invalid.

The *assignation* must specify the documents on which the plaintiff intends to rely at the time of its drafting, although most of these will be served on the defendant at a later stage. However, some expedited proceedings available in cases of urgency require that all the documents be served on the defendant with the *assignation*. Further, certain statements and formalities are required, depending on the nature or the object of the litigation.[73]

The service of a summons normally stays the operation of the applicable statute of limitation for the duration of the litigation.[74]

71. NCPC, Article 55.

72. NCPC, Article 684.

73. See Solus and Perrot, *Droit judiciaire privé*, 33, *procédure de première instance*, Sirey 1991, Numbers 143 *et seq*.

74. Most civil actions have a limitation period of 30 years, (Civil Code, Article 2262) while those relating to obligations arising out of business transactions have a 10 year limitation period (Commercial Code, Article 189 *bis*) and there are other shorter limitation period in special areas.

Other pleadings

An important part of French civil practice is the exchange of pleadings known as *conclusions*.

Time limits for such an exchange vary depending on the complexity of the case, its possible urgency and the caseload of the particular court. The plaintiff is supposed to have already stated his case in the *assignation* or *requête*, the initial pleading that was served at the beginning of the case. He should then produce the documents he intends to rely on so that the defendant can respond by serving a defence in the form of conclusions *en réponse*.

The plaintiff will normally in turn respond by serving *conclusions en réplique*, a reply to the defence. Even if the *assignation* sets out the plaintiff's claim, the absence of strict time limits allows the plaintiff to file amended pleadings and replies at least until an order is entered for, the closure of pleadings, the *ordonnance de clôture*. This marks the end of the investigatory phase of the proceedings. Pleadings filed and documents produced thereafter must be declared inadmissible by the court,[75] unless it is found necessary to revoke the closure of pleadings to allow the other party to comment or respond.

While the lack of subject-matter jurisdiction can be raised *sua sponte* in certain cases by the judge at any time during the proceedings,[76] objections in this respect made by the defendant must normally be made at the same time that the other procedural objections are raised and before any defence on the merits is served, after which such objections would be waived[77] — just as "affirmative defences" in United States litigation.

Incidental claims may be raised at any time and are, generally, made in the *conclusions*,[78] as in the case of additional claims by which a party modifies its initial claims,[79] and counter-claims by which the original defendant sets forth a claim against the plaintiff.[80]

Joinder of parties may be voluntary or involuntary.[81] In the case of an impleader, the third-party defendant is served with an *assignation*.[82]

OBTAINING INFORMATION PRIOR TO TRIAL

There is no such institution as pre-trial discovery in French civil litigation. Depositions, interrogatories, and the like are unheard of. Not only

75. NCPC, Article 783.
76. NCPC, Article 92.
77. NCPC, Article 74.
78. NCPC, Article 68.
79. NCPC, Article 65.
80. NCPC, Article 64.
81. NCPC, Article 66.
82. NCPC, Article 68.

is discovery totally unknown, as in many other Civil Law systems, but France has also reacted violently to Common Law type pre-trial discovery by adopting a so called "blocking statute" which prohibits the supply of information for the purpose of participating in pre-trial discovery.[83]

The main devices that can be used in certain respects as substitutes for pre-trial discovery are document production and expert investigations.

Document production

Prior to a hearing on the merits, the parties must exchange the documents on which they respectively intend to rely, so that each has the opportunity to analyse and elaborate on the other's evidence. Such document production must be spontaneous.[84]

In addition, parties have the legal right to request the court to order the production of a document held by the other party or even by a third party. However, the requesting party must be aware of the existence of such a document so that it may claim that it intends to rely on it.[85] Therefore, in practice, this right is exercised only for particularly important documents and is very rarely recognised by the courts.

In fact, besides the above-mentioned mandatory spontaneous production of documents by a party, most document production occurs in the framework of the investigations carried out by court-appointed experts.

Court-appointed experts

Expert evidence is not given by experts hired by the parties, but by neutral court-appointed experts. While parties are at liberty to appoint consultants to assist them in the analysis, development or presentation of their

83. French Law No. 82–538 of 16 July 1980 JO 1799, a translation of the law appears in *Société Nationale Industrielle Aérospatiale* v. *United States District Court*, 107 SCt. 2542 (1987); see generally, Mercier and McKenney, "Taking Evidence in France for Use in U.S. Litigation", 2 Tul. J. Int. L Comp. L. 91 (spring 1994); Article 1 of the 1980 law provides: "Subject to international treaties and agreements, all persons are prescribed from asking for, searching or communicating by writing, orally or in any other form, documents or information of an economic, commercial, industrial, financial or technical nature, meant for the establishment of evidence in a foreign jurisdictional or administrative proceeding are in relation thereof."

84. NCPC, Article 132.

85. NCPC, Article 138.

cases either to the court or to the court-appointed expert, this is not provided for by French law. A court is empowered to choose any person to carry out the duties of:

(1) Taking notice of certain facts;
(2) Giving an opinion to the court; or
(3) Providing the court with expert findings.[86]

As a general rule, investigations can only be ordered with respect to a fact that cannot be proved by the party that makes the allegation. Under no circumstances can a court order investigation measures to alleviate a party's burden of proof.[87]

Usually an expert is appointed to carry out (3) above. The courts establish lists of experts in the various technical areas whom they usually appoint. Once she has been appointed, the expert receives an advance on her fees, the amount of which is set by the court. The expert is empowered to require production by the parties of any documents she deems necessary to discharge her duties, and the court will order such production if necessary.[88]

The investigations of the court-appointed experts are said to be inquisitorial. This means that the expert must hear and take into consideration the observations of all the parties involved,[89] and accomplish this task independently from the parties. *Ex parte* meetings or other contact with any party are forbidden. Any contacts must be in the presence of all parties or their counsel.

Expert testimony is normally given to the court in the form of a written report, although the court may authorise the expert to provide oral testimony at the hearing.[90] In practice, the court will sometimes request the expert to attend the hearing in order to answer questions, or elaborate on the findings summarised in his report. While the court is never bound by the expert's findings, it does not usually have the information necessary to disregard them and, therefore, normally follows them.

The court may, *sua sponte* or on a party's request, order any investigation it deems proper,[91] in order to preserve or establish facts.[92]

It is possible to ask the court to request the appointment of an expert prior to and even without subsequently initiating a lawsuit. In practice,

86. NCPC, Article 232.
87. NCPC, Article 146.
88. NCPC, Article 275.
89. NCPC, Article 276.
90. NCPC, Article 282.
91. NCPC, Article 143.
92. NCPC, Article 145.

such possibility is widely used by potential litigants who take this opportunity to establish facts or obtain expert evidence that might become decisive in later litigation.[93] Such an order can be obtained in an expedited procedure known as *référé*[94] albeit there is no requirement that any urgency, or a serious dispute as to the right involved be shown at that stage.

INTERIM PROTECTION OF ASSETS PENDING TRIAL

There are two kinds of provisional attachments.[95] Provisional attachment (*saisie conservatoire*) may be authorised by the *juge de l'exécution* where the claim appears to be well founded and there are circumstances that might threaten the recovery of the debt.[96]

In certain circumstances, a creditor does not even need to ask the court for an attachment, for example, when he holds an enforceable judgment, a bill of exchange, a promissory note, checks or a debt for unpaid rent.

In other instances, the creditor must obtain the authorisation of the *juge de l'exécution* by a simple *ex parte requête*.

Strict deadlines apply. If the creditor proceeds to the attachment without an order on the basis of an executory title, he must file the appropriate proceedings within one month of obtaining this title. Where a court order was issued, the attachment must be effected within three months thereof.

Liens and mortgages may also be ordered by the court at a creditor's request. Their conditions are usually similar to those described above for attachment, although they may also be granted on the basis of stocks or transferable securities. There are strict requirements relating to publication.

SUMMARY JUDGMENTS

There is no procedural equivalent to Common Law summary judgment. This may be because it would be of little further advantage in a system without jury trials. Nevertheless, certain proceedings are expedited as indicated below.

93. NCPC, Article 145.
94. See below.
95. This is as a result of the reform of execution proceedings, which was recently brought about by Law No. 91/650 of 9 July 1991 and *Décret* No. 92–750 of 31 July 1992.
96. Law No. 90/650, Article 67.

Request for an order to pay a debt

The procedure known as *injonction de payer* allows a creditor of a determined sum of money to obtain within a short period of time — generally not exceeding four weeks — an order obliging the debtor to pay. This is available mainly in the case of debts based on contract, for example, liquidated damages, or on commercial paper that has been issued, accepted or endorsed by the debtor.[97]

Depending on whether the debt is civil or commercial, the *requête* is filed with either the *Tribunal d'Instance*[98] or the *Président du Tribunal de Commerce*.[99]

The proceedings are *ex parte* from the granting of the order to its service on the debtor, which must be effected within six months.[100] It will only become adversarial if the debtor files an opposition with the clerk of the court within one month from service of the order on him.[101]

The opposition is the only way the debtor may challenge the order, and gives rise to a full adversarial adjudication, which ends with the issuance of a judgment.[102] If, however, the debtor does not file an opposition within the one month period, the creditor requests the clerk for the order to be marked accordingly, and it then becomes executory, without any possibility of appeal.[103]

Summary proceedings for provisional orders

An increasing number of proceedings are filed to obtain fast provisional orders, called *ordonnances de référé* (*référé*). The main purpose of this procedure is to speed up the ordering of measures:

(1) To which no serious objection has been made; or
(2) Which are justified by the existence of a dispute.[104]

Even in the case of a serious objection, an *ordonnance de référé* may be issued to prevent immediate injury or to stop a manifestly unlawful

97. NCPC, Article 1405.
98. Whatever the amount claimed, even if it exceeds the limits of the *Tribunal's* usual jurisdiction, See Paris, 20 April 1988, D 1989, Som. 179, Obs. Julien.
99. NCPC, Article 1406.
100. NCPC, Article 1411.
101. NCPC, Articles 1415 and 1416.
102. NCPC, Articles 1417 to 1421.
103. NCPC, Article 1422.
104. NCPC, Articles 808 and 872.

disruption. Where the obligation cannot be seriously opposed, the payment of provisional compensation or strict performance may be ordered.[105] The appointment of an expert, as well as other investigatory measures, may also be ordered in *référé* proceedings.[106]

A *référé* is commenced by serving an assignation on the other party, and is thus an adversarial proceeding. The *Présidents* of both the *Tribunal de Grande Instance* and the *Tribunal de Commerce* have jurisdiction with respect to *référés*. Hearings are normally very brief — a few minutes at the most — and sometimes they take place very soon after service of the assignation — a few days or even a few hours.

Other expedited proceedings include default judgments and the more frequent "judgments deemed adversarial".[107] Default judgments are strictly reserved to instances where:

(1) The defendant has not been served in person; and
(2) The judgment cannot be appealed.[108]

Either event gives rise to a possibility of avoiding the judgment by filing an opposition.

Other judgments rendered in the *de facto* absence of the defendant to the proceedings are "deemed adversarial" (*réputés contradictoires*), so that only an appeal can be brought against them. However, full reconsideration of the matter is possible in appellate proceedings.

TRIAL

There is no jury in civil and commercial litigation in France. This probably partly explains the virtual absence of rules of evidence.

Hearing

It is generally not an individual judge who hears cases and renders judgment. The principle that the court should be composed of a plurality of judges — usually three — is considered to be a guarantee of justice and impartiality. Nevertheless, the need to expedite the resolution of simple matters has given rise to an increasing number of exceptions.

105. NCPC, Articles 809 and 873.
106. NCPC, Article 145.
107. NCPC, Articles 467 to 479.
108. NCPC, Article 473.

While there are usually three judges in the *Tribunal de Grande Instance* to consider a matter, the *Président* may refer a matter to a single judge,[109] subject to the right of any party to request that the case be referred back to a panel of judges.[110]

Likewise, in the *Tribunal de Commerce*, there is normally a panel of three judges to handle a ase. Again, however, a single judge who is entrusted with the duty of monitoring the preparation of the case[111] may also conduct the hearing alone unless any party requests that the matter be heard by a panel of judges.[112]

In addition, expedited proceedings such as the above discussed *référé*, as well as proceedings dealing with problems of execution are heard by single judges.

Setting the case for hearing

The exchange of pleadings — the conclusions — is most important in the preparation of the hearing as it exposes the various claims and arguments of the parties. Once the closing order is issued, there is normally no further communication between the parties and the case is referred for hearing.

Scope and order of the hearing

The hearing is significantly shorter than a hearing under Common Law procedure as it merely consists of the successive presentation of the arguments of counsel over a period of time that may vary from a few minutes to a few hours. The length of the main hearing on the merits in a civil or commercial dispute varies according to the terms and can last an entire court session of half a day.

Submission of evidence

In the *Tribunal de Commerce*, it is only in unusual instances, for example, in very complex cases that counsel will actually present a structured argument. Counsel is normally required, prior to the hearing, to provide the court with a file containing their written evidence to enable the court to ask a few questions at the hearing if necessary. These files

109. NCPC, Article 801.
110. NCPC, Article 804.
111. NCPC, Article 862.
112. NCPC, Article 869.

have become very sophisticated and structured and develop all of the parties' arguments to cover the evidence.

In the *Tribunal de Grande Instance* and the Court of Appeal, the file is left with the court at the end of the hearing as it is in the Court of Appeal.

Evidence

Nature and purpose of evidence

What may be the most striking difference between French and Common Law litigation is the almost absolute absence of testimonial evidence at the hearing. It is very rare to hear any testimonial evidence at all in a French court during civil or commercial matters. Further, wherever testimonial evidence is introduced, it will normally be in the form of a written affidavit rather than oral testimony.

Another major difference is the rather lax rules of admissibility. It is likely that the absence of a jury has curtailed the need for such safeguards against the abuse that could improperly affect the jury's opinion. It will be most surprising to Common Law parties in French litigation to find out that there are no rules as to the admissibility of hearsay, or of evidence, of remedial measures, or of settlement negotiations.

In the French civil justice system, the legal sanction of a contested right can only be obtained if evidence of the legal act or the fact that gave rise to it is produced. In order to prevail, the plaintiff must prove the facts of his case.[113] Obviously, once the plaintiff has established his allegations, the defendant can then put forward his defence. He then has the burden of proving it. Only contested facts need be proven, and a major part of the pleadings is devoted to this.

As a general rule, a legal act — such as a contract — must be proven by so called "legal" evidence such as documentary proof, whether notarised or not. Alternatively, a fact may often be established by testimonial evidence. In addition, proof is said to be freely admissible in commercial courts.

Kinds of evidence

DOCUMENTS

In general, documentary proof is only needed for those obligations exceeding 5,000 FF, and which are of a non-mercantile kind.[114] Written

113. NCPC, Article 9.
114. Civil Code, Article 1341.

evidence is given predominance in French litigation. For example, testimonial evidence is not normally permitted to contradict written evidence.[115]

On the other hand, corroborating written evidence is not required where some written proof is offered.[116]

TESTIMONIAL EVIDENCE

Testimonial evidence is normally not introduced and when introduced it is, generally, in the form of written affidavits of witnesses. The court has a discretion in determining the probative value of testimony.

Written affidavits of witnesses must satisfy certain formal requirements. They must only relate to facts that their author has personally witnessed.[117] The witness must state his full name, date and place of birth, address and occupation as well as, if any, his parenthood with the parties or whether he is employed by or has in any fashion a community of interest with them. Witnesses must be over the age of 18. The oath is mandatory except for persons having an incapacity to testify. Interestingly, the author of such a written affidavit must state that it is made with the purpose of being produced in court and that he is aware that the provision of inaccurate information would be perjury, and hence a criminal offence. The affidavit must be hand-written, dated and signed and a copy of an official identification signed and attached.[118]

In the very limited instances when live testimony is allowed, there is no such thing as direct examination and cross-examination. At most, French counsel merely suggests that the court may wish to consider questioning a witness on a particular subject. Indeed, any question or statement addressed by a party or his counsel to a witness must be stricken.[119] A French lawyer is strictly prohibited from having any type of contact whatsoever with a witness prior to or during the hearing and could be criminally and professionally sanctioned for so doing. A person giving oral testimony may not refer to or be prompted from notes or any other writings.[120]

PARTY TESTIMONY

Parties cannot testify in French litigation. They may appear in court and be heard at the court's discretion,[121] but they may not testify under oath

---

115. Civil Code, Article 1341.
116. Civil Code, Article 1347.
117. NCPC, Article 202.
118. NCPC, Article 202.
119. NCPC, Article 214.
120. NCPC, Article 212.
121. NCPC, Articles 184 and 185.

and the weight of their statement is regarded very suspiciously. In practice, the appearance of the parties is rather unusual.

If, however, they are summoned to appear in court and does not comply, any legal consequences can be inferred by the court,[122] which may, among other things, take this as sufficient evidence to render all kinds of proof admissible.

In a very special and unusual instance, a party can tender oath to his opponent; this is known as a "decisive oath".[123] Likewise, a court may tender oath to a party — this is known as "judicial oath".[124] The party to whom oath is tendered shall yield if he refuses to swear the oath and does not require the person who tendered it to him from taking it. In other words, where one who has tendered oath fails to return the challenge, he will be considered as having acquiesced. However, this kind of incident is most unusual and the risk involved in tendering the oath requires absolute certainty as to the outcome of such a challenge.

PRIVILEGES

French law forbids the use of certain facts in court. Facts known by counsel are absolutely privileged. The medical privilege, however, is the subject of discrepancy between the case law of the various courts. Also, the confidentiality of criminal investigations is all too often violated by communications to the press.

The attention of Anglo-American businesspersons and their lawyers should be especially drawn to the fact that in-house counsel does not enjoy any privilege in proceedings with French authorities. This includes lack of privilege from investigations by the authorities in charge of antitrust enforcement.

JUDGMENTS

A judgment is deemed final if it resolves all or part of the dispute on the merits or rules on procedural issue such as an affirmative defence.[125]

Judgments that resolve all or part of the dispute on the merits, order some preparatory measures — for example, appoint an expert — or a

122. Civil Code, Article 1347.
123. Civil Code, Articles 1325 to 1365.
124. Civil Code, Articles 1366 to 1369.
125. NCPC, Article 480.

provisional measure or resolve procedural incidents, such as with respect to jurisdiction, can be appealed immediately.[126]

In contrast, provisional judgments cannot be appealed immediately. This applies to those orders that have, as their subject matter, provisional measures such as the *ordonnance de référé*[127] and the *ordonnance sur requête*.[128]

POST-TRIAL MOTIONS

There is no possibility of obtaining a new trial in French litigation, probably as a result of the above-discussed lack of jury trial. Indeed, the main challenge to a judgment is by way of an appeal and will be dealt with below. Normally, the issuance of a judgment removes the case from the court.[129]

However, a party may file a request for interpretation of a judgment with the court that issued it, as long as an appeal has not been filed.[130] Likewise, a request for rectification of a material mistake or omission can be filed with the court that issued the judgment at any time.[131] Also, a court can be requested to complement a judgment with respect to a claim that it has admitted to adjudicate up to one year after the judgment has become final.[132]

A court also has jurisdiction to retract its judgment in several situations. Firstly, an objection may be filed by the defaulting party in the case of a judgment by default.[133] Secondly, a third party to the initial proceedings may file a *tierce opposition* where it is injured or damage to it is threatened.

Lastly, review *de novo* of a judgment can be sought in certain very limited circumstances. This is the *recours en révision*, which aims at the retractation of a final judgment so that full re-adjudication of all issues of fact and all issues of law would be undertaken.[134] A *recours en révision* can only be filed against a decision that is no longer subject to appeal. It is only available for two months[135] from the time when

126. NCPC, Article 544.
127. NCPC, Article 484.
128. NCPC, Article 493.
129. NCPC, Article 481.
130. NCPC, Article 461.
131. NCPC, Article 462.
132. NCPC, Article 463.
133. See above for the very strict conditions to be met for a judgment to be considered rendered by default as opposed to those judgments which are "deemed contested".
134. NCPC, Article 593.
135. NCPC, Article 596.

a party to the initial proceedings[136] learns of a valid ground for review. Grounds for review are limited to:

(1) Fraud discovered after the judgment and which has been determinant in the outcome;

(2) Discovery of decisive documents which had been withheld by another party;

(3) Judicial determination that documents which had a decisive impact on the outcome were forged; and

(4) Judicial adjudication that testimonial evidence given at the hearing was false.

In addition, the above circumstances are only grounds for revision if the moving party was unable to allege the corresponding fact before the judgment was issued.

ENFORCEMENT OF FOREIGN JUDGMENTS

The enforcement of judgments rendered in other European Community Member States is governed by the 1968 Brussels Convention on Jurisdiction and the Enforcement of Judgments in Civil and Commercial Matters.[137]

The Lugano Convention on Jurisdiction and the Enforcement of Judgments in Civil and Commercial Matters extends the rules of the Brussels Convention to parties in countries that are members of the European Free Trade Association (EFTA).[138] A judgment made in any Contracting State must be recognised in France without any special procedure. Under no circumstances can it be reviewed *de novo*. Instead, a party who wishes to avoid recognition can only raise the following limited grounds:[139]

(1) The recognition would be contrary to public policy in France;

(2) The defendant was not duly served or was not able to arrange for his defence and the judgment was given in default of appearance;

136. NCPC, Article 594.

137. This Convention was concluded on 27 September 1968 by the six founding Member States of the European Community and has been amended a number of times due to the accession of the other Member States. A codified version is published in OJEC Number C 189 of 28 July 1990, p. 2.

138. Convention 88/592, 31 OJEC (No. L 319) 9 (1988).

139. Brussels and Lugano Conventions, Articles 27 and 28.

(3) The judgment is irreconcilable with a judgment given in a dispute between the same parties in France;

(4) The court which rendered the judgment has decided a preliminary question concerning the status or legal capacity of natural persons, rights in property arising out of a matrimonial relationship, wills or succession, in a way inconsistent with the law applicable under French rules of conflict of laws;

(5) The judgment is irreconcilable with an earlier judgment given in a non-Contracting State, involving the same cause and between the same parties, which fulfils the conditions necessary for its recognition;

(6) The judgment conflicts with one of the provisions of the Convention relating to insurance matters and consumer contracts or those provisions designating courts with exclusive jurisdiction over certain subject-matters.

A French court may stay the proceedings with regard to recognition if an ordinary appeal against the judgment has been lodged.

The application must be submitted to the presiding judge of the *Tribunal de Grande Instance* of the place where the party against whom enforcement is sought is domiciled. If such party is not domiciled in France, jurisdiction is determined by reference to the place of enforcement. The applicant must attach the following documents to the application:

(1) A copy of the judgment which satisfies the conditions necessary to establish its authenticity;

(2) In the case of a default judgment, the original or a certified true copy of the document instituting the proceedings or with an equivalent document;

(3) Documents which establish that, according to the law of the State of origin of the judgment, it is enforceable and has been served;

(4) Where appropriate, a document showing that the applicant is in receipt of legal aid in the State of origin.

Enforcement may be refused only for the same reasons as non recognition cited above. Here again, the Convention prohibits the review of a foreign judgment as to its substance.

The party against whom enforcement is ordered may appeal against the decision with the Court of Appeal, in principle, within one month of service, and the judgment given on the appeal may be challenged in the *Cour de Cassation*. During the time specified for an appeal and until any such appeal has been decided, no measures of enforcement may be taken other than protective measures against the property of the appellant party.

No security, bond or deposit whatsoever is required of a party who applies for enforcement of a foreign judgment in France on the ground that he is a foreign national or that he is not domiciled or resident in France.

APPEAL

Contrary to challenges before the *Cour de Cassation*, which are extraordinary challenges of last resort, the Court of Appeal generally hears arguments on the entire dispute *de novo* and is not limited to specific grounds.

Appeals

Appeal of judgments (the ordinary challenge in the Court of Appeal) is widely available with few exceptions. Probably the most noticeable of such exceptions are with respect to judgments which:

(1) Do not resolve all or part of the dispute on the merits;
(2) Order some investigatory or provisional measure; or
(3) Put an end to the proceeding.[140]

As a result, the dispute may be transferred from the lower court to the Court of Appeals as a whole. The Court of Appeals will consider the entire matter again, both in fact and in law.[141] However, the dispute before the initial court fixes the boundaries for the scope of review in the Court of Appeals: the parties can only raise those claims that they had already made in the original forum.[142]

To this end, however, they are allowed to make new allegations and produce new documents or evidence.[143] In substance, while entirely new claims would be inadmissible in appellate proceedings, allegations and arguments are not deemed such new claims where they aim at the same purpose as those made in the first court, even though their legal bases differ.[144]

The scope of review of the Court of Appeals is sufficiently wide as to allow it to take full jurisdiction over disputes where the initial court has ordered

140. NCPC, Article 544.
141. NCPC, Article 561.
142. NCPC, Article 563.
143. NCPC, Article 563.
144. NCPC, Article 565.

investigatory measures or put an end to the case based on some affirmative defence. In such an instance, the Court of Appeal has discretion to resolve the dispute entirely and need not refer it back to the initial court.[145]

Pourvoi en cassation

The *pourvoi en cassation* is an extraordinary challenge before the *Cour de Cassation*, which aims at the cancellation of final decisions. In most instances, these are rulings from the Court of Appeal on strictly legal grounds.[146]

By contrast with appeals, the filing of a *pourvoi* does not stay the execution of appellate decisions that are the subject of such a challenge. Indeed, they must be executed before the *Cour de Cassation* will accept the filing of a *pourvoi*.

The grounds for *cassation* are breach of the law, abuse of authority, lack of jurisdiction, breach of a formality, inadequate reasoning, inconsistent judgments and lack of legal basis.

Another difference with the appeal is that, if the challenge is successful, the *Cour de Cassation* will only "quash" the decision it has reviewed, that is to say, cancel it.[147] The *Cour de Cassation* refers the case to another court of same level as the court from whose judgment the *pourvoi* was sought — for example, most usually a Court of Appeals — unless the *cassation* itself dispenses with the matters in dispute.

CONCLUSIVENESS OF JUDGMENT

As a general rule, a claim with the same purpose, the same basis and the same parties acting in their same respective capacities, as those in a former matter which has given rise to a final judgment is said to be barred by the *autorité de la chose jugée*.[148] As a matter of practice, the matter must have been specifically challenged in the first court.

This means that an action in contract could be filed where an action in tort has been unsuccessful.

---

145. NCPC, Article 568.
146. NCPC, Article 604.
147. This is the reason why one speaks of "casser" (to break) the judgment.
148. Code Civil, Article 1351.

CHAPTER 7

GERMANY

GEORG A. WITTUHN AND RALF STUCKEN
Huth Dietrich Hahn
Hamburg, Germany

ESTABLISHING JURISDICTION

Types of jurisdiction

Prior to discussing the different types of jurisdiction it is necessary to give a short overview over the different types of courts which — depending on the subject matter — have jurisdiction. There are two types of civil courts in Germany, namely the so-called ordinary courts and the labour courts. The latter deal with all law-suits arising out of labour or employment contracts. They have special rules of procedure, which are not within the scope of this analysis. This chapter deals exclusively with ordinary civil courts, which are competent to hear all other civil lawsuits.

A civil lawsuit will be heard in first instance either by the geographically competent Regional Court (*Landgericht*) or Local Court (*Amtsgericht*). The Local Court is the court of first instance for monetary claims if the value in dispute does not exceed German Marks 10,000.00 according to Section 23 Number 1 in connection with Section 71, Paragraph 1 of the Statute on the Constitution of Courts (*Gerichtsverfassungsgesetz* — GVG). Moreover, Local Courts are exclusively competent to hear disputes between landlord and tenant if the rented space is used for living purposes and not for commercial purposes, and they are competent to hear family law cases. In the Local Courts, all cases are heard and decided by one single, professional judge.

For all other cases, i.e., monetary claims exceeding 10,000.00 German Marks and non-monetary claims the Regional Courts are the courts of first instance. Except for specialised divisions for commercial matters, the divisions of the Regional Courts consist of three professional judges. According to Section 95 of the GVG, the special divisions for commercial matters are competent to hear:

(1) Conflicts between businessmen, commercial partnerships and companies arising out of their business;
(2) Conflicts involving bills of exchange, cheques and other commercial documents;
(3) Conflicts between partners of a partnership or shareholders of a company;
(4) Cases involving trade names or marks;

(5) Unfair competition claims;

(6) Admiralty; and

(7) Cases involving the issue of common stock.

These commercial divisions are composed of one professional judge and two lay judges who are members of the local business community. In Regional Courts and all higher courts, each party must be represented by an attorney admitted to the bar of this court.[1]

These courts have jurisdiction under the following circumstances described below. It must be noted that under German law the international jurisdiction follows the principles of the national jurisdiction, i.e., if jurisdiction is established under the following principles the question of international jurisdiction is automatically answered in the affirmative.

Jurisdiction over the parties of the action

NATURAL PERSONS

According to Sections 12 and 13 of the German Code of Civil Procedure (*Zivilprozeßordnung* — ZPO), the basic principle giving rise to the international jurisdiction of German courts is the fact that the defendant has his residence in Germany.

CORPORATIONS

According to Sections 12 and 17 of the ZPO, the same principle applies to corporations. The residence of a corporation is the place of its registered office.[2] If company branches have been created, lawsuits involving these branches may be filed at the place of business of the branch according to Section 21 of the ZPO.

Jurisdiction over the subject matter of the action

Property claims

Questions of title to real estate may be subject to jurisdiction in the place where the real estate is located. When questions other than title are involved, the location of the real estate may still be the place where jurisdiction is established.

1. ZPO, Section 78.
2. ZPO, Section 17.

Damage or violation of rights

If a tort has been committed, jurisdiction is established in the place where it occurred according to Section 32 of the ZPO. It should be noted that the *forum delicti commissi* covers both the place where the tort was committed and the place where the damages occurred.

Place of performance

The place of performance of a contract can establish jurisdiction according to Section 29 of the ZPO. The place of performance is to be ascertained by the *lex causae*, i.e., the law that governs the contract. If German law is applicable, it should be noted that the place of performance is generally identical to the domicile or place of business[3] of the debtor.

Stipulation with regard to international jurisdiction

Apart from the aforementioned factors that establish international jurisdiction under German law by operation of law, it is also possible to stipulate jurisdiction. The rules pertaining to the prorogation and derogation of jurisdiction are laid down in Sections 38 *et seq.* of the ZPO. Generally, it can be assumed that such a stipulation is valid under German law if at least one party to the contract is not domiciled or resident in Germany.

Submission to the proceedings

Finally, it must be mentioned that the defendant's submission to the proceedings establishes jurisdiction. This rule establishes German jurisdiction and is also applied in favour of foreign jurisdiction in recognition proceedings. If a defendant pleads to the merits in the foreign proceedings without raising any objection against the foreign court's taking jurisdiction, a German court will not hear his objection to the foreign court's jurisdiction.

This rule, however, does not apply if the defendant had no opportunity, according to the foreign procedural law, of effectively challenging the foreign court's jurisdiction or if it was foreseeable that the foreign court would not accept his argument.

3. German Civil Code (BGB), Section 269, Paragraph 1.

Article 3 of the Brussels Convention

If a defendant has neither domicile nor residence nor a place of business in Germany, jurisdiction is established at the place where he owns assets.[4] It is not necessary that the assets are sufficient to cover the whole claim. However, if the assets are not significant, German courts will decline to take jurisdiction.

Otherwise, no doctrine of *forum non conveniens* tempers this far-reaching jurisdiction. According to Article 3 of the Brussels Convention, Section 23 of the ZPO does not apply with respect to citizens of member states.

Venue

Under German procedural law the question of venue is not separated from the question of jurisdiction. The court, for example, competent under Sections 12 and 13 of the ZPO[5] has jurisdiction and venue. If the defendant is a resident of Hamburg and the law-suit involves an amount exceeding German Marks 10,000.00 the Regional Court of Hamburg is competent to hear the matter in the absence of a stipulation between the parties.

Service of summons of writ

General procedure under German law

Under German Civil Procedure Law the service is an official and certified act carried out by the court. The statement of claim as well as the statement of defence and any other statements of the parties containing formal motions must be served by the court. The party filing the statement in question hands it into the court. The court uses the postal service to deliver the documents in a formalised way.

The letter carrier must fill out and sign a document of service for certification. This document contains the time, place and manner of service. The document may be served on the party itself, its legal representative, employees at the office of an enterprise or members of the household. The service to a validly empowered attorney-at-law does not require this formally documented procedure.

4. ZPO, Section 23.
5. Residence of the defendant, see above.

In the event that neither the party nor any other person to whom the document can be served is available, the document can be deposited at the post office and the notice left in the mail box.

If neither the domicile of the party to whom the service is addressed nor a representative are known, the method of publication is available. In this case, the notice of service is published at the court's board in the court building.

Direct service by post or personal service through parties or their attorneys at law is not available under German law.

Service of summons of proceeding from outside Germany

Treaties

The service of proceedings that take place outside Germany is largely regulated by bilateral and multilateral treaties guaranteeing a service of writ in Germany.

The Hague Convention of 1954 on Civil Procedure is in force between Germany and Austria, Belgium, the Czech Republic, Denmark, Finland, France, Hungary, Israel, Italy, Japan, Lebanon, Luxembourg, Morocco, Netherlands, Norway, Poland, Portugal, Rumania, Sweden, Switzerland, Soviet Union, the Slovak Republic, Spain, Syria, Turkey, the Vatican and Yugoslavia. According to this treaty, service is generally carried out by consular channels.

The procedure is further facilitated by supplementary agreements with the following states: Austria, Belgium, France, Luxembourg, Netherlands, Norway, Sweden and Switzerland.

The Hague Convention on the Service Abroad of Judicial and Extra-Judicial Documents in Civil and Commercial matters of 15 November 1965 replaces the Articles 1–7 of The Hague Convention of 1954 between Germany and the following states: Barbados, Belgium, Botswana, Denmark, Egypt, Finland, France, Israel, Japan, Luxembourg, Malawi, Netherlands, Norway, Portugal, Sweden, Turkey, United Kingdom and the United States. As a consequence, consular channels need not be used but the competent court authorities help each other directly.

The Hague Convention on Civil Procedure of 17 July 1905 is in force between Germany and Iceland only.

In addition, bilateral treaties may apply in addition to the above-mentioned Hague Conventions between Germany and the following states: Australia, Canada, Greece, Tunisia, Turkey, United Kingdom, the United States and New Zealand.

AUTONOMOUS LAW

In the absence of a treaty of public international law, German authorities nevertheless generally lend their assistance to serving a writ. However, they will deny assistance to a foreign state that itself repeatedly denied its services to Germany. The procedure is regulated by Sections 57 and 66 *et seq.* of the Ordinance of Legal Aid (*Rechtshilfeordnung*). According to this ordinance the Local Court in the area in which the person to receive the document is domiciled or resident is competent to receive and to deal with the request. The service carried out under these circumstances, however, is only informal. This means that the document is served on the designated addressee only if he is voluntarily prepared to accept the document after having inspected it and being instructed that he need not accept it.

ASCERTAINING THE APPLICABLE LAW

Regional law and national law

Except for restricted areas of public law, the German legal system is completely unified. The different *Länder* (provinces or states) of the Federal Republic of Germany do not have legislative power in the field of civil or corporate law. As a consequence, questions of regional law do not arise.

Conflict of laws principles

Sources of conflict of laws

AUTONOMOUS LAW

The major source of the German conflict of law's principles are Articles 3–38 of the Introductory Code of the German Civil Code (*Einführungsgesetz zum Bürgerlichen Gesetzbuch* — EGBGB). This codification, however, is still incomplete in many aspects. A number of important areas are subject to case law.

TREATIES

Another important source of German conflict of laws principles are international treaties. Germany is a contracting party to a number of multilateral treaties in particular in the area of family law, inheritance law and transport law. In these areas it is also necessary to check whether the autonomous rules of the EGBGB or the case law are superseded by international treaties which according to Article 3, Paragraph 2, Sentence 1 of the EGBGB take precedence over the autonomous law. However, in view of the very specialised areas of these treaties it does not seem appropriate to discuss them in detail in the context of a manual of civil procedure.

Principles of autonomous law

NATURAL PERSONS

The capacity of a person to hold rights and to enter into legal transactions is, according to Article 7, Paragraph 1, Sentence 1 of the EGBGB, determined by the law of the country of which such person is a citizen.

The interests of German commerce and traffic are protected by the rule that a foreigner who enters into the legal transaction in Germany although he is incapable to do so under his personal law will be deemed to have capacity for this transaction if he would have such if German law were applicable, unless the contractual partner knew or should have known about the lack of capacity.[6] This exception from the rule of the law of citizenship does not, however, extend to family law and succession law transactions or the transfer of foreign real estate agreed on in Germany.

CORPORATIONS

There is no written rule in the EGBGB determining the law governing corporations. The courts unanimously hold that the actual business headquarters (seat of administration) is the appropriate connecting factor for the law of the corporation. This law determines the formation of the corporation, the beginning, the extent of its legal capacity and its end.

CONTRACTS

The EGBGB contains a detailed set of rules with regard to contracts. These rules, Articles 27–37 of the EGBGB, incorporate the Convention on the Law Applicable to Contractual Relations of 19 June 1980, the so-called Rome Convention.

According to Article 27, Paragraph 1, Sentence 1 of the EGBGB, a contract is governed by the law chosen by the parties.

The party autonomy is only restricted in two areas that are traditionally characterised by binding provisions, namely consumer contracts and

6. EGBGB, Article 12, first sentence.

employment contracts. According to Article 29, Paragraph 1 of the EGBGB a choice of law clause is valid unless it deprives the consumer of the protection granted by the binding provisions of the law of the state where he has his habitual residence in the following situations:

(1) If the closing of the contract was preceded by an offer or an advertisement in the state of the habitual residence of the consumer and if the consumer has accepted the offer in said state;
(2) If the contractual partner of the consumer or his agent has received the order in said state; and
(3) If the contractual partner of the consumer induces the latter to travel to another state in order to purchase goods.

Article 30, Paragraph 1 of the EGBGB provides that a choice of law in connection with employment contracts may not lead to depriving the employee of the protection granted by binding provisions of the law of the state where the employee has his habitual residence even if he has been sent temporarily to another state.

Article 27, Paragraph 1, Sentence 2 of the EGBGB provides that the choice of law may be either actual or implied. Factors indicating an implied choice of law are the agreement as to the place of jurisdiction, the agreement on a single place of performance, the agreement of arbitration before an institutional court of arbitration, the use of legal forms which are particularly tied to a certain legal system, the proceedings of both parties with the basis of one law in a court of law, the language of the contract or of the negotiations or the stipulated currency.

In the absence of a choice-of-law clause, the law of the state with the closest relation to the contract is applicable according to Article 28, Paragraph 1, Sentence 1 of the EGBGB. This provides that it is assumed that the contract is most closely related to the state where the characteristic performance is to be carried out.

The scope of the law ascertained according to the aforesaid rules governs the requirements for the conclusion and validity of the contract and all questions related thereto.

TORTS

The parties are also free to choose the law in disputes involving the law of torts. The choice may be either express or implied. It has been held on a regular basis by the courts that an implied choice of law is given if the parties start court proceedings arguing exclusively on the basis of the substantive law of the German forum without raising the question of the applicable law.

In the absence of a choice of law, the law of the place where the tort is committed applies. The place where the tort is committed is both the place where the wrong-doer has acted and the place where the protected legal interest has been injured. The injured person may proceed under the law most favourable to him. It must be noted that German law affords a privilege to German citizen insofar as a tortious action committed by a German citizen abroad will not give rise in Germany to more extensive liability than is provided by German law.[7]

PROPERTY

The courts follow the rule that the law applicable to a question of property is determined by the situs of the property. This rule — developed by case law and not included in the EGBGB — applies both to real estate and chattel.

COMMENCING THE ACTION

Complaint

Stating the essential elements and the relief sought

The minimum requirements for the statement of claim and the defence are laid down in Section 253, Paragraph 2 of the ZPO. According to this provision, the statement of claim must include a precise motion that sets out what the party seeks. It must be clear whether the performance of a certain act, a judgment for payment of a certain sum, a declaration of a certain right or something else is sought from the court. If, for example, a plaintiff asks for delivery of a car he must specify the make and the official registration number as well as other particulars. If the plaintiff asks for payment he must specify in principle the exact amount of money.

In theory, neither the plaintiff nor the defendant need to cite any provisions of acts or statutes or any court decisions. The old Roman principle of *iura novit curia* applies. In practice, however, the lawyers will refer to statutory provisions and cite case law favourable to their position.

If the motion is not precise enough the claim must be dismissed as inadmissible.

Furthermore the plaintiff must assert in detail all facts necessary to establish his case. Evidence should be offered for all questions for which a party bears the burden of proof. This does not mean that each and every piece of information available to the parties must be written down in the statement of claim. It is possible to wait and see which allegations are in dispute and amend the pleadings accordingly. In particular, the plaintiff is not obliged to anticipate the factual allegations and legal arguments of the defendant. However, the pleadings in Germany provide much more

7. EGBGB, Article 38.

information than in most other jurisdictions, especially the Common Law countries. This is necessarily so since the pleadings must enable the parties to evaluate their situation without the possibility of a discovery procedure.[8]

The plaintiff must assert as many facts as are necessary to allow the conclusion that he has the right he claims.

The key-word in this context is substantiation. Both the statement of claim and the defence must substantiate and identify what the case is about. This obligation may seem extremely hard to satisfy in cases where the defendant has all available information at his disposal. However, it must be kept in mind that the jurisprudence and case-law have developed duties of co-operation and changes in the onus of proof in certain situations.

The standard of relevancy and precision required for the statement of claim comes back to a basic principle of the German law of civil procedure, the prohibition of probing. This principle states that the court will only order the taking of evidence if:

(1) A precise material fact is at issue; and
(2) The evidence nominated by the party is material to the proof of such fact.

A mere allegation or the speculation by a party "in the blue sky" made in the hope that the taking of evidence will have some result or lead to new evidence, will not cause the court to order the taking of evidence.

This principle makes "fishing expeditions" virtually impossible.

For example, if a party requests the court to take evidence about an alleged contract or agreement by hearing a witness, this request will be rejected for lack of precision. The party must be able to substantiate the nominated evidence, e.g., by saying that the witness is to be heard about a contract and specifying when, where and between whom the alleged contract was concluded and why the witness has knowledge about the material facts.

The rationale for this principle is twofold. First, it promotes efficiency by preventing the waste of judicial time and effort. Second, it protects individuals and businesses from the nuisance, costs and interference of privacy rights that follow inevitably from the taking of evidence. Evidence will not be taken if the request for it is based on mere speculation.

An example may be helpful to clarify this principle:

In a case decided by the Federal Court of Justice (*Bundesgerichtshof* — BGH), the plaintiff had a contractual claim to be admitted to the administration and management of a company of which he was a shareholder. The defendants — the other shareholders — alleged that the plaintiff did not have the necessary qualifications and sought to prove this with a scientific test. The Federal Court of Justice ruled that such a test was inadmissible

---

8. See Obtaining Information Prior to Trial below.

as a pure fishing expedition in the absence of any other indication that the plaintiff was not fit for the job. The BGH specifically stated that the taking of evidence is not intended to provide the parties with material they do not have before and that nobody is obliged to provide his opponent with the material necessary to win at trial.

A limitation on this strict rule is to be found where the party that has the burden of proof cannot satisfy this burden whereas the other party could easily provide the information. In accordance with the general principles of the duties of the parties, a vague motion for the taking of evidence is admissible.

This principle governs all different kinds of evidence.

Action by stages

If a party is unable to specify and substantiate his claim right from the beginning, and if the opposing party is not obliged to provide this information under the principles set out below,[9] the only remaining possibility is to start an action by stages (*Stufenklage*) according to Section 254 of the ZPO.

If, for example, the plaintiff has a claim for information that will enable him to specify his "real" claim, the claim for information is followed in the first stage, and the real claim followed on the second stage. Such claims for information are granted by statute in most cases where the parties are involved in constant and narrow relationships.

Partners in a partnership, shareholders in a company or the spouses in divorce proceedings, for example, have far reaching claims for information. In the absence of such a special relation, the general claim for information according to Section 810 of the BGB applies. Under Section 810 of the BGB somebody who has reason to believe that somebody else is in the possession of documents that give him a case against such person may ask for the production of such document. However, the documents must be described in a very detailed way that satisfies the aforesaid principle of substantiation.

Types of answer

Denials

If the factual assertions are not sufficiently clear, the defending party does not even need to respond to the statement of claim because the judge has a duty to dismiss the claim as inadmissible without entering into the merits of the case.

9. See Types of Answer below.

From a practical perspective, however, it is a rather dangerous game not to react when faced with a deficient statement of claim, hoping that the judge will dismiss the claim. Generally, a lawyer will state in the defence that the statement of claim is considered not to be in accordance with the standards of precision of the ZPO. At the same time the judge will be asked to state whether he shares this opinion. If he does not, there is still an opportunity to plead to the merits.

Such extreme cases are very rare. In general, the statement of defence will be required to satisfy the same standards as the statement of claim. This means in particular that the principle of substantiation applies. It is not sufficient to simply deny the allegations of the plaintiff. The defendant must deny every single factual assertion and give reasons for such denial. Alternatively, the defendant may deny the facts stated by the plaintiff altogether by alleging a different set of facts. Facts that have not been denied are deemed to be admitted according to Section 138, Paragraph 3 of the ZPO.

Reply

The plaintiff is entitled to reply to factual assertions of the defendant. The court may determine whether a first hearing precedes the reply or whether further briefs are exchanged prior to the hearing.[10]

Amendments to pleadings

Facts

Another factor that encourages the parties to file complete briefs right from the beginning of the proceedings is the constant threat of being precluded with factual assertions and offers of evidence. According to Section 296, Paragraph 1 of the ZPO, assertions made after the specified time-limit has elapsed are only admissible if they do not delay the proceedings or if the party concerned can show that he did not act negligently. The decision of the court is a discretionary one. Time-limits are regulated in the ZPO or may be fixed by the court.

According to Section 296 II of the ZPO, assertions that have not been raised in time according to the general duty of the parties to promote the development of the proceedings are also inadmissible if the party acted negligently and the proceedings are delayed.

There is considerable dispute as to the meaning of the word "delay" in Section 296 of the ZPO. According to one opinion, "delay" only requires

10. See Trial below.

that the proceedings take longer if the additional assertion is taken into consideration. The contrary view is that one must ask whether the proceedings would take longer than if the assertions had been raised before the time-limit elapsed.

It is not necessary to enter into a discussion of these niceties of German procedural law in order to understand that Section 296 of the ZPO gives an extremely strong incentive to the parties to make complete and precise statements. This provision — together with possible cost sanctions — ensures that no trial by surprise occurs.

Section 528 of the ZPO contains similar provisions to ensure that new assertions are not raised in the court of second instance.

Change of motion

Once the statement of claim has been served on the defendant a change of the motion is only admissible if the defendant agrees to it or if the court considers it to be appropriate.[11]

Section 264 of the ZPO defines that the following situations are by operation of law not to be considered as a change of motion and therefore always admissible:

(1) If the legal or factual assertions of a party are amended or additional points are brought forward;

(2) If the motion is extended or limited, that is cases where at the beginning of the proceedings the plaintiff asked only for a partial amount and subsequently changes to the complete amount owed to him; and

(3) If the motion must be changed due to a change in the underlying facts; i.e., for example, situations where the action pursued initially the handing over of the possession of a good and such good is destroyed during the proceedings; in such a scenario the plaintiff may ask for damages without the consent of the defendant or the court considering the change of the motion to be appropriate.

The consent of the defendant to a change of the motion is deemed to be given if he argues to the merits of the new motion without stating that the change is inadmissible.[12]

If Section 264 of the ZPO does not apply and the defendant refuses to give his consent, the court may nevertheless deem the change of motion to be appropriate. The court has a relatively vast discretionary power in

11. ZPO, Section 263.
12. ZPO, Section 267.

this respect. The court is likely to deem the change of motion to be appropriate if it helps to finally settle the dispute between the parties and avoids fresh proceedings.

Supplemental pleadings

Other claims may be introduced in the proceedings, according to Section 260 of the ZPO,[13] against the same defendant if the court is competent to hear these claims as well. In addition the parties may at any time introduce or amend legal arguments. It is even possible for one party to adopt the legal arguments or factual assertions of the other party. If, for example, the plaintiff pursues an action based on a contract and the facts pleaded by the defendant justify a claim based on the concept of unjust enrichment, the plaintiff may adopt the defendant's argument.

Joinder of claims and parties

The only parties to the civil lawsuit in a legal sense are the plaintiff and the defendant. However, a joinder of parties as plaintiffs (*aktive Streitgenossenschaft*) or defendants (*passive Streitgenossenschaft*) is possible (*Streitgenossenschaft* or *subjektive Klagenhäufung*). A joinder of claims is given when the plaintiff pleads two or more claims in one action against the defendant (*objektive Klagenhäufung*).

Joinder of parties

A joinder of parties (as plaintiffs or defendants) is possible, when:

(1) The right in dispute is owned or owed jointly by the parties, e.g., joint and several debtors, co-owners or co-heirs;[14]
(2) The joint parties are entitled or committed to by the same cause in law or fact, e.g., joint buyers to a sales contract, injured parties of an accident;[15] and
(3) Similar claims or obligations that are founded on similar causes in law or on similar facts are subject matter of the action, e.g., claim of an insurance company against several policyholders for payment of the insurance premium.[16]

13. Also see Joinder of Claims below.
14. ZPO, Section 59, 1st alternative.
15. ZPO, Section 59, 2nd alternative.
16. ZPO, Section 60.

Apart from these specific prepositions the general procedural prerequisites must be fulfilled with respect to each joinder of party, e.g., the court must be locally competent for the claim against each defendant. If this is not the case — e.g., the court has no jurisdiction for one of the defendants — the action is inadmissible with respect to this joinder of party.

The joinder of parties means the consolidation of several actions for one trial and hearing of evidence. Only the litigation is consolidated, the joined parties remain legally independent and one party is not influenced by the conduct of the case by the other.[17] Accordingly, the joined parties may conduct the litigation differently or even contradictory. For example, one defendant may apply for the dismissal of the claim while the other defendant acknowledges the claim. Therefore, joinder of parties does not necessarily mean a uniform decision in favour of or against the joined parties.

Special rules apply if a compulsory joinder of parties (*notwendige Streitgenossenschaft*) is given. The joinder of parties is a compulsory joinder,[18] when:

(1) The right in dispute must be decided uniformly for the joined parties; or
(2) The joinder of parties is a compulsory joinder by other reasons.

Therefore, compulsory joinder of parties is given when the *res judicata* effect applies to all joined parties,[19] when the decision will change a legal right or a status with effect to all joined parties (e.g., action to set aside the resolution of the shareholders meeting of a joint stock company) or when the joined parties must hold and dispose of a right jointly under substantive law (e.g., community of heirs).

If a compulsory joinder of parties is given, the judgment must be uniform for the joined parties. To ensure a uniform judgment, contradictory acts in litigation by the joined parties are without effect, e.g., if one defendant applies for the dismissal of the claim while the other defendant has acknowledged the claim the court is prevented from rendering a judgment on acknowledgement against the defendant who has acknowledged the claim.

Joinder of claims

A joinder of claims is possible, provided that the same kind of proceedings is admissible and the same court is competent to hear all pleaded

17. ZPO, Section 61.
18. ZPO, Section 62.
19. See The Conclusiveness of Judgment below.

claims.[20] The several claims may be independent and pleaded with equal priority or as a main claim joined with an alternative claim that will only be decided if the main claim is dismissed.

Counterclaim

The counterclaim is an admissible means of attack for the defendant provided that all general procedural prerequisites for the counterclaim are fulfilled and the court is competent to hear the counterclaim in the pending proceedings. The consistent practice of the Federal Court of Justice furthermore requires a legal connection between claim and counterclaim,[21] and allows a counterclaim even against third parties if the third party consents or in view of the court it is appropriate to hear this claim in the same proceedings.[22]

Cross-claims

In German Civil Procedure, cross-claims in the sense of a claim by one plaintiff against another plaintiff or one defendant against another defendant are not admissible.[23]

Third party claims

Under Sections 72 *et seq.* of the ZPO, a party (plaintiff or defendant) may bring a third party into the action by serving a third party notice — third party claim (*Streitverkündung*).

A party may commence third party notice procedure if the third party would be liable to the party or might have a claim against the party in case of a detrimental judgment in the pending trial.[24]

The party will request with the notice that the third party to join in the trial for support. If the third party does join the trial the provisions on intervention[25] apply.[26] If the third party does not join in the trial will be carried on without respect to the third party claim. Notwithstanding

20. ZPO, Section 260.
21. BGHZ 40, 185, 187 *et seq.*; BGH NJW 1975, 1228 *et seq.*
22. BGHZ 69, 37, 44 *et seq.*; BGH NJW 1975, 1228 *et seq.*
23. Rosenberg/Schwab/Gottwald, *Zivilprozeßrecht* 15th Edition (1993) Section 98, Number 4.
24. ZPO, Section 72.
25. ZPO, Sections 66 *et seq.*; see also Intervention below.
26. ZPO, Section 74, Paragraph 1.

whether the third party has joined in the trial or not, the third party notice has the effect of an intervention under Section 68 of the ZPO.[27] Accordingly, in a later trial between the third party and the party who has served the third party notice, the third party cannot argue that the judgment (by the pending trial) is not correct or that the trial was conducted insufficiently or faulty by the party.

Impleader

A third party who is claiming a right or thing which is the subject matter of an action between the parties of a pending lawsuit may bring an action against both parties of this pending trial (*Hauptinterven-tion*).[28] In this (new) lawsuit both parties of the pending trial will be joined parties as defendants. On application by a party the court may suspend the pending trial until a final judgment in the action launched by the third party is made.

Interpleader

A defendant sued for payment of a debt may serve a third party notice on a person who is alleging to be entitled to the claim in dispute in the trial if the defendant is prepared to pay the debt but uncertain about the rightful claimant. If the third party does join in the trial the defendant will resign from the lawsuit on deposition of the amount in dispute and the proceeding will be carried on (only) between the plaintiff and the third party about their entitlement to the claim.[29]

The same or similar principles apply if a defendant is sued for the possession of a thing he is holding not as legal owner but, for example, as tenant or as depositary. The defendant may serve a third party notice if, in his opinion, he must return the possession to a third party other than the plaintiff. If the third party does join in the trial, the third party may take over the proceedings and continue the lawsuit about the entitlement to the possession with the plaintiff; the defendant will then resign from the lawsuit. If the third party does not join in the trial the defendant may acknowledge the claim and return the possession to the plaintiff. In this case the third party is excluded from any claim against the defendant with regard to the possession.[30]

27. ZPO, Section 74, Paragraph 3.
28. ZPO, Section 64.
29. ZPO, Section 75.
30. ZPO, Section 76.

Intervention

Under Sections 66 *et seq.* of the ZPO, a third party — the intervener — may join in a pending lawsuit in support of one party if the intervener has a legal interest in the success of the supported party.[31] The necessary legal interest is given when the decision in the pending trial would affect the legal position or status of the intervener, e.g., if the decision would prejudice his legal position, if he would be subject to the *res judicata* effect of the decision or if the supported party would have a claim against him in case of a detrimental decision.

Notwithstanding the fact that the intervener is not party to the lawsuit but only assisting to the party he supports, the intervener may plead all means of attack and defence unless they would be in contradiction to the conduct of the case by the supported party. An exception applies in case of an intervention under Section 69 of the ZPO (*streitgenössische Nebenintervention*) where the intervener has a more independent status and may even act in contradiction to the party supported. In so far as the supported party is precluded from the introduction of new facts or fresh evidence, the intervener is barred to the same effect.[32]

The judgment in the lawsuit will be rendered only between the plaintiff and the defendant but will cause the specific intervention effect between the intervener and the supported party. By this intervention effect, the intervener is barred in a later lawsuit against the supported party from using the argument that the judgment is not correct. He is furthermore precluded from asserting that the litigation was conducted in a faulty or insufficient way by the supported party unless at the point in time of his intervention the intervener was barred from introducing new facts and fresh evidence or means of attack and defence unknown by the intervener where not pleaded by the party intentionally or through gross negligence.[33]

OBTAINING INFORMATION PRIOR TO TRIAL

The German Code of Civil Procedure does not know any distinction between a "trial" and a "pre-trial" phase. As described above,[34] proceedings are started by a statement of claim (*Klagschrift*) in accordance with Section 253 of the ZPO. According to Section 277 of the ZPO, the statement of claim and the defence (*Klagerwiderung*) contain the factual assertions of the parties, an offer of evidence for those questions in respect of which the party has the burden of proof and — almost invariably — legal arguments. On the

31. ZPO, Section 66 — *Nebenintervention.*
32. ZPO, Section 67.
33. ZPO, Section 68.
34. See Commencing the Action above.

basis of these briefs, the court decides which questions are in need of evidence and fixes a day for the hearing, that is the trial, which will be described below.

INTERIM PROTECTION OF ASSETS PENDING TRIAL

In the ordinary proceeding, it may take years to reach a final judgment. Pending trial the debtor may dispose of his assets or jeopardise by other means the execution of the final judgment. Accordingly, there might be the need for the creditor to obtain temporary relief by summary judgment and/or the opportunity to execute the judgment before the ordinary proceedings have come to an end and the judgment is final.

Provisional attachment (arrest)

The arrest procedure — like interlocutory injunctions[35] — provides for temporary relief by summary judgment before ordinary proceedings have started or pending ordinary proceedings if the enforcement of the judgement on ordinary proceedings is jeopardised. The arrest is an executory title that secures the future execution of the judgment to be rendered in ordinary proceedings.

The arrest (provisional attachment)[36] is a court order in a special proceeding to obtain security for a future execution to satisfy a money claim or claim that may become a money claim.[37]

Arrest proceedings

An order for attachment will only be granted if without the order for attachment the execution of a judgment rendered in ordinary proceedings will be at risk or substantially complicated.[38] With his application for a writ of attachment, the applicant must establish *prima facie* evidence[39] for the existence of his claim and assumes the jeopardy of its enforcement. This application may be filed with the Local Court that has jurisdiction where the assets attached are located or with the competent court for the ordinary proceeding.[40]

35. See Interlocutory Injunction below.
36. ZPO, Sections 916 *et seq.*
37. ZPO, Section 916, Paragraph 1.
38. ZPO, Section 917, Paragraph 1.
39. For example, by affidavit; ZPO, Section 294.
40. ZPO, Section 919.

The court may decide the application for a writ of attachment without prior oral hearing by order or — at its discretion — on oral hearing by judgment.[41] The writ of attachment is an executory title. In its decision the court must declare that the debtor may prevent the execution by depositing a specified amount of money.[42]

Execution

The writ of attachment must be executed by the creditor by seizure of moveable assets or registration of a mortgage on land within one month of service of the writ of attachment on the debtor.[43] A further realisation of the pledge or the mortgage is not possible on the writ of attachment.

Interlocutory injunction

In distinction to the arrest, which secures a money claim, the interlocutory injunction[44] is a provisional order obtained from the court which may be issued in order to prevent a threatening change of existing conditions which may render impossible or substantially difficult the realisation of a right; or, if the interim adjudication of a controversy is necessary for the prevention of substantial damage or other reasons.[45]

Apart from minor deviations, the proceedings for an interlocutory injunction are similar to the arrest proceedings.[46]

Provisional enforceability

The execution presupposes an executory title. Besides the titles justifying the execution, which are listed in Section 794 of the ZPO such as settlement in court, enforceable default summons or enforceable deed, the most important executory titles are final judgments and judgments declared to be provisionally enforceable.[47] Under Section 704 of the ZPO, a judgment that is not final and unappealable may be executed if declared to be provisionally enforceable by the court.

41. ZPO, Sections 921 *et seq.*
42. ZPO, Section 923.
43. ZPO, Sections 928 *et seq.*
44. ZPO, Sections 935 *et seq.*
45. ZPO, Sections 935, 940.
46. ZPO, Section 936.
47. ZPO, Section 704.

In principle any judgment will be declared to be provisionally enforceable by the court *ex officio* unless the judgment is final and therefore executable without declaration, it is executable by operation of law (e.g., interlocutory injunctions) or the provisional enforceability is excluded by operation of law.[48]

The reversal of the judgment terminates its provisional enforceability.[49] If the provisionally enforceable judgment becomes final, all restrictions caused by the provisionality of enforceability[50] cease and the judgment becomes finally enforceable.

In its declaration for provisional enforceability the court must determine whether the provisional execution is admissible without security or on security only.

Provisional execution on security

In principle, the court must declare the judgment to be provisionally enforceable on security only.[51] The court must determine kind and amount of the security in its decision.[52] With respect to the amount of security the court must assess the possible damage for the debtor on an execution by the creditor if the judgment will be set aside on appeal. The order for security provokes that the creditor can commence the execution only when he has provided the security.[53]

Provisional execution without security

The only exceptions to the rule of provisional enforceability of judgments on security are specified in Section 708 of the ZPO. Thus, e.g., judgments on waiver of claim[54] or on acknowledgement,[55] default judgments,[56] and judgments by the Higher Regional Court on financial claims are to declare to be provisionally enforceable without security.

Apart from the cases where a judgment is to be declared provisionally enforceable *ex officio*, Section 710 of the ZPO provides for an application by the creditor to the court to declare a judgment which is

48. ZPO, Section 704, Paragraph 2: Judgment in parent and child cases.
49. ZPO, Section 717, Paragraph 1.
50. See next paragraphs.
51. ZPO, Section 709.
52. ZPO, Sections 108 *et seq.*
53. ZPO, Section 751, Paragraph 2.
54. ZPO, Section 306.
55. ZPO, Section 307.
56. ZPO, Sections 330 *et seq.*

provisionally enforceable on security only to be exceptionally provisionally enforceable without security when the requirement to provide a security would cause a fundamental detriment to the creditor (creditors' protection).

A judgment for payment that is provisionally enforceable on security may only be executed without providing the security if the execution is restricted to measures of safeguard, i.e., the seizure of moveable assets and the registration of a mortgage on land.[57]

Debtors' protection

The Civil Procedure Code provides for the opportunity of the debtor to prevent the execution of a provisionally enforceable judgment by lodging a security.

If a judgment is provisionally enforceable without security under Section 708 Numbers 4–11, of the ZPO the court must declare that the debtor may prevent the execution by providing a security unless the creditor himself is providing a security prior to commencement of execution.[58]

Under Section 712 of the ZPO, the debtor may apply for an order preventing the execution by providing a security even when the creditor has lodged a security if the execution would cause an irreversible detriment to the debtor. If the debtor can convince the court that the execution will cause an irreversible detriment to him, the court may further declare that the execution is restricted to measures of safeguard or even declare the judgment non-enforceable if the debtor is not in a position to provide a security.

Apart from these specific provisions for debtors' protection, Sections 719 and 707 of the ZPO provide for the opportunities to suspend the execution on or without security, to allow further execution only on security or to set aside enforcement measures on security by a court order if an appeal is lodged against the provisional enforceable judgment.

SUMMARY JUDGMENTS

Apart from the normal legal procedure, the Civil Procedure Code provides for summary proceedings and special means of termination of legal proceedings.

57. ZPO, Section 720 a.
58. ZPO, Section 711.

Adjudication without trial or by special proceedings

Sections 688 *et seq.* of the ZPO provide for summary proceedings without trial (*Mahnverfahren*) to obtain an enforceable default summons (enforceable order for payment — *Vollstreckungsbescheid*). These proceedings are admissible only for recovering a monetary debt.[59]

The proceedings start with an application for an order for payment of a debt (default summons — *Mahnbescheidsantrag*) to be filed with the Local Court that has jurisdiction for the legal domicile of the creditor/appellant.[60]

The court will only examine the admissibility of the application and then without a hearing and without examination of the claim issue the payment order (*Mahnbescheid*) in accordance with the application against the debtor/opponent.[61]

If the opponent raises opposition (*Widerspruch*) within two weeks of service of the payment order, the summary proceedings are suspended and the claim will be decided in ordinary proceedings on application.[62]

When no opposition is raised within two weeks of service, the court will issue an enforceable default summons.[63] The enforceable default summons becomes final if no objection (*Einspruch*) is raised within two weeks of service.[64] On an objection within these two weeks, the court will refer the case to the competent court of ordinary proceedings, which will examine the admissibility of the objection and — if the objection is admissible — decide the claim on the merits of the case.

Summary judgments

A summary proceeding with trial is the proceeding restricted to documentary evidence (trial by the record) according to Sections 592 *et seq.* of the ZPO. This proceeding is admissible only for claims for payment.

In these proceedings the plaintiff must provide the necessary evidence for his claim by documents and the defendant is restricted to defences he can proof by documentary evidence; counter-claims are excluded.[65]

The court will render a provisional judgment (*Vorbehaltsurteil*) in favour of the plaintiff if the trial by the record is admissible, the plaintiff can

---

59. ZPO, Section 688.
60. ZPO, Section 689.
61. ZPO, Sections 691 *et seq.*
62. ZPO, Sections 694, 696 *et seq.*
63. ZPO, Sections 699 *et seq.*
64. ZPO, Sections 700, 338 *et seq.*
65. ZPO, Sections 592, 595.

provide sufficient documentary evidence for his claim and the defendant does not defend to the claim at all or cannot support his defence by documentary evidence.[66] This provisional judgment is enforceable.

The defendant may appeal against the provisional judgment in summary proceedings or apply for the reversal of the provisional judgment in subsequent proceedings (*Nachverfahren*), which is the ordinary proceeding where all kinds of evidence are admissible.[67]

Default judgments

A further summary proceeding that the Civil Procedure Code provides for in Sections 330 *et seq.* is the default proceeding to obtain an enforceable default judgment (*Versäumnisurteil*).

The default proceedings take place if one party fails to attend the court hearing or does not plead in court and the other party applies for a default judgment.[68] The court must render a default judgment on request of the party attending the court hearing if the prerequisites for the admissibility under Section 335 of the ZPO (such as proper summons) and the specific requirements under Sections 330 *et seq.* of the ZPO are fulfilled.

If the plaintiff fails to appear in the court hearing the court will render a default judgment in favour of the defendant without examination on the merits.[69]

In case of default by the defendant the court must examine whether the claim is admissible and well-founded. For this purpose the assertions by the plaintiff are deemed to be conceded by the defendant.[70] As far as the claim is justified under these circumstances, the court will render the default judgment and dismiss the claim in other respects.[71] The default judgment is enforceable.

The default judgment is appealable by objection (*Einspruch*) in accordance with Sections 338 *et seq.* of the ZPO. An objection must be filed in writing within two weeks of service of the default judgment with the court that rendered the judgment.[72] If the objection is admissible the court will determine a new court hearing to decide on the objection and on the merits of the case.[73] If the court comes to the conclusion that

66. ZPO, Section 599.
67. ZPO, Section 600.
68. ZPO, Sections 330 *et seq.*
69. ZPO, Section 330.
70. ZPO, Section 331, Paragraph 1.
71. ZPO, Section 331, Paragraph 2.
72. ZPO, Section 339.
73. ZPO, Section 341 a.

the default judgment is not correct, it will reverse the default judgment and render a new decision on the merits of the claim. Otherwise the court will uphold the default judgment.[74]

Other means of termination

Voluntary dismissal

WAIVER OF A CLAIM

The plaintiff may make a waiver (*Verzicht*) of his claim at any time and stage in the proceedings.

On a waiver of the claim, the court must dismiss the claim without examination of the claim as being unfounded if the defendant applies for the dismissal.[75]

WITHDRAWAL OF THE ACTION

The plaintiff may also withdraw the action. The withdrawal (*Klagrücknahme*) will terminate the lawsuit without a decision on the merits. The withdrawal — for example, at the appeal stage — renders a decision in the same matter already made — for example, at first instance — ineffective.[76]

The defendant must consent to the withdrawal of the action when an oral court hearing has already taken place. Before the beginning of the oral hearing the plaintiff may withdraw the action without consent of the defendant.[77] The plaintiff may withdraw the action — if necessary with the consent of the defendant — at any stage of the proceedings until a decision in the same matter has become final.

After a withdrawal the plaintiff may take the case to court again provided he has reimbursed the defendant for the costs incurred in the proceedings terminated by the withdrawal.

Termination of the substantive dispute

During the proceeding, the dispute may become obsolete by intervening facts, for example, the defendant pays the claimed debt.

74. ZPO, Section 343.
75. ZPO, Section 306.
76. ZPO, Section 269, Paragraph 3, Sentence 1.
77. ZPO, Section 269.

In such a situation the plaintiff will not waive the claim or withdraw the action because on a waiver or withdrawal he would be obliged to pay the costs of the proceedings[78] notwithstanding the fact that his claim was (or might be) well-founded until the intervening fact occurs. The plaintiff will therefore make a motion to the court declaring the termination (*Erledigung*) of the dispute and ask the court for a cost order against the defendant.

If the defendant consents to the motion declaring the disposal of the dispute the lawsuit will be terminated without a decision on the merits by the cost order.[79]

If the defendant does not consent to the motion declaring the obsolescence of the dispute the court must decide whether the plaintiff's declaration of obsolescence is justified. If the action has been admissible and well-founded until the facts intervening rendered it obsolete, the court will declare the dispute obsolete and award the plaintiff his costs. Otherwise the court will dismiss the claim.

Settlement in court

The parties may settle their dispute in court. The court should aim for and support a settlement (*Prozeßvergleich*) at any stage of the proceedings.[80]

A settlement in court will be recorded in the court's minutes of the hearing. The settlement recorded by the court becomes an enforceable consent judgment on which a writ of execution may be granted.[81] As far as the settlement deals with the issue in dispute, the settlement terminates the suit without court decision and renders former court decisions in the same matter which have not become final inefficient.[82]

Acknowledgment

The defendant may acknowledge the plaintiffs claim at any time and stage of the proceedings.

On an acknowledgment (*Anerkenntnis*) of the claim, the court must find against the defendant without decision on the merits of the claim if the plaintiff applies for a judgment on acknowledgment.[83]

---

78. ZPO, Section 91, 269, Paragraph 3, Sentence 2.

79. ZPO, Section 91 a.

80. ZPO, Section 279.

81. ZPO, Section 794, Paragraph 1, Number 1.

82. BGH JZ 1964, 257.

83. ZPO, Section 307 — *Anerkenntnisurteil* provided that the claim is admissible and the acknowledgment not contrary to public policy.

The judgment on acknowledgement terminates the suit if the defendant has acknowledged the whole claim. Otherwise the court will make a part-judgment on acknowledgement (*Teil-Anerkenntnisurteil*) and proceed with the trial in other respects.

TRIAL

Trial stages

Since there is no distinction between "trial" and "pre-trial" under German law it is not possible to follow the structure recommended by the editors. Instead, some general remarks about the structure of a trial and the role of the parties and the judge in Germany are appropriate.

Adversary system and role of the judge

The German civil procedural law is, except for family and related matters, in essence adversarial. This is expressed in the basic procedural principle that only the parties themselves may introduce facts. The court may take into consideration only those facts and assertions that the parties have presented to it and may not seek out new evidentiary material on its own. This is the so-called "Verhandlungsmaxime". However, the German judge has a much greater role to play during the trial in general and especially in the process of the submission of evidence.

According to Section 139, Paragraph 1 of the ZPO, the presiding judge shall ensure that the parties make full explanations concerning all material facts and make the appropriate demands for relief, in particular that they supplement inadequate statements or asserted facts and designate sources of proof. In carrying out this duty the judge has the right to discuss the factual and legal aspects of the dispute with the parties and put questions to them. This so-called duty of clarification (*Aufklärungspflicht*) does, however, have restrictions. First, it must be underlined that the "duty of clarification" does not impose an independent duty on the judge to inquire into the case regardless of how the case has been pleaded. The court does not even have the right to do this but is strictly bound to questions, and inquiries are only possible on the basis of these assertions.

Recently the Federal Court of Justice stated that in all law-suits where the parties are represented by an attorney the duty of clarification is removed and generally left to the discretion of the judge. Since it is obligatory to be represented by an attorney whenever the value in dispute exceeds 10,000.00 German Marks, i.e., in the regional and the higher courts, the judge is only under this duty in minor cases. This decision has not been criticised by the bar, but only by authors who generally argue in favour of a greater role for the judge and a higher obligation of disclosure for the parties.

The judge does, however, have a right to assist the parties as long as he does not breach his obligation to be impartial. Though no statistical evidence can be given in this respect it may be useful to add that during the ten years of practical experience of the author it was only once that a judge exercised this right.

Setting the case for trial

Against the background of these general remarks the court has the — unrestricted and uncontrolled discretion — to proceed in the following alternatives:

The court may according to Section 275 of the ZPO appoint an early first hearing and fix the date of such hearing at the same time as the court orders the defendant to prepare the statement of defence. This alternative will be chosen either if the case seems to be straight-forward, or if the court expects that there will be a default judgment or an acknowledgement judgment or if there is a high probability for a settlement.

The alternative is the proceeding in writing according to Section 276 of the ZPO. Under this alternative the court will ask the defendant to submit within a specified time the statement of defence and decide thereafter whether additional briefs by either party are necessary to prepare the trial.

According to Section 273 of the ZPO, the court prepares actively the trial date by:

(1) Asking the parties to amend or explain their briefs as well as produce documents or objects they referred to within a time to be specified by the court;
(2) Asking authorities involved in the case — if any — for information;
(3) Ordering the personal appearance of the parties; and
(4) Ordering witnesses or experts to appear at the trial date in court.

Evidence

After the judge has finally decided which factual assertions require evidence — possibly after the exchange of several briefs from each party and several hearings — the evidence is taken.

The nature and purpose of evidence

According to Section 355 of the ZPO, the evidence is taken by the court. The taking of evidence may only be transferred to a member of the court or under certain restricted conditions according to Section 263 of the ZPO to another court. The purpose of the evidence is to prove the factual assertions to the court. Generally, each party must prove all facts favourable to it.

Kinds of evidence

The ZPO recognises five different kinds of evidence: Expert evidence, inspection by the court, evidence by witnesses, documentary evidence and — to a very limited extent — the evidence of the parties themselves.

WITNESSES

The powerful position of the judge becomes obvious when evidence is taken by way of witnesses. According to Section 396, Paragraph 1 of the ZPO the court must see that the witness relates his knowledge of particular events or circumstances in a continuous narrative. Afterwards, first the judge has the right to ask clarifying questions. Only then are the attorneys allowed to put additional questions.

EXPERT WITNESSES

Expert witnesses are chosen by the court according to Section 404, Paragraph 1, Sentence 1 of the ZPO. The parties may introduce expert opinions too, but the court will as a general rule follow the opinion of the independent expert appointed by the court. Experts must explain their written opinions to the court and the parties at trial. Again, the judge has the right to commence the questioning.

THE ROLE OF THE PARTIES

In principle the parties are not obliged to help each other or to help the court in finding the truth. There is no duty to reveal all documents, be they favourable or unfavourable, as, for example, in Common Law countries. Normally, no examination of the parties takes place. As the value of the testimony of a party is profoundly distrusted under German law, the parties are not considered to be witnesses. A party can only testify if the other party requests it according to Section 445 of the ZPO or if the court is convinced that it is impossible to find out the truth otherwise, according to Section 448 of the ZPO. In any event the testimony of a party is given less weight than other evidence.

According to Section 446 of the ZPO, a party cannot be compelled to testify. However, the court is free to evaluate such refusal in its consideration of the evidence. Again, no statistical evidence can be given, but testimony was never requested from one of the parties during the author's professional experience.

The situation is of course different when the parties are not represented by lawyers but act for themselves. However, even then their assertions are not considered to be testimony.

In the briefs in which the facts are stated, however, the parties are under a statutory duty of truth according to Section 138, Paragraph 1 of the ZPO.

This concept reflects the liberal views of the nineteenth century, when the ZPO was enacted. It shows a pure adversary system. Yet, this system would have led to unjust results in a number of situations if it had remained unchanged. Under circumstances where the plaintiff has little or no information and the defendant can provide this information without significant difficulties, it would seem unjust to dismiss the action because the plaintiff cannot state his case exactly. Therefore the courts have developed certain mechanisms to adjust the system.

One such mechanism is to shift the burden of proof. The general principle is that each party must allege and prove what is in his favour. In those cases where the plaintiff does not have sufficient information and is not aided by a shift of burden of proof or by an obligation on the part of the defendant, the defendant can block the action by simply denying the claim.

The interest of the plaintiff in establishing his case and the interests of the defendant — specific trade secrets, the desire not to be harassed by court actions — are considered to be of the same value. This is consistent with the general scheme of the ZPO and with the prohibition on probing and fishing expeditions in particular. It cannot be assumed that it leads to unjust results or hardship in any significant number of cases. It would be erroneous to focus solely on the needs and desires of the plaintiff without paying attention to the defendant. All court proceedings involve nuisance and harassment. Defendants should therefore be protected against claims that are so vague that it is difficult to answer them. It should be noted that a growing number of legal scholars are arguing *de lege lata* in favour of far more extensive obligations on the parties to help each other and the court to find the truth. However, these authors have so far had no significant impact on the development of the case law.

DOCUMENTS

Parties

First, it must be underlined that the ZPO departs from a narrow notion of documents, restricted to written texts. German procedural law does not contain any general obligation to disclose documents. A party is only obliged to disclose and produce documents under two circumstances.

According to Section 423 of the ZPO, an obligation of disclosure arises if the party has made reference to the document in question in the statement of claim, the defence or in a brief.

According to Section 422 of the ZPO, a party is obliged to produce documents to which the other party has a right according to the provisions of the material law. This means, for example, receipts under Section 371 of the BGB, or more generally, documents in which the other party has an interest.[84]

The latter provision applies mainly to documents that the party is obliged to gather by law, e.g., tax declarations or commercial books of account. Section 422 of the ZPO is, however, subject to the prohibition against probing. As a consequence, the desired document must be described precisely. There is no possibility that this provision could be used in order to obtain internal studies and documents of the opponent.

If a party does not produce documents despite having been ordered to do so by the court, the alleged content of the document is considered to be true. This presumption may only be rebutted in cases where the court is convinced that the party searched properly and simply does not have the document.

It must be mentioned that it has been proposed occasionally to introduce into the German civil procedure a general duty to disclose documents. This duty allegedly exists already under the duty of truth according to Section 138 of the ZPO. So far, this idea has not had any impact in practice and is upheld only by a very small minority of the scholars.

Non-parties

Non-parties are only under a duty to produce documents if the party who demands the documents has a right to these documents under the material law.[85] If the non-party refuses the production the party has no choice other than to start separate proceedings against the non-party. As for lawyers there is no risk at all that the opposing party might even try to "look into their briefcase" as this party does not have any material rights or claims against the lawyer.

84. BGB, Section 810.
85. ZPO, Section 429.

PRIVILEGE

German law does not consider the parties to be witnesses. As a consequence the privileges of parties and witnesses must be analysed separately.

Parties

The parties are in need of privileges only to a very restricted degree. Generally they need not provide their opponents with valuable information. Documents that have been prepared in contemplation of litigation need not be disclosed. There is no claim under German law that would require the disclosure of such documents. The practical importance of privileges is further diminished by the fact that the parties cannot be compelled to testify. Two problems, however, must be mentioned.

German law does not contain a general privilege against self-incrimination. In every case the interests involved must be weighed and analysed. In order to avoid the conflict between the testimony in civil procedure and possible criminal or administrative charges, the courts have developed the principle that the testimony cannot be used in criminal proceedings.

As far as the parties are concerned, no special privilege to protect trade secrets exists. The court can restrict the access to such secrets to lawyers, but the secrets are not privileged.

Again, it should be recalled that the obligation to make a precise statement and the prohibition on probing offer an effective protection.

Non-parties

Non-parties enjoy very far-reaching privileges under German law. According to Section 383, Paragraph 1, Numbers 1–3 of the ZPO, relatives and spouses are entitled to refuse to give any testimony. The same is true for priests,[86] journalists[87] and persons who are obliged to keep secrets according to their professional ethics.[88]

Lawyers fall into the latter category. Their privilege is construed broadly since the unjustified revelation of secrets entrusted to them is an offence according to Section 203 of the German Penal Code, punishable by up to three years imprisonment.

According to Section 384 of the ZPO, all witnesses can refuse to testify if the testimony would lead to economic loss, generate the danger of criminal prosecution or reveal business or trade secrets.

86. ZPO, Section 383, Paragraph 1, Number 4.
87. ZPO, Section 383, Paragraph 1, Number 5.
88. ZPO, Section 383, Paragraph 1, Number 6.

The notion of business secrets is extremely broad and comprises all data and information that is not available to the public and that the witness intended to be kept secret.

JUDGMENT AND KINDS OF RELIEF

Final judgment

Final judgment and interlocutory judgment

Once the trial has been closed, all necessary evidence has been taken and the parties have maintained their unwillingness to settle the case the judgment is rendered. An important decision must be made between final judgments[89] and interlocutory judgments.[90] Only final judgment may be attacked by means of appeal. The interlocutory judgment on the contrary does not lead to the end of the proceedings in the court that renders the interlocutory judgment. It only decides with a binding effect for the court that has rendered the interlocutory judgment one aspect of the claim. The interlocutory judgment is, for example, available if the foundation of the claim as well as the amount is in dispute. If, for example, the defendant allegedly caused an accident which allegedly lead to damages of 100,000.00 German Marks and the defendant denies his responsibility in the first place and argues that any possible damage may not be higher than 50,000.00 German Marks, then an interlocutory judgment with regard to the question whether the defendant is at all responsible for the damage may be rendered. It is in the free discretion of the court whether to deliver an interlocutory judgment or not.

Types of final judgment

Usually a distinction is made between judgments dealing with the merits of the case and judgments exclusively dealing with procedural questions (procedural judgment).

Procedural judgments are delivered by the court if it comes to the conclusion that the claim is for procedural or formal questions inadmissible.

Final judgments may either cover the whole dispute or decide only one aspect of it.[91] If, for example, the plaintiff pursues a claim for damages based in tort and a contractual claim for payment and the court is

89. ZPO, Section 300.
90. ZPO, Section 304.
91. Partial judgment according to ZPO, Section 301.

convinced that the contractual claim is well-founded whereas the claim based in torts requires further evidence to be taken a partial (final) judgment with regard to the contractual claim can be delivered.

Final judgment may be provisional according to Section 302 of the ZPO. The most important examples for provisional final judgments are summary judgments.[92]

Entry of judgment

Generally the operative provisions of the judgment are declared orally without stating any facts or the *ratio decidendi*. According to Section 310 of the ZPO, the judgment is either pronounced immediately after the end of the trial or in a separate hearing. This separate hearing must take place within three weeks after the end of the trial unless there are special reasons, especially the size or complexity of the case.

The written judgment must satisfy the conditions set out in Section 313, Paragraph 1 of the ZPO. Therefore it must include:

(1) The names of the parties, their legal representatives and their attorneys;
(2) The exact designation of the court and the names of the judges;
(3) The day the trial was ended;
(4) The operative provisions of the judgment;
(5) The facts of the case; and
(6) The *ratio decidendi*.

The judgment must be served on the parties according to Section 317, Paragraph 1 of the ZPO. The service is not a prerequisite of the validity of the judgment, however, the terms for an appeal only start once the written judgment has been served.

Kinds of relief

The kind of relief granted by the judgment is not determined by the procedural law but by the provisions of material law.

Specific performance

In this context it must be mentioned that specific performance is — unlike, for example, the Common Law countries — the regular relief granted.

---

92. See Summary Judgments above.

Substitution relief

Only to the extent that specific performance is not possible or the plaintiff exercised — if applicable — a choice in favour of a substitution relief, such relief is granted, for example, by a way of damages.

Constitution, transformation, rescission, declaration concerning legal relations

Finally, the judgment may also constitute or transform a legal relation. All judgments in favour of the defendants are *per se* declaratory judgments since they declare that the claim pursued by the plaintiff is not well-founded. However, declaratory judgment may also be pronounced in favour of the plaintiff, for example, if the plaintiff asked the court to declare a contract to be valid and existing. Standard examples for judgments that constitute or transform legal relations are divorce judgments or judgments by which companies or partnerships are dissolved.

POST-TRIAL MOTIONS

Attacks on judgments

Court decisions that have not become final and unappealable may be contested by ordinary appeals.[93] The ordinary appeals will be part of the ongoing (pending) proceedings.

Proceedings that have come to an end by a final and unappealable decision of the court may be reopened under certain circumstances on an action for a reopening of the proceedings, which is an extraordinary appeal under Sections 578 *et seq.* of the ZPO.

Grounds for a new trial

The Code of Civil Procedure provides in Section 578, Paragraph 1 of the ZPO for two kinds of action for a reopening of the proceedings:

(1) The action for annulment (*Nichtigkeitsklage*); and
(2) The action for restitution (*Restitutionsklage*).

If both proceedings are started at the same time, the court will suspend the proceedings for restitution until the decision of the action for annulment has become final and absolute.[94]

93. See Appeals, below.
94. ZPO, Section 578, Paragraph 2.

Both actions aim for the reversal of the contested decision and rendering a new decision by the court applied to. They only differ in the grounds for reopening the proceedings they can be based on.

Admissibility

Final judgments[95] and orders that terminate the proceedings[96] are subject to an action for a new trial.

ACTION FOR ANNULMENT

The grounds for an action for annulment are specified in Section 579, Paragraph 1 of the ZPO. These are serious infringements on procedural rules such as the incorrect composition of the court, the contribution of an excluded judge, incorrect or missing representation of the party in the proceedings.

Whether the contested decision was caused or influenced by the violation of these procedural rules is not decisive. Such serious violations of procedural rules are always reason enough for the reversal of the decision.

The action for annulment is inadmissible if the ground for the action specified in Section 579, Paragraph 1 Numbers 1 and 3 of the ZPO could have been pleaded with an ordinary appeal during the proceedings.[97]

Action for restitution

The grounds for an action for restitution are specified in Section 580 of the ZPO. These are on the one hand criminal offences during the trial like false statement under oath and falsification of documents. If the action for restitution is based on one of this grounds the conviction of these offences is further preposition for the action.[98]

On the other hand ground for an action for restitution is given under Section 580 of the ZPO if the basis of the decision has changed fundamentally or ceased to exist, e.g., the reversal of a decision the contested decision was based on or the discovery of a document which would have led to a decision in favour of the appellant.

95. ZPO, Section 578, Paragraph 1.
96. BGH NJW 1983, 883.
97. ZPO, Section 579, Paragraph 2.
98. ZPO, Section 581.

Unlike the action for annulment, the action for restitution can only be based on such grounds that have caused or influenced the decision.

The action for restitution is inadmissible if the ground it is based on could have been pleaded with an ordinary appeal or by notice of objection and the appellant has omitted this opportunity by negligence.[99]

Form

Both actions for a new trial must be filed in writing (statement of claim) with the competent court, which is the court that has rendered the decision against which the action is filed.[100] Thus, the Federal Court of Justice might decide in first instance the action for a new trial.

The statement of claim must specify the judgment against which the action is filed and must express the appellant's intention to bring an action for annulment or restitution. The statement of claim must include the assertion of a ground for the action under Sections 579 *et seq.* of the ZPO.

Time-limit

Both actions for a new trial must be filed with the court within one month of obtaining knowledge of the ground for reopening the proceedings, but not later than five years after the decision has become final and absolute.[101]

Proceeding and decision

The court must carry on an oral hearing and decide by judgment if the contested decision is a judgment. If the contested decision is an order, the court may decide without an oral hearing by an order.[102]

The court will dismiss the action for reopening the proceedings as inadmissible when the prerequisites of the action for a new trial are not fulfilled.[103]

The court will dismiss the action on the merits if none of the grounds for reopening the proceedings under Sections 579 *et seq.* of the ZPO is met.

---

99. ZPO, Section 582.
100. ZPO, Section 584.
101. ZPO, Section 586.
102. BGH NJW 1983, 883.
103. ZPO, Section 589.

The court must reverse the contested decision when it comes to the conclusion that a ground for reopening the proceedings according to Sections 579 *et seq.* of the ZPO is present. The reversal of the decision comes into force with retroactive effect when the decision for reopening becomes final. The reversed action then is deemed to be never made. Apart from the reversal of the decision, the court must reopen the proceedings and make a new decision on the merits of the case if it is appealable by the normally available appeals.[104]

ENFORCEMENT AND EXECUTION OF JUDGMENT

Internal provisions

If the unsuccessful party (debtor) does not follow the judgment the successful party (creditor) must take steps of forced execution. The core provisions are laid down in the ZPO.

Writ of execution and execution clause

Once the judgment has been served on the debtor the creditor may start steps of forced execution. Prerequisite to any measure of execution is the existence of an official copy of the judgment provided with an execution clause. Such a certificate of enforceability according to Section 725 of the ZPO is issued on motion by the clerk of the court that has delivered the judgment. The official copy with the execution clause is at the basis of the following steps of execution. The steps of execution and the state authority competent to deal with them depends on the object of execution.

Enforcement against chattels

The bailiff of the court is competent to carry out execution against chattel in the possession of the debtor.[105] The bailiff takes away or seizes the chattel by taking actual possession. In order to do this the bailiff is — subject to a special permission to be granted by the court — entitled to enter and search the debtor's house. The chattel seized by the bailiff is sold at public auction in accordance with Section 814 of the ZPO.

104. ZPO, Sections 590 *et seq.*
105. ZPO, Section 808, Paragraph 1.

Enforcement against realty, registered ships and aircraft

The court at the place of the realty, the registered ships or aircraft is competent to take steps of forced execution and not the court that delivered the judgment. On motion by the creditor the competent court may grant:

(1) Registration of a mortgage;
(2) Compulsory administration; or
(3) Compulsory sale.

The technical details of this procedure are laid down in the Forced Sale and Administration Act *(Gesetz über die Zwangsversteigerung und Zwangsverwaltung).*

Attachment of debts

The creditor may attach debts or other rights of the debtor by way of an application to the clerk of the court in the district where the debtor has his residence. The clerk will issue an order of attachment and transfer of the garnished claim pursuant to Section 829 of the ZPO. This procedure does not infringe on any rights of the third party debtor.

Declaration of will

No special steps of forced execution are necessary if the judgment orders the debtor to make a declaration of will, for example, the acceptance of an offer made by the creditor. When the judgment becomes final, the debtor is deemed to have made such declaration of will according to Section 894 of the ZPO.

Act or omission

If the debtor is ordered by the judgment to carry out a specific act and refuses to do so the creditor may file a motion for an order for substitute performance by a third party in accordance with Section 887, Paragraph 1 of the ZPO. The competent authority is the court that delivered the judgment.

If an omission is ordered the court may on motion of the creditor threaten and subsequently fix a penalty of up to German Marks 500,000.00 or a term of custody not to exceed six months.[106]

106. ZPO, Section 890.

Bankruptcy, liquidation, receivership

In case of bankruptcy, liquidation or receivership any steps of forced execution based on a distinct judgment come to a stand-still. The procedures to be followed then are laid down in the Bankruptcy Act and in the Receivership Act, which are not within the scope of this chapter.

Brussels Convention recognition and enforcement

Germany is a contracting country to the Brussels Convention of 27 September 1968 as amended on 25 October 1982. Articles 25 *et seq.* of the Convention facilitate the recognition and enforcement of judgments delivered by courts of countries that are parties to the Convention considerably.

Recognition and enforcement outside of the Brussels Convention

Treaties

Apart from the Brussels Convention, Germany is a party to the following multilateral treaties dealing with the recognition of foreign judgments:

(1) The Hague Convention on Civil Procedure of 1 March 1954 concerning the recognition of decisions with regard to the costs;
(2) The International Convention on the Transport of Goods by Railway;
(3) The International Convention on the Transport of Goods by Road; and
(4) The International Convention on the Transport of Persons and Luggage by Railway.

Moreover, there are bilateral treaties between Germany and the following countries that contain regulations with regard to the mutual recognition of judgments: Austria, Belgium, Greece, Israel, Italy, Netherlands, Norway, Switzerland, Tunisia and United Kingdom. With respect to Belgium, Italy, Netherlands and United Kingdom the Brussels Convention prevails within its scope of applicability.

Autonomous law

RECOGNITION

In the absence of international treaties a foreign judgment must be recognised according to Section 328 of the ZPO before execution can take place. Under Section 328 of the ZPO, foreign judgments will be recognised under the following conditions:

(1) The foreign court that rendered the judgment must have been competent to decide the matter. The question of competence is ascertained by application of the German rules of jurisdiction;[107]

(2) The foreign judgment can only be recognised if the writ was served properly on the defendant;

(3) The foreign judgment cannot be recognised if it is contrary to another foreign decision that was previously held or if it interferes with a pending litigation in Germany or a German decision;

(4) The foreign judgments will not be recognised if they contravene the German order public; and

(5) There must be reciprocity, i.e., the foreign judgment is only recognised to the extent that the foreign state recognises German judgments.

EXECUTION

The execution will take place if all condition of Section 328 of the ZPO are fulfilled and the foreign judgment is final and binding according to the law under which it was delivered.[108]

APPEALS

In German civil procedure, two kinds of appeals must be distinguished: The ordinary appeals such as appeal of first instance,[109] the appeal of second instance[110] and the (ordinary or immediate) complaint.[111]

Extraordinary appeals are the opposition,[112] objection,[113] motion for reinstatement[114] and the action for reopening the proceedings.[115]

107. See Establishing Jurisdiction above.
108. ZPO, Section 723.
109. *Berufung* — ZPO, Sections 511–544.
110. *Revision* — ZPO, Sections 545–566 a.
111. *Einfache und sofortige Beschwerde* — ZPO, Sections 567–577 a.
112. *Widerspruch* — ZPO, Sections 694, 700, 338.
113. *Erinnerung* — ZPO, Section 766.
114. *Antrag auf Wiedereinsetzung* — ZPO, Sections 233 *et seq.*
115. *Wiederaufnahmeklage* — ZPO, Sections 578 *et seq.*

Ordinary appeals always have a dual effect:

(1) They suspend the effect of the decision (*Suspensiveffekt*); and
(2) The superior court will be seized of the matter (*Devolutiveffekt*).

ISSUES SUBJECT TO REVIEW

The appeal of first instance and the complaint are appeals on questions of both fact and law. The appeal of second instance is an appeal on questions of law only.

As far as an appeal may be based on questions of fact as well, e.g., appeal of first instance and complaint, the appeal in principle may be based on the introduction of new facts and fresh evidence in the appeal proceedings. Regarding the complaint, this principle is valid without limitation while the possibility to introduce new facts and fresh evidence with the appeal of first instance is very limited. The appeal of second instance, which is an appeal on questions of law only, cannot be based on new facts or fresh evidence.

Prerequisites of an appeal

The court of appeal may only examine the validity of the grounds of appeal after ascertaining the compliance with all necessary prerequisites of an appeal. The five particular prerequisites of any appeal are:

(1) Admissibility of the appeal, e.g., the concrete appeal must be available against the contested decision;
(2) The appeal must be filed in the proper form;
(3) The appeal must be filed within the legal time-limit if the appeal is subject to a time-limit (appeal of first instance, appeal of second instance and immediate complaint);
(4) The appellant must be aggrieved by the contested decision. In pecuniary claims a certain amount which may differ between the different kinds of appeals must be exceeded to contest the decision; and
(5) The appellant has not waived his right of appeal.

Cross-appeal

Subject to the aforementioned prerequisites both parties may file ordinary appeals that are independent from each other. If the court, for example, has ruled that a claim for damages in the amount of 100,000.00 German

Marks is only justified in the amount of 50,000.00 German Marks, both parties may appeal against this judgment, the plaintiff to obtain a judgment in the amount of 100,000.00 German Marks and the defendant for dismissal of the action.

In distinction from such independent appeals of both parties one party may file a cross-appeal in defence of the appeal of the other parties. Such cross-appeals are admissible as an appeal of first instance,[116] an appeal of second instance[117] or a complaint.[118]

The formal requirements for a cross-appeal are basically the same as for an ordinary appeal, but there is no time-limit for the cross-appeal as for the ordinary appeal and a cross-appeal is admissible even where the party has waived its right to an (independent) appeal.[119] Furthermore, a cross-appeal is admissible even where the party is not aggrieved by the decision of the lower court.

On the other hand, the admissibility of the cross-appeal as an appeal which is dependent on the appeal of the other party is dependant on the admissibility of the appeal. Therefore, if the appeal is withdrawn by the appellant or dismissed by the court, the cross-appeal automatically becomes ineffective[120] unless the cross-appeal was filed during the time-limit of the appeal and the party has not waived its right to appeal; the cross-appeal will then be treated as an ordinary appeal.[121]

The appeal decision

The appeal court will dismiss an appeal as inadmissible unless all prerequisites of the appeal are given.

Only if all prerequisites for an appeal are given the court will examine the validity of the ground of the appeal. In this case the court may dismiss the appeal as unfounded when it comes to the conclusion that the contested judgment is correct.

If the court of appeal comes to the conclusion that the contested decision is not correct the court of appeal will set aside the judgment and refer the case back to the lower court or make a decision of its own on the merits of the case (judgment on appeal). The appeal decision has a dual limitation: It may neither award more to the appellant than

---

116. ZPO, Sections 521 *et seq.*
117. ZPO, Section 556.
118. ZPO, Section 577 a.
119. OLG Stuttgart NJW 1960, 1161.
120. ZPO, Section 522, Paragraph 1, and Section 566, Paragraph 2.
121. ZPO, Section 522, Paragraph 2, and Section 577 a.

he claimed for[122] nor may the appeal court alter the judgment of the lower court to the appellant's detriment.

Individual types of appeals

Appeal of first instance

SCOPE OF APPEAL

The appeal of first instance (*Berufung*) is an appeal on questions of fact as well as law. In principle, new facts and fresh evidence (new means of attack and defence) may be introduced with the appeal of first instance unless their introduction is excluded:

(1) New claims or an extention of the claim of first instance are admissible if the prerequisites for an amendment of action[123] are given;

(2) The defendant may launch a counter-claim or plead the defence of set-off if the plaintiff consents or the court decides that it would be appropriate to deal with the new matters raised;[124]

(3) New means of attack and defence which could not have been pleaded in the court of first instance are admissible. Such new means of attack and defence may only be refused by the court of appeal if they are not timely pleaded and their allowance would delay the appeal proceedings and the delay is not sufficiently excused;[125]

(4) New means of attack and defence which could have been pleaded in the court of first instance but have not timely been pleaded are admissible and can only be refused by the court of appeal if their allowance would delay the appeal proceedings and the delay in pleading the new means of attack and defence in the court of first instance is not sufficiently excused and there was gross negligence on the party in not pleading the new means of attack and defence in the court of first instance.[126] Any new means of attack and defence are excluded if they were rightly refused by the court of first instance;[127] and

122. ZPO, Sections 536 and 559.
123. *Klagänderung* — ZPO, Sections 263 *et seq.*
124. ZPO, Section 530.
125. ZPO, Sections 523, 282, 296.
126. ZPO, Section 528, Paragraphs 1 and 2.
127. ZPO, Section 528, Paragraph 3.

(5) The introduction of new facts or factual allegations which are not pleaded in the statement of grounds for appeal or in the defence or within a time-limit set by the court of appeal are excluded if their allowance would delay the appeal proceedings a nd the delay is not sufficiently excused.[128]

Prerequisites

The appeal of first instance is admissible only against judgments, not against other forms (e.g., orders) of court decisions. The appeal of first instance is given against final judgments of the Local Court (*Amtsgericht*), final judgments in first instance by the Regional Court (*Landgericht*) and against interlocutory judgments to be treated as equal.[129] The appeal of first instance against a default judgment is inadmissible if the extraordinary appeal by notice of objection (*Einspruch*) is given.[130]

The appeal of first instance must be filed in writing (notice of appeal) with the court of appeal. The notice of appeal must specify the judgment against which the appeal is filed and must express the appellants intention to appeal.[131] The appellant must give reasons for the appeal,[132] either in his notice of appeal or in a separate document (statement of grounds for appeal). The court of appeal for an appeal against a judgment of the Local Court is normally the Regional Court.[133] In cases concerning parent and child legal relationships or matters of family law it is exceptionally the Higher Regional Court (*Oberlandesgericht*).[134] Court of appeal for appeal of first instance against judgments of the Regional Court is always the Higher Regional Court (Section 119 GVG).

The appeal of first instance must be filed with the court of appeal within one month after service of the complete formal judgment by the court on the appellant, but not later than five month after the judgment was pronounced.[135] The statement of grounds for appeal must be filed within one month after filing the notice of appeal if not filed together.[136]

128. ZPO, Section 527.
129. For example, ZPO, Sections 280, Paragraph 2, 304, Paragraph 2 and 511.
130. ZPO, Section 513.
131. ZPO, Section 518.
132. ZPO, Section 519.
133. GVG, Section 72.
134. GVG, Section 119.
135. ZPO, Section 516.
136. ZPO, Section 519, Paragraph 2.

The sum of appeal in financial claims is currently 1.500.00 German Marks.[137] The grievance of the appellant by the decision of first instance must exceed this amount.

The appeal of first instance is inadmissible if the appellant has waived his right to appeal[138] or has withdrawn his appeal.[139]

Appeal judgment

The court of appeal has the two opportunities to decide about the appeal of first instance.

First if the appeal of first instance is inadmissible, the court will dismiss the appeal as inadmissible, at its discretion without an oral hearing by an order or after an oral hearing by judgment.[140] If the appeal of first instance is dismissed as inadmissible by a Regional Court, no appeal against this decision is given. If the Higher Regional Court has dismissed the appeal of first instance as inadmissible, its decision may be contested by immediate complaint or by appeal of second instance,[141] depending whether the Higher Regional Court has decided without an oral hearing by order or after an oral hearing by judgment.

Second if the appeal is admissible the court of appeal will always decide the merits of the case after an oral hearing by judgment.[142] The court of appeal will dismiss the appeal and will uphold the judgment of the lower court if it agrees to the result of this judgment, even if it disagrees to the reasons given by the lower court for its judgment.

The court of appeal will allow the appeal and reverse the judgment of the lower court if it comes to the conclusion that the judgment of first instance is not correct. In principle, the court of appeal will make an own judgment. Under certain circumstances the court of appeal may refer the case back to the court of first instance if the judgment successfully appealed against has not dealt with the matter at issue or if serious procedural mistakes were made by the lower court.[143] However, the court of appeal may not refer the case back if it can decide the entire case and hold that this would be appropriate.[144]

A decision on the merits by the Regional Court as court of appeal cannot be contested by a further appeal. The decision on the merits by the

137. ZPO, Section 511 a.
138. ZPO, Section 514.
139. ZPO, Section 515.
140. ZPO, Section 519 b.
141. ZPO, Sections 519 b, 547.
142. ZPO, Section 520.
143. ZPO, Sections 538 *et seq.*
144. ZPO, Section 540.

Higher Regional Court as court of appeal may be contested by the appeal of second instance, provided the below mentioned requirements are given.

The appeal of second instance

SCOPE OF APPEAL

The appeal of second instance (*revision*) is an appeal on questions of law only.[145] The court of second appeal is bound by the finding of facts by the lower court in principle.[146] The introduction of new facts or fresh evidence by the parties as well as new claims or an amendment of action are excluded.

Only in certain cases may the court of second appeal deviate from the finding of facts by the lower court, e.g., if the finding of facts by the lower court was influenced by procedural irregularity and this irregularity is asserted by the appeal of second instance.[147]

Only infringements of Federal Law or State Law whose application extends beyond the jurisdiction of one Higher Regional Court can be asserted in the appeal of second instance. Furthermore, the contested court decision must be based on this infringement of law if the second appeal shall succeed. A causal connection between the infringement of law and the court decision is necessary.[148]

Section 551 of the ZPO is stating certain serious violations of procedural rules, which are by statute valid grounds of appeal. If the appellant can show that at least one of these certain procedural rules has been violated, his appeal will be granted.

PREREQUISITES

The appeal of second instance is admissible only against judgments, not against other forms of court decision (e.g., orders). The appeal of second instance is given against final judgments of the Higher Regional Court in second instance[149] and against interlocutory judgments to be treated as equal.[150]

---

145. ZPO, Section 549.
146. ZPO, Section 561.
147. ZPO, Section 561, Paragraph 1, Sentence 2.
148. ZPO, Sections 549 *et seq.*
149. ZPO, Section 545, Paragraph 1.
150. ZPO, Sections 280, Paragraph 2, 304, Paragraph 2.

Furthermore, an appeal of second instance is possible against a judgment of the Regional Court in first instance under Section 566 a of the ZPO if the certain requirements are fulfilled (leap-frog appeal).

An appeal of second instance is inadmissible under Section 545, Paragraph 2 of the ZPO against default judgments and injunctions.[151]

The appeal of second instance must be filed in writing (notice of appeal) with the court of second appeal.[152] The appellant must give reasons for the appeal, either in his notice of appeal or in a separate document.[153]

In principle, the court of second appeal is the Federal Court of Justice (*Bundesgerichtshof*). Only in the state of Bavaria does the Bavarian State Court of Justice (*Bayerisches Oberstes Landesgericht*) have jurisdiction for certain second appeals.[154]

The appeal of second instance must be filed with the court of second appeal within one month of service of the complete formal judgment by the court of first appeal on the appellant, but not later than five months after the judgment has been pronounced.[155]

The statement of grounds for appeal must be filed within one month after filing the notice of appeal if not already filed together with the notice of appeal.[156]

The appellant must be aggrieved by the contested judgments. Further specific considerations for an appeal of second instance are:

(1) The appeal of second instance is always admissible if the Higher Regional Court has dismissed an appeal of first instance as inadmissible;[157]

(2) For pecuniary claims, the grievance of the appellant must exceed the sum of 60,000.00 German Marks.[158] However, even when this amount in dispute on appeal is exceeded, the court of second appeal may refuse the appeal if the case is not of fundamental legal importance,[159] and the appeal has no chances of success;[160]

(3) In pecuniary claims where the amount in dispute on appeal does not exceed German Marks 60,000.00 or in non-pecuniary

151. ZPO, Sections 513, 566.
152. ZPO, Section 553.
153. Statement of grounds for appeal — ZPO, Section 554.
154. EGGVG, Section 8 and EGZPO, Section 7.
155. ZPO, Section 552.
156. ZPO, Section 554, Paragraph 2.
157. ZPO, Section 547.
158. ZPO, Section 546, Paragraph 1, Sentence 1.
159. ZPO, Section 554 b.
160. Postulated by the Federal Constitutional Court BVerfGE 54, 277; 55, 206.

claims, the appeal of second instance must be explicitly admitted by the court of first appeal;[161]

(4) The court of first appeal will grant permission if the case has fundamental legal importance or if its decision deviates from a precedent decided by the Federal Court of Justice or by the Common Senate of the Federal Appeal Courts (*Gemeinsamer Senat der obersten Gerichtshöfe des Bundes*) and is based on this deviation;[162] and

(5) If the court of first appeal has admitted the appeal of second instance, the Federal Court of Justice is obliged to decide the appeal.[163] No appeal is given against the decision of the court of first appeal not to grant permission for the appeal of second instance.

THE JUDGMENT OF APPEAL

The Federal Court of Justice has the following opportunities to decide about the appeal of second instance:

(1) If the appeal of second instance is inadmissible, the court will dismiss the appeal as inadmissible by order (if no oral hearing has taken place) or by judgment (after an oral hearing);[164]

(2) If the appeal of second instance is admissible the Federal Court of Justice will always decide the merits of the case after an oral hearing by judgment;[165] and

(3) The court will dismiss the appeal and will uphold the judgment of the Higher Regional Court if it consents to the result of this judgment. If the Higher Regional Court has ignored or falsely applied rules of law, the Federal Court of Justice will dismiss the appeal if for other reasons the result of the judgment by the Higher Regional Court is correct.[166]

The appeal of second instance is well-founded if the judgment of the Higher Regional Court is based on an infringement of law. The Federal Court of Justice will then set aside the judgment of the Higher Regional Court.[167] At its discretion the Federal Court of Justice will make an

---

161. Higher Regional Court, ZPO, Section 546, Paragraph 1, Sentence 2.
162. ZPO, Section 546, Paragraph 1, Sentence 2.
163. ZPO, Section 546, Paragraph 1, Sentence 3.
164. ZPO, Section 554 a.
165. ZPO, Section 555.
166. ZPO, Section 563.
167. ZPO, Section 564.

own decision on the merits or will refer the case back to the Higher Regional Court,[168] depending whether the facts of the case are clear and it can decide on the whole case with or without taking further evidence.

Complaint

SCOPE

The complaint is an appeal on questions of both fact and law. New facts and fresh evidence may be introduced by the complaint without any limitation.[169]

TYPES OF COMPLAINTS

The Code of Civil Procedure provides for four types of complaints:

> (1) Ordinary complaint;[170]
> (2) Immediate complaint;[171]
> (3) Further ordinary complaint; and[172]
> (4) Further immediate complaint.[173]

Unlike the ordinary complaint, the immediate complaint is subject to a statutory time-limit. A further distinction between the ordinary and the immediate complaint is the opportunity of the court which decision has been appealed against by an ordinary complaint to grant the redress sought by the complaint by modifying the appealed decision on its own.

The further complaint is the appeal against the decision of the court in first instance about a complaint.

PREREQUISITES

The ordinary complaint is admissible either where explicitly provided for by law or against decisions that do not require a prior oral hearing and

168. ZPO, Section 565.
169. ZPO, Section 570.
170. *Einfache Beschwerde* — ZPO, Section 567.
171. *Sofortige Beschwerde* — ZPO, Section 577.
172. *Weitere einfache Beschwerde* — ZPO, Section 568.
173. *Weitere sofortige Beschwerde* — ZPO, Section 568 a.

dismiss procedural motions.[174] Basically orders and rulings are subject to complaint, not judgments. Decisions by the Regional Court as a court of appeal of first instance or by the Higher Regional Court are not subject to complaint in principle.[175]

The immediate complaint is admissible only where explicitly provided for by law, e.g., Section 99, Paragraph 2, 519 b, Paragraph 2 of the ZPO.

The further ordinary complaint is given against decisions by the court of appeal, provided that the appeal decision is setting a new and independent ground of appeal.[176] A decision that rejects the complaint as inadmissible is subject to further complaint. In principle, only appeal decisions by the Regional Courts are subject to the further complaint whereas appeal decisions by the Higher Regional Court are not subject to further complaint.

The further immediate complaint is admissible only against decisions by the Higher Regional Court, provided the specific requirements under Section 568 a of the ZPO are fulfilled.

The ordinary and immediate complaint normally must be filed in writing.[177] Unlike the appeal of first and second instance, the appellant is not obliged to give reasons for the complaint. However, in practice the appellant will always set out the grounds for his complaint.

The ordinary complaint must be filed with the court that has rendered the contested decision; only in urgent cases the ordinary complaint can be filed with the appeal court.[178] The immediate complaint may always be filed with the appeal court.[179]

The ordinary complaint and the further ordinary complaint are not subject to any statutory time-limit. The immediate complaint and the further immediate complaint are subject to a time-limit of two weeks after service of the decision on the appellant.[180]

THE DECISION

The court that has rendered the decision against which the ordinary complaint is filed can allow the complaint and amend its previous decision.[181] If it is not willing to amend its decision, the court must submit

174. ZPO, Section 567, Paragraph 1.
175. ZPO, Section 567, Paragraph 3.
176. ZPO, Section 568, Paragraph 2.
177. ZPO, Section 569, Paragraph 2.
178. ZPO, Section 569, Paragraph 1.
179. ZPO, Section 577, Paragraph 2, Sentence 2.
180. ZPO, Section 577, Paragraph 2.
181. ZPO, Section 571.

the complaint to the appeal court, which may allow the complaint if it is admissible and well-founded or dismiss the complaint as inadmissible or unjustified.[182]

The court that has rendered the decision against which the immediate complaint is filed is not entitled to remedy the complaint and to amend its previous decision. It must submit the complaint to the court of appeal, which will decide the complaint.

THE CONCLUSIVENESS OF JUDGMENT

Res judicata

The purpose of any judgment is to reach a final and binding settlement of the lawsuit by the decision of the court. A judgment is final and binding when it becomes unappealable and *res judicata*.

Finality

JUDGMENTS

Any judgment becomes non-appealable. Finality means that the judgement cannot be contested by ordinary appeals[183] or by opposition/objection under Section 338 of the ZPO (against default judgments). A non-appealable judgment may only be contested by extraordinary appeals such as an action for reopening the proceedings.[184]

A judgment becomes non-appealable when the statutory time-period for appeal has lapsed,[185] the parties have waived the right of appeal or an appeal against the judgment is inadmissible (e.g., exhaustion of appellate instances judgment of appeal of first instance by the Regional Court, judgment of appeal of second instance by the Federal Court of Justice).

ORDERS

Court orders that only exceptionally provide for a final decision do not always become non-appealable. Orders only become non-appealable when the finality is stated by law[186] or when the order is contestable by

182. ZPO, Sections 571, 573 *et seq.*

183. See Appeals, above.

184. See Post-Trial motions, above.

185. ZPO, Section 705.

186. For example, ZPO, Sections 281, Paragraph 2, Sentence 1, 707, Paragraph 2, Sentence 2.

immediate complaint and the statutory time-period has lapsed. Thus, orders that are contestable by ordinary complaint (complaint not subject to a time-limit) do not become non-appealable unless the parties have waived the right of complaint.

Res judicata

Res judicata means that the judgment is with final force and effect to the parties concerned. The res judicata provokes the finality of the decision by binding the parties concerned and the court in any further lawsuit where the res judicata is prejudicial.

The res judicata effect provokes that any further court proceeding and any further court decision on the issue that has been adjudicated is barred — ne bis in idem. The res judicata effect is restricted by objective, subjective and temporal limitations.

OBJECTIVE LIMITATIONS

The res judicata effect is restricted to the object at issue that has been adjudicated[187] and the adversaries ad litem. Whether the res judicata effect can be extended to the facts of the case, the legal relationships or defences that have prejudicial effect to the issue decided, is in issue and is declined by the prevailing doctrines.

SUBJECTIVE LIMITATIONS

The res judicata effect is further — in principle — restricted to the parties of the lawsuit.[188]

By operation of law the res judicata effect is extended to third parties with special relationship to the parties of the lawsuit, e.g., the legal successor of a party,[189] the reversionary heir[190] and the executor.[191]

Apart from these, statutory provisions, the res judicata effect may be extended to third parties in other cases within the meaning and for the purpose of the res judicata.[192]

187. ZPO, Section 322, Paragraph 1.
188. ZPO, Section 325, Paragraph 1.
189. ZPO, Section 325, Paragraph 1.
190. ZPO, Section 326.
191. ZPO, Section 327.
192. See Stucken, *Einseitige Rechtskraftwirkung von Urteilen im deutschen Zivilprozeß* (1990), pp. 43 et seq., 125 et seq.

TIME LIMITATIONS

The *res judicata* effect is restricted to the point in time of the last oral hearing in court. Therefore, a further litigation is not barred by the *res judicata* effect when the further litigation is based on facts that have been developed after the last oral hearing in court.

THE PROCEDURAL CONSEQUENCES OF RES JUDICATA

The *res judicata* effect — within its aforementioned limitations — in further litigation depends on the object at issue:

If the object at issue is identical, any further litigation is inadmissible and the further action will be dismissed by judgment on procedural grounds. The same applies if the object at issue in the further litigation is the adversarial to the issue that already has been adjudicated.

Where the object at issue in further litigation is neither identical nor adversarial but where the judgment is with prejudicial effect to the further litigation, the *res judicata* is binding for the court and the parties in the further lawsuit. In such cases the *res judicata* effect is not a bar to the further litigation as such but prevents any further decision about the already decided issue by the court, which must base its judgment on the *res judicata*.

EXCEPTIONS TO RES JUDICATA

According to the purpose of the *res judicata* exceptions are limited.

The exceptions to the *res judicata* by operation of law are the action for reopening the proceedings according to Sections 578 *et seq.* of the ZPO and the petition to modify a judgment to periodical payments according to Section 323 of the ZPO.

A further exception is recognised by the practice of the courts on the grounds of an action for damages under Section 826 BGB in cases where an incorrect judgment has been obtained by misrepresentation or is taken advantage of contrary to public policy.[193]

Besides the *res judicata* and the internal binding of the court under Section 318 of the ZPO, the court in its decision is in principle not bound to precedents and may decide according to any independent conviction without being bound by the practice of other courts or even its own practice in the past. Thus, no lower ranking court need to follow the decisions of a higher ranking court, not even the decisions of the Federal Court of Justice. German Civil Law is not based on binding precedents.

193. BGHZ 101, 380, 383 *et seq.*; 103, 44, 46 *et seq.*; BGH NJW 1991, 1362 *et seq.*

Only by operation of law in two cases must the court follow a decision by a higher ranking court: If the court of first or second appeal remands the decision to the lower court, the lower court must follow the reasoning of the remanding higher court.[194] The Regional Court as a court of appeal must follow the legal decision of the Higher Regional Court or the Federal Court of Justice in a lawsuit regarding the rent of living accommodation if the Regional Court is obliged under Section 541 of the ZPO to obtain the legal decision of the Higher Regional Court.

Note: Although Dr. Wittuhn and Dr. Stucken each prepared various of the sections of this chapter independently, both authors share the responsibility for the entire chapter. Due to the editorial restrictions on the length of the chapter both authors agreed to limit citations; also, outside Germany, most cited material would only be accessible in large university libraries. Both authors wish to thank their secretaries Ms. Dombrowski and Ms. Mertins for the dedicated co-operation in the preparation of this chapter.

194. See Appeals, above.

CHAPTER 8

GREECE

NIKOS FRANGAKIS, NASSIA KAZANTZI AND HARA SAOUNATSOU
Souriadakis, Frangakis & Associates
Athens, Greece

ESTABLISHING JURISDICTION

Types of jurisdiction

In modern Greek law, the terms "jurisdiction", "competence" and "locus standi" are used to describe three different aspects of the same notion: the court's power and/or duty to hear a case. The word jurisdiction either refers to the State's judicial power — to hear a case in contrast with the one of others — or to the tripartite division of judicial authority[1] among administrative, civil and criminal courts. Competence pertains to the allocation of judicial power within each jurisdictional division. Finally, capacity and standing to sue corresponding to *locus standi* refer to the capacity of a person to be a party and to conduct litigation in its own name.

Both jurisdiction and competence refer to a court's capacity to adjudicate a matter while locus standi refers to the parties' ability to bring a matter before a court.

As far as the third aspect of jurisdiction is concerned, the Greek Code of Civil Procedure (CCP) allows for three types of persons to be litigants in a trial so long as they are capable of holding rights. These are:

(1) Natural persons who enjoy the capacity to enter into judicial acts and thus have the capacity to conduct litigation in their own name. According to law, such persons should be above 18 years of age, and should not be interdicted or mentally ill. The latter persons may conduct litigation through their legal representatives;

(2) Legal entities, falling under any of the forms of entities provided for by Greek commercial and Civil Law. These entities are represented by their legal representatives; and

(3) Associations of persons which do not form a legal entity as in (2) above. These associations are represented by the persons

---

1. According to the Constitution, Article 93(1).

entrusted with their representation or contracting power. In relation to the above, it should be noted that, according to CCP, Article 94, litigants are obliged to appoint an advocate (*dikigoros*) in all civil courts, with the exception of Courts of the Peace (the lowest in the judicial hierarchy of courts), litigation for the interim protection of assets, and where absolutely necessary. In any event the court, even in the above cases, may ask a litigant to appoint an advocate.

The subject matter competence of a court depends, as a rule, on the amount in controversy[2] as it is set out in the complaint without taking into account any interest or other accessory claims. As currently determined by L2207/1994, demarcation between Courts of the Peace and Single-Member Courts of First Instance is drawn at the amount of 600,000 Drs. and between the latter and the Multi-Member Court of First Instance at the amount of 25-million Drs.

As an exception to the above rule, the CCP provides for a parallel criterion irrespective of the value of the dispute, by expanding the competence of the Court of the Peace and that of the Single-Member Court of First Instance in order to facilitate and accelerate the proceedings in respect of disputes with a strong local connection (such as in cases involving farming, restrictions on property, transportation or performance of some other services) or disputes of social interest (such as leases, employment, insurance and car accident disputes, claims of lawyers and some other professionals, as well as some family litigation and disputes concerning the internal operation of associations and cooperatives). The CCP expands the competence of the Courts of the Peace to include the former class and the competence of the Single-Member Court of First Instance to include the latter.

In contrast to the view taken by Common Law, the CCP's allotment of the above courts' competence does not take into account the division of disputes in damages or violation of rights actions or actions with a property claim.

Article 3 of the Brussels Convention makes an indicative reference to a number of provisions in the national laws of the contracting parties, among them Article 40 of the CCP[3] that have been abrogated by Sections 2–4 of the Convention.

The above stipulation is of minor importance in Greece since by virtue of Article 26 of the Constitution, international conventions or agreements entered into and ratified by Greece override conflicting provisions of national law.

2. CCP, Articles 7 *et seq.*

3. CCP, Article 40 provides that persons having property or movable assets in Greece may be litigants to proceedings opened before Greek Courts.

Venue

As a principle, the CCP links the venue of a dispute to the defendant's domicile as defined in Article 51 of the Greek Civil Code. According to substantive law, domicile is a person's main and permanent establishment, consisting of *corpus* and *animus*. Where a person does not have a domicile either in Greece or abroad, venue is defined by its residence, that is a person's main (though not permanent) establishment and in the absense thereof, by its last domicile in Greece or, in sequence, its last residence in Greece.

A person's professional address may equally, according to Article 2(2) of the CCP, serve as a basis for the "territorial"competence of a court. Further, the CCP provides for other bases of venue in cases where the defendant is a civil servant or an employee,[4] the Greek State, a legal entity,[5] an advocate or a notary public.[6] The legislator has deviated from the above system by laying down[7] other bases of territorial jurisdiction which are specific and in some cases exclusive.

Exclusive jurisdiction is granted in relation to:

(1) Disputes arising from the internal relationship of a company and its shareholders or between shareholders themselves;
(2) Disputes regarding the management of an entity on judicial order;
(3) Disputes with respect to rights *in rem* or those regarding matters of succession, proceedings opened in the occasion of other proceedings such as interpleaders and actions relating to a garantee contract; and
(4) Disputes between joinders of claimants or defendants.

Further in disputes as to a pecuniary interest, litigants may only alter a court's territorial jurisdiction by common consent.[8] Where, according to law, a court has exclusive territorial jurisdiction to deal with an action the litigant's consent regarding venue should be clearly stipulated, whereas such agreements regarding disputes that may arise in the future[9] are valid only if they are in writing and refer to a specific lawful relationship from which they will stem.

According to Article 42(2) of the CCP, a litigant's presence in proceedings opened before a court that does not have territorial jurisdiction to hear the case is deemed to be tacit consent to this court's competence.

4. CCP, Article 24.
5. CCP, Article 25.
6. CCP, Article 26.
7. CCP, Articles 27–40.
8. CCP, Article 42.
9. CCP, Article 43.

Service of summons or writs

Summons and writs are served by an authorised process server, appointed by the court in the jurisdiction of which the person to whom the summon or writ is to be served has his legal residence or, in case of a legal entity its seat.[10]

If, at the place where the summons or writ is to be served, no process server is appointed, the service will be effected by the process server of a criminal court or by the police.[11] Further, service may be effected by wire, should a judge so allow in cases of absolute urgency.

The summons or writ is served diligently according to an order that the litigant or his advocate has placed in writing on the complaint to be served.[12]

The CCP stipulates that the server may serve the complaint at any place where the addressee may be found, with the exception of a church in which a service is being held.[13] As to the time and the days that a summons or writ may be served, the CCP provides that it may only be effected on working days, between 7 a.m. and 7 p.m., except where the judge has permitted otherwise or where the addressee does not object.

The summons or writ is served on the addressee or his legal representative in the case of persons who lack the capacity to conduct litigation in their own name. The CCP, however, provides separately for service to persons who are absent at the time the server is serving the summons or writ for example, in prison, or hospital, aboard a merchant ship, or pursuing a career in the army or carrying out their military service and finally to persons or legal entities who have their residence or seat abroad.[14]

In relation to the latter category of persons, it should be stressed that Article 134 applies only to cases where The Hague Convention of 15 November 1965 or bilateral agreements on the service of summons and writs do not apply.

ASCERTAINING THE APPLICABLE LAW

In determining the applicable law to a specific case, the judge will seek for the forum closer to the elements of the case before him, and he should apply that forum's law. This may not be easy, especially where the case's connecting factors may tie it to several *fora*, thus leading to a conflict of

10. CCP, Article 122(1).
11. CCP, Article 122(2).
12. CCP, Article 123.
13. CCP, Article 124.
14. CCP, Articles 131, 132, 133, 134 respectively.

applicable laws. When a case *prima facie* may only be associated with the judge's forum, Greek law will be applied. In contrast, where the relevant elements are connected to more than one countries, the Greek judge will apply the rules stipulated in Articles 4–33 of the Civil Code, under the heading "Private International Law" and identify the applicable law, which may be the law of a foreign country.

In fact, Greek courts are quite receptive to the application of foreign law and, in accordance with CCP, Article 337, take it into account *ex officio* and without proof. This does not preclude an order for or offer of proof in aid of discovering foreign law's content. Further, it should be stressed that, according to Article 559 of the CCP, an error as to foreign law is treated the same way as one of domestic law for purposes of judicial review in cassation by the Supreme Court.

TRIAL

Commencing the action

A civil action (*agogi*) — regardless of its procedural — classification as an action for performance,[15] or for declaratory judgment[16] or for judicial modification of legal relationships[17] is commenced on the plaintiff's initiative:

(1) By filing the relevant legal document with the clerk of the competent court,[18] who fixes a date and time for the hearing of the case and registers it in the docket; and

(2) By serving on the defendant a copy of the action containing the place, date and time fixed for the hearing.[19] When service is accomplished, the action is considered commenced and the litigation pending.[20] Service must be made at least 30 days before the hearing.[21] If the defendant is domiciled abroad, service must be made at least 60 days before the hearing,[22] notwithstanding the provisions of the Brussels Convention.

15. *Katapsifistiki* — CCP, Article 69.
16. *Anagnoristiki* — CCP, Article 70.
17. *Diaplastiki* — CCP, Article 71.
18. Subject matter, territorial and functional competence; see above.
19. CCP, Article 215; see above.
20. CCP, Article 221.
21. In some proceedings, the judge may allow for a shorter period of time for the service to take place.
22. CCP, Article 228.

The introductory legal document of the action should mention:

(1) The court before which the case is brought and the elements in support of its competence;
(2) The full name and address of the litigants as well as of their proxies; in case of legal entities, their title and the place of their seat;
(3) A complete account of the events which substantiate, according to law, the action and explains its instigation by the plaintiff against the defendant;
(4) The subject matter of the action, in a clear, precise and succinct manner;
(5) A precise request for judicial relief, including the exact amount sought, if the claim is of a pecuniary nature; and
(6) The date and the signature of the plaintiff's advocate or of the plaintiff himself in cases where the presence of an advocate is not mandatory.[23]

EFFECTS OF THE ACTION

The commencement of the action has both procedural and substantive effects. On the procedural level:

(1) The plaintiff cannot extend or modify his action in the future, unless he withdraws the pending document of action and files a new one;[24] exceptionally, he can claim accessories of the main subject matter and/or a substitute instead of his original claim or seek a declaratory judgment instead of one for performance; and
(2) The pending litigation (*lis pendens*: *ekremodikia*) prevents any other court from being seized and hearing the same action.[25]

On the substantive level:

(1) The running of the period of limitation (*paragrafi*) is interrupted; and
(2) Interest accrues on all monetary claims on an action for performance.[26]

23. CCP, Articles 118, 216.
24. CCP, Articles 223 and 224.
25. CCP, Article 222.
26. CCP, Article 221; Civil Code, Articles 261, 346.

Further, the following procedural principles are relevant to the scope of an action's trial:

(1) The court may not award the plaintiff anything not requested nor go beyond the request submitted;
(2) The court has no authority to consider facts not submitted nor proven by a party;[27]
(3) All further procedural steps rely on the initiative of the parties while the court cannot, in principle, move by itself;[28] and
(4) The court is deemed to know the law, even the foreign one (*jura novit curia*). In case, however, the court is not familiar with the relevant provisions of the applicable foreign law, it can order the submission of evidence by the parties or collect official (for example, through the Institute of International and Foreign Law) or even unofficial information about it.[29]

The plaintiff is not allowed to modify the basis of his action. He may, however, complete, correct and clarify it until the first hearing of the case (in practice, through written pleadings).

The defendant, having lawfully been notified of the coming hearing, need not reply before that date to the plaintiff's action and will most probably wait until the first hearing of the case in order to develop in his pleadings his factual and legal stance.

Hearings and pleadings

The hearing of the action in open court begins with the reading of the names of the parties from the docket by the President of the Multi-Member Court or the judge of the Single-Member Court.

The advocates of the parties appear in court and present their oral pleadings, usually very briefly, making reference to their written ones. They are also allowed, for their convenience, wherever appearing physically is not mandatory, to file in advance a written statement of appearance in lieu of oral pleading, thus avoiding to appear during the hearing.[30]

During the hearing the clerk writes down the minutes which are signed by himself and the president or the judge of the Single-Member Court and constitute a full proof of their contents.[31]

27. CCP, Article 106.
28. CCP, Article 108.
29. CCP, Article 337.
30. CCP, Article 242.
31. CCP, Articles 258, 259.

The court may adjourn once during the hearing of the case if one of the parties requests it for a convincing reason.[32] The case may also be adjourned if the outcome of another trial, either civil or criminal, is a prerequisite for the outcome of the one under hearing.[33]

All means of attack and defence should be presented during the first hearing of the case, in each party's pleadings,[34] otherwise they are rejected *ex officio*, with the exception of those that arise at a later stage and those whose belated presentation is excusable.[35]

Reply

Each party must respond clearly and unambiguously, generally or specifically to the contentions, allegations and arguments of his opponent. If the truthfulness of an allegation has not been contested, it is within the discretion of the court, after evaluating all the arguments of the parties, to deduce whether there is an admission or a denial of the allegation.[36]

The pleadings (*protaseis*) of the parties should, at the risk of being declared inadmissible, be submitted at the latest to the bench on the hearing date of the case for proceedings taking place at the Multi-Member Court of First Instance, the Single-Member Court of First Instance (special proceedings) and the Court of the Peace.

At the Single-Member Court of First Instance (ordinary proceedings), the pleadings should be submitted three working days before the hearing date. In proceedings for the interim protection of assets, the judge appoints a day for the submission of the pleadings by the parties, which is usually the third day following the hearing date.

Types of answers

The defendant at first hearing of the case will submit his allegations regarding the admissibility of the complaint or his remarks on the merits. The omission of any of the required elements of the content of the complaint[37] renders the action inadmissible.

With respect to the merits of the action, the defendant may follow two lines of defence, either by denying the factual background of the complaint (*arnissi*) or by invoking additional facts that form the basis

32. CCP, Article 239.
33. CCP, Articles 249, 250.
34. CCP, Article 237.
35. CCP, Article 269.
36. CCP, Article 261.
37. See above.

of a right that either impedes the formation of the claim invoked by the plaintiff's right or its exercise, or abrogates it (affirmative defence — *enstasis*).

The borderline between denials and affirmative defences, although clearly drawn in theory, is not easily distinguishable in practice, since the former are most commonly followed by additional supporting facts, thus resembling the latter. The distinction, however, is crucial for the debate on the question of who bears the burden of proof of the respective allegations.

Amendments and supplemental pleadings

The parties have a last opportunity to reply to their opponents' allegations by submitting their supplemental pleadings by noon of the third day following the first hearing of the case. Again, proceedings before the Single-Member Court of First Instance (*ordinary procedure*) derogate from the rule, and supplemental pleadings should be submitted at the latest on the bench on the hearing date.

Joinder of claims and parties

The CCP provides for two kinds of joinder of claims by several plaintiffs or defendants in Articles 74 and 76. In Article 74, the code deals with the joinder of plaintiffs or defendants in cases where several persons share the right or duty in dispute or in cases where joint parties put forward or face claims based on similar causes of action (permissive joinder of claims, *apli omodikia*).

Article 76 deals with the joinder of plaintiffs or defendants in cases where several persons are required in order to bring or to defend a particular action or where no inconsistent judgments should be rendered as among them (compulsory joinder of plaintiffs or defendants, *anagastiki omodikia*).

The former kind of joinder serves the task of diminishing the expenses of several proceedings by the respective parties and creates a loose bond among them: each person in the joinder is acting independently of the others and his acts or omissions do not benefit or harm the rest of the group.[38]

In the compulsory joinder of Article 76, several persons form a group in order to pursue their common interest or to defend their common obligation through a single complaint, while in the permissive joinder, several complaints are contained in one action. The law differentiates the two by stipulating that the acts or omissions of each person in the

38. CCP, Article 75.

joinder have an impact on the others, thus requiring the presence of only one person or representative of the joinder in order for the trial to proceed.

Counterclaims

The defendant may oppose the plaintiff's complaint by filing a counter-complaint thus opening proceedings parallel to the main trial. A countercomplaint which could be described as an offensive means of defence is based on a denial or an affirmative defence and is accompanied by a claim against the plaintiff which requests the rejection of the complaint.

According to Article 268 of the Greek CCP, after the service of the complaint and before the date of the hearing of the case, the defendant may file a separate complaint at the secretariat of the court where the complaint was filed. The proper filing of the countercomplaint is dependant on its timely service eight days before the first hearing of the case. This is a separate complaint, although the law allows for the submission of a countercomplaint with the pleadings to the complaint provided they are serviced eight days before the first hearing to the other party.

Cross-claims

The Civil Code stipulates that reciprocal claims between two persons shall be extinguished by operation of set-off to the extent to which they cover each other.[39] Further, in regard to a contentious claim, set-off can be relied on if the counterclaim can be established forthwith at any stage of the proceedings or in the course of enforcement.[40] The relevant contentions may be submitted by the defendant in his pleadings at the pending proceedings or in the course of separate proceedings opened by a counter-complaint.

Third party claims

Very often third parties, although not litigants in pending proceedings, are individually affected by the case's outcome. In order for these parties to participate in the on-going proceedings or at least to have an opportunity to question the judgment rendered, the CCP permits their

39. Civil Code, Article 440.
40. Civil Code, Article 442.

intervention (*paremvasi*) on their own motion or on impleader (*prosepiklisi*) by the interested party and regulates the appeal of the rendered judgment. The intervention of the third party is regulated in Articles 79 to 85 of the CCP. Pursuant to the above, the intervention of a third party may take two forms:

(1) It will be exercised when the party who is external to the proceedings has a direct legal interest in one of the litigants' success; in this case the CCP refers to the additional intervention (*prostheti paremvasi*), which may take place at any stage of the proceedings until the issuance of judgment by the Supreme Court (*Areios Pagos*); or

(2) It will be the act of a person who claims for himself wholly or partially the subject matter of the dispute; in this case the CCP refers to the main intervention (*kyria paremvasi*), which may take place at any stage of the proceedings before the first instance or the Appeal Court (*efetio*).

The difference between the two forms of intervention may be explained as follows. If the trial in civil courts is a tripartite affair involving the plaintiff, the defendant and the judge then in the permissive form of intervention, the tripartite nature of the trial is not altered; the intervening party is subsidiary to either the plaintiff or the defendant. On the other hand, intervention under Article 80 enlarges the subjective limits of the trial, thus rendering it multi-party affair; the intervening person is is a new party, his interest being independant of that of the primary litigants.[41]

A third party may intervene on a litigant's impleader or on his own motion. Again a litigant's impleader may take the form of a forced impleader or that of an announcement (*anakinosi dikis*).

The term "forced impleader", in this text is used to describe the relevant written pleading of the litigant which, according to the CCP, has the minimum content of a complaint (action), is filed at the court's secretariat and notified to the person who is to intervene. The law provides for three instances where the forced impleader may be employed:

(1) Where the notifying person is a party to a compulsory joinder;[42]

(2) Where the defendant in the main proceedings is in possession of the chattel or the immovable asset that is the subject matter of the dispute or where he holds the relevant right in the name of someone else;[43] and

41. See Beis, *Civil Procedure*, Sakoulas ed., Athens 1985.
42. CCP, Article 86.
43. CCP, Article 87.

(3) Where the notified party is under the liability for any debt, money, goods or chattels in respect of which he is or expects to be sued by any of the parties to the main proceedings. The notified person in this case is free to intervene in the main proceedings, nevertheless in the case of defeat he will be bound by the rendered judgment, which may be enforced against him as well.

In contrast, the announcement of the pending proceedings to a third person, although similar in nature to the forced impleader, does not have the same consequences, namely, it does not create the obligation for the court to issue a separate decision (whereas the court has such an obligation in the case of a forced impleader), and the notifying person will not be directly bound by the rendered judgment but only to the degree that he shall not be able to file an appeal as a third person individually and directly concerned by it.

Appeal by a third person

The CCP regulates in Articles 586 *et seq.* the submission of an appeal by a third person (*tritanakopi*) that is personally affected by a judgment rendered by the Court of First Instance and that did not have the opportunity to participate in the proceedings for its revision.

This special appeal is filed at the court that rendered the decision or at the higher court where proceedings for its appeal are pending.

Evidence

Nature and purpose of evidence

Each party must prove the facts that invokes and that are necessary for the support of his claim or counterclaim and for the rejection of those of his opponent. The controversial facts constitute the matters of evidence (*apodeixi*) that the court must establish.

In ordinary proceedings, such as the ones for an action, the court must attain, through evidence-taking, full conviction only in cases specifically provided in the law. The burden of proof is considered objective, and the court may be satisfied only with probability.[44]

The Multi-Member Court orders evidence by issuing an interlocutory judgment in which, on a fully reasoned opinion, establishes the controversial facts, allocates the burden of proof between the parties and

44. CCP, Article 340.

specifies the accepted means of proof. It also fixes the place and time of evidence-taking and the period available for its completion, in view of the fact that it usually lasts (especially testimonies) for several sessions before the judge rapporteur (designated among the members of the panel, or an out-of-town judge if necessary or a Greek Consul, if the witness is domiciled abroad), escalated in a few months' time.[45]

Before the Single-Member Courts, parties must produce all their means of proof at the first hearing and, in principle, no interlocutory judgment for proof is rendered by the judge.[46]

Only the facts relevant to the outcome of the trial and contested by one party are the subject matter of proof.[47] Facts that are so widely and commonly known that there can be no reasonable doubt of their truth (such as historical events or geographical information) as well as proven facts known to the court from other cases may not be the subject matter of proof. The same applies to teachings of common experience.[48]

Kinds of evidence

Pursuant to CCP, Article 339, there are eight means of proof: confession,[49] autopsy,[50] expert's report,[51] documents,[52] examination of parties,[53] witness testimony,[54] party oath[55] and juridical presumptions.[56]

In practice, witnesses and documents are the most widely used means of proof invoked before Greek courts. Written proof is preferable and in many cases necessary; testimony is admitted as an affirmative defence, though a rather broad one, if the possession of documentary evidence is morally (e.g., in transactions between spouses) or practically impossible, or if the originally existing document is proven to be lost or destroyed; or in most commercial transactions or in all transactions where the value does not exceed the sum of 500,000 Drs.[57]

45. CCP, Article 341.
46. CCP, Article 270.
47. CCP, Article 335.
48. CCP, Article 336.
49. *Omologia* — CCP, Articles 352–354.
50. CCP, Articles 355–267.
51. *Pragmatognomosini* — CCP, Articles 368–392.
52. *Engrafa* — CCP, Articles 432–465.
53. *Exetasi ton diadikon* — CCP, Articles 415–420.
54. *Martyres* — CCP, Articles 393–414.
55. *Orkos* — CCP, Articles 421–431.
56. *Dikastika tekmiria* — CCP, Article 395.
57. CCP, Articles 393, 394.

Documentary evidence

The law distinguishes between documents drawn by public servants and other specially authorised officials (including notaries public) during the exercise of their competencies (*dimosia engrafa*), and instruments drawn privately (*idiotika engrafa*).

Documents of the first category constitute conclusive proof and may be contested only for falsification (*plastografia*). Instruments drawn by foreign public authorities have the same proof value. Documents drawn in a foreign language must be accompanied by an official translation into Greek.

Privately drawn instruments have a lesser probative effect, since the facts mentioned therein are considered as established by the party producing the instrument. A challenge for falsification is always possible.

Professional books and records kept by merchants, advocates, notaries, physicians and chemists as well as photographs, films, recordings and any mechanical reproduction in general are considered, for the purposes of civil procedure, as privately drawn documents. It should be mentioned that mechanical recordings such as photographs and tapes can only be produced and invoked if taken with the consent of the person against whom they are going to be used, unless the recorded event took place in public.

Copies and photocopies of documents, provided they are authenticated by duly authorised persons, may be used, with certain exceptions, as evidence.

Obtaining information prior to trial (sintiritiki apodixi)

Subject to CCP, Article 348, the court on the application of either party may order the taking of evidence prior to the commencement of the trial, under the following circumstances:

(1) In cases of imminent danger, where loss or destruction of a means of proof is involved, for example, in cases where the witness testimony is deemed to be necessary for the outcome of the litigation, the court may order the examination of the witness prior to trial if the attendance of the witness at the hearing is impossible for some compelling reason (for example, absence or illness);

(2) When it is deemed necessary that an object should be examined in its present state. Thus, in an action arising out of a breach of a sales contract due to the deterioration of goods, the court, in order to assess the damages, may order the examination of the deteriorated goods prior to trial, since the goods in question should be examined in their present state; and

(3) When the parties agree to call evidence before trial.

The aforementioned exceptional procedure of taking evidence facilitates the collection of evidence especially in cases where the controversial facts would otherwise be difficult to establish.

The application for provisionary evidence should first be submitted to the court which is competent to deal with the dispute in question. However, when the "danger" is obvious the application could be brought before any court which is deemed appropriate to decide on it immediately. The application should clearly stipulate the facts to be proved, the means of proof to be used, and the reason justifying the taking of evidence prior to trial.

As a rule, it is left to the discretion of the court to decide on the application and order provisionary evidence. This may only be done if the requirements set forth by the law[58] are satisfied. Thus, the taking of evidence prior to trial is ordered by a formal decision of the court, containing the subject matter of evidence, the allowed means of proof and the place and time of evidence-taking. If hearsay evidence is to be called pursuant to the aforementioned procedure, it should be confined solely to those facts specifically mentioned by the party in his application.

Evidence so taken before trial will be used at the hearing of the case and evaluated by the court in any way it deems proper.

INTERIM PROTECTION OF ASSETS PENDING TRIAL

Generally speaking, the remedy sought by the plaintiff in an action brought before a civil court is a final judgment against the defendant ordering the compensation or the relief claimed by the plaintiff. Greek law does, however, provide a range of provisional remedies (*asfalistika metra*) which have been come to enjoy increasing practical importance in Greece. In terms of practical significance, provisional remedies protect the plaintiff's substantive right against the defendant until the case is decided on its merits.

Cases where interim measures applicable

Under Article 682 of the CCP, the court may, on application of either party, grant provisional relief for each and every claim under the condition of an urgent need or in order to evade an imminent danger. Provisional remedies are generally available, provided that two requirements are met:

(1) The case must be urgent; and
(2) An underlying substantive right for seeking provisional protection is present.

58. CCP, Articles 348 and 349.

As a rule, provisional relief may be granted for all kinds of substantive rights, property matters, contract or tort cases. Thus, in an action for damages, the court may order the provisional attachment of the debtor's property in order to secure the future enforcement of an eventually affirmative judgment. Similarly, in cases of unfair competition the affected party may obtain an order against his competitor to block the distribution in the market of the product in question.

Whether a provisional relief should be granted is a matter of discretion of the court. As to that, the governing principle is that the court should first establish that the aforementioned two requirements set out by the law are met. Both requirements need only be shown as probable.

Jurisdiction

The court, in the exercise of its civil jurisdiction, may order provisional remedies either before the principal action is brought or during the pendency of any action before it.

Generally, provisional remedies are administered by the Single-Member Court of First Instance. However, should, according to the rules of subject matter jurisdiction, the principal action be brought before the Court of the Peace, the provisional remedies are ordered by that court. In exceptional cases, where the principal action is pending before the Multi-Member Court of First Instance, the provisional remedies are administered by that court.

Proceedings

The action claiming provisional relief should be commenced by an application filed to the secretariat of the competent court, and follows the ordinary course to judgment. Before the Court of the Peace, the application could also be filed orally before the secretary of the court. Finally, in cases where provisional relief is sought during the pendency of the trial, the application could be filed before the court together with any pleadings.

The application should contain an unambiguous specification of the provisional relief requested, the existence of the underlying substantive right requiring provisional protection and the existence of an imminent danger or an urgent case giving rise to the commencement of the aforementionded proceedings. Failure to allege sufficient facts to support the claim will lead to the dismissal of the application.

The defendant will then, on plaintiff's initiative, be served at his home or place of business with a copy of the application containing also the date and time fixed for the hearing. Service must be made a certain number of days before the first hearing as the judge may order. In very urgent cases, provisional remedies may even be granted on an application *ex parte*.[59]

Much of the value of the provisional remedies, and the whole of their interest from the point of view of procedure, lies in their use to protect the plaintiff's substantive rights against the defendant until the case has been finally decided by the judgment in the action. Thus, Article 691(2) of the CCP empowers the judge to issue immediately a provisional order on the filing of the application which should remain in force until the decision of the court on the provisional relief is rendered.

The taking of evidence should always take place at the first hearing on the motion for provisional relief. In addition, the court may, on its own initiative, collect all the evidence required to establish its decision. The factual allegations of the parties need only be *prima facie* assumed as substantiated. The decision of the court is usually rendered within a couple of weeks after hearing. As will be analysed below, the decision has a provisional effect and does not affect the court's final judgment on the principal action.

The decision rendered specifies the provisional remedies to be enforced as well as the substantive right seeking provisional protection. Whether the court should grant the kind of provisional relief requested by the plaintiff is a matter at its discretion, the governing principle being that the court has the discretionary power to order the kind of provisional relief that it thinks would be an adequate remedy for the plaintiff. In any case, the relief granted should not be excessively burdensome for the defendant.

It should be stressed that the scope of provisional remedies is solely confined to the provisional protection of the plaintiff's right and not to the satisfaction of it.

Subject to the provision of Article 693 of the CCP, the granting of provisional remedies may be combined with an order specifying a time limit, not less than thirty days, within which the plaintiff should bring the principal action before the competent court. In case of non-compliance, the provisional remedy expires as of right.

Normally, the decisions ordering provisional remedies or dismissing the application for them are not appealable. However, on application of the party who has not been duly summoned to the hearing, the court may revoke or modify the decision rendered.

Moreover, the court before which the main litigation is pending always has the power to modify or revoke the provisional remedies that have been ordered. Revocation becomes mandatory whenever the judgment on the principal action ripens into *res judicata*.[60]

---

59. CCP, Article 687(1).
60. CCP, Article 698(1).

If the plaintiff's principal action fails, he is obliged by law to pay reasonable compensation to the defendant for the expenses or damages incurred through the execution of the decision which ordered provisional remedies, provided that the plaintiff knew that his claim was groundless.

The decision ordering provisional remedies is enforced in accordance with the enforcement proceedings set out below. In Greece, provisional relief has been enjoying increasingly practical importance. The rather slow progression of ordinary proceedings adds to the attraction of provisional remedies and makes recourse to them highly desirable.

Kinds of provisional remedies

Provisional protection is now provided for with respect to the following kinds of provisional remedies:

(1) Guaranty (*egyodosia*);
(2) Registration of a mortgage foreclosure (*prossimiossi hypothikis*);
(3) Provisional attachment (*sintiritiki kataschessi*);
(4) Sequestration (*dikastiki messegiisi*);
(5) Provisional enforcement of a claim (*prosorini epidikasi apaitiseon*);
(6) Provisional preservation of the situation (*prosorini rythmissi katastasis*); and
(7) Sealing, unsealing and inventory.

Guaranty

Subject to CCP, Article 704, the court may, in order to secure a money claim or any other substantive right, order the defendant to pay the plaintiff a sum of money in satisfaction of a guaranty. Thus, the victim of a traffic accident may obtain an order against the tortfeasor for part of the damages suffered in an accident.

Registration of a mortgage foreclosure

Without prejudice to the provisions of the Civil Code, the court may order the registration of a mortgage foreclosure in order to secure a real property claim. The decision should specify the amount of the mortgage debts.

Provisional attachment

Any claim for the payment of a debt may be secured by an order for provisional attachment. On application, the court may order the provisional attachment of any movable or immovable property or any other property rights of the debtor, either being in his possession or in the possession of a third party. The court's decision ordering the provisional attachment of any movable or immovable assets should specify the amount due from the debtor.

As a rule, provisional attachment and garnishment are enforced in accordance with the rules applicable to enforcement proceedings subject to a few deviations. The proceedings start with the notification of a copy of the enforceable order of attachment to the debtor. An exception to this rule is provided for by Article 711 of the CCP, which does not require a notification of the order with respect to the provisional attachment of chattels.

In case of an affirmative final judgment, the provisional attachment or garnishment leads to a public auction of the destrained property and, in the meantime, suspends the debtor's or third party's power of disposal.

Sequestration

Real property litigation may support a grant of relief consisting in the sequestration of any movable or immovable property of the defendant. Thus, the court, on the application of the plaintiff, may order the sequestration of the land or the disputed movable property of the defendant.

The decision should specify the property to be sequestrated and direct a receiver to be appointed. The court may appoint as a receiver the plaintiff, the debtor or a third party. Finally, the court has the discretionary power to replace the receiver on application of either party.

Provisional enforcement of a claim

The court may order the provisional enforcement of a claim provided that the plaintiff brings the principal action before the competent court within 30 days from the date that the decision is rendered.

Claims eligible for provisional enforcement include claims for damages or compensation, claims for remuneration, and maintenance claims. Thus, the victim of a car accident may obtain an order against the tortfeasor for part of the damages. However, the amount of money which the defendant is ordered to pay should not exceed half of the amount claimed by the plaintiff.

Provisional preservation of the situation

Real property litigation between neighbours may equally support a grant of relief consisting in the provisional preservation of the current situation. Provisional preservation of the situation may also be ordered by the court in disputes concerning the relationships between parents and children.

Sealing, unsealing, inventory

The court may, on application of either party, order the sealing, the unsealing or the placing in inventory of the disputed property.

SPECIAL PROCEEDINGS

The CCP sets out the functions of special proceedings (*eidikes diadikasies*), along with those of ordinary civil proceedings. The latter are distinguished from the former essentially through a simpler and speedier procedure, accompanied by wider powers of the court.

Much of the value of the special proceedings and the whole of their interest from the point of view of procedure lies in the fact that the slow progression and the exaggerated formalities of ordinary civil procedure are considerably reduced. Accordingly, the Parliament expanded the scope of their application by increasingly assigning to them additional kinds of disputes.

Groups of special proceedings

Special proceedings are now provided for with respect to those kinds of disputes which are more frequently encountered in everyday life: matrimonial cases (divorce or annulment of marriage); relationships between parents and children; orders to pay debts on the basis of documentary evidence; disputes concerning negotiable instruments; disputes between landlords and tenants; labour cases; disputes related to the performance of independent services; car accidents; maintenance and custody cases and disputes related to the infringement of rights through the mass media.

Most of the rules applicable to special proceedings introduce common procedural features connecting all the aforementioned groups.

Thus, with regard to matrimonial cases and parent-child disputes, the most important deviation from the general principles of the civil procedure is provided for by Article 599 of the CCP, which stipulates that the parties may formulate their pleadings and produce all their means of proof until the last hearing of the case.

Further, Articles 611–613 of the CCP assign wider powers to the court which include a wider demarcation of international jurisdiction and a broader *res judicata* effect operating as against the world and not only as against the parties of the action. They also remove availability of the party oath and demote the statutory confession to the position of a non-conclusive means of proof. Finally, Article 607 of the CCP provides for the public prosecutor's potential participation in the trial as a party.

With regard to the other types of special proceedings, it should be stressed that labour cases should be regarded as their prototype. They share the following common procedural features:

(1) The parties may assume their defence themselves since the law does not require them to be represented by advocates; and
(2) Standing to sue is granted not only to the interested parties but also to professional chambers and trade unions.

As far as evidence is concerned, CCP, Article 671 grants an exception to the general rule by providing that the court may take into account "means of proof not complying with the terms of law". Thus, even unsigned private documents or depositions of biased witnesses may also be considered.

Further, the parties may formulate their pleadings and produce all their means of proof until the last hearing of the case. Defaulting parties should be regarded as fictionally or tacitly present, and the court is compelled to examine the merits of the case as if the parties were present.

In disputes between landlords and tenants, apart from the aforementioned rules which are applicable here as well, two more procedural peculiarities should be mentioned:

(1) Service of the application should be made to the defendant not more than 15 days and not less than eight days before the first hearing; and
(2) The time for reopening of defaults is eight days and the time for appeal, reopening of contested judgments and cassation is 15 days.

The beginning of the aforementioned exceptional terms is calculated in accordance with the generally applicable principles.[61]

Along with the legal peculiarity of special proceedings, particular rules apply to the collection of claims not exceeding the amount of 150,000 Drs.

---

61. See below.

Here, although the procedure deviates from the standard, this group of claims is not listed under the heading of special proceedings since a minor degree of deviation occurs.

Non-contentious proceedings

Along with the adjudication of disputes (*iurisdictio contentiosa*), the Greek civil courts are also statutorily assigned with the regulation of the so-called "affairs of voluntary jurisdiction" (*iurisdictio voluntaria*). The distinction between contentious and non-contentious matters (*ekoussia dikaiodosia*) is based in the nature of the subject matter of jurisdiction. Accordingly, non-contentious matters do not refer to relationships and violation of rights between persons, but to the individual's legal situation.

Practically, there are no actual parties, but only the person introducing the request. Functionally, therefore, *iurisdictio voluntaria* resembles more public administration than proper civil justice. According to the CCP, voluntary jurisdiction involves matters such as:

(1) Granting, retracting, annulling, revoking or amending a certificate of inheritance;
(2) "Publication" of a will; pronouncing the interdiction and guardianship or judicial supervision of persons;
(3) Adoption;
(4) Authorising the alienation of a thing pledged;
(5) Declaring a lost negotiable instrument as void; or
(6) Declaring a person whose death is strongly probable as an absentee, or revoking such a declaration.

With respect to non-contentious proceedings, the following procedural characteristics emerge: As a rule, the subject matter competence belongs to the Single-Member Court of First Instance; although in exceptional cases such as bankruptcy, adoption, interdiction and guardianship or judicial supervision of persons, the competent court is the Multi-Member Court of First Instance. Further, in non-contentious proceedings, a copy of the request is served to the public prosecutor or to such third parties as the judge may order.

In contrast with the ordinary civil proceedings, the person introducing the request in voluntary jurisdiction matters (*applicant*) may submit any factual allegations and plead additional facts until the last hearing of the case. Default by the applicant requires the court to cancell the hearing of the case, even if the third party which has been duly summoned is present. On the other hand, default by a third party requires the court to examine the merits of the case.

Final judgments are subject to revocation or modification on presentation of new facts. Appeal, reopening by interested parties and cassation are also available here, but it is important to note that the suspensive effect of the regular appeal does not accompany this method of attack *de lege*. The right to appeal the judgment is also given to persons who, although having participated in the proceedings, are not aggrieved by the court's decision. In non-contentious proceedings, the court exercises quasi-inquisitional powers in order to establish the relevant facts of the case.

JUDGMENT AND KINDS OF RELIEF

Drafting and contents of judgments

The judgment is drawn up by the trial judge within one or two months after the conclusion of the hearing. In Multi-Member Court of First Instance and Court of Appeal proceedings, the president or the presiding judge of the judicial panel appoints one of its members to be the rapporteur of the opinion. After the rapporteur has developed his opinion on the merits of the case orally in closed deliberations among the members of the panel, the judges vote in the reverse order of seniority. After judgement has been given and drawn up, the clerk of the court enters the index number and the date in which the judgment is rendered in the books kept for this purpose.

As far as the form of the judicial decision is concerned, there is a prescribed form required to be followed in the drawing up of the judgment. Thus, the text of the judgment opens by mentioning the composition of the judicial panel and the name of the judge who drafted the opinion. It indicates the parties and the statement of the claim and then states the fully reasoned opinion of the panel on the merits of the case. The operative part of the decision comes at the end.

Finally, the judgment contains directions as to costs of the proceedings, if they are claimed by the plaintiff. Without prejudice to the relevant provisions of the CCP, the general rule, as in most continental systems, is that the costs of the successful party should be borne by the unsuccessful one; nevertheless, the court has the discretion to excuse part or the whole of costs if it deems that the unsuccessful party had reasonable doubts as to the outcome of the trial.

Kinds of relief

The judgment may only give the plaintiff what he is seeking in a fairly specific way. Two points about the operative part of judgments require special mention. Firstly, where the judgment is for a sum of money, damages must be assessed or accounts or inquiries made before it is known precisely what is due from one party to the other. Secondly, if the judgment requires the defendant to do or avoid doing an act, it should specify the act and usually the time within which the act is to be done or avoided. Additionally, the judgment usually imposes a fine to the defendant in case of non-compliance with the order of the judicial decision.

Kinds of judgments

Greek civil procedure distinguishes between final (*oristiki*), non-appealable (*telesidiki*) and irrevocable (*ametakliti*) judgments; this distinction is closely connected with the function and distinctions of the methods of appeal. The functional consequences of such distinction lie with the effect of *res judicata* and the enforceability of judgments.[62]

A civil judgment is not automatically binding and enforceable. Where the law refers to final judgments, it means the decisions rendered either by the Court of the Peace or the Courts of First Instance after the hearing of cases subject to the ordinary methods of appeal, i.e., reopening of default and regular appeal.

As a rule, a final judgment is not automatically enforceable and genuinely binding on the parties unless the court orders the provisional enforcement of the judgment as long as one or the other ordinary method of appeal remains pending. Provisional enforcement of the judgment is pronounced by the court in certain groups of cases statutorily provided for by the law. *Res judicata* does not accrue to a final judgment unless it becomes non-appealable.

A non-appealable judgment is one which is no longer subject to ordinary means of attack, because the ordinary means of appeal have been exhausted either through denial or failure to apply for appeal within the time limitation provided by the law. Accordingly, such a judgment is automatically enforceable against the parties.

A non-appealable judgment becomes irrevocable when it is no longer subject to cassation (*aneressi*), that is, the extraordinary means of attack before the Supreme Court.

Conclusiveness of judgment res judicata

Res judicata (*dedikassmeno*) accrues only to non-appealable and irrevocable judgments. The general doctrine followed by the CCP is that *res judicata* effect is limited to the claim and issues determined in the first suit and the parties involved at the trial.

More concretely, the *res judicata* effect between the same parties produces a preclusion with respect to both the claim involved and the

62. See below.

procedural questions determined in the first suit. Claim preclusion requires a judgment on the merits and is restricted to the same cause of action, both in factual and legal terms. Therefore, if the plaintiff, after having lost the first suit, brings an action against the defendant with a new complaint based on different factual or legal allegations, no plea of *res judicata* effect can be entertained.

The *res judicata* effect also produces a preclusion with regard to the issues determined during the proceedings, insofar as they fall within the subject matter competence of the court, and their determination was necessary for the outcome of the litigation.

With respect to the parties' preclusion, *res judicata* effect is extended only to the parties of the action and their heirs or other successors. However, substantive relationships justify a broader conclusive effect of judgment which is depicted in the following rules. Accordingly, in real property litigation the *res judicata* effect is extended to non-parties holding the thing in dispute in their possession or custody.[63] Judgment for or against a legal person (e.g., a company) is also binding on its members (e.g., shareholder).[64]

Further, a judgment on the settlement of the dispute between the creditor and the principal debtor regarding the existence of the debt is conclusive also for the guarantor.[65] Finally, judgments in matters of succession, where the administrator of a vacant succession, the liquidator of an estate, or the executor of a will is a party, become *res judicata* also with respect to the heirs.[66]

As far as the time limits of *res judicata* are concerned, Greek rules adhere to the principle that even if reality turns out to be different from predictions, *res judicata* remains undistributed. However, Article 334 of the CCP grants an exemption to the aforementioned rule and allows the court, in cases of periodic performances, to modify the previous conclusive judgment for the future with respect to the price index.

POST-TRIAL MOTIONS

Functions of appeal

The law does not leave the exercise of the rights to appeal to the sole discretion of the judge. All methods of appeal are specifically provided by the CCP and constitute the only ways of reviewing a judgment.

---

63. CCP, Article 325(3).
64. CCP, Article 329.
65. CCP, Article 328.
66. CCP, Articles 326–327.

Greek civil procedure distinguishes between ordinary and extraordinary methods of appeal. The ordinary methods of attack (reopening of default and appeal) lead to a review of the judgment on both the facts and the law of the case in question, while the extraordinary methods of attack (reopening of contested judgments and cassation) lead to a review of the judgment on the law only.

This distinction is closely connected with the effect of *res judicata* and the enforceability of judgments. The *res judicata* effect and the enforceability of judgments come into play only after the ordinary methods of appeal have been exhausted. By contrast, the extra-ordinary methods of appeal do not suspend the *res judicata* effect nor the enforcement of a judgment.

Reopening of default

Article 501 of the CCP provides that if a party has not been duly summoned to attend the hearing of the case, he may demand the reopening of the decision. A reopening of default (*anakopi erimodikias*) decision is initiated by filing an application with the clerk of the court which rendered the default judgment within 15 days from the date of service of the default judgment, if the defaulting party is domiciled in Greece. If he is domiciled abroad or if his domicile is unknown, the application should be filed within 60 days from the date that the summary of the default judgment is published in two daily newspapers, one in the Athens area and the other in the district of the court which rendered the attacked judgment.[67]

The reopening of default decision is premised on the right of the defaulting party to be heard in court and does not produce a suspensive effect. However, a request for reopening of a default decision results in a stay of the execution of the default judgment until the decision of the court is rendered.[68]

Appeal

As a rule, an appeal (*ephesi*) may be taken from final judgments rendered by the Courts of First Instance (e.g., Court of the Peace, Single-Member Court of First Instance, Multi-Member Court of First Instance) and leads to the review of the judgment on the law and on the facts.[69] A request for

67. CCP, Article 503.
68. CCP, Article 504.
69. CCP, Articles 511–513.

appeal suspends the *res judicata* effect and results in a stay of the execution of the challenged judgment until the decision of the appellate court is issued.[70]

The Greek Code of Civil Procedure does not enumerate the grounds for appeal, as it does for cassation and reopening of contested judgments, however, the grounds for appeal may refer to questions of fact, to questions of substantive or procedural law, to the evaluation of the submitted evidence or to the procedural faults of the court.

Articles 516–518 of the CCP provide that anyone who was a party to the action as well as his successors and assignees may appeal the judgment rendered by the court within 30 days from the date of service of the judgment attacked if the appellant is domiciled in Greece, or within 60 days if he is domiciled abroad or if his domicile is unknown. If the judgment is not served, appeal should be filed within three years from the issuance of the judgment.[71] The application for an appeal should be filed with the Clerk of the court which issued the challenged decision and should specify the grounds for the appeal.

According to the provisions of the CCP, the appellate court has potentially the same powers as the trial court which issued the challenged decision. Consequently, if the appeal is granted, the appellate court retains the case and re-examines its merits. If, on the other hand, the court which rendered the challenged decision has not examined the merits of the case, the appellate court may, at its descretion, either decide the case on its merits or remit it to the trial court.[72]

However, the appellate court cannot decide issues beyond those which the appellant has appealed. Similarly, the appellate court cannot admit, except on special grounds, new claims and further evidence which have not been submitted during the proceedings before the first instance court which issued the challenged decision.[73]

Yet, a cross-appeal is allowed to the appellee but it should be confined to the challenged parts of the judgment or to those necessarily related to them.[74]

Reopening of contested judgment

A reopening of contested judgments (*anapsilaphisi*) may be taken from judgments rendered by the first instance courts, the Court of Appeal and

70. CCP, Article 521.
71. CCP, Article 518(2).
72. CCP, Article 535.
73. CCP, Article 525.
74. CCP, Article 523.

the Supreme Court, regardless of the availability of a cassation to the Supreme Court.[75] The grounds for the reopening of contested judgments are strictly enumerated by the law[76] and are limited to purely procedural deficiencies. Contested judgments may be reopened by reason of:

(1) The party's request in cases of the existence of inconsistent judgments;
(2) An improper method of service of process;
(3) A party's improper representation; or
(4) The absence of a power of attorney.

A request for the reopening of a contested judgment may also be filed in cases in which documentary evidence has been discovered after trial or the challenged judgment has been based on a judicial decision which has been irrevocably vacated.

A request for the reopening of contested judgments does not suspend the *res judicata* effect of the challenged judgment; there is no stay of its execution either.

Cassation

The main extraordinary means of contesting a judgment is cassation (*anairesi*). It consists of a request to the Supreme Court of Civil and Criminal Judicature (*Areios Pagos*) for the review of a judgment on the law only. Although precedent is not formally binding in Greek law, the impact of the jurisprudence of the Supreme Court is, obviously, considerable. A request for cassation may attack a judgment of a Court of the Peace, a Single-Member or Multi-Member Court of First Instance or, more frequently, a Court of Appeal,[77] provided that such judgment is not susceptible to either reopening of default or regular appeal.[78]

A request for cassation does not suspend the *res judicata* effect of the challenged judgment and there is no stay of its execution. Nevertheless, the Supreme Court may, on request of one of the parties, suspend its execution until the issuance of its own judgment if the execution may result in damage which would be difficult to repair.[79]

The grounds for review in cassation are strictly enumerated by law[80] and are limited avoiding the violation of either a provision of

75. CCP, Article 538.
76. CCP, Article 544.
77. CCP, Article 552.
78. CCP, Article 553(1).
79. CCP, Article 565(2).
80. CCP, Articles 559 and 560.

substantive law (including a foreign or international one), such a provision's improper interpretation, or violation of certain specified procedural rules pertaining mainly to the rules on evidence and its evaluation.

The evaluation by the lower court of facts and, in particular, of the contents of documents cannot be reviewed by the Supreme Court.[81] However, the demarcation between questions of law and fact is not always self-evident and subtle problems of interpretation emerge sometimes.

An application for cassation should be filed with the clerk of the court which issued the challenged judgment within 30 days from its service if the requesting party is domiciled in Greece or within 90 days if he is domiciled abroad or if his domicile is unknown. If the judgment is not served, cassation should be filed within three years from the issuance of the judgment.[82]

If cassation is admitted, the challenged judgment is quashed and the parties are returned to their previous positions.[83]

ENFORCEMENT PROCEEDINGS

Enforcement proceedings are of particular significance for the claimant who entrusts the satisfaction of his rights to the legal system. Enforcement proceedings are also of a highly technical nature and are linked to a desire for speed and efficiency.

Kinds of enforcement proceedings

The CCP, for systematic purposes, divides enforcement proceedings into two main parts:

(1) One containing rules common to all enforcement proceedings; and
(2) One containing rules applicable to each of several specific enforcement proceedings.

The former part comprises an exhaustive list of the instruments that, according to law, are enforceable by execution (*ektelesti titli*) and that constitute the foundation of enforcement proceedings. These are the non-appealable judgments of Greek courts that have been declared provisionally enforceable as well as acts of the court and orders for payment

81. CCP, Article 561(1).
82. CCP, Article 564.
83. CCP, Article 579.

issued by a judge, arbitral awards, notarial documents, foreign instruments of execution that have been declared enforceable under Greek law[84] and finally orders and acts that are deemed enforceable by law,[85] for example, notices for payment that the Social Security Foundation issues.

Process of enforcement

Enforcement proceedings begin with a formal notice of the creditor to the debtor to satisfy his claim. This notice (*epitagi*) is placed at the bottom of a certified copy of the enforceable instrument (writ of execution *ektelesto apografo*). A three-day time period is granted to the debtor after his notification in order to voluntarily perform his obligation. After the expiry of this period and within one calendar year from the notification to the debtor, the creditor may attempt the satisfaction of his claim through the enforcement of the writ of execution. The execution is performed by an authorised server who may seek the assistance of the competent authority for peace-keeping where he deems this necessary.

Any disputes arising as to the validity of the writ of execution, the enforceability of the claim or the observance of the rules of the execution proceedings are resolved by the Single-Member Court of First Instance of the place where the enforcement takes place and on the debtor's appropriate motion.

The CCP's provisions on specific enforcement proceedings regulate the enforcement of several claims providing the means for their execution in respect of each claim's nature. A distinction may be drawn between the direct specific performance and enforcement to satisfy a money claim.

Direct specific performance is provided in relation to claims for the duty to transfer the ownership of any movable or immovable asset, the transfer of securities, ships or airplanes, and finally for the duty of a person to perform, not to perform or not to oppose an act.

Enforcement to satisfy a money claim is based either on the attachment and auction of movable or immovable assets of the debtor or on two other means of execution of a money claim: the debtor's imprisonment (in certain cases narrowly prescribed by law) for a period of up to one year and the compulsory administration of the debtor's immovables or business by a court-appointed administrator.

The CCP does not regulate issues relating to bankruptcy or liquidation. These fall within the ambit of bunkruptcy law, which is included in the Code of Commercial Law.

84. For the enforcement of foreign judgments in Greece, see below.
85. CCP, Article 904.

Enforcement of foreign judgments in Greece

General

Greece is a party to several judgment enforcement treaties, most notably the multi-lateral Brussels Convention on Jurisdiction and Enforcement of Judgments in Civil or Commercial Matters and to the Protocol on its interpretation by the European Court of Justice and bilateral conventions with Austria and Yugoslavia. Where there is no specific treaty provision, enforcement of foreign judgments in Greece is governed by the Greek Code of Civil Procedure.[86]

Two provisions of the CCP are particularly important: Article 323 (finality of foreign judgments) and Article 905 (enforcement of foreign deeds).

Substantive legal issues

According to Article 905 of the CCP, a foreign judgment can be pronounced enforceable in Greece by the first instance court of the area of the debtor's residence barring any applicable convention on the subject. The CCP is guided by the principles of universality of justice and of international cooperation in that it provides for no review of the merits of the dispute and does not require reciprocity. Instead, it sets forth a test of enforceability based on five criteria:

(1) The foreign judgment must be final and enforceable according to the law of the state of its origin at the time when enforcement is sought in Greece. All procedural matters, such as adequacy of service, are reviewed according to that same law;

(2) The dispute must fall under the jurisdiction of the foreign court according to Greek law. Articles 22–44 of the CCP stipulate that jurisdiction can be based on the residence of the party against whom the suit is brought, on the place where a legal person (e.g., corporation) has its registered office, on the location of real property (for disputes concerning it), on the residence of the deceased (for inheritance disputes), on the fact that a contract was made in a certain place, on the existence of property of the party against whom the suit is brought (in the jurisdictional area), and on a special agreement between the parties (there are other grounds of minor importance);

(3) The party against whom the judgment was entered must not have been denied the right to defend itself and to take part in

---

86. Greece is also signatory to the New York Convention on Recognition and Enforcement of Foreign Arbitral Awards of 10 June 1958.

the proceedings in general, unless nationals of that State are also treated in this way;

(4) There must be no conflict with a similar final decision of a Greek court ("similar" means between the same parties and on the same subject as the foreign judgment); and

(5) The foreign judgment must not be contrary to the public order and the public policy of the Greek state or the good morals of the Greek community. This means that the enforcement of a foreign judgment is denied when it is presumed that it will run contrary to the basic principles guiding life in Greek society.

The public policy criterion is inherently vague. It is difficult to provide safe standards for its application, since it was conceived to be "concretised" on a case-by-case basis. This criterion is mainly used to deny enforcement to decisions on personal status, such as marriage, divorce or affiliation, rather than those on pecuniary claims. In practice, however, public policy concerns are extended to judgments issued in every kind of litigation, including antitrust, securities and tax cases.

Lack of adequate substantiation of the foreign judgment does not violate *per se* the public policy criterion. Where the foreign judgment is stated in a currency other than Greek currency, in principle, the applicable rate of currency on enforcement is the one of the date of payment by the debtor. Payments may only be enforced in Greek currency.

Procedure

Under Article 905 of the CCP, a judgment enforcement action must be in non-contentious proceedings. Notice to the debtor is not compulsory, but it is recommended. The debtor may then become a party in the dispute and contest the enforcement of the judgment. A decision pronouncing the judgment enforceable is appealable. If the debtor is not served with a notice and subsequently does not participate in the proceedings, he can file a so-called "opposition by a third party".

The party demanding the enforcement bears the burden of proof that the conditions of Articles 905 and 323 of the CCP are fulfilled, whereas the defending party has the right of counter-proof. The enforcement proceedings before the first instance court usually do not take more than three months, which is considerably less than would be required for an action on the merits. In case of an appeal, several months should be added.

The CCP allows the creditor to seek interim relief while the enforcement action is pending.

CHAPTER 9

INDIA

HEMANT SAHAI
J. Sagar Associates
New Delhi, India

INTRODUCTION

The law in India relating to the procedure to be followed by the courts of civil judicature has been codified in the "Code of Civil Procedure". The original Code was enacted in 1908 and was updated from time to time.

Major amendments were carried out in 1976. The Code of Civil Procedure applies to the civil courts in the whole of India, except for certain specified regions that have been exempted for various political and/or cultural reasons. These exempted regions have their own separate civil procedure codes, which are essentially variations of the 1908 Code.

The Code of Civil Procedure essentially consists of three broad divisions. The first division comprises of 158 Sections and is the substantive portion of the Act. These Sections define the powers of the courts as well as the principles governing diverse elements of procedural law.

The second division consists of "Schedule I" which is made up of 51 "Orders". The Orders in turn are further sub-divided into "Rules". Schedule I addresses the operative aspects of procedural law and defines the manner and form in which procedure is to be applied.

The third division consists of Appendices A to H, which give the suggested formats of diverse documentation, including pleadings, process, summons and notices. The Appendices are essentially a part of Schedule I, however, for ease of description, these are dealt with separately. Schedules II–V have been repealed.

The courts have inherent powers to make such orders as may be necessary to meet the ends of justice or to ensure that the court process is not abused by any person. These inherent rights have been specifically saved by Section 151 of the Code of Civil Procedure, which clarifies that no provision of the Code of Civil Procedure will limit or otherwise affect such inherent powers of the court. However, the inherent powers of the court cannot be invoked for any particular purpose where a specific provision exists in the Code of Civil Procedure for such purpose.

ESTABLISHING JURISDICTION

Subject matter jurisdiction

Sections 1–8 of the Code of Civil Procedure deal with preliminary issues, such as hierarchy of courts (i.e., High Courts, District Courts and Small Causes Courts), savings in respect of special local laws or provisions that will override the Code of Civil Procedure and the pecuniary jurisdiction of the courts.

The pecuniary jurisdictions of the Small Cause Courts and District Courts have been specified through local enactments by the various Federal States of India. Also, each Federal State of India has a High Court whose jurisdiction extends over the entire territory of the Federal State. Each High Court has diverse District Courts subordinate to it. The territorial jurisdiction of the District Courts is also defined. The various High Courts in turn are subordinate to the Supreme Court of India, located at New Delhi.

The courts have jurisdiction to entertain and try all civil suits subject to their territorial and pecuniary jurisdictions and any other restrictions under specific legislation. Certain specialised enactments have created special tribunals and fora for trying disputes arising under such enactments, and to this extent, the jurisdiction of civil courts is barred (e.g., customs, excise and other revenue-related enactments).

Place of suit

Every suit must be instituted in a court having pecuniary and territorial jurisdiction. The territorial jurisdiction of the courts is essentially determined on the principle that civil suits are to be instituted in the court in whose jurisdiction the cause of action arises or where the defendant resides or voluntarily carries on business. Cause of action includes "part of cause of action", and "defendant", where there is more than one defendant, will mean any one or more of the defendants.

Suits in respect of immovable properties will be instituted in the court within the local limits of whose jurisdiction the immovable property is situated. The territorial jurisdiction of all other suits not involving immovable properties will be determined on the principle "where the cause of action arises or where the defendant resides or voluntarily carries on business". A corporation must be deemed to carry on business at its principle place of business or where it has a subordinate office.

Parties to actions

All persons having a common cause of action and common question of fact or law may sue together as joint plaintiffs. Similarly, all persons against whom a right to relief arising out of a common cause of action exists may be joined in one suit as defendants.

One person may sue or defend a suit on behalf of all those having the same interest.

A suit will not be defeated on account of misjoinder or non-joinder of a party, i.e., if a person has been wrongly impleaded as a party or if a person who ought to have been a party has not been so impleaded. However, if a "necessary" party has not been impleaded then the suit may be dismissed. Before dismissing a suit for non-joinder of a "necessary" party, the court will give the plaintiff an opportunity to implead such "necessary" party in the suit. Only upon failure of the plaintiff to implead such "necessary" party will the suit be dismissed.

A "necessary" party is one whose presence is essential and in whose absence no effective decree at all can be passed. A "necessary" party is different from a "proper" party, and every "proper" party is not necessarily a "necessary" party. Failure to implead a "necessary" party can be fatal to the suit while failure to implead a "proper" party is not fatal to the suit.

The court has the power, whether on its own motion or on application by any person, to substitute or to add any person as a plaintiff or defendant in the suit where the court is satisfied that this is necessary to determine the real controversies in the suit. The court also has the power to remove any party as plaintiff or defendant if it is satisfied that such person has been incorrectly joined as a party to the suit.

Every suit must include the whole claim that the plaintiff is entitled to make in respect of the cause of action. The plaintiff is entitled to relinquish any part of his claim if he so wishes. On the other hand, the plaintiff may combine more than one cause of action against the same defendant(s) in one suit. This rule generally ensures that there is no multiplicity of proceedings, and particularly that the plaintiff cannot file more than one suit in respect of a single cause of action.

A party may appear before court in person or through his agent or recognised pleader (lawyer). Once a party has entered appearance through an agent or pleader, the court may order service of process, summons or notices on such party through his said agent or pleader.

Where a plaintiff sues for recovery of money and claims foreclosure of mortgage of immovable property, all persons having an interest either in the mortgage security or in the right of redemption will be joined as parties to this suit.

COMMENCING THE ACTION

Suits are instituted by presentation of a "plaint" in court. Upon filing of a suit, the court may issue summons to the defendants to appear and answer the claim. The summonses are to be issued in the prescribed manner.

Issue of summons

Once a suit is instituted a summons may be issued (with a copy of the plaint) to the defendant unless the defendant appears at the time of presentation of the plaint and admits to the plaintiff's claim.

The summons must be in the prescribed format and must be signed by the judge or officer appointed by the court. The summons must be served on each one of the defendants individually who will acknowledge receipt thereof. Service on the agent of the defendant is valid service.

If the defendant refuses to accept summons or cannot be found, the serving officer of the court will effect the service by affixing the summons on the outer door or some conspicuous part of the premises in which the defendant ordinarily resides or carries on business. The officer of the court will make a report to the court stating the circumstances in which the summonses are served.

Where the court is satisfied that there is reason to believe that the defendant is either deliberately avoiding service or for any other reason the summons cannot be served in the ordinary way, the court may order "substituted service". This could be either by affixation in the court house, affixation in some conspicuous portion of the premises where the defendant is last known to have resided or to have carried on business or in such other manner as the court thinks fit. The normal procedure adopted is by inserting an advertisement in a daily newspaper that is normally circulated in the locality in which the defendant is last known to have resided or carried on business.

Service on defendants residing outside India will be effected through post at the address where he resides, unless such defendant has an agent in India empowered to accept service, in which case service on such agent will be deemed to be adequate service.

Pleadings

A pleading must contain only statements of fact in a concise form, but not evidence by which to prove them. Pleadings are to be divided into paragraphs and should contain all details, including dates, sums and numbers where applicable. Pleadings generally should not contain any legal arguments.

Suggested forms of pleadings for different kinds of suits have been set out in Appendix A of the Code of Civil Procedure. These may be adopted with such variations as may be necessary.

Requirements

The pleadings must disclose all facts necessary to make out a complete case and/or defence. They must contain complete particulars including dates and material items. If the pleadings lack in material particulars, the court may order that the plaintiff or defendant, as the case may be, make a statement of further and better particulars as to the nature of claim or defence or any matter stated in the pleadings.

Every pleading must be signed by the party. Every pleading must also be verified at the foot of the document by the party. Such verification must specify by reference to the numbered paragraphs of the pleading what is verified as true to knowledge and what is verified as based on information received and believed to be true. This verification must be signed and dated by the person making the pleading.

Amendment

The court may at any stage of the proceedings allow the pleadings to be amended by addition or alteration, as may be necessary in the opinion of the court to determine the real questions in controversy between the parties. The powers of the court to allow amendments is very wide and the court may also take notice of events that have ensued subsequent to the filing of the suit. However, the parties are not entitled to set up by way of amendment an entirely new case that was not originally disclosed in the pleadings.

Plaint

The "plaint" must contain the following particulars:

(1) The name of the court in which the suit is brought;

(2) The name, description and place of residence of the plaintiff;

(3) The name, description and place of residence of the defendant, so far as they can be ascertained;

(4) Where the plaintiff or the defendant is a minor or a person of unsound mind, a statement to that effect;

(5) The facts constituting the cause of action and when it arose;

(6) The facts showing that the court has jurisdiction;

(7) The relief that the plaintiff claims;

(8) Where the plaintiff has allowed a set-off or relinquished a portion of his claim, the amount so allowed or relinquished; and

(9) A statement of the value of the subject matter of the suit for the purposes of jurisdiction and of court fees, so far as the case admits.

The plaint must disclose the defendant's interest and liability. The court will reject a plaint where:

(1) It does not disclose a cause of action;
(2) The relief claimed is undervalued, and the plaintiff, on being required by the court to correct the valuation within a time to be fixed by the court, fails to do so;
(3) The relief claimed is properly valued but the plaint is written upon paper insufficiently stamped, and the plaintiff, on being required by the court to supply the requisite stamp-paper within a time to be fixed by the court, fails to do so; and
(4) The suit appears from the statement in the plaint to be barred by any law.

For good reasons shown by the plaintiff, the court has the power to extend the time for correcting the valuation of the reliefs claimed and for affixing the proper court fees. However, if the plaint is rejected for any of the reasons aforesaid, the plaintiff is entitled to present a fresh plaint after removing these objections.

The principles for valuation of the reliefs claimed in the suit are contained in the Suits Valuation Act of 1887.

The plaintiff must produce all the documents in his possession or power on the basis of which the plaintiff makes out his case. If the documents are not within his power or in his possession, he must state in whose possession or power the documents are placed.

Answers

The defendant must file his defence, if any, to the claims by way of a written statement. This has to be filed at the first hearing, however, the court may allow the defendant further time for filing its written statement. The written statement must contain all the relevant facts that the defendant pleads in its defence. The defendant must also, along with its written statement, file any documents relied upon by the defendant in support of its defence, set-off, or counter-claim. If the documents relied upon by the defendant are not in its power or possession, then the defendant must state in whose possession or power they are in.

Every allegation of fact, if not denied in the written statement either specifically or by necessary implication, will be deemed to have been admitted. However, the court may, in its discretion, require the plaintiff to prove any fact otherwise than by such admission. The defendant is entitled to claim a set off against the plaintiff's demand for money. The set off should be for an ascertained sum of money legally recoverable by the defendant from the plaintiff and should not exceed the pecuniary jurisdiction of the court. The counter-claim will be treated as a separate suit and the defendant will have to pay the requisite court fee on the same.

If the defendant fails to present a written statement within the time permitted by a court, the court will pronounce judgment against the defendant or make such other order as the court may deem fit. On the pronouncement of judgment, a decree will be drawn up.

Admissions

A party to the suit may give notice of admission of truth of the whole or part of the case by his pleading.

Conversely, a party may call upon the other party to admit within 15 days from the date of service of notice any document saving all just exceptions. In case of refusal or neglect by the party to respond to the notice, the party refusing or neglecting to respond has to pay costs of proving any such document unless the court directs it as other- wise.

Similarly, a party may give notice to the other party to admit facts, within six days from the date of service of such notice. The consequences of failure or neglect to admit facts pursuant to such notice are the same as in the case of failure or neglect to comply with a notice to admit documents. The forms of the notices to admit documents and facts are specified in Appendix C.

The parties must produce all the documents of every description in their possession or power on which the party intends to rely. These documents have to be produced before the framing of issues. The parties cannot produce or rely on any documents not filed in court, prior to framing of issues as aforesaid, except with leave of the court and for good cause to be shown.

The admitted documents are endorsed and signed by the judge. The documents not admitted are rejected if these are not relevant. If any party seeks to rely on them, such party will have to prove these documents on the principles of the law of evidence.

OBTAINING INFORMATION

The court has the power to make orders relating to discovery of documents, answering of interrogatories, admission of documents and other steps to cut short and narrow down the controversies between the litigating parties. The court also has the power to summon witnesses and compel the attendance of such witnesses.

Interrogatories

Any party may, with the leave of the court, deliver interrogatories in writing for examination by the opposite party. The interrogatories must be in the form specified in Appendix C. The replies to the interrogatories will be in the form of a sworn affidavit. The form of the reply to interrogatories has also been specified in Appendix C of the Code.

Discovery of documents

Similarly, any party may apply to the court for an order directing the other party to make discovery on oath of documents that are or have been in possession or power of such other party and which relate to the matters in question in the suit. The court may allow the application, or if satisfied that discovery is not necessary at that stage, refuse or adjourn the same. The discovery will be allowed only if the court is satisfied that it is necessary for disposing fairly of the suit or for saving costs.

The reply to the application for discovery must be made by the party in the form specified in Appendix C of the Code. The court may order a party to produce the documents in court supported by an affidavit.

Any party may give notice to the other party to produce the original documents relied upon by him and mentioned in his pleadings, and such party will be entitled to inspect these documents and take copies thereof. If a party fails to produce the documents despite being put to notice as aforesaid, such party cannot later, except with the leave of the court, rely on these documents. The notice to produce documents as aforesaid must be in a form as specified in Appendix C of the Code.

Non-compliance

Where any party fails to comply with the orders of the court to answer interrogatories or for discovery or inspection of documents then such party will, if he be the plaintiff, be liable to have his suit dismissed for want of prosecution, and if he be the defendant, be liable to have his defence struck off. If a suit is dismissed in the above circumstances, the plaintiff is precluded from filing a fresh suit on the same cause of action.

INTERIM PROTECTION

Arrest and attachment

The court may issue a warrant to arrest the defendant and bring him before the court to show cause why he should not furnish security for his appearance if the court is satisfied by affidavit or otherwise:

(1) That the defendant, with intent to delay the proceedings, or to avoid any process of the court or to obstruct or delay the execution of any decree that may be passed against him:
   (a) Has absconded or left the local limits of the jurisdiction of the court; or
   (b) Is about to abscond or leave the local limits of the jurisdiction of the court; or
   (c) Has disposed of or removed from the local limits of the jurisdiction of the court his property or any part thereof; or
(2) That the defendant is about to leave India under circumstances affording reasonable probability that the plaintiff will or may thereby be obstructed or delayed in the execution of any decree that may be passed against the defendant in the suit.

However, if the defendant pays to the officer executing the warrant of arrest any sum specified in the warrant as sufficient to satisfy the plaintiff's claim, which sum will be deposited in court until further orders by the court, then the defendant will not be arrested.

The court may direct the defendant to either furnish adequate security to satisfy the decree that may be passed against him or to appear and show cause for his failure to furnish security if the court is satisfied by affidavit or otherwise that the defendant, with intent to obstruct or delay the execution of any decree that may be passed against him:

(1) Is about to dispose of the whole or any part of his property; or
(2) Is about to remove the whole or any part of his property from the local limits of the jurisdiction of the court.

If the defendant fails this, the court may order attachment of his property or such portion thereof which would be sufficient to satisfy any decree that may be passed against him.

The orders for arrest of the defendant or attachment of property may be passed at any stage of the suit.

Interlocutory orders and injunctions

The court may grant temporary injunctions to restrain any act, or dispossess the plaintiff or otherwise restrain any act calculated or likely to cause damage or injury to the plaintiff or any property in dispute in the suit, if it is satisfied by affidavit or otherwise:

(1) That any property in dispute in a suit is in danger of being wasted, damaged or alienated by any party to the suit, or wrongfully sold in execution of a decree;

(2) That the defendant threatens, or intends, to remove or dispose of his property with a view to defrauding his creditors; or

(3) That the defendant threatens to dispossess the plaintiff or otherwise cause injury to the plaintiff in relation to any property in dispute in the suit.

The court may also grant an injunction to restrain the commission, repetition or continuance of breach of contract or injury complained of. The injunction may be on such terms as the court thinks fit.

In case of disobedience by any person of any injunction granted, the court may order the property of the guilty person to be attached and may also order that such guilty person be detained in civil prison.

As a general rule, the court will not grant temporary injunctions without giving notice to the other party. However, if the court is satisfied that the object of granting the injunction would be defeated by the delay then the court may grant the injunction without giving notice to the other party, provided that in such case the court will record the reasons for granting such *ex parte* injunction and will require the applicant to deliver to the opposite party a copy of the affidavit and supporting documents and a copy of the plaint, immediately after the injunction order has been granted. The applicant is also required to file an affidavit stating that the above requirements have been complied with, not later than the day immediately following the day that the injunction was granted.

Where an injunction has been granted *ex parte*, the court will endeavour to finally dispose of the application within 30 days from the date on which the injunction was granted.

Appointment of receivers

The court may appoint a receiver to take charge of any property whether before or after decree, or to remove any person from the possession or custody of the property. The receiver will thereafter manage and have custody and control of the property.

RESOLUTION WITHOUT FULL TRIAL

Dismissal for non-appearance

The parties must appear on the day fixed in the summons issued to the defendant. The parties may appear in person or through respective pleaders and the suit will then be heard unless the hearing is adjourned for a later date.

If neither party appears on the day fixed for appearance in the summons, the suit will be dismissed. However, the plaintiff is entitled in such case to file a fresh suit or apply to the court giving reasons for non-appearance and if the court is satisfied that there was sufficient cause for his non-appearance, the court will set aside the dismissal and restore the suit and then appoint a day for proceeding with the suit.

If the plaintiff fails to take timely steps to effect service of summons on the defendant (i.e., pay the process fee and postal charges and furnish copies of the plaint to the court) and the plaintiff fails to satisfy the court that he has been diligent or that there is some sufficient cause for such failure, the court will dismiss the suit. However, this does not preclude the plaintiff from filing a fresh suit, subject to the laws of limitation.

If the defendant has been properly served in due time but fails to appear, the suit will be heard *ex parte* (i.e., in the absence of the defendant). However, if the defendant appears on or before the adjourned date of hearing and gives good cause for his earlier non-appearance, the court may allow the defendant to participate in the proceedings as if he had appeared on the day fixed for his appearance. The court, after hearing the case *ex parte*, may pronounce judgment in favour of the plaintiff. In any case in which an *ex parte* decree has been passed, the defendant may appear and if he satisfies the court that the summons were not duly served or that he was prevented by any sufficient cause from appearing when the suit was called on for hearing, the court will set aside the *ex parte* decree against the defendant.

Where only the defendant appears and the plaintiff does not appear when the suit is called for hearing, the suit will be dismissed unless the defendant admits, in whole or in part, the claim of the plaintiff. The court will pass judgment in respect of the claims admitted and dismiss the suit so far it relates to the remainder. In such case, the plaintiff is not entitled to file a fresh suit for the same cause of action, however, he may apply for setting aside the dismissal of the suit by showing that he had sufficient cause for his earlier non-appearance. The court may, if satisfied with the reasons assigned by the plaintiff for his non-appearance, set aside the dismissal and proceed with the suit.

In all the aforesaid instances, the court, while condoning any of the lapses, delays or non-appearances, may impose such terms as to costs or otherwise on the defaulting party as it sees fit.

Withdrawal and adjustment of suits

The plaintiff may at any time after the institution of the suit, abandon his suit or part of his claim. The parties may at any time compromise the suit and the court will pass a decree in terms of the compromise.

Summary procedure

Order 37 of the Code of Civil Procedure provides the procedure for "summary trials" Under this procedure, the defendant is not entitled to a defence as a matter of right. The provisions under Order 37 apply to the following classes of suits:

(1) Suits upon bills of exchange, *hundies* (a local form of negotiable instrument) and promissory notes;
(2) Suits in which the plaintiff seeks only to recover a debt or liquidated demand in money payable by the defendant, with or without interest, arising:
    (a) On a written contract; or
    (b) On an enactment, where the sum sought to be recovered is a fixed sum of money or in the nature of a debt other than a penalty; or
    (c) On a guarantee, where the claim against the principal is in respect of a debt or liquidated demand only.

A suit under Order 37 is instituted by presenting a plaint that specifically mentions that the suit is under Order 37 of the Code of Civil Procedure. Pursuant to the filing of such plaint, summons will be issued in the form specified in Appendix B. The summons together with copies of the plaint and Annexures thereto will be served on the defendant.

The defendant may enter appearance not later than 10 days from the date of service of the summons. Upon entering an appearance, the defendant must file in court an address for service of notices on him and must also give notice to the plaintiff of having so entered appearance.

Once the defendant enters an appearance in court, the plaintiff must serve on the defendant "summons for judgment" in the form prescribed in Appendix B. The summons for judgment must be supported by an affidavit verifying the cause of action and the amount claimed and stating that in the belief of the plaintiff the defendant has no defence to the suit.

The defendant may, at anytime within 10 days from the service of such summons for judgment, apply for "leave to defend" the suit by disclosing such facts as may be deemed sufficient to entitle him to defend the suit. The court may allow the application for leave to defend, either conditionally or unconditionally, if it is satisfied that the defendant has disclosed facts that give rise to a "triable issue" and that the defendant has a substantial defence. The court may grant the defendant leave to defend the suit either as to the whole or any part of the claim.

At the hearing of such summons for judgment, if the defendant has not applied for leave to defend the suit, or if applied, such application has been refused, then the plaintiff will be entitled to judgment forthwith. Alternatively, if the defendant has been permitted to defend the suit as to the whole or any part of the claim, the court may direct the defendant to furnish such security within such time as may be determined by the court and on failure of the defendant to furnish such security within the time specified, the plaintiff will be entitled to judgment forthwith.

The court may for sufficient cause shown by the defendant excuse the delay of the defendant, if any, in entering appearance or in applying for leave to defend, as aforesaid.

If the defendant is permitted to defend the claim of the plaintiff on the grounds disclosed in the application for leave to defend, then the suit will be converted into an ordinary suit and the procedure as applies to ordinary suits will be applicable.

Foreclosure actions

In a suit for foreclosure of a mortgage, if the plaintiff succeeds, the court will pass a preliminary decree. Pursuant to the preliminary decree, the principal amount and interest until the date of preliminary decree will be declared and the defendant will be allowed six months' time to pay such amount. If the defendant pays such declared amount, the plaintiff will hand over to the defendant all the documents in relation to the said mortgaged property and re-transfer the same to the defendant. If the defendant fails to make such payment of the declared amount, on or before the time fixed, the plaintiff may apply for a final decree to be passed and the defendant will thereafter be debarred from redeeming the said mortgaged property.

The time fixed for payment may be extended by the court on good cause shown by the defendant.

TRIAL

Framing of issues

Issues arise when a material proposition of fact or law is affirmed by one party and denied by the other. Material propositions are those propositions of law or fact that a plaintiff must allege in order to show a right to sue or a defendant must allege in order to constitute his defence.

At the first hearing of the suit, the court will frame issues on those material propositions of fact or law upon which the parties are at variance.

Therefore, the court will proceed and frame and record only those issues upon which the right decision of the case appears to depend. There may be more than one issue framed and the onus of proving one or more of the issues may be on the plaintiff and the onus of proving the remaining issues, if any, may be on the defendant.

After hearing the parties and considering the evidence on record, the court will pronounce judgment on all issues. However, if issues of law as well as fact arise in the same suit and the court feels that the suit can be disposed of on the issues of law only, the court may try that issue first which relates to jurisdiction of the court or a bar to the suit created by any law for the time being in force. The court may postpone the settlement of the other issues until this preliminary issue is determined.

The court may frame the issues based on all or any of the following materials:

(1) Allegations made on oath by the parties, or by any persons present on their behalf, or made by the pleaders of such parties;
(2) Allegations made in the pleadings or in answers to interrogatories delivered in the suit; and
(3) The contents of documents produced by either party.

The court may adjourn the framing of issues to a future date if it feels that examination of a person (not in court) or inspection of a document (not produced in the suit) is indispensable to the framing of issues, and may compel the attendance of such person or production of such document by summons or any other process.

Where the parties are not at issue on any question of law or fact, the court may at once pronounce judgment.

Summons of witnesses

Not later than 15 days after framing of issues, the parties must present a list of witnesses whom they propose to call either to give evidence or to produce documents, and the court will issue summonses to such persons to ensure their attendance in court. However, the parties are free to produce witnesses to give evidence or produce documents, without applying for summonses from the court. The parties may also produce any person to give evidence as an expert.

The court has the power to compel attendance of witnesses. This may be achieved by imposing a fine or ordering attachment of property of such witnesses, or by issuing a warrant for his arrest and production in court.

Hearing of suit and examination of witnesses

The general rule is that the plaintiff has the right to begin the hearing of the suit. However, if the defendant admits the facts alleged by the plaintiff and contends that either on a point of law or on some additional facts alleged by defendant, the plaintiff is not entitled to any part of the reliefs claimed, then the defendant has the right to begin the hearing of the suit.

At the hearing of the suit, the party entitled to begin will state his case and produce his evidence, if any, in support of the issues that he is bound to prove. The other party will then state his case and produce his evidence, if any, in support of the issues that he is bound to prove. The parties may then address the court generally on the whole case. The court may, for reasons to be recorded, direct or permit any party to examine any witnesses at any stage.

JUDGMENT

The court will pronounce judgment in the open court either soon after the case has been heard or at a later date, which it will specify and give notice of. The court will make every endeavour to pronounce the judgment within 15 days after the case has been heard. If this is not practicable, the court will ordinarily render judgment not later than 30 days after hearing. If court fails to pronounce the judgment within 30 days it will record the reasons for such delay and fix a future day on which judgment will be pronounced.

Where a written judgment is to be pronounced, it is sufficient if the findings of the court on each issue and the final order are read out. However, copy of the entire judgment should be made available for the perusal of the parties or the pleaders immediately after the judgment is pronounced.

The judgment can be pronounced by declaration in the open court to a stenographer. The resulting transcription will then be signed by the judge, and will bear the date on which it was pronounced and such judgment will form part of the record.

The judgment will contain a concise statement of the case, the points for determination, the decision thereon and the reasons for such determination.

While pronouncing judgment, the court may, where applicable, order interest at such rate as the court deems reasonable for the period prior to institution of the suit as well as *pendente-lite* and future interest, i.e., interest from the date of institution of the suit until the date of payment under the judgment. In commercial transactions, the court may award interest at prevalent commercial rates subject to a contractual rate of interest, if any.

SUPPLEMENTARY MOTIONS

Under Section 112 of the Code of Civil Procedure, any court may state a case and refer the same for the opinion of the High Court, and the High Court may make such order as it thinks fit.

Any person aggrieved by an order or decree from which an appeal is allowed but no appeal has been preferred or an order or decree from which no appeal is allowed, may apply for a review of the order or decree, to the same court that passed the decree or order.

Any party may file a revision in a High Court against an order or decree against which no appeal lies, where a court subordinate to the High Court decides a case and such subordinate court appears to have:

(1) Exercised a jurisdiction not vested in it by law;
(2) Failed to exercise jurisdiction vested in it; or
(3) Acted in the exercise of its jurisdiction illegally or with irregularity.

The powers of the High Court in revision are very wide. It can call for the records of the case from the subordinate court and decide the matter afresh. The expression "jurisdiction" used in the context of revision means powers of the subordinate court, which it either exceeds, fails to exercise or exercises illegally.

ENFORCEMENT

The decree prepared pursuant to the judgment of a court is executed through the court. However, where suits are merely for determination of status of parties, i.e., suits for declaration or for injunction to restrain defendant from committing or continuing to commit any act, no execution proceedings are necessary.

Execution of decrees and orders

All money payable under a decree must be paid either by depositing funds in court or directly to the decree holder or in such other manner as may be directed by the court.

A decree holder may apply to the court for execution of the decree. The application must contain, *inter alia*, the details of the decree and the mode in which the assistance of the court is required to execute the decree. The court may execute the decree by directing:

(1) Delivery of any property specifically decreed;

(2) Attachment, attachment and sale or sale without attachment, of any property;

(3) Arrest and detention in prison of any person;

(4) Appointment of receiver to take charge of any property; and

(5) Any other order as may be necessary in the facts of the case.

The Code of Civil Procedure contains detailed provisions in respect of attachment of various classes of properties, whether, *inter alia*, moveable, immovable, agricultural or salary.

Property attached or such portion thereof as may be necessary must be sold by public auction under the supervision of the court. The proceeds thereof will be paid to the party entitled under the decree to receive the same.

Foreign judgments

Section 13 of the Code of Civil Procedure lays down in negative language the principle on which foreign judgments are enforced in India. The rules enshrined in this Section are not merely procedural; they also contain substantive law.

The Section provides that a foreign judgment will be conclusive as to any matter thereby directly adjudicated upon between the same parties or between parties under whom they or any of them claim, except:

(1) Where the foreign judgment has not been pronounced by a competent court;

(2) Where the foreign judgment has not been given on the merits of the case;

(3) Where it appears on the face of the proceedings that the foreign judgment is founded on an incorrect view of International law or a refusal to recognise the law of India in cases in which such law is applicable;

(4) Where the proceedings in which the foreign judgment was obtained are opposed to Natural Justice;

(5) Where the foreign judgment has been obtained by fraud; and

(6) Where the foreign judgment sustains a claim founded on a breach of any law in force in India.

The Indian courts will presume upon production of a certified copy of the foreign judgment that the foreign court was of competent jurisdiction, however, this presumption is rebuttable.

Foreign judgments may be enforced in India either by:

(1) Execution proceedings; or

(2) By filing a suit in India based on the foreign judgment.

A foreign judgment does not bar a party from suing in India on the basis of the original cause of action.

The Code of Civil Procedure clarifies that aliens, i.e., persons who are not citizens of India, as well as foreign states can sue in Indian courts as if they were citizens of India.

APPEALS

Every decree passed by a court of original jurisdiction is appealable, unless specifically barred by any law for the time being in force, e.g., decree by a small causes court. However, a decree passed by consent of the parties is not appealable. The first appeal against a decree will lie to the next higher court.

A second appeal will lie to the High Court only on substantial questions of law.

On the other hand, all orders (as opposed to final decrees) of the court are not appealable. Only specified classes of orders are appealable. The remedy where an order is not appealable is by way of review or revision, as explained above.

Every appeal will be preferred in the form of a memorandum, which must be accompanied by a copy of the decree appealed from and a copy of the judgment on which the decree is founded.

The memorandum of appeal must set forth concisely the grounds of objection to the decree appealed from, without containing any argument or narrative.

If the appeal is against a decree for payment of money, the appellant must deposit the disputed amount or furnish such security in respect thereof, as the court thinks fit.

The court hearing the appeal will give notice of the filing of the appeal to the court that passed the decree against which the appeal is filed and the records of the case will be transferred to the appellate court. However, the appellate court may dismiss the appeal if it thinks fit, without giving notice to the court that passed the decree against which the appeal is preferred. Before dismissing the appeal, as aforesaid, the appellate court will hear the appellant or his pleader. If the appeal is not dismissed as aforesaid, the court will hear the respondent and in such case the appellant will be entitled to reply.

Upon hearing the parties, the court may allow or dismiss the appeal and thereafter pronounce judgment in open court. Thus, the judgment may confirm, vary or reverse the decree from which the appeal is preferred.

The other procedure relating to appearance of parties, serving of notices, dismissal of appeal due to non-appearance of appellant and reinstatement of appeal if dismissed as aforesaid, is similar to the procedure applicable to suits, as described above.

Appeals from appellate decrees passed as above, i.e., second appeals will only be to the High Court and the procedure in such second appeals is the same as applies to first appeals.

RES JUDICATA AND LIS PENDENS

Two important principles of procedure aimed at avoiding multiplicity of actions and ensuring that different courts do not give conflicting decisions, are enshrined in Sections 10 and 11 of the Code of Civil Procedure. The principle of *res sub judice*, under Section 10 of the Code of Civil Procedure, provides that no court shall proceed with the trial of any suit in which:

(1) The matter in issue is also directly and substantially in issue in a previously instituted suit;
(2) The party or parties under whom they claim are the same in the two suits;
(3) The court in which the earlier suit has been instituted is competent to grant the relief claimed in the second suit; and
(4) The earlier suit is pending in the same court in which the second suit is pending or in any other court in India or outside India having jurisdiction to grant the relief claimed.

Accordingly, if two suits having identical subject matter among same parties have been instituted, the trial of the suit instituted later will be stayed.

Similarly, the principle of *res judicata* as expressed in Section 11 provides: "No court shall try any suit or issue in which the matter directly and substantially in issue has been directly and substantially in issue in a former suit between the same parties."

"Former suit" means a suit that has been decided prior to the suit in question, whether or not such former suit was instituted prior to the suit in question.

CHAPTER 10

IRELAND

BILL HOLOHAN
GJ Moloney & Company
Cork, Ireland

INTRODUCTION

The territorial jurisdiction of Irish courts is confined to the 26 counties of Ireland[1] excluding the six counties of Northern Ireland, which falls within the jurisdiction of the courts of the United Kingdom. A Common Law system based on precedent and case law exists in the Republic of Ireland (Ireland), as opposed to a Civil Law system, which is found in most continental European jurisdictions. Within this system, general principles of law are derived from decisions in particular cases, as opposed to the Civil Law system where cases are decided in accordance with general principles.

Court structure

The court structure, in ascending order of authority, is the Small Claims court, the District Court, the Circuit Court, the High Court and the Supreme Court.

Small claims court

In the recent past, a small claims court has been established on a trial basis in some urban areas. The court is designated to cater for claims up to IR£500. Legal representation is not permitted and legal costs are not recoverable.

District Court

The District Court sits in most medium sized towns in Ireland. The country is divided into 24 Districts. Each District is further sub-divided into "District Court Areas".

1. *Bunreacht nah-Eireann* (The Irish Constitution), Article 3.

Circuit Court

The Circuit Court is superior to and hears appeals from the District Court. It is also a court of first instance. The country is divided into eight circuits.

High Court

The High Court is superior to and hears appeals from the Circuit Court. It is also a court of first instance. The High Court sits in Dublin. It also travels on circuit to cities around Ireland in order to hear personal injury actions and to hear appeals from the Circuit Court. It may also take references by way of appeal on points of law through a process known as "appeal by way of case stated".

There is an officer of the High Court known as the Master who sits in the Master's court and determines issues of procedure and practice. He also has limited judicial capacity. He generally deals with:

(1) Motions on notice between the parties relating to procedural matters;
(2) *Ex parte* applications regarding procedural matters; and
(3) Motions for Judgment in summary matters.

Supreme Court

The Supreme Court is superior to and hears appeals from the High Court. It is not a court of first instance. It hears appeals on points of law and points of fact.

Legal profession

The legal profession in Ireland is divided into solicitors and barristers (who are referred to collectively as "the Bar"). Solicitors are general practitioners and are regulated by the Incorporated Law Society. Barristers, generally, deal with the drafting of court proceedings and advocacy that is, presentation of cases in the courts.

Some barristers are experts in particular areas of law and often their advice (Counsel's Opinion) will be sought. Barristers accept instructions from solicitors. A distinction is drawn between senior counsels and junior counsels. Senior Counsels, generally, settle (that is approve) proceedings as drafted by junior counsels, and act as advocates in the High and Supreme Courts. An appearance by a Senior Counsel in a

Circuit Court although unusual is permissible. Senior Counsel's opinion on complex issues of law are often sought.

ESTABLISHING JURISDICTION

Jurisdiction over the parties of the action

Natural persons and the state

Distinctions may be drawn in law between different classes of person. Legislation may expressly provide that the State or other persons are not to be bound by the legislation.

Representative and class actions are also possible. It is essential that persons on whose behalf an action is taken have both a common interest and common a grievance and the relief sought is of benefit to all of them. In relation to a representative action, the proceedings must show on the face of them, the capacity in which the party sues or is sued.

Where a person is incapable of acting on his own behalf, then proceedings may be instituted or defended on that person's behalf by another person. Such a representative action would arise in instances where the party to the proceedings is an infant (that is, under the age of 18 years), a bankrupt, a ward of court or is of unsound mind.

Corporations

Few distinctions exist between the treatment of corporate personalities and individuals. While an individual may represent himself in court, a corporate personality must be represented by either a solicitor or a barrister.

Jurisdiction over the subject matter of the action

The District Court has no jurisdiction in actions for slander, libel, seduction, slander of title, malicious prosecution or false imprisonment. The Circuit Court has no jurisdiction in actions that would necessitate declaring the existence of a constitutional right or striking out a constitutional right that had previously been found to exist. The High Court has originating jurisdiction in all matters except malicious damage to property. The High Court may decline to exercise its jurisdiction if proceedings should more properly have been brought in a lower court.

Property claims

Jurisdiction in property disputes concerning land is determined by reference to a valuation system whereby all property in the State is given a rateable valuation. This rateable valuation system is used as the basis of calculating local taxes on commercial property. The Circuit Court has jurisdiction where the rateable valuation does not exceed IR£200.

Damage or violation of rights

DISTRICT COURT

The District Court has jurisdiction in all actions in contract and tort (including hire purchase claims), proceedings by the State and actions for ejectment where the monetary value of the claim does not exceed IR£5,000. Where the monetary value of the claim exceeds IR£5,000 and the plaintiff still wishes to bring the proceedings at District Court level, for example, due to reasons of speed and expediency, then the plaintiff may waive the excess of the claim over IR£5,000.

It is not possible to split one cause of action into two separate claims, each claim being below IR£5,000, in order to come within the jurisdiction of the District Court. As such, an action must be brought in the Circuit Court. In proceedings for the recovery of rates (levied on commercial properties) the District Court has no monetary limit on its jurisdiction.

CIRCUIT COURT

The Circuit Court has jurisdiction in claims concerning contract, tort or hire purchase where the value of the claim does not exceed IR£30,000. With the written consent of all the parties, the Circuit Court may be given unlimited jurisdiction. A claimant who obtains an award of IR£5,000 or less will only be entitled to such costs as would have been awarded had the case been taken in the District Court. The claimant may waive any portion of his claim that exceeds IR£30,000, or the defendant may consent to giving the court unlimited jurisdiction.

HIGH COURT

The High Court has unlimited jurisdiction to hear claims. If a Claimant obtains an award of IR£30,000 or less, then he will only be entitled to such costs as would have been awarded had the case been brought in the correct lower court.

Article 3 of the Brussels Convention

Article 3 of the Brussels Convention provides that persons domiciled in a contracting State must be sued in the courts of that State. In relation to Ireland, it specifically excludes the application of those rules that enable jurisdiction to be founded on the service of proceedings on a defendant during his temporary presence in the State.

Venue

General principles

The venue for the issue of and hearing of proceedings is determined by the geographical jurisdiction of courts as set out hereunder.

Ireland has also adopted the Brussels Convention on Jurisdiction of Courts and Enforcement of Judgments by means of the provisions of the Jurisdiction of Courts and Enforcement of Judgments (European Communities) Act, 1988. The rules regarding jurisdiction contained in the Convention are in force in Ireland.

Section 53 of the Courts of Justice Act, 1936 determines the rules for deciding jurisdiction in all courts. Proceedings which are founded on contract or tort, or in proceedings for ejectment, may be brought, heard, and determined (at the option of the plaintiff) either before the judge for the District or the Circuit where the defendant or one of the defendants ordinarily resides or carries on any profession, business or occupation, or alternatively before the judge of the District or Circuit where the contract is alleged to have been made, or where the tort which is alleged to have been committed was committed or occured, or where the lands which form the subject matter of the proceedings are situate.

DISTRICT COURT

Ireland is divided into 24 Districts, which are sub-divided into 249 District Court areas. The originating court document must cite the correct district and area of the court that is seized with jurisdiction in each particular case. Where civil proceedings are brought in the wrong District or Area, the proceedings will be struck out and costs awarded against the party who issued the same.

CIRCUIT COURT

The State is divided into eight circuits, which are subdivided into 26 counties. Every originating document must cite the particular circuit and county in which it is intended to be tried. The correct circuit and county is determined as follows:

(1) In probate actions — where the testator or intestate, at the time of his death, had a fixed place of abode;

(2) In actions relating to the title to land — where the land is situate;

(3) In contract or tort cases — at the election of the plaintiff, where the defendant or any one of the defendants resides or carries on any business, profession or occupation, or alternatively where the cause of action arose, that is, where the contract was made or where the tort was committed;

(4) In lunacy matters — where the person alleged to be of unsound mind ordinarily resides;

(5) In all other cases — where the defendant or any one of the defendants ordinarily resides or carries on any business, profession or occupation.

HIGH COURT

The High Court sits in Dublin, except in cases of personal injury and appeals from the Circuit Court when it also sits in the cities and towns of Cork, Limerick, Galway, Sligo, Dundalk and Kilkenny. In such personal injury actions, the plaintiff may elect for the case to be heard in either Dublin or such of the aforementioned cities as is convenient.

Transfer of venue

In order to transfer the venue of the proceedings, it is necessary to acquire the consent of all the parties to the proceedings or to obtain an order from the court transferring the said action. Obviously, an order of the court will only be required where the parties are not in agreement. Convenience or expediency, depending on the circumstances of the case, would be valid grounds for the making of such an order. It should be noted that the Circuit Court does not have the power to transfer an action out of the Circuit Court without:

(1) The consent of the Circuit Court which would receive the case; and

(2) The consent of the parties to the action.

Service of summons or writ

Irish law provides for several means of service. Although The Hague Convention on Service Abroad of Judicial and Extra Judicial Documents in Civil or Commercial Matters, 1965 has been signed by Ireland, it has not been ratified and consequently is of no effect within the jurisdiction of Ireland.

In respect of District Court and Circuit Court proceedings, following issue of the same, the original of the originating court document together with a declaration or affidavit of service, as is appropriate, must be lodged in the appropriate court office within 14 days of service. In High Court proceedings, the original document is retained and an affidavit of service is sworn as to service.

Post

Pursuant to Section 379 of the Companies Act, any document may be served on a company (irrespective of its nature) by posting a copy of the same to its registered office.

DISTRICT AND CIRCUIT COURTS

Unless personal service at the hands of a summons server is required, service must always be effected by way of recorded registered prepaid post addressed to the person to be served, at his last known place of residence or place of business in the state. If service cannot be effected by way of registered prepaid post, then an order of the court must be acquired before the originating document may be served by ordinary prepaid post (except when serving a company).

HIGH COURT

Personal service is required by the Rules. For proceedings at High Court level, service may only be effected by post (registered and/or ordinary) on the basis of an order of the court. Such order is not required when serving a company.

Personal service

DISTRICT AND CIRCUIT COURTS

If a court summons server has been assigned to a particular district, then service must always be effected by way of personal service by the summons server in that particular district. If a court summons server has not been assigned to a particular district, then service may only be effected by way of personal service (by a person other than a summons server) on the basis of an order of the court. There are now very few court summons servers as they are no longer being replaced following retirement.

HIGH COURT

Service of proceedings must always be effected by way of personal service in the High Court, unless an order to the contrary is obtained from the court.

Consular or diplomatic channels

Order 121, Rule 9 of the Rules of the Superior Courts (RSC) allows for service of legal documents on persons in Ireland:

". . . when in any civil or commercial matter pending before a court or tribunal of a foreign country, a letter of request from such court or tribunal for service on any person in Ireland of any process or citation in such matter is transmitted to the Master of the High Court by the Minister for Foreign Affairs, with an intimation that it is desirable that effect should be given to the same."

Further to the above, the powers of the District Court, Circuit Court and High Court respectively to make an order for substituted service are discretionary in nature and it would therefore be open to any such court to make an order effecting service through consular or diplomatic channels.

Publication

Service may only be effected by way of publication on the basis of an order of the court, in all courts of first instance.

ASCERTAINING THE APPLICABLE LAW

Sources

Ireland is not a Federal State. Laws made by the *Oireachtas* (Legislature) apply equally to all parts of the State, unless the legislation specifically provides otherwise.

Local authorities are empowered to make certain laws known as by-laws. However, these have little or no importance in relation to the institution and carriage of civil proceedings.

Sources of law are as follows:

(1) The Irish Constitution;
(2) Acts of the *Oireachtas*, (the Legislature);

(3) Laws which were in existence prior to the formation of the Irish Free State in 1921 and which are not repugnant to the Constitution;

(4) Statutory instruments;

(5) Local by-laws;

(6) Case law; and

(7) European Community legislation to the extent that it is directly applicable or to the extent that it has been incorporated into Irish Law.

Irish conflict of laws principles

Questions relating to civil status (such as marriage, matrimonial causes, and legitimacy) and moveable property, including succession and taxation, are decided on the basis of domicile. There are three types of domicile:

(1) Domicile of origin — a legitimate child born during the lifetime of its father has the domicile of origin of the country in which his father was domiciled at the time of his birth. An illegitimate child or a legitimate child born after its father's death has its domicile of origin in the country where its mother was domiciled at the time of birth);

(2) Domicile of choice — this is acquired by a person who resides in a country with the intention of continuing to do so permanently or indefinitely); or

(3) Domicile of dependency — (this describes minors and mentally ill persons regardless of their own intentions or wishes).

The domicile of a person will be determined according to Irish Law.

Whenever the whole subject matter of an action consists of land situate within the jurisdiction or whenever any act, deed, will, contract, application or liability effecting land or hereditaments situate within the jurisdiction is sought to be construed, rectified, set aside or enforced in an action, the applicable law is Irish law.

Whenever the action relates to the administration of the personal estate of any deceased person who, at the time of his death, was domiciled within the jurisdiction, or for the execution (as to property situate within the jurisdiction) of the trusts of any written instrument, of which the person to be served is a trustee, which ought to be executed according to the law of Ireland, then the applicable law is Irish law.

When the action is an action brought to enforce, rescind, dissolve, annul or otherwise effect the contract or to recover damages or other relief for or in respect of the breach of a contract, where any one of the following three conditions is fulfilled:

(1) The contract is made within the jurisdiction;
(2) The contract is made by or through an agent trading or residing within the jurisdiction on behalf of a principal trading or residing out of the jurisdiction; or
(3) The contract is stipulated by the terms or by implication to be governed by Irish Law or is one brought in respect of a breach of a contract entered into within the jurisdiction even though such breach was preceded or accompanied by a breach out of the jurisdiction, which rendered impossible the performance of the part of the contract, which ought to have been performed within the jurisdiction, then the applicable law is Irish law.

Where the action is founded on a tort committed within the jurisdiction, then the applicable law is Irish law. Where any injunction is sought as to anything to be done within the jurisdiction, or any nuisance within the jurisdiction is sought to be prevented or removed, whether damages are or are not also sought in respect thereof, then the applicable law is Irish law.

Where any person who is out of the jurisdiction is a necessary or proper party to an action properly brought against some other person duly served within the jurisdiction, then the applicable law is Irish law.

Where the proceedings relate to an infant or person of unsound mind domiciled in or who is a citizen of Ireland, then the applicable law is Irish law. Where the proceedings in question relate to interpleader proceedings relating to property within the jurisdiction, then the applicable law is Irish law. Where the proceedings relate to an arbitration held or to be held within the jurisdiction of the courts of Ireland, then the applicable law is Irish law.

Where the proceedings relate to the enforcement of an arbitrator's award or of obligations imposed by an award then the applicable law is Irish law.

COMMENCING THE ACTION

Complaint

District Court

Civil proceedings are instituted in the District Court by means of a "civil process". The facts forming the basis of the claim must be set out in the civil process together with the relief sought. Every civil process must show on the face of it the costs that would be payable by the defendant to the plaintiff if the defendant wished to settle the plaintiff's claim before entry of the proceedings. Each civil process must also cite the appropriate District, District Number and Area. It must also recite the facts that show that the court has jurisdiction.

There are three types of civil process:

(1) Summary civil process;
(2) Ejectment civil process; and
(3) Ordinary civil process.

Summary civil process is used in the pursuit of liquidated damages, for example, debt collection (excluding proceedings instituted in relation to hire purchase agreements or pursuant to the Money Lenders Act, 1933). Where it is permissible to use a summary civil process, judgment may be obtained against the defendant, without the necessity of attending court, if the defendant fails to defend the proceedings. This is known as obtaining judgment "in the office".

Ejectment civil process is used in order to recover possession of land where the rent is less than IR£5,000 per annum.

Ordinary civil process is used in all other circumstances.

The civil process is filed in the District Court Office — not sooner than 10 days after and not later than 14 days after service.

Where the amount of the claim might exceed the jurisdiction of the District Court (where the total damages in certain circumstances might exceed IR£5,000) and the plaintiff intends to abandon any amount in excess of the monetary jurisdiction, then this must be stated in the body of the civil process. Where the plaintiff sues in a representative capacity, this must also be stated in the civil process.

Circuit Court

Proceedings are instituted in the Circuit Court by way of a civil bill. The civil bill must contain an endorsement of claim which must state the nature and extent of the grounds on which the proceedings are brought, the relief sought, and if it is a money claim, the amount of the claim and the rate and amount of interest (if any) claimed. Where there is more than one claim, similar particulars must be given in respect of each claim and of each relief sought.

Where the amount of the claim might exceed the jurisdiction of the Circuit Court (IR£30,000) and the plaintiff intends to abandon any award in excess of the jurisdiction of the Circuit Court, this must be stated in the body of the civil bill. Where a plaintiff sues in a representative capacity, this must also appear in the body of the civil bill.

In actions claiming a debt or liquidated (specific) amount only, the endorsement of claim in addition to setting out the nature of the claim and the amount claimed for the debt must also state the costs, which will be payable by the defendant if the amount of the debt and costs are paid within six days after the service of the civil bill.

There are three types of civil bill. In equity proceedings, the civil bill will be headed "equity civil bill" and the body of the civil bill must contain such facts as may be necessary to show the jurisdiction of the court. In proceedings for ejectment on the title or proceedings issued for the purposes of establishing questions of title to land, the civil bill should be headed "title jurisdiction" and must contain a statement that the rateable valuation does not exceed IR£200 in order to show jurisdiction. All other civil bills should be headed "ordinary civil bill" and should be modified as the circumstances of each particular case require.

High Court

Proceedings in the High Court are instituted by way of originating summonses. There are three types of originating summons. These are:

(1) Summary summons;
(2) Special summons; and
(3) Plenary summons.

Each summons should contain an endorsement of claim, which indicates the general nature of the claim. A special summons must contain a special endorsement of claim, which is a statement of the general nature of the claim, and the facts supporting the claim. A plenary summons must contain a general endorsement of claim, which is a short statement of the nature of the plaintiff's claim. A summary summons sets out the facts, the nature and the amount of the plaintiff's claim. The summons is sometimes referred to as the "writ of summons" or simply as the "writ".

Proceedings are instituted by way of summary summons, pursuant to Order 2, Rule 1 of the Rules of the Superior Courts, in the following classes of claim:

(1) Actions for the recovery of a debt or liquidated demand in money payable by the defendant with or without interest; and
(2) Certain actions where a landlord seeks to recover possession of land, where the rateable valuation of the land is in excess of IR£200.00.

Proceedings are instituted by way of special summons pursuant to Order 3 of the Rules of the Superior Courts, in 22 classes of claim: The main classes of claim are as follows:

(1) The payment into court of any money in the hands of executors, administrators, or trustees;

(2) The determination of any question arising in the administration of any estate or trust;

(3) Applications for the taxation of bills of costs and for the delivery by any solicitor of deeds, documents or papers;

(4) Sale, delivery of possession by a mortgagor, or redemption, re-conveyance or delivery of possession by a mortgagee;

(5) Such other matters as the court think fit to dispose of by special summons.

The institution of proceedings by way of plenary summons is obligatory in all other cases, and include proceedings in respect of claims for tort, breach of contract and claims for personal injury.

Order 20, Rule 2 of the Rules of the Superior Courts provide that where proceedings are instituted by way of plenary summons, the plaintiff may deliver a statement of claim with the Plenary Summons or notice in lieu thereof, or at any time within 21 days from the date of service thereof. The statement of claim should state all the material facts on which the plaintiff relies and then claim the relief that he desires. It must give dates and details sufficient to inform the defendants specifically of the nature of the claim being made against him so that he will be able to decide whether he has a defence to the proceedings.

In certain types of claims, proceedings are commenced by way of petition instead of by way of originating summons. Examples of such types of claim are:

(1) Liquidation — proceedings to wind up companies pursuant to Order 74 of the Rules of the Superior Courts;

(2) Proceedings to make a person a ward of court pursuant to Order 67 of the Rules of the Superior Court;

(3) Bankruptcy — proceedings to adjudicate an individual bankrupt and wind up his estate and assets and distribute them among creditors.

Types of answer

Denials

DISTRICT COURT

The only obligation on the defendant is to give notice of his intention to defend. The nature of the defence need not be specified. The notice is served on the plaintiff's solicitor and on the court clerk.

CIRCUIT COURT

The defendant must enter an appearance within 10 days of service. This is merely a form of notice from the defendant to the court Clerk and to the plaintiff's solicitor indicating that the defendant has received the proceedings and intends to defend them. If the defendant fails to enter an appearance, the plaintiff may obtain judgment in default of appearance on foot of a motion.

The defendant must enter his defence within 10 days after the entry of appearance. The defence must refute every single fact and claim made in the civil bill if it is not admitted, even if only by way of general denial.

HIGH COURT

The defendant must enter an appearance to a summary or plenary summons within eight days of service. A defendant may enter an appearance to a special summons at anytime before hearing, but may not be heard in the proceedings, unless an appearance has been entered.

A defendant should deliver his defence (and counterclaim if any), within 28 days from the date of entry of the appearance, or the date of service of the plaintiff's statement of claim, whichever is the later.

The defendant must state in his defence every material fact on which he proposes to rely at the trial. He must deal specifically with every fact alleged in the statement of claim either admitting or denying it. He may plead further facts in answer to those he admits. He may object to the whole pleadings as not being sustainable in law.

In his defence, the defendant may also rely on a set-off or a counterclaim. All of these separate grounds of defence must be stated (as far as may be) separately and distinctly, especially where they are founded on separate and distinct facts. The defendants must deal specifically with each allegation of fact and claim that he does not admit as being true, except damages.

Denials — affirmative defences

DISTRICT COURT

It is not necessary to deny the plaintiff's claim at District Court level, a notice of Intention to Defend being sufficient to contest the plaintiff's claim.

There is a procedure whereby the defendant before the hearing may lodge, on notice to the plaintiff, a sum in court either with or without an admission of liability, in satisfaction of the plaintiff's claim. Should the plaintiff ultimately not obtain an order or an award for an amount greater than the sum of the lodgement, the plaintiff will be obliged to pay all costs of all parties after the date of lodgement.

CIRCUIT COURT

The defence to a civil bill must deal specifically with every fact and claim alleged in the endorsement of claim of the civil bill, either admitting the same or denying it. Further, the defence may plead further facts in answer to those facts that are admitted. The defendant may also set up a counterclaim or may claim a set-off. Such counterclaim or set-off would have the same effect as a cross action so as to enable the judge to pronounce final judgment on all the matters in the same action. If the defendant is setting up a counterclaim with the defence, the counterclaim should contain the same particulars of the defendant's claim as would be expected to be set out in the plaintiff's civil bill.

As in the District Court, there is a procedure whereby the defendant may make a lodgement with the defence. The effect of a lodgement in the Circuit Court is the same as that in the District Court, in relation to costs. After the defence has been filed, a lodgement may only be made with the permission of the court and, generally, the plaintiff will be awarded costs up to the date of any such order.

The defendant may also increase a lodgement previously made, but may only do so on one occasion.

HIGH COURT

The defence to a summons must deal specifically with every fact and claim alleged in the statement of claim or endorsement of claim (special or general) as the case may be, either admitting same or denying it. Further, the defence may plead further facts in answer to those facts that are admitted. The defendants may also set up a counterclaim or claim set off in his defence. If the defendant is setting up a counterclaim with the defence, the counterclaim should contain the same particulars of the defendant's claim as would be expected to be set out in the plaintiff's originating summons.

As in the Circuit Court, the defendant may at any time prior to defence, lodge a sum of money in court, on notice to the plaintiff, in satisfaction of the plaintiff's claim. If same is not accepted by the plaintiff and the plaintiff subsequently is not given an award greater than the amount of the lodgement, the plaintiff will be forced to pay all costs incurred by the defendant subsequent to the date of lodgement. There is a procedure whereby the defendant may increase a lodgement previously made, but may only do so on one occasion. A lodgement may only be made after a defence has been filed by permission of the court and, generally, the plaintiff will be awarded costs up to the date of the order.

Reply

As a defence is not required at District Court level, a notice of intention to defend being sufficient, a reply is not relevant at District Court level.

In the Circuit Courts and in the High Court, it is not necessary to reply to the defendant's defence, but a plaintiff may do so. A reply is rarely delivered, unless allegations of contributory negligence or a counterclaim are made in the defence.

Amendments and supplemental pleadings

In all courts, the possibility of amending pleadings is restricted. Pleadings may only be amended with the consent of all parties or on the basis of an order of the court. This also applies to the delivery of supplemental pleadings.

Joinder of claims and parties

A distinction should be drawn between joining causes of action, and in hearing separate causes of action at the same time. Joinder involves the consolidation of two separate actions into one. Separate cases may also be heard at the same time before the same judge as a matter of convenience where the same facts give rise to a separate cause of action. However, the claims remain separate and are not linked.

Joinder of claims by plaintiff

There are no provisions in the District Court rules for the joinder of actions by the plaintiff, however, this is possible in actions before the Circuit Court and the High Court.

CIRCUIT COURT

Where the plaintiff is in doubt as to the person against whom he is entitled to seek his remedy, he may join two or more defendants, such that the question to be decided may be determined as between all parties. It is not necessary that all the relief sought be sought from every defendant, or that every cause of action be against every defendant sought to be joined. The judge will, however, make such order as appears just in order to prevent any defendant from being required to attend any proceedings in which he has no interest.

HIGH COURT

Order 18 of the Rules of the Superior Courts provides for the joinder of causes of action. Order 18, Rule 1 provides that the plaintiff may join several causes of action in the same action, however, if it appears to the court that such causes of action cannot be conveniently tried or disposed of, the court may order separate trials to be had or to make such an order as may be necessary for the separate disposal thereof.

In general, no causes of action will be joined with an action for the recovery of land without leave of the court, except in certain specific situations. Order 18, Rule 8 of the Rules of the Superior Courts provides that any defendant who alleges that a plaintiff has united several causes of action, which cannot be conveniently disposed of together, may at any time apply to the court for an order confining the action, to such of the causes of action as may be conveniently disposed of together.

Joinder of claims by defendant

There are no provisions in the District Court rules for the joinder of actions by the defendant (or any other party), however, this is possible in actions before the Circuit Court and the High Court.

CIRCUIT COURT

Order 6, Rule 1 of the Rules of the Circuit Court provides that all persons may be joined in one action as plaintiffs in whom any right to relief in respect of or arising out of the same transaction or series of transactions, is alleged to exist, whether jointly, severally, or in the alternative, where if such persons brought separate actions, any common question of law or fact would arise, provided that if, on a motion or notice by any defendant, it appear that such joinder may embarrass or delay the trial, the judge may order separate trials, or make such other order as may be right and provided also that no person will be made a plaintiff without his consent.

Under Order 30, Rule 10 of the Rules of the Circuit Court, judgment may be given for one or more plaintiffs and against or in favour of one or more defendants. This gives the court the inherent power to determine what is at issue in any particular matter. As a pre-requisite, for the application of Order 30, Rule 10, the successful parties must be represented by the same solicitor and barrister and there should be no conflict of interest or tactical strategy between them. A person cannot be a plaintiff without his consent and if he is joined without his consent, he should apply to have himself struck out.

HIGH COURT

As in the joinder of claims by the plaintiff, claims may be joined by the defendant where such causes of action may be conveniently tried or disposed of together. Order 18, Rule 6 of the Rules of the Superior Courts provides that claims made by plaintiffs jointly may be joined with claims made by them or any of them separately against the same defendant.

Counterclaim

The defendant who wishes to make a counterclaim or who wishes to set off a claim against the claim of the plaintiff may do so by delivering a notice of counterclaim and/or set-off detailing the particulars of such counterclaim and/or set-off and sending same to the plaintiff and the court clerk, prior to the hearing. The defendant may waive the excess of any counterclaim, which is above the jurisdiction of the court or may issue separate proceedings in a higher court.

The defendant who wishes to make a counterclaim and/or set off a claim against the plaintiff's claim, may do so by incorporating the counterclaim and/or set-off, as part of his defence. This would have the same effect as if the defendant had issued separate proceedings. Any counterclaim in excess of the jurisdiction of the Circuit Court must be waived, unless the plaintiff consents to unlimited jurisdiction.

If the counterclaim does not arise out of the same facts or transaction as the plaintiff's claim, the plaintiff may apply for an order that the claim and counterclaim should be tried separately, on the basis that it cannot be conveniently tried by the same court or alternatively it cannot be tried at the same time as the plaintiff's claim.

Cross-claims

It is possible to have a cross-claim treated as a counterclaim to an action. Generally, cross-claims are used where separate causes of action lie between the same parties. Cross-claims as opposed to counterclaims must be brought where a successful application is made to the court for an order that a counterclaim be disposed of by way of independent action.

Third party claims

Such claims, generally, arise where a defendant in proceedings:

> (1) Claims against any person not already a party to any form of contribution or indemnity;

(2) Claims against such person, any relief or remedy in relation to or connected with the subject matter of the proceedings or substantially the same or some relief or remedy claimed by the plaintiff as against the defendant; or

(3) Requires that any question or issue relating to or connected with the original subject matter of the proceedings should be determined, not only as between the plaintiff and the defendant, but also as between either or both of them and such other person.

District Court

The District Court Rules provide that the defendant may serve a notice on the third party, within 10 days of the service on the defendant of the civil process as issued by the plaintiff, the third party notice containing a statement of the claim by the defendant as against the third party. A copy of the plaintiff's civil process must also be served and copies given to the plaintiff and to the court Clerk.

Circuit Court

There are no specific provisions under the Circuit Court Rules for joining of third parties. There is, however, a general provision that indicates that in the absence of specific rules in the Circuit Court Rules, the High Court Rules are to apply.[2]

High Court

Order 16 of the Rules of the Superior Courts deals with third party procedure. The application to join a third party is made to the court by way of motion on notice to the plaintiff, and the court may grant the defendant permission to issue the third party notice to the third party.

Impleader and interpleader

When goods or chattels have been seized in execution by a Sheriff or other officer charged with the execution of process and any claimant alleges that he is entitled to the goods or chattels by way of security for debt,

2. Accordingly, reference should be made to the following paragraph.

the courts may order the sale of the whole or a part thereof and direct the application of the proceeds of the sale in such manner and on such terms as may be just. The court may in any interpleader proceedings make such orders as to costs as in the circumstances may be just and reasonable.

When the execution creditor has given notice to the Sheriff or his officer that he admits the claim of the claimant, the Sheriff may thereupon withdraw from possession of the goods claimed, and may apply for an order protecting him from any action in respect of the said seizure and possession of the said goods, and the court may make any such order as may be just and reasonable in respect of same.

Where the execution creditor does not in due time admit or dispute the title of the claimant to the goods or chattels and the claimant does not withdraw his claim thereto by notice in writing to the Sheriff or his officer, the Sheriff may apply for an interpleader order, and the court may, in and for the purposes of such interpleader proceedings, make all such orders as to costs, fees, charges and expenses as may be just and reasonable.

Intervention

In the Circuit Court, intervention is only possible in actions for the recovery of land. In the High Court, it is possible to intervene in actions for the recovery of land, admiralty actions *in rem*, matrimonial causes and probate actions. A motion may be brought pursuant to Order 63, Rule 1(13) of the Rules of the Superior Courts for liberty to appear in any such proceedings.

OBTAINING INFORMATION PRIOR TO TRIAL

Types of discovery

Depositions

In practice, depositions are very rarely used in Irish civil law proceedings. Depositions may not be used in evidence without an order of the court. In the absence of oral evidence, practitioners rely on evidence taken by a "commissioner". Generally speaking, evidence is only taken on commission when the person giving the evidence is outside the jurisdiction and is not willing to attend before the court or where their attendance before the court would not be possible, for example, due to illness.

There are no provisions at District Court level for the use of depositions. At the Circuit Court and High Court levels, the court Rules provide that the courts may order the examination of any person and such examination or deposition may be given in evidence on such terms that the court may direct.

Interrogatories to parties

There is no provision in the District Court Rules for the taking of interrogatories. The Rules of the Circuit Court make no specific provision for the taking of interrogatories, but there is a provision that provides that in the absence of a specific rule as to any subject, the High Court Rules mentioned hereunder are to apply to the Circuit Court.

The Rules of the Superior Courts allow either the plaintiff or the defendant after delivery of the statement of claim or defence, as appropriate, to deliver interrogatories for the examination of the opposing party. Further, interrogatories may only be delivered with the permission of the court.

A party may ask the court to decide whether interrogatories are unreasonable or vexatious or should be struck out on the grounds that they are prolix, oppressive, unnecessary, irrelevant, unreasonable or scandalous. In the absence of any reply whatsoever, the parties seeking the reply may apply to court for an order directing the person to whom the interrogatories are addressed to reply to the same.

Discovery and production of property (physical evidence)

DISTRICT COURT

There are no provisions in the District Court Rules for the discovery of documents, but a party may compel the other party to produce documents at the hearing of the action by service of a notice to produce, which specifies the documents required to be produced, or by issuing a witness summons in the form of a *subpoena duces tecum*, which will require the person who is summoned to appear and to bring with him and to produce accounts, papers or other documents in his possession.

CIRCUIT COURT AND HIGH COURT

A party may make an application to the court for an order directing the other party to the proceedings to make discovery on oath by way of affidavit of all documents, which are or have been in that other party's possession or power relating to the issues in the proceedings. As a matter of practice, such order is granted if the party seeking the order has previously requested discovery on a voluntary basis. An order to allow the party seeking discovery to inspect the original documents referred to in the affidavit, is also granted.

A party may object to production of documents on the grounds that they are privileged, for example, communications between the client and lawyer. The affidavit must set out the nature of the documents in respect of which privilege is claimed, and the reason why such privilege is claimed. If there is any dispute as to whether or not a document is the subject of privilege, the court will decide.

A party who is inspecting documents, following discovery, is entitled to take copies of the documents. If a party fails to make discovery in response to an order made against it, the party in whose favour the order was granted may apply for an order of attachment. A party who fails to make discovery, may also find that the court will order its claim struck out (if it is a plaintiff) or its defence struck out, if it is a defendant.

There is no provision in the Rules of the Circuit Court allowing for discovery against a third party who is not a party to the proceedings. The method through which documents in the custody or control of a third party are produced is by way of a notice to produce or *subpoena duces tecum* — the same procedure that applies in the District Court.

The Rules of the Superior Courts allow for discovery against a third party not a party to the proceedings. If it appears to the Master of the High Court that such a third party is likely to have or has had in its possession, custody or power any documents that are relevant to the issue in the proceedings, or that such party is likely to be in a position to give evidence which is relevant to any issue in the proceedings, the court may order such third party to make discovery. The party seeking discovery will be liable to pay the costs incurred by the person making discovery.

Use of discovery at trial

Full use of discovery is allowed at trial. The authenticity of documents may be proved by one of the following methods:

> (1) Calling the writer of the document as a witness;
> (2) Calling a person who saw the document being executed;
> (3) Proving the handwriting;
> (4) Proving the attestation of a document; or
> (5) Securing an admission of authenticity from the opponent.

INTERIM PROTECTION OF ASSETS PENDING TRIAL

Jurisdiction to grant injunctions is vested in the High Court and in the Circuit Court. The various types of injunctions available are:

> (1) *Quia timet* injunction — where it is anticipated that a wrongful act will be committed, the court has equitable jurisdiction to grant an injunction to prevent the act being committed;

(2) Prohibitory — where the court orders the commission or continuance of a wrongful act or omission to cease;

(3) Mandatory — where the court orders the person to do something positive;

(4) Interlocutory injunction — an interlocutory injunction is granted to preserve the *status quo* until the plaintiff's claim for a perpetual injunction has been determined; and

(5) Perpetual injunction — this is a final injunction which is granted after a full hearing of the issues.

Provisional attachment

Provisional attachment is possible under Irish Law by way of:

(1) A *Mareva* injunction; or

(2) An *Anton Piller* order.

Mareva injunction

Where a plaintiff can show that the defendant has assets within the jurisdiction of the court and that there is real risk that the defendant will either remove such assets from the jurisdiction or will dissipate such assets, then the court may grant an injunction restraining the defendant from removing such assets from the jurisdiction or from dissipating such assets pending trial and/or execution.

Anton Piller order

An *Anton Piller* order is a mandatory injunction requiring the defendant to permit the plaintiff to enter into his premises in order to inspect and/or to remove any documents or items of property. Essentially, an *Anton Piller* order is an order in a nature of a search warrant.

The applicant for an *Anton Piller* order must have a very strong *prima facie* case and the potential or actual damage must be of a very serious nature. There must also be clear evidence that the defendant may dispose of or destroy evidence before any inter-parties application may be made.

Interlocutory injunction

Where the matter is sufficiently urgent, the court will grant an injunction on foot of an *ex parte* application. Such an injunction will normally only last until the next motion day where the arguments of both parties may be heard and such an injunction is known as an interim injunction. Following the granting of an interim order, the plaintiff may apply for an interlocutory injunction to bind the defendant until a full hearing can take place. The defendant is entitled to appear at such hearing and to show cause why an interlocutory order should not be made.

An interlocutory injunction is granted by the court where it is necessary to preserve the *status quo* until the plaintiff's claim for perpetual injunction has been adjudicated. In order to obtain an interlocutory injunction, the plaintiff must show that there is a serious question or issue to be tried, and the court must then proceed to consider whether the balance of convenience lies in favour of granting an injunction or not.

It should also be noted that an injunction will only be granted where damages are an inadequate remedy. Further, the plaintiff must give an undertaking to compensate the defendant if it is decided, after a full trial that an injunction was unwarranted.

SUMMARY JUDGMENTS

Adjudication without trial or by special proceedings

A procedure exists in all courts of first instance whereby claims for a debt or liquidated money demand may be adjudicated without trial.

District Court

If the defendant fails to enter a notice of Intention to Defend, the plaintiff may then proceed to obtain summary judgment once the specified court date has expired. The plaintiff may apply for judgment after the specified court date by lodging with the District Court Clerk the District Court Decree — this is the instrument of judgment and execution (the document that enables the plaintiff to enforce his judgment).

If the defendant does enter a notice of intention to defend, then the matter proceeds to a full plenary hearing.

Where the defendant has defaulted in entering an appearance or a defence as the case may be, the plaintiff may apply for judgment to be entered against such defendant and the said application will be supported, *inter alia*, by an affidavit of debt, verifying the plaintiff's claim.

Where the defendant does enter an appearance and a defence, the plaintiff may either:

(1) Bring a motion to strike out the defence, where the defence is vexatious and is merely entered for the purposes of delaying proceedings; or

(2) Serve a notice of trial and upon which he may proceed to a full hearing of the issue.

High Court

If the defendant fails to enter an appearance, the plaintiff may obtain summary judgment against him by lodging documents in the Central Office of the High Court, including the plaintiff's affidavit of debt.

If the defendant does enter an appearance, then the plaintiff may apply by way of a motion to the Master grounded on an affidavit, for liberty to enter final judgment against the defendant. If the Master decides that the defendant does not have a *prima facie* defence, then he will grant the plaintiff liberty to enter final judgment.

If the Master of the High Court is satisfied that there is an arguable case and that the defendant may have a defence, then the Master will refer the matter to plenary (full) hearing before a High Court judge. The defendant will be allowed to enter his defence. A notice of trial is then served and in due course the case will go on for full hearing before a High Court judge.

Default judgments

District Court

If the defendant does not enter a notice of Intention to Defend in summary proceedings, judgment may be entered in default in the office. In all other types of cases, even if the defendant fails to enter an appearance, the plaintiff must still prove his case to a District Court judge, although the defendant might not be allowed to appear or to defend the case.

Circuit Court

In summary proceedings, it is possible to obtain judgment in default of appearance or defence. In all other types of proceedings, the plaintiff must bring a motion for judgment before a Circuit Court. On the first occasion of a motion for judgment, the court will usually allow the defendant further time to enter an appearance and defence.

If, however, the defendant continues to be in default of appearance following the first order, judgment will usually be granted on bringing a second motion for judgment in default. Even where the plaintiff succeeds in obtaining judgment in default of appearance, he still must appear before the court in order to prove his claim. The defendant will not be allowed to appear, however, in order to defend the same.

High Court

In summary proceedings, it is possible to obtain judgment in the office in default of appearance.

Once an appearance has been entered in summary proceedings, it is not possible to obtain a judgment in the office. The plaintiff must then apply by way of a motion.

In non summary proceedings, the plaintiff is obliged to bring a motion for judgment in default of appearance or defence where the defendant had not filed a defence within the appropriate time. Even if the plaintiff obtains judgment in default, he must still prove his claim. However, the defendant will not be allowed to appear in order to defend the same.

Other means of termination without plenary trial

Other means of termination without plenary trial in Ireland are voluntary dismissal and dismissal for failure to prosecute. Judicially assisted settlement does not occur in Ireland.

Voluntary dismissal

DISTRICT COURT

The District Court Rules do not provide any formal means for terminating proceedings by the plaintiff prior to the trial. In practice, the court will strike out the proceedings if requested to do so.

CIRCUIT COURT AND HIGH COURT

The plaintiff may at any time by notice in writing wholly discontinue his action against all or any defendants (or withdraw any part or parts of his alleged cause of complaint) and thereupon pay such defendant's costs of the action, or, if the action is not wholly discontinued, the costs occasioned by the matter so withdrawn.

Dismissal for failure to prosecute

DISTRICT COURT

As the plaintiff is not obliged to serve any further proceedings subsequent to the civil process being served, there are no District Court Rules dealing with the issue of failure to prosecute. If the plaintiff continually adjourns proceedings to such an extent that the defendant is prejudiced in his defence of the action, the defendant can apply at trial stage to have the claim struck out or the court may take it on itself to do so.

CIRCUIT COURT AND HIGH COURT

The defendant may, apply to the court by notice of motion to dismiss the proceedings, with costs, for want of prosecution. Where the plaintiff or defendant fails to comply with an order for discovery, he will be liable for attachment and will be liable to have his action dismissed (if a plaintiff) or his defence struck out, if a defendant. As a matter of practice, the court will not dismiss an action for want of prosecution until approximately two years have elapsed, since the last step in the proceedings was taken.

TRIAL

Setting the case for trial

District Court

A return date (that is a date for hearing) is specified on the civil process, which is served on the defendant. Depending on the practice of the District Court in any particular district, the case will either be heard on the return date or a date for hearing will be assigned to the case. No additional steps are necessary to set the case down for trial.

Circuit Court

The Rules provide that when a defence has been duly entered, the plaintiff or the defendant may serve notice of trial. A notice of trial is the document that sets a case down for hearing, and enters the case in a list for hearing.

High Court

There is a difference between serving a notice for trial and setting a case down for hearing. Notice of trial will be given before setting down the action for trial. Unless within 14 days after the notice of trial is given, the action will be set down by one party or another, the notice of trial will be no longer in force. The party desiring to set down the proceedings for trial will do so by delivering to the court office a copy of the notice of trial together with two copies of the whole of the pleadings, one of which will be for the use of the judge at the trial.

Scope and order of trial

The court has the power to determine all issues in any cause or action. The plaintiff will first present his case. After any witness has given his evidence, the witnesses are then cross-examined. The plaintiff may then re-examine the witnesses as to any matters that arose out of the cross-examination. Once the plaintiff has finished presenting his case, the defendant will then present his defence. All witnesses for the defence are first examined, then they may be cross-examined and re-examined by the defendant in respect of anything arising out of the cross-examination. The plaintiff must prove his case on the balance of probabilities in a civil case.

Submission of evidence

In practice, most proceedings are conducted in English. A litigant has a constitutional right to conduct his case in the Irish language or in the English language, but does not have a right to have the entire proceedings heard in either Irish or English. Every person has a right to seek the assistance of an interpreter.

Any party may serve a notice to submit facts calling on the other party to admit, for the purposes of the cause, matter, or issue only, any specific fact or facts mentioned in such notice. An admission for the purposes of the trial only is not binding at a new trial. Failure to respond to a notice to admit facts is not an admission of the said facts. Any admissions, if not made during the hearing, will be in writing. Otherwise an admission may be made orally by a party in court. A formal admission is binding so that any other evidence to prove the fact is unnecessary. However, the admission must be clear and unambiguous.

The burden of proof rests on a party to prove any allegation made by him. The plaintiff must firstly prove those material facts that entitle him to relief and the defendant must then disprove the plaintiff's entitlement to relief.

The burden of proving certain specific facts is alleviated by accepted principles such as judicial notice and presumptions. Judicial notice refers to common-sense matters that do not require expert evidence and which the judge will know from his everyday life, (for example, that cars in Ireland drive on the left hand side of the road). There are a large number of presumptions of law in existence, which have been created either by statute or by Common Law. Some of the presumptions are general presumptions, while other presumptions depend on proof of a particular fact before coming into operation.

The effect of a presumption is to operate so as to shift the burden of proof from one party to the other. One example of a presumption relates to proceedings arising out of road traffic accidents where the driver of a vehicle, which is involved in a road traffic accident, is not the owner of the vehicle. The driver is presumed to be the servant or agent of the owner and consequently the owner of the vehicle may be made liable for the activities of the driver.

In the absence of any agreement in writing between the solicitors of all parties, the witnesses at the trial of any action will be examined *viva voce* in an open court. The court may at any time, for good and sufficient reasons, order that any particular fact or facts be proved by affidavit, or that the affidavit of any witness be read at the hearing or trial on such conditions as the court may think reasonable or that any witness, whose attendance in court ought for some sufficient cause to be dispensed with, be examined by interrogatories or otherwise before a commissioner or examiner.

The role of the trial judge in the presentation of evidence

The trial judge decides whether evidence is admissible (relevant to the facts that are at issue) and may as a matter of practice, ask any witness such questions as he thinks necessary in order to determine the issue. The judge has no inquisitorial role, the proceedings being accusatorial in nature.

Evidence

Nature and purpose of evidence

The purpose of evidence is to support the claims made by either party in the action. Evidence may be admissible or inadmissible. Evidence is admissible if it is not excluded by some canon of the law of evidence, such as the rule against hearsay.

Evidence is receivable if it is both admissible and relevant to the facts in issue. Direct evidence is evidence that proves a fact directly, if accepted. Primary facts are facts proved by direct evidence. Circumstantial or indirect evidence is evidence that is probative of a fact, but not conclusive in and of itself. Generally, circumstantial evidence is capable of proving a fact in civil proceedings.

Kinds of evidence

DOCUMENTS

All documents material to a fact at issue are admissible provided:

(1) They can be authenticated; and
(2) They are not privileged.

A document may be authenticated by:

(1) Calling the writer of the document as a witness;
(2) Calling a person who saw the document being executed;
(3) Proving the handwriting;
(4) Proving the attestation of the documentation; and
(5) The parties agreeing to admit the document.

The contents of a document may be proved by secondary evidence if the original has been destroyed or cannot be found after due search. Similarly, such contents may be proved by secondary evidence if production of the original is physically or legally impossible. At Common Law, secondary evidence may also be used to prove the contents of public documents if production of the originals would entail a high degree of public inconvenience.

A number of statutes provide for the proof of the content of various public and judicial documents by secondary evidence, which takes the form of an examined, certified or office copy. An examined copy is a copy signed and certified to be accurate by an official who has custody of the original. An office copy is a copy made in the office of the court and authenticated with the seal of the court.

PRIVILEGE

Privilege in civil proceedings arise in the following situations:

(1) Privilege against self-incrimination (where a witness in civil proceedings is asked a question which, if answered, could lead to criminal proceedings being brought against him);
(2) Marital privilege;
(3) Lawyer-client privilege or legal professional privilege; and
(4) "Without prejudice" communications.

In general, however, the only types of privilege relevant to civil proceedings in Ireland are lawyer-client privilege and "without prejudice" communications.

There are two basic aspects to legal professional privilege relating to:

(1) Communications between client and his solicitor; and
(2) Communications with third parties.

Communications between a client and his solicitor may not be given in evidence without the consent of the client. In order to attract this legal professional privilege, however, the communication must occur in the course of a professional legal relationship. The privilege belongs to the client who may waive or not waive the privilege as he sees fit. Under Irish law, it is permissible for the parties to the litigation to testify at the hearing of the said action.

The second aspect of legal professional privilege relates to communications between client and third parties or between legal advisors and third parties that are made for the purpose of pending or contemplated litigation. Pending litigation refers to a situation where legal proceedings have been issued. Contemplated litigation refers to a situation where it is expected that legal proceedings may be issued. It is not required that litigation be the sole purpose of communication. It is only required that litigation be the dominant purpose of the communication.

The privilege only attaches to "communications". Communications in this sense may be oral or in writing. Privilege does not extend to cover physical evidence, or, for example, to questions relating to the client's demeanour or appearance. The privilege may be lost by waiver. A party cannot tender only part of a document as this would result in disclosure of parts that were merely favourable to that party. The whole of the document must lose its privilege, if it is to be admitted in evidence.

There is a qualification in relation to the legal professional privilege, and this is where third parties gain access to information that is in fact privileged. The privilege only relates to the production of the evidence. In other words, privilege prevents the litigant's opponent from demanding access to the evidence. However, if the opponent obtains the evidence, then the question of privilege becomes irrelevant as the evidence is now in the hands of the opponent. It should be noted, however that Irish courts will refuse to admit evidence when they see fit because of the manner in which it was obtained.

"WITHOUT PREJUDICE" COMMUNICATIONS

If a party to litigation makes an offer in settlement of the proceedings, such admission might possibly weaken his position should the offer be refused and the action proceed to hearing. The rule therefore evolved that any offer made "without prejudice" cannot be entered in evidence without the consent of the maker and the receiver.

Should an agreement be reached between the parties, then the privilege ceases to apply and "without prejudice" communications may be looked at to determine if agreement was in fact reached and as to the terms of that agreement. The position is best summed up by stating that "without prejudice" means "without prejudice to the offeror's position should the offer be refused".

JUDGMENT AND KINDS OF RELIEF

Final judgment

Not all judgments in any particular case are final judgments. It is also possible for interim judgments to exist in any cause or matter prior to the determination of the final judgment.

After a full plenary hearing of any cause of action, the trial judge will give final judgment (subject to an appeal) in relation to the same. The trial judge may decide to give judgment immediately after the hearing of the case, or he may decide to wait and give judgment at a later date after contemplating all the issues. The trial judge may give a written or oral judgment. If the trial judge gives a written judgment, the judgment will be read in court.

Entry of judgment

It is only necessary to enter judgment at High Court level in summary proceedings. Where the defendant has entered an appearance, the plaintiff must bring a motion for liberty to enter final judgment.

Kinds of relief

SPECIFIC PERFORMANCE

Specific performance is an equitable remedy and hence discretionary. However, the discretion is exercised in accordance with settled principles. It will not usually be granted where damages are an adequate remedy and it may also be refused on grounds such as hardship, laches, or inequitable conduct on the part of the plaintiff. In order to obtain a decree of specific performance, it is necessary to establish that there is in existence a binding and valid contract. There must also be consideration for the promise sought to be enforced (even where the contract is under seal) as under Irish law, equity will not come to the aid of a volunteer.

Specific performance is most frequently sought and given in contracts for the sale of land. Specific performance is not normally granted in a contract for the sale of property other than land as damages would be a sufficient remedy. If, however, the subject matter is a unique or rare object such as a particular painting, specific performance may be granted. The courts will not grant a decree of specific performance where its enforcement would require constant supervision by the court.

Courts will not grant a decree of specific performance if the contract is only capable of being enforced against one of the parties. In general, specific performance will not be granted where only part of the contract can be enforced.

Specific performance may be refused on the grounds that the contract was induced by misrepresentation or a mistake contributed to, however, innocently, by the plaintiff. The court will not grant specific performance where performance of the contract is impossible. Nor will the court grant specific performance of a contract where, to do so, would be futile. The relief may also be refused if it appears to the court that the plaintiff has been substantially in breach of his obligations under the contract or is not ready or willing to perform his obligations thereunder.

DECLARATION CONCERNING LEGAL RELATIONS

An order taking the form of a declaration simply states what the rights of the parties are in law. There is nothing to prevent a declaration being granted without any accompanying relief in an appropriate case. However, this rarely, if ever, occurs. Certain statutes exclude the courts, either expressly or by implication, from granting declaratory relief. Declaratory relief may also be refused because the order sought would effectively determine the guilt or innocence of a person charged with a criminal offence.

POST-TRIAL MOTIONS

Attacks on judgments

The only way in which it is possible to attack a judgment by way of motion is through an application for judicial review. The leave of the court must first be obtained before an application for judicial review can be made. An application for leave to apply for judicial review must be made promptly and will be made within three months from the date when grounds for the application first arose, or six months where the relief sought is *certiorari*, unless the court considers that there is good reason for extending the period in which the application will be made.

The High Court may grant orders of *certiorari*, *mandamus* and prohibition in civil proceedings. *Certiorari* will lie to challenge an order for error or informality or for some abuse of jurisdiction or procedures in making the order. *Mandamus* directs the court to do some particular thing, while prohibition will restrain a court from exercising jurisdiction of a judicial character not within, or in excess of, powers conferred.

The High Court may also grant an order for *quo warranto* in civil proceedings. *Quo warranto* will lie against the person who claims any office, franchise, liberty or privilege of a public nature, directing him to show by what authority he supports his claim to that position in order to determine his right to do so.

The essential point about invoking judicial review is that this question of jurisdiction only is dealt with by the court and therefore the case is not re-heard.

Grounds for a new trial

The court may, on hearing an application for judicial review, order a re-hearing of the cause or matter where it grants an order of such *certiorari*, *mandamus*, prohibition or *quo warranto*. It should be noted, however, that a re-hearing will usually only be ordered following an appeal.

The mistake and/or excusable neglect of one party or his legal representatives will not be sufficient grounds to obtain a new trial.

Newly discovered evidence would not be sufficient grounds to bring a motion for judicial review. Newly discovered evidence may be admitted with the court's permission.

The fraud of a party to proceedings will not be a sufficient ground to bring a motion for judicial review. Fraud would, however, be a sufficient ground for an appeal where a judgment was obtained by deceit, for example, where the defendant was not aware of the existence of the proceedings.

ENFORCEMENT AND EXECUTION OF JUDGMENTS

Remedies

Writ of execution

The District Court decree is the writ of execution at District Court level. The Execution Order is the writ of execution at Circuit Court level. The *fi fa* is the writ of execution at High Court level.

Writs of sequestration, attachment or garnishment

Section 8 of the Debtors (Ireland) Act, 1872 provides that sequestration is available against a judgment debtor who cannot be arrested, or to enforce an order against any human or corporate person. A writ of sequestration is extremely harsh and is sparingly used. In general, the courts will not grant an order of sequestration if it can be avoided. When issued, a writ of sequestration binds all the properties of the person, both real and personal. The sequestrator is obliged to retain possession of the property until the owner has purged his contempt.

A judgment requiring any person to do any act, other than the payment of money, or to abstain from doing anything may be enforced by an execution order by way of attachment or committal. Attachment of earnings is also possible in matrimonial proceedings.

Rules of court provide that the courts, with the exception of the District Court, may order that all debts owing from a third person (the garnishee) to a debtor will be attached and that the garnishee will pay such debts to the person who has obtained judgment instead of paying the same to the judgment debtor. By the same or any subsequent order, the garnishee may be ordered to appear before the court to show cause why he should not pay to the person who has obtained such judgment or order the debt due from the garnishee to such debtor, or so much thereof as may be sufficient to satisfy the judgment or order. If the garnishee disputes his liability to the debtor, the judge may, instead of making an order that execution will issue, order that any issue necessary for determining the garnishee's liability be tried or determined accordingly.

Bankruptcy or liquidation

Bankruptcy — a debtor may be adjudicated a bankrupt by order of the High Court. A creditor is entitled to petition the court for the debtor to be adjudicated a bankrupt if the debtor fails to satisfy a demand for payment of the debt, even though the creditor has not obtained judgment. Bankruptcy is, generally, regarded by the court as a remedy of last resort. The court therefore, in practice, will not adjudicate a debtor bankrupt, unless the plaintiff has already obtained judgment and has already attempted to recover the debt by all other means open to him.

If the debtor has committed an act of bankruptcy (other than failing to satisfy a bankruptcy summons) a petition to adjudicate a debtor bankrupt may be grounded on that act of bankruptcy within three months prior to the presentation of the petition. Eight of the acts of bankruptcy are specified in Section 7 of the Bankruptcy Act 1988.

The effect of adjudication in bankruptcy is that all the estate (both real and personal) of the debtor vests in a court officer, the official assignee in bankruptcy, to be realised for the benefit of the debtor's creditors. In a bankruptcy, the secured creditors are paid first out of any security that they hold. Preferential creditors then receive the payments due to them and if there is any balance remaining, this is then divided proportionately among the unsecured creditors.

Liquidations — Section 213 (e) of the Companies Act, 1963 provides that a company may be wound up by the court if the company is unable to pay its debts. Also, the company may be wound up for other specified reasons on the application of the company or its members or directors. In practice, a court liquidator as distinct from a voluntary liquidator only arises in the situation where the debtor company is incapable of paying its debts when they fall due.

Section 212 of the Companies Act, 1963 provides that only the High Court will have jurisdiction to wind up any company.

It should be noted, however that the winding up order does not terminate the company's existence. The company remains in existence until the court makes an order under Section 239 of the Companies Act, 1963, dissolving the company.

On making a winding up order, the court appoints a liquidator or liquidators to carry out the winding up. The court directs what remuneration the liquidator is to receive. The liquidator is an agent of the company, with fiduciary obligations arising from his office and with statutory obligations imposed on him by the acts. It is the function of the liquidator to wind up the company and to distribute such assets as are available among the creditors.

Receivership orders

It is possible for receivership orders to be made in three situations:

(1) Over a limited liability company;
(2) Receiver by equitable execution; and
(3) Under the Conveyancing Acts.

LIMITED LIABILITY COMPANIES

The function of a receiver appointed by a creditor who holds a debenture mortgage is to receive all of the assets of a company subject to the debenture mortgage on behalf of the creditor whom he represents and to dispose of these assets in order to pay off the amount due together with interest. As a matter of practice, the debenture mortgage also gives him the power to manage the company's affairs with power to carry on its business for as long as is necessary.

RECEIVER BY WAY OF EQUITABLE EXECUTION

Equitable execution is a process that allows execution against an interest in property (which cannot be done under the normal methods of enforcement). Receiver by way of equitable execution is appointed over an interest in property. The effect of the appointment of a receiver by way of equitable execution is very limited. It does not transfer the property concerned to the judgment creditor, nor does it even give him a charge in it. A receiver by way of equitable execution may be appointed by an Irish court over money payable by a person resident outside the jurisdiction to a person resident within the jurisdiction.

RECEIVER APPOINTED UNDER THE CONVEYANCING ACTS

Various statutes confer on mortgagees the power to appoint a receiver over land. Section 19(1) of the Conveyancing Acts, 1881 confers the power to appoint a receiver on mortgagees whose mortgages are created by deed. This covers most legal mortgages and registered charges. It also applies to an equitable mortgage or charge where the mortgage or charge is created by deed. Otherwise, the equitable mortgagee or chargee must apply to the court for the appointment of a receiver, on such terms as it thinks fit, where it appears to be just or convenient to do so. The power to appoint a receiver arises when the mortgage money is due but remains unpaid.

Arrest

A procedure exists at District Court level for the making of an order for the payment of a monetary judgment granted by any court, by one or more instalments, and if the debtor fails to comply with the same, then he may be liable to arrest and imprisonment and for contempt for failing to obey the order. This procedure is known as the Enforcement of Court Orders Act Procedure.

Only the District Court has jurisdiction, irrespective of the amount of the judgment or the court in which the judgment was originally obtained. If the debtor fails to pay the instalments due, it is possible to apply for a committal order, for a maximum period of imprisonment of three months. It should be noted that the imprisonment of the debtor does not operate as satisfaction or extinguishment of the debt or any part thereof.

It should also be noted that a debtor may be imprisoned under the Bankruptcy Acts for absconding from the jurisdiction or for failing to assist in an investigation of his affairs. Similar provisions apply under the Companies Acts.

Brussels Convention

The Brussels Convention on Jurisdiction and the Enforcement of Judgments in Civil and Commercial matters was enacted into Irish law by the Jurisdiction of Courts and Enforcement of Judgments (European Communities) Act, 1988. Consequently, any order of the Master of the High Court allowing a foreign judgment to be enforced is treated as if it were an Irish court judgment.

APPEAL

All issues dealt with in the court of first instance are subject to review in an appeal. In general, a full review of the facts is permissible in all appeals. An appeal on the facts of the case lies from the District Court to the Circuit Court; from the Circuit Court to the High Court and from the High Court to the Supreme Court. It should be noted that in an appeal from the High Court to the Supreme Court new evidence may only be introduced if it was not available at the time of the original hearing and with the consent of the court. All parties may request review of any decision of a court of first instance as of right.

District Court

An appeal lies from any decision of the judge of the District Court to the Circuit Court judge. The appeal may be taken by any party and the appellant obtains a new hearing of the case. A judge of the Circuit Court, when hearing an appeal from the District Court, is bound by the same jurisdictional limitations as are imposed on the District Court and the order made on appeal must be one that could have been validly made in the District Court.

Circuit Court

In appeals from the Circuit Court, where the case was heard without oral evidence, the appeal is to a judge of the High Court in Dublin. In any other case, the appeal is by re-hearing to the High Court on circuit. Any party may appeal, and it is possible to appeal against a specific part of the judgment. An appeal will not operate as a stay of proceedings on the judgment or order appealed from unless the Circuit Court judge or on appeal the High Court sitting in Dublin, will so order, and then only on such terms (if any) as the court will think fit.

High Court

An appeal lies from the High Court to the Supreme Court. The appellant may appeal against the whole or part of any judgment or order. Where there has been a trial by jury, every notice of appeal will include an application for a new trial and such other relief as may be sought.

The notice of appeal will in every case set out the grounds for appeal and the relief sought. The Supreme Court has the power to order a new trial.

Where an *ex parte* application has been refused in whole or in part by the High Court, an application for a similar purpose may be made *ex parte* to the Supreme Court within four days from the date of such refusal, or within such enlarged time as the Supreme Court may allow. Discretionary review is available by way of judicial review.[3]

CONCLUSIVENESS OF THE JUDGMENT

Res judicata

Under Irish law, the actual decision on the facts of a case is only binding on the parties to that particular action. It is possible to make a plea of *res judicata* under Irish law.

Law of the case

Under Irish law, the doctrine of precedent (*stare decisis*) is binding on the courts. A decision of a District Court judge cannot create legal precedent. The decision of a Circuit Court judge is binding on all lower courts (namely the District Court) and on other Circuit Court judges. A decision of the High Court creates legal precedent and is binding on all lower courts (namely, the District Court and the Circuit Court) and on other High Court judges. A decision of the Supreme Court is binding on all lower courts (namely, the District Court, Circuit Court and High Court). Such decision is also binding on the Supreme Court itself.

3. Already dealt with under Post-Trial Motions above.

CHAPTER 11

ITALY

MARIO BELTRAMO
Studio Legale Beltramo
Rome, Italy

INTRODUCTION

Civil proceedings in Italy are governed by the Code of Civil Procedure, approved by Royal Decree Number 1443 of 28 October 1940 as amended by a very large number of subsequent provisions.

As originally conceived, the Code was divided into four books: Book I entitled "General Provisions", Book II on "cognisance proceedings", Book III on "enforcement proceedings" and Book IV on "special proceedings". Book I contains titles on judicial organs, on the public prosecutor, on the parties and counsel, on the initiation of proceedings, on the powers of the judge and on procedural acts. Book II contains titles on proceedings before tribunals, on proceedings before the pretore and conciliator judges, attacks on decisions and on labour proceedings. Book III contains titles on executable titles, on forcible expropriation, on execution by delivery, on enforcement of obligations to perform or refrain from an act, on oppositions to executions and on the suspension and termination of execution. Book I contains titles on summary proceedings, precautionary measures, on status and family law matters, on public records, on succession, on joinder of actions, on release of charges on land, recognition and enforcement of foreign judgments, and on arbitration.

The most important amendments were brought about by Law Number 581 of 14 July 1950, Presidential Decree Number 857 of 17 October 1950 and Law Number 533 of 11 August 1973, which replaced in its entirety Title IV of Book II setting forth provisions on labour disputes. By 1990, the volume of ever more complex statutes and regulations resulting in a multiplication of litigation threatened the court system with paralysis. This inspired the government of drastic procedural reform. Law Number 353 of 21 November 1990 contains "Urgent Rules for Civil Proceedings" and Law Number 274 of 21 November 1991 establishes a new first instance court, the Justice of Peace (*Giudice di Pace*) to replace the lowest existing first instance court, the Conciliator Judge (*Giudice Conciliatore*). After a transitional period, these new provisions all entered into full force in April 1995.

The present chapter deviates from the organisation of the Code in many respects. It adheres generally to the systematic outline imposed throughout the chapters in this book, dealing with the (i) judicial system,

(ii) the initiation of proceedings, (iii) precautionary measures, (iv) trial, (v) the decision of disputes, (vi) summary proceedings, (vii) proceedings before special tribunals, (viii) certain special proceedings, (ix) attacks on decisions and, finally, (x) enforcement proceedings. This compromise represents an effort to reconcile the structure of the source of the law with a convenient and uniform presentation. The reader should note that those matters dealt with under (ii), (iv), (v), (vii) and (ix) related primarily to normal, that is cognisance, proceedings while (iii), (vi), and (vii) fall mainly under the regulation of "Special proceedings" in Book IV, and (x) encompasses both matters regulated in Book III and Book IV (recognition of foreign judgments).[1]

JUDICIAL SYSTEM

Jurisdiction

In the Italian system, jurisdiction (*giurisdizione*)[2] means the authority of the State to exercise its judicial functions through agencies (the courts) aimed at ensuring the actual implementation of the rules established in a general and abstract manner by the legislator.

Jurisdictional authority is subject to certain distinctions depending on the nature of the matter involved and is exercised through a variety of courts. As a rule, all matters falling within the scope of the Civil Law come under the jurisdiction of the ordinary courts (*giurisdizione Ordinaria*), which also embraces disputes against the public administration when subjective rights are involved. If legitimate interests, as opposed to substantive rights, are involved and the public administration is a party to the dispute, the matter comes under the jurisdiction of the administrative courts, which include the Regional Administrative Tribunals (*Tribunale Amministrativo Regionale* — TAR) and the Council of State (*Consiglio di Stato*) or other special courts, such as the Court of Accounts (*Corte dei Conti*) which, in addition to auditing the accounts of the State and of certain other public entities, exercises jurisdictional functions in matters of government pensions, the Tribunal of Public Waters (*Tribunale delle Acque Pubbliche*) and the Tax Boards (*Commissioni Tributarie*).

The courts comprised in *Giurisdizione Ordinaria* are: the Justice of Peace (*Giudice di Pace*), the *Pretore*, the Tribunal (*Tribunale*), the Court of Appeal (*Corte d'Appello*), located throughout the national territories,

1. The following are the provisions of the Code of Civil Procedure only entered force in April 1995: Article 168–*bis*, Par. III, IV, V; Article 178, Par. II; Article 184–*bis*, Article 187, Par. IV; Article 208; Article 240, Article 268, Article 269, Article 271, Article 274–*bis*, Article 348, Article 350, Article 352, Article 356, Par. I; Article 447–*bis*.

2. The dangers of translating legal terms of art have induced me to make frequent use of Italian terms in italic type and in brackets to avoid possible misinterpretation.

and the Court of Cassation (*Corte di Cassazione*), which sits in Rome. The first two are monocratic courts, while the others are in panel form even though, pursuant to Law Number 353/90, the Tribunal operates normally as a monocratic court and makes rulings in panel form only in cases expressly contemplated by law (appellate proceedings, partitions, proceedings in chambers etc.).

The Code of Civil Procedure imposes a limitation to the civil jurisdiction authority by providing in Article 4 that a foreign citizen can be named a defendant in the Italian courts in certain contexts only, without prejudice to the provisions of the 1968 European Community Brussels Convention concerning the jurisdictional competence and the enforcement of judgments in civil and commercial matters.

In view of these jurisdictional limitations and distinctions, questions may arise with respect to the existence of jurisdiction of the ordinary courts in respect of a given dispute.[3] These may be raised by the courts *ex officio* at any stage of the proceedings, and are considered and resolved in the manner indicated in the Code of Civil Procedure, Article 187. The relevant decisions are subject to appeal and to review by the Court of Cassation in joint chambers.[4] Furthermore, the parties, until a decision on the merits in first-degree proceedings is made, are entitled to submit immediately these jurisdictional issues to the Court of Cassation acting in joint chambers.

Pending review by the Court of Cassation, the court can suspend the proceedings only if it feels that the application for review is not manifestly inadmissible or that the challenge to jurisdiction is manifestly unfounded.

The proceedings must be resumed within six months from notification of the decision affirming the jurisdiction of the ordinary court.[5]

Competence

Competence (*Competenza*) is the sphere of jurisdictional authority actually vested in each court with respect to a given dispute. Competence is regulated by Articles 7 *et seq.* of the Code of Civil Procedure on the basis of criteria concerning the value, the subject matter and the territorial venue of the litigation. The general rule is that the value criterion applies in all cases unless otherwise provided by rules concerning the subject matter of the litigation.

The value of a dispute, for the purposes of competence, is determined on the basis of the claim asserted. If more than one claim is asserted in the same proceedings against the same person (so-called objective cumulation), the claims add to one another. If more than one person claims the fulfilment

3. Code of Civil Procedure, Article 37.
4. Code of Civil Procedure, Articles 360–362.
5. Code of Civil Procedure, Article 367, Par. II.

of a portion of a single obligation (so-called subjective cumulation), competence by value is measured by the total obligation, even if not all debtors or creditors are represented in the proceedings.

The Justice of Peace has competence over cases relating to movable property not exceeding 5-million lire, unless they are by law reserved for the competence of another court; over cases concerning damages resulting from the circulation of vehicles or vessels having a value not in excess of 30-million lire; and over cases of opposition to injunctions referred to in Law Number 689/81[6] not exceeding 30-million lire in value. The Justice of Peace is competent by subject matter without limitations of value in proceedings relating to the settlement of boundaries and observance of distances; in those relating to the extent of and procedures for the use of condominium services and relationships between holders or users of dwelling premises in respect of discharges, noises, etc.; in proceedings to object to administrative sanctions as provided in Article 75 of Decree of the President of the Republic Number 309 of 9 October 1990.[7]

The *Pretore* is competent over cases, even if relating to immovable property, of a value not exceeding 20-million lire that are not within the competence of the Justice of Peace as well as over those referred to in Article 8, Par. II, Code of Civil Procedure. The *Pretore*, acting as a labour court, is competent over individual disputes in employment matters and over disputes concerning compulsory social security and health insurance.

The Tribunal is competent over all cases exceeding in value 20-million lire that are not attributed, by way of subject matter, to the *Pretore* or the Justice of Peace. Furthermore, the Tribunal is always competent in cases dealing with taxation, in cases relating to the status and capacity of persons, or to rights to honourable titles, in incidental proceedings concerning the falsity of documents in civil matters and, in general, in cases whose value cannot be determined.

Competence by territory constitutes the criterion of distribution of cases among courts of the same type; it is determined on the basis of the connection between the territory and the court that exercises its jurisdiction thereon and, it being established in the interests of the parties, is generally derogable by an agreement between them evidenced by a written document and referring to one or more specific matters.

The judicial agencies competent by territory (venues) are divided into: general venue (*foro generale*), which is that where a party may be summoned

6. Law No. 689 of 24 November 1981 makes provisions for the collection of certain administrative penalties through the issuance of injunctions similar to a *decreto ingiuntivo* and the related opposition procedure.

7. Decree of the President of the Republic No. 309 of 9 October 1990, Article 75 provides for certain administrative sanctions in matters of unlawful possession of drugs.

as a defendant in any dispute which is not expressly attributed to another venue under the law, and which, with respect to individuals, is the venue where the defendant has his residence or domicile or abode while, with respect to juristic persons, it is where the legal address, or an establishment or a representative authorised to appear in court is located; special venues (*fori speciali*), which are inderogably fixed by the code only for certain specific disputes. Failure to observe the rules on competence may be raised by the parties and by the court not later than the first hearing; if it is an infringement of rules on derogable territorial competence, the issue may be raised only by the defendant in his answer brief: if the objection is not timely raised, it is barred under the law.[8]

If a conflict arises between two or more courts with respect to the competence to deal with a given dispute, the so-called petition for competence settlement (*regolamento di competenza*) to the Court of Cassation is made. An issue on competence may be raised *ex officio* or *ex parte* and, in the first instance, the court to which the dispute has been submitted is called on to determine it. If the court finds that it is competent, it affirms its competence either expressly, by a judgment, or impliedly through its decision on the merits; if it finds itself not to be competent, it so rules and refers the parties to the court that it deems to be competent. The latter court, if it does not deem itself competent, will promote *ex officio* the above-mentioned proceedings to settle competence. The competence settlement proceedings may also be instituted by the party who feels injured by the ruling on competence of the court to which the dispute has been submitted.

INITIATION OF PROCEEDINGS

Proceedings commence with the issuance of the citation (*citazione*)[9] whereby the plaintiff exercises his right to sue. The citation has the dual function of summoning the defendant to appear before the court (*vocatio in ius*) and to submit the claim to the court, thus determining the subject matter of the proceedings (*editio actionis*).

The citation must contain:

(1) The designation of the court to which the claim is being submitted;

(2) The given-names, the surnames and the residences of the plaintiff, of the defendant, and of the persons who act as their representatives or caretakers;

(3) The subject matter of the claim (*petitum*);

8. Code of Civil Procedure, Article 38.
9. Code of Civil Procedure, Article 163.

(4) A description of the facts and legal grounds for the remedy sought (*causa petendi*);

(5) An indication of the evidence and documents that the plaintiff intends to introduce;

(6) A request that the defendant enter an appearance no less than 20 days prior to the first hearing, with an express warning that failure to observe this deadline will result in the forfeiting of the right to assert a counterclaim and to raise objections that would not be susceptible of being raised by the court *ex officio*; and

(7) The Christian and family names of the attorney for the plaintiff and a reference to the power of attorney.

If the defendant is a juristic person or an association, the citation must contain the name and indication of the person or persons having the authority to act for it in court. The citation must be signed by the attorney or by the plaintiff, if the appointment of an attorney is not required.

Pursuant to the Code of Civil Procedure, Article 164, a citation is null and void if the designation of the court, the identification of the parties or the subject matter of the claim are missing or altogether unclear; if the period allowed to the defendant to enter an appearance is shorter than required under the law or if the indication of the date of the first hearing is missing; if the warning to the defendant of the consequences of his failure to enter a timely appearance is missing or a description of the facts on which the claim is based is not included. The nullity of the citation is cured if the defendant does enter an appearance, or the court having raised the deficiencies *ex officio* orders that the citation be renewed.

Service

The claim is brought to the attention of the defendant by service (*notificazione*) of the citation effected by a process server (*ufficiale giudiziario*). From that point in time, the proceedings are in existence and pending.

If service of process is null because of omissions by the process server,[10] it can be cured by the appearance of the defendant or by a renewal of service on order of the court. Such nullity does not extend to the citation itself. However, defective service concerning the identity of the destinee or the location where service should have been effected results in a nullity of the citation as well, which is incapable of attaining its normal effect.

10. Code of Civil Procedure, Article 160.

Appearance

A formal contact between the parties and the court is not established by the simple citation but only through their formal appearance (*costituzione delle parti*). The plaintiff must enter an appearance (*costituzione dell' attore*) within 10 days after service of the citation by filing with the clerk's office a request for entry in the docket and a file containing the original citation and the documents offered in evidence.[11]

The defendant must enter an appearance (*costituzione del convenuto*) at least five days prior to the first hearing by depositing his own file with an answer and any documents. In the written answer, the defendant must state his position as to the facts laid down by the plaintiff in the citation, must submit under penalty of forfeiture his counterclaims and those procedural and substantive objections which cannot be raised by the court *ex officio*, must indicate the evidence which he intends to submit, set forth his prayer for relief and, as the case may be, declare his intent to join a third person in the proceedings at the first hearing.[12] Pursuant to the Code of Civil Procedure, Article 171, if none of the parties enters an appearance within the required time limits, the proceedings are stricken from the docket. If the plaintiff does not appear within the period contemplated by law or at the first hearing, the court may, on the defendant's motion, provide for the continuation of the proceedings in the plaintiff's absence (*contumacia*). If the defendant does not appear within the period contemplated by law or at the first hearing, the court provides for the continuation of the proceedings in the defendant's absence (*contumacia*).[13]

After the entry of appearances, the parties usually act through their counsel, on whom process must be served and notices given in the course of the proceedings, except in particular cases specified by the law.[14] From this time on, the clerk becomes the custodian of the files of the parties, enters the case in the general docket and compiles the official court file (*fascicolo d'ufficio*), into which all records of the case must be inserted.[15]

Parties

Parties to the proceedings are the plaintiff (*attore*) and the defendant, (*convenuto*). The status of a party is acquired as a result of the institution

11. Code of Civil Procedure, Article 166.
12. Code of Civil Procedure, Articles 166, 167.
13. Code of Civil Procedure, Article 171, Par. II.
14. Code of Civil Procedure, Article 170.
15. Code of Civil Procedure, Article 168.

of the action, joinder in pending proceedings or succession into the position of one of the original parties. Those having legal capacity, in other words individuals and juristic persons, to associations, committees, business companies and some estates, such as a bankruptcy and an unclaimed inheritance,[16] to which particular autonomy is recognised in the Italian system, are eligible to be a party to the proceedings.

Not all those eligible to be a party have the capacity of appearing in the action, that is, to validly perform procedural acts: Incompetent persons must appear in the proceedings through a representative, acting in the name and on behalf of the represented party, while emancipated and disabled persons appear in the proceedings with the assistance of a curator and juristic persons through those who have the authority to represent them. A procedural substitute (*sostituto processuale*) is a person who acts in the proceedings in his own name, but for somebody else's right, and since the results of the action affect also the holder of the right, substitution is possible only in those cases contemplated by law.[17]

A party may appear in civil proceedings before the Justice of Peace personally in cases whose value does not exceed 1-million lire and when authorised by the court in view of the nature and the scope of the case, in labour disputes and in those involving compulsory social security and health insurance not exceeding in value Italian lire 250,000[18]. Otherwise, the law requires the parties to be represented by counsel to act in legal proceedings. Except in proceedings before the Justice of Peace, counsel (*difensore*) must be an attorney duly admitted to the bar and, in proceedings before the Court of Cassation, a member of a special register. Counsel is normally appointed by the party by means of a general power of attorney (*procura ad lites*) or special power of attorney (*procura ad litem*). A party destitute of financial means may obtain legal assistance at the charge of the State.

Public Prosecutor

The Public Prosecutor (*pubblico ministero*), as an authority of the State established to guarantee the implementation of the law in those matters where the protection of general or social interests that cannot be left to the sole initiative of private persons, may initiate the action as a plaintiff where expressly provided for by law.[19] He is under an obligation to join not only in the actions that he himself could institute, but also in

16. Civil Code, Article 528.

17. For example, a creditor may, in a subrogation action, exercise the rights and patrimonial actions that belong to his debtor *vis-à-vis* third parties.

18. Code of Civil Procedure, Articles 417 and 442.

19. Code of Civil Procedure, Article 69.

matrimonial disputes (including those of personal separation of the spouses and dissolution of the marriage), in those relating to the status and legal capacity of individuals and in the other cases contemplated by the law.[20] The Public Prosecutor is entitled to join in any other action, where he deems it appropriate for the protection of public interest.

Multiple parties

A *litis consortium (litisconsorzio)* occurs when there are several parties to the proceedings. The litisconsortium may be mandatory (*litisconsorzio necessario*)[21] when the judgment cannot be rendered except *vis-à-vis* several parties participating in the substantive relationship asserted in the proceedings, or optional (*litisconsorzio facoltativo*)[22] when several actions are exercised within the same context to reduce the number of proceedings and to avoid conflicting decisions. In the latter case, as the aggregation of proceedings is not imposed by the law, each case retains its autonomy and cases may be separated on the concurrent motion of all parties or if the court believes that the aggregation would entail delays or make the proceedings too onerous.

Joinder

A joinder (*intervento*) occurs when proceedings already initiated are entered by a strange party (other than the original parties, i.e., by a third person). The latter may join the proceedings of his own initiative, so-called voluntary joinder (*intervento volontario*), or at the initiative of one of the parties or of the court, so-called compulsory joinder (*intervento coatto*).[23]

A voluntary joinder[24] is based on the possibility that a judgment handed down *inter alios* may produce indirect consequences on the interests of a third person. The joinder will be classified as a principal joinder (*intervento principale*) if the intervenor asserts a right of his own, in conflict with both the plaintiff and the defendant; it will be classified as an autonomous supporting joinder (*intervento adesivo autonomo*) if the intervenor although retaining his own autonomy, takes a position equal or parallel to that of one of the parties; and as a dependent supporting

20. See Code of Civil Procedure, Article 70.
21. Code of Civil Procedure, Article 102.
22. Code of Civil Procedure, Article 103.
23. See "Consolidation" below.
24. Code of Civil Procedure, Article 105.

joinder (*intervento adesivo dipendente*) if the intervenor, although not vested with autonomous eligibility to act or to resist, has nevertheless an interest in the success of one of the litigants.

A compulsory joinder may occur at the instance of one of the parties[25] who deems the case to be common to the third person or wants to be indemnified by the latter, or by an order of the court[26] requiring one of the parties to summon the third person into the proceedings.

Change of parties

In the course of the proceedings, two events may occur which involve the change of one or more parties:

(1) A succession in the proceedings (*successione nel processo*),[27] when a party ceases to exist (e.g., a merger of companies, the winding up of a juristic person, by death or another reason); and

(2) The right being disputed is transferred individually rather than in the context of a universal transfer of rights.

In the first case, the universal successor assumes the proceedings and if there is more than one successor they enter the proceedings as co-claimants. In the second, a distinction must be made between a transfer occurring by a transaction *inter vivos* where the proceedings continue between the original parties and their effects extend also to the successor, and a case in which the transfer occurs *mortis causa,* where the proceedings are continued by or against the successor.

PRECAUTIONARY MEASURES

Nature

Precautionary measures (*procedimenti cautelari*)[28] discharge an instrumental function, since they are aimed at securing the outcome of cognisance or enforcement proceedings. Indeed, in view of the often excessive length of those proceedings, it may well happen that the defendant's financial or factual conditions change, at the risk that the plaintiff may not ultimately obtain satisfaction of his claim. The technique of precautionary protection consists in enabling the party to apply to the

25. Code of Civil Procedure, Article 106.
26. Code of Civil Procedure, Article 107.
27. Code of Civil Procedure, Article 110.
28. These are "special proceedings" regulated in Book IV of the Code.

court for the issuance, on completion of a summary examination, of a provisional measure when two conditions prevail:

(1) *Fumus boni juris* (the reasonable appearance of a lawful right), to wit, the probable existence of the right which will be the object of normal litigation on the merits; and

(2) *Periculum in mora* (risk in delay) to wit, the likelihood of a damage that may be incurred by the plaintiff as a result of the length of normal litigation on the merits.

The main feature of precautionary protection is its provisional nature: The measure issued by the court will not definitively settle the issue at stake.

Procedure

Pursuant to the amendments introduced by Law Number 353/90, the entire subject matter of precautionary measures has been rationalised. Pursuant to the new rules set forth in Articles 669–*bis* to 669–*quaterdecies* of the Code of Civil Procedure, three distinct phases can be identified in the proceedings:

(1) An authorisation phase in which the court, having verified the existence of the conditions justifying the action, grants or denies, by an order or decree, as the case may be, the precautionary measures;

(2) An implementation or enforcement phase which is conducted before the same court as issued the precautionary measure or before the enforcement court; and

(3) A phase of attack of the precautionary measure, which is quite novel in the procedure and is conducted before a court different from that which issued the measure.

Request for the precautionary measure is made by an application filed in the clerk's office of the court that is (or would be in the event of measures requested before instituting litigation or in the context of an arbitration clause) competent to take cognisance of the merits. Following submission of the application, the court may:

(1) Require both parties to enter an appearance and, omitting all formalities which are not deemed essential, proceed in the most suitable manner with an examination of the matter; and

(2) Where prejudice to the implementation of the precautionary measure must be avoided, issue such measure by a decree *inaudita altera parte* (without hearing the opposite party), subject, however, to making summary inquiries.

In the case of (2) above, the court appoints in the same decree a hearing for the personal appearance of the parties and a deadline within which the applicant must serve it on the other party. In either case, the proceedings are concluded by the issuance of a court order rejecting or granting the application. An application that has been rejected may be submitted again when there are changes in circumstances or new grounds in fact or at law are alleged. If an application submitted prior to the institution of normal litigation proceedings is granted the court's order must set a peremptory deadline not exceeding thirty days in order to commence litigation on the merits. The precautionary measure loses its effect in the following cases:[29]

(1) When litigation on the merits is not commenced within this deadline or, after having been commenced, is extinguished; or

(2) When the bond required by the court against possible damages has not been posted; and

(3) When the right for whose protection the precautionary measure had been granted is declared to be non existent by a judgment, even though it has not become *res judicata*.

A precautionary measure can be granted by the Italian court even if the merits of the case fall within the jurisdiction of a foreign court or are to be adjudicated by arbitration in Italy or abroad pursuant to a valid arbitration clause. In these cases the precautionary measure loses its effect if the party who applied for it does not seek enforcement in Italy of the foreign judgment or arbitration award within the peremptory time-limits provided for in the law or by international treaties; or when a foreign judgment or arbitration award is handed down declaring the non-existence of the right for whose protection the measure had been issued.

Supervision

Two types of supervision can be exercised over precautionary measures:

(1) The court before which litigation on the merits is pending may, on an *ex parte* request, issue an order amending or revoking the precautionary measure, even if issued prior to the institution of the action, but only if there have been changes in circumstances;[30] or

29. Code of Civil Procedure, Article 669–*novies*.
30. Code of Civil Procedure, Article 669–*decies*.

(2) An attack that permits a new evaluation of the lawfulness or advisability of the measure issued, can be submitted to a court different from that which issued the measure within 10 days from the date of notice of the order, and the attack proceedings are conducted in chambers.[31]

The court after summoning the parties, issues not later than 20 days after the filing of the attacking petition, an order not subject to appeal confirming, amending or revoking the precautionary measure.[32] The presiding judge of the panel vested with the adjudication of the attack, when measure causes serious damage for supervening reasons, may provide for the suspension of its enforcement or condition it on the posting of an adequate bond.

Specific precautionary proceedings

Subject to a few details, the above procedure applies to various specific precautionary measures.

Sequestration

Sequestration (*sequestro*) is a preventive form of protection that allows the preservation and prevents the disposition of specified property for the period necessary for a settlement of the dispute or the satisfaction of the claimant's rights. The Code of Civil Procedure contemplates two types of sequestration:

(1) Judicial sequestration (*sequestro giudiziario*), aimed at ensuring the custody of movable and immovable property or universalities of assets whose ownership or possession is disputed, or of books, registers or other things which are intended to be offered in evidence when a party's right to obtain their exhibition or disclosure is being disputed and it is advisable to provide for their custody;[33] and

(2) Preserving sequestration (*sequestro conservativo*) aimed at freezing unspecified property of the debtor, to prevent its

---

31. Code of Civil Procedure, Article 669–*terdecies*.

32. The court ruling on the challenge will be the Tribunal, against the measures issued by the *Pretore*; the panel against measures issued by an individual judge; another chamber of the Court of Appeal or, in the absence of it, the nearest Court of Appeal against the measures issued by the Court of Appeal.

33. Code of Civil Procedure, Article 670.

removal or alteration, which constitutes, in a sense, an advanced attachment founded on the reasonable appearance of a rightful claim (*fumus boni juris*) and on the risk of the justifiable fear of losing the security of the claim (*periculum in mora*).

The precautionary function of sequestration is fully discharged when judgment on the merits ascertains the foundation of the claimant's right. Thus, in the case of judicial sequestration of specified property, the sequestrating creditor acquires an autonomous possession of the property, while in a case of preservative sequestration, sequestration is converted into attachment when an enforceable judgment is rendered.

Denunciation of new work or feared damage

Denunciation of new work (*denuncia di nuova opera*) is aimed at preventing dangers or limitations in the enjoyment of property resulting from activities undertaken by others on the neighbour's property.[34] The action cannot be instituted if the work is completed or if more than one year has elapsed from its commencement.

Denunciation of feared damage (*denuncia di danno temuto*) is aimed at preventing the risk of serious and immediate damage originating from a building, tree or other things already existing in the neighbour's property. Both actions can be brought by the owner or the holder of another real right of enjoyment or by the possessor of the property affected by the new activity or the risk of the feared damage. If the party bound by the precautionary measure infringes the prohibition to perform the damaging action or to change the existing conditions, the court may, on request of the other party, order the original conditions to be restored at the cost of the infringer. Possessory proceedings are intended to provide a fast remedy for the restoration of a pre-existing situation of possession, independently of the underlying right of ownership.

Possessory proceedings

Possessory proceedings provide a fast remedy for the restoration of a pre-existing situation of possession, independent of underlying proprietary rights.

34. Civil Code, Article 1171.

A repossession or spolium action (*azione di reintegrazione di spoglio*) is the action by which a possessor deprived in a violent or clandestine manner of his possession demands that it be restored to him.[35]

A maintenance action (*azione di manutenzione*) is the action intended to protect from a disturbance in fact or at law a person who has possessed immovable property or a universality of immovables for at least one year.[36] The possessor or *detentore* (he who detains) of property is entitled to bring the action. The action can be brought against the moral or material author of the *spolium* or disturbance.

Urgent measures

Article 700 of the Code of Civil Procedure is a kind of catch-all provision intended to ensure provisionally the effect of a subsequent decision on the merits. It is of a temporary and ancillary nature. The prerequisites for the issuance of an urgent measure (*provvedimenti d'urgenza*) under Article 700 are a well founded reason to fear that one's right will not be satisfied (*periculum in mora*); imminent and irreparable prejudice threatening the right during the time required to assert it through normal litigation. Since Article 700 is resorted to when no other specific remedy is applicable in the circumstances, the contents of the measures issued thereunder can be of a most varied nature and are actually left to the imagination of the plaintiff and of the court as long as they are suitable to provide an anticipation of the ultimate juridical relief sought by the plaintiff without prejudicing the decision on the merits.

Typical examples of Article 700 urgent measures are: in domestic disputes, the measures in respect of the custody of children, pending a separation of the spouses; in matters of support, a provisional determination of its amount; in matters of competition, an injunction to refrain from using similar trademarks; in matters of personality rights, an order to refrain from using unlawfully another person's name and causing prejudice to him. The instrumental nature of urgent measures in the context of litigation on the merits results in such measures being automatically voided when they are replaced and absorbed by a decision on the merits that has become *res judicata*.

The use of the Code of Civil Procedure, Article 700 procedure has expanded to what may be termed an excessive extent in the last few years, clearly in view of the courts' desire to find a fast method to overcome, if only provisionally, the stagnation of ordinary litigation. Actually, this trend resulted in "urgent measures" often frustrating the

35. Civil Code, Article 1168–1169 and Code of Civil Procedure, Article 703.
36. Civil Code, Article 1170 and Code of Civil Procedure, Article 703.

due process envisioned for civil litigation. The recent amendments to the Code of Civil Procedure, concerning mainly the possibility of reviewing urgent measures issued pursuant to Article 700, are intended to restore an adequate balance between curing provisionally prejudicial situations in urgent cases and of ensuring a fair and non-precipitous consideration of the litigants' rights.

TRIAL

Initial hearings

The first stages of trial are *trattazione* and *istruzione*. *Trattare* means to handle an affair or a piece of business. Thus, the expression *trattazione* can roughly be translated to "handling" and refers to the conduct of the proceedings from the conclusion of the introductory phase to the phase immediately preceding the decision. The handling includes a phase known as "examination" (*istruzione*, or *istruzione probatoria*), devoted mainly to the taking of evidence and arguments on the admissibility of the relevant motions and other procedural issues. Responsibility for both the *trattazione* and the *istruzione* of the case is vested in a single judge, in case of a monocratic court such as the Justice of Peace or the *Pretore* or, if the dispute falls within the competence of the Tribunal, in a member of the panel appointed by the President to act as examining judge (*giudice istruttore*).

Examining judge's role

The Code of Civil Procedure, Article 175 provides that the examining judge will exercise all powers for the most expeditious and loyal development of the proceedings. It is his duty to conduct the proceedings from the conclusion of the introductory phase up to the pleadings before the panel, of which he becomes a member in the capacity of the reporting judge.

Such function is substantially of a preparatory nature and will be radically changed with the implementation of the amendments introduced by Law Number 353/90 whereby an examining judge who considers the case to be ready for decision may proceed directly to handing down the judgment. Only certain categories of cases exclusively reserved for a panel decision[37] would be excluded from this possibility.

37. Royal Decree Number 12 of 30 January 1941 "Rules on the judicial system" Article 48 as amended by Law Number 353/90.

The measures adopted by the examining judge are usually in the form of an order (*ordinanza*), which may be revoked or amended[38] by the examining judge or by the panel.

The examining judge in charge of the case is also vested with the authority to order payment of pecuniary penalties,[39] to require the posting of a bond by a party and to issue precautionary measures in the course of the proceedings.

Preliminary stage

The handling of the case may not commence unless at least one of the parties is present. If none of the parties appears at the first hearing, the examining judge orders the case to be stricken from the docket and unless the proceedings are resumed within one year, orders their extinguishment. If only the plaintiff appears, the proceedings continue in the absence of the defendant. If only the defendant appears and expressly moves for a continuation of the proceedings, the examining judge will provide for such continuation or, in the absence of the defendant's appearance or motion, will order the case to be stricken from the docket and declare the extinguishment of the proceedings.

Furthermore, the examining judge will preliminarily verify the regularity of the appearance of the parties and the compliance with the rules concerning representation, custodianship and authorisations.

First hearing

These activities of the judge are preliminary to the actual holding of the first hearing, in which the examining judge will freely interview the parties present and, when the nature of the case permits, try to promote a settlement.[40] Failure of the parties to appear without a justifiable reason constitutes conduct that can be taken into account for the purposes of the decision of the case.

Based on the facts alleged by the parties, the examining judge asks them for appropriate clarifications and points out the matters which can

38. Except in the cases listed in the Code of Civil Procedure, Article 177: when orders have been issued upon the agreement of the parties if the issue concerns rights which can be disposed of by the parties although these orders may be revoked by the examining judge or the panel if all parties are in agreement; when they have been expressly declared non-attackable by law; when special means of attack are contemplated under the law; when a complaint has been submitted to the panel pursuant to Code of Civil Procedure, Article 178.

39. Code of Civil Procedure, Article 179.

40. Code of Civil Procedure, Article 183.

be raised *ex officio* and which he considers appropriate to be dealt with; no amendments to the prayers for relief, objections and conclusions already submitted are permissible, unless authorised by the examining judge.

Pre-award measures

In order to meet immediate requirements and to discourage delaying tactics, Law Number 353/90 contemplates that the examining judge may pass awards in the course of the proceedings, which may anticipate wholly or in part the effects of a possible judgment.

Indeed, Article 186–*bis* of the Code of Civil Procedure provides that up to the moment of the submission of the final prayers for relief, the examining judge may on an *ex parte* motion order the payment of the sums not disputed between the parties. The order is without prejudice to the decision of the case, and its foundation may be contested in the final pleadings.

Pursuant to Article 186–*ter* of the Code of Civil Procedure, the examining judge may, in the course of the examination phase, issue an order to pay a sum or to deliver a specified item of movable property if the conditions which are required for the issuance of a "*decreto ingiuntivo*" under the terms of Articles 633 *et seq.* of the Code of Civil Procedure prevail. If the order to pay or deliver relates to the entire subject matter of the claim and the defendant does not appear or does not file an opposition, the proceedings are concluded and the order becomes final.

It is in this perspective that the order must assess the costs of the proceedings. However, if the order does not relate to the entire subject matter of the dispute or if the defendant files an opposition, the proceedings will continue and the order may be revoked or amended and is without prejudice to the ultimate decision on the merits.

If the proceedings are extinguished, the order to pay or deliver does not lose its effect and becomes enforceable, if not enforceable already.

Setting for judgment

In the order setting forth the conclusive measures of the preliminary handling, the examining judge will appoint a hearing for the continuation of the examination of the case. If the case appears to be ready for a decision without need to take additional evidence (e.g., if the dispute hinges only on a point of law), the examining judge will refer the case to the panel, unless he must decide it as a single-judge court. If the case entails preliminary issues, the examining judge will determine in his discretion whether the resolution of such issues should be postponed until the time of the final judgment, proceeding in the meantime with the taking of evidence, or whether the parties should be referred to the panel for a separate decision on such preliminary issues.[41]

Introduction of evidence

If no preliminary issues arise and it appears necessary to take evidence, the examining judge will usually allow the introduction of such evidence as he considers relevant for the purposes of the judgment. Resolving the issues concerning the introduction of evidence may require adequate arguments, and each party may move for a postponement of the hearing. If so, the examining judge will allow one party a peremptory time limit for the exhibition of documents and the submission of new evidence and the other party another time limit (also peremptory) to move for the introduction of opposite evidence.[42]

Failure to meet these time limits results in a preclusion of the motions to introduce evidence. Accordingly, after the second hearing no new evidence can be introduced, unless the examining judge acknowledges that the party failed to observe the time limit for reasons beyond his control, or when the introduction of new evidence by a party becomes necessary because it was admitted by the court *ex officio*.

Taking of evidence

The examination includes the taking of the evidence (*istruzione probatoria*) necessary for the decision of the issues identified and argued in the handling process. The introduction of evidence is often a crucial phase of the proceedings, in that under the terms of Article 2697 of the Civil Code, "one who asserts a right in judicial proceedings must prove the facts on which the right is based" and "one who asserts the invalidity of such facts or claims that the right has been modified or extinguished, must prove the facts on which the defence is based" (*onere della prova*). If the party fails to offer such proof, he loses the case. This burden of proof only falls on the defendant if the plaintiff proves the facts on which the claim is based. The parties may reverse or modify the burden of proof by express agreements when the issue concerns rights that can be disposed of by the parties or when the reversal or modification does not make the exercise of the right exceedingly difficult.[43]

41. Code of Civil Procedure, Article 187.
42. Code of Civil Procedure, Article 184.
43. Civil Code, Article 2698.

Evidence can be taken by the examining judge alone or with the assistance of an expert; by the *Pretore* of the location where the evidence must be taken, on delegation by the examining judge; or by the panel, when deemed necessary. Provisions for the taking of evidence are made by an order fixing the time, location and procedure. Allowing evidence to be introduced assumes its admissibility and relevance.

The court cannot base its decisions on facts that have not been proved by the parties or, when applicable, by the prosecutor. The court may, however, proceed on its own initiative with inspections and take into account facts that are of generalised common knowledge. The court may also infer elements for its decisions from the behaviour of the parties in the proceedings. Once the evidence has been collected, the court will freely evaluate it in its prudent appraisal except in the case of the so-called "legal evidence" by whose results the court is strictly bound.[44]

In the Italian legal system, evidence is a matter of substantive law to the extent that it ensures the certainty and protection of rights[45] but plays of course a fundamental role in the procedural law and is, therefore, also governed by the Code of Civil Procedure.

Documentary evidence

Documentary evidence (*prova documentaria*) is contained in a document already existing prior to the commencement of the proceedings. Two types of documentary evidence are identified in the Civil Code:

(1) A public act (*atto pubblico*),[46] which is an instrument drawn up with the required formalities by a notary or another public official authorised to clothe such an instrument with public reliability; and

(2) A private writing (*scrittura privata*),[47] which is any document not drawn by a public official but signed by the party.

Subject to an action to establish its falsity, a public act constitutes full proof that it was drawn by the public official it represents as having been

44. Such as in the case of an oath or confession; Civil Code, Articles 2736 *et seq.* and 2730 *et seq.*

45. Civil Code, Book VI, Title II.

46. Civil Code, Article 2699.

47. Civil Code, Article 2702.

drawn by, as well as of the declarations and facts which the public official attests having taken place in his presence or having been performed by him.[48]

Subject to an action to establish falsity, a private act constitutes full proof of the origin of the declarations set forth therein, but only if the person against whom it is asserted recognises in court the signature or if the signature is legally deemed to have been recognised. A signature that has been authenticated by a notary or by another authorised public official is treated as having been recognised. If the party against whom the writing is asserted does not recognise the signature, the party who still intends to avail himself of such document must request that the authenticity of the writing or of the signature be verified, by introducing such evidence as he deems appropriate. A decision on confirmation of the authenticity is made by the panel decision.

In order to ascertain the falsity of a public act or of a recognised, authenticated or verified private writing, a citation may be submitted known as a "*querela di falso*" (complaint of falsity) at any stage of the proceedings. The decision on the complaint is made by a judgment of the panel, which will order the document to be returned and the complainant to pay an administrative penalty if the complaint is rejected, or which will issue provisions for the cancellation or amendment of the document if it ascertains its falsity.

Evidence to be established

The main types of evidence that are not pre-existing (*prove costituende*) but that are to be formed during the trial are confession, oath and testimony. Their common characteristic is the fact that they consist in an oral statement concerning the facts of the dispute.

CONFESSION

A confession (*confessione*)[49] is a declaration made by one party stating the truth of facts unfavourable to him and favourable to the other party. The confession must be made personally by the party and is ineffective if it is not given by a person competent to dispose of the right to which the facts confessed relate. A confession not made in judicial proceedings (i.e., an extra-judicial confession) will be proved in court; a judicial confession has full evidentiary value — it is binding for the court in its judgment and makes the evidence conflicting with it ineffective.

48. Civil Code, Article 2700.
49. Civil Code, Article 2730.

OATH

An oath (*giuramento*) is a statement made in solemn form as contemplated by law, whereby a party asserts the truth of a fact favourable to him. There are two types of oath:

(1) A decisory oath (*giuramento decisorio*),[50] which is that referred by one party to the other to cause the dispute to be totally or partially decided on the basis of the oath; or
(2) Supplemental oath (*giuramento suppletorio*),[51] with which the judge *ex officio* charges one of the parties for the purpose of deciding the case when the claim or the defences have not been fully proved, but are not totally without proof.

A particular type of supplemental oath is the valuation oath (*giuramento estimatorio*), i.e., an oath used to ascertain the value of the subject matter of the claim if it cannot be otherwise determined. The oath is taken personally by the party and if the party fails to appear to take the oath or, having appeared, does not take it, he loses the case with respect to the fact that was the subject matter of the oath. An oath is a most effective form of legal evidence, since the court must declare the victory of the party who took it and the defeat of the other party, who is not allowed to prove the contrary, but can only claim damages if the party who took the oath is convicted of perjury in penal proceedings.

TESTIMONY

Testimony (*prova testimoniale*) or proof by witnesses is a narration of the facts in the dispute made before the court by persons that are not parties to the proceedings and do not have an interest in the dispute.[52] Since testimony does not provide a type of evidence of indisputable reliability, the law has set certain limits on its admissibility[53] and made it subject to the free valuation of the judge who must appraise the facts disclosed and the actual reliability of the witnesses. Proof by witnesses is not allowed in the following cases:

(1) When the dispute concerns an act in respect of which the written form is required as a matter of substance;

50. Civil Code, Article 2736, Par. I.
51. Civil Code, Article 2736, Par. II.
52. Code of Civil Procedure, Article 246.
53. Civil Code, Articles 2721 *et seq.*

(2) When the subject matter of the testimony is a contract, a payment or a remission of a debt having a value higher than 5,000 lire;[54] and

(3) When, irrespective value, the subject matter of the testimony are covenants added to or contrary to the contents of a document, and it is alleged that they were stipulated prior to or concurrently with the document.[55]

Proof by witnesses is always allowed, pursuant to the Civil Code, Article 2724:

(1) When there is *prima facie* written evidence;

(2) When it has been morally or materially impossible for the contracting party to secure written evidence; and

(3) When the contracting party has, without fault, lost the evidentiary document.

The party wishing to introduce proof by witnesses must name specifically the witnesses to be interviewed and the facts on which each of them will testify and opposite proof must be moved for by the other party in the first answer.[56] The court will then issue an order ruling on the admission or rejection of the testimony.

INSPECTION

Another form of evidence which the court may obtain *ex officio* is judicial inspection (*ispezione giudiziale*) by which the court may — possibly with the assistance of an expert it appoints — inspect a thing or a location with a view to acquiring full knowledge of its characteristics.[57] The examining judge may, pursuant to the Code of Civil Procedure, Article 261, provide for casts, imprints and (also photographic and when necessary cinematographic) reproductions to be made of objects, documents and locations. He may also order the reproduction of an event to determine if

54. Nevertheless, the court may allow proof by witnesses over and above such limitation, taking into account the quality of the parties, the nature of the contract and any other circumstances: Civil Code, Articles 2721 and 2726.

55. Civil Code, Article 2722; when it is alleged that the added or conflicting covenant was stipulated after the formation of the document, a court may allow proof by witnesses only if, in consideration of the character of the parties, the nature of the contract and any other circumstances, it appears likely that additions or modifications have occurred: Civil Code, Article 2723.

56. Code of Civil Procedure, Article 244.

57. Code of Civil Procedure, Articles 258–262.

it may have occurred in a given manner (so-called "test"), and he may cause it to be photographically or cinematographically recorded.

When necessary, the examining judge may appoint one or more *ex officio* technical consultants (*consulenti tecnici d'ufficio*) to perform certain acts or for consultation throughout the proceedings. He may choose them from persons with particular technical knowledge in a given field. If such a consultant is appointed, the parties may in turn appoint their own *ex parte* technical consultants (*consulenti tecnici di parte*)[58] to attend the sessions of the *ex officio* technical consultant and to comment on the latter's report. The *ex officio* technical consultant must discharge his duties under oath and report on the specific questions submitted to him by the Examining Judge.

The accounting (*rendimento dei conti* or *rendiconto*) cannot be classified as evidence but is a special procedure to which general rules on the burden of proof and proof-taking means are applicable. If the court orders the submission of an accounting, the accounting must be deposited in the clerk's office, together with supporting documents. If the examining judge accepts the accounting, he will order payment of the amounts due. If a party challenges the accounting, the examining judge will proceed with the examination of the case, which will be referred to the panel for final decision.[59]

JUDGMENT

Crystallising the issues

On completion of the examination, the examining judge, whether he will continue the case before him alone (in the capacity of a single-judge court) or submit it to a panel decision for judgment on the merits (*decisione della causa*),[60] directs the parties to make their final prayers for

58. Code of Civil Procedure, Article 201.

59. Code of Civil Procedure, Article 263.

60. In the cases referred to in Article 48 of Royal Decree Number 14/1941, as amended by Article 88 of Law Number 353/9. A panel decision is mandatory: in appellate proceedings; in proceedings where the attendance of the Public Prosecutor is mandatory; in proceedings assigned to specialised sections of the court; in proceedings whose decision is handed down in chambers; in opposition, attack and revocation proceedings arising from a late proof of claim; in proceedings for the approval of the composition of creditors in bankruptcy or for the composition before bankruptcy; in liability proceedings brought against administrative or controlling bodies, directors and liquidation commissioners and in any other proceedings relating to internal relations in companies, mutual insurances and co-operative companies, joint ventures and syndicates; in proceedings referred to in Code of Civil Procedure, Articles 784 *et seq.*; in proceedings referred to in Law No. 117 of 13 April 1988.

relief (*conclusioni*). Such conclusions are nothing but a restatement, in a precise and synthetic form, of all demands and defences made by each party in the first phase of the proceedings (i.e., the citation for the plaintiff, the answer and possible counterclaim for the defendant and the joinder brief for a joining third party) taking, however, into account, the elements disclosed during the course of the trial and the results of the evidence submitted.

Then, if the decision of the dispute pertains to the examining judge in his capacity of single-judge court, Article 190–bis of Code of Civil Procedure provides that the examining judge should appoint deadlines of respectively 60 and 20 days from the date of referral of the case for decision[61] for an exchange of two written briefs by each party: a final brief (*comparsa conclusionale*) and a reply brief (*memoria in replica*).

The parties are still entitled to deliver oral pleadings at a hearing to be appointed by the judge, but in such case they will lose the possibility of submitting reply briefs.[62] The Code then accords the judge 60 days to deposit his decision in the clerk's office. It should be noted that the 60-day deadline is not peremptory, so that if a decision is deposited after its expiration, its validity and effectiveness will not be affected.

In the cases that cannot be decided by single-judge court,[63] the examining judge, after submission of the final prayers for relief, will refer the dispute to the panel for a decision.[64] The panel will be comprised of three members: a presiding judge and two judges, one of whom acted as the examining judge.

In such case, there will still be an exchange of final briefs and reply briefs and possibly, in addition thereto, oral pleadings at a special panel hearing on request of any party to be made concurrently with the filing of the final prayers for relief. The hearing is open to the public and the examining judge makes an oral report on the proceedings, whereupon the parties proceed with the oral pleadings.

The decision is handed down in chambers by the majority vote of the judges who attended the oral pleadings. The decision is signed by the judge who wrote it and by the presiding judge and must be published by deposit in the clerk's office within 30 days from the date the decision was made in chambers. The clerk notifies the parties' respective counsel by a notice containing the conclusive ruling of the decision.

61. Code of Civil Procedure, Article 190.
62. Article 190–*bis*, Par. II, Code of Civil Procedure.
63. Royal Decree Number 14/1941, Article 48.
64. Code of Civil Procedure, Article 275.

Types of judgments

The provisions made by the court (whether a panel or a single-judge court) in the decision may fall within three categories:

(1) Definitive judgments (*sentenze definitive*), which conclude the proceedings and may be issued when the court decides the dispute in its entirety or, by resolving questions of jurisdiction or competence, declares its lack of jurisdictional competence or considers that a review of the merits of the case is precluded by a prejudicial or preliminary issue;

(2) Non-definitive judgments (*sentenze non definitive*), which do not conclude the proceedings but provide for their continuation in order to obtain the issuance of a definitive decision; and

(3) Procedural orders (*ordinanze*), to wit, provisions by which the court, without deciding the dispute, rules simply on questions relating to the examination of the case not ripe for a decision yet.

Non-definitive judgments are *interim* decisions issued when the court rejects an objection of lack of competence or jurisdiction or objections on prejudicial or preliminary issues on the merits or, having reached a finding of liability (the so-called *an debeatur*), makes provisions for a continuation of the proceedings to determine the amount (*quantum*) of damages deriving from such liability or, when a decision is sought on more than one claim, issues a non-definitive decision on some of them which are already mature and provides, by a separate order, for the examination steps which it deems necessary in respect of the other claims.

By its publication through the deposit in the clerk's office, the decision acquires the effectiveness of an official pronunciation of the court, even though it may not yet be operative materially, in view of the several procedures for attack contemplated by the legal system to obtain an amendment or cancellation of the decision. When such remedies are exhausted or precluded, the decision becomes no longer contestable, in that the determinations set forth in it "are binding"[65] for all purposes between the parties and their successors in interest, without, however, affecting such actions as might be brought by third parties with respect to the same subject matter under an autonomous entitlement.

In a sense, the immutability of a decision that has become *res judicata* is not absolute, in that exceptional circumstances may still arise permitting the institution of extraordinary remedies. Nevertheless, further

65. As provided by Civil Code, Article 2909.

objections on the issue decided are precluded, and the proceedings must be regarded as definitively concluded. The institution of such extraordinary remedies would entail the opening of new proceedings.

As to the enforceability of judicial decisions, the recent reform of the Code of Civil Procedure has made all first instance decisions provisionally enforceable[66] even if they have not yet become *res judicata*. This provisional enforcement is subject to suspension, which may be granted for serious reasons by the appellate court at the request of the party concerned.[67]

Omissions, material errors or miscalculations inadvertently made by the court in drawing up the decision may be corrected, at the request of the interested party, by a decree or order of the judge that rendered the decision.[68]

ABBREVIATED PROCEEDINGS

Consolidation

A consolidation of proceedings (*riunione*) may be ordered when more proceedings relating to the same dispute or to connected disputes are pending before the same court.

If separate proceedings are instituted in respect of the same dispute before the same court, Article 273, Par. I of the Code of Civil Procedure provides that the court must, even *ex officio*, order a consolidation of the proceedings, while if different proceedings are pending before different judges or different chambers in the same court, their consolidation will be ordered by the presiding judge.[69] On the other hand, if identical disputes are pending before two different judges who are not members of the same court, a transfer of competence governed by Code of Civil Procedure, Article 39 occurs and one dispute only continues, while the other is stricken from the docket or resumed before the court that is competent under the law.

Likewise, when more than one connected dispute (namely, disputes having at least one element in common: the *petitum*, the *causa petendi* or the parties) are brought before the same court, the court will order their consolidation even *ex officio*;[70] if connected disputes are pending before different judges in the same tribunal, the presiding judge will order the disputes to be called before the same judge for such action

66. Code of Civil Procedure, Article 282.
67. Code of Civil Procedure, Article 283.
68. Code of Civil Procedure, Articles 287 and 288.
69. Code of Civil Procedure, Article 273, Par. II.
70. Code of Civil Procedure, Article 274, Par. I.

as he may deem appropriate. Thus, in this case, a consolidation will be ordered only if deemed appropriate.

In the event, however, that the connected disputes are pending before different courts, the shifting of competence governed by Code of Civil Procedure, Article 40 will occur and a deadline will be set for the parties to resume the secondary dispute (*causa accessoria*) before the court vested with the principal dispute (*causa principale*) and in other cases before the court previously approached.

It may also happen that with respect to connected disputes, initiated jointly as provided by Articles 103, Par. I and 104, Par. I Code of Civil Procedure or consolidated at a later date, it is determined that their joint handling is inappropriate. In this event, Articles 103 and 104 Par. II of the Code of Civil Procedure, provide that the examining judge or the panel may, during the trial or in the decision, order the separation (*separazione*) of the actions cumulated in the same proceedings either on the motion of all parties or when the continuation of the joint handling would delay or make them more cumbersome.

Non-appearance

If one of the parties fails to enter an appearance, the rules governing proceedings *in absentia* (*procedimento in contumacia*) will apply. A declaration of the relevant parties' failure to appear must be made by the examining judge, usually at the first hearing,[71] but the declaration cannot be made without prior verification.

If the party whose failure to appear should be declared is the plaintiff, the law provides that the defendant should expressly state his intent to continue the proceedings, failing which the case is immediately stricken from the docket and extinguished.

If the party whose failure to appear should be declared is the defendant, the law considers the possibility that his failure to appear derives from a lack of knowledge of the institution of the action as a result of irregular service of process. The examining judge will check into the regularity of service and, if he finds it defective, provide for its renewal within a peremptory deadline.

Once a party's failure to appear is declared, the proceedings will continue in the normal manner except that certain communications, expressly listed in Code of Civil Procedure, Article 292, must be served on the absent party personally. The absent party is permitted to enter a late appearance until the moment when the case is taken up for decision.

71. Code of Civil Procedure, Article 171, Par. III.

If the defendant applies for an authorisation to cure the late appearance,[72] by proving that he was unable to participate in the proceedings for reasons beyond his control, the examining judge may allow him to perform the activities which would have been precluded to him. Otherwise, he can only accept the proceedings in their current state.

Suspension of proceedings

The proceedings may be suspended (*sospensione del processo*) by the court when the decision of the case is dependent on the definition of another case[73] or when all parties apply for suspension. If the court fails to appoint a date for the resumption of the proceedings, the parties must apply to the court for the setting of a new hearing. This application is to be submitted not later than six months from the parties' obtaining knowledge that a cause for mandatory suspension no longer exists or, in the case of optional suspension, no less than 10 days prior to the expiration of the agreed suspension period.

Interruption of proceedings

An interruption of the proceedings (*interruzione del processo*) occurs when events impair the active participation of the parties, their legal representatives or their counsel. Such events may consist in the death of a party or loss of his legal capacity by reason of interdiction, disability, bankruptcy, or the death, loss of capacity of a legal representative; the death, disablement or the suspension of counsel.[74]

The proceedings must be resumed not later than six months after the cause for interruption has become known, by a citation to be served by the most diligent party. If resumption is not effected within this period, the proceedings are extinguished.

Extinguishment

Extinguishment (*estinzione*) is an advanced termination of the proceedings for a reason that prevents their continuation. Two reasons for extinguishment are contemplated in the Code of Civil Procedure:[75]

72. Code of Civil Procedure, Article 294.
73. Code of Civil Procedure, Article 295.
74. Code of Civil Procedure, Articles 299 *et seq.*
75. Code of Civil Procedure, Articles 306 *et seq.*

(1) A waiver of suit, which must be made by the party personally or through a special attorney-in-fact and must be accepted by the other parties in the proceedings, who might have an interest in continuing the litigation; or

(2) The inactivity of the parties, which takes effect when proceedings are not resumed within one year from the time when they are stricken from the docket or when the parties entitled to continue, resume or integrate them fail to do so within the peremptory deadline set by the law or the court.

The proceedings before the *Pretore* or the Justice of Peace (*Giudice di Pace*) do not differ in their essential features from those before the Tribunal acting as a single-judge court and are regulated by the same rules insofar as applicable.[76] Pursuant to Articles 312 and 313 of the Code of Civil Procedure, the *Pretore* or Justice of Peace may proceed *ex officio* with the introduction of proof by witnesses when the parties, in reciting the facts, have made reference to persons who appear likely to know the truth. Furthermore, when a complaint of falsity is advanced, the *Pretore* or Justice of Peace may suspend the proceedings and refer the parties to the Tribunal if he deems that the challenged document is relevant to decide the case, but may, on an *ex parte* motion, continue the handling of the case in respect of those claims that may be decided independently of the attacked document. The formalities to be followed in the conduct of proceedings before the *Pretore* are now identical to those applying to proceedings before the Tribunal.

SPECIAL TRIBUNALS

Pretore proceedings

The Code of Civil Procedure, as amended by Law Number 353/90, accords the *Pretore* two options for the decision of the case:

(1) The *Pretore*, having completed the handling and examination of the case, directs the parties to submit the final prayers for relief, to exchange final briefs and reply briefs and then deposits the decision in the clerk's office within 30 days from the deadline for the submission of the reply briefs;[77] and

(2) If the *Pretore* has taken no action pursuant to Article 314, he may direct the parties to proceed immediately with the oral pleading of the case, and render forthwith the decision, reading

76. Code of Civil Procedure, Article 311.
77. Code of Civil Procedure, Article 314.

to the parties the ruling (*dispositivo*) and a concise recital of the factual and legal grounds of the decision.[78]

Justice of peace proceedings

Law Number 374/91 instituted a new type of single-judge court, known as the Justice of Peace, to replace the Conciliator. The rules laid down in Articles 316–322, of the Code of Civil Procedure are intended to simplify the proceedings before this court. The claim may be advanced in writing or also orally to the Justice, who causes a record to be drawn appointing a date for the hearing, and requiring the plaintiff to effect service. The parties need not be represented by counsel in disputes whose value does not exceed 1-million lire or even in cases of a greater value, if authorised by the Justice.

The case is dealt with in no more than two hearings. At the first hearing the Justice interviews the parties and attempts to reach an amicable settlement, a record of which is dressed up and can be enforced by the levying of execution. If no settlement is reached, the proceedings continue and when the Justice feels that the case is ready for decision, it directs the parties to submit their final prayers for relief and to argue the case and deposits the decision in the clerk's office within 15 days.

When the Justice of Peace makes a decision on a fair and equitable basis, in cases whose value does not exceed 2-million lire, the decision cannot be appealed. A procedure for conciliation of the dispute without formal litigation is also contemplated. It involves the submission of an application, even orally, and the dressing up of a *procès-verbal*. If the dispute falls within the jurisdiction of the Justice of Peace, the *procès-verbal* is enforceable. If not, it has the effect of a private writing recognised in judicial proceedings.[79]

Labour proceedings

Characteristics

A special procedure, which was enacted by Law Number 533 of 11 August 1973 and resembles the amendments introduced into the Code of Civil Procedure by Law Number 353 of 1990, governs litigation in individual labour disputes and in disputes concerning social security and compulsory medical insurance. This procedure is characterised by measures aimed at expediency, consolidation and oral pleadings.

78. Code of Civil Procedure, Article 315; this is altogether new.
79. Code of Civil Procedure, Article 322, and Civil Code, Article 2702.

With a view to reducing judicial litigation, Code of Civil Procedure, Article 410 provides for an optional conciliation system before a special board. Those who intend to sue in connection with these matters may initiate, directly or through a union or employers' association, an attempt at conciliation. The conciliation board consists of the Director of the Provincial Labour Office, acting as chairperson, four representatives of employees designated by the most representative national unions and four representatives of the employers.

Whether the attempt at conciliation is successful or not, a *procès-verbal* of the proceedings must be drawn up, filed in the office of the clerk at the court and made enforceable by a decree of the *Pretore* either in its general ambit or with respect to the portion concerning the employee's claim on which the parties agreed. Alternatively, an attempt at conciliation can also be made before the unions and the employers' associations.

Subject matter and competence

The *Pretore* has exclusive functional jurisdiction in all first instance labour disputes. Second instance proceedings fall within the jurisdiction of the Tribunal. Territorial jurisdiction lies with the court in whose district the employment relationship originated, or where the business of the branch to which the employee was assigned is located.[80] If the employer is an individual, a subsidiary venue is that of the place where the defendant has his residence, domicile or abode.

The rules governing individual labour disputes apply to all disputes relating to:[81]

(1) Private subordinate employment relations, even if not connected with the operation of a business;
(2) Farming employment contracts, except those falling within the jurisdiction of specialised agricultural chambers;
(3) Commission agency, marketing representation and other co-operation relations resulting in the rendition of continuing and co-ordinated services, prevailingly of a personal nature, even though not falling in the category of subordinate work;
(4) Employment relations of employees of public entities engaging solely or prevailingly in economic business operations; and
(5) Employment relations of employees of public entities, other than those engaging in economic operations, such as the State and other local public entities, provided that they are not attributed under the law to the jurisdiction of other courts.

80. Code of Civil Procedure, Article 413.
81. Code of Civil Procedure, Article 409.

Procedure

The proceedings are conducted orally, the only written materials being the petition, the defendant's reply and the decision. The proceedings in a labour dispute are introduced through a petition (*ricorso*), which is first submitted to the judge, and then served on the defendant. The petition must contain a reference to the court, the particulars of the claimant and the defendant, the appointment of an address by the claimant in the commune where the court is located, a description of the subject matter of the claim and of the facts and the claim's legal basis, together with the prayer for relief and a specific indication — subject to forfeiture — of the evidence that the claimant intends to introduce and — in particular — of the documents exhibited.

The *Pretore* will set the date of a hearing at the bottom of the petition, which will then be served on the defendant. The defendant must enter an appearance no less than 10 days prior to the date of the hearing, filing in the clerk's office a reply brief in which, in addition to appointing an address in the commune where the court is located, he must — subject to forfeiture — submit any counterclaim and any procedural or substantive objections; take a precise position as to the facts alleged by the claimant; raise all of his defences in fact and at law; describe specifically — subject to forfeiture — the evidence which he intends to introduce and in particular the documentary proof, which he must concurrently exhibit. If the defendant submits a counterclaim, he must ask the court in the reply brief to appoint a new hearing for appearance.

Normally, the parties are represented by counsel, but they may plead their case personally if the value of the dispute does not exceed 250,000 lire.[82] The hearing for oral arguments fixed by the court is the crux of the whole proceedings. It serves the purpose of a first contact between the parties and enables the court to intervene and freely examine the parties on the facts at stake and to attempt an amicable settlement of the dispute.

This is why the Code requires a party's obligation to appear personally at the hearing. The court may draw conclusions from the parties' failure to appear.

During the hearing the parties may amend the claim, the defences and prayers for relief previously submitted, but only if serious reasons exist and subject to the prior authorisation of the court.[83] No new claims can be introduced. At the hearing, the court will rule on the admission of evidence offered by the parties. The court is accorded ample authority for the conduct of labour proceedings. Accordingly, it may:

82. Code of Civil Procedure, Article 417.
83. Code of Civil Procedure, Article 420, Par. I.

(1) Call the attention of the parties at any time to the irregularity of pleadings and documents capable of being cured, setting a time limit to do it;[84]

(2) Allow *ex officio* at any time the introduction of evidence, even beyond the limits set forth in the Civil Code, except a decisory oath;[85]

(3) Order, if necessary, on an ex parte motion, a survey of the work location and the examination of witnesses at such location; and

(4) Request written or oral information or observations from the unions and employers' associations designated by the parties.

After completing the collection of evidence, the *Pretore* asks the parties to deliver their oral arguments and to submit final prayers for relief. He hands down the decision at the end of the hearing, reading the conclusive part containing the award. Under Code of Civil Procedure, Article 431 the conclusive part of the decision is immediately enforceable if it awards relief to the employee. However, the employer may obtain from the tribunal, acting as an appellate court in labour disputes, a suspension of enforcement if most serious prejudice would derive from it and on condition that the levying of execution involves collection of sums in excess of 500,000 lire. Following the amendment to Code of Civil Procedure, Article 431 introduced by Law Number 353 of 1990, judgments rendered in favour of the employer are also immediately enforceable. In this case, enforcement may be wholly or partly suspended when serious reasons prevail.

The same features of expediency, consolidation and prevalence of oral pleadings apply also in appellate proceedings, where all activities must be conducted before the panel. All first instance decisions issued by the *Pretore* in disputes exceeding 50,000 lire in value can be appealed to the Tribunal.[86] Decisions of a lower value can be attacked only by a petition for review by the Court of Cassation.

Social security and compulsory health insurance proceedings

The same special procedure for individual labour disputes also applies to all proceedings dealing with social security and compulsory health inurance disputes.[87] The procedural rules are the same except that jurisdiction lies only with the *Pretore* sitting in the principal town of the Tribunal's district where the plaintiff resides and that the petition cannot be prosecuted

84. Code of Civil Procedure, Article 421, Par. I.
85. Code of Civil Procedure, Article 421, Par. I.
86. Code of Civil Procedure, Article 440.
87. Code of Civil Procedure, Article 442.

as long as proceedings prescribed by special legislation can be instituted for the settlement of disputes at administrative level.

SPECIAL PROCEEDINGS

Special proceedings (*procedimenti speciali*) are characterised by the differences that they present in the substance and in the procedure from normal litigation proceedings. They are mostly regulated in Book IV of the Code of Civil Procedure under Articles 633 *et seq.*, and in part by special laws or in the Civil Code. They can be divided into three groups:

(1) Summary proceedings (*procedimenti sommari*), which can be compared to normal litigation, except that the initial phase of the examination is conducted in a summary manner, the court issuing a provisional decision after having examined the case in an abridged form;

(2) Voluntary jurisdiction proceedings (*volontaria giurisdizione*) or proceedings in chambers (*procedimenti in camera di consiglio*), where the parties simply submit a written petition to the competent court and the rest of the proceedings is conducted orally; and

(3) Other special proceedings that cannot otherwise be grouped on the basis of a common element.

Summary proceedings

Injunction proceedings

Injunction proceedings are a special and abridged form of litigation providing for a summary examination of the claim by the court, which results in the issuance of a decree requiring the debtor to pay an amount of money or to deliver a specified item of personal property (*decreto ingiuntivo*). The decree is issued directly on the creditor's application, without an appearance of the debtor. However, the debtor can file an opposition against the decree, thereby instituting proceedings that are conducted with all safeguards of normal litigation. Hence, litigation is left to the initiative of the party who receives the *decreto ingiuntivo*. Competent to issue the decree is the court that would be competent in ordinary litigation.

PROCEDURE

The following parties are entitled to obtain a *decreto ingiuntivo* pursuant to Code of Civil Procedure, Article 633: the creditor of a sum of money which is liquidated and mature for payment; he who is entitled to the delivery of a given quantity of fungible things or specified item of movable property; lawyers, court clerks, process servers and any person having performed work in connection with legal proceedings in order to obtain payment of his fees or a refund of disbursements; notaries and other persons practising a free profession or trade in respect of which a legally approved tariff exists, in order to obtain payment of their fees and refund of costs. As a rule, the creditor must prove the existence of his right by written evidence. In particular, appropriate written evidence consists of policies, unilateral promises by private writings and telegrams as well as certified extracts of accounting records in respect of claims for the supply of goods and the provision of money made by entrepreneurs engaging in a commercial activity.

A *decreto ingiuntivo* is applied for by means of a petition filed in the clerk's office together with the supporting documentation. The court issues its decision on the basis of the documentary evidence submitted and, if the conditions contemplated by Code of Civil Procedure, Article 633 prevail, issues a decree setting forth the reasons, whereby it orders the other party to pay the sum or to deliver the property or the amount of property required within a deadline of 20 days, with an express warning that an opposition can be submitted within the same deadline, failing which forceful enforcement will be levied. The deadline for payment or delivery is not always accorded, since the court may, on the petitioner's application, authorise the provisional enforcement of the decree[88] if the claim is evidenced by a bill of exchange or promissory note, a bank cheque or cashier's cheque, a stock exchange certificate or an instrument drawn up by a notary or another public official or if delay entails a risk of serious prejudice. The decree together with the petition must be served on the debtor and the 20-day period for opposition or payment runs from the date of service. The decree becomes ineffective if it is not served within 40 days after the date of its issuance.

OPPOSITION

Opposition is the vehicle by which the debtor who considers the decree unfair attacks it, summoning the creditor to appear before the same court that issued the *decreto ingiuntivo*. In opposition proceedings, the parties' roles are inverted. The parties are the creditor granted the injunction, who assumes the role of an opposed-party defendant and the debtor (enjoined party), who assumes the role of an opponent-plaintiff. The opposed party may offer any proof of his right, the requirement of written evidence described for the issuance of the decree being no longer applicable.

88. Code of Civil Procedure, Article 642.

In the course of litigation the Examining Judge may order provisional enforcement of the decree (if the opposition is not based on written evidence and the party applying for provisional enforcement offers to post an adequate bond) or may suspend provisional enforcement for serious reasons. If no opposition is advanced within the established deadline, or if the opponent fails to enter an appearance or if the opposition is rejected, the decree becomes automatically enforceable. The same happens if the court issues an order declaring the extinguishment of the proceedings.

Lease termination and ejectment proceedings

NATURE

These proceedings (*procedimento per convalida di sfratto*) are aimed at obtaining from the court a decision validating the notice of termination or ejection for default in payment of the rental and declaring the dissolution of a lease. The procedure applies to all leases, including those of farming land and agricultural contracts although practically it is mostly followed in the lease of business or dwelling premises. Three possibilities are contemplated by the law:

(1) A notice of termination of the lease which is given prior to the expiration of the contract to prevent it from being automatically renewed;
(2) An ejection, which is notified after the expiration of the contract; and
(3) An ejection by default, which is notified when the lessee fails to pay rental on the dates provided.

PROCEDURE

In all three cases, the procedure is initiated by a request served by the lessor on the lessee to release the immovable and the concurrent summoning of the lessee to appear and hear the validation of the request. The first hearing is of particular importance in this procedure since it may involve the following situations:

(1) If the defendant fails to appear or, having appeared, fails to resist the notice of termination or the ejection, the court will validate the notice or ejection and grant an enforcement order;
(2) If the lessee appears, he may oppose the request, in which case the proceedings are converted into normal litigation, which,

however, is conducted before the *Pretore* observing the special procedure applicable in labour disputes.[89]

Ejection by default in the payment of rentals has the following additional peculiarities: The validation of ejection is conditional on the confirmation given in court by the lessor that the default is continuing; if the lessor so requests, the court may issue a *Decreto Ingiuntivo* for payment of the outstanding rentals and of those maturing until the premises are surrendered;[90] if the defendant contests the amount of the claim, the court may order payment of the undisputed amount allowing a period not exceeding 20 days to pay, failing which it will validate the ejection and issue a *Decreto Ingiuntivo* for payment of the rentals.[91]

Voluntary jurisdiction

The Code of Civil Procedure gives no definition of voluntary jurisdiction proceedings (*volontaria giurisdizione*), but confines itself to grouping them in a single title under the heading proceedings in chambers (*procedimenti in camera di consiglio*). They may to some extent be compared to what is known in American law as non-adversary or *ex parte* proceedings. Through voluntary jurisdiction the State co-operates in the formation of a legal relationship that could not come into existence by itself by the simple declaration of intent of the private party. Here, the court does not override the actions of the parties, but operates side by side with them with a view to integrating the establishment, amendment or extinguishment of legal positions within the scope of private law.

The procedure is initiated by an application submitted to the competent court, which issues a decree by a decisional process in chambers. Both the parties and the public prosecutor can submit an opposition to the higher court. This step, however, must be taken within a peremptory period of 10 days from notice of the decree. The decree becomes effective on the expiring of said period, unless the court made provisions for its immediate effectiveness in urgent cases. The decree, although continuing in effect, is not susceptible of becoming final and can be amended or revoked at any time, without prejudice to the rights acquired in good faith by third parties. Furthermore, the decree is not subject to review by the Court of Cassation.

Particularly relevant among the various types of voluntary jurisdiction proceedings to be found in the Civil Code and in the Code of Civil Procedure, in addition to those concerning minors and incompetent persons,[92]

---

89. Code of Civil Procedure, Article 667.
90. Code of Civil Procedure, Article 664.
91. Code of Civil Procedure, Article 666.
92. Code of Civil Procedure, Article 732; Civil Code, Article 320.

the acceptance of an inheritance with benefit of inventory,[93] a declaration of absence or of presumed death of an absentee,[94] are those concerning personal separation of the spouses and interdiction and disability. Proceedings for the personal separation of spouses (*procedimento per la separazione personale tra coniugi*) tend to obtain a decision ordering separation with the effects contemplated by Civil Code, Article 156 There are two types of separation:

(1) A judicial separation (*separazione giudiziale*), if it is applied for by one party against the other; and
(2) A separation by agreement (*separazione consensuale*), when both parties apply for it, having agreed the terms.

In judicial separation, the proceedings are in the nature of litigation and are settled by a judgment. The competent court is the tribunal in the location where the defendant spouse has his or her residence or domicile. The proceedings are divided into two phases: an initial phase held before the presiding judge of the tribunal, and another possible phase held before a designated Examining Judge. During the initial phase, the presiding judge must first of all attempt to persuade the parties to a reconciliation, failing which he must order such provisional and urgent measures as he deems appropriate in the interests of the spouses and the children; he must, furthermore, appoint an Examining Judge, and fix a hearing for the appearance of the parties before him. Thereafter, the proceedings continue in the ordinary form.

In separation by agreement, the proceedings, after an initial phase before the presiding judge, which is conducted in the same manner as just described, continue in chambers and are concluded by a decree of the panel ratifying the separation agreement between the spouses. The decree is in the nature of a voluntary jurisdiction measure.

Proceedings for interdiction or declaration of disability (*procedimenti di interdizione ed innabilitazione*) are aimed at establishing a status of interdiction or disability in the interests of a person incapable of understanding and intending. The proceedings are initiated by a petition submitted to the tribunal in the location where the person to be interdicted or disabled has his domicile or residence. The spouse, relatives within the fourth degree, in-laws within the second degree, a guardian or curator, and the public prosecutor are eligible to submit the petition. If the person to be interdicted or disabled is under parental authority or one of his parents has been appointed curator, only such parent or the prosecutor is entitled to submit the petition.[95]

93. Code of Civil Procedure, Article 778.
94. Code of Civil Procedure, Article 772.
95. Civil Code, Article 417.

The first phase of the proceedings is handled by the presiding judge of the tribunal, who will verify the prima facie foundation of the petition in order not to commence a wholly unfounded process. If the presiding judge does not reject the petition he will appoint an Examining Judge and fix a hearing for the appearance of the petitioners, the person to be interdicted and such other persons from whom he may deem it advisable to obtain information. The petitioners must cause the application and the decree to be served on such persons and notice of the decree will be given to the public prosecutor. The examining judge will then continue the proceedings, examining the person to be interdicted or disabled, to ascertain the status of his intellectual ability, obtaining the opinion of the persons summoned and, finally, taking all such evidence as is deemed advisable for the purposes of a decision. On completion of the examination, the matter will be referred to the panel and the proceedings will be closed by a judgment.

Arbitration

Arbitration proceedings are regulated by Articles 806–840 of the Code of Civil Procedure. While important amendments to the Code of Civil Procedure provisions on arbitration were introduced by Law Number 28 of 9 February 1983 to make the Code consistent with certain international conventions on arbitration,[96] Law Number 25 of 5 January 1994 has further materially amended such provisions by the addition of two new chapters (VI and VII) consisting of nine articles on "International Arbitration" and on the "Recognition and Enforcement of Foreign Arbitral Awards" respectively.

DOMESTIC ARBITRATION — RITUAL AND INFORMAL

This section deals with arbitration proceedings as regulated in the Code of Civil Procedure, commonly called "ritual arbitration" (arbitrato rituale). However, Italian practice also contemplates a peculiar form of arbitration commonly called "informal arbitration" (arbitrato irrituale). While in ritual arbitration the arbitrators actually substitute the ordinary courts and their award is directly enforceable like a normal judgment — subject

---

96. For example, Geneva Protocol signed on 24 September 1923 relating to arbitration clauses; New York Convention signed on 10 June 1958 relating to the recognition and enforcement of foreign arbitral awards; Geneva Convention signed on 26 September 1927 relating to the enforcement of foreign arbitral awards; European Convention on international commercial arbitration, signed in Geneva on 21 April 1961; Washington Convention on litigation relating to investment between states and persons belonging to other states, signed on 18 March 1965.

only to a verification by the Pretore that the agreement to arbitrate and the award meet the formal prerequisites set forth in the Code, in informal arbitration, the arbitrators are deemed to act as agents to whom the parties have delegated the function of settling the dispute by means of a document (the award) which is in the nature of a settlement agreement rather than a judicial decision. Informal arbitration is not subject to the Code of Civil Procedure or any other specific statutory rules and a decision rendered by informal arbitrators cannot be enforced with the same procedure as a ritual award, but must be "sued on" like a contract and is carried into effect through the enforcement of the judgment rendered on it.

Parties may choose the arbitral jurisdiction instead of the ordinary one whether after or before the dispute has arisen. The agreements by which such choice is made *after* or *before* the beginning of the dispute are called, respectively, "submission agreement" or "agreement to refer existing dispute" (*compromesso*) and "arbitration clause" or "agreement to refer future disputes" (*clausola compromissoria*). Identical rules apply to *compromesso* and *clausola compromissoria* as to their form and contents. In no case may disputes concerning the status of persons, the separation of spouses, or labour and social security and health insurance disputes, and other disputes involving rights that the parties are not authorised to dispose of be referred to arbitration. Labour disputes, however, may be assigned in advance to arbitral jurisdiction on a non-binding basis, provided that the applicable labour collective bargaining contracts allow it, that the arbitrators are not granted the power to decide on a fair and equitable basis (*secondo equità*) and that the award is not expressly defined as non-attackable.

Any *clausola compromissoria* entered into in violation of such requisites is null and void. *Compromesso* and *clausola compromissoria* must be made in writing under penalty of nullity.[97] The prerequisite of written form is considered to be met if the *compromesso* or the *clausola compromissoria* is entered into by means of telegraph or teleprinter. In addition, a *compromesso* must specify, under penalty of nullity, the actual dispute to which it refers; on the other hand, in case of a *clausola compromissoria* such specification cannot obviously be made, since the clause refers to future disputes. Nevertheless, the *clausola compromissoria* is contained in a contract (or in a separate document to which the contract refers), and a basic limitation of the *clausola's* scope — in the absence of any specific indication by the parties — is implied in the scope of the contract itself.

If the parties intend to challenge the arbitrators' jurisdiction in respect of a specific dispute on grounds that it does not fall within the scope of the *compromesso* or of the *clausola compromissoria*, they must do so in the

97. Code of Civil Procedure, Articles 807, 808.

course of the arbitration proceedings subject to forfeiting their right.[98] Moreover, the validity of the *clausola compromissoria* will be treated and evaluated independently of the validity of the contract in which it is inserted or which refers to it; nevertheless, the power to enter into such contract includes the power to agree to the *clausola compromissoria*.[99]

Both *compromesso* and *clausola compromissoria* are considered and treated as acts exceeding business in the ordinary course. *Compromesso* and *clausola compromissoria* must indicate the number of arbitrators — whose number must be odd — and the procedure for their appointment.[100] Failing an indication by the parties, the dispute will be referred to a panel of three arbitrators. Detailed provisions apply to the appointment of arbitrators and to the power of the court to supplement or correct the parties' incomplete or defective arrangements in respect thereof,[101] and of the substitution of arbitrators.[102] In particular, the presiding judge of the Tribunal competent over the location of the arbitration, or that where the *compromesso* or the agreement containing the *clausola compromissoria* was made, (or the presiding judge of the Tribunal of Rome if such location is abroad) will have the authority:

(1) To appoint an additional arbitrator if the parties have indicated or appointed an even number;
(2) To appoint, on petition of the most diligent party, any arbitrator who should have — and has not — been appointed by the other party or by the arbitrators already appointed by the parties;
(3) To substitute any missing arbitrator or any arbitrator who did not fulfil his obligations;[103] and
(4) To rule on challenges of the arbitrators raised by the parties on the grounds set forth in Code of Civil Procedure, Article 51.[104]

Both Italian and foreign citizens may be appointed arbitrators. Minors, interdicted persons, bankrupts and anyone who has been barred from public office cannot act as arbitrators.[105] Arbitrators must accept their appointment in writing; they will render their award (which is called *lodo*) within the period established by the parties or by law — i.e., according to Code of Civil Procedure, Article 820, within 180 days from acceptance (or, if more than one arbitrator, from the last acceptance) of

98. Code of Civil Procedure, Article 817.
99. Code of Civil Procedure, Article 808.
100. Code of Civil Procedure, Article 809.
101. Code of Civil Procedure, Article 810.
102. Code of Civil Procedure, Article 811.
103. Code of Civil Procedure, Article 813, Par. III.
104. Code of Civil Procedure, Article 815.
105. Code of Civil Procedure, Article 812.

office — and are liable for damages if the award is annulled on grounds of non-observance of the time limit for its issuance, or if they resign without any justifiable reason their office after acceptance. However, a party who intends to avail himself of such failure as a ground for nullity must notify the other parties and the arbitrators accordingly before the award is handed down and signed by a majority of the arbitrators.[106] The period may be extended by the arbitrators only once for no more than 180 days, in connection with different occurrences. Notwithstanding this limitation, the parties may always consent to one or more extensions of the period by written agreement.[107] Arbitration proceedings must take place in the territory of the Republic of Italy in the place agreed between the parties or determined by the arbitrators. The parties or the arbitrators will have also the power to establish the rules applicable to the proceedings, preserving the equal right of the parties to plead (the principle of *contraddittorio*).

The arbitrators may examine witnesses[108] but have no authority to issue attachments or other precautionary measures,[109] nor may they decide or examine any incidental matter affecting their decision which is excluded by law from their jurisdiction.[110] In such case, the arbitral proceedings are suspended until a final decision on such matter is made by the competent judge and served on one party by the other. Arbitral jurisdiction is not excluded by the connection of the dispute submitted to arbitration with another dispute pending before an ordinary court.[111]

An arbitral award will be rendered according to law, unless the parties have granted the arbitrators the power to decide on a fair and equitable basis.[112] The form and contents of the award are regulated by Code of Civil Procedure, Article 823, which mainly provides that the award must be in writing, must contain certain references and must be executed at least by the majority of the arbitrators (provided that, in the latter case, the award includes an acknowledgement that it has been resolved by personal conference of all the arbitrators and an express statement that the others did not intend or were unable to execute it). The award is effective from the date on which the last signature was affixed. It may be corrected by the arbitrators in case of omissions or of material or calculation errors.[113] The arbitrators will give notice of the award by delivering

106. Code of Civil Procedure, Article 821.
107. Code of Civil Procedure, Article 820.
108. Code of Civil Procedure, Article 819–*ter*.
109. Code of Civil Procedure, Article 818.
110. Code of Civil Procedure, Article 819.
111. Code of Civil Procedure, Article 819–*bis*.
112. Code of Civil Procedure, Article 822.
113. Code of Civil Procedure, Article 826.

an original to each of the parties also by means of registered mail within 10 days from the date of the last signature.

An award rendered by ritual arbitrators may be given the authority and effectiveness of a judgment by depositing it together with the *compromesso* or the document containing the *clausola compromissoria* with the competent *Pretore* at any time. The *Pretore*, after having ascertained the formal regularity of the award, declares it enforceable by a decree; the clerk's office gives notice to the parties of the deposit and of the decree. The decree denying enforceability of the award may be attacked before the tribunal within 30 days starting from this notice.[114] An arbitral award can be attacked[115] before the Court of Appeal having territorial competence over the place of arbitration within 90 days from service of the award, or within one year from the date of the last signature, if service has not been effected.

Such attack, known as "attack on grounds of nullity" (*impugnazione per nullità*), is allowed and may be lodged, notwithstanding any waiver, if:

(1) The *compromesso* is null;

(2) The arbitrators have not been appointed pursuant to the above described rules, provided that such issue has been raised during the arbitration proceedings;

(3) The award has been rendered by a person ineligible to be an arbitrator;

(4) The award decided matters *ultra vires*, i.e., outside the scope of the *compromesso* or of the *clausola compromissoria*, or did not decide a matter submitted to the arbitrators in the *compromesso* or contains contradictory provisions;

(5) The award does not indicate or contain the reasons for the decision, its *dictum*, the place of the arbitration and the place or manner in which the award has been made, and the signature of all, or the majority of, the arbitrators;

(6) The award has been made after the lapse of the available period;

(7) Any formality prescribed under penalty of nullity has not been observed in the course of the proceedings, provided that the parties had agreed that it should mandatorily be observed and the nullity has not been cured;

(8) The award is contrary to another award not subject to attack or to a final judgment rendered between the parties, provided that the relevant defence was raised during the arbitration proceedings; and

(9) The principle of the parties' equal right to plead has not been observed.

114. Code of Civil Procedure, Article 825.
115. Code of Civil Procedure, Article 829.

An arbitral award can also be attacked if the arbitrators did not observe the rules of law, unless the parties had granted them the authority to decide on a fair and equitable basis or had agreed the award not to be attackable or, in respect of labour disputes, in case of an infringement or wrongful interpretation of the collective bargaining contracts.[116]

The Court of Appeal may declare the nullity of the entire award or of a divisible part thereof, and in either case, if it believes that no further examination is required, may decide the merits of the case, unless otherwise agreed among all parties. If the court believes that a further examination is necessary, it will refer the case to the Examining Judge.[117] An arbitral award is also attackable by revocation for the reasons indicated in Article 395, Numbers 1, 2, 3 and 5 of the Code of Civil Procedure and by a third party opposition pursuant to Code of Civil Procedure, Article 404. Both revocation and third party opposition must be filed with the Court of Appeal competent over the place of arbitration.

INTERNATIONAL ARBITRATION

All the above-described rules on domestic arbitration apply to international arbitration except as amended by the provisions of Articles 832 to 838 of the Code of Civil Procedure. An arbitration is "international" when it concerns disputes between parties at least one of whom was at the time of signing of the *clausola compromissoria* or of the *compromesso* a foreign resident or had its actual place of business abroad, or when a relevant part of the obligations originating from the relationship to which the dispute refers is to be performed abroad. These provisions of the Code of Civil Procedure are without prejudice to the applicability of any international convention.

A *clausola compromissoria* contained in standard conditions of contract or in forms need not be specifically approved in writing.[118] A *clausola compromissoria* contained in standard conditions of contract incorporated in a written agreement between the parties is valid if the parties knew of the *clausola compromissoria* or should have known of it using ordinary diligence.[119] The parties are free to agree the rules to be applied by the arbitrators to the merits of the dispute or to instruct them to adjudicate it on a fair and equitable basis. In the absence of any determination by the parties, the law applicable will be that to which the relationship is most closely linked. In both cases the arbitrators will

116. Code of Civil Procedure, Article 829.
117. Code of Civil Procedure, Article 831.
118. Civil Code, Articles 1341 and 1342.
119. Code of Civil Procedure, Article 833.

take into account the indications in the contract and the usage of the trade.[120]
The arbitrators will also have, failing agreement between the parties, the
power to choose the language of the arbitration in relation to circumstances.

Unless otherwise agreed in each case between the parties:

(1) The arbitrators may be challenged according to Code of Civil
    Procedure, Article 815;[121]
(2) The award will be resolved by the arbitrators convened in personal
    conference, even by videophone, and will then be drawn up in
    writing;[122] and
(3) The award is not attackable on the grounds of nullity if the arbitra-
    tors did not observe the rules of law, nor by way of revocation,
    nor third party opposition, nor will the Court of Appeal have
    the authority to adjudicate the merits of the dispute[123] in case of
    an attack for nullity.

FOREIGN ARBITRAL AWARDS

Two additional Articles of the Code of Civil Procedure apply to the
recognition and enforcement in Italy of foreign arbitral awards. Anyone
who intends to avail himself of a foreign arbitral award in Italy must file
an application with the presiding judge of the Court of Appeal of the
place of residence of the other party — or if such party is not a resident
of Italy, with the presiding judge of the Court of Appeal of Rome —
together with an original or certified true copy of the award, of the
compromesso or of the equivalent document, and, if necessary, a sworn
translation of such documents. After its formal regularity has been ascertained, the award is declared enforceable in Italy by a decree of the
President of the Court of Appeal, except when:

(1) The dispute could not constitute the subject matter of a com-
    promesso under Italian law; or
(2) The award contains provisions contrary to Italian public
    policy.[124]

The decree according or denying enforceability of an award in Italy
may be opposed by serving on the other party a citation before the Court

120. Code of Civil Procedure, Article 834.
121. Code of Civil Procedure, Article 836.
122. Code of Civil Procedure, Article 837.
123. Code of Civil Procedure, Article 838.
124. Code of Civil Procedure, Article 839.

of Appeal within 30 days after the date of notice of the decree that denies the enforceability or the date of service of the decree that grants it. The relevant proceedings must follow to the extent applicable the procedural rules set forth in Articles 645 *et seq.* of the Code of Civil Procedure. The recognition or enforcement of the award is denied if the party against whom the award is intended to be used proves the following circumstances:

(1) That the parties to the arbitration agreement were not competent under the law applicable to them, or that the arbitration agreement was not valid under the law chosen for it by the parties or, in the absence of such choice, under the law of the place where the award was rendered;

(2) That the party against whom the award is to be used was not informed of the appointment of the arbitrator or of the arbitration proceedings or that it was not possible for him to assert his defence in the proceedings;

(3) That the award ruled on matters not contemplated by or outside the scope of the *compromesso* or *clausola compromissoria*, provided that, if the rulings of the award concerning matters submitted to arbitration can be separated from those concerning matters *not* submitted to the arbitral jurisdiction, the former rulings can be recognised and declared enforceable;

(4) That the constitution of the panel of arbitrators or the arbitral proceedings were not conformable to the parties' agreement or, in the absence of such agreement, to the law of the place of the arbitration; and

(5) That the award has not yet become binding on the parties or has been annulled or suspended by the competent authorities of the State where, or pursuant to whose law, the award has been rendered.

If a request for amendment or suspension of the award is submitted to the authorities, the Court of Appeal may suspend the proceedings for the recognition and enforcement of the award, and may, on request of the party who has applied for enforcement, order the other party to provide a satisfactory guarantee. The recognition and enforcement of foreign awards are obviously denied if:

(1) The dispute could not constitute the object of a *compromesso* under Italian Law; or

(2) The award contains provisions contrary to Italian public policy.[125]

125. Code of Civil Procedure, Article 840.

These provisions are without prejudice to the applicability of international conventions.

Other special proceedings

Among non-adversary proceedings, some are substantially aimed at the implementation of potestative rights. The peculiarity of such proceedings lies in the fact that they relate to rights that do not involve a claim of their holder against an opposite party but simply his ability of producing certain legal effects independently of other persons' intent. In these proceedings the function of the court is not that of settling a dispute but simply of implementing the intent of the holder of the right.

Dissolution of common ownership

Proceedings for the dissolution of common ownership (*procedimenti di scioglimento della comunione*) are related to the rule that "each participant can always demand the dissolution of common ownership",[126] and that if partition is not made in agreement with all participants, each of them may institute the appropriate action. Proceedings are initiated by an application served on all parties concerned (a typical case of compulsory co-litigation). If no disputes arise, provisions for partition are made by an order of the Examining Judge.[127] If, however, no agreement is reached among the parties, normal litigation ensues and is concluded by a judgment of the panel.

Release from mortgage

Proceedings for the release of property from mortgages (*procedimento di liberazione degli immobili dalle ipoteche*) are related to the right of a third person purchaser of mortgaged property who has transcribed his purchase instrument and is not personally bound to pay the mortgagee creditors, to release the property from any mortgages recorded prior to the transcription of such instrument by offering the creditors the price agreed in the contract or, failing that, the value of the property.[128] To achieve the release of the property from mortgages, an offer of the third person purchaser is not sufficient, but special proceedings are required, regulated by Articles 792–795 of the Code of Civil Procedure, ending up

126. Civil Code, Article 1111.
127. Code of Civil Procedure, Article 785.
128. Civil Code, Article 2889.

in an order of the court which, having verified the regularity of the procedure, provides for the cancellation of mortgages and the distribution of the price to the creditors.

ATTACKS ON DECISION

Attacks on decisions are the remedies that the law makes available to the parties to obtain reconsideration of the judgment issued by the court which first dealt with the dispute, and whose decision may be affected by errors either of fact or of law. As a rule, this reconsideration is made by a court other than the one that issued the attacked judgment, although exceptionally (in the cases of revocation or third party opposition) it may be made by the same court. The means of attack that can be used against judgments, as specifically contemplated and limited by the law, are appeal (*appello*), review by the Court of Cassation (*ricorso per cassazione*), revocation (*revocazione*) and third party opposition (*opposizione di terzo*). Similar to the latter is the *regolamento di competenza* (special procedure for settlement by the Court of Cassation of issues on competence).

In view of the principle requiring certainty in legal relations, attacks on judgments are subject to certain time limitations. After the lapse of the period provided for by the law — 30 days in all cases except review by the Court of Cassation where the period is 60 days[129] — without the judgment having been challenged, the attack is no longer admissible and the judgment acquires legal stability, becoming *res judicata*. Two general prerequisites must exist to justify the attack:

(1) The decision must be susceptible of being attacked under the law; and
(2) Except in the case of someone entitled to advance a third party opposition, the attacked party must have been a party in the previous phase of the proceedings and have been defeated.

Regardless of the lapse of time limitations, an attack may be barred by the losing party's express or implied acquiescence to the judgment.[130] Express acquiescence consists of a declaration of waiver by the party interested in bringing the attack, while implied acquiescence can be inferred from acts incompatible with the attempt to bring the attack (e.g., the *spontaneous compliance* with an as yet unenforceable judgment). At

129. Code of Civil Procedure, Article 325.
130. Code of Civil Procedure, Article 329.

any rate, the existence of an acquiescence must be asserted by the interested party and cannot be raised by the court *ex officio*.

A fundamental concern of the Italian legislator was that of preserving unity in proceedings for an attack against the same judgment. Thus in the event of a plurality of parties the law provides that all those who were parties to the first instance proceedings, except for divisible cases, participate in the second instance phase. However, all attacks of the same type that can be asserted against the same judgment by the two or more parties who participated in the previous phase should be brought in the same proceedings. If the first instance proceedings involved a plurality of parties (*litis consortium*), the Code of Civil Procedure expressly provides that all attacks asserted separately against the same judgment must be joined, even *ex officio*, in single proceedings.[131]

A distinction must be made between two different situations. First, if the judgment was rendered in a non-divisible (i.e., within a mandatory *litis consortium*) or interdependent case, and the judgment was not attacked *vis-à-vis* all parties, the court will order the missing parties to be joined in the proceedings and set the hearing at which they should appear as well as a time limit for the joinder order to be served on them. If no party complies with summoning of the missing parties, the attack will be declared inadmissible.[132] Second, if a judgment was rendered in divisible cases (e.g., in cases joined only by way of optional joinders), and an attack has been advanced only by some of the parties or *vis-à-vis* some of the parties, the court will order that notice of it be served on the other parties. Nevertheless, if service of the notice is not made, the proceedings must be suspended until the lapse of the time limits provided for the attack.[133]

One further rule reflects the principle of the unity of attack proceedings. It relates to those cases where the party against whom an attack has been asserted (or who has been served with the above-mentioned notice pursuant to Articles 331 or 332 of the Code of Civil Procedure) also intends to attack the judgment. Code of Civil Procedure, Article 333 provides that the new challenge must be asserted — subject to forfeiture — ancillarily in the first appearance in the same attack proceedings.[134] The incidental nature of the attack is evidenced also in respect of the further and very important rule codified in Code of Civil Procedure, Article 334 "Late incidental attacks" which provides that the parties against whom an attack has been advanced and those called on to participate in the proceedings pursuant to Code of Civil Procedure, Article 331 can bring an incidental attack notwithstanding that the time limitation

131. Code of Civil Procedure, Article 335.
132. Code of Civil Procedure, Article 331.
133. Code of Civil Procedure, Article 332.
134. Code of Civil Procedure, Articles 343 and 371.

has expired for an independent attack or that they have acquiesced in the judgment. This allows a partially defeated party to accept the judgment subject to his adversary's acceptance without prejudicing his own rights to attack the judgment.

The effects of the decision on the attack vary: The decision may replace the judgment rendered in the previous proceedings as in the case of an appeal; or it may quash it, as is the case with Court of Cassation proceedings. The law makes it clear that reversal on appeal or quashing by the Court of Cassation results in the immediate lapse of the measures and the execution acts performed pursuant to the attacked judgment, even before the attack decision becomes final.

The recent reform of the Code of Civil Procedure introduced a substantial change by making all first instance decisions provisionally enforceable.[135] However, the party in interest may apply for a suspension of the provisional enforcement, which will be granted only if the application for suspension is supported by serious grounds or, in the case of Court of Cassation proceedings, only if the court that issued the judgment under attack holds that serious and irreparable damage may result from enforcement.[136]

Appeal

Scope

Appeal (*appello*) is the broadest means of ordinary attack, since it accords a total reconsideration of the dispute resolved by the first instance court, even though limited to the claims and objections that have been expressly resubmitted on appeal. Consequently, as to the issue resubmitted, the appealed decision is intended to replace the first instance judgment in establishing a new settlement of the controversy.

The appeal is intended as a *revisio prioris istantiae*, so that the subject matter of the proceedings is, to the extent claims and objections are resubmitted, only that of the first instance litigation. No new claims (i.e., different parties, *petitum* or *causa petendi*) are permissible on appeal, except those which constitute a logical and chronological development of claims previously submitted such as interest, fruits or other accessories that have matured after the judgment.[137] Infringements of this prohibition can be detected by the court also *ex officio* and will entail a declaration of non-admissibility of the new claims.

135. Code of Civil Procedure, Article 282.
136. Code of Civil Procedure, Articles 373, 401, 407.
137. Code of Civil Procedure, Article 345, Par. I.

No new defences (except those that would be detectable *ex officio* anyhow) and no new evidence[138] can be allowed in appellate proceedings. The prohibition concerning new evidence does not apply if the full panel of the court considers it indispensable for the decision of the case or if a party shows that it could not be submitted in the first instance proceedings for reasons beyond that party's control. Finally, any claim or objection submitted in the first instance and either not allowed or not considered must be expressly resubmitted, failing which it will be deemed to have been waived.[139]

Appealable decisions

Generally, all decisions rendered in the first instance are eligible for appeal.[140] The non-appealability is an exception and must be expressly contemplated by the law. Such is the case in respect of decisions rendered under equitable principles by the Justice of Peace in cases not exceeding 2-million lire in value; of those that have settled an individual labour or social security and compulsory health insurance dispute not exceeding 50,000 lire in value;[141] those dealing with an opposition to enforcement acts (*opposizione agli atti esecutivi*)[142] or those pronounced in accordance with fair and equitable principles pursuant to Code of Civil Procedure, Article 114. Furthermore, no appeal can be instituted if the parties have stipulated to submit a first instance decision directly to the Court of Cassation for review. However, in such case, the review may be requested only on grounds of an infringement or false application of the rules of law[143] or when the decision contains a ruling relating only to competence. A further distinction concerning the submission of an appeal against a first instance decision must be made between definitive and non-definitive decisions.[144] The former must be appealed within the prescribed time limit of 30 days. As to the latter an appeal may immediately

---

138. Except decisory oath; see Code of Civil Procedure, Article 345, Par. II, III.
139. Code of Civil Procedure, Article 346.
140. Code of Civil Procedure, Article 339.
141. Code of Civil Procedure, Articles 440 and 442.
142. Code of Civil Procedure, Article 618.
143. Code of Civil Procedure, Article 360, Par. II.
144. The following example will help understanding the difference between a definitive and non-definitive decision: A sues B for damages in a third-party liability case resulting from a traffic accident. A asks the court to first decide whether or not B is liable for the accident. The court finds that A is liable (non-definitive decision) and remands the case to the Examining Judge to rule (definitive decision) on the nature and amount of damages sustained by A. A has an option to appeal the non-definitive decision immediately or to wait for the issuance of the definitive decision to lodge a global appeal, subject to having made an express reservation of the right to appeal.

be lodged within the prescribed time limit, or the party can make an express reservation to appeal them, together with the definitive decision.

Appeal procedure

Insofar as applicable, the rules laid down for first instance proceedings before the tribunal must be observed in the appellate proceedings.[145] The parties are he who submits the appeal (the appellant) and he who resists it (the appellee or defendant on appeal), but the latter may also play the dual role of defendant and cross-appellant. All parties who participated in the first instance proceedings may be parties to the appeal. However, a joinder in appellate proceedings by a third party is not possible, except by a party entitled to assert a third party opposition (*opposizione di terzo*).[146]

The tribunal is competent to hear appeals against the decisions of the Justice of Peace and the *Pretore* within its circuit, and the Court of Appeal is competent to hear appeals against the tribunal's decisions.[147] An appeal is taken by causing a citation to be served on the opponent like in first instance proceedings, setting forth the specific grounds for the appeal.[148] The rules concerning the appearance of the parties are very similar to those applicable in first instance proceedings. Any cross appeal must be submitted by the appellee in his answer to the appeal, failing which he will forfeit his right to the cross appeal.[149]

Appeal decision

Pursuant to the reform of the Code of Civil Procedure enacted by Law Number 353 of 1990, appellate proceedings that used to be handled by a member of the panel (the Examining Judge), like in first instance proceedings, are now conducted before the full panel. Thus, the full panel is competent to dismiss the appeal by declaring it *inammissibile* or *improcedibile* as the case may be. An appeal is declared *inammissibile* whenever it has been submitted after the lapse of the time limit prescribed, or the appeal is incompatible with the appellant's acquiescence to the first instance decision or when the conditions to appeal did not prevail and, further, if the appellant failed to comply with a court order to summon

145. Code of Civil Procedure, Article 359.
146. Code of Civil Procedure, Article 404.
147. Code of Civil Procedure, Article 341.
148. Code of Civil Procedure, Article 342.
149. Code of Civil Procedure, Article 343, Par. I.

into the proceedings parties to whom the case is common. An appeal will be declared *improcedibile*, even *ex officio*, when, even though the appeal would have been admissible, the appellant failed to enter an appearance within the deadline prescribed or was absent at the first hearing and at the adjournment of it fixed by the panel.[150] At the first hearing, the panel also takes action (by an order which cannot be attacked) on the motion for suspension of enforcement or enforceability of the first instance decision, which motion must be expressly submitted concurrently with the appeal or the cross-appeal.[151] The formalities for the decision of an appeal, such as the submission of final prayers for relief, the presentation of final briefs and reply briefs, and the oral pleadings are similar to those applicable in the first instance proceedings. The panel's decision may be definitive or non-definitive. It is definitive when the panel definitively decides the merits of the case affirming or amending the appealed judgment; it is non-definitive when the panel, amending the appealed judgment, decides preliminary issues and makes provisions by an *ad hoc* order for further proof-taking activities, which will be conducted by the appellate court. Articles 353 and 354 of the Code of Civil Procedure set forth the cases where the second instance court is required to remand the cause to the first instance court. These are, however, but apparent exceptions, since actually they relate to situations where the first instance proceedings either did not validly develop or did not attain a conclusive result. When a case is remanded to the first instance court, the parties must resume the action within six months, failing which the proceedings will be extinguished.

Review by the Court of Cassation

Nature

The review by the Court of Cassation (*Ricorso per Cassazione*) prevents a decision from becoming final (*res judicata*) without, however, introducing a total re-examination of the dispute. It may not, therefore, be regarded as third instance proceedings. The review by the Court of Cassation is confined to the existence or non-existence of such procedural or judicial errors denounced by the party requesting the review. When granted, a request for review by the Court of Cassation leads to a quashing of the decision attacked, and the referral or remanding of the case to another court. Only in exceptional cases, when no further investigations are required that may the Court of Cassation not only cancel the previous decision but actually produce a definitive decision

150. Code of Civil Procedure, Article 348.
151. Code of Civil Procedure, Article 351.

on the merits.[152] The review by the Court of Cassation is essentially aimed at verifying the precise application of the law by the courts rather than by the parties.

The Court of Cassation, while supervising the accurate observance of the law in specific cases, should ensure the uniform interpretation of legal rules on a national scale. Indeed, the decisions of the Court of Cassation, which are systematically condensed in syllabi (*massime*) constitute precedents which, even though not binding on the courts called on to resolve the same issues of law, ultimately guide, not only on the strength of their legal reasoning, but also in view of the authoritativeness of the court from which they emanate and to which those issues might eventually be submitted.

With a view to this function, the Code of Civil Procedure[153] contemplates a peculiar form of petition for review by the Court of Cassation. When the parties have forfeited their power to attack the decision because of the lapse of a deadline or of a waiver of the attack, the Chief Prosecutor (*procuratore generale presso la Corte di Cassazione*) sitting with the Court of Cassation may submit a "petition for review in the interests of the law" (*ricorso nell'interesse della legge*).[154] A decision rendered on it does not affect the relationship between the parties and is promoted for the sole purpose of obtaining decision of the Court of Cassation for guidance in future cases.

Finally, it is worth noting that a petition for review by the Court of Cassation, like an appeal, does not work a suspension of the decision challenged and that only if enforcement of that decision may result in serious and irreparable damage does the law[155] allow the court of origin (i.e., the court that handed down the decision attacked by a petition for review by the Court of Cassation), on an *ex parte* application, to suspend enforcement by an order which is not capable of being attacked.

Reviewable decisions

A petition for review by the Court of Cassation is allowed against four categories of decisions.[156] The first two categories include decisions rendered in appellate proceedings and those rendered by an ordinary court in a single instance. Hence, even those decisions that under the law are non-appealable may be reviewed by the Court of Cassation. A third category of decisions includes first instance decisions that, while normally

152. Code of Civil Procedure, Article 384.
153. Code of Civil Procedure, Article 363.
154. Code of Civil Procedure, Article 363.
155. Code of Civil Procedure, Article 373.
156. Code of Civil Procedure, Article 360.

incapable of being submitted directly to the Court of Cassation, may exceptionally by-pass the appellate stage (*revisio per saltum*) — only on grounds of infringement or misapplication of rules of law — if the parties are in agreement.[157] Furthermore, Article 111, second paragraph, of the Italian Constitution allows the submission of a petition for review by the Court of Cassation against all decisions of ordinary or special courts (except the Council of State and the Court of Accounts) on grounds of infringement of the law. This means on all those grounds set forth in Code of Civil Procedure, Article 360. In this respect, the Court of Cassation has taken the firm view that the provisions of Article 111 of the Constitution would apply not only to measures that are in the form of an actual judgment but also to any other measure issued in any other form, as long as it affects subjective rights, is in the nature of a decision and cannot be attacked otherwise. The admissibility of a petition for review by the Court of Cassation is not only conditional on the fact that the decision be objectively attackable before the Court of Cassation, but is also subject to the condition that the petition complain of a specific error or defect that has affected the outcome of the proceedings and falls within one of the categories expressly mentioned by way of limitation in Code of Civil Procedure, Article 360 under the heading "grounds for petition" (*motivi del ricorso*). Such grounds are usually divided into two groups:

(1) Procedural errors (*errores in procedendo*), pertaining to the observance of the legal rules regulating the development of proceedings; and
(2) Errors in judgment (*errores in judicando*),[158] which may have been made by the court in identifying and applying the rules of substantive law governing the legal relationship that was the subject of the proceedings.

Some procedural errors cause the nullity of procedural steps, which extends to the subsequent steps dependent on the previous ones up to the judgment.[159] Others[160] pertain to jurisdiction or to an infringement of rules on competence, when no competence or jurisdiction settlement procedure is required. A particular type of *error in procedendo* is the lack of, insufficient or contradictory reasoning concerning a decisive point of the dispute raised by the parties or capable of being identified by the court *ex officio*.[161]

157. Code of Civil Procedure, Article 360, last paragraph.
158. Code of Civil Procedure, Article 360, Number 3.
159. Code of Civil Procedure, Article 159.
160. Code of Civil Procedure, Article 360, Numbers 1 and 2.
161. Code of Civil Procedure, Article 360, Number 5.

Cassation procedure

Proceedings before the Court of Cassation take place in a form quite different from that typical of the merits stages of the proceedings. The most remarkable difference consists in the total absence of an examination phase, except only the filing of instruments and documents not previously submitted concerning the nullity of the attacked decision and the admissibility of the petition and cross-petition for review.[162] Cassation review proceedings are instituted by a petition (*ricorso*) addressed to the court and signed by a lawyer registered in the special list of counsel licensed to plead before the Court of Cassation, appointed by a special power attorney. In the absence of these conditions the petition will be declared not admissible.[163] The petition will be served by the petitioner on the opponent within 60 days after service of the judgment, prior to being filed with the court, and will, subject to being declared inadmissible, contain the names of the parties and a reference to the judgment or decision being attacked; a summary recital of the facts; the grounds on which Cassation review is sought, with a reference to the rules of law on which they are based; a reference to the power of attorney, if it was granted by a separate instrument.[164] The party on whom the petition was served (the opponent) may, if he so desires, remain inactive up to the oral pleading, in which case he may equally participate in the pleading[165] but may not submit a written memorandum. If he intends to contradict he must draw up and serve on the petitioner a counter-petition (*controricorso*) i.e., a document, having the same formal prerequisites as the petition, which can only set forth the defences against the grounds laid down in the petition and deal with such questions as the court may take up even *ex officio,* but cannot contain criticism of the decision attacked, for which a cross-petition (*ricorso incidentale*) would be required. A cross-petition must be submitted in the same document as containing the counter-petition and must be advanced both by a party losing in respect of one of the items of the decision (*ricorso incidentale autonomo*) and by a party who, although having been fully successful in the litigation, may wish subordinately or subject to the allowance of the main petition to resubmit issues of a prejudicial or preliminary nature unfavourably resolved, even though implied by the court of merits (*ricorso incidentale condizionato*). On completion of the introductory phase, the case is argued before the panel at a hearing appointed by the chief presiding judge. Cases are normally decided by an individual chamber of the court with a panel consisting of five members, but the law provides that a

162. Code of Civil Procedure, Article 372.
163. Code of Civil Procedure, Article 365.
164. Code of Civil Procedure, Article 366.
165. Code of Civil Procedure, Article 370, Par. I.

decision by joint chambers with a panel comprised of nine members may be made when the petition relates to questions of jurisdiction or conflicts of competence or when so provided by the chief presiding judge if the petition deals with a question of law previously decided in a conflicting manner by individual chambers or with a question of principle of particular relevance.[166]

Effect of cassation

Cassation proceedings have a particularly rescissory effect, and tend to quash the decision of the court of merits, so as to make it possible for the dispute to be reconsidered (i.e., *giudizio rescissorio*).

The decisions of the Court of Cassation may provide either for the dismissal of the petition for procedural improprieties or for its rejection: in both cases the judgment attacked becomes *res judicata;* they may also provide for the correction of the reasoning of the attacked judgment, if the Court of Cassation finds that the lower court erred in its reasoning but nevertheless reached the correct result. In this case, too, the lower court's decision becomes *res judicata*. The decisions of the Court of Cassation may also allow the petition and reverse the judgment attacked.

Two types of reversal are possible: a reversal without remand (*cassazione senza rinvio*) and a reversal with remand (*cassazione con rinvio*). Reversal without remand (*cassazione senza rinvio*) occurs when the Court of Cassation, while resolving a question of jurisdiction or competence, acknowledges that the court whose decision has been attacked and any other court lack jurisdiction or that, for any reason, the case could not be submitted or the proceedings could not be continued before the court of merits;[167] another possibility of reversal without remand was introduced by Law Number 353 of 1990 which, in amending Article 384 of the Code of Civil Procedure, provides that the Court of Cassation, when allowing the petition on grounds of infringement or misapplication of a rule of substantive law, lays down the principle of law with which the remand court should comply or decides the case on its merits if no further determination of the facts is required. This is the only case in which the Court of Cassation is permitted to adjudicate the merits of the dispute. The rationale of such amendment is the advisability of avoiding useless and costly continuation of the proceedings before the remand court and of precluding the institution of further and unfounded petitions for Cassation review aimed at delaying the decision from becoming *res judicata*. In all other cases the Court of Cassation provides for reversal with remand (*cassazione con rinvio*), quashing the decision of the lower court

166. Code of Civil Procedure, Article 374, Par. II.
167. Code of Civil Procedure, Article 382, Par. III.

and designating the court before which the proceedings should be resumed. As a rule the court designated is not the same, but at the same level as that which rendered the original judgment. Usually, the choice will fall on a court geographically close to that which rendered the reversed judgment, but often a different chamber of the same court of appeal may be chosen for the remand. If the remand is based only on the detection of a logical error,[168] the court to which the case is remanded will confine itself to repeating the logical itinerary of the judgment on the merits, avoiding the error detected by the Court of Cassation. If the remand was justified by an infringement or misapplication of a rule of substantive law,[169] the Court of Cassation will formulate the rule of law which must be applied to the issue of the judgment by the remand court. The decisions of the Court of Cassation are not usually capable of being attacked in any manner.

The procedure for revocation (*revocazione*) of decisions can also apply in respect of a decision of the Court of Cassation if the Court in its judgment incurred a revocatory error of fact under the terms of Article 395, Number 4 of the Code of Civil Procedure. Pursuant to this Article, material errors and calculation errors contained in a Court of Cassation decision may be corrected by proceedings initiated through an application to be served not later than 60 days from service of the decision or one year after its publication.

Remand proceedings

Remand proceedings (*giudizio di rinvio*) are initiated by the party interested in continuing the litigation by means of a citation to be served on all those who participated in the Court of Cassation review. If the proceedings are not reactivated within the peremptory deadline of one year after publication of the Court of Cassation's decision, the whole process is extinguished and any previous pronunciation loses its effect, except only that concerning the enunciation of the principle of law by the Court of Cassation which must be complied with by such other court as might be requested to adjudicate the claim in new proceedings.[170] Remand proceedings are regulated by the procedural rules applicable before the court to which the case has been remanded.[171]

The law does not expressly regulate the powers of the remand court, but from the function of the remand proceedings it may be inferred that the court, even though bound to confine its review to the portions of the

168. Code of Civil Procedure, Article 360, Number 5.
169. Code of Civil Procedure, Article 360, Number 3.
170. Code of Civil Procedure, Article 393.
171. Code of Civil Procedure, Article 394.

attacked decision which were quashed, has full autonomy and is subject only to the binding effect of the ruling of the Court of Cassation, whether requiring the performance of certain procedural steps or stating a principle of law. The remand court has in any case the power to interpret the decision of the Court of Cassation and the judgment rendered by it on remand can be attacked by a new petition for Cassation review.

Revocation

Revocation (*revocazione*) is a remedy accorded in respect of exceptional situations deemed to have prevented the correct formation of a judgment. By an application for revocation, the same court that has rendered the attacked decision is requested to quash it and replace it on the assumption that it is vitiated by defects that escaped its cognisance. Pursuant to Article 395, Par. I of the Code of Civil Procedure, the decisions that may be attacked by revocation are decisions rendered on appeal or not appealable as well as, pursuant to Article 391–*bis* of the Code of Civil Procedure, Court of Cassation decisions rendered on petitions based on Article 360, Number 4 of the Code of Civil Procedure, where the court made a revocable error of fact under the terms of Article 395 Number 4 of the Code of Civil Procedure.

The reason why revocation can be exerted only in respect of appellate decisions is that the grounds for revocation relate to the merits of the case and could form the object of appellate proceedings, so that the legislator has excluded the remedy of revocation as long as a normal appeal can be instituted. The Code of Civil Procedure, Article 395 contemplates six grounds for revocation which may be divided into two groups: those set forth in Article 395, Numbers 4 and 5, which are the basis for the so-called ordinary revocation (*revocazione ordinaria*) and those set forth in Numbers 1, 2, 3 and 6, which are the basis for the so-called extraordinary revocation (*revocazione straordinaria*).

Grounds for ordinary revocation (*revocazione ordinaria*) are either an error of fact evidenced by the record or documents of the proceedings which occurs when the court by an oversight or omission relies on a fact whose truthfulness is undoubtedly excluded or when the judgment attacked is contrary to a prior judgment having the force of *res judicata* between the parties. The deadline to apply for revocation is 30 days from the date of service of the decision.

The first ground for extraordinary revocation is fraud of a party which substantially affected the outcome of the litigation; the second ground is when a judgment was rendered on the basis of evidence which is recognised or declared to be false after the judgment; the third ground is when one or more decisive documents are found after the judgment, which could not be exhibited during the proceedings by reason of *force majeure* or of the opponent's behaviour; the fourth ground is when the decision is the result of fraud by the court, ascertained by a judgment that has become *res judicata*. The deadline for the institution of extraordinary revocation proceedings is 30 days from the date on which the fraud or falsity or collusion was discovered or documentary evidence was found or from the day when the judgment found fraudulent by the court became *res judicata*. For revocation of a decision by the Court of Cassation, a petition for revocation must be served not later than 60 days from the date of service of the attacked decision or one year from its publication.

The party eligible to submit a petition for revocation is the party that lost the litigation. The Public Prosecutor can also institute revocation proceedings, when the judgment was handed down without seeking the Prosecutor's opinion or was the result of collusion of the parties aimed at circumventing the law.[172]

The petition is submitted to the same court that issued the attacked decision. Such submission does not entail a suspension of the period to apply for a Court of Cassation review or of the related proceedings. Nevertheless, the court vested with the revocation petition may, if it does not consider the petition altogether unfounded, suspend either period on an *ex parte* motion until service of the decision rendered on the revocation petition. The procedure is the normal one and consists of two phases: A first phase to determine whether a reason for revocation exists and a second phase to decide the merits of the case. The revocation of a judgment is effective between the parties, restoring the situation that existed prior to the revoked decision, but has no effect *vis-à-vis* good faith third parties. A revocation decision is subject to the same attacks as could be brought against the decision now revoked, but is not subject to revocation.[173]

Third party opposition

A third party opposition (*opposizione di terzo*) is an extraordinary means of attack, since it can be advanced even if the judgment has become *res judicata*. It is accorded to a third party to remove the prejudicial effects that inure on him from a decision rendered *inter alios*. The Code of Civil Procedure contemplates two types of third party opposition:

(1) An ordinary opposition (*opposizione ordinaria*)[174] available to any third party against a judgment that became *res judicata* or enforceable and is prejudicial to his rights;

172. Code of Civil Procedure, Article 397.
173. Code of Civil Procedure, Article 403.
174. Code of Civil Procedure, Article 404, Par. I.

(2) A revocatory opposition (*opposizione revocatoria*)[175] available to creditors or to successors in interest of either party who would suffer prejudice when a judgment unfavourable to their debtor or predecessor in interest was issued to their detriment as a result of fraud or collusion between the parties.

A third party opposition must be submitted to the court that handed down the attacked decision.[176] The procedure is that ordinarily applicable before that court. While there is no time limit for the institution of an ordinary opposition, a revocatory opposition must be initiated not later than 30 days from the date on which the third party became aware of the fraud or collusion.[177] A third party opposition does not have *per se* a suspensive effect so that a possible motion for suspension and its handling are treated in the same manner as one in connection with Court of Cassation proceedings.[178] A third party opposition is decided by a judgment, with the only peculiarity being that if the opposition is declared inadmissible or is rejected for lack of grounds, the court will also order the opponent to pay a pecuniary penalty.[179]

ENFORCEMENT PROCEEDINGS

General rules

Enforcement proceedings are regulated by Book VI, Title IV of the Civil Code and Book III of the Code of Civil Procedure. They are aimed at the forced material satisfaction of the creditor's claim, based on a judgment or other enforceable instrument (*titolo esecutivo*). Enforcement proceedings may have a different structure depending on the type of substantive rights to be enforced. Some common characteristics are:

(1) The parties to the proceedings are, on one side, the enforcement authority operating under the supervision of the court and, on the other, the creditor and the debtor, i.e., respectively, he who demands or he against whom judicial protection is sought;

(2) The enforcement authority is the process server (*ufficiale giudiziario*) literally "Judicial Officer". He is a government employee

175. Code of Civil Procedure, Article 404, Par. II.
176. Code of Civil Procedure, Article 405, Par. I.
177. Code of Civil Procedure, Article 326.
178. Code of Civil Procedure, Article 407.
179. Code of Civil Procedure, Article 408.

attached to the court and charged with the function of serving process, attaching property, and the like;

(3) The court supervising enforcement or "the enforcement court" (*giudice dell'esecuzione*) is the *Pretore* if levy of execution is exercised on movables or the tribunal if the object of forced execution are immovables;

(4) The action is initially unilateral, and the debtor does not have the position of a defendant; it is only when the debtor institutes an opposition that bilateral litigation ensues as to the form of execution;

(5) An application to the enforcement authority is normally submitted orally; and

(6) The activities of the enforcement authority consist of taking a number of steps, while those of the court consist of the issuance of regulatory orders or decrees.

Types of enforcement action

Three fundamental actions may be brought in enforcement proceedings:

(1) Forced execution (*espropriazione forzata*) for the collection of pecuniary claims or "generic forced execution", consisting in enforcement proceedings aimed at taking property forcefully away from the debtor and converting it, again forcefully, into money in order to satisfy the creditor's rights;

(2) Execution for delivery or release (*esecuzione per consegna o rilascio*), consisting in enforcement proceedings aiming at letting the creditor obtain the physical availability of a given movable or immovable asset, intended to be delivered or released; and

(3) Forced execution of an obligation to do or not to do something (*esecuzione forzata di obblighi di fare o non fare*), consisting in proceedings aimed at the enforcement of a judgment requiring the defendant to do or to refrain from doing something.

A typical feature of enforcement proceedings are certain steps that must be taken prior to the commencement of the actual execution, with a view to informing the debtor of the creditor's intent to proceed with forced execution on the basis of an enforceable instrument in satisfaction of the right mentioned therein. These steps enable the debtor to discharge his obligation and avoid forced execution and the related costs, and to be apprised of the elements of the announced execution and possibly to contest its lawfulness. Accordingly, pursuant to Code of Civil Procedure, Article 479, forced execution will be preceded by service of the enforceable instrument and of a formal notice known as "precept" (*precetto*).

Enforceable instruments

An enforceable instrument (*titolo esecutivo*) is the instrument ascertaining or constituting the creditor's right to be satisfied by way of execution and showing the existence of a claim: certain (*certo*), that is whose existence is certain to the extent deemed necessary by law; liquid and liquidated (*liquido*), that is for a definite amount; and collectible (*esigibile*), that is not subject to a condition or to the lapse of time. Execution cannot be initiated without such instrument (*nulla executio sine titulo*). Production of the instrument proves the underlying right, until the instrument is challenged.

Enforceable instruments of a judicial nature[180] are judgments and other provisions to which the law expressly attributes executive force (for example, certain orders to pay a fine[181] under *procès-verbal* of conciliation, summary judgments or eviction orders). Enforceable instruments of an extra-judicial nature are promissory notes and other negotiable instruments as well as other instruments to which the law attributes the same executive force (for example, the *procès-verbal* of conciliation in litigation proceedings) and instruments drawn up by a notary or other official, but only in respect of the pecuniary obligations set forth therein.

Precept

A precept under the terms of the Code of Civil Procedure, Article 480 is a formal intimation to comply with the obligation set forth in the enforceable document within a time limit of no less than 10 days, and a warning that, failing compliance, forced execution will ensue. A precept is without effect unless it is brought to the knowledge of the destinee. Accordingly, it must be served personally on the party pursuant to Articles 137 *et seq.* of the Code of Civil Procedure, subsequent to or concurrently with service of the enforceable document. The precept loses its effect if forced execution is not commenced within 90 days of service.

Forced execution

Forced execution (*espropriazione forzata*) consists of a series of steps aimed at taking compulsorily from the debtor some of its assets and converting them into money, in order to satisfy the creditor. Depending on the property on which it is exercised, forced execution may be:

180. Code of Civil Procedure, Article 474.
181. Code of Civil Procedure, Article 179.

(1) Movable (*mobiliare*), if exercised against the debtor's money or movables in his possession in which case it falls within the competence of the *Pretore*;

(2) Third party (*presso terzi*) if exercised over the debtors movables in the possession of a third party or over obligations owed to the debtor by a third party; or

(3) Immovable (*immobiliare*), if exercised over immovable property in which case it falls within the competence of the Tribunal.

Since a debtor is liable for the discharge of his obligations with all of his present and future assets,[182] the creditor is entitled to levy execution on the debtor's property. The levy of execution is supervised by the court competent for execution proceedings,[183] i.e., a member of the Tribunal, for immovable execution, and the *Pretore*, for movable execution or for execution on property in the possession of third parties. The judge supervises execution throughout the proceedings and cannot be substituted except in cases of absolute impediment.

The judge hears the interested parties at a hearing set by him which must be attended by the creditor levying execution, any joining creditors, the debtor, and any other interested parties[184] and may, on the motion of the parties, issue orders that may be revoked and amended until they have been carried into effect. Forced execution begins with an attachment (*pignoramento*),[185] which consists in an order by the process server (*ufficiale giudiziario*) to the debtor to refrain from any action aimed at removing the assets attached as security of a given claim and their fruits.[186]

Attachment is an act of the process server, performed at the request of the creditor and subject to the prior exhibition of the enforceable instrument and to due service of the precept. It creates a legal charge on the assets to be expropriated, voiding *vis-à-vis* the attaching creditor and the joining creditors any act of assignment or disposition made by the debtor on the attached assets, without prejudice to good faith possession of movable assets not recorded in public registries.[187] An attachment may be imposed both on specified assets selected by the creditor among all those owned by the debtor[188] and assets owned by third parties, when they are pledged as security for the claim or deriving from a transaction that has been set aside as having been performed to the prejudice of the creditor.[189]

182. Civil Code, Article 2740.
183. Code of Civil Procedure, Article 484.
184. Code of Civil Procedure, Article 485.
185. Code of Civil Procedure, Article 491.
186. Code of Civil Procedure, Article 492.
187. Civil Code, Article 2913.
188. Civil Code, Article 2010, Par. I.
189. Civil Code, Article 2910, Par. II.

However, when the creditor is the beneficiary of a pledge or mortgage over specified assets, he has no freedom of choice and must levy execution on the asset pledged or mortgaged or subject to another lien.[190] A debtor confronted with an attachment may alternatively:

(1) Avoid the attachment by paying to the process server the amount of the claim and costs;[191]
(2) Apply for a conversion of the attachment, i.e., the substitution for the attached assets of a sum of money equal to the amount of the costs and claims of the attaching creditor and the joining creditors: such sum is fixed by the judge by an *ad hoc* order. However, to prevent this procedure from resulting in a merely dilatory manoeuvre, an amendment to Code of Civil Procedure, Article 495, introduced by Law Number 353/90 provides that an application for conversion may be submitted only once, by depositing in the clerk's office one-fifth of the amount of the claims for which the attachment has been made and that the debtor cannot pay by instalments the sum in substitution for the attached assets;
(3) Apply for a reduction of the attachment when the value of the attached assets exceeds the amount of the costs and claims.[192] An attachment loses effect after the lapse of 90 days since its date without an application for sale or assignment having been submitted.[193] The running of this time limit is suspended in case of opposition to the execution.[194]

"Joining creditors" (*creditori intervenuti*) are all those creditors who intend to satisfy their claims in the same proceedings and have applied to join in the proceedings after the creditor who initiated them (the so-called "proceeding creditor"). A few rules apply in this connection: only one execution proceeding is permissible on the same asset; the joining creditors, if holding an enforceable instrument, may cause individual steps of forced execution to be taken if the proceeding creditor fails to do so; in the distribution of the proceeds of execution, all creditors are entitled to an equal treatment based on the "*par condicio creditorum*" principle, except those holding preferred claims. In order to satisfy his claim, the proceeding creditor or any joining creditor must liquidate the assets under execution, either by forced sale or direct assignment to the creditor based on a pre-established value. The competent judge sets a hearing to authorise the sale or the assignment.

190. Civil Code, Article 2911.
191. Code of Civil Procedure, Article 494.
192. Code of Civil Procedure, Article 496.
193. Code of Civil Procedure, Article 497.
194. Code of Civil Procedure, Article 628.

The last phase of execution proceedings consists in the allocation of the proceeds. If there is only one creditor, the judge, having heard the debtor, provides for payment to the creditor of the sums owing to him, applying the proceeds to principal, interest and costs. If the creditors who have proceeded with or joined in the same attachment are more than one, a distribution plan must be mutually agreed, subject to the approval of the judge, or imposed by the judge. The plan must observe legitimate priorities. The balance of proceeds, if any, must be delivered to the debtor or to the third party suffering the enforcement. Disputes arising in connection with distribution[195] are examined by the enforcement court if they fall within its competence, or referred to the court competent according to the value of the highest claim contested.

Movable forced execution from the debtor

Movable forced execution from the debtor *(espropriazione forzata presso il debitore)* concerns movable assets which the process server, producing the enforceable instrument and the precept, may trace and attach in the debtor's home or in other locations the debtor controls or even on the debtor's own person, without injuring his dignity.[196] If authorised by the *Pretore*, the process server may also attach specified items that are not in locations the debtor controls, but which the debtor may directly dispose of. The process server will prefer to attach easily marketable items such as cash, jewels and securities.

After identifying the assets to be attached within the limits of the claim and the presumable costs, the process server must make a description of the assets and determine their approximate value in the *procès-verbal*. Thereupon, he will order the debtor to refrain from any disposition of the attached property and appoint a custodian for the preservation and, possibly, for the management of the attached assets.[197] Not later than the first hearing appointed for the authorisation of sale or assignment, anyone having a claim certain, liquidated and collectible may join in the execution proceedings. After the lapse of 10 days from the attachment, the attaching creditor or any joining creditor may apply for the distribution and the sale of all other assets. They may also apply for the assignment of securities and other assets whose value is reflected in the quotations of the stock exchange or commodities market.[198] On application of the attaching creditor, the *Pretore* sets a hearing to interview the parties who may submit observations concerning the procedures for the sale and

195. Code of Civil Procedure, Article 512.
196. Code of Civil Procedure, Article 513, Par. I.
197. Code of Civil Procedure, Article 521.
198. Code of Civil Procedure, Article 529.

must, subject to forfeiture, assert an opposition to enforcement acts (*opposizione agli atti esecutivi*). If no oppositions arise or if the parties present are in agreement, the *Pretore* issues an order, making provisions for the assignment or sale. If oppositions arise, the *Pretore* resolves them by a judgment, and issues an order making provisions for the assignment or sale.[199]

A simplified procedure was introduced by Law Number 353/90 with regard to movable forced execution when the value of the attached assets does not exceed 10-million lire.[200]

Forced execution from third parties

Forced execution from third parties (*espropriazione presso terzi*) deals with movable assets owned by the debtor but in the possession of third parties or claims of the debtor against third parties. In these cases, the attachment is aimed at the dual purpose of preventing the third party from paying or delivering the asset to the debtor and of ascertaining the actual existence of the debtor's claim or of the asset owned by him. It is served personally on the third person and the debtor.[201] Following service of the attachment, the third person becomes subject to the obligations of a custodian[202] with respect to the property or sums due, thereby undertaking a personal liability to the attaching creditor.

By a statement made at the hearing personally or through a special attorney, the third person must specify which sums he owes, of which property he is in possession, when he must deliver such property or pay such claims; the sequestrations and attachments previously made against him and the assignments that may have been served on him or that he accepted.[203] Such a statement is an integral part of the attachment failing which the attachment is not perfected. If the third person fails to appear at the hearing or, even though appearing, refuses to make the statement, or if a dispute arises on the contents of the statement, the execution proceedings are suspended by operation of law and, at the instance of the interest party, a regular action is commenced at the end of which if the debtor's right is found to exist, the court appoints a deadline for the continuation of the execution proceeding.[204]

199. Code of Civil Procedure, Article 530.

200. Code of Civil Procedure, Article 525, last paragraph, as amended by Law Number 353/90.

201. Code of Civil Procedure, Article 543, Par. I.

202. Code of Civil Procedure, Article 546.

203. Code of Civil Procedure, Article 547.

204. Code of Civil Procedure, Article 549.

Immovable forced execution

The target of immovable forced execution (*espropriazione immobiliare*) is immovable property with its appurtenances and real rights of enjoyment in immovable property. The choice of the property to be attached is not made by the process server at the time of the attachment, but rather by the creditor who, having chosen this type of forced execution, must already know what property is owned by the debtor and its approximate value. The only limitation concerns a mortgagee creditor who cannot attach other property without first attaching the mortgaged assets.

The first of two different stages, each having its own specific legal effect,[205] is the service on the debtor of an instrument signed by the creditor containing a description of the assets and real property rights on which execution is intended to be levied and a warning to refrain from any action that may interfere with their function as security of the claim. On such service the attachment is perfected *vis-à-vis* the debtor. The second is a transcription of the attachment in the real property records which makes the lien to which the property has been subjected effective *vis-à-vis* third parties.

By the attachment the debtor is made a custodian of the attached property, but the court of the enforcement proceedings may appoint another person as custodian. The debtor (or the third party custodian) has limited power to dispose of the property. In order to lease it out, he must obtain the court's authorisation. The concurrence of enforcement proceedings against the same property is regulated in a manner similar to that applicable to other types of enforcement. Such concurrence is permissible also in favour of creditors who hold a claim not yet due, such as one not yet matured or subject to a condition precedent.

After the lapse of 10 days from the attachment, the attaching creditor and each joining creditor, holding an enforceable instrument, may apply for the sale of the attached immovable. The court, after setting a hearing to interview the parties and on completion of the opposition proceedings, if any, may order the sale, which usually does not involve an auction[206] but rather occurs through one or more individual tenders filed in the clerk's office, unless the court deems it appropriate to provide for an auction sale.[207]

Specific enforcement

Specific enforcement (*esecuzione in forma specifica*) can be obtained whenever the right of the creditor may be realised by delivery of the

205. Code of Civil Procedure, Article 555.
206. Code of Civil Procedure, Articles 570–575.
207. Code of Civil Procedure, Article 576.

property or the performance of the activities or services that the creditor is entitled to receive from the debtor.

Specific enforcement of judgments, which require the delivery to the creditor of a specific item of property, whether movable (*esecuzione per consegna*) or immovable (*esecuzione per rilascio*), can be obtained forcefully under the authority of the *Pretore* in the location where the movable or immovable property is situated. Actually, the proceedings are primarily conducted by the process server (*ufficiale giudiziario*), while the judge will intervene at the instance of the parties only in case of particular difficulties in connection with the delivery or the assessment of costs. Execution pursuant to Code of Civil Procedure, Article 605, must be preceded by a precept setting forth, in addition to the information provided for in Code of Civil Procedure, Article 408, also a summary description of the property.

Enforcement of obligations

Enforcement of obligations to do or not to do something (*esecuzione forzata degli obblighi di fare e di non fare*) is aimed at enabling the creditor to obtain the specific performance of an act to which he is entitled or elimination of the infringement by the debtor of his obligation not to do something. If a party fails to comply with an obligation to do something, the party entitled to the performance may require it to be discharged at the expense of the debtor[208] in the manner provided by the Code of Civil Procedure. If a party fails to comply with an obligation not to do something, the party entitled may require that whatever was done infringing the prohibition be destroyed at the expense of the debtor.[209] Nevertheless, if such destruction would be detrimental to the national economy, it may not be ordered and the claimant may only obtain compensation for damages.

As a rule, the enforceable instrument is a judgment. Nevertheless, this type of execution can be applied also in connection with precautionary measures such as those in matters of denunciation of new work and feared damage (*denunzia di nuova opera e danno temuto*)[210] and with urgent measures (*provvedimenti d'urgenza*).[211] The procedure is initiated by the submission to the *Pretore* of an application whereby the claimant, after having caused a precept to be served, requests the procedure for enforcement to be laid down. The *Pretore,* after hearing the obligor, issues an order providing for the time and procedures of enforcement and

208. Civil Code, Article 2931.
209. Civil Code, Article 2933.
210. Civil Code, Articles 1171 and 1172.
211. Code of Civil Procedure, Article 700.

designates the process server who will proceed with the execution, as well as the persons who must materially effect the completion of the work not performed or the destruction of the work performed. The process server supervises the activities of these auxiliaries, seeking if necessary the assistance of the police and may apply to the *Pretore* for such provisions as may help overcome the material obstacles that may arise during enforcement.

Precautionary measures

Oppositions

An opposition (*opposizione*) is the remedy to which the debtor or a third party may resort when complaining that his rights have been injured as a result of an attempt at unjust enforcement. An opposition results in regular litigation (*cognizione*) aimed at a declaratory judgment. The execution proceedings may be suspended until a decision on the opposition is rendered. In opposition proceedings, the party who takes the initiative of submitting an opposition, whether the debtor or a third person, takes the position of an opposing party and as such has the status of a plaintiff, while the status of a defendant is assumed by the creditor or the party who initiated or announced the initiation of enforcement proceedings.

The oppositions that may be advanced by the debtor or by a third person subjected to enforcement may relate to enforcement as such or to enforcement acts.

Opposition to enforcement

Opposition to enforcement (*opposizione all'esecuzione*) consists of the contestation by the debtor of the creditor's right to proceed with forced execution. It substantially touches on a question of merits in that the opposing party, in alleging the injustice of enforcement, contests the existence of the conditions precedent to the levy of execution. Such conditions may relate to the very foundation of the executory action, i.e., the existence of a right capable of enforcement, or the object of the execution, i.e., capacity of an asset to be subjected to execution. The opposition may be brought by the debtor or the third person subjected or even one of their subrogated creditors. The creditor (or other creditors, joining voluntarily or compulsorily in the proceedings) may resist the opposition.

The opposition may be advanced at the inception of the execution, as an opposition to the precept by a citation to appear before the court having jurisdiction, or during the execution proceedings by a petition to the execution court. The opposition proceedings are concluded by a judgment that may either grant or reject the opposition and that is subject to the normal second instance remedies. A judgment rejecting the opposition may require payment of damages if the execution was resisted in bad faith or with gross negligence[212] and entails in any case the continuation of enforcement proceedings. A judgment granting the opposition entails instead the avoidance of all enforcement acts performed and the termination of their effect.

Opposition to enforcement acts

Opposition to enforcement acts (*opposizione agli atti esecutivi*) consists of the contestation by the debtor of the formal regularity of the enforceable instrument, the precept or the other acts of the enforcement proceedings[213] and raises merely procedural issues. It may be raised by the debtor, a third party owner subjected to enforcement, an attaching creditor and the joining parties, if any, as well as such third persons as are involved in the enforcement proceedings. The defendant is the party that performed the challenged act.

The opposition must be submitted not more than five days after the date on which the act opposed has been performed or served. The enforcement court orders such provisions as it deems undeferrable and proceeds with the examination of the case which is then decided by a panel judgment, which may only be reviewed by the Court of Cassation on grounds of infringement of the law pursuant to Article 111 of the Constitution.[214] A special type of opposition that can be raised by the debtor, the third party subjected to enforcement or the creditors is available to settle disputes arising in respect of the allocation of the proceeds of forced execution.[215]

Third party opposition

Third party opposition (*opposizione di terzo*) can be raised by a third party claiming to be the owner or to have another real right (e.g., usufruct, use, dwelling or servitude) in the attached property,[216] a pledge or a right in intangible property (e.g., likeness, trade name or trademark). The defendants in a third party opposition are the attaching

212. Code of Civil Procedure, Article 96.
213. Code of Civil Procedure, Article 617.
214. Code of Civil Procedure, Article 618.
215. Code of Civil Procedure, Article 512.
216. Code of Civil Procedure, Article 619.

creditor, the debtor or a third party against whom execution is being levied, who must all be summoned to participate in the proceedings from the outset.

As to the deadline for the submission of a third party opposition, a distinction should be made between timely opposition and late opposition. A timely opposition is one raised before the sale or the assignment of the asset and up to the moment of its transfer. A late opposition is one submitted thereafter, in which case the third party's rights may be asserted on the proceeds from the forced sale until they have not been distributed to the creditors.[217]

The petition for opposition must be submitted to the court competent having regard to the value of the disputed property and to the location where enforcement is being levied. Pursuant to the opposition, the court may, on an *ex parte* motion and having interviewed the parties in interest, totally or partially suspend enforcement, if serious reasons exist. In such case the court may require the opponent to post a bond.

To avoid collusion between the debtor whose property is being subjected to enforcement and the third party opponent, Article 621 of the Code of Civil Procedure imposes a serious probatory limitation by providing that the third party opponent cannot prove by witnesses his right to property attached in the debtor's home or business premises, unless the existence of such right is credible in the light of the profession or trade in which the third party or the debtor is engaged. Opposition proceedings are decided by a judgment that may be attacked through normal attacking procedures. If the opposition is granted, enforcement is definitively frozen and all previous enforcement acts based on it are cancelled.

Suspension and extinguishment of enforcement proceedings

Suspension consists in holding in abeyance the proceedings and may be ordered by the court where:

(1) There is an opposition to enforcement;
(2) A dispute arises concerning the existence of movables in a third party's premises or the ownership of property which is intended to be attached;[218]
(3) In case of forced execution against undivided property, a partition of the property must be proceeded with;[219] or
(4) The parties jointly apply for suspension.

217. Code of Civil Procedure, Article 620.
218. Code of Civil Procedure, Articles 548–549.
219. Code of Civil Procedure, Article 601.

An application for suspension can be submitted even orally and, if granted, prevents the performance of any act, unless otherwise provided by the court. When the reasons for suspension no longer exist, the proceedings must be resumed within the deadline set by the court and, in any event, not later than six months since the first instance judgment becomes *res judicata* or since notice of the appellate decision rejecting the opposition.

Normally, the extinguishment of enforceable proceedings coincides with the creditor's obtaining satisfaction of his claim. However, the law contemplates also other anomalous ways of extinguishment such as a waiver of action by the creditors,[220] a prolonged inactivity of the parties,[221] the parties' failure to appear at a hearing,[222] or when an opposition to enforcement is granted or the enforceable instrument or the property involved in forced execution ceases to exist. If the exstinguishment occurs prior to the sale or assignment, it results in the ineffectiveness of the acts previously performed. If it occurs afterwards, the proceeds of the sale are turned over to the debtor.

Recognition of foreign judgments

Proceedings for the recognition of foreign judgments (*procedimento di delibazione delle sentenze straniere*) are regulated in Book IV, Title VII of the Code. They enable, subject to the verification of certain conditions, a foreign judgment to be validated for the purposes of enforcement in Italy and "to acquire any other effect typical of a judicial act".[223] Validation proceedings are instituted by means of a citation served by the party in interest on the opposite party,[224] summoning it to appear before the Court of Appeal in the location where the foreign judgment is to be enforced. In order to validate a foreign judgment, the Court of Appeal will verify that the following prerequisites exist:[225]

(1) That the foreign court which rendered the judgment was competent to take cognisance of the case under the principles of jurisdictional competence in force in the Italian state;

220. Code of Civil Procedure, Article 629.
221. Code of Civil Procedure, Article 630.
222. Code of Civil Procedure, Article 631.
223. Code of Civil Procedure, Article 796.
224. When bilateral treaties guarantying reciprocity permit, the validation of a foreign judgment may be requested through diplomatic channels, in which case if the party in interest has not appointed an attorney in Italy, the presiding judge of the Court of Appeal upon request of the Public Prosecutor may designate a special attorney to institute the validation proceedings.
225. Code of Civil Procedure, Article 797.

(2) That the citation to appear before the foreign court was served in accordance with the law of the place where the proceedings were held, and that it accorded the defendant a reasonable period to enter an appearance;

(3) That the parties entered an appearance in accordance with the law of the foreign location or that a default was ascertained and validly declared in accordance with such law;

(4) That the foreign judgment became *res judicata* under the law of the location where it was rendered;

(5) That the foreign judgment is not in conflict with another judgment rendered by an Italian court;

(6) That other proceedings between the same parties, having the same subject matter and instituted before the foreign judgment became *res judicata* are not pending before an Italian court; and

(7) That the foreign judgment does not contain any provision contrary to Italian public policy.

Participation of the Public Prosecutor in the recognition proceedings is mandatory in view of the public interest involved in the matter. The Court of Appeal accords or denies the recognition by a judgment. If, notwithstanding due service of the citation to appear in the foreign court and adequate time having been allowed for the appearance, the defendant did not enter an appearance in the foreign proceedings, he is entitled to obtain a review of the merits of the case from the Court of Appeal.

Besides several bilateral treaties concerning mutual assistance and reciprocal enforcement of judgments, two multilateral conventions[226] are of particular relevance in the context of enforcement of foreign judgments in the other contracting States. Both the Brussels and the Lugano Conventions lay down rules on the jurisdictional competence of domestic courts in litigation involving parties of one or more contracting States, in ample derogation from the domestic rules applicable in each country, and provide that a judgment rendered in the court of a contracting State under jurisdictional rules contemplated in the convention is automatically recognised in the other contracting States without necessity for the institution of validation proceedings, subject only to the following exceptions:

(1) When the foreign judgment is contrary to public policy in the state where enforcement is sought;

226. The EEC Convention concerning Jurisdictional Competence and the Enforcement of Judgments in Civil and Commercial Matters signed in Brussels on 28 September 1968 and made effective in Italy by Law No. 804 of 21 June 1971 and the Convention concerning Jurisdictional Competence and the Enforcement of Judgments in Civil and Commercial Matters signed in Lugano on 16 September 1988 and made effective in Italy by Law No. 198 of 10 February 1992.

(2) When the citation to appear before the foreign court was not served on the defendant in a proper manner and without allowing him a reasonable period to enter an appearance;

(3) When the judgment is in conflict with another judgment rendered between the same parties in the state where recognition was requested; and

(4) When the court, in rendering a judgment relating to the status or legal capacity of persons, financial settlements between husband and wife, wills and inheritances, has infringed a rule of international private law. It is important to note that Article 54–*ter* of the Lugano Convention provides that its application is without prejudice to the applicability of the Brussels Convention and of the Luxembourg Protocol signed on 3 June 1971, relating to the interpretation of the latter.

Note: More than one word of appreciation goes to Sabrina Cherchi, Giuseppe Schiavello and Marina Savastano, three enterprising young people who have lent me a charitable hand in this venturesome effort.

CHAPTER 12

MEXICO

JUAN FRANCISCO TORRES-LANDA R. AND HUMBERTO ZACARÍAS F.
Barrera, Siqueiros y Torres-Landa, S.C.
Mexico City, Mexico

INTRODUCTION

There are 31 states and a Federal District in Mexico, and each has its own Code of Civil Procedure. The Code of Civil Procedure of the Federal District (CCP) has traditionally set forth the guidelines and trends that the rest of the State Codes tend to follow. While the CCP is generally followed, each state has its own procedural rules, and (depending on the venue of a case) local statutes of limitations, procedural rules and other requirements may need to be checked necessarily contemplate. The general principles on procedural law summarised here apply in most respects in all states of Mexico.[1]

This chapter focuses on the analysis of the ordinary civil process. There are other, different proceedings for housing lease agreements, probate, family law, commercial, bankruptcy and other matters, as well as administrative, tax, labour and Constitutional litigation that merit specific analysis.

ESTABLISHING JURISDICTION

Types of jurisdiction

Jurisdiction over the parties of the action

"Jurisdiction" is, on the one hand, the sovereign territorial function of the tribunal or court whereby legal rules are applied to a case in dispute

---

1. Mexico is a party to several relevant international treaties: Interamerican Convention on Letters-Rogatory; Interamerican Convention on Taking of Foreign Evidence; Interamerican Convention on Conflict of Laws in the Subject Matter of Letters of Exchange, Promissory Notes and Invoices; Interamerican Convention on International Commercial Arbitration; Interamerican Convention on the Legal Regime of Powers-of-Attorney to be used Abroad; Interamerican Convention on Conflict of Laws in the Subject Matter of Commercial Companies; Interamerican Convention on General Rules of Private International Law; Interamerican Convention on the Address of Individuals in Private International Law; Interamerican Convention on Procedural Efficiency or Foreign Judgments and Arbitration Awards; Washington Protocol of the Uniform Legal Regime of Powers-of-Attorney; United Nations Convention on the Recognition and Enforcement of Foreign Judgments and Arbitration Awards.

to resolve it, the ruling thus being binding and enforceable against the parties involved, even against their will. Jurisdiction is also intimately related with competence. Competence is understood as the scope of authority where the jurisdiction may be enforced by the jurisdictional authority.

The parties to a legal action subject their disputes to the competence of a tribunal, so that it may assert its jurisdiction, by setting the case for trial, rendering judgment and its enforcement. The type of jurisdiction that a court asserts depends entirely on its competence: Local courts have local jurisdiction; federal courts have jurisdiction. As a rule, once the competence has been defined, the court's jurisdiction is the exercise of its authority within those limits.

NATURAL PERSONS

Generally, the competent court will be the one that the parties have expressly agreed on to resolve the dispute. If there has been no forum selection, then it will be the court of the defendant's domicile or that of the place where the specific duties are to be performed that will be competent. The exeption to this is for real estate matters where the court of the site will be competent.

CORPORATIONS

There are no other specific guidelines in terms of asserting jurisdiction over natural persons or corporations. Corporations are deemed domiciled at their principal place of business, unless otherwise having conventional addresses where they agree to be subject to jurisdiction or where they perform business activities giving the courts of those places jurisdiction.

Jurisdiction over the subject matter of the action

PROPERTY CLAIMS

Claims on real property fall within the competence of courts of the site where those properties are located. On the other hand, jurisdiction may be asserted by different courts depending on the nature of the matter being litigated. Section 48 of the Organic Law of the Tribunals of the Local Forum of the Federal District (Organic Law), establishes the following courts:

(1) Courts of Real Estate Leases have jurisdiction over matters related to disputes of real estate leases, regardless of the use of leased premises;[2]

2. Organic Law, Section 60–D.

(2) Civil Courts have jurisdiction over any voluntary or litigious proceedings that is not otherwise within the competence of any of the other courts;[3]

(3) Family Courts resolve any consensual proceedings dealing with family law as well as contentious proceedings dealing with marriage, divorce, family estate matters, kinship, alimony, child support, parenthood, adoptions and similar matters. They also have jurisdiction over probate proceedings, handicapped and mentally ill persons rights and representation, and other matters in this area of law; and

(4) Civil Courts have residual jurisdiction including property claims that are actions *in rem*, that is, where the issues involved deal with real property, matters other than leases.

Damage or violation of rights

In the case of violation of rights, jurisdiction is normally asserted by the court where the defendant is domiciled. Unless a forum selection clause has been agreed on or a different special cause for jurisdiction exists, then the plaintiff must sue the defendant where the latter resides. This issue is further explored in the next section.

Venue

General principles

Venue under Mexican law should be understood as the possibility of a court, being considered as having jurisdiction over a particular matter, to exercise its dispute settlement authority by taking cognisance of a claim filed by a plaintiff and opposed by a defendant, resolving it and enforcing a ruling.

Traditionally, there have been four criteria to determine the correct venue: the subject matter, territory, degree and amount. Subsidiarily, two other criteria may be applied: rotation and prevention.

SUBJECT MATTER

In regard to subject matter, the jurisdiction of a court is determined by the specific areas of law that it enforces, which, in civil matters, results in the distinction of several classes of courts.[4]

3. Organic Law, Section 54.
4. See above.

TERRITORY

Territory refers essentially to the geographic area where the court may exercise its jurisdiction. Thus, a judge in the Federal District will have no jurisdiction in the State of Morelos and *vice versa*.

DEGREE

The criterion of degree assumes the existence of different levels of hierarchy within the judicial system. The superior courts will usually act as the organ to review the actions of the lower courts, the decision of the former binding the latter. In civil matters, the Chamber Courts of the Superior Tribunals in each state have authority over first instance Civil Courts.

AMOUNT

Pursuant to the Organic Law, there are two classes of Civil Courts: those of First Instance and of Mixed Peace; the former will handle all cases dealing with matters where the amount in controversy exceeds 182 times the minimum wage in the Federal District, while the latter resolves all other cases.

ROTATION

According to the Organic Law, a common filing office exists for all Civil Courts through which a computer system randomly selects the specific court where a claim will be processed. The goal of this system is to prevent the plaintiff from selecting the specific court that will handle a case.

PREVENTION

According to Section 258 of the Organic Law, the court that will have jurisdiction over a particular matter is the one that first rules on the admittance of a claim filed by the plaintiff.

Regardless of the foregoing criteria, the competence of a court is determined according to the rules set forth by Section 156 of the Organic Law, which in general terms establishes that the competent court will be:

(1) The court which the defendant has indicated as the one to be judicially required to perform its obligations;
(2) The court at the place where the agreement calls for the performance of the duties in dispute;

(3) The court at the place where the land is located in the case of real property claims, or in the case of claims related with lease agreements on real property;

(4) The court at the defendant's domicile in the case of actions over assets, or personal claims. If there are several defendants, the plaintiff will determine the court that will assert jurisdiction by filing the claim therewith;

(5) In the case of probate proceedings, the court of (in the following order) the decedent's last address, of the location of the probate's properties or of the place of death of the deceased;

(6) In the case of actions contesting probate rulings, the court of the judge that heard those proceedings;

(7) In bankruptcy proceedings, the court where the bankrupt person is found;

(8) In non-contentious proceedings, the court of the applicant's address, but for real estate matters it must be the court of the property's location;

(9) For the designation of guardians of minors and retarded persons, the court of the place where they reside, and if a guardian exists, then the court of the latter's address;

(10) For matters related to matrimony, disputes between spouses or matrimonial nullity, the court of the matrimonial residence;

(11) In divorce cases, the court of the matrimonial residence; or

(12) In alimony cases, the court of the plaintiff's residence or the defendant's residence, at the plaintiff's choice.

Transfer of venue

If we consider that the competence is the scope where a court can exercise its jurisdiction over a particular case, then the venue can be transferred if the scope of the court that will have jurisdiction is changed. Therefore, according to the CCP only competence by territory is extendible, meaning that, unless the law restricts their choice (property claims, family law matters, etc.), the parties may freely include a forum selection clause that will render a particular court competent over any dispute that may arise between them.

Service of summons or writs

Section 111 of the CCP recognises the following methods of serving notices to parties in a court procedure. The means of notice included do not necessarily reflect a preference order. Each method has different requirements that must be met.

By mail

Postal service is only used to serve court experts and witnesses not involved as parties to the suit. The use of certified mail is required, and the expenses incurred must be borne by the party that proffers the corresponding evidence.

Personal service

For personal service, Section 114 of the CCP sets forth the cases in which it is required that personal service be performed:

(1) The service of process on the defendant and in any event of the first notice of the suit, even in a preparatory stage;
(2) The ruling that orders the deposition of any of the two parties, or the recognition of a document;
(3) The first ruling issued if the proceedings ceased for whatever reason for a period of over six months;
(4) In the event of an urgent matter;
(5) The ruling whereby a party is required to perform a specific act;
(6) The ruling requiring a tenant to vacate the premises leased; and
(7) All other cases expressly indicated by the law as requiring personal service.

In each of the above cases, the CCP provides specific rules and requirements that must be followed to perform personal service.

By consular or diplomatic channels

Service by consular or diplomatic channels is governed by Sections 604 et seq. of the CCP that indicates in the chapter on international procedural co-operation that any service made by way of letters rogatory must follow these rules:

(1) The court requested to perform the service under a letter rogatory must do so according to the CCP and should abide by the foreign tribunal's request unless Mexican public policy is infringed; and
(2) Courts requesting or processing foreign court service requests must deliver them in two copies and keep a copy in the records as evidence of what was processed.

It is clear that according to the above, all notices that relate to foreign service must be carried out through authorised courts, with the diplomatic or consular channels only serving as the means to deliver those documents. Service of process may be carried out as well as preparation of evidence or discovery.

Publication

The only notices that are allowed by publication are given through the *Judicial Bulletin*. This *Bulletin* is published by the Superior Court of Justice and contains the data of any proceedings where a ruling has been issued, with the purpose of informing the interested parties to go to the relevant court to receive a copy of the ruling. According to Section 123 of the CCP, the parties must appear at the court within three days following the publication date. Otherwise, pursuant to Section 125 of the CCP, the parties will be deemed as duly notified within the 12 hours following the last day of the referred three-day term.

In practice, the *Judicial Bulletin* is used by litigants as a method to determine if any ruling has been issued in the lawsuits that they are participating in.

Once parties have been alerted as to the existence of any ruling, they must appear at the court and request to see the file to get a copy of the ruling. The notice will be considered effective in the terms set forth by Section 125 of the CCP, except for when the notice is conditioned to be personal, in which case the file may not be seen unless an affidavit of notice is delivered by the corresponding party.

Only in those cases in which by errors or omissions the particular lawsuits are not identifiable will a party be able to challenge a notice made by publication in the *Judicial Bulletin*.[5] Every court will keep a sample of its publications in the *Judicial Bulletin* for clarification purposes when any notice is challenged.

In practice, an error in the publication will constitute a cause for the notice to be deemed null, thus requiring that another publication be made. To this end, according to Section 127 of the CCP, the court clerks will include in every ruling a legend regarding the exact publication data in the *Judicial Bulletin*.

Edicts

The CCP also contemplates this edict notice. Edicts are defined as the public notice made by an administrative or judicial order for the notified parties to be made aware of any resolution they are expected to know or

5. CCP, Section 126.

to perform accordingly. Section 122 of the CCP provides that notices must be made by edicts in the following cases:

(1) In the case of unknown parties;
(2) In the case of persons whose address is unknown, once a police report has been secured; and
(3) When real estate is being awarded to notify any person that may be prejudiced.

In the first two cases, the edicts are published three times, once every three days in the *Judicial Bulletin* and in the local newspaper that the court selects. The edict will indicate that the corresponding parties must appear in court within a period that cannot be less than 15 days nor more than 70 days. In the third case, the edict will be published once in the *Federal Official Gazette*, in the *Judicial Bulletin*, in the *State Official Gazette* and in a major newspaper.

The Hague Convention

Mexico is not a party to The Hague Convention and the mechanisms set out therein are therefore not available with respect to actions or parties in Mexico.

ASCERTAINING THE APPLICABLE LAW

Regional law

Every one of the 31 States in Mexico has its own Code of Civil Procedure, the statute that governs the judicial process in the respective territory of each state. Save for some few provisions, these Codes are almost identical to the CCP, the latter being the Code that sets the trend followed by the rest.

According to Section 104 of the Constitution, those matters that have not been expressly granted to the federal powers are understood to have been kept under each state's jurisdiction. This Constitutional provision indicates then that Federal Courts have jurisdiction over:

(1) Any civil or criminal dispute as to the enforcement of or compliance with federal laws or international treaties entered into by Mexico; or
(2) Those matters in which the Federation is a party.

In all other cases not contemplated as under federal jurisdiction, the State Courts will have adjudicatory competence. Hence, when State Courts exercise their jurisdiction, the relevant process will be governed by the corresponding Code of Civil Procedure.

National law

The Federal Courts are governed by the Federal Code of Civil Proceedings of 1936. This Code is outdated in many respects, the impetus for its reform not being as great as in the case of the State Codes because the number of proceedings before the Federal Courts is considerably smaller. The Federal Courts dedicate most of their time to the adjudication of constitutional suits (*Juicio de Amparo*), proceedings over which they have exclusive competence and which are governed by a specific law (*Ley de Amparo Reglamentaria de los Articulos 103 y 107 de la Constitución Política de los Estados Unidos Mexicanos*).

Conflict of laws principles

Section 12 through 15 of the Civil Code for the Federal District (CCFD) set forth the general criteria about conflict of laws rules in the territory of Mexico. The basic conflict of laws rule is contained in Section 12 of the CCFD that indicates that Mexican laws will govern all acts performed in Mexico, all persons located in its territory and in all those cases where any parties have expressly submitted to its jurisdiction. However, under the CCFD the application of foreign law is permissible when expressly indicated by Mexican law or when required by operative international treaties ratified by Mexico.

Under Section 13 of the CCFD, legal situations validly created in any of the States of the Republic or in a Foreign State according to its own laws must be recognized. Legal status and capacity of individuals is governed by the laws of the place where they reside. The creation, effect and extinction of real rights, as well as lease and temporary use agreements regarding such things, and the movable goods will be governed by the laws of the place where they are located, even if their holders are foreigners. The form of legal acts will be governed by the laws of the place where they are executed. Nevertheless, those acts may comply with the forms set forth by the CCFD if the act is to have effects within the Federal District or anywhere in Mexico regarding federal matters. Subject to the foregoing rules, the legal effects of acts and contracts will be governed by the laws of the place where they must be performed, unless the parties have validly agreed upon the application of a different law.

The application of foreign law is governed by Sections 14 and 15 of the CCFD (recently amended to conform to the guidelines of the Ineteramerican Convention on the Application of Foreign Law). Foreign law will be applied as it would be by the foreign judge, therefore the judge may avail himself of the necessary information about the text, validity, sense and scope of that law. Only the substantive foreign law must be applied, except when given the special circumstances of the case, exceptionally the foreign conflict of laws rules indicating application of the substantive rules of Mexico or another State (*renvoi*). The fact that Mexican rules do not provide for specific rules or essential procedures for the applicable foreign rule will not be an impediment for its application if there are analogous rules or procedures. The prior, preliminary or incidental matters that may surface with regard to a principal matter need not be resolved according to the provisions ruling the latter. Whenever several aspects of the same legal relationship are governed by several laws, these laws should be applied in a harmonious manner, trying to attain the goals sought by each of those laws. The difficulties caused by the simultaneous application of such laws will be resolved taking into consideration the fairness requirements of the specific case. This provision shall be applied whenever the laws of another State of this country are applicable.

Foreign law may not be applied when fundamental principles of Mexican law have been artificially avoided (the Judge must find fraudulent intent behind the avoidance) and when the foreign law rules or the result of its application are contrary to Mexican public policy, fundamental principles or institutions.

Regarding Mexican law, a conflict of laws occurs in those cases where two or more statutes allow, order or restrict the same conduct of one or more persons that may not be simultaneously applied or observed. Therefore, it is possible for two statutes to be consistent with each other, because the conflict is not in their existence but in their simultaneous application. Courts must determine the applicable law, for which purpose they must follow certain criteria.

Chronological order

Newer law prevails over the older law. On being published, the new laws establish a mechanism for their coming into effect in what are known as their "Transitory Articles". These articles not only refer to the date when that law will become effective but also include reference to the statutes or norms that are repealed or modified, as well as any other rule required for its implementation. Retroactive effect is banned by Article 14 of the Constitution. While these Articles may miss some of the possible statutes that will be considered as annulled or modified, the criteria of this principle still applies to any statute that is inconsistent with the new law enacted.

Specialty order

The special law will prevail over the general law, and likewise special provisions will prevail over general provisions. This principle is clearly applied in lease lawsuits that deal with households because they will be governed by the special provisions of the Civil Code dealing with housing leases, and not those of the general lease agreements. This principle will also then apply in any case in which a specific matter is governed by some special provisions that will then take precedence over general rules that apply to general cases.

Hierarchy order

The higher hierarchy statute will prevail over the lower one. This principle is contemplated by Section 133 of the Constitution, which says that the Constitution, along with Federal Laws and International Treaties constitute the Supreme Law of the Union. The Constitution will prevail over any other statute in Mexico, and in fact any law issued by the Federal or State Congresses must be consistent with the Constitution. State Courts must abide by the Bill of Rights set forth by the Constitution. State Codes of Civil Procedure must be consistent with the Constitution by establishing courts that are created prior to the disputes being adjudicated where due process rules must always exist.

Competence order

The conflict most often presented is the competence between courts to assert their jurisdiction. The CCP establishes in this case the rules to determine the competent court and therefore the applicable procedural law. According to Section 163 of the CCP there are two manners in which to challenge the competence of a court, by "inhibition" or by "declination".

INHIBITION

The "inhibition" defence is filed with the court that is deemed competent within the nine days following service of process, requiring the court deemed to be incompetent to deliver the file records to the superior court that will rule on the competence issue at stake.

DECLINATION

The "declination" motion is filed with the court deemed to lack competence requesting that the file be forwarded to the competent court. The motion is ruled on by the superior court so that the file is delivered to the competent court to continue the suit.

In both of these cases the suit is not suspended. If the motion is declared valid, all acts performed until then are considered null and void save for the complaint and the answer. The incompetence motion is then deemed a defence and must be filed at the time the defendant files its answer.

While a court may not rule on competency issues, it may refuse to handle a suit on valid conflict of interest rules. If one or more courts refuse to assert jurisdiction over a particular case, the affected party may then request the Superior Court to issue a ruling to order a court to proceed with the adjudication of the matter.

COMMENCING THE ACTION

Complaint

The complaint is the written procedural act whereby a suit is filed and the claims and relief sought by the plaintiff from one or more persons that will act as defendants are established. It contains the essential elements of the suit. Pursuant to Section 255 of the CCP a complaint must state:

(1) The court where it is being filed;
(2) The name of the plaintiff and the address to receive notices;
(3) The name of the defendant and its address;
(4) The list of the relief sought or things being sued for and its accessories;
(5) The facts on which the plaintiff bases its claim, listing and stating them in a concise and clear manner, allowing for the defendant to file its answer thereto;
(6) The type of action being filed and the legal provisions that govern the process and the cause of action; and
(7) The amount of the relief sought, if relevant to determine the competent court.

Additionally, Sections 95 and 96 of the CCP require that the following documents be attached to the complaint:

(1) When the plaintiff is being represented by another person, the power of attorney to evidence the capacity of that representative;
(2) The documents that support the claim and that entitle the plaintiff to the cause of action; and
(3) Copies of the complaint and its exhibits to serve process on the defendant. If these copies are not filed, the court will require the plaintiff to file them within a certain time under threat of the complaint being dismissed.

The complaint must be prepared in Spanish, and documents in other languages must always be filed with their official Spanish translation prepared by experts authorised by the Superior Court of Justice. No abbreviations or unclear corrections in the text of the documents will be allowed or accepted.

The complaint's description of the remedy sought and the facts surrounding the case must be clear. If errors or inconsistencies exist in the complaint's text, then the court will require the plaintiff to correct or complement them within a three-day period.

Stating the remedy

The CCP requires that the description of the remedy being sought be consistent with the description of the facts included in the complaint. The complaint must list all the remedies being sought, because pursuant to Section 31 of the CCP, omitting any remedy will be considered a waiver by the plaintiff to seek it at any other time; any cause of action stemming from the same facts against the same defendant must be resolved in a single action, all others being automatically waived.

Likewise, Section 34 of the CCP states that once the complaint has been accepted, it cannot be altered or modified.

Stating the type of action being filed is not an absolute prerequisite that the plaintiff must comply with as long as the description of the remedy sought and the facts of the case are clear enough so as to allow the court to interpret the type of action being filed (this follows the general judicial principle that the parties deliver the facts and the court determines the law).

Types of answer

In principle, the answer must fulfill the same formal requirements for the complaint, in addition to the defences and counterclaim that may be included in it.

Denials

Section 266 of the CCP provides that in the answer the defendant must refer to each of the facts included in the complaint. The defendant must either admit the facts (accepting that they are true) or deny them and stating those that are ignored or are not relevant to the suit. Silence or inconsistency by the defendant will be understood as admission of those facts. This rule applies in all cases save for suits on family matters or disputes on housing leases.

Generally, the defendant may use one of the following approaches to respond to the facts alleged in the complaint:

" The fact being answered is true and therefore there is no dispute in that regard."
" The fact being answered is false and is therefore denied, stating that . . . ." or
" The fact being answered is neither affirmed nor denied as not being part of the suit."

Denials and affirmative defences

The affirmative defences (defences) are the answer that the defendant makes with regard to the facts or cause of action set out in the plaintiff's complaint. These may attack procedural or substantive issues, with the purpose of the court releasing the defendant from liability for the relief sought by the plaintiff.

These defences must be filed at the same time as the answer, except for those supplementary defences that may arise in the course of the suit, the latter being understood as those existing by virtue of circumstances unknown by the defendant at the time the answer was filed or because the fact arose after the answer was filed. In these cases, the defendant may claim the defence before the final judgment is issued and within the three days following the date when he becomes aware of their existence.[6]

As in the case of the type of action, the defences are valid even if they are not expressly named in the answer provided the facts on which they are based are clearly set out.

None of the defences will suspend the proceedings. On the defences being admitted by the court, the plaintiff will be granted a three-day term to make any statement it deems necessary.

The defendant may claim two types of defences: dilatory and peremptory defences. Dilatory defences refer exclusively to procedural matters and have as their goal to thwart the action filed by the plaintiff but do not attack the substance of the action. These defences are ruled on in the final judgment and if any of them is ruled applicable, the court will not rule on the substance of the suit but it will be dismissed, the plaintiff's rights surviving. Only the defences on lack of competence, joinders, pending claim and *res judicata* must be resolved at a prior hearing to avoid hearing an unfeasible process. Peremptory defences are meant to defeat the cause of action claimed by the plaintiff, thus attacking the substance of the claim. These defences are ruled on in conjunction with the issues at stake in the suit when the final judgment is issued.

Reply

When the answer to the complaint is filed by the defendant, the reply must relate to the facts asserted by the plaintiff. The plaintiff will have a three-day period to make its statements regarding the answer and the defences filed, and will have time to produce its answer if a counter-claim is filed by the defendant.[7]

6. CCP, Section 273.
7. See below.

Amendments to pleadings

Section 34 of the CCP does not allow corrections to the pleadings once they have been filed with the court. This rule facilitates the flow of the process and prevents parties from bringing new issues that will delay the issuance of the final judgment.

Supplemental pleadings

For the same reasons stated above under Section 34 of the CCP, it is not possible to file supplemental pleadings. Therefore, the plaintiff and the defendant must be consistent and thorough on preparing their pleadings because a second chance to include claims or counterclaims will not exist.

Joinder of claims and parties

The joinder of claims or suits in the Mexican civil procedure system may be obtained through two different motions: "connection of the cause" or "pending lawsuit". In both cases the purpose of the procedural formula is to consolidate the corresponding lawsuits and to prevent different judgments from being issued regarding the same cause between the same parties.

In this sense, the "connection of the cause" is a dilatory defence, which, pursuant to Section 39 of the CCP, has as its goal the transfer of the case from the court where the defence has been filed to the court that first participated in the connected cause. The connection of the cause defence is used when the causes are identical. The things in dispute and the parties may be different as long as the actions stem from the same cause.

Section 37 of the CCP determines that a "pending lawsuit" defence is appropriate when another court is already handling the same suit for which process is brought against the defendant. The defendant must clearly indicate the court where the first suit is being handled. If the defence is granted, the file is forwarded to the court that first participated in the cause if it is in the jurisdiction of the same appellate court as the forwarding court. If it is not in the same jurisdiction, the latter procedure is simply concluded and dismissed.

The difference between the "connection of the cause" and the "pending lawsuit" defences is that the first brings about a joinder of the suits because of a cause that is common to the suits regardless of whether the parties and the things are the same. The second defence applies when there is a complete identity between the two suits, the result being not really a joinder but rather an extinction of the second suit.

In the connection defence, the joined suits are processed in separate files, but are resolved in a single final judgment to prevent contradictory rulings. This defence is not applicable:

    (1) When one of the suits is being heard by an appellate court;

    (2) When the courts handling the suits belong to jurisdictions of different appellate courts; or

    (3) If one of the suits is being processed by a foreign court.

Pursuant to Section 41 of the CCP, the defendant filing the connection defence must produce a copy of the complaint and the answer from the first suit. Likewise, the only evidence required for this defence is the inspection of the other court's file.

The connection defence is not applicable if service of process has not been made, based on the principle that serving the defendant has the effect of granting that court competence to hear the suit between those parties. If the connection exists, the suits will be joined with the court that first served process.

Joinder of claims by the plaintiff

Only the defendant can file to obtain a joinder of a claim. Plaintiffs are not entitled to file for a joinder of claims because the motions are filed as defences, which only the defendants have the right to request. The plaintiff decides where to file the original complaint and can thus thereafter not claim that a joinder should be made. If a new suit is filed elsewhere, it is the defendant in that new suit that can file the corresponding defence.

Counter claim

The counterclaim is the complaint that the defendant files against the plaintiff and must be prosecuted in the same suit on filing its answer to the complaint.

Section 260 of the CCP indicates that along with the answer a counterclaim may be filed by the defendant. Section 272 of the CCP makes it clear that the defendant may not file a counterclaim after filing its answer to the complaint.

The counterclaim must fulfil the same requirements that are set forth for the complaint pursuant to Section 255 of the CCP. The plaintiff will have a nine-day period to answer the counterclaim.

Section 261 of the CCP provides that the counterclaim will be discussed and ruled on in the final judgment simultaneously with the original complaint. The counterclaim avoids having to hold two separate suits to resolve issues between the same two parties. Therefore, whenever a counterclaim is filed, there are two suits being handled in a single file, the parties having the exact opposite status in both suits as plaintiff and defendant, respectively.

Cross-claims

A cross-claim is defined by the procedural rules as the action that a defendant files against its plaintiff in the same file. The existence of the cross-claim is justified as a manner in which all issues pertaining to a specific relationship between both parties are settled in a single final judgment.

If the defendant were to decide to file its action in a different suit, then the original plaintiff could file a connection of cause defence. The cross-claim will be handled by the same court and will be subject to the same procedural steps required for the original suit. However, both actions will be resolved in a single judgment that determines the validity of each party's claims.

Third party claims

Only certain limited third party motion and interventions are contemplated under the CCP and the general procedural rules in Mexico. Third parties have a right to participate in suits that may affect their rights. Third party claims as such do not exist as independent actions. When a third party files a claim within an existing lawsuit, the third party designation ceases and it becomes a party to the action.

To avoid prejudice without prior adjudication in those cases, third parties have a procedural right to intervene and seek court relief. Third parties may file actions to extract properties or other rights that they enjoy from the encumbrance of legal disputes between other persons.

Impleader

There are two types of third parties: those that are called to participate in the suit but are alien to the cause of action (i.e., witnesses and experts), and those that participate because they have some kind of interest in the outcome of the suit.

An impleader motion occurs when according to Section 652 of the CCP third parties are called to participate in an ongoing lawsuit where they have an interest different to that of the plaintiff and the defendant. If the third party were to have a shared interest, then it would be joined as a co-plaintiff or co-defendant.

The impleader third party appears in a "third party action" that according to Section 653 of the CCP must be formulated in the same terms as the initial complaint before the judge who is hearing a case. This action will be resolved by the same judge as an ancillary issue to the principal suit.

Generally, third party actions may have as their aim either to assist or to exclude. Assisting actions are those whereby the third party participates to collaborate with one of the parties because he or she has an interest that coincides with the latter's. The third party may file this motion at any stage before final judgment is issued. The third party may perform all acts necessary to defend the corresponding right, and may even continue the claim if the party that originally begun the process withdraws.

Excluding actions refer to motions that seek to withdraw a given property or right claimed by third parties as those legitimately entitled thereto. The third party must prove that he has a better right to those properties or rights in order to obtain a favourable ruling. The third party must file the documents necessary to evidence its right so that the other parties may have an opportunity to challenge this right, and so that the judge may rule on the motion.

Interpleader

Pursuant to Section 32 of the CCP no person can be compelled to start an action or file a motion except in the following cases:

(1) When a party has a cause of action or a defence that depends on the action that another party is entitled to, the latter can be required to exercise it so that the issue may be settled. If the second party refuses to file the action, then the other party may proceed with its own action to seek adjudication; and

(2) When a third party claim is filed for an amount exceeding the original court's competence, this forces the remission of the matter to a court with proper competence and obliges the third party to pursue the action before the new court.

OBTAINING INFORMATION PRIOR TO TRIAL

Types of discovery

The information that may be obtained prior to the trial is always retrieved as part of a judicial process. Unlike in Common Law countries where it is customary for the parties to seek evidence through proceedings where the courts only participate in a secondary and limited manner, Mexican procedural rules require that all evidence be gathered and prepared under the close scrutiny and participation of the courts. Only such evidence as has been offered before a court, admitted by that court and prepared accordingly may constitute proper evidence for the final judgment.

In the purest theory, no discovery takes place under Mexican procedural law. What happens is that as a procedural stage in a lawsuit after the basis of the suit is formed (complaint and answers are filed), both parties are allowed to file their evidence, requesting their admission and their preparation to be warranted.

Depositions

Extra-judicial depositions as such are not supported nor do they form part of Mexico's procedural rules. Private interviews and records of discussions have no validity as a statement by a party if they are not made as part of an existing suit and with the participation of the court.

Those depositions that are admissible are in fact taken before the court, and take the form of testimony or confessional evidence, depending on whether the person being deposed is a witness or a party to the proceeding.

Interrogatories to parties

Interrogatories to parties in a lawsuit are the basic elements of a confessional evidence. This evidence is analysed in the corresponding section of this chapter.[8]

Discovery and production of physical evidence

Pre-trial production of physical evidence as such is not a procedural step that is contemplated under the CCP and the general procedural rules in Mexico. Notwithstanding this, the CCP does set forth certain cases in which it is possible to file motions before the lawsuit begins that are known as "preparatory motions". These motions are judicial instances to obtain declaratory confirmation of a set of facts or circumstances that are necessary to use in a possible successive lawsuit.

The different preparatory motions regulated by the CCP include preparatory motions for a general lawsuit and preparatory motions for an enforcement action.

Preparatory motions for a general lawsuit are available:

(1) To request the delivery of a movable good that will be the subject of a suit (action *in rem*);
(2) To request the delivery of goods among which the applicant has the right to choose from;
(3) To request the delivery of a will under which the applicant believes to have a right as an heir, co-heir or legatee;
(4) To request delivery of the title to goods that were subject to a title transfer, regardless of whether acting as the seller or the purchaser;

8. See Admissions below.

(5) To request that witnesses be interrogated by the court when they are of elderly age, in imminent danger of dying, or soon to leave to places where communications may be difficult or unduly complicated; and

(6) In general, to request the examination of witnesses or statements required in proceedings handled by a foreign court.

To begin a preparatory motion, the applicant must clearly indicate the goal being sought on its submission and the reasons why that motion cannot wait until the relevant suit is filed.

According to the CCP, the person being requested to deliver goods, documents or information in a preparatory motion must act with speed and diligence. If that person refuses to act the court may impose sanctions, and if the documents or information are destroyed, the requested party must indemnify the requesting party for damages caused, independently from the criminal liability that may derive from the former's neglect.[9]

Preparatory motions for an enforcement action are regulated by Section 201 of the CCP. The enforcement action may be prepared by requesting the defendant to acknowledge the existence of a certain debt. The court will set forth a given day and hour for the hearing to take place. The debtor must be personally served and duly notified of the purpose of the hearing, the amount being claimed and the origin of the cause. If the debtor fails to appear at the first call, a second notice will be delivered and a fine imposed and a warning that the party will be declared as accepting the existence of the debt.

If the debtor fails to appear without just cause after a second notice is filed, the court will rule that the debt is valid and exists in the amount claimed by the creditor. The goal of this preparatory motion is that when the admission or the ruling on the existence of the debt is made, the creditor may then use that statement as the basis to file the enforcement action (instead of an ordinary lawsuit).

Use of discovery at trial

Use of preparatory motions in trial is meant to provide the evidence about exact facts that have been referred to in those motions, the same that need not be evidenced again when the final suit is filed.

The notion of discovery has a very limited scope in Mexican procedural rules. That private parties may freely seek to secure information that may be relevant during the suit is contrary to the general thrust legal

---

9. CCP, Section 200.

procedure in Mexico. Mexican courts govern the evidence accumulation stage and monitor the preparation of proof during the proceedings.

INTERIM PROTECTION OF ASSETS PENDING TRIAL

Provisional attachment

The provisional attachment of goods is a precautionary measure that Section 235 of the CCP allows to be utilised on limited occasions. The cases in which a provisional attachment may be ordered are the following:

(1) When it is feared that goods potentially subject to a collection action may be withdrawn or given away; or
(2) When it is feared that the defendant does not have other assets with which to pay and that the existing ones may be withdrawn or given away.

The provisional attachment may be requested before or during the lawsuit. The court will review the merits of the case to decide if the attachment is necessary. On requesting provisional attachment, the value of the claim must be indicated, so that the court may set the exact amount that needs be secured when the provisional attachment is made against the debtor's assets. If the request for the attachment is made other than with a recognised document, the requesting party must deliver a bond to guarantee possible damages if the attachment is revoked or if the defendant is subsequently released from any liability.

The performance of the provisional attachment will not be carried out or the debtor may request release if he proves to have other property with which to secure the debt. The debtor may post a security instrument to release the attachment once it has been imposed. The debtor may also challenge the order through an appeal if it is deemed not to be justified.

If the attachment is made prior to the lawsuit, the requesting party must file the suit within three days from the day the attachment is made if the suit is to be heard in that same location. If it is to be heard elsewhere, that term will be extended according to the judge's discretion and depending on where the action is to be filed. If the suit is not filed within the time set and confirmed by the court, then the attachment will be released immediately.

Interlocutory injunction

Interlocutory injuctions are not a procedural step contemplated under the CCP and the general procedural rules of Mexico.

SUMMARY JUDGMENTS

Under the CCP and the general procedural rules of Mexico, there are only certain possibilities for adjudication without full trial.

Summary judgments

Generally, summary proceedings have been eliminated from Mexico's civil procedure system. However, there remain special proceedings or trials (special trials) that consist of privileged proceedings different from the ordinary proceedings and aimed at accomplishing a more expeditious adjudication of disputes. These include the enforcement action, the special foreclosure action and the eviction action.

Enforcement action

This enforcement action is supported by the existence of an instrument that is self-executing and permits the attachment of assets to exercise the rights evidenced by such instrument at the very moment of serving process.

The following are the executory instruments listed by Section 443 of the CCP:

(1) The first authenticated copy of a public deed issued by the judge or notary public before whom such instrument was granted or the subsequent copies issued by judicial order;

(2) Other public instruments that are fully evidentiary;

(3) Any private document after it is acknowledged by the person who issued it or caused its issuance. For this purpose, it is sufficient that the person acknowledges the signature affixed in the instrument as his or her own, even if he or she denies the underlying debt;

(4) The confession by the debtor or his/her legal representative of the debt before the presiding judge;

(5) The settlement agreement executed by the parties or third parties involved in the proceedings before the presiding judge;

(6) The original drafts of contracts executed with the intervention of a public broker; and

(7) The accountants' uniform opinion acknowledged or approved by the presiding judge.

Furthermore, Section 444 of the CCP deems as executory documents the following: final judgments, judicial agreements, agreements executed before the Federal Consumer Protection Agency and the awards granted by such agency.

Enforcement actions may be carried out with documents that evidence the obligation to pay, perform or deliver. The purpose of the enforcement action is to enforce the right evidenced by the instrument that is the main cause of action.

When the enforcement action is filed to claim payment of a liquid debt and once the complaint is admitted, the court will order the debtor to pay the debt. If a debtor refuses to comply with the order issued by the court, the latter will issue a further order for the attachment of the debtor's assets sufficient to guarantee the outstanding amount. The debtor has a period of nine business days thereafter to appear before the court either to pay the debt or to make the necessary pleas or allegations in his or her defence.

The enforcement action is divided into two parts. The first part ("principal book") will take cognisance of the complaint, the answer to the complaint and the final judgment. The second part ("execution book") will include the attachment of the debtor's property and all acts related to such attachment.

Finally, after the attachment of the debtor's property, the enforcement action will be handled according to the rules relating to ordinary actions.[10]

If the judgment reached in the enforcement action favours the plaintiff, then the court will issue an order for the institution of a public auction on the attached property and the proceeds of such auction will be delivered to the creditor.[11]

Special foreclosure action

This proceeding is held for the creation, extension, severance or registration of a mortgage, as well as demanding and securing its cancellation or acceleration of payment of the credit guaranteed by the mortgage.

If the proceeding is held for the demand and securing of payment of the credit, it is required that the mortgage be evidenced through a public deed duly registered with the Public Registry of Property of the place where the property is located. Likewise, such mortgage shall be past due.[12] The public deed evidencing the mortgage must be attached to the complaint.

On filing of the complaint, the judge shall order the issuance and registration of a mortgage bond. The court shall serve the debtor who thereafter shall have a period of nine business days to appear before the court to make the necessary pleadings and to present any relevant defence to the complaint. After the foregoing steps are taken, the proceeding will follow the rules related to ordinary actions.

In connection with the mortgage bond, such document shall include a brief description of the public deed evidencing the mortgage. Likewise, the mortgage bond shall include an order to the public or any authority

10. CCP, Section 453.
11. CCP, Section 461.
12. CCP, Section 468.

not to foreclose, take possession or take any other action on the mortgaged property that might interrupt the course of the proceeding or violate the rights acquired by the creditor plaintiff.

For publication purposes, the mortgage bond shall be registered with the Public Registry of Property.

The person in possession of the property will be the legal depository. All the benefits or products resulting from and any object found on the property shall be kept with the property. For these purposes and if solicited by the debtor, the court shall keep an inventory of all the benefits, results or objects found related to the property and stored by the depository.

On delivery of the judgment and if the latter is resolved in favour of the creditor plaintiff, the court shall order the public auctioning of the property.

Eviction proceeding

This special proceeding is held when a tenant defaults on two or more monthly rent payments. The plaintiff must always attach the lease agreement to the complaint as grounds for the action.

Once the complaint has been filed and admitted, the judge will order the defendant to pay the outstanding rents or to present evidence that he has paid them. If the defendant fails to evidence payment of past due rents, then enough of his or her assets are attached to secure payment of the debt. Simultaneously, the plaintiff will be notified to vacate the premises within 30 days if it is a living quarter, 40 days if it is a commercial or industrial establishment, and 90 days if it is a farmland, and warned of forced eviction otherwise. In that same act the defendant will be served notice that a defence must be filed at the court within a period of nine days.

If the defendant provides evidence of currency in the payment of rents with the corresponding receipts, or provides an affidavit of having deposited them with a court, or pays them on that occasion, once the acknowledgement of receipt has been made by the plaintiff, the suit will be dismissed.[13]

On the other hand, if during the term for the vacancy of the premises referred to above, the tenant delivers the documents to evidence being current in the payment of rents or pays them in full, then the suit will be dismissed. However, if these amounts are paid or the documents produced after the eviction term elapses, the defendant will be required to pay attorneys' fees and litigation expenses.

If the defendant files defences, they will be subject to objections filed by the plaintiff, and the court will open an evidence period, after which a final judgment shall be issued. If the final ruling declares the eviction, the tenant shall be required to vacate the premises, unless the outstanding rents are paid at that moment.

13. CCP, Section 491.

Default judgments

The CCP sets forth in Sections 637 through 651 the rules for default judgments. These rules provide for both cases where the defendant is present or absent. In all cases, the court will make a statement that the suit is being handled with a defendant not appearing in the process.

Section 637 of the CCP provides that in all suits where the defendant does not appear before the court after being served, no further notice will be delivered to summon him or her. All rulings issued thereafter will be notified by publication in the *Judicial Bulletin*.

Rulings ordering commencement of the evidence period or hearings to prepare evidence offered, as well as those giving the final judgment must be published twice by the court at a three-day interval in the *Judicial Bulletin* and at the court's discretion in a major newspaper of that area.

Finally, as an additional measure in these proceedings, based on the plaintiff's request, the judge may order that an attachment of assets of the defendant be made until the suit ends. If service of process was performed by publication, the final judgment will be enforced after three months from the last publication unless the defendant posts a bond to guarantee possible damages.

Regarding the procedure when the defendant is present, the latter may appear at any stage of the proceedings, but without being able to re-enter in the proceedings, the rebel party being considered as having been party to the suit all along.

If the rebel defendant appears during the evidence period he or she will have the right to submit evidence for a peremptory defence (those referring to the substantive arguments of the claim), provided that the defendant proves that he or she was prevented by *force majeure* from appearing in the proceeding at an earlier stage.[14]

Other means of termination without plenary trial

Voluntary dismissal

There are two different classes of dismissal:

    (1) Dismissal of the action; and
    (2) Dismissal of the proceedings.

The legal effect of dismissal of the action is that the plaintiff waives at its own prejudice all rights against the defendant for the cause of action being exercised through the suit filed with the corresponding court.

14. CCP, Section 646.

Dismissal of the action may be performed at any stage of the process, and the defendant does not need to consent to the dismissal for its operation. However, if the dismissal is filed after service of process is carried out, the plaintiff must pay the attorney's fees and litigation costs unless agreed otherwise.

Dismissal of the proceedings has, as its legal effect, the fact that the plaintiff waives in its own prejudice the complaint filed, but without waiving the right to sue its counterpart in a new procedure. Consequently, the dismissal of the procedure, also known as the dismissal of the complaint, renders things to their status before the suit was filed.

If the dismissal of the proceedings is made after service of process was carried out, the plaintiff must pay the attorney's fees and litigation costs unless agreed otherwise. Likewise, if the dismissal is filed after service of process was made, the defendant must consent to it, otherwise the procedure must continue.

Dismissal for failure to prosecute

The expiration of the proceedings (*Caducidad de la Instancia*) is governed by Section 137–*bis* of the CCP, which provides that the proceedings will be declared as dismissed at any stage if no act is performed by either party within a period of 180 working days. The term for this dismissal is interrupted by any act filed by the parties or by a court's act.

This cause for dismissal is a matter of public order, is non-waivable and may not be subject to agreement by the parties. The judge may declare the dismissal directly or at the request of either party. This dismissal extinguishes the proceedings but not the cause of action. Thus, the plaintiff may file a new suit subject to the statute of limitations.

Dismissal for failure to prosecute will render void all acts performed during the dismissed proceedings except for final rulings as to competence, existing suits, connection of the cause, authority and capacity of the parties. During appellate proceedings, this dismissal will cause the appealed rulings to be considered final.

This dismissal cause does not apply in bankruptcy or probate proceedings, nor in non-contentious proceedings, nor in family law action or in those pursued before Justices of the Peace.

Judicially assisted settlement

Judicial settlements are those agreements that the parties enter into within a procedure to solve a conflict and that are ratified in the presence of the court presiding over the cause. The court will review the agreement to make sure that it contains no provision contrary to the law, after which it will be approved and granted the status of a final judgment, binding on both parties as *res judicata*.

If the judicial agreement is not complied with by any of the parties in conflict, the other party may request enforcement through a court as if it were a final judgment issued by a court. The enforcement action will be conducted in a summary procedure.

TRIAL

Hearing

Setting the case for trial

Setting the case for trial means that only those facts that have been contested by the parties will be adjudicated by the court. Those facts indicated by the plaintiff that are not challenged by the defendant — silence or evasive comments will be considered to be acceptances — will be declared as valid, and only the remaining ones will be subject to proof by each party in the evidence stage.

From the contents of the defendant's answer, one may then determine the points in conflict. If the only conflict is with regard to the application of the law and not with facts, the court may summon the parties to an arguments hearing to issue a final ruling. Otherwise, the evidence stage will be opened if the parties so request or if the court deems it necessary.

Scope and order of trial

The trial has as its goal the settlement of a dispute between the parties in conflict. The judgment issued by the court will be considered a public order (ruling) that will bind both parties and that must be complied with. The trial cannot encompass issues other than those raised by the complaint and the answer. The court will rule only on those issues and will not file an order on different matters.

Submission of evidence

In ordinary civil proceedings, parties have a 10-day period to offer evidence commencing from the date that the relevant ruling of the court to open the evidence period is issued.

The courts have great freedom in evaluating the evidence. To discover the truth about the cause of the litigation, the court may take into account the testimony of any party in the action or of a third person or any thing or any document, be it in one of party's possession or not, with no limits other than legal restrictions and moral limitations.[15]

The parties will assume the burden of proving the facts on which they base their claims. The party denying a fact must prove the assertion implied by such denial only when there is no other way to ascertain the true facts.

Only factual issues, and not the law, are subject to evidentiary proof. The exception is foreign law.[16] Notorious facts need not be proven and the court may refer to them in its determinations. Parties may not waive their rights to offer evidence. Parties may only offer evidence suited to prove facts based on the parties' allegations.

The role of the trial judge in the presentation of evidence

The judge, under Mexican procedural law, plays a prime role during the evidence stage. While it is the parties that offer evidence to prove their assertions, the judge is allowed and expected to gather any and all evidence necessary to find the truth about the disputed facts.

At any stage and regardless of the nature of the claim, the judge may order any act that is necessary to find the truth about issues in dispute. In these acts, the judge will act as he or she deems fit in order to obtain the best results without harming the parties' interests, and based on an equal treatment of their rights. While the judge may perform these additional acts, the parties have the principal burden of proving their allegations.

The judge must accept all evidence filed by the parties that is authorised by law and relevant to the matters in dispute. The courts then have full authority to compel third parties to testify or produce any type of evidence required to find the true facts. To this end they may employ all the required sanctions to compel co-operation.

Evidence

Nature and purpose of evidence

The goal of evidence is to determine the truth about the facts contested by the parties, so that a final judgment on the applicable legal rules may be issued. Therefore, the evidence period involves the process and steps performed by the parties, third parties and the court to find the truth about the contested facts so that a final judgment may be issued.

There are several aspects related with evidence: the party that offers the evidence, the fact being proven, the burden of proof, the preparation

15. CCP, Section 278.
16. CCP, Section 284.

of the evidence, the method to assess the value of the evidence. Likewise, there are different types of evidence that can be offered by the parties: confessional, witnesses, documents, expert testimony, etc.

Kinds of evidence

All means that may show the truth about the challenged facts may be offered as evidence.[17] Without limiting other means, the CCP lists as possible means of evidence admissions, documents, expert testimony, judicial inspection, witnesses' testimony, other means of capturing data (photographs, photostats, etc.) and legal presumptions.

ADMISSIONS

Admissions always involve the deposition of one of the parties, be it the defendant or the plaintiff. They must refer to facts connected with the party being deposed. The nature of this evidence is to accept or recognise facts that the party being deposed may know.

This means of evidence may be offered from the date the evidence offering period begins and until the allegations hearing before final judgment is held.[18]

The party to be questioned must be personally summoned at his/her address to appear before the court. The questions that the deposed party must answer (positions) must meet the following requirements set forth by Section 311 of the CCP:

(1) They must be formulated in clear terms;
(2) They can only include one fact and must relate to the party being deposed;
(3) They cannot be confusing or misleading or try to get an admission of a fact contrary to the reality;
(4) They must be formulated in a positive sense and never involve a denial of a fact; and
(5) They must only relate to facts of the dispute between the parties.

Regarding the preparation of this evidence, the following rules must be observed. Once the evidence has been offered, the court will designate a specific date and time for the confession to take place. The counterpart will be personally summoned and warned about being declared as accepting the facts being questioned if failing to appear without a justified cause.

17. CCP, Section 289.
18. CCP, Section 308.

After the party has been notified, on the date for the hearing, the judge will open the envelope with the questions. The judge will review the questions to determine which of them, if any, meet the requirements, and will dispense with those that do not.

After this is done, the party will be requested to sign the interrogatory, and after stating his or her general data, will be warned to answer truthfully under penalty of perjury. The party making the admissions may not be aided by an attorney, representative or any other person, and will not be given a copy of the interrogatory, or time to discuss them. However, if the confessing party is foreign, then a translator appointed by the court may assist.

Thereafter, the judge will ask the party to answer the questions asked in a categorical affirmative or negative way, and subsequently add the explanations that he or she may deem convenient or those that the judge may require.

If the confessing party refuses to answer or answers evasively, the judge will warn that party that he or she will be deemed to have accepted the facts if he or she persists. The judge may apply a penalty to the party being questioned if he or she continues with such conduct.

Questions may be asked orally and directly during the presentation of the evidence. Nevertheless, it is better to submit a questionnaire prior to the deposition hearing because if the confessing party fails to appear without cause, the court may then declare that party as having accepted those questions that have been admitted by the court. If no questionnaire is filed before the hearing, there would be no questions to be declared answered and no declaration of acceptance or admission.

Answers will be transcribed literally in a separate document which for this effect will be prepared during the hearing at the court. Once the examination is finished and having read the document where this examination was recorded, the confessing party will sign in the margin and at the bottom of such document.

If the party does not agree with what is reproduced in the examination document, he or she may ask the judge to correct it. The judge will decide which corrections should be made. Nevertheless, once the document is signed by the confessing party, it cannot be modified.[19]

DOCUMENTARY EVIDENCE

There are two types of documentary evidence based on the different sources they may come from:

(1) Public documents are issued by public authorities in the exercise of their functions and within the jurisdiction provided by law.

19. CCP, Sections 319 and 320.

Section 327 of the CCP enumerates these types of documents. This evidence is regulated in Sections 308–328 of the CCP.

(2) Private documents are documents written, signed or caused to be written and signed by private parties or by public officials not in the exercise of their authority.

Parties have two different opportunities to deliver documents. The first is when the complaint (or the answer — as the case may be) is filed. The second is at the time the 10-day period to offer evidence is granted by the court. If the documents are not directly available to the party offering them, the interested party will name the file or place in which the originals are located.[20]

After the periods expire, no additional document may be filed by the plaintiff or defendant, unless:

(1) The document was issued at a subsequent date;
(2) The interested party had no knowledge of the document's existence at the time of the filing; or
(3) It was not possible to obtain the document before due to reasons not within the control of the interested party.[21]

Documents that are essential to the parties' cause of action or defence must be filed together with the complaint or answer. Parties may object to the use and evidentiary value that the offering party pretends to give to the documents. If a public document is challenged, the court may proceed to order its certification by the authority that issued it.

EXPERT TESTIMONY

Expert testimony is given by a third party whose participation has been requested by the parties or by the judge, and who has specific knowledge of an item or science related to the matter being tried.

The parties may agree to appoint a common expert. If they fail to name a common expert, each of the parties must name its own. The parties are required to present their experts so that they may accept the appointment before the court. Once they have accepted their nomination, they should give their expert opinion as to the issues touching on their area of expertise, according to their own knowledge and understanding.

The experts' opinions can be objected to on the basis of their contents, but not on the basis of the knowledge or techniques used by the expert.

In the event that experts' opinions are inconsistent, the judge will name a third expert to decide, whose opinion will stand as correct regarding the

20. CCP, Section 96.
21. CCP, Section 98.

questions involved. The third expert may object to the other experts' opinions and issue his or her own.

Under no circumstance will the parties be left without the assistance of an expert and if this appears imminent, the judge will name one on behalf of the party. The experts' fees are covered by each party and the third expert's fees are covered by both parties.

JUDICIAL INSPECTION

Judicial inspection consists in the direct examination by the judge of the real estate, goods or persons involved in the action in order to determine their status, location, situation or any other fact related thereto that might be relevant to the action.

Subjective considerations may not apply during the judicial inspection. The court will keep a record of the inspection, which shall be signed by everyone in attendance. Likewise, the court may accept any additional documents that might better serve the record, such as photographs or descriptions of the place where the property or the goods are located.

TESTIMONY OF WITNESSES

Testimony of witnesses is evidence brought by third parties not linked to the trial, and who have knowledge of the facts that the parties are required to prove. The testimony is given in court on the date and hour determined by the judge, and only in special cases (e.g., elderly or sick witnesses or public officials) may it be given at the witnesses' domiciles.

The parties have the obligation to bring before the court their own witnesses. However, when it is not feasible for a party to present its own witness before the court, the party will declare that circumstance under oath so that the court may then issue an order for the witness to appear before the court under a penalty of fifteen days incarceration for failure to appear.[22]

Sometimes, testimonial evidence is offered for the sole purpose of slowing down the trial, giving false or imprecise addresses or using other mechanisms that might make it difficult to find the witness. If this is the case, the party providing incorrect information may be fined and the evidence will be declared as not presented.

The questions made to witnesses will be direct and oral, never written. The questions must be directly related to the issues involved in the trial, and they must be clear and specific, making sure that each question deals with one fact only.[23]

22. CCP, Section 357.
23. CCP, Section 360.

In addition to the general information and the witness' oath, the witness will be asked the following:

(1) Whether he or she is a relative, close friend, dependant or employee of any of the parties; and
(2) Whether he or she has a direct or indirect interest in the trial.

These questions have the purpose of establishing the suitability of the person as a witness and to prevent a biased declaration that might benefit a party to the detriment of the other party.

Witnesses may deal with questions regarding time and place and circumstance that are directly related to the issues involved in the trial, so that these persons may share his or her knowledge with the court. Testimony may never include subjective considerations, since it is understood that witnesses know and are sure about the stated facts. Thus, words such as "I think, I believe, they told me, I guess" or any other similar formulations have the consequence that it will be presumed that the witness does not know or is unsure of the facts being declared.

Witnesses will be examined separately and successively. A witness may not be present during the taking of testimony of any other witness. The court will establish a single day for the presentation of witnesses.

Witnesses' answers will be reproduced in a separate document that will be kept with the trial record, and in case there are contradictions or ambiguities, the parties can call this to the attention of the judge in order to make the necessary clarification.[24]

At the end of the examination, each witness should explain the basis for its statement. This consists of an explanation of the origin of its knowledge as declared in the testimony given. The statement will be reflected in the corresponding document.

In the case of witnesses that have their addresses outside the jurisdiction of the judge in charge of the trail, the taking of the evidence will be done through letters rogatory sent to the judge that has jurisdiction at the witness' place of residence. For such taking of the evidence, a written questionnaire and cross-examination questionnaire will be included with the letter rogatory. The letter rogatory will be sent with the questionnaires, to be processed in terms of the Civil Procedure Law of the corresponding state.

The witness offered by a party can also be cross-examined by the other party. This means that new questions may be formulated with respect to the answers given by the witness to the original questions posed.

24. CCP, Section 365.

REPRODUCTION EVIDENCE

Sections 373–375 of the CCP also regulate cinematography, videos and any other photographic reproductions. All other types of *dactyloscopic*, audio registers and other elements that serve to attest to a state of affairs are admissible evidence. The party that presents this evidence should provide the court with the equipment or elements necessary for the evaluation of such evidence.

PRESUMPTIONS

The presumption is the consequence that the law or the court deduces from a known fact to discover an unknown fact. Both legal presumptions (by operation of law) and human presumptions (by the reasoning of the court) are permitted.[25]

JUDGMENT AND KINDS OF RELIEF

Final judgment

The final ruling that settles the dispute by resolving the issues in controversy is the substantive judgment. It is not final until it is no longer subject to appeal or other recourse. This ruling is issued once the evidence stage has expired and the hearing on the allegations (an opportunity for each party to make a summary the arguments that support the judge in issuing its final determination based on the merits of the case) has been concluded.

Entry of judgment

Section 79 of the CCP provides that there are different types of rulings: those that are issued throughout the suit and that may simply command the developments, those that decide interim issues, those that may be decided on peremptory matters that put an end to the process, and the final judgment that ends the suit by settling the dispute between the parties.

Pursuant to Section 14 of the Constitution, all rulings must be properly based on legal provisions or principles that justify the application of those rules. Judges may not vary or modify their rulings after they are signed but may clarify some concept or complete any omission as to an issue in dispute. These clarifications may be made directly by the court within

25. CCP, Sections 379 to 383.

the working day following the publication of the corresponding resolution or at the request of one of the parties within the day following the notification. In this case the court will rule as deemed adequate.

Kinds of relief

The judgment is the act that settles the dispute of the matter subject to adjudication. Therefore, the judgment may either rule for or against the defendant based on the analysis that the court performs of the evidence offered by the parties, which must have a direct relation with the plaintiff's action or the defences filed by the defendant.

The judgment may rule against the defendant as long as the plaintiff has proven the veracity of the facts on which the action was based and the defendant did not prove his defences. The defences considered valid will defeat the plaintiff's action. Where the defences may have been only partially proven, and depending on the type of action and the relief sought, the court may partially rule against the defendant.

Judgments must be consistent with the points being litigated. If the defendant loses, the extent of the judgment will depend on the type of relief requested, and the actions to enforce that relief.

In principle, the judgment will grant the defendant a period, usually five working days depending on the relief granted, for voluntary compliance with the ruling. If the ruling is not complied with in accordance with its terms, then enforcement may be carried out pursuant to the plaintiff's request. Normally the parties must exhaust all actions and appeals that the laws allow (local and federal) before the ruling is considered final. The judgment becomes final and firm because the law mandates so or because the parties do not exhaust all available remedies within the statute of limitations.

With regard to enforcement of the judgment against the defendant, when the defendant does not voluntarily comply, the plaintiff must seek enforcement through the court's forces pursuant to Sections 500 to 533 of the CCP. Measures such as pre-cautionary attachment or others are available in this process for enforcement of the judgment. Therefore, Section 500 of the CCP provides that forceful enforcement is required before the same court that issued the judgment, for which purpose the complete file must be returned to that court if it is being held by the Court of Appeals.

Specific performance

If the judgment orders the specific performance of an act, the court will grant a reasonable period to comply with the act. If the term elapses without compliance, the following steps will be adopted:

(1) If the act was strictly personal and is not complied with, the court will administer all measures necessary (fines or arrest) to force compliance, without prejudice to the claim for the corresponding damages;

(2) If the act was not strictly personal, the court will appoint a person to perform the act at that party's cost; and

(3) If the act was the granting of any instrument or the execution of a specific act, the court will perform it for the rebel party, indicating in the document that it was granted in default.

In general, most of the matters filed with the courts fall within the categories listed above, but there may be other acts, such as the rendering of accounting records, the division of an asset or the obligation not to perform or to repossess personal property or real estate.

Monetary awards

The CCP indicates that when the judgment awards a cash amount, enough assets will be attached without a prior notice to the defendant. If the assets attached are liquid funds, the plaintiff will be immediately paid, and if different assets they will be appraised and publicly auctioned. It may happen that the ruling has different relief granted, but the cash award would be immediately satisfied if the defendant's cash were attached.

The interested party must file an enforcement request with a list of the cash against which enforcement is sought, which the other party will have the opportunity to review for three days to argue in its favour. The court will rule based on the arguments filed by both parties, but also based on the contents of the final judgment. This ruling may be appealed but will not stop execution.

All expenses incurred in connection with enforcement of the judgment must be paid by the obliged party, stressing that the law grants a term of 10 years to request enforcement of the judgment, from the date when the term for voluntary compliance expired.[26]

Construction, transformation or rescission

Based on the relief sought by the parties and the contents of the judgment, the court may rule on the rescission of obligations between them, or the interpretation of what should be considered as a valid obligation between them. The process for enforcement is the same as described above in case any specific act is required of the obliged party.

26. CCP, Section 529.

Declaration concerning legal relations

The court's judgment may simply decide the status of the legal relations between the parties, based again on the contents of the complaint and the answer. The court may communicate the terms of the ruling to third parties as may be necessary for the proper enforcement and satisfaction of the awarded relief.

POST-TRIAL MOTIONS

Attacks on judgments

Judgments can only be challenged through an appeal.[27] Depending on the type of proceedings, the final judgment may permit other attacks, but only the appeal truly addresses the substance of the ruling. The first instance court cannot revoke its own determinations.

Grounds for a new trial

Under Mexican procedural rules, a suit and the corresponding judgment will preclude the possibility of a new trial as to those issues that have been adjudicated. No new trials will be allowed, and whatever the plaintiff originally claims in its complaint will be considered a waiver of any other relief or benefit sought from the defendant for that specific cause of action.

Thus, for example, a motion for a new trial due to mistake and excusable neglect on the part of one of the parties is not a procedural step contemplated under the CCP and the general procedural rules of Mexico. This restrictive approach also applies to evidence that is discovered after judgment.

Once the final judgment has been issued it cannot be modified or revoked by the court that issued it. Any newly discovered evidence must be submitted during the proceedings, that is, from the time the complaint is filed and until the court orders the file to be prepared for the issuance of the final judgment.

Although newly discovered evidence is not a ground for a new trial, it may disclose or prove important facts that were unknown to the parties and it may facilitate the court's decision. Newly discovered evidence that was not otherwise available or known by the parties might be admissible in appeal proceedings.

The court will assist the parties in securing the additional evidence by ordering its release from the Registry or location where it is being kept.

27. See below.

According to Section 98 of the CCP, neither party will be allowed to file documents after the original complaint and answer are filed except where:

(1) They came into being at a later date;
(2) They are stated under oath not to have been known earlier; or
(3) It is stated under oath that they could not be gathered before for causes not within that party's control.

After the file is sent by the court for issuance of the final ruling, then no additional evidence will be admitted and anything filed by either party will be rejected. Any new evidence that is filed in a timely manner will be subject to the other party's objections and arguments to affect its evidentiary impact.

Even in the case of fraud, retrying the case is not foreseen. When making any filings with the court or making any statements, the parties are doing so under oath. A false statement could be made in the personal hearings or when the parties personally appear in court for the main hearing. If this occurs, it may constitute sufficient grounds to initiate criminal proceedings and possibly a civil action for damages. While this is the subject of a different suit, it would surely effect the way the court adjudicates the original suit if the deceit were discovered prior to its judgment. Such frauds, however, are seldom prosecuted in practice because it is often difficult to evidence the deceit.

ENFORCEMENT AND EXECUTION OF JUDGMENTS

Writs of execution

This is the order that the court issues to instruct the parties to comply with the terms of the final judgment.[28] The court is allowed to order attachment of assets to guarantee enforcement of the judgment when the parties do not voluntarily comply with its terms.

Bankruptcy or liquidation

The court that issued the final judgment will not have the authority to declare a party bankrupt or subject to liquidation if on enforcement it is clear that such party is insolvent. The interested party may, however, request certified copies of the circumstances at that juncture so that a bankruptcy or liquidation action may be declared applicable. Some of

28. This process is discussed above in more detail.

those actions may lie within the competence of Commercial Courts that will need to adjudicate the need for the bankruptcy or liquidation of the party that has not met its duties according to the original enforcement order.

Administration orders

An administrator is normally appointed by the court to administer the business of a party that is required to make payments in a given suit and is believed to be prone to hide its assets.

The administrator will have the duty to keep the records of the debtor. However, this is only the case where a judgment may order payment of a cash amount that is to be satisfied by the debtor's business proceeds and as a consequence of the attachment of the debtor's assets.

Arrest

Arrest is not a part of the judgment or relief included therein, but a way in which to achieve enforcement of the court's ruling. Generally, the CCP does contemplate the possibility of imposing arrest as a measure to sanction a party's non-compliance with enforcement of the judgment. However, the court may order a domicile arrest. The judgment debtor is not allowed to leave the premises until the judgment is fully complied with. This measure could be applied in the case of judgments that order specific, personal performance of an act by the obliged party.

International cooperation

The Sections 604–608 of the CCP deal with international cooperation including the taking of evidence, the enforcement of foreign judgments and arbitration awards, and other acts whereby a Mexican Court will assist a foreign court in its jurisdictional activities as they may have an impact in parties located in Mexico.

Generally, the Mexican court will according to letter-rogatory pursuant to the instructions received and the authority referred to by the foreign court. The Mexican court, however, will only act based on local procedural requirements and not according to foreign law.

Regarding the enforcement of foreign judgments and arbitration awards these will be generally recognized and accepted by the courts of the United Mexican States without retrial or examination of the merits of the case, provided all requirements set forth by the CCP and the Federal Code of Civil Procedures are met. Thus, *inter alia*, the foreign judgment must not violate Mexican public policy; it must be filed before a Mexican court in documents complying with all formalities clearly evidencing their authenticity (duly certified by an official whose signature is legalized by the Mexican Consulate nearest to the place of issuance); the matter and issue dealt with in the ruling issued abroad must not derive from an action *in rem*; the foreign court must have validly asserted jurisdiction according to internationally accepted principles as recognized by Mexican law; the defendant must have been duly served of process to avail the Constitutional right of evidence and prior defense before being judged; the foreign judgment must be final and not subject to any review or legal recourse (*res judicata*); and the issue resolved by the ruling not be one currently being decided among the same parties in an Mexican Court, provided in the latter process the foreign party was duly served.

Even if all requirements above are met, the Mexican Court can deny enforcement if evidenced that the country where the judgment was issued would not reciprocate if asked to enforce a Mexican Court judgment.

APPEAL

The appeal action asks the superior court to either confirm, revoke or modify the ruling of the inferior court. Section 689 of the CCP provides that the parties may appeal a ruling if it is considered to have suffered a violation of legal rights. The right to appeal is also granted to third parties that may be prejudiced by the particular judicial ruling. A partial appeal of the ruling is acceptable. A party that has obtained all relief sought may not appeal a ruling.

The appeal action must be filed in writing, even when the law contemplates the possibility of a verbal appeal. The time for filing the appeal is within five working days from the date on which the notification of the corresponding ruling is deemed effective. Once that term elapses, it is understood that the parties have accepted the ruling and the opportunity to appeal has expired with prejudice, and consequently the ruling becomes final.

The appeal will be processed by the court immediately above that which issued the ruling. Rulings issued by Civil Courts will be appealed before the Chambers of the Superior Justice Tribunal of the corresponding state. Once the appeal is filed, the court will rule on whether the action is admissible and will order initiation of appeal proceedings before the Superior Court.

Appeals may be submitted in two different manners:

(1) On a return basis, which means that the principal suit will not be suspended during the appeal process. Nonetheless, if the appeal is ruled on favourably, then anything done inconsistent with the appeal will automatically be revoked and lose validity; and

(2) On a suspension basis, which means that while the appeal is in process, the principal suit will be suspended and a complete stay of execution is mandated.

The CCP indicates the cases in which the appeal must be admitted on a suspension basis. Section 700 of the CCP indicates that, among others, appeals against the following rulings will be admitted on a suspension basis:

(1) Final judgments (except family law matters in general);
(2) Rulings that make the continuation of the principal process impossible; and
(3) Interim judgments that paralyse the principal suit.

All other appeals are only accepted on a return basis.

Once the court rules on the admission of the appeal, it will then rule on whether it should be processed on a suspension or return basis. If accepted on a suspension basis the original file will be sent to the Superior Court, and if admitted only on a return basis, copies of the relevant portions of the file will be prepared and sent to the superior court.

When the appeal is filed, it is not necessary to include the arguments challenging the ruling; these are subsequently presented to the superior court. When the file or the corresponding copies reach the superior court, the latter will decide the admission of the appeal and the basis on which it was admitted by the lower court. If the appeal is ruled inadmissible, the file will be returned; if only the basis is changed, an exchange of documents between the lower and the superior court will need to take place to adjust to the correct basis.

The superior court's ruling admitting the appeal will give the appealing party a period of six days to file the appeal arguments. If the arguments are not filed within the allotted period, the appeal will be dismissed and the appealed ruling declared final and *res judicata*.

In the event that the appellant files the appeal arguments within the allotted term, then the other party will have a subsequent six-day period to file its comments to the arguments. Once the appeal file is complete, it is sent to one of the three judges of the superior court to prepare the draft of the ruling. The draft of the ruling will be analysed by the other two judges. The ruling requires approval in a majority vote.

It is necessary to clarify that in the appeal of final judgments, the parties may only offer new evidence if it is relevant to a supplementary defence that is not alien to the subject matter of the dispute.

Issues subject to review

The superior court will only review the records of the proceedings with the lower court. No additional elements may be put forward for review as that would extend the matter beyond the lower court judgment that is to be confirmed, revoked or modified.

The superior court must review each and every part of the original case according to the appeal arguments filed by the appellant. If a party fails to make an argument as to an issue that is to its prejudice, the superior court may not remedy that deficiency *ex officio*; it must rule solely on the basis of the appeal documents.

Review of proceedings

The review of facts will cover the proceedings from the initial complaint up to the last act by the parties in the arguments hearing before the judgment is issued. The appeal arguments may deal with facts throughout the process. However, if there were procedural violations that should have been appealed during the proceedings, these may not be challenged in an appeal against the final judgment. All unchallenged acts must be considered final and not subject to a new review.

Further appeal

Once the appeal is resolved and the superior court issues its determination, the Appeal Ruling is only subject to a Constitutional Suit (*Juicio de Amparo*) that may be filed by either party before the Federal Courts. These Constitutional Suits are governed by a federal statute and follow very specific procedural rules for a final ruling by a Circuit Court that will not be subject to any further appeal action.

THE CONCLUSIVENESS OF JUDGMENT

Res judicata

Pursuant to Section 426 of the CCP, a judgment is considered *res judicata* when it is subject to no further appeal or revocation action. Likewise, by provision of law, the following judgments become final:

(1) Rulings issued in lawsuits where the amount in dispute does not exceed 182 times the minimum wage in force in the Federal District, save for those rulings issued as regards to lease agreements for domestic premises. These cases are handled by the Courts of Mixed Peace;

(2) Judgments issued by a superior court whereby appeals are finally resolved;

(3) Rulings that resolve a complaint against a judge (action to seek a sanction against a judge for improper or unfair conduct); and

(4) Rulings that resolve a competition defence, and those that by law are not challengeable through an appeal action.

The CCP treats these acts as final rulings because they are not challengeable through an appeal action. These acts can only be challenged through Constitutional Suits (*Juicio de Amparo*) that may be brought before Federal District Courts or Circuit Courts depending on the act being challenged. These Federal Courts will review the lower courts acts to determine their consistency with the principles and bill of rights contemplated under the first 29 Articles of the Constitution.

Additionally, based on a specific judicial declaration pursuant to Section 427 of the CCP, a judgment or other ruling may be declared *res judicata* in the following cases:

(1) Rulings that have been expressly consented to by the parties or their representatives expressly authorised to that effect;
(2) Rulings that after notification are not challenged by the parties within the statute of limitations; and
(3) Rulings that having been challenged are not processed, or the corresponding appeal is withdrawn.

The judicial declaration of *res judicata* can be made directly by the court or at the express request of a party. This resolution cannot be appealed except for a special action against the court itself.

The law of the case

The Mexican legal system, as any major Civil Law system in the world, is not based on the *stare decisis* doctrine. The courts are expected to resolve issues based on the provisions included in the Codes enacted by the Legislature. The decisions issued by the courts have generally no binding power over other courts and set no precedent for future cases.

However, there is a concept known as "jurisprudencia" that is understood as the criteria applied to solve a particular issue that should be used by all lower courts. In the Mexican judicial system, only the Supreme Court of Justice of the Nation and the Collegiate Circuit Courts are authorised to set these criteria of interpretation. At the local level there is no similar concept nor any specific precedence theory that applies.

The jurisprudence is published in the *Federal Judicial Weekly Gazette*, a publication of the Supreme Court of Justice of the Nation. Jurisprudence is valid when there are five uninterrupted rulings on the same issue by the same level of Courts. Before the five consecutive rulings are issued that would require to be followed by lower courts, these isolated judgments may be referred to by those courts but need not be applied.

CHAPTER 13

SPAIN

ANTONIO VIÑAL
Antonio Viñal & Co.
Madrid, Spain

ESTABLISHING JURISDICTION

Organic Law Number 6/1985 on the Judiciary (LOPJ), dated 1 July 1985, and amended by Organic Law Number 16/1994, dated 9 November 1994, regulates the extent and limits of Spanish jurisdiction, i.e., the so-called international judicial competence of Spanish courts, under its Sections 21 and 22. These are clearly inspired by the Brussels Convention on Jurisdiction and the Enforcement of Judgments in Civil and Commercial Matters, dated 27 September 1968.[1]

Specifically, Section 21 recognises that everyone is entitled to the right of jurisdiction, regardless of nationality, whether Spaniards or foreigners. Nevertheless, it subordinates this jurisdiction to two requirements:

(1) That the actions, whether only between Spaniards, only between foreigners or between Spaniards and foreigners, arise in Spanish territory; and

(2) That these actions should, additionally, be in accordance with the provisions of the LOPJ and those of the conventional norms incorporated by Spain into its national legislation.

Section 22 of the LOPJ includes a classification that is not without its criticism due to technical flaws and its having an attributive character rather than a distributive one.[2] The criteria determining the

1. Almagro Nosete *et al.*, *Derecho Procesal, Tomo I* (Volume I), *Parte General Proceso Civil (I)*, Valencia, 1986, p. 110.

2. Abarca Juncos, "Extensión y Límites de la Jurisdicción Internacional de los Juzgados y Tribunales en el Orden Civil. Regulación en la Ley Orgánica del Poder Judicial y en el Convenio de Bruselas", *La Ley*, 1987-1, pp. 1108 *et seq.* Supreme Court Decision (*Sentencia del Tribunal Supremo* — STS) 18 June 1990; Almagro Nosete *et al*, *Derecho Procesal, Tomo I* (Volume II), *Parte General Proceso Civil* (I), Valencia, 1986, p. 114; Amores Conradi, "La Nueva Estructura del Sistema Español de Competencia Judicial Internacional en el Orden Civil: Art. 22 LOPJ" *Revista Española de Derecho Internacional*, 1989, Volume XLI, p. 125.

jurisdictional attribution to the Spanish courts in the civil sphere groups them into five large blocks of legal rights, namely:

(1) Exclusive rights;
(2) General rights;
(3) Subsidiary rights;
(4) Special rights; and
(5) Preventive rights.[3]

As opposed to the previous attributive system for jurisdiction, referred to in Sections 51 and 70 of the Law on Civil Procedure (LEC) — considered confusing and contradictory by one doctrinal sector,[4] and lacking in legal regulation by another one[5] — the present system of Section 22 of LOPJ — adopted under the aegis of the 1978 constitutional norms — presents "a new and complete regulation, with pretensions to being effectively systematic and coherent".[6] In spite of everything, the regulation under Section 22 has been unable to avoid the corresponding criticism.

Such criticism includes, *inter alia*, the fact that this regulation of international court jurisdiction is separate and independent of the internal territorial jurisdiction and that such separation and independence are accompanied by a lack of co-ordination between one and the other, with the result, in some cases, that it is impossible, even where the Spanish courts have international jurisdiction, to establish which court is territorially competent.[7] In many cases, the result of this is that the court proceedings for the establishment of international judicial jurisdiction have to be undertaken in light of the norms for the verification of internal territorial jurisdiction.[8]

3. Amores Conradi, "La Nueva Estructura del Sistema Español de Competencia Judicial Internacional en el Orden Civil: Art. 22 LOPJ", *Revista Española de Derecho Internacional*, Volume XLI, pp. 113 *et seq.*

4. Pecourt García, "Las Normas de Competencia Judicial Internacional en el Derecho Español", *Anuario Ihladi*, 1963, p. 207.

5. Amores Conradi, "La Nueva Estructura del Sistema Español de Competencia Judicial Internacional en el Orden Civil: Art. 22 LOPJ", *Revista Española de Derecho Internacional*, 1989, Volume XLI, p. 115.

6. Amores Conradi, "La Nueva Estructura del Sistema Español de Competencia Judicial Internacional en el Orden Civil: Art. 22 LOPJ", *Revista Española de Derecho Internacional*, 1989, Volume XLI, p. 114.

7. Amores Conradi, "La Nueva Estructura del Sistema Español de Competencia Judicial Internacional en el Orden Civil: Art. 22 LOPJ", *Revista Española de Derecho Internacional*, 1989, Volume XLI, pp. 121 *et seq.*

8. Amores Conradi, "La Nueva Estructura del Sistema Español de Competencia Judicial Internacional en el Orden Civil: Art. 22 LOPJ", *Revista Española de Derecho Internacional*, 1989, Volume XLI, p. 123.

Types of jurisdiction

Jurisdiction over the parties of the action

NATURAL PERSONS

The Spanish courts are competent in those cases where the parties, either tacitly or expressly, have submitted to them. This jurisdiction is general in character and is known as extended jurisdiction due to the decisive will of the parties for establishing it.

Section 22, Paragraph 2, of the LOPJ regulates this extended jurisdiction but does not develop the conditions for applying it. Such conditions are detailed in the regulations on internal territorial jurisdiction and may, as in other cases, be transposed to the delimitation of international jurisdiction of Spanish courts.

In this sense, as far as express submission is concerned, Section 57 of the LEC requires two main constraints:

(1) Surrender of one's personal privilege of forum; and
(2) The indication of the judge to which the parties submit, with the possibility being admitted, with reference to the renunciation of the personal privilege that this may be done implicitly.[9]

As for tacit submission, the LEC, this time in Section 58, requires that the action be presented by the plaintiff and that the defendant should do something more than merely appearing. In this respect, Spanish jurisprudence considers, in an interpretative clarification of this action, that the requests for a longer period for replying to the suit or for the suspension of the proceedings constitute such additional activity.[10]

Within this context, the jurisprudence includes, as strictly exceptional, those cases where Spanish authorities are not competent with a view to jurisdiction following a provision of submission to a foreign court, provided that there are no doubtful circumstances that make it null and void.[11] This is so because there are subject matters, such as those included in Section 22, Paragraph 1 of the LOPJ, in which the surrender (*derogatio*) of jurisdiction of the Spanish courts will not be admissible.

Similarly, Spanish courts are competent in those cases where the defendant has his domicile in Spanish territory. This privilege, *actor sequitur*

---

9. Supreme Court Decisions 18 June 1990; 30 April 1991; 15 February 1992; 18 February 1993; and 19 February 1993.

10. Camacho Ortega, "La Competencia Judicial Internacional de los Juzgados y Tribunales Españoles en el Orden Civil: Breves notas en torno al problema de la sumisión tácita", *La Ley*, 1991–3, p. 1001. SSTS 1 October 1978; 21 March 1981; 9 May 1983; and 5 December 1984.

11. STS 10 July 1990.

forum rei, is general in character like the preceding one. It has its origin, on the one hand, in the rules for internal territorial jurisdiction[12] and, on the other hand, the Brussels Convention.[13]

CORPORATIONS

Spanish courts have special, in this case not general but exclusive, jurisdiction in questions of the incorporation, validity, annulment or dissolution of companies or bodies corporate domiciled in Spanish territory, as well as with regard to the decisions and agreements of their administrative organs.[14]

This exclusive privilege of forum, also inspired by the Brussels Convention, in its triple exclusivity (exclusive territorial jurisdiction, the impossibility of agreement between the parties and non-recognition of foreign judgments which conflict with its jurisdiction) is without a doubt one of the most eye-catching aspects of the new regulations.[15]

Spanish courts also have special jurisdiction, bearing in mind the nature of the matter giving rise to the suit, in conflicts concerning the exploitation of a branch office, agency or commercial establishment, when this is located in Spanish territory. However, for bankruptcy proceedings, these are governed by their regulations.[16]

Jurisdiction over the subject matter of the action

CLAIMS FOR PROPERTY

When a real action is undertaken to reclaim the property of an item, one must, in principle, distinguish between movable and real property. In the case of real estate, as it is a question of real rights over estate, the Spanish courts will be competent, and exclusively so, provided that the real estate in question is located in Spanish territory. This is most clearly deduced from Section 22.1 of the LOPJ.

For any kind of action on movable estates, the Spanish courts will be competent provided that the estate in question is located in Spanish territory when the action is initiated. Nevertheless, this jurisdiction is not exclusive, which means that the parties may, tacitly or expressly,

12. LEC, Sections 62 *et seq.*
13. Brussels Convention, Section 2.
14. LOPJ, Section 22.1.
15. Amores Conradi, "La Nueva Estructura del Sistema Español de Competencia Judicial Internacional en el Orden Civil: Art. 22 LOPJ", *Revista Española de Derecho Internacional*, 1989, Volume XLI, p. 127.
16. LOPJ, Section 22.4.

submit to the courts of another state. They may also take up the case before the courts of the defendant's domicile.[17]

DAMAGES OR VIOLATION OF RIGHTS

In claims for damages where an action is begun to obtain fulfilment of an extra-contractual obligation, the Spanish courts have jurisdiction in two kinds of situation, namely when the fact from which the harm arises has occurred in Spain and when both the author of the harm and the victim habitually reside in Spanish territory.[18]

When the infringement of a right represents a breach of a contractual obligation, the jurisdiction of Spanish courts extends to all those cases in which the obligation arises or should be performed in Spain. This, however, is not a forum that excludes express or tacit submission nor does it prevent an action before the court of the defendant's domicile.[19]

Among the obligations arising out of a contract, one has to distinguish the specific cases set out in the LOPJ where the Spanish courts will, therefore, have jurisdiction:

(1) In matters of consumer contracts, if they concern instalment plan sales of corporal movable estate or of loans intended to finance their acquisition, when the purchaser has his domicile in Spain;[20]

(2) In matters of insurance, when the insured party and the insurer have their domiciles in Spain;[21] and

(3) In those cases of any other contract for the rendering of services or in connection with movable estates, when the execution of the contract must have been preceded by a personal offer or of advertising effected in Spain or the consumer must have effected in Spain the actions necessary for the execution of the contract.[22]

Article 3 of the Brussels Convention

The Spanish LOPJ draws its principal inspiration from the Brussels Convention. Yet, there are some basic differences between them, such as the

17. LOPJ, Section 22.3.
18. LOPJ, Section 22.3.
19. LOPJ, Section 22.3.
20. LOPJ, Section 22.4.
21. LOPJ, Section 22.4.
22. LOPJ, Section 22.4.

general rules on jurisdiction. The Brussels Convention refers only to the defendant's domicile,[23] whereas the Spanish LOPJ to the express or tacit submission.[24]

Furthermore, when considering contractual obligations, the LOPJ confers competence on the Spanish courts when these obligations have arisen or will be performed in Spain,[25] but such an alternate criteria is not incorporated in the Convention, which only takes up the latter.[26]

The Convention deals with certain contracts (insurance, consumer) in a more extensive and detailed way than the LOPJ. Thus, according to Section 8 of the Convention, an insurer domiciled in a Contracting State may be sued in the courts of the state where he is domiciled or in another Contracting State, in the courts for the place where the policy-holder is domiciled. Also, on the other hand, the insurer may bring proceedings only in the courts of the Contracting State in which the defendant is domiciled.[27]

Venue

General principles

The existence of a variety of courts in Spain poses the problem of distributing among them the various cases arising in Spanish territory. This diversity of courts, fundamentally included in Section 26 of the LOPJ, allows four jurisdictional orders to be established: civil, criminal, contentious-administrative, and company matters.

In principle, the civil courts will, in accordance with Section 9.2 of the LOPJ, deal with the matters corresponding to them as well as, residually, all those which are not specifically assigned to any jurisdictional order. These Civil Courts are: Courts of the First Instance;[28] Provincial Courts of Justice;[29] Civil Chambers of the Superior Courts of Justice;[30] Civil Chamber (First) of the Supreme Court.[31] The fact that there is a variety of court institutions with different degrees of jurisdiction and that there are, in short, various organs involved, obliges the following

23. Brussels Convention, Section 5.
24. LOPJ, Sections 57 and 58.
25. LOPJ, Section 22.3.
26. Brussels Convention, Section 3 in connection with Section 5.
27. Brussels Convention, Section 11.
28. LOPJ, Section 85.
29. LOPJ, Section 82.3 and 4.
30. LOPJ, Section 73.1 and 2.
31. LOPJ, Section 56.

criteria to be considered in order to establish which of these courts will deal with the matters mentioned above.

OBJECTIVE JURISDICTION

The nature of the plaintiff's intention is one of the criteria for establishing jurisdiction, as is the amount, as established in Section 54 of the LEC. In the first case, the assignation of jurisdiction is done on a casuistic basis and in the second case by reference to the amount that is the object of the suit.

In view of this criterion on amount, the current rules establish that there are four ordinary level declarative actions, namely that of "larger claims" for claims of an economic interest in excess of 160-million pesetas;[32] that of "lesser claims" for actions with an economic interest of between 800,000 pesetas and 160-million pesetas;[33] the so-called declaratory proceedings for claims where the economic interest exceeds 80,000 pesetas but does not exceed 800,000 pesetas and the oral proceedings for claims with an economic interest of less than 80,000 pesetas.[34]

At times, as with Sections 483 and 484, the LEC itself combines both the criteria of the subject matter of the action and that of the amount, and sets out that the actions for honorific rights of the person must be decided in "larger claims",[35] and those connected with filiation, paternity, maternity, capacity and marital status of individuals must be dealt with through "lesser claims" as well as all those cases where the amount is impossible to estimate or where no other provision is specifically made.[36]

In those cases where no specific amount is involved, the legislator has provided a series of rules to calculate the value of the actions and in this way be able to determine the amount and the kind of hearing. Thus, among other things, the amount of the proceedings for actions on movable and real property will be their current market value;[37] for actions regarding leases of property, the amount of one year's rent;[38] and in actions for money where the amount is not specified, the actions will be deemed to be for an amount unable to be estimated and will be dealt with through the procedures for petty amount hearings and before the Courts of First Instance.[39]

32. LOPJ, Section 483.1.
33. LOPJ, Section 484.1.
34. LEC, Section 486.
35. LEC, Section 483.2.
36. LEC, Sections 484.2 and 484.3.
37. LEC, Section 489.1.
38. LEC, Section 489.10.
39. LEC, Section 489.8.

FUNCTIONAL JURISDICTION

The most significant feature of functional jurisdiction, as some authors have remarked, is its derivative nature, i.e., that in order to establish jurisdiction one must always start from a situation of an action begun before a specific jurisdictional organ and substantiated through certain measures but currently pending resolution. The major manifestations of such jurisdiction are the attribution of cognisance for devolutive remedies (appeals, petitions in error, and motions to vacate) or that of investigation of the rejection of judges and magistrates or the decision on the joinder of actions being heard by different courts.[40]

TERRITORIAL JURISDICTION

The norms for territorial jurisdiction are determined through the criteria known as "rules" which may be conventional, established through the submission of the parties to an organ of jurisdiction or legal, established by law as mandatory. These latter rights are subdivided into general and special rights, including in the first case those associated with the defendant's domicile and the other cases in the latter. The legal rights may be exclusive, whereby the legislator establishes a single forum, or concurrent in which several fora are established for the cognisance of a matter.

Transfer of venue

The rules on territorial jurisdiction, as distinct from the rules on objective and functional jurisdiction, can be extended, as recognised in Section 54 of the LEC. Thus, the parties may by agreement choose any court and pursue civil proceedings before it, provided that such a court exercises ordinary jurisdiction in accordance with the provisions of Section 56 of the LEC and has such jurisdiction for the cognisance of the same kind of hearings and in the same degree.

Notwithstanding, there are cases in which jurisdiction is established in a definitive and non-extensible fashion. Among others, this happens in proceedings for leases, in which the only competent judge is that of the place where the property is located;[41] or for proceedings to challenge the agreements of a company, where the only competent judge is that of the company's registered office;[42] or with suits regarding rights to registered trade marks or patents.[43]

40. Almagro Nosete *et al*, *Derecho Procesal, Tomo I* (Volume II), *Parte General Proceso Civil* (I), Valencia, 1986, pp. 230 *et seq.*
41. Law Number 29/1994 of 24 November 1994 on Urban Leases, Section 38.
42. Law on Joint Stock Corporations, Section 118.
43. Patent Law, Section 125.

In these latter cases, the judge must refrain from judgment at his own initiative whenever he considers himself to be without jurisdiction on the basis of Section 9.6 of the LOPJ or else under Section 51.2 of the same Law. Otherwise, the defendant may challenge such jurisdiction through two specific routes, known as "demurrer to the jurisdiction" and "plea for inhibition". However, in any case, proceedings undertaken where a lack of territorial jurisprudence exists are not void.[44]

To return then to the regulations defining the standard for territorial jurisdiction, this must be established with respect to specific rules. The first of these is the verification of a possible express submission of the parties to a particular court. Only in default of this express submission, or where there is some tacit submission, will the rules established in detail by Sections 62 and 63 of the LEC be applicable.

Before analysing these precepts, it is appropriate to point out that tacit submission is not so much a rule to determine jurisdiction as a technical expedient to prevent controversies from arising on the question of jurisdiction. The plaintiff tacitly submits by the simple act of lodging the action[45] before a judge with objective jurisdiction, regardless of the rules on territorial jurisdiction (i.e., the rules making provisions not prohibitions). However, true tacit submission is that of the defendant that arises through merely effecting any matter before the judge chosen by the plaintiff, other than the submission of a demurrer to the jurisdiction.[46]

Once submission has occurred, the defendant may no longer challenge the jurisdiction of the judge through a demurrer or plea for inhibition as these faculties are then precluded. The demurrer to the jurisdiction is lodged by the defendant before the judge chosen by the plaintiff and which the former considers to have no jurisdiction in the case. The judge is requested to disqualify himself from investigation of the case and to send it to the judge appointed by the defendant, which the latter considers to be the only court with jurisdiction. The plea for inhibition is submitted to the judge whom the defendant considers to have jurisdiction so that he may address the judge actually investigating the matter to request that the proceedings be remitted to him.

For the resolution of both matters, the corresponding judge (the investigating judge in the demurrer or else the judge requesting remission at the instance of the defendant, or even a superior court of both, in the case of the plea for inhibition) will decide with regard to the rules for attribution of jurisdiction.[47] Should the defendant have lodged in due form the

44. LOPJ, Section 238.1, interpreted *contrario sensu*.
45. LEC, Section 58.1.
46. LEC, Section 58.2.
47. Express and tacit submission and LEC, Sections 62 and 63.

demurrer or plea for inhibition, thus avoiding tacit submission, it is necessary to resort to the criteria for determination of territorial jurisdiction.

The first rule or privilege of forum to be applied by the deciding judge is, where appropriate that of express submission, *pactum de foro prorogato*. This consists in the clear and determinant agreement of wills by the parties to the effect that they renounce the fora to which they are legally entitled and appoint the judge with jurisdiction for the cognisance of the actions that might later arise between the parties.

If there is no express or where appropriate tacit submission or this cannot be proved, the judge must have recourse to the rules established in the LEC on jurisdiction. First, the so-called special rules found in Sections 63 and 1431 of the LEC are applicable together with those other procedural regulations not included therein.

Classified by the most significant rules, for the purposes of the present study, jurisdiction lies:

(1) In actions concerning the presentation and approval of accounts by an administration, with the judge of the place where such presentation is to be made or, if lacking, with the judge of the domicile of the owner of the property or the judge of the place where such presentation is to be made;

(2) In hearings for eviction or redemption, with the judge of the place where the object is located or with that of the defendant's domicile (at the plaintiff's option);

(3) In bankruptcy or insolvency proceedings, if voluntary, with the judge of the debtor's domicile; if compulsory, with the judge of the place where any of the execution measures are being dealt with;

(4) In proceedings to challenge the agreements adopted by General Shareholders' Meetings of Corporations, with the judge of the place where the meeting has been held; and

(5) In cases of preventive distraint, with the judge of the place where the property to be distrained is situated.

In the absence of any applicable special rule, the so-called general rules of Section 62 of the LEC come into play. These rules refer to the kind of action (personal, real or mixed) being undertaken, as shown below:

(1) In personal actions, jurisdiction lies, as a general rule, with the judge of the place of fulfilment of the obligation; and

(2) In real actions, jurisdiction is with the judge of the place where the real property is to be found, if appropriate. If the action is pursued relative to movable or semi-movable goods, the judge of the place where they are located or that of the defendant's domicile are the two alternative venues, at the plaintiff's choice.

The last two rules of court mentioned are also those corresponding to mixed actions (where these are considered to be those so classified since ancient times, such as the division of common property), as well as those real and personal actions which are pursued in joinder.[48]

Finally, in default of express or tacit submission, special or general privilege, the natural jurisdiction that operates is that of the defendant's domicile, even where this is not expressly referred to in law.

Service of summons or writs

By post

Notifications are judicial acts whereby a judicial decision or a measure arranged by the Secretary to the Court must be made known to the parties and to those concerned either by reference or through prejudice to their interests, as provided for by Section 271 of the LOPJ and Section 260 of the LEC.

Spanish regulations divide these communicable events in the proceedings into notifications in the strict sense (communication of a decision), summonses (indication of the date and time for the person to appear in order to carry out some part of the proceedings), arrangements (initiation of a period of time during which some part of the proceedings can be completed) and injunctions (court notification to do or cease to do something ordered therein, either immediately or within the time specified).

Section 261 of the LEC foresees the despatch of notifications through registered mail with an acknowledgement of receipt for those notifications effected outside the precincts of the court. Whenever particular circumstances or the requirements of additional speed make it necessary, the notifications may be made by telegram or by any other appropriate method of communication. The LOPJ, in Section 271, also refers to these methods.

Personal service

If 15 days should pass following the despatch by registered mail without receiving any reply, and also in the case where the communication is negative and this communication is addressed to someone who is or must be a party to the case and whose participation in the action depends on such

48. SSTS 5 December 1961; 8 May 1971; 4 March 1972; and 27 January 1982.

communication (with this communication normally adopting the form of an injunction), then the "ordinary" system for notifications is employed.

The so-called "ordinary system" of the LEC[49] foresees the possibility of notification in the offices or premises of the jurisdictional organ established for this purpose. There, the secretary or court official must read the decision and deliver a literal copy of it to the person notified who is obliged to sign the annotation documenting such a decision.

One special form of notification (but not an infrequent one) is domiciliary notification in those cases where neither the addressee of the notification (*notificando*) nor his or her proxy appears in person. Should the *notificando* not be located at his domicile, the notification will be effected through the delivery of a summons to a relative, servant or neighbour in the manner set out in Sections 266 *et seq.* of the LEC.

Consular or diplomatic channels

The regime for requesting the notification of judicial actions to individuals abroad is foreseen in The Hague Convention on civil proceedings dated 1 March 1954, of which Sections 1–7 were amended by The Hague Convention dated 15 November 1965. This latter international text foresees more rapid methods for the notification of judicial proceedings abroad but does not prevent the use of the consular or diplomatic route when the states involved consider it the most convenient.

In very general terms, the system foreseen by The Hague Convention operates briefly as follows: the Consul of the State requesting notification (the State issuing the letters rogatory) addresses its request to the authority appointed for this purpose by the State receiving them. The request must state the authority whence the document to be notified has originated, the name and condition of the parties, the address of the final addressee and the nature of the document, which must be written in the language of the authority receiving the letters rogatory.

After the petition is received, the authority requested will remit the notification to its final addressee. It may simply remit the document to the addressee for its voluntary acceptance, unless the State issuing the letters rogatory has specified that the request be executed in any particular way. This authority will then remit to the Consul of the State issuing the letters rogatory the document certifying the delivery of the notification or indicating the fact that has prevented it from being delivered.

In its tendency to simplify things, the Convention dated 15 November 1965 considers the possibility that the notification may be delivered directly in

49. Sections 262 *et seq.*

another subscribing State by the consular or diplomatic authorities of a participating State who are accredited in the former (unless the State concerned has expressly declared its opposition, which may not in any case affect the notifications from the original State of the diplomatic or consular authority effecting the notification).

Publication

Should there be, *ab initio*, no record of the domicile or location of the addressee of the notification, such notification will be effected through proclamations. In this form of notification, the summons (containing a literal copy of the decision and other details of the action and the person to be notified) is affixed to the court's notice-board and is inserted in a newspaper. When considered necessary, it may also be published in the *Official State Gazette*.

Apart from the general case, mentioned above, notification by proclamation (known as "courtroom notification") is foreseen in special cases when the identity and number of the persons addressed have not been established. This notification involves the reading aloud of the decision to be notified in public session. However, due to a certain mistrust of this system, the LEC provides that the writs and decisions thus notified and the summonses should be published in the form of proclamations. For this hypothesis, the proclamations are to be fixed specifically "on the door of the place where the judges and magistrates hold the hearings" and the dispositions of the definitive judgments are to be inserted in the official publications.

Methods provided by The Hague Convention

The Convention attempts to avoid the problems arising out of the notification system established by the 1954 Convention on civil procedure. Specifically, it attempts to speed up the proceedings while preserving the procedural guarantees of the addressee of the notification.

The Convention foresees that the States should appoint a central authority to receive all the letters rogatory, a role assumed in Spain by the Office of the Technical Secretary-General of the Ministry of Justice. It is up to the ministerial or court authorities themselves to address the notification petition directly to this central authority of the State receiving the letters rogatory. Without prejudice to this innovation in the Convention, the States may opt, if they find it appropriate, to use the consular or diplomatic route or even direct communication between the respective authorities if the States involved so decide. Moreover, it is possible to effect notification directly by post through authorised public servants of the ministries or courts in the State of destination.

The request for notification must conform to the formula in the model contained in an appendix to the Convention and requires no legalisation.

The process for dealing with the notification request must be conducted in accordance with the manner foreseen by the regulations of the State receiving the request and the document may be drafted in or translated into the official language of that State. Notification may be effected in the manner specified by the requester if this is not incompatible with the legislation of the State receiving the request.

In order to protect the procedural guarantees of the final addressee of the notification, it is foreseen that, should the defendant, despite a notification of an action having been effected in accordance with the Convention, not put in an appearance, the judge of the State making the request will suspend proceedings until such time as a certification is provided that the notification of the action has been conducted in accordance with the manner laid down in the Convention.

Such suspension may only be avoided if three conditions are concurrently fulfilled, namely:

(1) That the document has been despatched in accordance with the terms of the Convention;
(2) That at least six months have passed since the despatch of the document; and
(3) That it has not been possible, despite having taken the appropriate steps before the competent authority in the State receiving the request, to obtain any certification.

The exemption from the periods of time allotted for the presentation of appeals is also foreseen for those defendants who have not received the notification of the action which should have been delivered in accordance with the rules of the Convention (or who received it late), provided the following conditions are fulfilled:

(1) That the delay or lack of notification is not attributable to the defendant himself;
(2) That his allegations are not totally unfounded; and
(3) That the exemption has been requested within a reasonable period of time following his knowledge of the decision (this term must not be less than one year).

ASCERTAINING THE APPLICABLE LAW

Regional law

The court regulations in Spain may be described as complex or "plural" as the Spanish Constitution (CE) of 1978, in Section 2, allows, at the same time as it recognises and guarantees the right to autonomy of the nations and regions making up the indissoluble unity of the Spanish nation, the Autonomous Communities to draft their own legislation on civil and special matters, and questions of rules.

The legislative power of the Communities is, however, a derived power, as for the organisation and distribution of jurisdiction it requires the recognition by each respective Statute of Autonomy. A study of each of the Statutes of Autonomy, drafted within the general framework of the distribution of jurisdiction effected by the Constitution, would exceed the purposes of the present paper.[50]

In this regard, let it suffice to recall that the State's legislative power has exclusive jurisdiction, among other topics, over legislation concerning companies, crimes and prisons;[51] over legislation on procedures, without prejudice to the special cases deriving out of the peculiarities of the laws on substantiation in each Autonomous Community;[52] and over labour laws;[53] over civil legislation, without prejudice to the conservation, amendment and development of the respective special, civil and privilege legislation by the Autonomous Communities, as appropriate;[54] and over the legislation referring to intellectual and industrial property.[55]

However, in some cases the Autonomous Communities may, within the scope of the laws on business which are an exclusive jurisdiction of the State, issue regulations for their legislative development within the respective territory, as in the case of regulations on credits, banking and insurance, or may take care of their execution, as happens with the laws regarding stockbrokers, insurance brokers or industrial property agents.[56]

National law

In view of the provisions of Section 8 of the Civil Code, which introduces the regulations on questions of International Private Law contained in Chapter IV, the laws on crimes, the police and public safety are binding on everyone in Spanish territory. Moreover, by virtue of the territoriality of the laws on court procedure, the only laws applicable to cases being

50. There are 17 Autonomous Communities, and they are subject to their respective autonomy statutes.
51. CE, Section 149.6ª.
52. CE, Section 149.6ª.
53. CE, Section 149.7ª.
54. CE, Section 149.8ª.
55. CE, Section 149.9ª, CE.
56. CE, Section 150.2 CE.

substantiated in Spain will be the Spanish procedural laws, without prejudice to the remissions which these laws might make to foreign regulations regarding acts of the court which must be effected outside Spain.

The basic regulation of contracts is included in the Civil Code. Nevertheless, this body of law will be applied as a supplement in all those cases where a more specific law is applicable, as is the case with all business contracts, as these are affected by the Commercial Code or some of the special Commercial Laws. In those hypotheses where there is a parallel regulation of the contract in both civil and commercial laws, the latter will be applicable whenever a trader or businessperson is involved (this may be a company provided it has been incorporated as a trading company).

The special commercial laws are nowadays very numerous, due to their proliferation to cover inadequacies in the Commercial Code. As a merely illustrative list, one might mention here the Consolidated Text of the Law on Joint Stock Corporations, dated 22 December 1989; the Law on Limited Liability Companies, dated 17 July 1953; the Law on Insurance Contracts, dated 8 October 1980; the Stock Exchange Law, dated 28 July 1988; the Law on Bills of Exchange and Cheques, dated 16 July 1985; the General Law for the Defence of Consumers and Users, dated 19 July 1984; the General Law on Advertising, dated 11 November 1988; the Law for the Defence of Competition, dated 17 July 1989; and the Law on Unfair Competition, dated 10 January 1991.

Conflict of laws principles

When a legal relationship has connections with several different state legal systems, where each of them has its own rules on the jurisdiction of the courts and legislative powers, the private agent involved may choose the legal system by which he is to regulate his behaviour (choice of law). The regulations contained in Sections 8, 9 and 10 of the Civil Code apply to this choice, attributed to the rules on legislative jurisdiction or applicability, known as "rules on the conflict of laws" or "connections".[57]

These rules are not, however, the only sources for conflicts of laws as there are also others which, although conventional in nature, are equally binding in Spain and which, by virtue of the provisions of Sections 95 and 96 of the Spanish Constitution, will be applied in preference over the internal laws. In this regard, let it suffice to mention as examples the

57. Spanish Constitution (CE), Section 3; Organic Law Number 7/85, of 1 July, on the Rights and Freedoms of Foreign Citizens in Spain, Section 51; LEC, Sections 4, 21.1 and LOPJ, Section 23; STS 23 October 1992.

Convention dated 4 May 1971, on the law applicable to road traffic accidents, the Convention dated 2 October 1973, on the law applicable to third party liability deriving from products, and the Convention dated 19 June 1980, on the law applicable to contractual obligations.

Form of the acts

As doctrine would peacefully have it, all legal acts imply a form.[58] This implication highlights the profound connection between the essence of a matter and the form it takes. At the same time. it underlines the significance of the formal aspects, such as the legal guarantees of the certainty of an action, and the authenticity of indispensable requisites. Thus, the regulation of these aspects and the solution given to this regulation, either through recourse to the formula of *locus regit actum* or that of *auctor regit actum*, is decisive when it comes to considering their validity.[59]

Under Spanish law, the form of the acts is regulated by Section 11 of the Civil Code (CC). In its first Paragraph, Subsection 1, this body of law recognises a plurality of points of connection by establishing that "the forms and other legal acts will be governed by the law of the country in which they take place" but that:

". . . nonetheless, those celebrated in accordance with the forms and solemnities required by the law applicable to their content as well as those celebrated in accordance with the personal law of the grantor or the common law of the parties must also be valid."

This Article, no matter which of the three connections is chosen, *lex loci*, *lex causae* or *lex personae*, thus accepts that all of them have the same capacity to validate the form of a legal act, although in this respect, and following some other authors, let us admit that the rules of the forum vest themselves with a certain conceptual priority, which is due to historical deep-rootedness both in Spanish positive law as well as in international doctrine and practice.[60]

On the other hand, and complementary to the basic rule expressed above, Section 11 of the Civil Code accepts, in part, the formula of *auctor regit actum*, by establishing in its Subsection 3 that "Spanish law will be applicable to the contracts, testaments and other legal acts authorised by Spain's diplomatic or consular officials abroad" and, in the final clause of Paragraph 1, Subsection 2, the rule of *lex rei sitae*, by determining that "those acts and contracts concerning real property

---

58. Perez Vera, *Derecho Internacional Privado. Parte Especial*, Madrid, 1980, p. 290.
59. Perez Vera, *Derecho Internacional Privado. Parte Especial*, Madrid, 1980, p. 291.
60. Perez Vera, *Derecho Internacional Privado. Parte Especial*, Madrid, 1980, p. 294.

must be valid if granted in accordance with the forms and solemnities of the place in which the same is located".

The question concerning the form of the legal acts carried out aboard ships and aircraft is considered in the first Paragraph, Subsection 2 of the said Section 11, with complementary rules on the formula of *locus regit actum*, by considering that "the acts carried out aboard ships or aircraft during their voyages or flights will be deemed to have been celebrated in the country whose flag they bear and in which they are registered" which means in short that the law of the vessel's nationality is applicable in the same cases as the *lex loci*.

Finally, Section 11 of the Civil Code, in its Paragraph 2, prescribes that ". . . if the law regulating the contents of the acts and contracts should require for them to be valid that they respect a certain form or solemnity, this will always be applied, even where these acts or contracts are granted abroad" in an evident and imperative enshrinement of the application of the law of the matter to its form. This implies that certain acts, in which the importance of their consequences is exceptional, can only be granted in the terms prescribed by law and these must, therefore, be respected even when they are granted abroad.

Contractual obligations

In the case of contractual obligations, as opposed to extra-contractual ones, the legislative power has recognised that the wills of the parties have a certain margin for action when it comes to choosing the criteria for connection, in line with the controlling system of private independence within the scope of purely internal contracts. Thus, the positive Spanish system, in which the basic rule is to be found in Section 10, Paragraph 5, Subsection 1 of the Civil Code, formally recognises the principle of party autonomy wills, although it is subject to limits.

In effect, this precept provides in this respect that "contractual obligations will be subject to the law to which the parties have expressly submitted themselves, providing that there is some connection with the matter in question" enshrining autonomy as the main connection. Next, it foresees certain subsidiary connections completing the previous system by establishing that:

". . . in its absence, the national law common to the parties [must be applied]; in its absence that of the common regular residence will apply and finally, the law of the place where the contract was celebrated."

Apart from these general systems, the same Section 10 of the Civil Code contains other special systems, depending on the object of the contract in some cases (real property) and the type of contract in other cases. Thus, with regard to real property, Section 10, Paragraph 5, Subsection 2 provides that:

". . . notwithstanding the provisions of the preceding Paragraph, in the absence of express submission, the law of the place where the property is located must apply to contracts concerning real property."

Later, this same Subsection foresees, in connection with corporeal personal property that its sale carried out on business premises will be governed by the law of the place in which it is located.

All of these rules refer to the *lex contractus*, i.e., the overall law governing the contract. Given the existence, within the same system, of rules on the conflict of law referring to other matters, such as the capacity of the parties[61] or the form of the acts,[62] such a unifying intent is not feasible. This is, moreover, corroborated by the existence of imperative laws that affect the life of the contract. Thus, together with the rules that must be observed in the *lex causae* and the *lex fori*, the Spanish legislator also declares certain provisions of the *lex loci executionis* to be applicable.

In fact, Section 10, Paragraph 10 of the Civil Code, after proclaiming the submission of performance to the law of the contract in Subsection 1, acknowledges in its Subsection 2 that "the law of the place of execution will, nevertheless, be applied to those forms of the execution which require judicial or administrative intervention" a wide-ranging circle, as some authors have pointed out, in which all material rules relating to a State's foreign trade could be included and if they were not respected then the successful conclusion of the contract would become impossible.[63]

Extra-contractual obligations

By way of clarification of preliminary concepts, when considering extra-contractual obligations, these may be deemed to include both obligations *ex delicto* as well as those *ex quasi-delicto* and subsumed within the generic notion of quasi-contracts. The first of these categories is governed under Spanish law by the provisions of Sections 1092 and 1102 of the Civil Code. The second of them is ruled by Sections 1093, 1103 and 1902 *et seq.* of the Civil Code. Finally, the third category is governed by the provisions of Section 1887 of the Civil Code.

The applicable law for *ex delicto* liability, as dealt with in Section 10, Paragraph 9, Subsection 1, sets out that "the extra-contractual obligations must be governed by the law of the place where the fact whence they derive took place". This solution adopted by the Spanish legislator, enshrining the rule of *lex loci delicto commissi* has been the object of

61. Civil Code, Section 9.
62. Civil Code, Section 11.
63. Perez Vera, *Derecho Internacional Privado. Parte Especial*, Madrid, 1980, p. 343.

numerous criticisms by legal scholars, who have criticised, among other things, the lack of exceptions and clarifications which would allow the functional scope of the classical rule to be moulded and updated.[64]

In Section 10, Paragraph 9, Subsection 2 of the Civil Code, the Spanish legislature determines the law applicable to the management of third parties' affairs, foreseeing that such management will be governed by the law of the place where the manager carries out the main activity. In this case, the applicability of the *lex loci* would be based not only on the concern to avoid the owner being arbitrarily removed from the normal rule of applicable law but also on the wish to make him comply with all the obligations imposed by such laws.[65]

Finally, Section 10, Paragraph 9, Subsection 3 of the Civil Code concludes with a rule on conflicts of law whereby "unjustified enrichment will be subject to the laws by virtue of which the value of the wealth was transferred to the person enriched". In light of the jurisprudence, which has developed an expansive interpretation, illicit enrichment by a principal either through an increase in wealth (*lucrum emergens*) or else through a non-reduction of the same (*damnum cesans*) with the proportional impoverishment of a third party lies at the heart of all quasi-contracts.

COMMENCING THE ACTION

Complaint

Under Spanish law, all persons are explicitly granted the right to effective jurisdictional protection of their legitimate rights and interests. From a subjective viewpoint, this right applies to all types of persons, whether public law or private law, Spanish or foreign, whether individuals or juristic persons. From an objective viewpoint, the right is protected by the courts, before whom such persons may appear, i.e., they are entitled to be parties to proceedings and to judgments in law.[66]

The capacity to be a party to the proceedings is a procedural presupposition, which, as doctrine accepts without controversy, implies the generic ability to be the subject of the action, i.e., the active or passive bearer of the rights or obligations under contention in the action.[67] For

---

64. Carrillo Salcedo, "Comentario al artículo 10", 9, *Comentarios al Código Civil y Compilaciones Forales*, Jaén, 1978, p. 368.

65. Perez Vera, *Derecho Internacional Privado. Parte Especial*, Madrid, 1980, pp. 356–357.

66. Almagro Nosete *et al.*, *Derecho Procesal*, Tomo I (Volume II), *Parte General Proceso Civil* (I), Valencia, 1986, p. 362.

67. Espinar Vicente, *Derecho Procesal Civil Internacional*, Madrid, 1988, p. 74.

some authors, this concept, linked to that of juridical subjectivity, is synonymous with the latter, while others feel that this connection does not represent an absolute identity as it is possible for someone who is completely capable of being a party to proceedings not to enjoy juridical capacity.[68]

Procedural capacity is the ability of a subject to appear in court, to effect valid acts in the proceedings or for such acts to be effected regarding this person. This capacity may be equivalent to capacity for action even though in this case there is also no complete identity between the two concepts, as certain persons without full capacity to exercise their rights, such as the emancipated minor, still enjoy full procedural capacity.

While generally the party's personal law is applied to verify its procedural capacity, in the case of foreign plaintiffs or defendants, it is the law applied to the merits of the claim which is applied — in the absence of any legally established criterion — to determine this capacity. This same law applied to the personal procedural capacitation is also applied to substitutive capacitation through substitution, whereby those persons who are not the bearers of the right on which the actions are based may effect procedural actions.[69]

Enjoying the different types of capacity and legitimation mentioned above is not always sufficient to be able to act before the courts, where, because of the complexity of the matters to be argued and the formal and technical nature of the proceedings, the participation of legal counsel is necessary. The *lex fori* governs this participation. In the case of Spanish law, it is governed by Sections 3, 4 and 10 of the LEC.

Section 3 sets out that "the appearance in court must be through a solicitor legally empowered to act before the court hearing the case and with powers declared sufficient by a lawyer". Section 10 provides that "the litigants must be directed by a a solicitor legally empowered to act before the court hearing the case".[70]

Thus, the general rule is to require representation by a solicitor and participation by a barrister. In the first case, this representation is merely formal in nature, while in the second the participation involves the study, preparation and drafting of the written documentation to be presented by the litigant, or presence at the acts and appearances with oral declarations.[71] In this context, the main problem that may arise is that the

---

68. Almagro Nosete *et al.*, *Derecho Procesal, Tomo I* (Volume II), *Parte General Proceso Civil* (I), Valencia, 1986, p. 268.

69. Espinar Vicente, *Derecho Procesal Civil Internacional*, Madrid, 1988, p. 80.

70. Royal Decree 2046/82, of 30 July, on the General By-Laws for Spanish Solicitors.

71. Royal Decree 2090/82, of 24 July, on the General By-Laws for Spanish Barristers.

powers have been granted in a foreign country. The question arises as to whether it is sufficient for the formalities required by this foreign country to be fulfilled or whether it is necessary to observe the sufficiency and legality demands set out in an imperative fashion by Section 533.3 of the LEC. In this sense, the powers must comply, in formal terms, with the conditions required in the country of origin (*locus regit actum* rule) as well as with those presented in Sections 600 and 601 of the LEC.

The powers must be reflected in a public instrument, as prescribed by Section 1280.5 of the Civil Code, whether they are general powers for representation in court or the special powers as required in Section 1713 of the Civil Code (for cases involving certain matters) and Sections 410.1 and 846.2 of the LEC (in order to abandon appeals).

Stating the essential elements

The complaint (*demanda*) is the procedural step originating in the plaintiff and initiating the action. As this is the formal vehicle for the exercise of the action, it determines the objects of the dispute and particularly the contents of the judgment. It is presented in writing, even in the "verbal" proceedings, in the form of the "writ". Sufficient copies of the writ must be presented all similarly signed for each of the defendants.

The writ begins with a generic invocation to the judicial organ that has to deal with the case and contains a presentation in which the solicitor identifies the defendant (*demandado*), as expressly required by Section 524 of the LEC, his client and himself with reference to the deed of appointment. which will be enclosed with the writ. Moreover, it enunciates the kind of action (declaratory, prosecution or test action) and the kind of hearing through which the case should, according to the plaintiff, be substantiated.

Following this, in another section, the text includes the statement of the facts with numbered paragraphs presenting these in a clear and concise fashion, linking them together. Should the lawyer not present this exposition clearly, he will be in breach of the provisions of Section 524 of the LEC, and the dilatory plea of Section 533, Paragraph 6, of the LEC will be applicable, as can be seen in many repeated cases of the jurisprudence with regard to this legal defect in the presentation of the writ.[72]

In practice, however, this plea will rarely prosper. This is not only because of the difficulty involved in its application (how to determine when the facts have been sufficiently clearly expressed), but also because the writ can comply with this requirement by indicating what is being

---

72. SSTS 28 February 1978; 24 May 1982; and 8 March 1991.

sought in such a way and with the precise characteristics so as to allow the defendant to undertake what is requested.

Following the facts, the legal foundations will be set out succinctly. It is sufficient to indicate the rules supporting the plaintiff's plea (*demandance*) but it is appropriate for these to be related to the facts narrated above so that the desired judicial consequences can be inferred. Neither the judge nor the plaintiff are bound by the legal considerations presented in the writ, in accordance with the principle of *iura novit curia*.

The specific petition of the court's protection will be presented by the plaintiff in the last part of the writ, known as the "supplication" (*suplico*). The precise specification of the remedy being sought (the *petitum* or prayer for relief) is the most important requirement of the writ as well as the most obvious. Its omission would ensure the success of the plea mentioned above and contained in Paragraph 6 of Section 533 of the LEC, although the Supreme Court (*Tribunal Supremo*) has held that this plea is not valid when the plaintiff's *petitum* can be clearly deduced from the writ as a whole.

Stating the relief sought

The *petitum* determines the kind of court protection that the plaintiff is requesting and thus allows the action to be divided into three categories: "prosecutions", in which the judge is invited to order the defendant to perform a certain act; merely declaratory actions, in which the plaintiff attempts to obtain the court's declaration that a particular right or a specified legal relationship exists, does not exist or how it is to be interpreted; and test actions, in which the plaintiff attempts to obtain the creation, modification or rescission of a right or legal relationship.

Types of answer

The defendant answers the writ whenever he adopts any active posture regarding the same. If the writ is the formal vehicle for the exercise of the action, then the answer is the formal vehicle whereby the defendant confronts the plaintiff's action. In this situation, the answer shares the main characteristics, structure and nature of the complaint, as indicated in Section 540 of the LEC.[73]

Thus, the answer must adapt to the formal requirements of the complaint. This means that the facts must be clearly distinguished from the

73. STS 20 June 1981.

legal foundations and the section setting out the remedy sought. Moreover, he answer must be accompanied by the same documentation as the original writ, listed in Sections 503 and 504 of the LEC, namely:

(1) Powers accrediting the personality of the solicitor;
(2) Documents accrediting the character with which the litigant is appearing in court; and
(3) Documentation on which the party bases its rights.

Denials

In the answer, the defendant may simply deny the facts included in the complaint and even if he does so with no further explanation, then the burden of proving these facts will lie with the plaintiff. However, it is possible that the defendant may admit the truth of the facts alleged by the plaintiff while denying the legal effects that the plaintiff had attempted to deduce from these events.

In the latter situation, provided there is total agreement on the facts, the proceedings are greatly simplified. The litigation will be limited to the consideration and legal scope of the facts that have been admitted by both parties, thus making it unnecessary to go through the presentation of evidence and even the second instance (in the hearings for large and petty amounts and ejectment proceedings).

Denials and affirmative defences

The kinds of answer to the complaint examined so far presuppose that the defendant adopts a posture with regard to factual statements and legal considerations contained therein. Nevertheless, the most common situation is where the defendant includes in his answer certain facts that are new to the case and which it will be up to him to prove. This latter kind of defence is known as "exceptions".[74]

Exceptions are not only the allegation of new facts introduced by the defendant. They may also include facts that the judge is aware of or should be aware of and, if true, would negate the plaintiff's right to the requested protection of the court or else would deny him the right to have the judge decide on the feasibility of such protection (i.e., they would deny the plaintiff the right to sue).

In connection with the foregoing, a distinction must be drawn between procedural and material defences. The procedural exceptions attempt to deny the plaintiff's right to have the judge decide the action undertaken.

74. LEC, Section 542; STS 7 March 1990.

The admission of a procedural exception carries with it the acquittal of the defendant without the judge having begun to examine the merits of the case (the plaintiff's right to the suit undertaken).

Within the scope of procedural exceptions, there is a group of exceptions known as "dilatory exceptions"[75] which may only be lodged in the case of the large amount hearings at the beginning of the suit. They suspend the proceedings until they are resolved.[76] When one of these exceptions is admitted as valid, the defendant is released from answering the complaint. In any case, apart from the lesser claim cases, the defences must be included in the answer to the complaint.

As opposed to the procedural exceptions, the so-called material exceptions are new facts that, if proved, will produce a judgment of acquittal regarding the merits (in recognition of the fact that the plaintiff was not entitled to the protection of the court that had been requested). The introduction of new facts into the case must not imply any change in the object of the proceedings as, if this happens, one would be facing not a defence but a counterclaim.

As in the preceding case, within the scope of material exceptions, it is normal to distinguish two kinds of exceptions known, respectively, as proper and improper exceptions. The proper exception is characterised by being a counter-right or faculty of the defendant,which, when pleaded, allows him to avoid a conviction which in any other case would be certain. The typical example of this kind of exception is that of prescription or limitation, which if pleaded successfully, allows the defendant to avoid fulfilling the compulsory action.

The proper exceptions must be pleaded for them to be taken into account, whereas improper exceptions must be appreciated by the judge *ex officio*. This is so because these latter exceptions attempt to show that the suit undertaken by the plaintiff never existed (for instance, because the contract was null and void) or else that it has already been extinguished (because payment has been made). Nevertheless, the Supreme Court deems that the judge's obligation to the duty of congruity prevents him from appreciating impediments or facts extinguishing the suit which have not been pleaded by the defendant.[77]

Reply

The Spanish court system includes two kinds of hypothesis in which the plaintiff may respond to the defendant's answer. First, the plaintiff may

75. LEC, Section 533.

76. LEC, Section 535.

77. Almagro Nosete *et al*, *Derecho Procesal, Tomo I* (Volume II), *Parte General Proceso Civil* (I), Valencia, 1986, p. 296.

respond to the defendant whenever the latter's answer contains or constitutes a counterclaim. In fact, there is no real reply to the defendant's response, as the counterclaim is a new suit, to which the plaintiff will respond in his capacity as defendant.[78]

The true response by the plaintiff to the defendant's answer is the "reply", foreseen in the case of large amount hearings.[79] This is not a necessary pleading (as are complaint and answer) but a step which the plaintiff may renounce expressly or implicitly (e.g., by letting the term assigned for the reply pass unanswered).

In the same reply, the plaintiff may respond to the counterclaim, if appropriate, or he may also renounce his right to reply and respond solely to the counterclaim. The latter choice can be understood if one bears in mind that the defendant acquires the right to a rejoinder if the reply is presented. Should the plaintiff renounce his right to reply, or fail to present the same within the period of 10 days appointed by law, then the defendant may not make use of the right to a rejoinder.[80]

Amendments to pleadings

The reply and rejoinder documents may contain various pleas with the sole purpose of clarifying and specifying the facts and requests in the complaint and the answer. In the lesser claim hearings, the possibility of clarifying the facts and requests may take place in the so-called "prior appearance" of the parties before the judge in an oral proceeding that precedes the presentation of evidence.

As in the answer, silence regarding the allegations of the other party and evasive responses may be taken into account in the judgment as recognition of the facts to which they refer. In this sense, the burden of negation means that those facts which, although not admitted, have not been denied, do not need to be proved, as the judge may, on the basis of Section 549 of the LEC, find in this fact the legal effect claimed by the party so pleading without the necessity for it to be proved.

In any case, one must bear in mind the prohibition of altering the complaint, as included in Section 548 of the LEC. This prohibition is infringed when the parties alter their original requests, complaints or answers during the pleadings referred to above. The jurisprudence of the Supreme Court has upheld this principle,[81] although changing it slightly by accepting the introduction of clarifying or complementary requests in

78. LEC, Section 542.
79. LEC, Section 546.
80. LEC, Section 547.
81. STS 7 July 1978.

addition to the originals, provided that they are compatible and coherent with the latter and do not alter their essence.[82]

Supplemental pleadings

In spite of the prohibition against altering the complaint, the Spanish system for court procedure does allow the addition of supplemental pleadings by either the plaintiff or the defendant under very specific circumstances. The method for adding these pleas is the so-called "extension writ", referred to in Section 563 of the LEC. According to this statute, this writ is possible following the celebration of the replies and rejoinders, should any fact of outstanding influence for the resolution of the case come to light or should the parties become aware of a similar fact from an earlier period that they swear they had no prior knowledge of. This writ must be despatched to the other party so that it may deny or admit the facts, or even plead others that cancel out those of the extension writ.[83]

This writ must be distinguished from the extension of the complaint. The extension of the complaint refers to a form of joinder of actions and is subject to its constraints.[84] Thus, it is only possible to extend the complaint lodged before reception of the answer from the defendant.[85] If the plaintiff varies his pleas after this point in the proceedings, this would represent an alteration in the plea.

Joinder of claims and parties

In Sections 153 *et seq.*, the LEC regulates the joinder of actions and allows that various objectives be substantiated simultaneously for resolution in the same judgment when there is a clear connection between the topics. The characteristic feature is that a single plaintiff exercises, in his complaint, two or more actions against a single defendant.

Joinder of claims by plaintiff

The plaintiff may join claims into one single complaint either initially or else following the presentation of the complaint but before the presentation of the defendant's answer. This latter case is known as the extension of the complaint.

82. STS 26 October 1931.
83. LEC, Section 564.
84. LEC, Sections 154 *et seq.*
85. LEC, Section 157.

The initial joinder of causes of action may be "objective" (*acumulacíon de acciones*) when various actions are joined against a single defendant,[86] or "subjective" (*liti consorcio necesario*) where the actions joined are addressed to various defendants or are lodged by various plaintiffs. In the latter case, apart from a joinder, there is also joint litigation.[87]

This distinction is not, however, conclusive, in that all subjective joinders represent an objective joinder of causes of action since these are actions that might have given rise to separate proceedings but are being tried together and will be resolved in a single judgment. As a result, the "subjective" joinder must always comply with the requirements established in Section 154 of the LEC for the objective joinder of causes of action.

The objective joinder of causes of action is a privilege (never an obligation) of the plaintiff. The actions may be joined in two ways: in simple joinder or contingency joinder. The simple joinder is feasible for those actions that are completely different from one another or for those with a juridical relationship, so that the admission of one of them would mean the admission of all the others. The contingency joinder occurs with two or more actions that are incompatible with each other but which are exercised jointly so that the judge may begin to analyse the merits of the second case only after the first has been dismissed.

The requirements for objective joinder are as follows:

(1) That the same plaintiff exercises various actions against the same defendant;[88]
(2) That the judge before whom the action is raised has jurisdiction over each of the actions;[89]
(3) That the actions must be substantiated in a procedure of the same nature;[90] and
(4) That the actions that the plaintiff wishes to join are not incompatible with each other.[91]

The joinder of causes of action that a person may have against various other persons, or various plaintiffs against one person (subjective joinder) is applicable when the requirements of Section 154 of the LEC are fulfilled and when they "arise out of a single title or are based on the same cause

---

86. SSTS 11 March 1935; and 16 March 1944.
87. STS 22 March 1982.
88. LEC, Section 153.
89. LEC, Section 154.2.
90. LEC, Section 154.3.
91. LEC, Section 154.1.

of action".[92] This requirement for a certain connection between the actions refers to the voluntary subjective joinder but this may, on occasions, be necessary.

The so-called joint litigation process takes place as a result of the precept that obliges an action to be conducted simultaneously against several persons, as, for example, with regard to indivisible obligations[93] or to the payment of hereditary debts.[94] Supreme Court jurisprudence has extended the requirement of joint actions against several persons to other situations, such as persons who might be directly affected by the judgment, or who have an evident legitimate interest in the outcome of the case, or are involved in a legal relationship which, through being indivisible, only allows of a single decision.

The practical consequence of the obligation to join the causes of action in a subjective joinder is that the trial activity of each of the members of the joint litigation will be to the benefit of the others (although the prejudicial acts effected by any of the others will have no effect, for example, a settlement reached by one of the parties).

When the plaintiff effects the joinder of actions following the presentation of the complaint (extension of complaint), then, as mentioned above, this must always be done before the complaint is answered. The only special feature of this kind of joinder is that the term for responding to the complaint begins to be counted from the moment at which the extension writ is despatched to the defendant.

In view of the provisions of Sections 160 *et seq.* of the LEC, it is necessary to distinguish between a joinder of actions in general and the joinder of proceedings, which occurs when two separate proceedings, already under way and pending, are combined to be tried together and resolved through a single judgment.

Counterclaim

Counterclaim (*reconvención*) has been defined here as a new action to be exercised by the defendant against the plaintiff, to be tried in the same proceedings and to be resolved by the same judgment as the original complaint. As for the counterclaim itself, the plaintiff will become the defendant and the defendant will be the plaintiff, but they will conserve their original positions with regard to the complaint that originated the process.

In Spain, counterclaims can be filed very easily without any requirement of connection with the object of the proceedings. This is due to the

92. LEC, Section 156.
93. Civil Code, Section 1139.
94. Civil Code, Section 1084.

scarce and fragmentary nature of the legal regulations that have led the doctrine and jurisprudence to accept not only irrelevant counterclaims but also implied counterclaims.[95]

This latter situation has been developed by the jurisprudence through interpreting that the counterclaim exists whenever the defendant includes in his answer any request that goes beyond the petition of his acquittal.[96] As a result, the defendant always lodges a counterclaim whenever his answer includes allegations that represent a new object other than that which gave rise to the suit (claiming compensation, for instance). Nonetheless, the Supreme Court has also pointed out that the counterclaim must be set out with some clarity.

As for the form of the counterclaim, in the absence of legal regulation, it must be held that it corresponds to the requirements of any plea. In spite of being part of the written answer,[97] it must be distinguished from this; it contains its own sections on facts, legal foundations and supplication.

There is a logical limitation to the lodging of a counterclaim in that there must be a relationship between the counterclaim and the original cause of the complaint in those trials that are intended to deal with certain specific matters, even when the normal declaratory trial proceedings are used for substantiation. In connection with this, it is necessary to recall that the counterclaim must be capable of being heard in the same procedural channel through which the main complaint is being dealt with.[98]

The judge dealing with the main complaint must have authority to decide the counterclaim. This is expressly required in statutes for both the jurisdiction of matters[99] and the amount.[100] In the case of counterclaims, as opposed to the procedure for joinder of cause of actions, the amounts of the two complaints are not added together to determine the question of jurisdiction.

Finally, within the topic of counterclaim requirements, one must include the obligation that the defendant (or co-defendant, if there are more than one) must direct the counterclaim against the plaintiff and not against a third party. Later, the possibility of the defendant lodging a counterclaim against a co-defendant will be examined.

The counterclaim must fulfil all of the requirements of trial procedure, although it can be assumed that those referring to the counter-claiming defendant have already been met through having been admitted as a party

95. Marquez Romero, *La Reconvención*, Granada, 1994, p. 34.

96. Handed down in STS 30 January 1974.

97. LEC, Section 542, Paragraph 2.

98. LEC, Sections 689 and 715, and Decree on the Declaratory Proceedings, dated 21 November 1952, Section 46.

99. LEC, Section 542, Paragraph 3.

100. LEC, Section 63, Paragraph 4.

to the main complaint. The plaintiff may oppose the counterclaim if there is some procedural flaw that prevents it, for instance, a question of *lis pendens*.

The counterclaim may be lodged as a contingency, so that the judge may begin to consider the question only if the proposed defences are dismissed. On occasions, the defendant pleads certain facts for his defence that might constitute a defence as well as a counterclaim. At the practical level, the choice is an important one: So long as the defendant pleads defences, the plaintiff has no right to answer these allegations (except for the possibility of reply considered in cases of large amounts), but the plaintiff will always have the opportunity to respond to the counterclaim.

Cross-claims

Cross-claims involve those claims made against co-defendants or co-plaintiffs but not against a person involved in the other side of the litigation. The cross-claims against co-defendants have been admitted by Spanish jurisprudence and are treated as counterclaims. Cross-claims between co-plaintiffs are not expressly considered in Spanish legislation yet there seems to be no obstacle to a person in the position of co-plaintiff presenting a new suit against a fellow plaintiff. If any of the parties were interested and the other necessary requirements are met, it would also be possible to decide the resolution of both cases by the same judgment.

Third party claims

Under current Spanish rules, two forms of third-party involvement can be admitted. This participation is the recourse placed at the disposal of third parties in order to defend their rights or allow them to prevail in the face of *lis pendens*. For third party claims (*tercerías*) to be admitted, they must be exercised by a true third party, i.e., someone who is not a direct party to the dispute — and who has not been placed in a similar legal situation to any of the parties, but who has some relationship with the rights being dealt with in the case.[101]

Third party claim to ownership

The third party claim to ownership is a court process through which the third party attempts to have the attachment on particular property lifted

---

101. STS 29 October 1984.

because this third party is the owner of the property and not the person in whose possession property has been attached or through which the third party protects a right over the property which would be harmed in the case of mandatory foreclosure. The *petitum* of the third party claim would be limited to requesting that the judge lift the attachment and the object of the claim would be the discussion of errors in the assignation of ownership of the attached property.[102]

The right pleaded by the third party must be current and must have been consolidated prior to the attachment. Nevertheless, third party claims to ownership may be founded on rights other than possession but which are in opposition to the attachment or future disposal of the property (rights over property *in re aliena*, such as usufruct, or a right to a sum for the conveyance of attached premises). As there is a clear analogy with actions for recovery, the third party claimant will have to accredit the right he invokes.[103]

The third party claim may be lodged as soon as the property in question has been attached (even if the attachment has been effected by virtue of a preventive attachment). Third party claims will be admitted until such time as the sale of the property in question is consummated or the same is adjudged in payment.

Paramount right of a third party

The paramount right of a third party claim is the procedure whereby a third party creditor may make his preferential right prevail in an action for foreclosure by a single creditor.[104] It therefore corresponds to the existence of credits classified as preferential because they entitle their bearers to collect payment before the other creditors of the same debtor.[105]

In the third party claim for a paramount right, two joined actions must be exercised according to legal imperative. One is against the foreclosed debtor, a personal action for prosecution based on a real, due and payable debt. This is a only a procedural step in that it exhausts its effectiveness within that sphere. It is not infrequent, however, for the third party claimant's right to be already reflected in an entitlement to execution or even in a decision pronouncing judgment. Even in these cases and until such time as there is no firm decision, the judge must analyse the creditor's claim to the debt.

---

102. SSTS 1 February 1990; 25 February 1991; 30 January 1992; 17 February 1992; 26 January 1993; and 2 November 1993.

103. LEC, Section 1537.

104. LEC, Section 1532.

105. STS 21 May 1963.

The third party claimant must also exercise an action against the foreclosing creditor aimed at stopping the executing creditor from recouping his debt (plus interests and legal costs) through the sale of the attached property and regardless of the existence of the debtors' other creditors.[106] The exception to this precept is specifically expressed in Section 1520, which says that the product of the disposal of the attached property may not be applied to any other purpose that "has not been declared preferential in foreclosure proceedings". This allows the judge, if the plea is made in time and the other executing creditor can prove his preferential right so that it is reflected in a judgment, to change the destination of the amount produced through the disposal of the property in order to satisfy this preferential credit.

The judge's decision requires the comparison of the third party creditor's entitlement to execution with that of the executing creditor in order to determine whether the former's title is executable and preferential to that of the latter and, in short, to proceed with the organisation of the credits in order of preference as provided in Sections 1921 to 1929 of the Civil Code and in other legal texts.[107]

Third party claims to ownership or to paramount rights may be undertaken at any stage of the foreclosure process. The first will not be admitted, in accordance with Section 1533 of the LEC, once the deed has been formalised or the sale has been completed for the disposal of the property in question, or once it has been adjudged to the executing creditor in payment, with the third party's right to deduct it from whom and how he can remaining safeguarded. The second claim, still in accordance with the aforementioned Section 1533 of the LEC, will not be admitted after payment has been effected to the executing third party.

Main procedural features common to third party claims

The most outstanding points of third party claims are the specific precautions established by the legislator to prevent third part claims being lodged with purely dilatory intentions. Thus, for the judge to proceed with the claim, the claimant is first of all required to present a document providing *prima facie* evidence of the existence and validity of the third party claimant's right. In this respect, the jurisprudence has admitted various kinds of documents (sales contracts, loan deeds, declaration of facts found proven in a criminal judgment), but it rejects, in general, those documents drafted unilaterally by the third party claimant.[108]

---

106. LEC, Section 1520.

107. Workers' Statute (ET), Section 32 and Commercial Code (Ccom), Sections 375, 376, 665 *et seq.*

108. STS 29 October 1984.

The second requirement worthy of note is that the third party claimant must address his claim simultaneously against the debtor and the executing creditor. This is, therefore, a form of joint litigation, which brings with it the possibility of pleading the absence of one of the parties to prevent the judge from handing down judgment. The judge may also appreciate this fact *ex officio* and refrain from dictating a judgment.

If the executing creditor and the foreclosed person should reach agreement on the third party claim or if both of them should fail to reply to the claim, then the judge, without further ado, will declare the proceedings ready for the formal hearing and will summon the parties to hand down the judgment, which may be appealed against in both effects, as established in Section 1541 of the LEC. Even where the lack of a response to the third party claim might in principle be deemed a tacit agreement, what is true is that, in those cases where there are two or more co-defendants, acceptance by one of them cannot prejudice the others, as otherwise the situation would mean the division of the case's consistency, and it cannot be forgotten that the third party action is indivisible.

Impleader

In certain circumstances under Spanish law, one of the parties in a trial is allowed to call in a third party who has previously been uninvolved in the case in order to form part of the same. This *litis denuntiatio* or "call to a third party" may be used to obtain the third party's assistance for the defendant, or to create a factual situation on which other rights such as guarantees or reparation may depend.

First, there is the call for a guarantee, which the purchaser makes to a seller when a third party outside the contract of sale claims ownership of the item transferred. The sued purchaser calls in the seller in order to assist him in the proceedings to prevent the loss of the item sold because of a firm judgment based on a right that pre-existed before the sale. When the seller (third party) receives the notification that the trial is pending, a notification made by the judge at the defendant's request, he can adopt two postures that will lead to different consequences. If the third party decides to appear and answer the claim, he will be admitted as a party and the purchaser-defendant will retain his same situation as a party. If he does not put in an appearance, then the litigation will proceed against the defendant, but should the latter lose the case and also the object sold, then he will be entitled to demand reparation from the seller for the eviction.[109]

Secondly, it is possible for an immediate possessor (lessee or usufructuary) to call in the owner to be a party to the case against the defendant,

---

109. Civil Code, Section 1481.

in which the owner's rights might be affected. This possibility derives from the general principle whereby the immediate possessor must communicate to the owner all those acts of third parties that might be able to affect the rights of ownership. Logically, these acts affecting ownership are deemed to include the lodging of a complaint against the immediate possessor (even though the statutes do not expressly consider the point). If the owner attends the call by the usufructuary or lessee, he must be admitted to the proceedings as an associate in joint litigation.

A third situation worth mentioning occurs when one of the heirs is sued by a creditor for a debt of the decedent's estate. As the Civil Code allows the creditor to claim the entire debt from any of the heirs (except those who accepted the legacy with benefit of inventory), it also allows the defendant to ask for the joint heirs to be summonsed (unless the defendant has alone been made liable for the payment of the debt). Any joint heir who appears will do so in the capacity of joint litigator.

Interpleader

Under Spanish positive law, there is no procedural institution which in all respects coincides with the concept of interpleader, which is more specific to the law of the English-speaking world. If, however, one considers its essence, by virtue of which the party sued by two or more persons may claim that he has no interest in claiming the property and request that the question of ownership should be investigated and that he should be relieved of all liability, one might assimilate this institution to that of a counterclaim studied above, in that it extends the initial objective of the suit.

Intervention

The intervention of a third party in a suit may correspond to several different intentions and consequently receives different names under Spanish law. Apart from forced intervention, the result of a call made by one of the parties to the suit involving a third party, there is another form of intervention which is not regulated by statute but which has been accepted by the jurisprudence, known as voluntary intervention. In this case the third party requests of the judge authorisation to become a party to a case involving others in order to support the legal position of one or other of the parties.

For lack of statutory regulation, there are still questions open, such as the status in the suit of the intervening party. Part of the doctrine and the jurisprudence[110] holds that the third party must be accorded the same

110. STS 17 October 1961.

procedural faculties as the party it supports as otherwise it would be liable to possibilities of fraud, which is precisely what the third party is trying to avoid by its intervention.

Together with the two kinds of intervention mentioned above, there is a third kind which Spanish legal terminology refers to as intervention with an independent claim, characterised by the fact that the third party lodges a claim simultaneously against both of the parties to a suit, requesting a legal tutelage which is incompatible with the interests of those parties. The articulation of these three suits (the main complaint plus the ones addressed by the third party against the plaintiff and defendant simultaneously) is plagued with problems and, basically, two imperfect solutions have been devised in the German and Italian legal systems.

This situation is not regulated under Spanish law but its advantages could be achieved through the resolution of the proceedings with a single judgment (by joining the suit between A and B to those addressed by C against A and B simultaneously). At times, one of the sectors of the doctrine has attempted to assimilate the circumstances of intervention as principal to those produced as a result of the intervention of a third party claimant. Nonetheless, there are clear differences if one goes a little deeper into both of these figures and one recalls that the third party claim is a procedure designed exclusively for foreclosure suits, while intervention occurs in declaratory processes.

OBTAINING INFORMATION PRIOR TO TRIAL

Types of discovery

According to Spanish law, the trial can be prepared in accordance with the procedural steps provided in Section 497 of the LEC generally called "committal proceedings" (*diligencias preliminares*). In their strict sense, these proceedings, as some authors point out, are more "initiative acts" of the process than "preparatory acts" of it, because they are a judicial practice of law in which, according to the provisions of Section 1937 of the Civil Code a stay of proceedings should be recognised.[111]

These committal proceedings are a group of procedural steps intended to clarify the questions that could emerge before the main action arises, such as the personality or the passive legitimation of the defendant, the relevancy or irrelevancy of the questions posed to that end, or the discovery and, when appropriate, the production of property, being the judge capable of knowing the proceedings and, accordingly, capable for the preliminary trial.

111. STS 9 September 1949.

Deposition

Any person seeking to bring an action can ask for a statement made on oath to the person against whom he intends to bring the action, regarding any fact related to his personality, and in absence of which an action cannot be taken. In such case, according to the provisions of Section 498 of the LEC, actions must be in the form established for the deposition in trial, until the judge, if necessary, declares the party to have confessed.

Interrogatories to parties

Interrogatories to parties can only be done, normally, after the action has been brought before the court. Therefore, the provisions of Section 502 of the LEC, which admit such interrogations in cases of witnesses of an advanced age, facing an imminent threat to their lives or an impending stay in a place in which communications are difficult or belated, are an exception to the rule that prohibits declarations from witnesses before the hearing.

Discovery and production of property

The discovery and production of the property (physical evidence) that if appropriate, will become the object of the real or mixed action to be brought against the person holding the property, is one of the most common and important committal proceedings for a trial. It is regulated in Section 497.2 of the LEC, and has a preventive intention. Its purpose is that the future defendant should remain in a situation similar to the one of the depositary. The defendant is warned to keep the property until the resolution of the court.

If the person required to produce the property refuses to do it at the time of the proceedings or at any later time, once the judgment of exception has been given against him, the judge has no other coercive way of compelling him, and so the petitioner may sue for damages in the future main action[112] or in a different one brought for that purpose.

Use of discovery at trial

In the case of a statement made on oath, as provided in Section 497.1 of the LEC, actions will be taken as established for the confession in trial,

---

112. LEC, Section 501.

until the self-confessed declaration is attained.[113] In the case of interrogation of parties as provided in Section 502 of the LEC, it will be conducted as established in Sections 637 to 659 of the LEC. Also, finally, in the case of discovery and production of property, which is the same the plaintiff intends to claim, the property must be described in the writ.

Given that this description in the writ, referred to in Section 499 of the LEC, mentions the discovery and production of property, it has to be considered applicable to the interrogation to parties, for it is so expressly provided in Section 502 of the LEC and by interpretative extension of these provisions, to the statement made on oath of the defendant, even if this case is not expressly mentioned in Section 497,1 or Section 498 of the LEC.

INTERIM PROTECTION OF ASSETS PENDING TRIAL

In Spanish law, there is a precautionary, provisional justice, which includes measures similarly called precautionary, provisional measures. As one author correctly points out, that does not mean to say there is a specific concept of precautionary, provisional measures as such. Rather, the concept is developed in a scattered way through different laws such as the LEC, the Real Estate Mortgage Act (REMA), the Commercial Code (CCom), and the Civil Code (CC).[114]

These may be defined as measures that are approved in a process already underway or which is about to begin within the statutory term for doing so, for the purpose of securing the effectiveness of pending or future judgments which may have a financial content or may call for a party to do or refrain from doing something, or of providing or preserving a necessary or legally appropriate position in the relevant proceeding.

The basic reason for these measures is to prevent a debtor who is acting in bad faith from escaping performance of an obigation, becoming insolvent or hiding away the things to which the process refers, squandering his wealth or even disappearing. Therefore, these measures are aimed at protecting the creditor's rights and, at the same time, preventing the debtor from doing anything that might hamper execution of the relevant judgment.

These precautionary measures are mainly provisional measures, as they last only as long as the main process that is pending or is to be initiated. As such, these measures anticipate the final result of the main

---

113. LEC, Section 598.

114. Viñal, "Chapter 25. Spain", *Attacking Foreign Assets*, Edited by Dennis Campbell, London, 1992, pp. 403–406.

process, making timeliness prevail over security considerations, on the grounds that a belated judgment may in many cases involve a denial of justice.

The foregoing notwithstanding, these measures are normally conditional on the party that requests them providing security in the form of a bond, to answer eventually for any damages that may be caused thereby to the other party, particularly where the party who requested the measures loses the main suit. Sometimes, the requirement of posting a bond is so prohibitive, as in the case of provisionally executing a judgment that is pending appeal for dismissal or reversal[115] that it may prevent the precautionary measure from being ordered.

The actual type of precautionary measure is normally chosen according to the purpose it is intended to serve, e.g., to guarantee the effectiveness of judgments having a financial content to call for doing or not doing something, to be ordered in pending or future processes, or else to provide or preserve a necessary or legally appropriate position in such proceedings.

Apart from the breakdown of precautionary measures given above, which is certainly one of the most typical, there are others in which the measure known as precautionary embargo is set apart, in a category of its own, with the rest falling under the general description of provisional security measures without any further methodological distinctions.

Among the precautionary measures that guarantee the effectiveness of judgments, the main ones are preventive embargo,[116] provisional annotation of a complaint at the Real Estate Registry[117] and seizure.[118] Among those which provide or preserve a given position in the proceedings, there is the appellant's bond for securing leave of appeal to both effects where permission to appeal has been granted to a single effect,[119] provisional execution of judgment[120] and stay of execution of a judgment pending review.[121]

The provisions governing preventive embargoes, which are significant in practice, are regulated in Sections 1397 et seq. of the LEC. These require that a document proving that the debt exists be submitted on requesting a preventive embargo,[122] and that the debtor is a foreign

---

115. LEC, Section 1722.
116. LEC, Sections 1397 et seq.
117. REMA, Section 42.1.
118. LEC, Section 499 and Civil Code, Section 1785.
119. LEC, Section 1476.
120. LEC, Section 1722.
121. LEC, Section 1803.
122. LEC, Section 1400.1; Decision of the Territorial Court of Barcelona of 30 September 1985.

person who has not acquired Spanish citizenship by naturalisation, or that the place of domicile of the foreign non-naturalised person is unknown, or that such person does not own any real estate, or a farming, manufacturing or commercial enterprise at the place where payment of the debt may be claimed.[123]

Even given these circumstances, a precautionary embargo may be ordered where the debtor has disappeared from his place of residence or business without leaving anyone in charge or where, having left someone in charge, such person is not aware of the debtor's whereabouts. It may also be ordered, where the debtor hides away, or there are reasons to believe that he will hide away or squander his assets in prejudice of his creditors.[124]

Thus, the fear of a person absconding or the fact that the person is foreign are two important considerations when it comes to interpreting the above-mentioned subjective requirements and ordering a preventive embargo. Where a creditor's request for an embargo is based on *prima facie* evidence of his claim, such as a public document, a bill of exchange, a promissory note or a cheque, or any lawful bearer or registered securities or written commercial contracts, such subjective requirements are not necessary pursuant to the provisions of Section 1401 of the LEC, read together with the provisions of Act Number 96/1966 of 23 July 1966, on the competence of municipal or local judges.

Where the above requirements are met and the preventive embargo is granted, this is not put into effect if, at the time of doing so, the party against whom the embargo has been ordered pays, deposits the sum owing or posts a bond covering the sum being claimed.[125] Otherwise, the embargo is put into effect and then the main process is undertaken, at which time the creditor must request that the embargo be confirmed[126] by filing the relevant demand within a term of 20 days after the embargo becomes effective, and the debtor may oppose it on the grounds that it is contrary to law and not admissible.[127]

SUMMARY JUDGMENTS

Expiry

The conclusion of the process in the first instance may come about through expiration of term. This expiration is deemed to be the effect

---

123. LEC, Section 1400.2; Decision of the Territorial Court of Caceres of 2 March 1975.
124. LEC, Section 1400.2.
125. LEC, Section 1405.
126. LEC, Section 1411.
127. LEC, Section 1416.

produced by operation of the law when certain terms transpire without the litigants formulating requests for the continuance of the proceedings, either because the case has been concluded by other means or because the judgment is not required or desired by any of the parties.

According to the provisions of Section 411 of the LEC, the proceedings in all kinds of cases will be reputed to have been abandoned and will lapse in law if their continuation is not urged within the term of four years, while the case is still in first instance; of two years, if it were in second instance; of one year if the case stands pending a repeal, with this term and all of the others being counted from the date of the last notification made to the parties.[128]

The effect of expiry, resolved by writ[129] and always declared *ex officio* by the judge,[130] is the conclusion of the trial. Then, the documentation is archived if the lapse takes place in the first instance, or the judgment acquires definitive status if the expiry of the period occurs in the second instance or during a repeal procedure.[131] The conclusion of the process in the first instance leaves the claim unjudged and it may be exercised anew if the plaintiff so wishes.[132]

Summary judgments

The courts may render their decisions in the form of a judgment not only when they definitively resolve the matters in dispute in a case at any instance or on extra-ordinary appeal, but also when their decision on a defence conclusively determines the object of the claim or where they find that a litigant may no longer be heard because of non-appearance.[133]

Similarly, another kind of judicial declarations, the rulings, may resolve the incidents arising during the trial and requiring a decision independent and separate from the definitive judgment, or else when they need not be handed down in the form of a judgment. Thus, as an example, the dilatory defences proposed in the trials of larger amounts constitute an incident that might put an end to the trial and can be resolved through a Ruling.[134]

128. SSTS 7 December 1943; 30 April 1949; and 29 June 1993.
129. LEC, Section 416.
130. LEC, Section 413.
131. LEC, Sections 414 and 415.
132. LEC, Section 418.
133. LEC, Section 369.
134. LEC, Section 538, Paragraph 3.

Default judgments

Once the time period established in the arrangement has transpired, if the defendant summonsed does not appear in person or through his next of kin or the relative who had been found in the household, then default occurs, a legal situation which is contrary to appearance in the proceedings.[135] This absence, which is a legal default not a material one, as the latter does not imply contempt as the former does, is concluded by the party's appearance in the trial.

In this sense, the LEC establishes in Section 766 that regardless of the status of the suit in which the defaulting party appears he will be admitted as a party to the suit and the substantiation of the case will take him into account, even though some rulings cannot be effected through having lapsed. Thus, it will not be possible to answer the claim[136] and, with regard to evidence, this stage may be completed during the second instance if the appearance occurs after its conclusion.[137]

Default, as accepted in Sections 281, 527 and 762 of the LEC only produces effects when it has been declared by the legal authority. For this declaration to have an effect, it must be notified to the person concerned and it converts the *de facto* situation into a *de iure* one. It is independent of whether or not the defendant wishes to appear in the trial as it responds to objective data. There is, in short, no need for the plaintiff to request this declaration of default, as provided for in Section 1462 of the LEC as it is made without the plaintiff making known the absence of the defendant.

The declaration of default means that the defaulting defendant[138] may not effect any procedural action while affected by this situation.[139] This does not imply any repercussion for the plaintiff on his burdens or possibilities, as he is in the same situation as if there were no default. Nor does it imply for the defendant any acceptance of the claim nor admission of the facts, not even a *ficta confessio*.

The judgment handed down in a situation of default produces an effect of *res judicata*, although in certain circumstances, such as those set out in Sections 773 *et seq*. of the LEC, it may be subject to a special rescission process, the extraordinary remedy of a hearing for the defaulter when, for example, the declaration has not been delivered to him in person. Thus, until such time as the terms foreseen for the

---

135. LEC, Section 527.

136. LEC, Section 527.

137. LEC, Section 862.

138. And not the plaintiff according to accepted Spanish legal doctrine.

139. Almagro Nosete *et al*, *Derecho Procesal*, *Tomo I* (Volume II), *Parte General Proceso Civil* (I), Valencia, 1986, p. 374.

lodging of the aforementioned remedy, the legislation prevents the disposal of the property obtained through execution.[140]

Other termination without plenary trial

Through a series of procedural acts such as acceptance of the claim, abandonment, waiver or judicial compromise, the parties may conclude the trial directly or indirectly and thus precipitate the corresponding court decision either in the form of a judgment or in the form of a ruling. In all these cases, the trial is therefore interrupted, without the proceedings having been completed.

Voluntary dismissal

The acceptance of the claim is a declaration made by the defendant at any point in the proceedings whereby he accepts what the plaintiff is requesting in the claim, thus recognising that the latter's pretensions were well-founded. In principle, this produces the termination of the trial and the subsequent condemnatory judgment, unless this involves renouncing public interest or public order or implies damages to third parties,[141] in which case the trial will continue until its normal conclusion.

This procedural act does not imply that the legal costs must necessarily be charged to the defendant. Specifically, if this voluntary dismissal occurs before the claim is answered, then there is no question of assessing the defendant for costs.[142] Nevertheless, if the plaintiff has had to lodge his claim due to the fault of the defendant, i.e., if there has been bad faith on the defendant's part, then costs will be assessed.

As opposed to this acceptance of the claim, where the process is concluded through a causal action by the defendant, in a voluntary dismissal there is a unilateral declaration of the plaintiff through which he abandons the litigation without waiving the claim, and this is recognised through a ruling or decree that leaves the merits of the case unjudged.[143]

Dismissal does not require the consent of the defendant to be valid but if the latter has answered the claim and opposed it, and his interest in the trial's continuance until the end can be deduced, then it would seem appropriate for such consent to be requested, but this would not happen if such interest does not exist.

140. LEC, Sections 787 and 788.
141. Royal Decree dated 21 November 1952, Section 41.
142. LEC, Section 523.
143. LEC, Section 848.

Dismissal for failure to prosecute

In abandonment, the plaintiff abandons the trial but does not waive the claim. In waiver, on the other hand, the plaintiff signs a statement to the effect that the claim is unfounded and by doing so he waives the right to the court's protection, thus determining an absolutory judgment with authority of *res judicata* which is handed down without any requirement for the trial to continue as, regardless of its situation, the judgment will always be absolutory.

The waiver, like the abandonment, requires that the solicitor have special powers of attorney. The general powers granted by the plaintiff for legal representation will not be sufficient. In the absence of such powers, the waiver can be ratified by the plaintiff later. However, the waiver does not require, as the abandonment does, the defendant's consent in any case as this is effected by the plaintiff's act of waiver.

Judicially assisted settlement

As opposed to the acceptance of the claim and the waiver that conclude the trial through a judgment, finding the defendant either guilty or innocent, the compromise concludes it without requiring a judgment. So that this effect can be produced, it is necessary for the judge to be present and he is thus a party to this process. If the compromise is reached outside the proceedings, then it does not conclude the trial nor avoid the judgment as it is not then a judicial compromise.

The compromise must be reached in a meeting held before the judge and must be signed by the judge, the secretary and the parties, except in the latter case where the solicitor has special powers of attorney and is able to sign it directly himself, and this is true in the predominantly oral proceedings (petty amounts, cognisance, verbal) as well as in the large amount proceedings, in spite of the fact that the law makes no provisions regarding this.

The compromise does not produce the effect of *res judicata* as this result is reserved for those judicial acts that decide the merits. As it is a legal question that produces material effects, it determines solely and exclusively the relations between the parties. On the other hand, it has executive efficacy as the law establishes it as an entitlement to execution which can be carried out through the procedure for execution of judgment.

TRIAL

In Spanish civil suits, the dominant principle governing the procedure for suits is that it is up to the parties to bring before the courts the facts and to develop the evidence for these facts. Thus, as opposed to the practice in other legal systems which stress the principle of investigation, the judge has no independence to introduce facts or evidence which have not been proposed by the parties, and his role is as a result limited to the legal consideration of these elements in accordance with the idea underlying the Roman maxim of *Da Mihi Factum, Dabo Tibi Ius*.

The obligation of the parties to present the facts is materialised in the original writs and the answers to the complaint, depending on the positions of the plaintiff and defendant, respectively and also in the development of the evidence during the periods for proposal and practice of the probatory phase, during which the judge may direct or organise the measures to be taken, accepting or rejecting particular forms of evidence[144] or questions to witnesses[145] if he considers them impertinent or useless.

When it comes to bringing evidence before the court and its proof, Spanish civil proceedings rest on the principle of provision by the parties and in the case of valuing the evidence, on the principle of assessed evidence, whereby the legislator has established a closed system of forms of evidence including formal interrogations,[146] presentation of public instruments[147] and — to a lesser extent — on evidence from witnesses.[148]

This rigid and closed classification has made it enormously difficult to bring into the proceedings other forms of evidence despite the fact that with the progress of technology over the years these have become much more common, such as audio and video recordings among many others, and only the jurisprudence has been capable of regulating in a flexible and gradual manner.[149]

The probatory proceedings are divided into two stages, proposition and practice, within the periods of 20 days for the first stage and 30 days for the second,[150] except where the evidence is to be obtained from abroad, in which case the legislation grants a period of four months for evidence to be effected in Europe and six months for the rest of the world,[151] taking into account the inherent difficulties involved in obtaining such evidence.

144. LEC, Section 566.
145. LEC, Sections 639, 649.
146. LEC, Sections 579 *et seq*.
147. Civil Code, Section 1718.
148. LEC, Sections 637 *et seq*.
149. Constitutional Court Decision (STC) Number 114/1984, dated 29 November 1984.
150. LEC, Section 553.
151. LEC, Section 556.

In order to be able to take advantage of this extraordinary period for evidence, the legislation first requires that it be so requested within the three days following the notification of the initiation of the probatory stage; secondly that the events have occurred in the foreign country in which the evidence is to be obtained;[152] thirdly that the witnesses live abroad;[153] and fourthly that the addresses of the witnesses, the archives containing the documents to be attested[154] and the person to respond to interrogation be stated.[155]

Evidence

Documents

The LEC and the Civil Code regulate the probative value of documents, both public and private.[156] They refer to what for procedural purposes are considered documents that is, a representation of a thought written in a paper, but not to any other representation thereof, such as cassettes and videotapes as indicated before, there public and private documents.

Public documents must be issued by notaries or authorised public officials,[157] and include solemn public documents, notarial documents, judicial documents and administrative documents.[158] These documents prove, against third parties, the fact that motivated their granting and their date; the statements of the contracting parties; and the name of the authorised notary or public official.

Although there is no specific definition of private documents, the LEC established that, when acknowledged under oath before the judge by the party they prejudice, they have the same probative value as public deeds.[159] For the rest, private documents may only be used as evidence against the person who has written them, and with respect to the facts stated therein. If drafted to amend the contents of a public document, they are not binding on third parties.[160]

---

152. LEC, Section 557.
153. LEC, Sections 557 and 558.
154. LEC, Section 557.
155. LEC, Section 592.
156. LEC, Sections 596 et seq. and Civil Code, Sections 1215 et seq.
157. Civil Code, Section 1216.
158. LEC, Section 596.
159. LEC, Section 1225.
160. Civil Code, Section 1230.

Depositions

The deposition, defined in accepted doctrine as "any statement by the parties in the trial which serves as evidence"[161] and intended to determine for the purposes of the judgment the truth or otherwise of the facts in which the party making the deposition has been directly involved,[162] may in certain cases exclude other forms of evidence, such as that of direct testimony.[163]

The part making the deposition must do so on its own account and not through its representative or proxy and therefore must enjoy not only capacity to be a party to the suit but also the legal capacity to make the statement in question. In the case of bodies corporate, the depositions will be taken from their corresponding legal organs, their legal representatives.

In this kind of evidence, the party making the deposition is liable to three main obligations, which if not complied with, will lead to the party being deemed to have confessed:

(1) Attend the citation by the judge;[164]
(2) Reply to the questions posed; and[165]
(3) Reply directly to the questions affirming or denying the questions posed by the opposing party.[166]

Depositions may be requested and effected not only during the probatory period but also at any point following the initiation of the probatory stage until the intimation that the court is ready to pronounce judgment.[167] Each party requesting that a deposition be effected prepares its own questions all eliciting an affirmative response ("State whether it is true that . . .") and presents them in a sealed envelope prior to the celebration of the deposition or in an open envelope at the moment when this takes place.[168]

Although, in principle, the party making the deposition may only answer "yes" or "no" without resorting to evasive answers, the law in fact admits that the party may add comments to its statement to specify

---

161. Almagro Nosete *et al.*, *Derecho Procesal, Tomo I* (Volume II), *Parte General Proceso Civil* (I), Valencia, 1986, p. 440.
162. Civil Code, Section 1231.
163. LEC, Section 637.
164. LEC, Section 583.
165. LEC, Section 583.
166. LEC, Section 586.
167. LEC, Section 579.
168. LEC, Section 582.

the scope and contents of the affirmations or negations by providing the explanations which it, or the judge, considers appropriate.[169]

Apart from being able to request additional explanations to the statements made, the judge also appoints the date and time for the celebration of the deposition;[170] he accepts or rejects, without possible recourse, those questions which do not conform to the conditions of clarity, precision and specificity determined by statute; and finally he adopts the normal precautions when various different people are to make statements on the same facts.[171]

Finally, it must be added that the deposition is made under an oath or promise to tell the truth;[172] that the party making the statement does not require the assistance of solicitor or barrister;[173] and that, once the statement has been taken, a written record of the events occurring and the statement made is drafted and signed by those present.

Party testimony

Witnesses — third parties not involved in the suit — are not required to have capacity for trial nor the capacity to act. They merely need natural capacity, i.e., the ability to narrate the events they have personally experienced. As a result, lunatics and the insane are not allowed to be witnesses through natural incapacity, nor are the blind and the deaf where the testimony depends on sight and hearing respectively, nor children under 14 years of age. Legal incapacity bars those persons with a special relationship to the parties to the suit or with the object of the case.[174]

The procedure for this evidence involves the presentation of a written request for it to be admitted, accompanied by the list of questions to be posed for the judge to be able to assess them and reject those which are not clear and precise or which are not pertinent because they fail to refer any of the matters under litigation.[175] As a complement to the questions, there are in due course the cross-examination questions prepared by the other party and which must also be answered by the witnesses.[176]

Once the statement by witnesses and the questions to be answered have been admitted by the court, the party proposing the same must then

169. LEC, Sections 586 and 588.
170. LEC, Section 586.
171. LEC, Section 590.
172. LEC, Section 580.
173. LEC, Sections 584 and 588.
174. Civil Code, Sections 1247 and 126.
175. LEC, Sections 638 and 639.
176. LEC, Section 641.

submit a list of the full names and addresses of the witnesses, which the judge may not reject, within the ten days following the notification of the admission of evidence by witnesses.[177]

The witnesses must make their statements separately under an oath or promise to tell the truth and are interrogated first, by the judge in order to establish their identity and to determine whether or not their is any cause for them to be disqualified as witnesses;[178] and then, following the list of questions and cross-questions previously admitted.[179]

Causes for disqualification of witnesses may be indicated during the four days following the completion of their statements through a procedure known as "impeachment of witnesses" which will be resolved as part of the definitive judgment.

JUDGMENT AND KINDS OF RELIEF

Final judgment

The judgment (*sentencia*) is the final act which, provided that it resolves the dispute among the parties, the plaintiff and the defendant, puts an end to the prosecution, estimating or dismissing the claim, i.e., finding the defendant guilty or innocent, as provided in Section 359 of the LEC. At times, the judgment may be partly estimative and partly dismissive, whenever an action contains different proceedings, some of which are reasonable and some of which are not.

The judgments may be classified according to different criteria, nevertheless, for the purpose of this work, only three of them are necessary:

(1) According to the aim of the contents, they may be condemnatory, merely explanatory, and constitutive;
(2) According to the jurisdiction in which they are ruled, of first instance, of appeal, and of repeal; and
(3) According to the subsequent conditions they may have, absolute or open to appeal.[180]

Leaving the two first categories aside and focusing on the third — absolute and open to appeal judgments — absolute judgments may be defined as those which may not be subject to any ordinary or extraordinary appeal, because of their nature or because they have been accepted

---

177. LEC, Section 640.
178. LEC, Section 648.
179. LEC, Section 649.

180. Gomez Orbaneja-Herce Quemada, *Derecho Procesal Civil, Tomo I, Parte General*, Madrid, 1969, pp. 300–301.

by the parties,[181] while open to appeal judgments are those which are not absolute, except for those from the Supreme Court of Justice.

Finally, one may differentiate absolute judgments from final judgments. The latter is meant to solve the problem posed in the appeal or the request, giving a definitive solution to the matter in dispute, while the first, as mentioned above, is a judgment that cannot be subject to any appeal, precluding all means of appeal whatever their nature may be.[182]

Entry of judgment

As soon as the judgment is absolute, it must be enforced, according to Section 919 of the LEC, at the request of one of the parties, by the judge or the court who held the trial at first instance. In cases of appeal, as soon as the inferior court has received the attestation containing the absolute judgment, execution will be agreed and the parties will be notified so they can act as they consider appropriate.[183]

Kinds of relief

The classification of the judgments with regard to their aim in condemnatory, merely declaratory and constitutive judgments goes together with that of the actions, and the later with the different ways adopted by the legal actions in their prosecution, i.e., explanatory or of knowledge, executive and enforceable. The first of them, explanatory or of knowledge, can be subdivided into condemnatory, merely explanatory and constitutive actions.

Specific performance

According to the doctrine, condemnatory actions are the most common way of legal protection as they request a formal declaration of a compensatory sum, which must be provided by the defendant, so that whatever comes from the jurisdictional report is an entitlement for making it effective. Therefore, the purpose of a condemnatory action, which is applied for in the claim and obtained in the judgment, is a double one: an executive entitlement of the obligation and the acknowledgement of a material claim.

181. LEC, Section 369.
182. LEC, Section 369 and LOPJ, Section 245.
183. LEC, Section 920.

If the judgment imposes the payment of a fixed and net amount, according to Section 921 of the LEC, the goods of the defendant will be seized, without being necessarily a previous personal injunction, in the way and order established in the executory process. If the judgment imposes the payment of a debt in a foreign currency, proceedings will also be taken in accordance with the dispositions contained in the executory process.

Substitution relief

In accordance with Section 926 of the LEC, whenever by reason of the judgment real or personal property has to be handed over to the party who won the case, proceedings will be taken to pass the tenure of the goods onto such party, taking the steps the interested party may request. If the handing over of the personal property was impossible because such property did not exist at the time delivery was requested, the enforcement of the judgment should be directed towards the corresponding compensation for damages as a substitution relief.[184]

In the same manner, if it had become impossible to hand over real property because, for example, it had been conveyed to a third party by public deed, Sections 926 and 928 will also be applicable, as regards the compensation for damages of the interested party. Questions referring to the declaration of damages and their compensation are of fact, and, therefore, the ascertainment of damages is to be made by the court, who has the option of leaving its ascertainment to the stage of the enforcement of the judgment.[185]

According to the provisions of Section 924 of the LEC, if the person condemned to do something does not carry it out for the enforcement of the judgment within the period of time established by the judge, it will be done at his expense; and, in case the act was so personal it could not be done this way, it will be understood that he chooses the compensation of damages.[186] If the judgment specifies what these damages amount to in case of failure, proceedings will be taken in accordance to the provisions of Section 921 of the LEC; if not, in accordance to the provisions of Sections 928 et seq.

Constitution, transformation or rescission

Even though the purpose of the constitutive actions is to enforce a right of the plaintiff for the constitution, transformation or rescission of a legal

184. STS 29 June 1985.
185. STS 29 March 1993.
186. STS 25 March 1981, STS 8 March 1951.

relation, in the estimative judgments of such actions, when a right is acknowledged, it is nevertheless recognised that it could not have otherwise arisen. The contents of the right is obtaining the change of the situation through the judicial statement.

In this sense, and according to Section 923 of the LEC, if the judgment contained an obligation of doing or not doing something, or of handing over any thing or net amount, it will be enforced using all necessary means for this purpose. If the judgment cannot be immediately served, whatever the reason may be, goods may be seized at the petition of the creditor to an amount that ensures, in the opinion of the judge, the coverage of the principal and the costs of the enforcement. However, the debtor may avoid this situation by providing sufficient surety to the judge's satisfaction.

Declaration concerning legal relations

The only purpose of explanatory judgments is to declare the existence or non-existence of a right or a legal relation and, as for the case of constitutive judgments referred to above, there is no executory action. However, the fact that it is not executory, which only corresponds to the condemnatory judgments, does not mean, as some authors point out that the judgment is not absolute. An absolute judgment is not the same as an executory judgment.

On some occasions, when the *petitum* of the claim has not been determined as regards the "quantum" and the estimative judgment, not being able to determine it, contains a "generic" or "pending" penalty, the judgment may become a merely explanatory one, because its "execution" will only proceed through a condemnatory action in the trial for settlement, based on the first judgment.[187]

POST-TRIAL MOTIONS

Attacks on judgments

Judgments may be incongruent, or contain a defect of form or content, upon which an appeal may be based. Incongruence, regulated in Section 359 of the LEC, is measured by the difference between the findings of the judgement and the terms in which the parties have brought their claims, so that the judgment may not grant any more than has been

187. LEC, Section 360, Paragraph 2; SSTS 11 June 1983; 27 April 1990; and 25 May 1993.

claimed for, nor less than what the defendant has accepted, or grant something different to what has been claimed.

If such deflection means a complete change of the terms in which the prosecution was carried out, as some authors point out, an infringement of the principle of repugnancy may have occurred, and in addition, of the right of defence contained in Section 24 of the CE.[188] Therefore, the incongruence of a judgment leads to a conflict with this right whenever, besides this incongruence, a lack of proper defence prohibited by Section 24 of the CE[189] exists.[190]

In view of these facts, there are basically three types of incongruence in a judgment:

(1) *Ultra petita* incongruence (whenever the plaintiff or the defendant has been granted something that exceeds the petitions of the claim);

(2) *Extra petita* incongruence (whenever the petitioner has been granted with something different from what he claimed); and

(3) *Citra petita* incongruence (whenever no judgment has been given).

According to some authors, the third is more an infringement of a duty established in the CE, Section 24 and Civil Code, Section 1.7 than an incongruence.

For determining this procedural error of incongruence in the judgment, and not in the legal grounds upon which the judgment was given, the factors which may be taken into account are the comparison between the petitions of the main documents of the prosecution and the decisions contained in the judgment, because the incongruence arises from the difference between the petitions contained in the claim and debated in the suit, and the decisions of the judgment.

Grounds for new trial

The LEC, when regulating the different types of appeals, only establishes the reasons it will be based upon in one of them, the repeal. For the other types, no matter if they do not seek for a return, such as the appeal of reinstatement and the rogatory, or if they do seek for it, such as the remedy, the LEC does not establish anything in that respect. Therefore,

188. Brocá-Majada, *Práctica Procesal Civil, Tomo I, Disposiciones Comunes*, Barcelona, 1988, pp. 485 *et seq*. Constitutional Court Decisions (SSTC) 88/92, of 8 June 1992; 44/93, of 8 February 1993; 172/94, of 7 June 1994.

189. See above.

190. STS 12 June 1986.

the doctrine, while studying the jurisprudence, has generally considered that for any appeal to be genuine "the petitioner must have an interest, levy, damage or injury".[191]

Therefore, focusing on the repeal, one finds that in Section 1692 of the LEC, there is a whole series of established causes on which the repeal may be based such as the misuse of authority in the exercise of jurisdiction;[192] the incompetency or unsuitability of the process;[193] the existence of fundamental procedural errors in the trial;[194] the wrong weight of evidence;[195] and the violation of rules of the legal system or the jurisprudence applicable for determining the dispute.[196]

ENFORCEMENT AND EXECUTION OF JUDGMENTS

Spanish provisions on recognising and executing foreign judgments have been strongly criticised by some authors, who consider them not only insufficient, incomplete, and hollow but also unsystematic, because the rules on recognising and executing such judgments are not grouped together in a single code of law.[197]

Besides, the lack of clear rules leads these authors to consider that the term "judgments" used in the applicable Spanish laws has to be construed broadly, as meaning not only "judgments" as such but also "writs of execution", "decisions" and "decrees" as well as those delivered by jurisdictional courts and courts of arbitration.

In the same sense, these authors take the view that any other similar foreign instruments proving a right of execution should carry similar weight in Spain, provided only that they carry the relevant "executive clause". Then, taking into account both Spanish legislation and the international treaties that are effective in Spain, the authors give the following list of judgments, writs of execution, decisions and decrees that may be recognised in Spain:

(1) Final, non-appealable judgments handed down by foreign courts or in foreign countries;
(2) Decisions on court costs;

191. Prieto-Castro Ferrandiz, *Derecho Procesal Civil, Volumen 1°*, Madrid, 1984, pp. 246 *et seq*.
192. LEC, Section 1692.1.
193. LEC, Section 1692.2.
194. LEC, Section 1692.3.
195. LEC, Section 1692.4.
196. LEC, Section 1692.5.
197. Viñal, "Chapter 25. Spain", *Attacking Foreign Assets*, Edited by Dennis Campbell, London, 1992, pp. 406–410.

(3) Arbitration decisions;

(4) Decisions handed down by jurisdictional courts or courts of arbitration, emergency or precautionary measures and documents which provide *prima facie* evidence of a claim; and

(5) Final, non-appealable decisions.

In order for such foreign judgments, decisions, and decrees to be fully effective for procedural purposes in Spain, i.e., in order to be recognised and executed, Spanish law calls for them to meet the requirements foreseen in any of the exequatur systems in force: the conventional system,[198] the reciprocity system[199] and the conditions system.[200]

These three systems are ranked, with the conventional system prevailing over the other two, and the reciprocity system prevailing over the conditions system. Despite being the lowest-ranking and of a supplementary nature, the conditions system is generally considered the most practical of the three. It dates back to 1881, but has hardly changed over time, save for the amendments introduced by way of conventions.

The conventional system applies under Section 951 of the LEC. Under the provisions of Section 951, final, non-appealable judgments handed down in foreign countries will have such force in Spain as is foreseen in the respective treaties. Thus, the duty of the judge or court that has to decide on the matter is to examine the requirements foreseen in the convention on which the petition for recognising and executing the foreign judgment is based, and then decide whether or not the petition, or more specifically the decision which according to the petition should be recognised and executed, meets such requirements.

There are very few such conventions, and their number has only grown modestly since 1945 as a result of the growing cross-border flows of persons and property and the underlying need to regulate these flows. Under virtually all of the conventions, recognition of the foreign decision is conditional on the court in which the decision originated having the necessary competence.

It is advisable to clarify the meaning of three key terms mentioned in Section 951 of the LEC, by reference to Section 369 thereof. The three terms are: "judgment" (*sentencia*), "final, non-appealable judgment" (*sentencia firme*), and "writ of execution" (*ejecutoria*). In that sense, a "judgment" is a court decision that finally decides the questions raised in a suit; a "final, non-appealable judgment" is one that is not or may not be appealed, and a "writ of execution" is a public and solemn document in which the final, non-appealable judgment is set forth.

198. LEC, Section 951.

199. LEC, Sections 952 and 953.

200. LEC, Section 954.

Thus, in the face of a foreign final, non-appealable judgment and of a petition that the judgment be recognised and executed in Spain, the judge or court which has to decide on the matter reviews the document carrying the judgment to determine if it meets the requirements foreseen in Section 600 of the LEC, and particularly the most problematic of all that of legalisation. Since The Hague Convention of 5 October 1961 was ratified, thus eliminating the requirement that foreign documents be legalised, the question has become much simpler: All that is required is an apostile by the relevant authority of the country of origin.

Apart from the conventional system there is the reciprocity system, governed by the provisions of Section 952 of the LEC, according to which, where there is no special treaty with the country in which the judgment in question has been handed down, this judgment will have similar force in Spain to that which a writ of execution issued in Spain has in the other country.

Apart from that positive reciprocity there is a negative reciprocity, provided for in Section 953 of the LEC, under which, if writs of execution issued by Spanish courts are not recognised in the decisions handed down by the courts of the other country, the writs of execution from that country will have no force in Spain.

Finally, the conditions system applies once it has been shown that there is no treaty with the country of origin, that the positive reciprocity system does not apply, and that the writ of execution comes from a country whose courts do not recognise writs of execution issued by Spanish courts. In that case, the foreign judgment will be recognised if it meets the requirements laid down in Section 954 of the LEC, which are as follows:

(1) That the writ of execution has been issued as a consequence of a personal action being brought;
(2) That it has not been issued in default;
(3) That the liability to be performed under the writ of executions is lawful in Spain; and
(4) That the writ of execution must meet the requirements in force in the country in which it has been issued in order to be considered authentic, and must meet the requirements of Spanish laws for being a valid document in Spain.

Authors, in general, take a rather dim view of the Spanish exequatur system, not only because it is not well suited to the characteristics of current legal practice but also because of the problems found in applying it, particularly in the case of the reciprocity system, in both its positive and negative or retortion forms, on account of the former being a vestige of the past and the latter playing an unjustified role in the system.

Besides these problems, which in most cases have to be solved by resorting to the doctrine of authors and previous court decisions, the procedure for recognising and executing foreign judgments in Spain is comparatively simple. Thus, a written petition for a judgment to be recognised and executed is addressed to Section One of the Supreme Court,[201] accompanied by a document attesting to the decision, which must carry the apostile set out in The Hague Convention. These documents must be duly translated,[202] either before they are filed with the Supreme Court[203] or later on during the proceedings.

In line with the rule that parties must furnish the evidence necessary to a decision, the condemned party or the party affected by a declaratory judgment is given nine days in which to appear before the court to be heard.[204] For the said party to be able to appear, the relevant certificate is issued to the responsible Spanish and foreign authorities according to the relevant judicial assistance arrangements. Once the term has elapsed, the court will go ahead with the proceedings even if the person who has been summoned does not appear.

After hearing the government attorney, the court declares whether the writ of execution will be recognised or not. If the court does not recognise the writ of execution, this is returned to the party who has filed it. If recognised, it is forwarded to the High Court (*Audiencia*), which orders the judge of first instance of the district where the condemned party has his domicile or the judgment is to be executed to put this into effect.[205]

The procedure for recognising the writ of execution has an erroneous consequence according to some authors, as it only provides for the inexorable result of execution (exequatur) and, in sum, for condemnatory judgments, leaving aside merely declarative judgments, constitutive judgments, and decisions on taking precautionary and provisional measures. Thus, the provisions of Section 958 of the LEC have to be interpreted as appropriate in case the petition is not to the effect that a judgment be recognised, but to some other effect.

APPEAL

Types of appeal

The amendment of a judicial decision can only be obtained, as provided in the LEC and the LOPJ, by the attack against a judgment known as appeal

201. LEC, Section 955.
202. LEC, Section 956.
203. LEC, Section 601.
204. LEC, Section 956.
205. LEC, Section 958.

(*apelación*). These appeals, which are predicated on the existence of a higher court with legal and functional authority to examine the judgment of the inferior court, may or may not seek for a remand. Those seeking for a remand are the "remedy" and the "repeal" those which do not are the "appeal of reinstatement" and the "rogatory".

Besides these appeals, there are others that, even though considered as such by the current law and practice, are not included by a doctrinal sector because they are not strictly a attack against a judgment. These "appeals" in the ample sense are the "appeal of responsibility" the "appeal for clarifying the judgment", the "appeal of knowledge by force", the "appeal of protest", the "appeal of annulment of proceedings" and the "appeal of jurisdictional defect".[206]

Appeals not seeking a return

The appeal of reinstatement (*recurso de reposión*) is made against the orders and decisions of the judge of first instance. It must be made according to Sections 377 and 380 of the LEC within the three following days, specifying the rule of the LEC that has been contravened. The only appeal that can be made against the decisions upon these appeals is the remedy, which must be settled together with the main appeal.[207]

These appeals of reinstatement are basically legal or "procedural" remedies, just a formality, a "material arrangement of the prosecution" and are intended to obtain a "replacement" or "reform" of the judgment by the judge. As soon as the appeal is submitted, a copy must be delivered to the party or parties concerned; the party or parties may contest the appeal, if considered appropriate, within a period of three days.[208] If there are several parties involved, the period must be applicable to all of them.

Nevertheless, whenever the court decisions involved are not merely procedural, or do not decide appeals of reinstatement, dilatory objections or occurrences, the law does not impose the requisite of quoting the rule that has been contravened. On the other hand, the period for contesting is extended to five days, in consideration of the greater importance of the objection.[209]

The rogatory appeal (*recurso de súplica*) is basically similar to the appeal of reinstatement, but it is made against decisions of the Territorial Courts

206. Prieto-Castro Ferrandiz, *Derecho Procesal Civil, Volumen 1°*, Madrid, 1984, p. 243.

207. LEC, Section 381.

208. LEC, Section 378.

209. LEC, Sections 416 and 417.

of Appeal and the Supreme Court. For merely procedural court orders, proceedings will be taken only against the corresponding Territorial Court of Appeal, however, for court orders that are not merely procedural, the rogatory appeal is recognised for a period of five days. A repeal can be made against the court decision whenever it is a final one.[210]

Appeals seeking a return

The appeal of remedy (*recurso de apelación*) gives rise to the second instance, and through it:

"... the matter upon which a decision of a court in first instance exists is submitted to a new review by the High Court because the appellant considers that the decision, not taking partly or totally into consideration his petitions at first instance, causes him a damage."

The purpose of this review is to evaluate if the contested judgment is pertinent or not with the material taken into account in the first instance.

Therefore, the possibilities of adducing new evidence or facts and of using new methods of attack or defence are very much restrained. New claims may not be made, and the submission of further evidence is restrained to the fact that they must have occurred at a later time and must be of influence for the court decision, or have occurred previously but had been unknown to the parties concerned.[211] Besides, the carrying out of new evidence is subject to the declaration of new facts, except for the case of a party being in contempt of court who appears in any of the instances; in such cases all forms of evidence considered pertinent will be admitted and carried out.[212]

The courts capable of hearing the appeals for remedy are the Provincial Courts, except for the specific cases of the Civil and Criminal Courts of the Supreme Courts of Justice of the Autonomous Regions. In this respect, Section 82 of the LOPJ provides that in the civil matters, the Provincial Courts will hear:

"The appeals established by law made against the decisions of the courts of first instance of the province. The civil or criminal matters which may arise between courts of the province which do not have a higher court in common. The objections to its Judges whenever the specific court appointed to that end in the Supreme Courts of Justice is not capable in such matter."

The repeal (*recurso de casación*), in the opinion of a great sector of the doctrine, has three main characteristics:

210. LEC, Section 402.
211. LEC, Sections 862.3 and 862.4.
212. LEC, Section 862.5.

(1) It is a jurisdictional appeal, as the organs meant to solve it are the Supreme Court or the High Courts of Justice of the Autonomous Regions;

(2) It is an extraordinary appeal, as it is only possible against some decisions and because of reasons perfectly regulated;[213] and

(3) Nevertheless, it is not a third instance, because it is not meant to sit upon the claims of the parties, but upon the misstatement of an inferior court, and because except for the provisions of Section 1724 of the LEC, it does not admit the acceptance of new facts.

The decisions subject to contention before these courts are the final judgments given in second instance by the Provincial Courts in those suits exceeding a certain amount, and in some cases, in those of less than the limiting amount;[214] the court orders given for an appeal, in the proceedings for the enforcement of the judgments of the suits above mentioned; the judgments of the Provincial Court in specific suits for eviction or pre-emption;[215] and the decisions for which this appeal is expressly granted.[216]

The application for appeal must be based upon one of the causes expressly regulated in Section 1692 of the LEC, which have been already mentioned in this document, and besides, has to be limited to a decision that may be contested. With the compliance of these requisites, the High Court will consider it valid, and consequently will send it to the First Division of the Supreme Court. In the mean-time, notice will be given to the parties concerned within the period of 30 days.[217]

The party who has prepared the appeal must submit to the said Division the written application, within the period of 30 days from the date of notice; upon expiry of the time limit without submitting the application of appeal, the judgment contested will become final.[218] If the appeal is accepted, once the prosecutor and judge appointed as rapporteur have given preliminary rulings, a copy of them must be handed over to the party or parties concerned, in order to allow the said parties to appeal against them within the period of 20 days.[219] Upon expiry of the time limit, whether the appeals have been submitted or not, the court

---

213. STS 29 October 1981.
214. LEC, Section 1687.1.
215. LEC, Section 1687.3.
216. LEC, Section 1687.4.
217. LEC, Section 1696.
218. LEC, Section 1704.
219. LEC, Section 1710.2.

will fix, within a period of 90 days, the date and time for the hearing and, if appropriate, for the veto and the judgment.[220]

CONCLUSIVENESS OF JUDGMENT

Res judicata

The material *res judicata*, in contrast to the formal *res judicata*, sometimes identified as the estoppel, is the "procedural effect of the judgment which establishes its immovable condition, its permanence in time".[221] Therefore, according to the Roman proverb *"res judicata pro veritatae habetur"*, the *res judicata* becomes an essential factor for the achievement of the legal certainty and security, avoiding the possibility that later judgments contravene previous ones.

Absolute judgments are the only ones that cause the effects of the *res judicata*. Therefore, *res judicata* can only refer to judgments that decide upon fundamental problems.[222] This fact brings about some problems when the effect of the *res judicata* is considered for judgments given in the executory prosecution, in interjunction, or temporary maintenance actions,[223] since these actions may be subject to the opening of a further proceeding.

Leaving the previous considerations aside, both the objective and the subjective limits of the *res judicata* have to be taken into account. Most important among the former is the fact that the *res judicata* only refers to the judgment, and not to the facts and issues that must be decided before trial, and, among the second, is that the *res judicata* refers to the parties to the suit and so its effectiveness is limited to the *erga omnes*.

Law of the case

The Civil Code, while establishing in Section 1 the legal sources, devotes Paragraph 6 to the jurisprudence, and establishes that:

". . . jurisprudence will complete the legal system with the doctrine provided repeatedly by the Supreme Court while interpreting and applying the law, the practice, and the basic principles of law."

220. LEC, Section 1711.
221. Almagro Nosete *et al, Derecho Procesal, Tomo I* (Volume II), *Parte General Proceso Civil* (I), Valencia, 1986, p. 490.
222. Civil Code, Section 1252.
223. LEC, Sections 1479, 1617, 1658 and 1677.

Therefore, the Civil Code and to some extent the LEC[224] confer to jurisprudence a function of support or integration in the legal system.[225]

This complementary function consists in supporting the legal system in all such matters where there is a lack of regulation or where the sense of it is mistaken.[226] For the jurisprudence to become a valid rule, it is necessary that:

(1) The criterion of a judgment has been uniformly repeated;[227]
(2) The facts of the preceding judgments are substantially similar to the ones of the new case;[228] and
(3) The *ratio decidendi* of the cases settled and of those brought up remains the same.[229]

224. Section 1692.5.
225. STS 27 May 1985.
226. STS 27 July 1987.
227. SSTS 8 November 1946; and 27 March 1952.
228. STS 15 February 1982.
229. STS 15 February 1982.

CHAPTER 14

SWEDEN

BO G. H. NILSON AND JONAS H. WESTERBERG
Rydin Carlsten Advokatbyrå AB
Stockholm, Sweden

ESTABLISHING JURISDICTION

Types of jurisdiction

Apart from international conventions, most notably the Lugano Convention, there are no statutory rules on when Swedish courts will take jurisdiction over international matters.

Jurisdictional issues are instead, generally, resolved by analogous application of the provisions in the Swedish Code of Judicial Procedure (the Code) on venue. If venue can be found under these provisions, the Swedish court identified will have jurisdiction over the matter.

There are exceptions to this rule, and the precise limits of its application are unclear. Notable exceptions are that Swedish courts may, under the Lugano Convention, not apply those forum rules which are "exorbitant" and that Swedish courts will even when forum can be found not hear matters where exclusive jurisdiction for the courts of a certain state follows from the subject matter of the dispute, for example, disputes over real property located in a foreign state or disputes concerning the validity of patents and trademarks registered abroad or disputes arising from the application of foreign public law; and that they will not hear cases against a foreign sovereign based on *acta jure imperii*. On the other hand, even if no venue can be found under the Code, Swedish courts will hear certain cases connected to arbitrations conducted in Sweden (in which case the Stockholm District Court will be competent).

The following are the bases on which the Swedish courts will find themselves competent to take jurisdiction over a matter mentioned. The outline below is a description of the various provisions on venue in the Code. The distinction between jurisdiction *in personam* and *in rem* is not entirely familiar to Swedish law, and it should be noted that the attempt in this chapter to make such distinction may not be entirely successful.

Jurisdiction over the parties to the action

NATURAL PERSONS — FORUM DOMICILII

The general forum of natural persons is the general court of first instance (the District Court — *tingsrätten*) of the defendant's place of domicile.[1] If the defendant is registered in the Swedish civil registration, the place set forth as residence in such register as of 1 November, the year preceding the year in which litigation is commenced is considered the place of domicile under the Code.

The estate of a deceased falls under the jurisdiction of the court of the deceased person in question. A claim against a person who does not have a known residence, in Sweden or abroad, could be pursued in the court of the place in Sweden where he stays. If such a person is a Swedish citizen and is staying abroad, or if his whereabouts are unknown, an action against him can be brought in the court of the place in Sweden where he last resided or stayed.

LEGAL ENTITIES — FORUM DOMICILII

The general forum of legal entities is the District Court of the place where the legal entity's registered seat is or, if no such seat exists, the place from where the legal entity's activities are managed.

ALTERNATIVE FORA

For both natural persons and legal entities, alternative fora for actions *in rem* and *quasi in rem* are possible. Alternative fora may also be based on the *forum re sitae* and the *forum contractus*. If the defendant has no known residence in Sweden or, in the case of legal entities, no registered seat there, a claim can be pursued in the District Court of:

(1) The place where the assets of the defendant are located, provided that the claim is a monetary claim;[2]
(2) The place where the disputed movable property is located;[3] or
(3) The place where the defendant entered into the disputed contract (or other transaction), or otherwise incurred the obligation in dispute.[4]

1. Code of Judicial Procedure, Chapter 10, Section 1.
2. Code of Judicial Procedure, Chapter 10, Section 3.
3. Code of Judicial Procedure, Chapter 10, Section 3.
4. Code of Judicial Procedure, Chapter 10, Section 4.

A natural person or legal entity engaging in farming, mining, manufacturing or other similar business with a fixed place of business may be sued in the District Court of such fixed place of business, if the disputed claim has arisen out of the business.[5]

Jurisdiction over the subject matter of the action

PROPERTY CLAIMS

A claim can be pursued in the District Court of the place where the disputed movable property is located if the defendant has no known residence in Sweden, or in the case of legal entities, if the defendant has no registered seat in Sweden.

With respect to real property, exclusive jurisdiction in actions concerning title, leasehold, easement or other specific right to real property or possession thereof is vested in the District Court of the place where the real property is situated.[6] Such a court also has non-exclusive jurisdiction over:

(1) An action regarding purchase money for real property or other similar claim relating to the transfer of real property;
(2) An action against the owner of real property regarding personal liability for a debt for which the real property has been pledged as security, if payment is simultaneously sought from the pledge;
(3) An action regarding damage to or other encroachment on real property;
(4) An action regarding reimbursement for work on real property; or
(5) An action regarding damages based on breach of the assignor's responsibility for having valid title to real property disposed of.[7]

For the purpose of the foregoing, buildings belonging to a third party (that is, a party who is not the owner of the land) are considered to be real property.[8]

ACTIONS IN TORT

A claim against a tort-feasor may be pursued in the court of the place where the tortious act was committed or where the damage occurred.[9]

---

5. Code of Judicial Procedure, Chapter 10, Section 5.
6. Code of Judicial Procedure, Chapter 10, Section 10.
7. Code of Judicial Procedure, Chapter 10, Section 11.
8. Code of Judicial Procedure, Chapter 10, Section 12.
9. Code of Judicial Procedure, Chapter 10, Section 8.

CONTRACT — FORUM PROROGATUM

With exception to the rules on exclusive jurisdiction, the Code[10] allows parties to a contract to refer future disputes to a certain court. By analogy, a Swedish court is, in principle, willing to give effect to a contractual clause conferring jurisdiction over disputes arising out of a contract on the "courts of Sweden". The precise limits of this principle and its application where venue cannot be found under the Code are uncertain.

Lugano Convention

Pursuant to Article 3 of the Convention, Sweden has in cases falling under the Convention given up the right to apply its rules of "exorbitant" jurisdiction. The Convention expressly mentions Chapter 10, Section 3 of the Code (*forum rei sitae*). Also, Chapter 10, Section 4 of the Code (*forum contractus*) is considered exorbitant in the sense of the Convention.

The Swedish Act[11] implementing the Convention expressly provides that if no Swedish court is competent under Chapter 10, when Swedish courts have jurisdiction under the Convention, then action may be brought before the District Court of Stockholm.

Venue

General principles

With respect to general principles, the Code's rules on venue are the basis of the uncodified rules on jurisdiction discussed above.

Transfer of venue

The proper venue is decided on the basis of the factual circumstances at the time of serving the summons application on the defendant. Subsequent changes in these circumstances do not affect the venue.[12] However, if in a certain case there are practical reasons, as laid down in the provisions on joinder of claims and parties in Chapter 14, Sections 1–6, for transferring the case to another court, the Supreme

10. Code of Judicial Procedure, Chapter 10, Section 16.
11. SFS 1992 : 794.
12. Code of Judicial Procedure, Chapter 10, Section 15.

Court could, on application of one of the parties or courts concerned, decide on such a transfer pursuant to Chapter 14, Section 7 a, of the Code. Such a transfer is not possible if it contravenes the Code's rules on exclusive jurisdiction.

Service of summons or writs

The general rules on service in connection with court proceedings are set forth in the Act on Service,[13] to which the Code refers. Service is normally effected by the court unless a party requests to effect service itself, which request the court normally grants.

By post

The usual way to serve summons or writs is to send the documents by ordinary mail with a receipt to be signed and returned to the court. Registered mail with requested return receipt is an alternative.

With respect to subsequent writs in the proceedings the court could use simplified service. In such case, the relevant writ is mailed to the party and a separate message informing of the mailing of the writ is sent at least one day later. No receipt is then required.

Personal service

In cases where it is not possible to serve summons by ordinary or registered mail (often indicated by the failure to obtain the defendant's receipt for the summons) the court can decide to serve summons by special postal service (involving personal delivery by postman of the writ) or by use of a process server. Such a process server could either be a police officer, a police authority appointed process server or an official of the executive authority (*Kronofogdemyndigheten*).

Consular or diplomatic channels

Sweden is a party to the 1965 Hague Convention on Service of Documents in matters of civil and commercial Nature pursuant to which a Swedish court can request assistance from foreign authorities for service

13. SFS 1970 : 428.

abroad and *vice versa*. A special convention applies between Sweden, Denmark, Finland, Iceland and Norway.

Pursuant to internal Swedish legislation,[14] a court, other authority or private person can file a request for assistance with service abroad with the Swedish Foreign Ministry.

Publication

Service by publication is used if either:

(1) The person to be served lacks known residence and his whereabouts cannot be established; or
(2) The person to be served or other adult member of his household who could give receipt for the writ cannot be found at his known residence and there is reason to believe that the person to be served attempts to avoid service. In the latter case, the writ can also be left in a sealed envelope in the relevant person's residence or attached to the door of such residence.

Service on an undefined group of persons must be made through publication. Such method can also be used when a large number of persons are to be served and ordinary service on each of them would be unreasonably costly or cumbersome.

Substituted service

Substituted service could be used if the natural person to be served, or a representative of the legal entity to be served, is not to be found at the time of the process server's visit. The use of substituted service on an individual with respect to summons, as opposed to other kinds of writs, requires that there is reason to believe that the person in question tries to avoid personal service. Service on a natural person could be effected by leaving the documentation with an adult member of his household or, if he lives in a residential unit, with the landlord or janitor of the residential unit.

Service may be effected at the workplace of a natural person by leaving the documents to certain individuals representing his employer.

If the person to be served maintains an office in his line of work, service could be carried out at such office by delivering the documents to an employee during ordinary business hours. Office service on a

14. Ordinance 1933 : 618.

legal entity may be carried out in the aforesaid manner if no authorised representative of such entity is present during ordinary business hours.

A non-resident party in a lawsuit can be ordered to appoint counsel in Sweden or other state within the European Economic Area authorised to receive service the first time he appears in the case. If such party fails to do so, the court is entitled to effect service by mailing the documents to the party's last known address.[15]

Methods provided by The Hague Convention

Service of a writ pursuant to a request from a foreign court will be carried out in accordance with the internal Swedish rules on the subject, as outlined above, unless the request for service designates another method. In the latter case service should, if possible, be carried out in the requested manner.

ASCERTAINING THE APPLICABLE LAW

Sweden is not a federal state and thus has no specific regional legislation. The Swedish conflict of laws rules are mostly based on general principles, expressed in case law.

Actions in tort

Swedish courts are inclined to apply the law of the country where the tortious act was committed.

Actions in contract

According to the general principles of Swedish conflict rules with respect to contracts, the parties are free to choose the applicable law. In the absence of any agreement between the parties, Swedish courts have in some cases tried to establish what law the parties would have chosen, had this issue been dealt with in the contract. Such deliberation on the fictitious intention of the parties in practice comes close to the alternative principle of closest connection, meaning that the law of

---

15. Code of Judicial Procedure, Chapter 33, Section 8.

that state to which the contract has the closest connection will govern. This principle is the one favoured lately.

Relevant factors in establishing the state with the closest connection are the domicile of the parties; the place where the contract was entered into; the place of performance of the obligation, in kind, under the contract and the language of the contract.

With respect to certain international sales of goods, Sweden has enacted legislation on the determination of the applicable law[16] based on the corresponding Hague Convention of 1955. The Act states the basic principle that the parties to the contract have the power to agree on the law of their contract by including a provision on the subject. If no such provision exists and the parties' intention in this respect is not otherwise clear from the contract, the law of the state of the seller will apply, unless the seller received the order for the goods in the state of the buyer. The Act is consistent with the general principles of Swedish conflict of laws rules.

Since it is not yet a member of the European Union,[17] Sweden has not acceded to the 1980 Rome Convention on the Choice of Law for Contracts. However, Articles 1 to 13 and 25 to 88 of the 1980 United Nations Convention on Contracts for the International Sale of Goods have been enacted as Swedish law as of 1 January 1989. This Act does not apply if both parties to the transaction have their place of business in either Denmark, Finland, Iceland, Norway or Sweden.

Rights in rem

Issues regarding rights *in rem* are generally decided pursuant to the law of the State in which the disputed property is located or was located at the time of the relevant transaction, for example, a pledge. However, a security right that is valid pursuant to the law of the state in which the goods were located at the time of the creation thereof could, pursuant to Swedish rules on applicable law, become invalid following the importation of the goods to Sweden — the new *lex rei sitae*.

Legal entities

Questions regarding the constitution and legal capacity of legal entities, regarding their dissolution and their internal operation and

16. Act 1964 : 528.

17. This chapter was written in December 1994, prior to Sweden's accession to the EU.

similar questions are considered to be governed by the law of the state of incorporation of the relevant legal entity.

COMMENCING THE ACTION

Complaint

Stating the essential elements

The summons application must, in addition to formalities to identify the parties and facilitate service of process contain:

(1) A precise prayer for relief;
(2) A detailed statement of the facts invoked as a ground for the relief sought;
(3) A statement of the evidence (written and oral) invoked; and
(4) The basis for the competence of the court (with respect to the venue rules in the Code) unless this is clear from other statements made.

The requirement with respect to (2) above is based on the "theory of substantiation" From this theory, it follows that the complaint must contain a statement of the material facts from which follow the legal consequence, to which the claim corresponds.

If, for instance, the plaintiff asks the court to declare that a contract is invalid, the complaint must set forth the factual circumstances that give rise to the invalidity. Generally, the standard enforced by the courts with respect to the statement of facts is rather modest.

With respect to the legal grounds (that is the legal rule from which follows the remedy sought), these need not be asserted in the complaint or even later in the proceedings if the subject matter can be determined under Swedish law. This follows from the principle of *jura novit curia*. It is another matter in cases of any complexity in respect of the legal issues involved, in that it is often advisable to invoke case law and legal writings in connection with the closing argument or at an earlier stage of the proceedings.

With respect to evidence, it is in practice rarely possible to make a conclusive statement already at the time of filing the summons application. It is therefore common and accepted practice for the plaintiff to submit copies of essential documentation together with the summons application and otherwise reserve his right to state his evidence once it has been established to what extent the alleged circumstances are contested by the defendant.

Stating the relief sought

The prayer for relief could be either for a declaratory or for a performance judgment and should be formulated as to reflect the precise content
of the judicial decision that the plaintiff wishes to obtain. Pursuant to
Chapter 17, Section 3 of the Code, the courts may not render judgment
in excess of the relief sought, and thus a prayer, for example, "such other
relief as the court deems just" is not meaningful.

There is no requirement for consistent pleading or compliance with
technical form. Relief in the alternative or of several different types may
be requested, in different counts.

Answer

In principle, the defendant could be ordered to answer orally, at the first
preliminary hearing of the case. However, in practice the courts almost
invariably require the defendant to submit his answer in writing. The
answer must state:

(1) Any procedural objections the defendant wishes to raise;
(2) To what extent the plaintiff's prayer for relief is admitted or
    contested;
(3) If the plaintiff's prayer for relief is contested, the basis therefore
    and a statement regarding the circumstances invoked by the
    plaintiff and any further circumstances which the defendant
    wishes to invoke; and
(4) The evidence which the defendant wishes to invoke.

With respect to (1) above, it should be noted that many jurisdictional
objections are considered waived unless raised at first appearance, that is,
normally in the answer. This also applies to the right of the defendant to
request that the plaintiff furnish security for the litigation costs, where
applicable.[18]

Three kinds of defences have been distinguished by Swedish legal
writers. Firstly, a denial of all or some statements of fact in the complaint;
secondly, an affirmative defence invoking additional facts which "neu-
tralise" the facts invoked by the plaintiff; and thirdly, a defence based on
the view that the legal consequences of the facts invoked by the plaintiff
are other than as appear from the prayer for relief.

A defendant's failure to deny certain facts is not equivalent to an
admission of these facts. The court will, however, normally require an
express statement as to whether relevant facts are denied or admitted.

18. Cf. below.

Reply and rejoinder

The exchange of writs between the parties can, particularly in complex cases, continue in several steps, starting with the plaintiff's filing of a reply with his comments on the answer, but the courts more frequently decide to take the matter to a preliminary hearing after the filing of the answer.

Amendments to and supplemental pleadings

The Code[19] states the basic principle that "claims filed may not be amended". However, there are several exceptions to this rule:

(1) A plaintiff may change the kind of performance sought based on circumstances that have occurred or become known to the plaintiff during the proceedings. An example of this is that the plaintiff might originally have petitioned for a judgment ordering the defendant to deliver a certain car. During the proceedings, the plaintiff is informed that the defendant has disposed of the car. The plaintiff could then instead claim damages for breach of contract;

(2) The plaintiff may also amend his pleading in order to obtain a declaratory judgment regarding a disputed right or obligation on which the validity of the original claim depends, and claim interest or other incidental obligations which follow from the main claim; and

(3) Finally, the plaintiff may put forward a new claim for relief which is based on essentially the same ground as the original claim. An example of such an amendment is a lessor claim claiming additional rents that have fallen due during the proceedings.

An amended claim according to (2) and (3) above could be dismissed by the court of first instance if it is made when the case has already been brought to a main hearing or otherwise is about to be adjudicated. Such amendment is not allowed on appeal.

With respect to changes in the grounds for relief, as opposed to the prayers themselves, the Code provides that such adjustments are allowed as long as the new grounds do not involve a change of the "subject matter" of the case.[20]

There are, of course, great difficulties in drawing a line between permissible and impermissible amendments under such a general rule. In

19. Code of Judicial Procedure, Chapter 13, Section 3.
20. Code of Judicial Procedure, Chapter 13, Section 3 in fine.

Swedish legal writings, guidance has been sought from the reasoning in
res judicata issues. The question to be asked is, then, whether it would be
possible for the plaintiff to have a claim based on the new ground, tried
in a subsequent proceeding, should the first claim have been invalidated.
If the answer to this question is affirmative, this would indicate that the
new ground involves a change of the subject matter. Since the determination of a *res judicata* issue often in itself is a complex matter, it is
frequently not possible to draw firm conclusions from such reasoning,
however.

In precedent cases, the Supreme Court has taken a liberal view on
amendments of the grounds.[21]

Supplemental pleadings

As exceptions (1) and (3) to the prohibition against the amendment of
claims set out above make clear, the plaintiff can supplement his pleadings
regarding matters that have occurred since the original pleadings were
filed.

Joinder of claims and parties

Mandatory joinder

If a plaintiff simultaneously files several claims, and thus several suits,
against the same defendant, the claims will be joined and heard in the
same case if they are based on essentially the same ground.[22]

The same rule applies if one plaintiff simultaneously commences actions against several defendants or several plaintiffs commence actions
against one or several defendants.[23] A counterclaim should be heard in
the same case as the main claim.[24]

If a third party wishes to file a suit against one or both parties to a
commenced action regarding the disputed subject matter, the third party's
claim will be joined in the case.[25] If the claim of the third party is filed at
the time of the main hearing or otherwise when the case is about to be
adjudicated, such a claim could be heard separately if it would be inconvenient to have it joined in the original case.[26]

21. Cf. NJA 1988 p. 161.
22. Code of Judicial Procedure, Chapter 14, Section 1.
23. Code of Judicial Procedure, Chapter 14, Section 2.
24. Cf. below.
25. Code of Judicial Procedure, Chapter 14, Section 4.
26. Code of Judicial Procedure, Chapter 14, Section 7.

General prerequisites for the joinder of parties and claims pursuant to the aforesaid provisions are that the different suits are filed with the same court. Such court is competent to hear all suits and the same trial procedure applies to all suits.[27]

With respect to venue, a plaintiff is entitled to sue all defendants in a multi-party litigation in a court where any of them could be sued, provided that the plaintiff's claims against the different defendants are based on essentially the same ground and that the suits are filed at the same time.[28]

Optional joinder of claims and parties

Pursuant to the general rule in Chapter 14, Section 6, the court in its sole discretion has the option to join parties and claims to be heard as one case, provided that such handling benefits the investigation of the matters before the court. The different cases can be separated again at a later stage if this should prove more efficient.

It is also possible to join parties and claims from different courts into one court.

Counterclaims

The general rule is that the defendant has the possibility of bringing a counterclaim against the plaintiff and have it heard in the same case, if the counterclaim concerns the same matter as the main claim or a matter related thereto or could be set-off against the main claim.[29] The Code's rules on venue also provide that a counterclaim will be heard by the court seized with the main claim.[30] The general prerequisites for the joinder of claims are that the same trial procedure will apply to the claims joined, and must also be met in the case of a counterclaim.

In this context, it should be noted that the defendant has the option to invoke a counterclaim for set-off against the main claim as a defence rather than as a separate and independent suit. A counterclaim invoked as a defence will not result in an enforceable judgment with respect to that part of the counterclaim that exceeds the main claim, if any. At the same time the defendant is barred from raising the counterclaim in a new

27. Code of Judicial Procedure, Chapter 14, Section 7.
28. Code of Judicial Procedure, Chapter 10, Section 14.
29. Code of Judicial Procedure, Chapter 14, Section 3.
30. Code of Judicial Procedure, Chapter 10, Section 14.

action if it is invalidated as defence in the first trial.[31] Thus, it is not advisable to invoke a counterclaim as defence only, if it considerably exceeds the main claim.

Impleader

If a party foresees that in the event of losing in a litigation claim, he will have a claim for indemnification and recovery of damages or similar claims against a third party (for example, against a co-tort-feasor), then he is entitled to have a suit against such a party joined to the original litigation.[32] This also applies to a third party who, depending on the outcome of a pending litigation, wishes to file suit against one or both of the original parties.

Interpleader

Interpleader relief is not set out in the Code. However, under the Swedish Act of Deposition of Funds with the Authorities,[33] a debtor who has valid reasons to be uncertain as to who is legally entitled to receive payment can discharge his payment obligation by depositing the amount due with the County Authority. The debtor must then notify the possible claimant(s) of the deposit.

If the reason for the debtor's uncertainty is the existence of several competing claimants, with each asserting an exclusive right to receive payment, the County Authority is prohibited from dispensing the deposited funds until the matter has been resolved by a final judgment or out of court settlement.

Intervention

Under the Code, intervention is possible for anyone who asserts that the subject matter of the pending suit affects his legal rights and can give probable cause for such assertion. An example is an insurer.

An ordinary intervenor does not have standing as an independent party in the action. The intervenor must not make any dispositions in the proceedings that interfere with or contravene those of the party on whose side he intervenes.

31. Code of Judicial Procedure, Chapter 17, Sections 4 and 11.
32. Code of Judicial Procedure, Chapter 14, Section 5.
33. SFS 1927:56.

A third party who would be bound directly by the judgment is eligible to intervene as an independent intervenor. An independent intervenor thus must stand in a relationship of privity to one of the parties to the suit for *res judicata* purposes. Examples of this kind of relationship include a partner when his partnership is sued by a partnership creditor or an association member in a lawsuit between other members and the association regarding the validity of an association resolution.

An independent intervenor's standing as a party in the proceedings includes the right to appeal.

OBTAINING INFORMATION PRIOR TO TRIAL

Types of discovery

Discovery proceedings as they exist under, for example, the rules of United States civil procedure have no equivalent under the Code in Sweden. Instead, the fact finding stage is handled by the parties' counsels, out of court, when preparing for the trial.

Once the litigation has commenced, documentary production can be ordered by the court on petition of one of the parties, but is then confined to rather specific documents identified by the party seeking the production.

Depositions of testimony can only be obtained in order to secure evidence for a possible future trial that otherwise could be lost, for example, hearing testamentary witnesses who might be deceased at the time the validity of the will may become disputed.[34]

INTERIM PROTECTION OF ASSETS PENDING TRIAL

General

A petition for provisional attachment or interlocutory injunction can be filed separately, in anticipation of the filing of a suit (or commencement of arbitral proceedings). A suit must then be filed within one month of the date of the grant of the provisional attachment or interlocutory injunction.

Normally, the adversary must be heard over an application for provisional measures, but if a delay appears to entail danger of loss to the plaintiff, the court may issue a temporary order *ex parte*.

The plaintiff is obliged to provide security for any damage that the adversary could incur due to the court's grant of provisional measures.

---

34. Code of Judicial Procedure, Chapter 41.

The sufficiency of the security is determined by the court unless accepted by the adversary. The security is normally provided in the form of a bank guarantee but could also be provided as other surety or pledge.

Provisional attachment

The prerequisites for provisional attachment are fulfilled in two different situations. A court can issue an order for provisional attachment if:

(1) A plaintiff shows probable cause for the existence of a money claim which is or is likely to become the object of court or similar proceedings (e.g., arbitration), and further it can reasonably be assumed that the debtor-defendant by escaping, hiding assets or otherwise will avoid the payment of the money claim in question; or

(2) A plaintiff shows reasonable cause for superior title to certain assets, which are or are likely to be the object of a court procedure or similar proceedings (e.g., arbitration); and it can reasonably be assumed that the defendant will hide the assets, substantially lessen their value or otherwise make dispositions with the assets that would adversely affect the plaintiff.

An order for provisional attachment pursuant to (1) above will normally not identify particular property of the debtor-defendant, but be rendered for a value corresponding to the amount of the asserted money claim. It is then for the enforcement authority to identify individual assets to be seized.

Finally, a specific court order restoring possession is possible. If it becomes obvious during the proceedings in a suit regarding superior title to certain property that one of the parties has unlawfully deprived the other party of his possession or otherwise taken any unlawful action with the property in question, the court can issue an order for immediate restoration of the possession of the property or other measures to cure the unlawful situation.

Interlocutory injunction

Outside the scope of the rules on provisional attachment, the court can issue an interlocutory injunction against one of the parties or prospective parties to a lawsuit.

An interlocutory injunction usually involves the prohibiting of the (prospective) defendant under penalty of a fine from taking action that would prevent or render difficult the exercise of the plaintiff's alleged right. Such order could also mean that the defendant must undertake certain actions, for example, preserve the condition and/or the value of the disputed property or a disputed right. The court generally has the discretion to draft the contents of the interlocutory injunction as to fit the circumstances in each specific case.

SUMMARY JUDGMENTS

Adjudication without trial or by special proceeding

Unfounded claims for relief

Should the court find that the plaintiff's claim for relief lacks legal merits or if it is otherwise obvious that the claim for relief is unfounded, the court may immediately, and without issuing summons, dismiss the case with prejudice.[35]

Judgment through executive authority proceedings

There are three types of summary proceedings before the executive authorities with respect to civil claims: Dunning proceedings, proceedings regarding ordinary authority assistance and proceedings regarding special authority assistance.

DUNNING PROCEEDINGS

The relief available in Dunning proceedings is an order for the debtor to pay a civil money-claim that is due. If the money-claim is secured by a mortgage in real property, a ship or ship being built, or a floating charge that has been pledged in writing as security, the relief could also include that the debt must be satisfied by the realisation of the property in question. Dunning proceedings are not possible against a debtor who resides in a foreign State that has acceded to the Lugano Convention.

The application for relief is filed with the executive authority in the county in which the debtor resides or where the debtor possesses property or where enforcement of a decision would otherwise be convenient. The written application for a decision only needs to state the claim, that is, the amount claimed, the due date and the interest claimed, and the grounds invoked as a basis therefore.

35. Code of Judicial Procedure, Chapter 42, Section 5.

After a formal review by the authorities, the application is served on the debtor. From the date of service of the application, the debtor has a time period fixed by the executive authority, normally not longer than two weeks, to submit a response to the claim. If the debtor contests the claim, it is enough for him to simply state this in his response. It is then up to the applicant to request that the case be referred to a District Court for trial. Such request must be submitted within three weeks of the applicant's receipt of the debtor's response from the executive authority.

If the debtor has not responded to the application within the time period set forth by the executive authority, the authority must issue an order in accordance with the applicant's prayer for relief. The applicant is also entitled to (a modest) reimbursement for costs. The order issued is subsequently enforced automatically by the executive authority, unless the applicant has declined enforcement in his application.

The debtor may apply for a reopening of the matter by filing an application with the executive authority within one month of the date of the order. The matter will then be referred to a District Court for further hearing. An applicant who is not content with the issued order has the right to appeal to the relevant District Court within three weeks of the order.

If no request for reopening or appeal is filed, the order becomes final and has the same value, with respect to *res judicata*, as an ordinary judgment.

ORDINARY AUTHORITY ASSISTANCE

Ordinary authority assistance may be requested with respect to evictions and the performance of obligations other than payment obligations, provided that the obligation in question is due. The rules on Dunning procedures as described above apply *mutatis mutandis* in this kind of proceeding.

SPECIAL AUTHORITY ASSISTANCE

A request for special authority assistance may concern an order for the adversary to remedy a situation, for example, if the applicant's possession has been interfered with or other unlawful action has been taken with respect to real or personal property or if the applicant's rights to certain property are otherwise obstructed.

Special authority assistance may also be applied for when the right to such assistance follows from certain special statutory provisions.

The procedure, generally, follows the rules applied in Dunning proceedings, but with a more comprehensive exchange of writs between the parties and an obligation for the parties to submit evidence to the executive authority in support of claims and allegations.

The executive authority must also render a decision with respect to the requested assistance and the case can thus not be referred to an ordinary court for trial. Another difference is that the applicant can request an immediate interim order *ex parte* from the executive authority for the time until the final order has been issued. No security needs to be furnished in order to obtain such *ex parte* order.

An order issued on the basis of an application for special authority assistance is not subject to reopening and has no *res judicata* effect, which means that either of the parties can file suit in order to have a question resolved, for example, which of the parties has valid title to the property in question.

Summary judgment

If the fact investigation in a case does not call for a main hearing and neither of the parties demand such, the court may render its judgment directly during the preliminary stage of the trial.[36] The option of a judgment without main hearing is in the hands of the court and contingent on the consent of the parties.

Default judgments

A default judgment could follow if the defendant does not answer the summons application within the time limit set by the court. It is also a sanction against a party who fails to appear at a preliminary or main hearing. If the defendant fails to file an answer to the summons application, a default judgment will be given as a matter of course unless the plaintiff resists it.

In case of non-appearance, the adverse party must move for such judgment. If the party present does not petition for a default judgment, the case will be dismissed without prejudice unless the plaintiff — when the defendant is absent — moves for a postponement of the preliminary hearing or the party present at the main hearing moves for a main hearing despite the absence of the adverse party.

A default judgment could be "appealed" to the same court that rendered it by an application for reopening of the case. Such application must be filed within one month of the date of service of the default judgment on the defaulting party.

36. Code of Judicial Procedure, Chapter 42, Section 18, Item 5.

Other means of termination without a plenary trial

Voluntary dismissal

Before the defendant has filed his answer, the plaintiff can withdraw his action without restrictions. However, once the defendant has submitted his answer, he has the right to judgment even if the plaintiff withdraws. Thus, the possibility of voluntary dismissal without prejudice at a later stage of the proceedings depends on whether the defendant accepts such dismissal.

Dismissal for failure to prosecute

There is no specific rule in the Code on dismissal for failure to prosecute. Under the Code, the court is charged with the responsibility to see to it that the facts and evidence of the subject matter of the dispute are satisfactorily presented prior to the main hearing so that such hearing can be carried out without interruptions and delay.

If the plaintiff fails to present his case, in other words, his prayer(s) for relief, the facts and evidence in full within the time limits set forth by the court, the court has the option to set one last "grace period" within which the plaintiff must finally state his case.[37] Once this deadline is passed, the plaintiff is barred from amending or supplementing his prayer(s) for relief and invoking any further circumstances or evidence, unless he can give a valid excuse for his omission to do so earlier.

By setting a final grace period, the court can thus force the case to a main hearing and any defects in the preparation of the case that might result in the invalidation of the claims then become the plaintiff's risk.

This rule on a final grace period applies equally to the defendant.

Judicially assisted settlement

The Code expressly provides that the court must investigate the possibilities for a settlement of the dispute during the preparatory stage.[38] The court can also arrange for mediation through a court appointed mediator.[39] How much effort the court will put into promoting settlement discussions very much depends on the individual judge responsible for the preparation of the case.

37. Code of Judicial Procedure, Chapter 42, Section 15.
38. Code of Judicial Procedure, Chapter 42, Sections 6 and 17.
39. Code of Judicial Procedure, Chapter 42, Section 17.

Should the parties come to a settlement, they can jointly petition for the court's confirmation thereof.[40] Such confirmation is given in the form of a judgment setting forth the terms of the settlement. A judgment on a settlement is subject to general rules for appeal, and has the same *res judicata* effect as an ordinary judgment.

TRIAL

Setting the case for trial

When the preparatory stage of the proceedings concludes, the court must set a time for the main hearing, if possible after having heard the parties' preferences in this respect.

By this time, the parties must have specified all prayers for relief, the circumstances invoked and all written and oral evidence that they intend to put forward during the main hearing. The court may disregard any subsequent amendments in this respect that are made during the main hearing, if it can be assumed that such amendments are made in an attempt to surprise the adverse party, stall the proceedings or otherwise made in bad faith or are due to gross negligence.[41]

With the consent of the parties, a main hearing can also be held in a simplified form immediately following the preliminary hearing at which the preparation of the case was concluded (or within 15 days of such a preliminary hearing provided that the same judge hears the case).

If the outcome of the case is evident, the consent of the parties is not required in order for a simplified hearing to be held. Everything that has occurred during the preliminary hearing immediately preceding the simplified main hearing is deemed to have occurred also during such a main hearing and need thus not be reiterated.

Scope and order for trial

A civil case is normally heard by three judges, one of which chairs the trial. With the parties' consent, the case can be heard by one judge. Sweden has no true jury system, other than in matters regarding the freedom of the press under Swedish constitutional law, but in matrimonial and criminal matters, laypersons participate in the court.

The scope of the trial is defined by the parties prayers for relief and the invoked circumstances and evidence.

40. Code of Judicial Procedure, Chapter 17, Section 6.
41. Code of Judicial Procedure, Chapter 43, Section 10.

Three basic features of the Swedish trial system are:

(1) "Orality";
(2) "Immediacy"; and
(3) "Concentration".

Pursuant to the principle of orality, the parties are prohibited from submitting or reading writs or other written statements during the main hearing, unless the court considers this facultative to the just resolution of the matter, for example, how spoken words were understood.[42]

The principle of immediacy entails that judgment may only be based on what has occurred during the main hearing.[43] Claims and allegations made during the preparatory stage of the proceedings are excluded from consideration unless reiterated during the main hearing.

The principle of concentration means that the main hearing should be held in one session until the case is ready to be adjudicated. However, in large cases, the court can decide to sit on three or, if special reasons can be invoked, two days each week.

If it nonetheless becomes necessary to adjourn the main hearing, one or several times, the hearing will on each new occasion continue from where it was left off. If the total delay exceeds 15 days, the entire main hearing must start anew.

The main hearing starts with an investigation by the chairperson of the court as to whether there is any obstacle to the main hearing taking place. If no such obstacle is presented or if an obstacle is envisaged to be removed before the end of the hearing, the trial commences by the plaintiff stating his prayers for relief and the defendant stating his position, admitting or contesting the relief requested.

Thereafter, the parties deliver their respective opening speeches and comment on what has been stated by the adverse party. Frequently, the presentation of written evidence is to some extent integrated into the opening speeches.

Submission of evidence

After the opening speeches, oral evidence is taken. If the parties or their legal representatives are to be heard, the taking of such oral evidence is done before the taking of testimony by witnesses.

The Code sets out that the questioning of the parties and the witnesses must be handled by the court, but in practice this is primarily handled by the counsel with the judge(s) posing supplemental questions.

42. Code of Judicial Procedure, Chapter 43, Section 5.
43. Code of Judicial Procedure, Chapter 17, Section 2.

The main examination of a witness is conducted by counsel for the party that has called the witness. Leading questions are in principle prohibited at this stage, and the preferred order is for the witness to be requested initially to state his testimony in his own words. However, with respect to witnesses who are unable to give a coherent account, the examination may be carried out on a question and answer basis. In practice, the latter is the only possible examination method in matters of greater complexity.

After the main examination, counsel for the adverse party has the opportunity to cross-examine. During the cross-examination, leading and argumentative questions are allowed in order to put pressure on the witness and thereby verify the validity of his earlier statements. The parties have an unlimited right to re-examination of the witness.

After hearing witnesses, the taking of oral evidence continues with any experts who have been called to testify. The procedure is the same as is the case with the examination of ordinary witnesses.

According to the principle of orality, the written evidence that has been invoked should be read into the record aloud during the main hearing. This can be done during opening speeches, in connection with witness examinations or separately, depending on what is more practical. However, with the consent of the parties it is possible and in practice common for the court to decide that parts of the written evidence should be considered taken down at the main hearing, without having been presented orally *in extenso*.[44]

Closing speeches

The main hearing is then concluded with first counsel for the plaintiff(s) and then counsel for the defendant(s) each giving a closing address (the "final pleading").[45]

The final pleadings focus on legal and evidential questions — emphasising those parts of the evidence presented that support the facts alleged by the respective parties and criticising the evidence of the adverse party. With respect to questions of law, the parties usually present precedent cases and preparatory works to the relevant statutory rules at issue. The court is not bound by the parties' arguments with respect to questions of law and is thus free to apply a legal rule which neither party has invoked (according to the principle of *jura novit curia*). However, the parties' arguments are an important source of information for the court if they are of an adequate professional standard.

44. Code of Judicial Procedure, Chapter 43, Section 8.
45. Code of Judicial Procedure, Chapter 43, Section 9.

Evidence

Nature and purpose of evidence

The Code adopts the principle of free evaluation of evidence: "The court shall after a thorough examination of everything that has occurred decide what has been proven in the case".[46] This means that "evidence" could be defined as anything that supports the existence and correctness of the circumstances alleged by a party.[47]

The purpose of the evidence is, of course, to support and substantiate the allegations as to circumstances, scientific theories, the contents of the foreign law that might be applicable and other relevant facts invoked by a party. Each party is obliged to submit a statement of evidence during the preliminary stage of the proceedings, setting forth for each item of evidence what the party wishes to prove by the evidence in question — the "theme of evidence".

The requirement for the theme of evidence to be stated has at least two functions. Firstly, it facilitates the adverse party's assessment of what counter-evidence he may need to produce; and secondly, it provides the court with an opportunity to assess the relevance of the evidence for the case and, if irrelevant, refuse its presentation.[48] The production of evidence lies with the parties. The court has a subsidiary right to take initiative in order to obtain evidence in a case "if necessary". However, in a commercial case this right to initiative is limited to recalling a witness who has been heard at the request of one of the parties.

Kinds of evidence

ORAL EVIDENCE

Witnesses

The general rule is that any one who is not a party to the suit may be heard as a witness. However, if the witness is under 15 years of age or suffers from mental disorder, the court will decide whether he or she should give testimony.

Anyone who can give testimony is under a statutory duty to do so, and could be forced to testify on the penalty of a fine or, ultimately, under threat of custody.

46. Code of Judicial Procedure, Chapter 35, Section 1.
47. Cf. below regarding the different kinds of evidence expressly set forth in the Code.
48. Code of Judicial Procedure, Chapter 35, Section 7.

Close relatives of a party are exempt from the duty to testify. Such relatives include anyone who is or has been married to the party, is in a direct lineal blood relation with the party or is or has been married to a person who is a sibling of a party or is close to a party in a way similar to those described (for example, cohabits with a party without being married).

With respect to legal privilege, it should be noted that a member of the Swedish bar (an *Advokat*) is exempt from the obligation to give testimony regarding matters entrusted to him unless the client in question gives his approval.

Also, certain groups of professionals, for example, physicians, dentists, nurses, psychologists, and psychotherapists, are exempt from the duty to testify as regards matters that they have gained knowledge of in their practice, unless the individual concerned gives his approval. Priests cannot be heard on such matters — even if consent is given.

As to the facts that a witness could be compelled to reveal, it should be noted that a witness is not obliged to make statements which would disclose trade secrets, unless special reasons can be invoked, or reveal that the witness or any of his close relatives committed a criminal offence or other dishonourable act.

A witness is generally heard under oath with the exception of individuals under 15 years of age or suffering from mental disorder.

Party testimony

A party, natural person or representative of a legal entity, may give testimony either under oath or without being sworn.

Expert witness

The general rule of the Code is that an expert witness is retained by the court and on its initiative, if the adjudication of the matter before it requires access to specific professional knowledge in a certain field. Before the appointment of an expert witness, the court should seek the advice of the parties as to whom to appoint. Where the parties agree on someone to be appointed, the court should follow their recommendation unless there are reasons not to do so.

Those who are eligible for appointment are public authorities or officials assigned to render opinions on the subject matter in question and private individuals known for expertise in the relevant field.

However, a party is also free to retain a private expert witness of his choice beside the one appointed by the court, if any. In practice, privately retained experts are probably more common than court-appointed ones.

During the preparatory stage of the proceedings, an expert witness must submit a written opinion containing his findings and conclusions on the subject matter which requires his expertise. The expert is also heard during the main hearing if the court finds it necessary, or if requested by one of the parties and such examination does not appear superfluous.

WRITTEN EVIDENCE

A document that is invoked as written evidence must be submitted to the court in original or as a certified copy.

Anyone who possesses a document that could be used as written evidence is obliged to provide such a document.[49] On request of one of the parties, the court can issue an order under the penalty of a fine for production of the document in question. The court can also choose to have the document produced with the assistance of the executive authority.

The party requesting documents to be produced must clearly identify the documents and establish their relevance as evidence in the case. Should the party not be able to give an adequate description of the documents in question, the court can examine particular witnesses under oath in order to obtain more precise information in this respect.

The duty to provide documentation does not extend to written messages between a party and his relatives or between such relatives.[50] Nor does it include documents possessed by an *Advokat* or other professional if the contents of the documents could be assumed to be of such nature that the *Advokat* or other professional could not be heard as a witness in this respect. If such exempted documentation is held by a party in the litigation, the party in favour of whom the aforementioned duty of secrecy applies is not obliged to produce the documentation in court.

The exemption from the duty to testify with respect to circumstances that might reveal that the witness has committed a criminal offence or might disclose a trade secret applies *mutatis mutandis* to the duty to produce documents with such impact.

Notes taken for personal use are not covered by the duty to produce documents, unless there is exceptional cause for demanding such notes to be submitted.

TANGIBLE EVIDENCE

The Code sets out rules on production of tangible evidence, which correspond to those regarding documents outlined above.

49. Code of Judicial Procedure, Chapter 38, Section 2(1).
50. For the definition of relatives, see under Witness above.

In order to examine real property or objects that cannot be moved to the court, a hearing may be held at the place of the property in question.

JUDGMENTS AND KINDS OF RELIEF

Final judgment

If the court has been composed of more than one judge at the main hearing, it will convene for deliberation on the judgment within the same day as the main hearing or the following work day. Should the nature of the case call for additional time for deliberation, the court could decide for an extension of the time within which the judgment will be rendered. Such extension must not exceed two weeks unless the court could invoke severe hindrance for the rendering of judgment.[51] In practice, the work loads of the courts cause further delays, but usually such delay does not exceed one month.

If the court, during the deliberation on judgment, find that it is necessary to complete the investigation in some respect, it can decide on a continued or new main hearing, or, if the necessary completion is uncomplicated, to obtain further information under hand.[52]

Piecemeal judgments

With respect to several individual claims for relief that are handled in the same case, the court may render a separate (partial) judgment over any of them. However, separate judgments must not be given on a main claim or a defendant's claim for set-off.

If the defendant partly admits a claim, the court can render a separate (interim) judgment regarding the admitted part.

The court is also free to adjudicate one of the several threshold issues in a separate (interim) judgment if this would expedite the hearing of the case. The threshold issue could concern both factual circumstances and legal issues. If the court issues an interim judgment, it can stay the proceedings until such judgment that can be appealed separately, has become final.

Entry of judgment

A judgment is issued in writing and should set out the following:

51. Code of Judicial Procedure, Chapter 17, Section 9.
52. Code of Judicial Procedure, Chapter 43, Section 14.

(1) The court, the time and place for rendering the judgment;
(2) The parties and their counsels;
(3) The judgment order;
(4) The parties' prayers for relief and objections, and the circumstance invoked as a basis therefore; and
(5) The judgment's opinion and the court's findings as to evidentiary facts of the case.[53]

The judgment is ordinarily rendered by being made available at the office of the court.[54] In simple cases, it can be rendered orally and documented in writing later.

Kinds of relief

Specific performance

A general prerequisite for the admissibility of a claim for specific performance is that the underlying claim is due.

However, a claim for specific performance of an obligation not yet due is allowed in the following situations:

(1) If the claim concerns a recurring obligation which is not contingent on any counter performance, and part of such obligation is due;
(2) If and when another obligation, which is also covered by the prayers for relief in question, is not timely performed;
(3) If the obligation is the duty to pay interest until there is full settlement of a due debt or other incidental obligation which follows from the main obligation claimed;
(4) If timely performance of the obligation is of extraordinary importance for the plaintiff and there are specific reasons to assume that the defendant will fail to perform in time; and
(5) If the right to claim specific performance of an obligation not due follows from statutory provisions.

Declaratory judgments

A claim for a declaratory judgment is a request that the court should establish the existence or non-existence of a certain legal right or obligation.

53. Code of Judicial Procedure, Chapter 17, Section 7.
54. Code of Judicial Procedure, Chapter 17, Section 9.

In order for the court to allow a claim for a declaratory judgment, the plaintiff must show that there is uncertainty as to the existence of a legal right or obligation and that such uncertainty is detrimental to the plaintiff.

It is not permissible to seek advisory opinions from the court on hypothetical legal issues, such as the proper interpretation of a certain statutory provision, nor to obtain declaratory judgments on solely factual questions, for example, the authenticity of a painting.

Costs

General principles

The basic rule is that costs follow the event. If the case results in a judgment which is only partly in the claimant's favour, the court will divide the costs pursuant to intricate principles, the main idea of which is to reflect the measure of success each party has had.

If an action is dismissed without prejudice, the relevant claimant is considered to be the losing party. A party withdrawing his action is also liable to reimburse the defendant's costs unless special reasons can be invoked. In case of a settlement, each party bears its own costs, unless otherwise agreed.

Costs eligible for reimbursement from the losing party include attorney's fees, work done by the party himself in order to prepare the case and costs for evidence.

A claim for costs must be put forward before the hearing of the case is concluded by the court in question. The relevant point of time is normally the end of the main hearing, after the parties have delivered their closing arguments.

Apportionment of costs

Costs may be apportioned as a remedy against party negligence. A party who is eventually found to have initiated legal proceedings without sufficient cause therefore, for example, if the claim is undisputed and the defendant is ready to perform, or who has otherwise intentionally or negligently brought an unmotivated action — is liable to reimburse the adverse party for his costs, regardless of the outcome the litigation.

Non-appearance at court hearings, failure to abide by the court's procedural orders, unfounded assertions or contentions made in bad faith or negligently, causing of delay in the proceedings or otherwise causing unnecessary costs for the adverse party could also make the party at fault liable to stand any additional costs caused by him, regardless of the outcome of the case.

Security for the defendant's litigation costs

Pursuant to a separate Swedish Act,[55] a foreign claimant is obliged to furnish security for the defendant's potential claim for litigation costs at the request of the defendant. The defendant must request for such security at the time of his first appearance, or the right to claim security is forfeited. Foreign claimants from states that have acceded to certain conventions are exempt from the duty to furnish security.

The rationale behind the obligation for foreign claimants to furnish security for litigation costs is the limited enforceability of a Swedish judgment on costs outside Sweden (where the foreign claimant's assets are presumed to be located).

Because of Sweden's accession to the Lugano Convention, this rationale has no bearing on foreign plaintiffs from states that have also acceded to the Convention. However, the Swedish Act that sets out the requirement to provide security for litigation costs has not yet been amended in order to exempt foreign plaintiff's from states who have acceded to the Lugano Convention.

Furthermore, the Lugano Convention does not contain any general non-discrimination provision, but only touches on the issue of furnishing security in connection with the rules on exequator in its Article 45. In a recent lawsuit, this issue came in focus. The Court of Appeal found in favour of the foreign plaintiff and noted that the Convention purported to treat parties domiciled in Contracting States in the same manner so that a party could not be discriminated on the grounds of citizenship or nationality.

The Court also found that since according to the Lugano Convention a judgment given by a Swedish court would be enforceable in the plaintiff's country, there was no need for the furnishing of security. The Court, thus, found that the application of the relevant Act on furnishing of security contravened the Convention and gave the Convention priority over the Swedish internal provisions. This case is currently before the Supreme Court on appeal.

POST-TRIAL MOTIONS

The Code provides three different means of obtaining a re-trial even when a judgment has become final pursuant to the ordinary provisions on appeal. These are:

(1) Relief for substantive defects;
(2) Restoration of time expired; and
(3) Relief for grave procedural error.

55. SFS 1980 : 307.

Relief for substantive defects

Relief for substantive defects is available on the following grounds:

(1) If new circumstances or evidence are invoked and such circumstances or evidence would have lead the court to a different conclusion in its adjudication of the case, provided that the claimant shows a valid excuse for his failure to invoke the circumstances or evidence earlier;

(2) If a written document which has been invoked as evidence proves to have been forged or if testimony proves to have been false and such false documentary evidence or statements may be assumed to have affected the outcome of the case;

(3) If the application of the law in the case has been manifestly wrong; and

(4) If a member of the court or a court official is guilty of criminal conduct or breach of duty which relates to the case, or a counsel or a legal representative of a party is guilty of criminal conduct which relates to the case, provided that the criminal conduct or breach of duty may be assumed to have affected the outcome of the case.

Relief is sought by making an application to the relevant Court of Appeal if the attacked judgment has been rendered by a District Court, while in other cases the application is filed with the Supreme Court. Such an application must be filed within one year of the date at which the applicant became aware of the circumstances on which his application for relief is founded, or in the alternative, if the ground for relief is criminal conduct of a relevant person, within one year from the date when a verdict against such person became final. An application based on erroneous application of the law must be filed within six months from the date when the attacked judgment became final.

If the relief is granted, the court must order a new trial but, it may, if the case is clear, directly adjust the judgment.

Restoration of expired time

This relief opens the possibility of having the time limits for appeal or application for reopening of a case restored if a party can invoke a valid excuse for not having filed the appeal or application in time.

The concept of "valid excuse" is defined in the Code as:

". . . when someone due to an interruption in the ordinary means of communication, illness or other circumstance, which he ought not have reasonable foreseen or the court otherwise finds to constitute a valid excuse, has been kept from fulfilling his obligations."

A party can invoke a valid excuse on the part of his counsel provided that he did not have the time to retain new counsel.

An application for restoration of expired time must, if concerning a case entertained by a District Court be filed with the relevant Court of Appeal. Otherwise such an application must be filed with the Supreme Court.

Relief for grave procedural error

This relief can be sought by anyone whose rights are affected by a judgment. The grounds on which the relief can be sought are:

(1) If the case has been entertained despite the existence of a procedural hindrance which, on appeal, a higher court is obliged to consider on its own initiative;

(2) If the judgment has been given against or affects someone not properly summoned, or who has not appeared in the case;

(3) If the judgment is ambiguously drafted or incomplete such that it is not clear how the court has adjudicated the subject matter of the case; or

(4) If during the proceedings a grave procedural error occured which may be assumed to have affected the outcome of the case.

An application for relief must be filed with the relevant Court of Appeal if the judgment has been given by a District Court. Otherwise the application must be filed with the Supreme Court. The application must be filed within six months from the date when the attacked judgment became final. If the applicant has not appeared in the case, this time period runs from the date when he became aware of the judgment in question.

ENFORCEMENT AND EXECUTION OF JUDGMENTS

General remarks

The statutory provisions on enforcement of judgments are set out in the Code on Execution of Judgments. An application for enforcement of a judement is filed with the executive authority in the County where the defendant resides. The judgment forming the basis of the application must be enclosed with it. A judgment regarding a money-claim that is still subject to appeal, or has been appealed against, may be enforced as a final judgment unless the defendant provides security for his future performance according to the judgment. A non-final judgment regarding repossession of personal property may also be enforced if the applicant provides security for the return of the relevant property, including any yield thereof.

Remedies

The available remedies are attachment, eviction and "other kinds of enforcement".

Attachment

Attachment is the general remedy for the enforcement of money-claims. An application for attachment is filed with the executive authority of the County where the defendant resides or where his assets are located. Attachment on aircraft or ships may also — if available — be sought with the executive authority of the County to which the relevant aircraft or ship is expected to arrive. With respect to ships, a further alternative is the executive authority of the place where the ship is registered.

Attachment on a claim or other right may also be sought with the executive authority of the place where the relevant debtor or obligee is residing. Attachment on salary payments or other attachable benefit may be sought with the executive authority of the place where the employer or the one who performs the payment of the benefit resides. Following an application for attachment, the executive authority undertakes an investigation as to the existence of attachable assets of the defendant.

All the assets of the debtor that are not excluded under law can be subject to attachment. The Code on Execution of Judgments sets out a list of certain kinds of personal property that are exempt from attachment and the minimum amount of cash that must be reserved for the debtor.

It should be noted, however that an asset pledged as security for a debt can be subject to attachment for the satisfaction of such a debt regardless of the aforesaid exemptions.

Attachment is secured by either having the property in question taken into the custody of the executive authority or by marking it with a legend evidencing that it is subject to attachment.

Current salary payments and social security benefits of various kinds are also subject to attachment so long as they exceed what the debtor must have to support himself and his family and also to fulfil other maintenance obligations. The executive authority decides the amount that must be paid in directly to the executive authority by the employer or state agency administrating the social security benefits. The time period for attachment must not exceed six months in any one calendar year or exceed six consecutive months if the period of attachment overlaps the year end.

Eviction

The application for eviction must be filed with the executive authority of the County where the defendant resides or where the eviction will be carried out.

Eviction is carried out either with the assistance of officials from the executive authority or by the issuance of an order to the defendant to handle the eviction himself. Such an order requires the consent of the applicant and can be coupled with a penalty of fine.

Other kinds of enforcement

Enforcement other than attachment and eviction is carried out through the executive authority's issuance of an order for the defendant to perform the obligation in question or adhere to a prohibition or other direction or by the direct assistance of the executive authority. On request from the applicant, the executive authority may, if it is considered appropriate, allow the applicant to undertake the necessary measures himself pursuant to its instructions.

An order by the executive authority may be coupled with a penalty of a fine.

Provisions in a judgment as to the method for enforcement are not binding on the executive authority if it is necessary to apply an alternative measure in order to have the judgment enforced. An application for enforcement of the kind now discussed must be filed with the executive authority of the place where the defendant resides, or where the property concerned is or where the conditions for enforcement otherwise are advantageous.

Bankruptcy

The enforcement of a judgment could eventually result in the defendant being declared bankrupt. The Bankruptcy Code sets out different legal presumptions of insolvency, one of them being that it must be established through attachment proceedings that the defendant lacks sufficient assets to satisfy the debt for which attachment has been sought. A petition for bankruptcy may then be filed with the court of the place where the defendant resides within six months from the date of the executive authority's finding as to the insufficiency of the assets of the defendant.

Lugano Convention

The text of the Lugano Convention has *in extenso* been enacted as law in Sweden through an Act after Sweden's accession to the Lugano Convention,[56] which entered into force on 1 January 1993.

An application for enforcement must be filed with the Svea Court of Appeal. If the application is approved, the foreign judgment is enforceable to the same extent and in the same manner as a final Swedish judgment, but subject to Article 39 of the Lugano Convention regarding prohibition of enforcement during the time limits for appeal of the decision to grant enforcement. If the foreign judgment concerns provisional measures, the Code of Execution provisions on enforcement of such measures will apply.

A decision to grant enforcement will be deemed to include a decision on provisional measures pursuant to Chapter 15, of the Code. This rule is motivated by the need for the applicant to secure the future enforcement of the judgment during the time period for appeal set out in Article 36 of the Lugano Convention.

APPEAL

Issues subject to review

The Swedish court system is a three-tier system with courts of first instance — District Courts, Courts of Appeal — six Courts of Appeal, and the Supreme Court.

The Courts of Appeal undertake a full review of a case on appeal — including legal, factual and evidentiary aspects thereof. One existing limit on the Courts of Appeals' power to amend a lower court's judgment is the "credibility rule" which means that the Courts of Appeal may not amend a lower court's judgment without re-examination of oral evidence, if the outcome of the case in the lower court was based on the credibility of such evidence. The rule on *reformatio in pejus* also applies meaning that the Courts of Appeal must not amend a judgment to the disadvantage of the appellant, unless there is a cross-appeal.

Certain restrictions on appeal of District Court judgments apply if the value of the disputed subject matter does not exceed certain statutory amounts.

The role of the Supreme Court is mainly to provide precedent cases on issues of law. The right to have a case tried in the Supreme Court is accordingly subject to the Supreme Court's grant of dispensation for review. A dispensation can be granted if:

56. SFS 1992 : 974.

(1) It is of importance for guidance on the application of law that the case be heard by the Supreme Court; or

(2) There are exceptional reasons such as the existence of grounds for relief for substantive defects or grave procedural error or that the outcome of the case in the Court of Appeal clearly has been caused by a gross mistake.

Thus, the court system in most cases consists of only two instances.

Procedures for appeal

An appeal against a lower court judgment, or a decision by which (part of) an action is dismissed is filed as a regular appeal (*vad*), while an appeal against other kinds of lower court decisions is filed as a limited appeal (*besvär*).

A default judgment is not appealable (but on application the case could be reopened by the court that has issued the default judgment).

An appeal against a judgment or decision of a District Court must be addressed to the relevant Court of Appeal, but it must be filed with the District Court that rendered the judgment. The appeal must be filed within three weeks from the date of the judgment. An appeal against a judgment of a Court of Appeal must be filed, within four weeks of the date of the judgment, with the Court of Appeal that rendered the judgment.

CONCLUSIVENESS OF JUDGMENT

The Code contains an express provision on the *res judicata* effect of a final judgment, and states that the subject matter adjudicated through the judgment must not be heard anew.[57]

The *res judicata* effect manifests itself in two different situations. The first is that a court must dismiss, on its own motion, a suit regarding a subject matter adjudicated through an earlier judgment. The *res judicata* effect also extends to grounds for relief granted or invalidated through the judgment or alternative grounds for contesting the relief sought other than those actually invoked by the parties and tried by the court in rendering the judgment. However, a claim for set-off is not covered by this extended *res judicata* effect.

The second aspect of *res judicata* is the prejudicial effect of a judgment, which means that a court in a subsequent litigation where the claim is not the same must base its conclusion on the contents of the prior judgment.

57. Code of Judicial Procedure, Chapter 17, Section 11.

An example of this is that an earlier judgment declaring that a certain contract is valid is binding on the parties and the court in subsequent proceedings regarding the payment of the purchase sum under such contract. It should be noted, however that it is only the judgment order as such which has this effect and not the findings of the court on which the judgment order is based.

CHAPTER 15

SWITZERLAND

Markus Wirth, Thomas Müller, Ueli Huber,
Franz Hoffet and René Bösch
Homburger Rechtsanwälte
Zürich, Switzerland

ESTABLISHING JURISDICTION

Preliminary remarks

A number of factors distinguish the jurisdictional system in Switzerland.

Irrelevance of service of process within the country

Whether service of process can be effected on a defendant within Switzerland is irrelevant for the determination of jurisdiction by the Swiss courts. Instead, other determinants such as attachment with respect to the parties to a lawsuit or the subject matter of the claim are determinative. In this respect, the jurisdictional system is the same as in all other continental European jurisdictions but fundamentally different from the English one.

Multiple set of jurisdictional rules

The Federal Constitution basically attributes legislative competence in civil procedure to the cantons (of which there are 26 in Switzerland). Accordingly, the jurisdictional rules applicable to domestic civil and commercial disputes are to be found in the cantonal codes of civil procedure (CCP).

"Domestic disputes" means disputes between parties domiciled or resident in Switzerland. Article 59 of the Federal Constitution intervenes by providing that a solvent debtor must always be sued for personal matters before the court of the canton where he has his habitual residence. Federal legislation further supersedes the cantonal jurisdictional rules in special areas of law where it was thought necessary to provide for unified federal jurisdictional rules to secure the implementation of private substantive law. Such areas include intellectual property law and unfair competition law.

Separately, the Federal Act on Private International Law (PILA) determines jurisdiction in international civil and commercial disputes. "International disputes" means disputes where one of the involved parties is not domiciled or resident in Switzerland. The rules of the PILA largely conform with the cantonal jurisdictional rules (applicable to domestic litigation); where they do not, the PILA rules prevail in international disputes.

With respect to disputes involving residents from European Union or EFTA countries, the jurisdictional rules set forth in the Convention on Jurisdiction and Enforcement of Judgements in Civil and Commercial Matters of 16 September 1988 (the Lugano Convention) apply. These rules prevail over the rules of the PILA otherwise applicable in international civil and commercial litigation.

Different aspects of jurisdiction

Which court has jurisdiction over a defendant in a civil or commercial dispute must be determined under three different aspects: Under territorial aspects it must be determined in terms of district, canton or country, where a defendant must be sued. Depending on the subject matter of the claim, it must be determined before which court of a specific territory a defendant must be sued and, again depending on the subject matter of the claim and the type of relief sought, it is either a single judge, the presiding judge or a collegiate judicial body that is competent to rule.

The following will concentrate on the determination of jurisdiction under territorial aspects as this is the primary determinative element. Once the place where a suit must be brought is determined, it follows from the applicable cantonal code of civil procedure which court, within the applicable district or canton, is the proper forum.

Jurisdictional rules in domestic civil and commercial disputes

Natural forum — defendant's domicile

According to all cantonal codes of civil procedure, actions in civil and commercial matters must generally be brought before the courts at the place of the defendant's domicile.[1] The domicile of a person, natural or corporate, is generally determined in accordance with the rules of the Swiss Civil Code (CC).

Article 23 of the CC defines the domicile of a natural person as the place where a person resides with the intention of settling. The distinction in English law between domicile of origin and domicile of choice is unknown to Swiss law.

1. For example, Zürich CCP, Section 2 I.

Where a defendant has given up his previous domicile without establishing a new one, or if he does not have a domicile in Switzerland, an action can be brought against him at the place of his habitual Swiss residence.[2]

The domicile of a corporation or other legal entity is the domicile registered with the commercial register or, if there is no such registration, the domicile designated in the corporation's articles of incorporation or association.[3] The same applies to partnerships (insofar as they have standing to be sued, i.e., the action must not be brought against the partners directly).

Constitutional guarantee of the judge of the domicile

Article 59 of the Federal Constitution intervenes by providing that a solvent debtor must be sued for personal matters before the judge of the place where he has his domicile. This so-called constitutional guarantee of the natural judicial forum delimits jurisdiction between the cantons. In other words, it only defines the canton competent within the inter-cantonal relationship and not the court competent within the canton itself.

The guarantee is only applicable in the case of claims arising from the Code of Obligations (CO) and not with respect to actions *in rem* or disputes concerning family law or the laws of succession. The guarantee can only be invoked by a debtor who is still solvent and who has a domicile in Switzerland. Article 59 of the Federal Constitution prevails over contradictory cantonal rules but has no effect *vis-à-vis* federal legislation, providing for a special forum other than at the place of the defendant's domicile. This is so because in Switzerland federal legislation cannot be judicially examined as to its conformity with the Constitution.

Special forums

Apart from the natural forum, the cantonal codes of civil procedure and federal legislation provide for various special fora. Depending on the subject matter of the claim, the special fora may be subsidiary, i.e., exist only if there is no natural forum in Switzerland (the defendant has no Swiss domicile). In other cases, the special fora are alternative *fora,* meaning that the plaintiff can choose between the natural forum and the special forum according to his preference. Certain special fora are exclusive, i.e., prevail over the natural forum.

2. For example, Zürich CCP, Section 2 II.
3. CC, Article 56.

The following enumeration lists the most important special fora with respect to civil and commercial claims. Some may not be available in all cantons.

PLACE OF A DEFENDANT'S BRANCH OFFICE

Actions relating to the business operations of a defendant's branch can be brought at the place where the branch is located. This forum is not exclusive; actions can also be brought at the place of the defendant's domicile.[4] With respect to corporations, federal law[5] explicitly provides for the special forum of the branch: Actions relating to the business activities of a branch can be brought either at the corporation's domicile or at the place of the branch as recorded in the commercial register or, if the branch is not recorded, at the actual location of the branch provided the branch has a certain independence in terms of its organisation and its way of operation.[6]

ELECTED DOMICILE FOR THE PERFORMANCE OF AN OBLIGATION

Where a party has elected, in writing, a special domicile for the performance of an obligation, such party can be sued before the courts of the elected domicile.[7] Some cantonal codes of civil procedure provide for restrictions in that a special forum can only be created by an elected domicile if the party has otherwise its domicile or a branch in the respective canton, or if the electing party is a Swiss citizen domiciled abroad.[8]

PLACE OF A DECEASED'S LAST DOMICILE

Actions by the creditors of a deceased's estate against the estate must be brought before the courts of the deceased's last domicile as long as the estate has not been divided among the heirs and the heirs have not yet formed a community of property.[9]

Federal legislation[10] provides that actions for the invalidation or modification of a last will or for the delivery up or division of the estate must

4. Zürich CCP, Section 3.
5. CO, Article 642, para. 3.
6. BGE 103 II 201.
7. Zürich CCP, Section 4.
8. Zürich CCP, Section 11 II.
9. Zürich CCP, Section 5.
10. CC, Article 538.

also be brought before the courts of the deceased's last domicile. This special forum is an exclusive one. Case law has extended this special forum to actions of a legatee for delivery up of the legacy.[11]

PLACE OF LOCATION OF PROPERTY (FORUM REI SITAE)

Actions *in rem* involving real estate must be brought before the courts at the place where the real estate is located. This is an exclusive special forum. Actions for the performance of contractual rights relating to real estate can, but need not, be brought before the courts at the place where the property is situated.[12]

The special forum of the property's location does also exist, as an alternative forum, for actions *in rem* relating to movable property, or actions relating to claims secured by collateral in the form of movable property.[13]

PLACE OF DEBT COLLECTION, INSOLVENCY AND ATTACHMENT

The Swiss Federal Act on Debt Collection and Bankruptcy (Debt Collection Act) provides for special actions in relation to money claims, many of which are dealt with in summary or expedited proceedings. These actions must be brought at the place of debt collection or insolvency (usually the debtor's domicile). An action for the granting of an attachment order for the purpose of securing a mature money claim must be brought at the place where the property to be attached is situated. Where an attachment order is granted and property can subsequently be attached, the principal claim on the merit can be brought before the courts at the place of the attachment (*forum arresti*).[14]

PLACE OF FACTUAL CONNECTION

Several actions against the same defendant can, if they are closely connected with each other, be brought together before any court that has territorial jurisdiction over any of the actions. Where two actions against the same defendant are related in the sense that one qualifies as the principal and the other as the subsidiary one, the actions must be brought at the place of the principal claim.[15]

11. BGE 66 I 48 *et seq.*, 105 II 15.
12. Zürich CCP, Section 6.
13. Zürich CCP, Section 7.
14. *Forum arresti*, Zürich CCP, Section 9.
15. Zürich CCP, Section 13.

PLACE OF PRINCIPAL ACTION FOR COUNTER-CLAIMS

In ordinary proceedings brought against a defendant, the latter can, subject to the restrictions hereinafter explained, raise a counter-claim irrespective of whether the court would otherwise have jurisdiction to hear the counter-claim.

Counter-claims may be raised if either the counter-claim has a close factual or legal connection with the principal claim or if it may be set off against the principal claim.[16] The latter condition is of particular importance with respect to money claims. Pursuant to Article 120 of the CO, any debtor, absent a contractual agreement to the contrary, can set off any claim he has against the creditor against such creditor's claim. Where the principal action is for the payment of money, a counter-claim likewise for money can, therefore, in most instances be raised irrespective of the grounds of the counter-claim or of any connection with the principal claim.

AGREED FORUM

The cantonal codes of civil procedure allow the parties to contract out of the jurisdictional rules otherwise applicable to an existing or potential commercial dispute and select a forum by agreement. As a rule, the agreement must be in writing,[17] i.e., signed by each party that waives an ordinary forum (though the parties' signature must not necessarily be on the same document).

If consumers are involved, forum selection clauses must be conspicuous, such as in bold letters. Where an agreement provides for the jurisdiction of the courts at a specific place, it is generally assumed that the parties meant to agree on the exclusive jurisdiction of those courts.[18] Where contractual claims are assigned, the assignee is, as a rule, deemed to be bound by a jurisdictional clause agreed to by the assignor.[19]

Forum agreements are subject to certain restrictions: First, such agreements must, in principle, be limited to the selection of a specific territorial jurisdiction; normally it is not possible to select which court (for example, commercial court, district court, single judge, etc.) should be competent at the selected place.

Second, a majority of the cantonal codes of civil procedure provide that their courts are not required to accept actions brought before them on the basis of a forum selection agreement, unless one of the parties

16. Zürich CCP, Section 15.
17. Zürich CCP, Section 11.
18. ZR 89/1990, Number 83.
19. ZR 80/1981, Number 69.

involved in the dispute is domiciled or resident in the canton.[20] Third, forum selection agreements are only valid to the extent that federal (or cantonal) legislation does not provide for mandatory jurisdictional rules from which the parties cannot derogate by contract. This is the case, for example, with respect to actions for divorce, which must be brought at the place of the plaintiff spouse's domicile[21] or as regards several of the actions provided for under the Debt Collection Act.

JOINING AN ACTION WITHOUT RESERVATION

Where proceedings are brought against a defendant before a court lacking territorial jurisdiction and the defendant joins the proceedings without reservation as to the court's lack of jurisdiction, the court becomes competent to rule on the matter. However, the majority of the cantonal codes of civil procedure again provide that competence can only be so created if one of the parties is domiciled or resident within the canton. The idea is that a canton's own courts should not be at the free disposal of parties who have no connection whatsoever with the canton.

Jurisdictional rules in international civil and commercial disputes

Swiss Federal Act on Private International Law

Jurisdiction in international civil and commercial disputes is generally governed by the Federal Act on Private International Law (PILA), subject to bilateral state treaties and the Lugano Convention. The PILA provides for the following deviations from the above stated jurisdictional rules applicable to domestic disputes.

NATURAL FORUM: DEFENDANT'S DOMICILE

With regard to international disputes, the PILA confirms the general rule that, unless otherwise provided, the courts at the defendant's domicile will have jurisdiction. This means that a foreign party can bring an action in Switzerland if the defendant has a Swiss domicile, and in such case the courts at the place of such domicile will have jurisdiction. Contrary to the jurisdictional rules applicable to domestic disputes, the PILA, however, does not refer back to the definitions of "domicile" as stipulated in the Swiss Civil Code; it sets forth it own definitions:

20. For example, Zürich CCP, Section 11 II.
21. CC, Article 144.

According to Article 20 of the PILA, "a natural person has his domicile in the state in which he resides with the intention to remain permanently". If a person has no domicile according to this definition, his habitual residence will be determinative. A habitual residence is deemed to exist in the state where a person "lives for an extended period of time, even if this time-period is limited from the outset".

According to Article 21 of the PILA, corporations and partnerships have their domicile at the place specified in the articles of incorporation or the partnership agreement. In the absence of such designation, their domicile is deemed to be at the place where a corporation or partnership is actually managed.

SPECIAL FORUMS

Place of performance of an obligation

If a defendant has neither a domicile nor a habitual residence nor a branch in Switzerland, an action for breach of contract can be brought against him before the Swiss courts at the place where the contract is to be performed.[22]

Place of location of property (forum rei sitae)

As in domestic disputes, an exclusive special forum at the place of the location of the property exists with respect to actions *in rem* involving real estate.[23] On the other hand, contrary to the rules applicable to domestic disputes, actions for the performance of contractual rights or actions in tort relating to real estate cannot be brought before the courts at the place where the real estate is located. The latter claims are subject to the jurisdiction of the courts at the defendant's Swiss domicile or habitual residence or, if no such Swiss domicile or residence exists, of the court at the place of performance or at the place of tort.

Actions *in rem* relating to movable property can only be brought before the Swiss court at the place of the property's location if the defendant has neither a domicile nor a habitual residence in Switzerland.[24] If the defendant has a Swiss domicile or habitual residence, the action must be brought there.[25]

22. PILA, Article 113.
23. PILA, Article 97.
24. PILA, Article 98, para. 2.
25. PILA, Article 98, para. 1.

Place of principal action for counter-claims

A counter-claim can only be brought at the place where the principal claim is pending if it is closely and directly linked to the principal claim.[26] Contrary to the rules generally applicable to domestic disputes, the mere fact that a claim may be set off against the principal claim is not sufficient to establish the jurisdiction of the court dealing with the principal claim.

Agreed forum

Under Article 5 of the PILA the parties may by agreement select a forum for an existing or a future dispute concerning pecuniary claims arising from a specified legal relationship. The term "pecuniary claims" in this context is meant to include all kinds of financial or monetary interests connected to contractual, quasi-contractual, commercial or civil matters, whether arising under domestic or foreign law.

The agreement on the selection of a forum may be in writing or by any other means of communication that evidences the terms of the agreement by a text. Contrary to the rules generally applicable to domestic disputes, a signed agreement thus is not necessary. As an example, the acceptance by letter or telefax of an unsigned contract offer that contains a clause on jurisdiction creates a valid forum agreement. Unless an agreement provides otherwise, the chosen court has exclusive jurisdiction.

Forum selection is subject to a few specific limitations, for example, for actions *in rem* relating to real estate[27] and regarding consumer claims.[28] Also, a forum selection agreement may be disregarded if under the specific circumstances it appears abusive.[29]

The Swiss court of the agreed forum may not decline its jurisdiction if one party has its domicile, place of habitual residence or business establishment in the canton of the court agreed on, or if Swiss law is applicable to the dispute.[30] As regards the last mentioned ground, it is disputed whether a simple choice of Swiss law by the parties is sufficient to bring the acceptance rule into operation[31] or whether Swiss law must be applicable by operation of a conflict of laws rule set forth in the PILA.[32]

26. PILA, Article 8.
27. PILA, Article 97.
28. PILA, Article 114, para. 2.
29. PILA, Article 5, para. 2.
30. PILA, Article 5, para. 3.
31. So affirmed by Schnyder, *Das neue IPR-Gesetz*, 2nd ed., Zürich 1990, p. 24.
32. According to Vogel, *Grundriss des Zivilprozessrechts*, 3rd ed., Berne 1992, Section 21 N 85 a.

Joining an action without reservation

In line with the rules applicable to domestic disputes, a defendant's appearance in court without raising a defence of lack of jurisdiction is to be construed as a tacit submission to jurisdiction of the Swiss court concerned thereby establishing the court's jurisdiction. Also, in line with domestic rules, the Swiss court concerned can only decline its jurisdiction if none of the parties has a domicile, residence or business establishment in the canton of the respective court or, as a new additional ground, if Swiss law is not applicable to the dispute.[33]

Place of tort

If the defendant has neither a domicile nor a habitual residence nor a business establishment in Switzerland, an action in tort may be brought before the Swiss court at the place of the tortuous act or the resultant injury.[34] The place of the tortuous action is deemed to be the place where the tort-feasor has committed the act or has omitted to perform an act that he should have performed. The place of injury is the place where the consequences of the tort-feasor's actions are suffered.

Place of plaintiff's domicile in consumer and employment matters

In line with the emerging federal substantive law on consumer protection, the PILA provides for the jurisdiction of the Swiss court at the consumer's domicile or habitual residence with respect to consumer claims arising from contracts relating to the provision of ordinary goods and services intended for the personal or family use of the consumer and which are not associated with the professional or commercial activities of the consumer.[35] A consumer cannot in advance waive the jurisdiction of the court at his domicile or place of habitual residence.[36]

As regards actions arising in connection with employment contracts, the Swiss courts at the domicile of the defendant or the place where the employee habitually performs his work will have jurisdiction. In addition, in the case of actions brought by an employee, the Swiss courts at the employee's domicile or place of habitual residence will have jurisdiction.[37]

33. PILA, Article 6.
34. PILA, Article 129, para. 2.
35. PILA, Article 114, para. 1 lit. a.
36. PILA, Article 114, para. 2.
37. PILA, Article 115.

Place of provisional remedies

Provisional remedies (such as preliminary injunctions and temporary restraining orders) may be obtained from the Swiss courts at the place where the requested relief may be effectively implemented, notwithstanding the lack of jurisdiction of Swiss courts over the claim on the merits.[38]

LIS PENDENS

The PILA also addresses the issue of competing jurisdiction between foreign Swiss courts. If an action concerning the same object is already pending abroad between the same parties, the Swiss court will stay the proceeding if it may be expected that the foreign court will, within a reasonable time, render a decision that will be recognisable in Switzerland. The Swiss court will dismiss the action as soon as a foreign decision is submitted to it that can be recognised in Switzerland.[39]

EMERGENCY JURISDICTION

Finally, the PILA provides for Swiss emergency jurisdiction with respect to actions sufficiently connected with Switzerland. If proceedings abroad are impossible or cannot reasonably be required to be brought, the Swiss courts at the place with which the facts of the case are sufficiently connected will have jurisdiction notwithstanding that there would otherwise be no forum in Switzerland.[40]

Lugano Convention

Jurisdiction in international disputes involving parties domiciled within the European Union and EFTA (i.e., the Contracting States) is governed by the Lugano Convention. The most notable modifications imposed by the Lugano Convention on the above discussed jurisdictional rules set forth in the PILA are as follows:

PLACE OF PERFORMANCE OF AN OBLIGATION

Article 5 Number 1 of the Lugano Convention generally provides that in matters relating to contracts, the courts at the place where the contractual

38. PILA, Article 10.
39. PILA, Article 9.
40. PILA, Article 3.

obligation must be performed will have jurisdiction. In view of the Swiss constitutional guarantee of the court of the domicile, Switzerland has reserved the right to refuse the recognition and enforcement of foreign judgments based on that forum against defendants who are domiciled in Switzerland. This reservation will not apply to the extent that at the time recognition or enforcement is sought, Article 59 of the Swiss Federal Constitution has been modified or lifted. In any case, the reservation will cease to have effect by the end of the year 1999.

PLACE OF LOCATION OF PROPERTY

In line with the concept of the PILA, proceedings that have as their object rights *in rem* in immovable property can exclusively be brought before the courts at the place where the property is situated.[41] On the other hand, contractual claims relating to real estate may only be brought at the *forum rei sitae* if the claim may be combined with an action against the same defendant in matters relating to rights *in rem* in immovable property.[42]

EXCLUSION OF FORUM ARRESTI

Pursuant to the prohibitions against exorbitant *fora* set out in Article 3 para. 2 of the Lugano Convention, it will no longer be possible for Swiss courts to claim jurisdiction over a defendant domiciled in a contracting state on the basis that assets of the defendant have previously been attached in Switzerland. On the other hand, the *forum arresti* continues to exist with respect to defendants domiciled outside of the European Union and the EFTA.

PLACE OF PRINCIPAL ACTION FOR COUNTER-CLAIMS

The Lugano Convention narrows the premise under which a counter-claim may be brought in the court in which the principal claim is pending. The latter forum is only available if the counter-claim is arising from the same contract or facts on which the principal claim is based.[43]

AGREED FORUM

In a more liberal approach than the PILA, the Lugano Convention admits agreements on forum selection not only if they are in writing or evidenced

41. Lugano Convention, Article 16, Number 1(a).
42. Lugano Convention, Article 6, Number 4.
43. Lugano Convention, Article 6, Number 3.

by a text but also if they are in a form which conforms to former practice between the parties or, in international trade or commerce, to a usage known to the parties or of which they should be aware and which in the trade or commerce concerned is widely known and regularly observed.[44]

A forum selection clause may be concluded for the benefit of only one of the parties. In such a case, that party will retain the right to bring proceedings in any other court that is competent pursuant to the Lugano Convention. Agreements on forum selections will have no legal force if the courts whose jurisdiction they purport to exclude have exclusive jurisdiction by virtue of the Lugano Convention.[45]

Bilateral treaties

Switzerland has bilateral treaties regarding the recognition and enforcement of foreign judgments with Austria, Belgium, Germany, Liechtenstein and Spain. These treaties relate to jurisdiction insofar as they determine the jurisdictional premises under which judgments will be mutually recognised. The aforementioned treaties will become ineffective once the Lugano Convention comes into force in these countries.

Service of summons or writs

Under the Swiss concept of law, service of process is deemed to be an official act of the state. There is, therefore, no direct service between the parties to a lawsuit. Summons or writs are exclusively served to the parties by the competent court, usually by registered mail return receipt requested.

Any foreign court, authority or private person attempting to effect service of process by mailing the relevant documents from abroad directly to the recipient residing in Switzerland or by serving him directly in Switzerland is deemed to be interfering with Swiss sovereignty and is punishable according to Article 271 of the Swiss Criminal Code.

Service of process from abroad to a Swiss resident must be effected as a general rule through diplomatic channels. According to The Hague Convention of 1 March 1954 on Civil Proceedings, service of process may take place between the Consul of the requesting state and the competent authority of the requested state or, if so agreed, between two member states, directly between the courts of the respective countries or by mediation of the competent authorities. Switzerland has concluded relevant treaties, for instance with Austria, Belgium, France, Germany and Italy.

44. Lugano Convention, Article 17, Number 1.
45. Lugano Convention, Article 17, Number 3.

ASCERTAINING THE APPLICABLE LAW

National law

Under Swiss legal principles, it is a matter for the court and not for the parties to find and apply the law applicable to a certain matter. In doing so, the court is in no way bound by the legal considerations set forth by the parties in their briefs and must itself research the relevant precedents and/or legal writing in connection with rendering the judgment.

Foreign law

Article 16 of the PILA establishes the general principle that Swiss courts have the duty to find and apply the applicable foreign law *ex officio*. However, the court may formally request the parties for their assistance, for example, by providing copies of certain relevant statutes, precedents or legal commentaries. In this context, it is important to note that Swiss courts in ascertaining foreign law may not only rely on the services rendered by the Swiss Institute on International and Comparative Law in Lausanne but also on a relevant treaty which was ratified by a number of European countries (European Convention on Information about Foreign Law of 7 July 1968).

If, despite all efforts, the Swiss court is unable to ascertain the content of the foreign law, Article 16, para. 2 of the PILA provides for the application of Swiss substantive law. In case of disputes relating to monetary claims (*vermögensrechtliche Ansprüche*), the court may, as an exception to the general principle described above, decide from the outset to put the burden of proving the content of the applicable foreign law on the party claiming to have rights based on such law.[46]

Conflict of laws principles

The Swiss conflict of laws rules are set forth in the PILA. The PILA is divided into 13 chapters whereby the first chapter,[47] sets forth certain basic principles such as scope of application of the PILA, rules on international jurisdiction, recognition and enforcement of foreign judgments as well as certain basic rules on the application of foreign law. Chapters 2 to 10 contain special provisions on various areas of law such as matrimonial law, property law, company law, tort law, contract law, antitrust law and intellectual property law. Each chapter includes provisions on jurisdiction,

46. PILA, Article 16, para. 1.
47. PILA, Articles 1–32.

applicable law and recognition and enforcement. Chapter 11 deals with international bankruptcy and composition law, and Chapter 12 with international arbitration.

As a general rule, the conflict of laws rules of the PILA rely (with only a few exceptions in family law matters) on the principle of the domicile[48] as opposed to the principle of citizenship.

In addition, the decisive factor underlying most of the specific conflict of laws provisions of the PILA is the closest connection between the factual basis of a dispute and the law of a particular country. Finally, one of the main features of the PILA consists in its principle of conferring on the parties, to the utmost extent possible, discretion to mutually determine the substantive law that will control their relationship. Only where public interests are at stake or where the statute provides for the protection of "weaker" parties (such as employees, injured persons, children) does the PILA restrict or exclude the choice of law by the parties.

COMMENCING THE ACTION

Conciliatory proceedings

Before being able to lodge a civil action with the competent court, most Swiss cantons require the parties to most (but not all) types of actions to first present their claims to the Justice of Peace or Conciliation Official. These are public magistrates, independent of the court, who have the task of trying to settle disputes or to convince a party not to file an action that is likely to be unsuccessful or which is obviously without merits. Thus, the main purpose of the conciliatory proceeding from the point of view of the legislator is to avoid, if possible, unnecessary litigation.

In the context of commercial disputes, the conciliation proceeding quite frequently is only a formality, because prior to taking the decision to litigate the matter the parties are likely to have engaged in settlement discussions. As a consequence, the efforts of the Conciliation Official or Justice of Peace to bring about a settlement of complex commercial disputes are often useless.

Usually, the procedural codes require that the parties to the dispute be present at the conciliation hearing in person or, in the case of companies, through authorised officers. Frequently, outside counsel are not allowed to be present or to participate in the conciliation hearing. Exemptions to these rules exist if one or both parties are not domiciled at the place where the action is brought. In such circumstances, representation by outside counsel is permitted, even if the opposite party is in fact domiciled at the place of litigation.

48. As defined in PILA, Articles 20 *et seq.*

In addition, if the claimant party has the right to be represented by an outside counsel it may waive attendance of the conciliation hearing and instead submit a written brief to the Conciliation Official or Justice of Peace whereupon the other party may also choose to submit a written brief. In such a case, it becomes evident that the conciliation proceeding is only a (necessary) formality prior to submission of the case to the court.

Should the conciliation be unsuccessful, the Justice of Peace or Conciliation Official, at the request of the claimant, must issue an official document confirming that the conciliation attempt has failed. The Justice of Peace or Conciliation Official must also ensure proper wording of the application in relation to the relief sought by the claimant.

In some cantons, certain types of disputes are expressly exempt from the otherwise mandatory conciliation proceeding. In the canton of Zürich, this is, for instance, the case in connection with trademark, patent or copyright claims that may be brought directly to the competent court.[49] The same is true in the canton of Zürich for claims to be dealt with in accelerated proceedings (*beschleunigtes Verfahren*) or claims under employment contracts.[50]

In three cantons (Fribourg, Vaud and Ticino) the conciliation proceeding in most cases is not mandatory. In some other cantons (Zug, Berne, Schaffhausen, Aargau), the conciliation proceeding may be waived with the consent of both parties.

Commencement of the conciliation proceeding has, among others, the following effects:

(1) Interruption of the running of the statute of limitation.[51] Generally, the time when the request is handed over to a Swiss post office is controlling;[52]

(2) As a rule, compliance with time limits set by the federal substantive law for the filing of claims. According to the practice of the Federal Supreme Court, submission of a request for conciliation is only sufficient compliance with a time limit provided by federal law if:

(a) The Conciliation Official or Justice of Peace must forward the confirmation document to the court on his own; or

(b) If the claimant must submit the confirmation document to the court within a time limit specified in the relevant procedural code.[53] The Federal Supreme Court has ruled that the filing of a request for a temporary restraining order or a preliminary

49. Zürich CCP, Section 103.
50. Zürich CCP, Sections 104 and 105.
51. CO, Article 135 II.
52. BGE 65 II 166.
53. BGE 98 II 181.

injunction does not, however, suffice for the compliance with statutory deadlines set by federal law;[54] and

(3) In connection with litigation in an international context, a claim is pending in Switzerland at the time when an application for conciliation is filed with the competent Conciliation Official or Justice of Peace.[55] As this is a provision of federal law, a uniform solution exists throughout Switzerland with regard to the issue when a claim is deemed to be pending in Switzerland when either one or both parties are not domiciled in Switzerland. As a consequence, cantonal procedural law no longer applies in this context.

Starting the main proceeding

General principles of Swiss procedural law

The main proceeding is designed to provide to the litigant parties the opportunity to submit to the court their allegations, in particular, all essential facts and circumstances of the matter. One of the main basic principles of Swiss procedural law imposes on the parties involved in civil litigation the obligation to submit to the court, within the procedural frame-work provided, any and all allegations, factual statements, arguments and defences which it deems might be relevant to decide the matter (*Eventualmaxime*).

Thus, if a particular procedural code provides, for instance, that each side has the right to file two briefs, the parties are generally excluded from making further factual and legal allegations or defences once they have filed their second brief.[56] Only under exceptional circumstances, for instance, if a new piece of evidence is discovered later without the party's negligence or if the court asks for some specific information may new allegations be made or additional evidence be submitted subsequent to the filing of the second brief or after the time limit set by the court for the submission of evidence has elapsed.[57]

The courts in civil proceedings (except in divorce or family law matters) normally do not become involved on their own in investigating the factual background of a matter brought to their attention. It is solely for the parties to present and prove those facts and circumstances on which they wish the court to apply the law (*Verhandlungsmaxime*). As a consequence, the court may base its judgment exclusively on factual allegations made either by the claimant or defendant.

54. BGE 110 II 387.
55. PILA, Article 10.
56. Zürich CCP, Section 114.
57. Zürich CCP, Section 115.

The evidence for factual allegations that are contested must be furnished by the parties. No evidence-taking will take place with regard to factual allegations that are not contested.[58] Under exceptional circumstances the court has the duty, however, to clarify allegations that are unclear or incomplete (*richterliche Fragepflicht*). Also, the courts have the option and are free to consider facts that are in the public domain irrespective of whether they form part of the allegations or not.

As the extent of the duty of the court to clarify the factual background of the matter is not clearly defined and as courts generally show considerable reluctance to exercise this right in the context of commercial disputes, in particular when attorneys are involved, the complaint should be as precise and as comprehensive as possible from the outset. It must contain a clear request as to the relief sought and should, to the extent possible, be accompanied by such documentary evidence already available or, at least, contain an indication of the kind or type of evidence the claimant intends to use to prove its allegations.

It is of utmost importance for the claimant to clearly state the relief sought. It is a basic principle of Swiss procedural law that in a civil matter no one can be forced to seek enforcement of his rights in court or to seek such enforcement earlier than is his intention (*Dispositionsmaxime*).

According to this principle, the party that initiates civil litigation is free to withdraw such litigation and *vice versa*. The defendant is (except in divorce or family law matters) free to acknowledge a civil claim brought against him. Furthermore, according to the above principle, the court may not award to the claimant more or something different from what he had applied for.

Finally, the *Dispositionsmaxime* imposes on the judge in an appeal procedure the duty not to exceed the requests made by the party appealing a judgment. In a few Swiss cantons (Zug, Basel, Baselland and Valais), a party against whom another person has expressly alleged to have a right may set a time limit to such person for the filing of a court claim failing that the right alleged is forfeited (*Klageprovokation*).

However, it is meanwhile generally accepted[59] and has been confirmed by the Federal Supreme Court that the right to force another person to file a court claim violates federal law. However, as far as the application of cantonal substantive law is concerned, the Federal Supreme Court considers the *Klageprovokation* to be admissible.[60] Finally, with the possibility of filing a claim for a negative declaratory judgment, it is possible for a party to achieve the same result as with a *Klageprovokation*.

Another fundamental principle of Swiss procedural is the principle of *iura novit curia*, which is considered to be a principle of federal law.

---

58. BGE 113 Ia 435.
59. Vogel, *Grundriss des Zivilprozessrechts*, 3rd ed., Berne 1992, Section 30 N 13.
60. BGE 92 II 110 f.; 110 II 23 f.

According to this principle, it is solely for the court to apply the law irrespective of the legal positions taken by the parties in their pleadings. Thus, the courts are completely free to interpret the law and are in no way bound by the legal arguments brought forward by the parties. However, if the court arrives at legal views that substantially differ from what the parties had argued in their pleadings and submissions, then the court prior to rendering the judgment must grant both parties the opportunity to comment on the legal views expressed by the court.[61]

The last fundamental principle of Swiss procedural law is the principle of due process of law. This principle has its basis in Article 4 of the Federal Constitution and is transformed into numerous provisions contained in the various procedural codes as well as in decisions handed down by the Federal Supreme Court.[62]

The principle of due process according to Article 4 of the Federal Constitution, among other things, grants all parties the right to be heard, the right to attend court hearings, the right to be represented by counsel, the right to have access to and review the files, the right to have the relevant pieces of evidence considered by the court and the right to receive reasons from the court for its judgment.

Ordinary proceeding

As procedural law in Switzerland (with certain exceptions) is regulated by the cantons, a vast variety of procedures exist in the courts of first instance. Typically, in the French-speaking part of Switzerland (Geneva, Vaud, Neuchatel, Jura, Fribourg, Valais) the procedural rules are influenced by the French system. This gives the judge a comparatively strong role, particularly in gathering the necessary evidence.

By contrast, in the German-speaking cantons, the codes leave the procedural burden somewhat more in the hands of the parties. However, here too, it is the judge and not the parties who has a decisive role in directing the proceedings and this contrasts sharply with the procedural principles applicable in Common Law jurisdictions. Most Swiss cantonal procedural codes divide the ordinary proceeding of first instance into four different stages:

(1) Conciliatory proceeding;
(2) Main proceeding;
(3) Evidence-taking proceeding; and
(4) Decision proceeding.

61. Vogel, *Grundriss des Zivilprozessrechts*, 3rd ed., Berne 1992, Section 30 N 42.

62. See for example, BGE 96 I 323 containing a summary of the practice developed by the Federal Supreme Court.

Whereas the conciliatory proceeding always marks the beginning, and the decision proceeding always marks the end of civil litigation, the main and the evidence-taking proceedings may overlap depending on the particular code of civil procedure. This means that in certain cantons, the gathering of evidence may come before the main proceeding; in other cantons the main proceeding will be interrupted by the taking of evidence and, finally, in certain cantons (such as Zürich) the gathering of evidence will, in principle, take place subsequent to the completion of the main proceeding.

COMPLAINT

The complaint is the request submitted to the court to request it to grant legal protection to a person or entity through issuance of a judgment.[63] The complaint comprises four essential elements, namely:

(1) The name of the claimant;
(2) The name of the defendant;
(3) The exact relief which is sought from the court; and
(4) The description of the factual basis of the matter including an indication of the means of evidence which will support the factual allegations in case they are contested by the defendant.

The request for relief must be precise and must be worded in such a way that it can be used as judgment if the claim is decided in favour of claimant. In case of claims for the payment of money, the amount sought must, generally, be exactly defined in the complaint. Exceptions to the above principle exist in the following cases:

(1) Where unspecified claims are expressly allowed in a statute (for instance Article 73 II of the Patent Act);
(2) Where the damages suffered may not be exactly proved or where future damages may not be exactly calculated.[64] In both cases Article 42 para. 2 of the CO provides for the judge to make his best estimate of the amount of damages to be awarded; and
(3) Where, at the time when the claim is submitted to the court, the claimant does not have sufficient evidence available to exactly specify the amount of his claim (for example, when such specification requires access to the books of the defendant). In cases

---

63. Vogel, *Grundriss des Zivilprozessrechts*, 3rd ed., Berne 1992, Section 33 N 1.
64. BGE 114 II 256.

of this nature, the claimant must specify his claim subsequent to completion of the evidence-taking procedure.

Once the claim is legally pending the claimant may, in principle, no longer change the relief sought. However, in the majority of the cantons it is admissible to change the claim provided that this does not unduly delay the proceedings and the revised claim is closely connected with the original claim.[65]

It is important to note that, if a complaint is divisible, it may also be submitted only in part (*Teilklage*). This is the result of the *Dispositionsmaxime*. There may be certain advantages in resorting to a partial claim such as the reduction of costs. Also, when launching a so-called test case it is advantageous to resort to partial claim if it is difficult to make a sound risk assessment or to exclude the competence of a certain court. Using the partial claim to achieve such goals is deemed not to constitute an abuse of rights.[66]

One must bear in mind, however, that in case of a partial claim the defendant always has the option to apply by way of counterclaim for a negative declaratory judgment so that then the entire claim is pending and must be decided by the court.

Usually, the complaint must be submitted to the court in writing. In the Canton of Zürich, for instance, the main proceeding in civil matters calls for oral pleadings if the litigation value is below a threshold of SFR 12,000 or if oral pleadings are expressly provided for in the statute (in particular family, divorce and employment matters).

However, if the claimant chooses to submit a written brief, then the defendant has the right (but not the duty) to file a written answer to the complaint as well. If in such a situation both parties have filed written submissions, only the second part of the main proceeding (namely rejoinder and duplication) will be oral. If the court should be of the view that the matter is likely to be too complex for an oral hearing, it has the authority to order the main proceeding to be conducted entirely in writing.

Once a claim has been submitted the court must immediately proceed to check whether certain prerequisites are met which are necessary for the court to be in a position to continue its proceedings (*Prozessvoraussetzungen*). Such prerequisites are, for instance, whether a sufficient interest to sue exists, whether conduct of a proper conciliation proceeding took place, whether the claimant is capable of suing, whether an identical claim between the parties is already pending elsewhere (*lis pendens*) or whether another court has already rendered a judgment on the identical claim between the parties in question.

65. Vogel, *Grundriss des Zivilprozessrechts*, 3rd ed., Berne 1992, Section 39 N 51 *et seq.*

66. ZR 83/1984, Number 104; Vogel, *Grundriss des Zivilprozessrechts*, 3rd ed., Berne 1992, Section 34 N 47.

Although these are issues the court must consider *ex officio*,[67] the court will, for all practical purposes, frequently be in a position to rule on these issues only once the answer to the complaint has been filed. With regard to jurisdiction, the court has the duty to check immediately after having received a complaint whether mandatory jurisdictional rules are complied with.

Inasfar as the defendant may submit to the jurisdiction of a court that would otherwise not be competent to hear the matter, a ruling on the possible lack of jurisdiction may be made only on the defendant expressly raising the defence of lack of jurisdiction.[68]

ANSWER TO THE COMPLAINT

Generally, the answer to the complaint in ordinary proceedings must also be in writing. It must be submitted by the defendant within the time limit set by the court. In the answer to the complaint, the defendant should, in detail, deal with the claims and allegations made by the claimant in his complaint. In particular, the defendant must take a clear position as regards the relief sought by the claimant, i.e., whether the claim should be fully rejected or partially rejected or, in the alternative, whether the claim is fully or partially acknowledged.

In addition, the defendant must expressly contest those allegations made by the claimant that in the defendant's view are incorrect, because otherwise the court may deem such uncontested allegations as being true (*Verhandlungsmaxime*). The defendant in his answer to the complaint is not restricted to simply contest the allegations made by the claimant. He may also submit to the court his own factual allegations in an attempt to rebut or render less likely the factual allegations made by the claimant. This includes affirmative defences such as lapse of the statute of limitation, the set-off defence or failure by the claimant to meet statutory exclusion time limits. The defendant may submit any pieces of evidence which:

(1) Are designed to rebut the factual basis of the claim; or
(2) Serve to support the defendant's counter allegations.

In addition, it is of utmost importance for the defendant to file a motion for dismissal of the case due to lack of jurisdiction of the court in his answer to the complaint because this is required by most cantonal procedural codes and because otherwise the defendant runs the risk of being deemed to have submitted to the jurisdiction of the court (joining the action without reservation or *Einlassung*).

67. Vogel, *Grundriss des Zivilprozessrechts*, 3rd ed., Berne 1992, Section 12 N 43 *et seq.*; ZR 88/1989, Number 43; BGE 112 II 27 2.
68. Vogel, *Grundriss des Zivilprozessrechts*, 3rd ed., Berne 1992, Section 36 N 79.

Einlassung may only be assumed if the defendant unconditionally demonstrates to the court his willingness to enter into the substance of the matter.[69] Participation in the conciliation proceeding does not constitute submission to the jurisdiction of a court.[70]

Furthermore, any motions as to *lis pendens* or existence of a final judgment in the identical matter (*res judicata*) should also be raised at this stage of the proceeding, although not strictly required by the law. However, substantial unnecessary costs can be avoided if these issues are brought to the attention of the court as early as possible. Finally, counterclaims generally must be submitted to the court at the latest with the answer to the complaint.

REPLY

Most of the cantonal procedural codes provide, in principle that the reply will be made orally in court.[71] However, the various procedural codes also allow the court in complex cases to order written submissions for reply and duplication. The reply, in principle, is the last opportunity for the claimant to make factual allegations. In the reply, the claimant will, in most instances, exclusively deal with the allegations made by the defendant in his answer to the complaint. If the defendant has raised a counterclaim, the claimant's answer to the counterclaim will be incorporated in the reply brief.

DUPLICATION

The duplication is the last pleading of the defendant. It is normally oral, unless the court has directed that a written submission be made. The duplication is the last opportunity for the defendant to make new factual allegations. In case of a counterclaim, the duplication brief incorporates the defendant's reply with respect to the counterclaim.

SUPPLEMENTAL PLEADINGS

If a counterclaim has been raised, the claimant will always have the opportunity to submit his duplication with regard to the counterclaim. If the defendant in his duplication has made new factual allegations as to the claim, the court must give the claimant the possibility to file an additional brief, restricted to submitting his comments to such new

69. BGE 87 I 58; 87 I 133 *et seq.*
70. Vogel, *Grundriss des Zivilprozessrechts*, 3rd ed., Berne 1992, Section 22 N 82.
71. Vogel, *Grundriss des Zivilprozessrechts*, 3rd ed., Berne 1992, Section 55 N 47.

allegations. Depending on the further development of the case, the court may at any time order that additional submissions be made, in particular in connection with the allegation of new facts by either party after the main proceeding has been closed.

Joinder of claims and parties

Under certain circumstances, depending on the applicable substantive law and on the legal basis of the claim, the claimant must sue several persons or several claimants must sue one defendant in order for their claim to be valid. This situation is called *notwendige Streitgenossenschaft* (mandatory litigation association).

Generally, this is the case when the dispute on a legal relationship must be decided uniformly *vis-à-vis* any and all persons involved because any and all persons involved will necessarily be uniformly affected by the court's judgment. Examples of mandatory litigation associations are claims filed by or against a community of heirs. The same applies in case of claims involving simple partnerships or in certain cases of martial community property matters.[72] The several claimants and/or defendants usually must act in concert in the course of the proceedings because otherwise their acts and submissions are deemed to be invalid (exceptions in Zürich, Berne, Schwyz and Obwalden).

Furthermore, several persons may sue or be sued:

(1) If the legal or factual basis for their rights and/or obligations are substantially identical; and
(2) If the court has jurisdiction for all defendants involved and if all claims may be dealt with in the same type of proceeding (*einfache Streitgenossenschaft* — "simple litigation association").

Although legally each person conducts its litigation separately and independent from the other parties, the courts normally will join the various claims with the purpose of avoiding inconsistent judgments. In connection with particularly close relationships (*echte einfache Streitgenossenschaft*), the courts do not only have the right but the obligation to join the various claims that must necessarily be decided by the same court.[73]

72. For further examples see Vogel, *Grundriss des Zivilprozessrechts*, 3rd ed., Berne 1992, Section 26 N 49 *et seq.*; Sträuli/Messmer, *Kommentar Zürich Zivilprozeßordnung*, 2nd edition, Zürich 1982, Section 39 N 6 *et seq.*

73. Vogel, *Grundriss des Zivilprozessrechts*, 3rd ed., Berne 1992, Section 26 N 61 *et seq.*

Counterclaims

Counterclaims are claims raised by the defendant against the claimant and are, in principle, admissible under Swiss procedural law. Counterclaims may also be raised conditionally that is, the counterclaim must only be dealt with in case a judgment in favour of the claimant is handed down by the court. Prerequisites for the admissibility of a counterclaim are as follows.

The court seized with the main claim must also have jurisdiction for the counterclaim. All cantonal procedural codes expressly provide that the court seized with the main claim is competent to deal with counterclaims. These provisions are compatible with the constitutional forum guarantee of Article 59 of the Federal Constitution provided that the main claim and the counterclaim are connected, that is if a factual connection exists or if both claims are based on the same legal relationship.[74]

The same type of procedure applies for main claim and counterclaim (for example, summary proceeding, ordinary proceeding).

The counterclaim becomes pending only if and at the time the main claim is validly pending.[75] Thus, if the court decides to dismiss a case due to lack of a procedural prerequisite (for example, lack of jurisdiction) the counterclaim does not become pending. On the other hand, pendency of the counterclaim will not be affected in case of withdrawal or acknowledgement of the main claim.[76]

Some cantonal procedural codes expressly provide for counterclaims to be mandatorily submitted in the course of the conciliation proceeding (Obwalden, Nidwalden, Glarus, Appenzell Ausserroden, Appenzell Innerroden, Graubünden and Thurgau). In all other cantons, counterclaims must be filed at the latest simultaneously with the answer to the complaint, but may be raised during conciliation.

Third party claims

Under specific circumstances defined in the various cantonal procedural codes, a third party may have the right to join proceedings pending between two other parties as claimant or defendant at a later stage of the proceeding (*Prozessbeitritt*). This constitutes an exception from the otherwise strict principle that the parties to the proceedings may not be altered once the claim has become legally pending.

74. BG E 71 I 346; 93 I 552; Vogel, *Grundriss des Zivilprozessrechts*, 3rd ed., Berne 1992, Section 22 N 90 and Section 35 N 53 *et seq*.

75. BGE 87 I 130.

76. Vogel, *Grundriss des Zivilprozessrechts*, 3rd ed., Berne 1992, Section 35 N 64.

Impleader

Impleaders are notices of pending litigation and requests for litigation support by parties to a pending litigation directed at third parties (*Streitverkündung*). In most cases, impleaders are raised if the main party wishes to sue a third party or fears to be sued by a third party in case the court renders an unfavourable judgment against it. Impleaders may be served on the third party either directly or through the assistance of the court, depending on the applicable cantonal procedural code. Otherwise, no legal interest for serving an impleader must be demonstrated to the court or the third party. It is a matter for the main party and not for the court to inform the third party on the course and the status of the proceedings.

If the third party decides to support the main party, various options exist such as:

(1) Internal support to the main party without officially joining the proceeding;
(2) Representation of the main party by the third party in the proceedings;
(3) The third party joins the litigation by way of intervention; or
(4) The main party entirely delegates the conduct of the litigation to the third party whereby formally the main party remains a party to the litigation.

The legal effects of an impleader and of the kind of support rendered (or not rendered) by the third party are entirely determined by substantive law. Generally, according to Swiss substantive law[77] and in case an impleader was timely made, a judgment rendered against the main party has effect also against the third party.

Intervention

Under Swiss procedural law one must distinguish between ancillary third party intervention (*Nebenintervention*) and main third party intervention (*Hauptintervention*). In principle, a third party may intervene at any time in a pending litigation prior to the judgment by way of ancillary intervention in order to facilitate a judgment in favour of one of the main parties to the litigation.

The intervening party has the duty to demonstrate to the court a sufficient legal interest in the outcome of the proceeding due to the fact that the judgment will directly affect its rights and/or obligations. In some cantons, the court must decide on the presence of such interest *ex officio*

---

77. CO, Article 193.

prior to allowing the intervention. In other cantons, the courts must check such interest only on request by one of the main parties.

Once the court has admitted the ancillary intervention, the intervening third party may submit briefs and file appeals in support of the main party. However, the intervening third party may not contradict the main party in whose support the intervention was made. Although a third party intervention has been made, the main party still has the right to terminate the proceedings by withdrawal, acknowledgement or settlement.[78] It may even withdraw appeals which had been filed by the intervening third party.[79] An important consequence of any ancillary third party intervention is that such third party subsequent to the intervention may not be heard as witness.

In case of the main third party intervention a third party alleging to have a better right to the subject matter in dispute may intervene by filing a claim against both parties to a pending litigation. Thus, the intervening third party becomes the claimant party in a new law suit against both other parties of the pending main litigation, the defendants in the new suit. In case of a main third party intervention, the court may either stay the pending main litigation or join the main and the intervention proceeding.[80]

OBTAINING INFORMATION PRIOR TO TRIAL

In Swiss procedural law, the taking of evidence such as depositions of witnesses, the production of documents or the carrying out of inspections prior to or during litigation is entirely under the control of the judge. Parties or counsel to the parties are not allowed to cross-examine the other party or witnesses. Pre-trial discovery proceedings known under the Anglo-Saxon legal systems do not exist in Switzerland since, as a rule, evidence taking is performed in the course of the main proceeding. Nevertheless, all cantonal codes of civil procedure allow for the taking of evidence and the obtaining of information prior to commencing with litigation under certain exceptional circumstances.

Usually, the party seeking to obtain the information or to secure the evidence must sufficiently demonstrate to the court that a particular piece of evidence might be lost or no longer be readily available and that it would suffer irreparable harm if the evidence were not immediately secured. If the motion is granted, then the court (and not the parties) will undertake the necessary steps designed to obtain the information or secure the evidence.

---

78. As to the exceptions in certain cantons, see Vogel, *Grundriss des Zivilprozessrechts*, 3rd ed., Berne 1992, Section 27 N 74 *et seq*.

79. Vogel, *Grundriss des Zivilprozessrechts*, 3rd ed., Berne 1992, Section 27 N 76.

80. Vogel, *Grundriss des Zivilprozessrechts*, 3rd ed., Berne 1992, Section 27 N 91.

In some cantons, the court that would have jurisdiction in the main claim is also competent for the preliminary securing of evidence. In other cantons, the court in which the particular piece of evidence is located has jurisdiction for the securing of evidence prior to commencing litigation.

By contrast, a party may also have the right to obtain information from another party based either on substantive law or based on a contract. In these cases, the party may ask for the information directly from the other party whenever the legal prerequisites to do so are fulfilled. If the other party refuses to comply, the party seeking the information may enforce this information right either in a summary proceeding or, in the alternative, in an ordinary proceeding.

INTERIM PROTECTION OF RIGHTS AND ASSETS

Where a party needs expedient and urgent protection of its entitlements and rights, interlocutory relief may be available before the commencement of ordinary proceedings. The most important types of such relief within the framework of commercial disputes are provisional injunctions and attachment orders.

Provisional injunctions

Requirements

Provisional relief may, as a general principle, not lead to an anticipated enforcement of a claim for specific performance.[81] A provisional injunction thus typically takes the form of a restraining order or an order maintaining a *status quo*, respectively. The defendant is ordered to refrain from certain actions, for instance from the infringement of a patent or copyright, from an act of unfair competition or from the disposition of specific pieces of assets.

The requirements for obtaining such provisional relief are set forth in a general manner in the cantonal procedural laws.[82] Federal legislation also contains relevant provisions, particularly in respect to the protection of intellectual property rights. The prerequisites are described in varying terms although the leading principles remain essentially the same. The plaintiff:

(1) Must establish with reasonable probability the entitlement or right which the provisional relief sought is intended to protect (*prima facie* case);

81. ZR 85/1986, Number 38.
82. For example, Zürich CCP, Section 222(3).

(2) Must further demonstrate with reasonable probability that there is an impending injury to his entitlement or right; and

(3) Must show that the resulting detriment could not easily be remedied.

As a general rule, more than potential monetary loss is needed to be shown as the probable result of the defendant's actions, such as irreparable damage to the reputation of the plaintiff or of his products, or a general confusion to the public that will result in injury, the effect of which is difficult to assess in monetary terms.[83]

Procedure

Provisional injunctive relief may be obtained before commencement of ordinary proceedings (pre-trial relief) or within the framework of ordinary proceedings. In the second case, competence to grant provisional relief lies with the court dealing with the principal action. Provisional injunctive relief before commencement of ordinary proceedings (pre-trial relief) is typically granted by way of summary proceedings. These usually are conducted before a single judge of a cantonal judicial body. Depending on the canton and the area of law involved, this may be the single judge of a district court, or of a cantonal superior court or of a special commercial court.

Proceedings for provisional relief are started by a petition to the single judge, usually in writing, although oral petitions are also admissible. Where a plaintiff can demonstrate particular urgency, relief may be granted *ex parte* (temporary restraining order).[84] In such a case, the party against whom the provisional injunction is directed will subsequently be heard and the judge will thereafter decide whether the relief is maintained (preliminary injunction) or lifted.

The means of evidence admissible in summary proceedings are, as a general rule, restricted. In the Canton of Zürich, for instance, typically only documents and written reports from third parties (including experts) are produced as evidence in summary proceedings for provisional relief although witness depositions are also possible, provided they do not cause undue delays.[85] Noteworthy is the judges' practice, particularly in respect to relief sought for alleged violation of patent rights, to obtain a short opinion from a court-appointed expert on the question of whether there exists a *prima facie* violation of the plaintiff's patent rights.[86] Very often, these opinions become a decisive factor in the outcome of proceedings.

83. BGE 108 II 230/31; 114 II 370.
84. Zürich CCP, Section 110 II.
85. Zürich CCP, Section 209.
86. ZR 89/1990, Number 54.

Security

Another special feature of provisional relief proceedings is that the judge may require the plaintiff to post a bond in order to secure payment of any costs or potential damage caused by the restraining order applied for. The judge may request such a bond as a precondition for an injunction to become effective. In some cantons, he may request security only on respective application of the defendant.[87]

However, pursuant to the majority of cantonal codes of civil procedure and the federal law providing for injunctive relief, the judge may order security at his own discretion, i.e., *ex officio*. An offer by a plaintiff to provide adequate security does not dispense with the need to show that all requirements for provisional relief, as explained above, are met.

Where a plaintiff is seeking provisional relief, and the defendant offers adequate security to cover the damage resulting from the alleged impending injury to the plaintiff's rights, the judge may abstain from granting a provisional injunction or revoke an injunction that has already been granted.[88] This rule is, however, not very often applied in practice: A plaintiff will and can only apply for provisional relief if the impending detriment to his rights is not easily remedial; and that means that more than mere impending monetary loss must be shown. Accordingly, a security provided by the defendant to cover monetary loss will generally not sufficiently protect the plaintiff against all possible consequences of the alleged impending injury to his rights.

Necessity to file ordinary action

Provisional relief granted before the commencement of ordinary proceedings will only remain effective if an ordinary action is filed in due time before the court with proper jurisdiction in respect of the right or entitlement that was to be protected by the provisional relief sought.[89] Normally, the principal action must be filed within thirty days after the granting of injunctive relief, failing which the injunction will automatically cease to be effective.

Intellectual property and unfair competition law

Frequently, provisional injunctions are sought for the protection of intellectual property rights and in relation to unfair competition practices.

87. Zürich CCP, Section 227 I.
88. Zürich CCP, Section 227 II.
89. Zürich CCP, Section 228.

The requirements for obtaining provisional relief in these areas are defined by federal law, namely the various federal acts on the protection of intellectual property rights including, in particular, patents and trademarks, and the Federal Act on Unfair Competition. The requirements are basically the same as set out above.

It is worth being noted that litigation in the areas of intellectual property rights and unfair trade practices are often and almost typically commenced with requests for pre-trial injunctive relief since the parties concerned usually have a special interest in the expedient (at least provisional) determination of their rights and obligations.

Often the parties then rely on the single judge's decision in the pre-trial relief proceedings either to shape their future commercial activities or to negotiate a settlement of the matter in dispute. Hence, the single judge's decisions, particularly in the area of intellectual property law, usually have great practical importance. As a reaction, the judges sometimes tend to transform the pre-trial summary proceedings into something close to ordinary proceedings, for example, by ordering repeated exchanges of written briefs and by applying time-consuming procedures for the obtaining of expert opinions. The consequences are frequently considerable delays until decisions are rendered.

Attachment

Availability to secure enforcement of money claims

Special interlocutory relief is available to secure the enforcement of a claim for payment of money: The Debt Collection Act accords creditors the remedy of attachment. Attachment is temporary seizure, without prior notice, of the debtor's assets located in Switzerland for the purpose of provisionally securing the enforcement of a money claim prior to adjudication of that claim.[90]

Attachment may be levied on both tangible and intangible property. For the purpose of determining whether such properties are located within Switzerland, the following rules apply: With reference to tangible properties, the place of their physical location is decisive. Intangibles, such as debtors' claims *ex contractu* or *ex delicto* against third parties, are deemed to be located at the debtor's place of residence, if the debtor is resident in Switzerland.[91]

If the debtor's residence is in Switzerland, however, attachment of assets is only available under very limited circumstances. If the debtor is

90. Cf. Markus Wirth, "Attachment of Swiss Bank Accounts: A Remedy for International Debt Collection", *The Business Lawyer*, Volume 36, (1981) Number 3.

91. BGE 64 III 130, 73 III 102 E2, 75 III 26, 76 III 19.

not resident in Switzerland or has no fixed residence, such claims are deemed to be located at the place of residence of a third person against whom the debtor has a claim.[92] Swiss patent rights of a debtor residing outside Switzerland are deemed to be located at the seat of the Swiss patent office.[93]

Statutory requirements

As a requirement for obtaining an attachment order, the plaintiff must establish with reasonable probability:

(1) That he has an unsecured and, in general, mature money claim against the debtor; and
(2) That one of the five grounds for attachment as specified by the Debt Collection Act exists.[94]

The five grounds are:

(1) The defendant has no fixed residence anywhere;
(2) The defendant, with the intent to evade payment of his debts, removes assets, absconds, or engages in preparations to abscond;
(3) The defendant is in transit through Switzerland;
(4) The defendant has no residence in Switzerland; and
(5) The plaintiff creditor holds certificates of unsuccessful former enforcement in respect of undischarged debts of the defendant debtor (*Verlustschein*).

The most important ground for attachment in the framework of international commercial litigation is the debtor's lack of residence in Switzerland. Specifically, the money claim that the creditor seeks to secure through attachment over a non-resident debtor's assets need not be related to the Swiss property attached and also need not have any other contacts with Switzerland.

According to the pending project for a revision of the Debt Collection Act, a sixth ground for attachment will be introduced: The plaintiff creditor holds a title declared enforceable by a court of first instance.

92. BGE 63 III 44, 75 III 26, 76 III 19, 80 III 126, 91 III 22.
93. BGE 38 I 704, 62 III 59.
94. Debt Collection Act, Article 271.

This new ground for attachment is designed to incorporate into the Debt Collection Act the creditor's entitlement to interlocutory relief pursuant to Article 39 of the Lugano Convention.

Procedure

An attachment order is usually applied for in the same manner as a pre-trial interlocutory order, but it may also be obtained at any time after the filing of the principal action. The order is obtained by way of summary proceedings before the court of first instance in the district where the attachable assets are located. The order is always granted *ex parte*, and the rejection of an unsuccessful application will not be notified to the debtor.

The creditor obtaining an attachment order is liable to the debtor for the damage that the latter may suffer as a result of an attachment that subsequently turns out to be unjustified.[95] Hence, the judge in charge may request the plaintiff creditor at any time, *ex officio* or on motion from the defendant debtor, to provide adequate security against such potential damage. The judges have large discretion in so deciding and, accordingly, their practice varies considerably. While the Zürich judges decide on a case-to-case basis, the practice in other cantons (for example, Geneva) is to routinely impose a bond of approximately 10 per cent of the principal money claim secured by the attachment.

Again, the attachment order will only be upheld if the plaintiff creditor pursues, within ten days after obtaining the order, the principal money claim by way of the collection proceedings as provided for by the Debt Collection Act.[96]

A successful attachment over a debtor's assets will generally serve to establish jurisdiction of the Swiss court at the place of attachment for the subsequent principal action on the money claim at issue (*forum arresti*). An exception applies to defendant debtors resident in the European Union— or EFTA— countries. With respect to such debtors, the Lugano Convention has done away with the *forum arresti*.[97] In these cases the principal money claim must, thus, be pursued before the court(s) having jurisdiction according to the rules of the Lugano Convention.

95. Debt Collection Act, Article 273.
96. Debt Collection Act, Article 278.
97. Lugano Convention, Article 3.

SUMMARY PROCEEDINGS

Introduction

In Switzerland, summary proceedings serve various purposes. If certain prerequisites are met they serve as a quick trial to reach a final and enforceable judgement. Further, summary proceedings are special purpose proceedings serving different purposes mainly in the field of debt collection and for the hearing of special requests, particularly based on the CC and the CO, i.e., in civil law matters. Finally, courts in summary proceedings hear requests for pre-trial interlocutory relief when they are dealing with enforcement matters.

Unlike in certain other jurisdictions, in Switzerland default proceedings are not summary proceedings. If the defendant defaults, there are special provisions in the various Codes of Civil Procedure simplifying further proceedings. The case will, however, not be transferred to summary proceedings.

Ordinary summary judgment

A number of cantonal Codes of Civil Procedure allow the claimant to obtain a final and enforceable judgment by way of summary proceedings if two prerequisites are met:

(1) The legal issue is clear; and
(2) The facts are not in dispute or easily provable.

The legal issue is clear, for example, if a rule contained in a body of law such as the CC or the CO is doubtlessly applicable to a given situation. In addition, the legal issue may be clear if a court, especially the Federal Supreme Court, has already ruled on it.

The prerequisite much harder to meet and much more difficult to assess prior to commencing proceedings is the question whether facts will be considered to be easily provable. This is practically only the case if the claimant can demonstrate the relevant facts by unequivocal and clear documents.[98]

There are three possible outcomes of this type of summary proceedings: The claimant may prevail, in which case the judgment is *res judicata* and may be enforced against the defendant. The court may also come to the conclusion that the plaintiff's claim has no merits, in which case the judgment is also *res judicata* and effectively bans the plaintiff from pursuing its claim in other proceedings.

---

98. Walder, *Zivilprozessrecht*, Zürich 1983, Section 37 N 21.

If, however, the court comes to the conclusion that one of the prerequisites of a clear legal situation and undisputed facts is lacking, then the defendant prevails in summary proceedings. However, the judgment is not *res judicata* and the plaintiff may pursue its claim in ordinary proceedings, where all means of evidence are admitted.

EVIDENCE-TAKING PROCEEDING

Submission of evidence and the role of the court in the presentation of the evidence

Evidence may be taken by the court prior, during or subsequent to the main proceeding, depending on the cantonal code of civil procedure applicable. It is the judge and not the parties who are in control of the presentation of evidence.

In the canton of Zürich, evidence taking in principle takes place subsequent to the main proceeding and is initiated by an order of the court identifying those of the alleged facts and circumstances it considers to be essential and, therefore, must be proved by the respective party. The parties at this stage will have the opportunity to submit or offer any evidence that they deem to be relevant in connection with the facts and allegations identified by the court in the said order. However, if it is deemed to be appropriate or advisable under the circumstances, the court may initiate the (partial) gathering of evidence already during the course of the main proceeding. Courts will make use of this possibility, in particular, in cases where the gathering of evidence could require considerable time, such as in the case of expert opinions or when evidence must be gathered abroad.

Sometimes, the evidence-gathering will be initiated early when the court feels that the taking of a few pieces of evidence (for instance the interrogation of one key witness) might help to allow for a quick disposal of the case. On completion of the evidence-taking, the parties usually have the right to comment on the results of the evidence-taking, either in a final written submission or in a final oral pleading. Thereafter, the court will go on to render the judgment.

The gathering of evidence and the interrogation of witnesses is firmly in the hands of the court. Cross-examination by the parties is not allowed.

Means and nature of evidence

General principles

The evidence-taking is designed to establish the factual basis of the case — to the extent that it is disputed or contested. Only if the factual basis of the matter is clarified can the court determine the legal consequences in a judgment. Proof means that a certain factual allegation (whether relating to an internal or an external fact) made by one party is in the opinion of the court deemed to be true.

Also subject to evidence-taking and proof are the causal links between the occurrence of certain events and results or the likely course of certain alleged events. In this context, the judge frequently must rely on the opinion of scientific experts. Finally, under certain circumstances a party may be required to furnish proof for the content of foreign law, unwritten customary law or usages of trade. According to Article 16 of the PILA the duty to furnish proof for the content of foreign law may only be imposed on the parties in case of commercial disputes and only if the court is unable to determine the content of the foreign law *ex officio*.

Only factual allegations that have been contested by the other party must be proven. Factual allegations not contested are deemed to have been proven in accordance with the *Verhandlungsmaxime*. No proof is necessary also for factual allegations expressly admitted to be accurate by the other party and for facts that either are public or common knowledge or which are otherwise known to the court.[99]

The distribution of the burden of proof is regulated by federal law in Article 8 of the CC. According to Article 8 of the CC, the burden of proof rests with the party who asserts to have certain rights due to the existence of certain factual circumstances. As a result, the party who alleges to have a right must prove the facts which allegedly form the basis for such right. On the other hand, the party who is contesting the existence of certain rights bears the burden of proving those facts whose existence results in the non-existence of certain rights alleged by the plaintiff.

Apart from the general rule set forth in Article 8 of the CC, federal and cantonal substantive law contain numerous provisions on the allocation of the burden of proof in certain specific situations.[100] In those cases in which the existence of a right depends on the non-existence or absence of certain facts (negative proof) the burden of proof is shifted to the other party in case such negative proof is considered to relate to unspecified circumstances.[101] The burden of proof is also shifted:

(1) If one party has taken steps with a view to rendering the proof impossible or more difficult for the other party; or

99. BGE 117 II 323.

100. For examples, see Vogel, *Grundriss des Zivilprozessrechts*, 3rd ed., Berne 1992, Section 45 N 38.

101. For instance, lack of use of a trademark during a period of time by the other party, BGE 66 II 147; 81 II 54; 95 II 233.

(2) In case of legal presumptions provided for in certain statutes as well as in case of so called natural presumptions.[102]

Under Swiss procedural law, the principle of free assessment of the evidence value applies (*freie Beweiswürdigung*), i.e., the judge is free to determine in consideration of all facts and circumstances whether or not proof has been furnished for certain factual allegations. In other words, no formal procedural rules exist as to the relative value of the various means of proof, which in principle have all the same weight and which are all admissible. Thus, the judge may consider a factual allegation to be proven if he personally is convinced beyond reasonable doubt that such fact exists.

Whether or not means of evidence that have been obtained illegally may be validly used as evidence in an ongoing litigation is disputed. The prevailing view appears to be, however, that such means of evidence are not generally excluded but may be considered if, under the circumstances, the need for clarification outweighs the illegality in having obtained such evidence.

Means of evidence

Swiss procedural law recognises the following means of evidence: documents, witness depositions, judicial inspection, expert opinions, written reports by public authorities or agencies and interrogation of the parties.

DOCUMENTS

Swiss procedural law distinguishes between private documents and public documents. Public documents are documents issued by a public authority or a notary public. Such documents, according to Article 9 of the CC, are deemed to be authentic and to furnish full proof, unless evidence is successfully furnished that the content of the public document is inaccurate or untrue. Private documents are documents written or issued by private persons.

The party who bears the burden of proof can demand edition of documents either from the opposing or from third parties through the assistance of the court. With the exception of the possibility of obtaining evidence or information on a preliminary basis and within very narrow limits, edition of evidential documents can only be demanded after the claim is pending with the court. If edition of documents is demanded from third parties, such third party must not submit a document to the court if the document contains facts for which that party would have a right to refuse testimony.

102. For examples, see Vogel, *Grundriss des Zivilprozessrechts*, 3rd ed., Berne 1992, Section 45 N 44 *et seq*.

WITNESSES

Witnesses are persons who are interrogated as to certain factual events that they witnessed. Normally, only witness statements as to their own findings may furnish full proof for factual allegations whereas depositions of so-called hearsay witnesses may serve to convince the judge of the accuracy of other witness statements. Thus, hearsay testimony is legally possible under Swiss law.

In principle, anybody may, unless specifically disqualified as a witness, be called as a witness. Specific codes of civil procedure certain persons from testifying, such as children under 14 years of age; close relatives of a party in the litigation; and conciliation officials or priests. The parties, intervening parties, counsel to the parties and, in case a company or partnership is a party, the company's executives normally may not be called as witnesses.

Only in the cantons of Zürich and Schwyz may company executives be called as witnesses, if their company is involved in the dispute. Anyone summoned as a witness must appear in court and must give testimony, although certain persons such as husbands, wives, close relatives, attorneys, physicians and priests may have the right to refuse to testify if the cantonal procedural code so provides. The protection of business secrets or the banking secrecy laws cannot generally be invoked in order to refuse testimony or to submit documents, but on request by one party or a third party the court may order measures for the protection of confidential information that must be divulged to the court.

Under Swiss law, affidavits sworn either by the parties or by third parties do not have any special weight and do not furnish proof of any allegation, a fact that is of particular significance in the context of applications for provisional relief.

JUDICIAL INSPECTION

Judicial inspection (*Augenschein*) is the inspection of persons or things by the court or, in case of persons, by an expert. Parties and third parties must tolerate the inspection. Only if third parties may invoke reasons that would give them the right to refuse testimony must the court refrain from performing an inspection.

EXPERT OPINION

Experts are persons who have special expertise in a certain area. Experts may be appointed by the court if requested by one party in order to obtain an opinion on the existence or the interpretation of certain facts or rules within their field of expertise. Opinions by private experts mandated by the parties do not have special weight but qualify merely as allegations made by one party. However, a few cantonal codes of civil procedure, which were recently revised (Aargau and Appenzell Ausserroden), allow the judge also to take into account such private expert opinions in connection with assessing whether proof has been furnished or not.

The court-appointed expert must be completely independent from the parties to the proceedings. He must restrict himself to answering the questions submitted to him by the court or the parties and does not have authority to make judgments as to issues of proof or the existence or non-existence of rights.

INTERROGATION OF PARTIES

Interrogation of the parties is a formal deposition of the parties with the purpose of getting information on certain facts. The so-called simple party deposition, which is not made under the threat of criminal penalty, may not furnish proof in favour of (but against) that party. The party deposition in the sense of Article 306 of the Criminal Code is made under the threat of severe criminal sanctions in case of an inaccurate or untrue deposition. It may only be performed subsequent to having had simple party depositions and may furnish proof also in favour of the deposing party.

JUDGMENT AND KINDS OF RELIEF

Types of judgments

Interlocutory and final judgments

Procedural interlocutory decisions (*Prozessleitende Entscheide*) are rendered in order to advance the procedure.[103] These types of decisions deal with procedural matters such as, for instance, the setting of time limits to file briefs, the opening of evidence-taking proceedings, etc. These types of decisions are usually rendered in the form of a decree by the presiding judge.

As opposed to procedural interlocutory decisions, another group of decisions is dogmatically defined as decisions setting an end to a procedure (*Prozesserledigende Entscheide*). Among this group, one may distinguish between decisions setting an end to the procedure in one particular instance (final judgment, *Endurteil*) and decisions by which a procedure is finished only partially (preliminary or partial judgment,

---

103. Vogel, *Grundriss des Zivilprozessrechts*, 3rd ed., Berne 1992, Section 37 N 93.

Vor- oder Teilurteil). Both types of decisions are usually rendered by the court in the form of a judgment (*Urteil*).

Judgments in the subject matter and procedural decisions

Within the group of decisions setting an end to a procedure two main groups are distinguished:

JUDGMENTS ON THE SUBJECT MATTER

A judgment on the subject matter (*Sachurteil*) usually contains a court's or judge's decision regarding the merits of the claims. However, a judgment on the subject matter does not necessarily put an end to the procedure as a whole. Rather, a judgment in the subject matter may only deal with a question of prejudicial matter for the case such as, for instance, the questions of standing or of a statute of limitation. In most cantons, such decisions are possible in the form of preliminary judgments.[104] Furthermore, partial judgments (*Teilurteile*) are possible in the event that a judge or a court renders a decision only with respect to a part of the claims before him (for instance, only about the question of the existence and validity of a contract).

A judgment on the subject matter may be based on the court's own findings or, in the event of a settlement, an abandon of an action or a recognition of the claims by the defendant, based on the parties' declarations. A decision based on the court's own findings is usually rendered in the form of a judgment (*Urteil*), a decision based on the parties' declarations in the form of a resolution (*Beschluss*, if rendered by a court) or a decree (*Verfügung*, if rendered by a single or presiding judge).

PROCEDURAL DECISIONS

As opposed to interlocutory procedural decisions by which the judge advances the procedure, a judge may also set an end to a procedure by a procedural decision (*Prozessurteil*). This may be the case in the event that certain procedural prerequisites (*Prozessvoraussetzungen*) are not met, for instance in the event of lack of jurisdiction, non-payment of a bond by the plaintiff, or lack of standing. The procedural decision is final in the event that the court determines that the procedural prerequisite is not met.

The decision may have interlocutory character in the event that procedural claims of a party (i.e., the alleged lack of standing of the opposite

104. *Vorurteile*, cf. Zürich CCP, Section 189.

party) are rejected by the court. A procedural decision is usually rendered on the basis of the court's own findings (for example, lack of jurisdiction).

Exceptionally, a procedural decision may be rendered on the basis of a party's declaration (for example, abandon of an action with the explicit reservation of a new action).

Rendering of judgments

As soon as a particular case is ready for decision the court will render its judgment. As a general rule, the case is decided based on the facts as of the date when the judgment is rendered.[105] In the event that a court (and not a single judge) must decide, the deliberations are usually prepared by one judge who will present the case and his pleas as to the suggested decision.[106] Thereafter, the other judges submit their respective positions. The presiding judge speaks last. In the event that, after discussion, dissenting opinions remain, a decision is rendered by majority vote.[107] Abstaining from the vote is not permitted.

Depending on the cantonal legislation, the instance and the subject matter in question, deliberations are either held in chambers (for instance in family matters) or in public (for instance, in the Zürich Court of Appeals or in the Federal Supreme Court).

The written judgment is usually edited by the clerk of the court under the supervision of the presiding judge.

The judgment in general is notified to the parties in writing some time after the deliberation. In the event that the parties are present during the deliberations of the court, the court may, in addition to the written notification, inform the parties about its decision orally.[108]

Form of judgments

The final judgment is notified to the parties in writing. In the event that a party is represented by an attorney, the judgment is notified to the attorney. If notification in writing proves to be impossible the court may also notify a party by publishing the judgment in the *Official Gazette* or other newspapers.[109]

105. Cf. Zürich CCP, Section 188.
106. *Referentensystem*, of the Zürich Code on the Constitution of Courts (CCC), Section 137.
107. Zürich CCC, Section 138.
108. Zürich CCC, Section 184.
109. Zürich CCC, Section 183.

A written judgment usually consists of the following parts:[110]

(1) Introduction (*Rubrum*): This section contains the indication of the court including the names of the judges and the clerk, the date when the judgment was rendered, indication of the parties with names, addresses, name and address of the attorneys, description of the subject matter and the relief sought by the parties.

(2) The court's grounds for its decisions (*Begründung*): This part usually consists of a summary description of the relevant facts, the determination of the sum in dispute (in the event of money judgments) and a detailed explanation by the court of the grounds for the decision rendered and the results of the evidence-taking.

(3) The decisions (*Dispositiv*): This part summarises the enforceable decisions of the court (for instance:"Defendant will pay the sum of SFR 10,000 to plaintiff"). In addition, this part of the judgment contains decisions regarding the amount of the court's fees and expenses and their allocation between the parties, as well as the indemnification owed by the losing party to the winning party for attorneys' fees. Finally, this part of the judgment consists of a list of those persons to whom the judgment is notified and of information regarding the possibility of an appeal as well as the time limit for the filing of such appeal.

Kinds of relief

Swiss procedural law dogmatically distinguishes between:

(1) Claims for performance (including claims for money judgment and specific performance);

(2) Claims for declaratory judgment; and

(3) Claims for modifications of the legal status or contractual relationships.[111]

These distinctions are in line with the different objectives of claims and the different rights that are awarded to individuals and legal entities by the CC, the CO and other statutes. With a view to procedural aspects there are clear distinctions between:

110. Zürich CCC, Section 157.

111. For example, claims for judicial dissolution of a partnership or judicial extension of a lease term, Guldener, *Schweizerisches Zivilprozessrecht*, 3rd ed., Zürich 1979, pp. 205 *et seq.*

(1) Claims for interlocutory relief;
(2) Claims for money judgment;
(3) Claims for performance (specific performance and/or injunctive relief);
(4) Claims for declaratory judgment;
(5) Claims for modification of legal status or contractual relationships; and
(6) Claims for enforcement of foreign judgment and arbitration awards.

Claims for money judgment

Neither Swiss substantive law nor the cantonal procedural laws differentiate between original monetary claims (such as for repayment of a loan, payment of a purchase price, etc.) and derivative, i.e., compensatory, monetary claims (such as claims for damages for breach of contract).

The proceedings to pursue money claims are partially governed by the Debt Collection Act. In the context of the Debt Collection Act, proceedings commence with the creditor demanding from the debt collection office at the debtor's domicile that it issue a writ of payment to the debtor.[112] The Debt Collection Act offers certain possibilities to obtain an enforceable judgment against the debtor by way of summary proceedings.[113]

If the creditor is not in a position to use summary proceedings, he must commence an ordinary law suit against the debtor in order to set aside the objection lodged by the debtor. Once the creditor is awarded a final judgment in his favour and the debtor does not pay, the creditor must enforce the judgment by commencing debt collection proceedings as described above.

Specific performance and injunctive relief

Where a defendant is supposed to perform specific acts, a claim for specific performance may be available. Where a defendant should refrain from certain acts, a claim for negative injunctive relief may exist. The basis for both types of claims may be either contractual or statutory.

Claims for specific performance and injunctive relief are basically to be pursued in ordinary proceedings. However, where time is of the essence, injunctive relief may be sought on a provisional basis by way of summary proceedings before commencement of ordinary proceedings. In addition, the cantonal procedural laws usually also provide for the availability of

112. Debt Collection Act, Articles 67 et seq.
113. Details are set out below.

summary proceedings in the event that indisputable and conclusive evidence for the factual basis of a claim can immediately be produced and a clear legal situation exists.[114] For obvious reasons such proceedings can very rarely be successfully resorted to in commercial disputes.

Although the respective provisions may vary slightly from one canton to the other, the different types of relief available are usually the same all over Switzerland. The relief granted will generally include an order against the defendant to perform, or refrain from, a specific act.[115] This order is either combined with a notice to the defendant that, should he not comply with the order, he would be referred to the criminal judge for conviction based on Article 292 of the Swiss Criminal Code or with any other measure which might be necessary to secure enforcement of the decision.

In addition, the court may also authorise the plaintiff (or a third party) to perform specific acts that the defendant is found to be under an obligation to perform.[116] Such authorisation may be combined with an order against the defendant to fully reimburse the plaintiff for the costs of such substitute performance.

In the event that the defendant, according to his contractual obligation, is supposed to perform a declaratory act (for example an entry in the land registry), the judge may order the defendant to perform the act within a certain time limit, failing which the court order will stand in place of the declaratory act required.[117]

Claims for declaratory judgment

Where compensatory or specific relief is inadequate or inefficient, a claim for declaratory judgment may be available. Such claims are for the binding adjudication of disputed rights or of the disputed status of litigants, without seeking further relief. The claim may, for example, be for a judicial determination that the disputed patent validly exists or that the plaintiff's patent has been infringed[118] or that a contract is void.

The remedy of declaratory judgment is typically subsidiary to all other types of claims. In order to have a court hear a motion for declaratory judgment, a plaintiff must establish:

(1) That there is an actual legal controversy; and
(2) That the controversy cannot be resolved by any other means.

114. Cf. Zürich CCP, Section 222 (2).
115. Cf. Zürich CCP, Section 223 (1).
116. Cf. Zürich CCP, Section 307.
117. Cf. Zürich CCP, Sections 307/308.
118. Cf. Federal Act on Patents, Article 74.

The Swiss courts have ruled that a claim for declaratory judgment is basically not available when a controversy is purely dogmatic in nature and bears no relationship to an actual dispute over the existence of one party's rights.[119] There exists, in other words, no right to have a court give a legal opinion in the absence of an actual dispute.

Second, the plaintiff must establish a "sufficient interest" in order for the court to settle the controversy by declaratory judgment.[120] Substantive statutory law sometimes specifies situations where such sufficient interest is legally presumed.[121] In all other instances, the plaintiff must establish that:

(1) Either no other remedy is available to him; or
(2) Monetary or specific relief would be inadequate or insufficient in the given circumstances.

If either of the two mentioned requirements is not satisfied, the court must dismiss the claim without considering it on its merits. In the context of disputes for which the Lugano Convention applies, it might be necessary for the Swiss courts to revise their rather restrictive attitude toward claims for declaratory relief.

Where the above mentioned requirements are met, there is basically no restriction on the possible content of a claim for declaratory judgment. The most common types of such claims include:

(1) Claims for the determination of the existence or non-existence of intellectual property rights or for a declaration that such rights are infringed;
(2) Claims for declaration that the defendant's business conduct violates anti-trust or unfair competition laws;[122]
(3) Claims for judicial determination that the defendant's acts infringe the plaintiff's rights or personality;[123] and
(4) Claims for determination of the validity of a contract.

In addition, a claim for a declaratory judgment may serve as an effective defensive device in the form of a counterclaim. If, for instance, a plaintiff has brought a claim for damages, but has only specified a part of the damages to be awarded (reserving the right to subsequently bring a claim for additional damages), the defendant may oppose such reservation

---

119. BGE 80 II 366.

120. BGE 110 II 354.

121. Vogel, *Grundriss des Zivilprozessrechts*, 3rd ed., Berne 1992, Section 34 N 24.

122. Federal Act on Cartels, Article 8, para. 1 and Swiss Federal Statute on Unfair Competition, Article 9 c.

123. CC, Article 28a (3).

by filing a counterclaim. With the counterclaim he may ask the court to render a declaratory judgment to the effect that the plaintiff has no or no further claims with respect to the subject matter in dispute.[124]

Claims for the modification of legal rights or status

Federal substantive law, in some instances, provides for a party's right to have a specific legal relationship or status established, modified or terminated by judicial decision. Claims granting such relief include, among others:

(1) Claims for the rescission of contracts for valid reasons;[125]
(2) Claims for the dissolution of a partnership[126] or corporation[127] for reasons defined by the law; or
(3) Claims for the voidance of shareholders' resolutions.[128]

The special element that characterises this type of claim and distinguishes if from claims for declaratory judgment is the effect of a respective judgment. On the rendering of the final judgment, the establishment, modification or termination of the legal relationship or status as sought by the claim becomes effective *ipso jure*. Neither the enforcement of such award nor the undertaking of any additional action is necessary to give effect to the judicial decision, which is self-executing.[129]

POST-TRIAL MOTIONS

Post-trial motions versus appellate remedies

With the rendering of the final judgment by the court, the proceedings come to an end. At the same time, the parties generally will be deprived of their right to file motions relating to procedural or substantive issues. Consequently, if a party is not willing to accept the judgment due to substantive reasons or for reason of alleged procedural irregularities, it may only take a formal appeal against such judgment.

124. Vogel, *Grundriss des Zivilprozessrechts*, 3rd ed., Berne 1992, Section 34 N 29 *et seq.*
125. CO, Articles 20 *et seq.*
126. CO, Article 545, para. 7.
127. CO, Article 736, para. 4.
128. CO, Articles 706 *et seq.*
129. Vogel, *Grundriss des Zivilprozessrechts*, 3rd ed., Berne 1992, Section 34 N 41.

Most cantonal codes of civil procedure do, nevertheless, grant the parties the right to file certain motions in respect of these issues, but with the handing-down of the judgment these motions are terminated. Such motions may either aim at lodging some kind of protest against certain procedural decisions taken by the court (objection, *Einsprache*) or against the court's behaviour during the proceedings (complaint, *Aufsichtsbeschwerde*) or may request that a judgment be explained and clarified by the court (request for explanation or rectification, *Erläuterung, Berichtigung*). All those motions have in common the fact that they do not embody the right to have a judgment be re-examined on its merits and eventually be set aside; such a result can only be accomplished by way of appellate remedies.

Types of post-trial motions

Request for explanation or rectification of a judgment

A majority of the cantons (incl. Zürich, CCC, Sections 162–165) do grant the parties the right to demand that a judgment whose text is either ambiguous, unclear or contradictory be clarified and, if necessary, rectified. The request for explanation or rectification will always be filed with the court that has rendered the judgment. If it is justified, then the court will amend the text of the judgment so to remove any inconsistencies or ambiguities. However, it will be noted that the court must in no instance change the substance of the judgment on such a request.[130]

If the court has, on demand, issued an amended or rectified judgment, then the time period for filing an appeal starts anew.

Objection

Judgments may often be handed down in proceedings in which one party, for whatever reasons (for example, unknown whereabouts of a party, lack of interest to be present), was not present and not represented. As a general rule, such judgments do come in full force and effect (subject to their review on reasons of due process). In a number of cantons (for example, in the cantons of Lucerne, Basel and Geneva), however, a party that without its fault has not been present or represented in a lawsuit has the right to object to a judgment that has been rendered in its absence. The effect of such objection, if granted, is to have the judgment be set aside without considering its merits and have the proceedings started all over again.

130. Cf. Walther J. Habscheid, *Schweizerisches Zivilprozess- und Gerichtsorganisationsrecht*, 2nd ed., Basel 1990, Section 63 N 775.

In some cantons (for example, Zürich), the objection remedy is available only against decisions taken by the presiding judge instead of the whole panel. Examples include decisions about injunctive relief, about the payment of an advance for the court's costs etc. In such instances a party may, by way of an objection, demand that the whole panel instead of the presiding judge render such decision.

Complaint

The complaint is not aimed at changing a particular judgment or decision of a court but rather at the court's or a judge's behaviour during the proceedings. It may be lodged (always with the court's superior authority) already during the proceedings to protest against an undue delay in the proceedings or may be filed after the judgment has been rendered to either protest against an undue treatment of either party by a judge or to notify the superior authority of violations by a judge of the code of conduct. The decision about a complaint results in disciplinary action against a judge only; it never has an influence on the decision or judgment that the judge or court has already rendered.

ENFORCEMENT AND EXECUTION OF JUDGMENTS

Introduction

General

In Switzerland, a judgment may be enforced once it has become final and enforceable, i.e., once an ordinary appellate remedy is no longer available and provided that an extraordinary appellate remedy is not granted suspensive effect.

Of the three types of judgments known in Swiss procedural law, only one needs to be enforced in case the defendant does not voluntarily submit to it: Declaratory judgments are not open to enforcement. Status judgments, such as divorce decrees, judgments on the resolution of a company, etc., are self-executing and no enforcement is necessary. Only judgments for performance (i.e., judgments ordering a party to do or not to do something) need to be enforced if the defendant does not voluntarily comply with the judgment.

Judgments for performance

Judgments for performance are enforced in two different ways: If the judgment orders a party to pay a sum of money (money judgment), the enforcement proceeding follows exclusively the rules of debt collection proceedings as provided for in the Debt Collection Act. As this is a Federal Statute, the steps necessary to achieve enforcement are identical all over Switzerland. If, however, the judgment is not a money judgment, but orders a defendant to perform or refrain from certain acts, then enforcement of such judgment is governed by the cantonal civil procedural laws.

Judgments eligible for enforcement

All final judgments rendered by Swiss courts can be enforced within Switzerland. Article 61 of the Federal Constitution explicitly provides that final and enforceable judgments rendered in one canton must be enforced all over Switzerland.

With respect to foreign judgments, a variety of relevant legal bases exists. First, foreign judgments stemming from a court in a country that has ratified the Lugano Convention must be recognised and enforced in application of that Convention. Second, Switzerland is a party to a number of bilateral treaties that govern the recognition and enforcement of foreign judgments. Third, with respect to judgments rendered by courts of foreign countries that are not parties to an international treaty, recognition and enforcement is governed by the PILA.

The above-mentioned treaties generally do not cover the recognition and enforcement of arbitral awards. However, Switzerland is a party to the New York Convention on recognition and enforcement of foreign arbitral awards and applies it to all foreign arbitration awards, whether stemming from a Convention Country or not.

Enforcement of Swiss non-monetary judgments

General

The enforcement of non-monetary judgments for performance is a matter of cantonal law. In general, enforcement must be sought at the ordinary place of jurisdiction of the defendant, i.e., its domicile. If enforcement is directed against a thing, then the place where such thing is located determines the competent jurisdiction.

If enforcement measures have not already been provided for in the judgment itself, enforcement must be sought in summary proceedings as already described in this chapter.

The rules applicable to the enforcement proceedings are the general rules of summary proceedings, including the right of the defendant to be granted its day in court. Further, the appellate remedies available against enforcement judgments are the remedies available against summary judgments. One-time fines (*Ordnungsbussen*) are not open to appeal or petition of nullity. This limitation does, however, not apply to revolving daily fines (*astreintes*).

The defendant has the following defences available against Swiss judgments stemming from a canton other than the canton in which enforcement is sought:

(1) The judgment was not issued by a competent court; competence is decided based on the law of the canton in which the judgment was rendered;

(2) Service of process was improper or the defendant was not properly represented; and

(3) The judgment has not become final and enforceable according to the law of the issuing court.

Measures

In the canton of Zürich the summary judge has the following enforcement measures available:

(1) He may order the defendant to do or not to do whatever the judgment provided for and may include in such order the condition that in case of non-compliance the defendant will be fined (one-time fine, *Ordnungsbusse*);

(2) He may order that the non-complying defendant will be punished in accordance with Article 292 of the Swiss Criminal Code according to which a defendant in contempt may be fined or imprisoned;

(3) He may issue a daily fine (*astreinte*) for each day of non-compliance;

(4) If the defendant has been adjudged to do something that may also be performed by a third party, the judge may ask such a third party or the plaintiff to do whatever is necessary to achieve compliance with the judgment. The costs of such act must be borne by the defendant;

(5) The judge may use force against the defendant or against things in his possession. For example, he may order a thing whose possession has been awarded to the plaintiff to be taken away from the defendant and be handed over to the plaintiff. Such force is exercised by the competent local authority, if necessary by the police; and

(6) Finally, if the defendant has been ordered to render a declaratory act, such as a consent to the execution of an agreement, the summary judge may rule that the enforcement judgment itself will substitute such act. This especially applies to entries in the land registry concerning title to real estate or limited rights to real estate.

If neither of the above leads to the result provided for in the judgment, the plaintiff may request damages for non-performance. The amount of damages to be paid are fixed in summary proceedings if this has not already been provided for in the original judgment.

Enforcement of Swiss money judgments

The enforcement of money judgments is governed by the Debt Collection Act.

Debt collection in Switzerland is a mixture of administrative-type acts together with court proceedings, the next step to be undertaken by the claimant always depending on the reaction of the defendant. The typical case of debt collection undergoes the following stages.

Introduction of debt collection

Debt collection is commenced by a request for the commencement of debt collection proceedings (*Betreibungsbegehren*), which must be filed with the competent debt collection office. The debt collection office, on receiving such a request and the respective advance payment, will then serve on the debtor a writ of payment (*Zahlungsbefehl*), granting the debtor a delay of 10 days either to pay or to lodge an objection (*Rechtsvorschlag*). Except in special cases, no reason must be given for such objection. Because it is so easy to stall debt collection proceedings by lodging an objection, there is hardly ever a case in which a debtor does not oppose to the writ of payment. The debt collection officer will now advise the creditor of the objection and the creditor will must decide whether to pursue the claim. The next step in debt collection proceedings accordingly would be the setting aside of the objection.

Setting aside of objection

A claimant may decide to start debt collection prior to having obtained a final and enforceable judgment. If this is the case, the debtor's opposition will effectively bring the debt collection proceedings to a halt. The creditor must obtain a judgment first and, to that effect, must commence an ordinary law suit (claim for money judgment).

If, however, the claimant is already in possession of a final and enforceable Swiss judgment or an acknowledgement of debt set forth in a public deed or bearing the debtor's original signature (*Schuldanerkennung*), he has the possibility to commence summary proceedings to set aside the objection (*Rechtsöffnungsverfahren*). If these proceedings are based on a final and enforceable judgment, he requests the judge to set aside the objection in a definite manner (*definitive Rechtsöffnung*).

The debtor's defences are limited. If debt collection proceedings are based on a judgment rendered in the same canton, then the debtor may only raise the defences of payment, stay or statute of limitation. The defences of payment and stay are valid only if the debtor is able to produce respective documentation. The same defences are available in case of a Federal Judgment. If the judgment has been rendered within Switzerland, but in another canton, then the debtor may raise, in addition to the defences of lack of jurisdiction of the court who rendered the judgment, improper service or improper representation. A confirmation by the issuing court that the judgment is final and enforceable may only be ignored if this is obviously incorrect. The setting aside of opposition in case of a Swiss judgment is subject only to a petition for nullity to the cantonal superior court, to the extent such a remedy exists, and to a Federal petition for nullity to the Federal Supreme Court.

If the summary proceedings designed to set aside the objection are based on a written acknowledgement of debt, on the other hand, then the basis is only a so-called provisional title.[131] Based on such title the judge may set aside the debtor's opposition provisionally (*provisorische Rechtsöffnung*). However, the debtor may, within 10 days, file an action in ordinary proceedings for a declaratory judgment determining that the debt in dispute does not exist.

Despite the fact that in this event the debtor is the plaintiff, the burden of proof for the existence of the debt in dispute is not reversed. It remains with the creditor-defendant. The action for negative declaratory judgment serves to provoke the creditor into legal proceedings that lead to a final and enforceable judgment on the money claim in dispute.

Continuance of debt collection

Once the debtor's opposition is set aside in one way or the other, and if the debtor still does not pay, the claimant may continue debt collection proceedings by filing with the debt collection office a request for continuance (*Fortsetzungsbegehren*). On receipt of this request, the debt collection office will continue the proceedings.

If the debtor is a natural person, it will serve on the debtor a notice of seizure (*Pfändungsankündigung*). If again the debtor does not pay, the debt collection office will seize goods belonging to the debtor that are sufficient to cover the claim that is prosecuted. If the debtor is a corporation, it will receive a notice of bankruptcy declaration (*Konkursandrohung*).

131. Debt Collection Act, Articles 82 *et seq.*

If the debtor does not pay within 20 days since receipt of this notice, the creditor may request, in summary proceedings that the debtor be declared bankrupt.

The judge's bankruptcy declaration is subject to appeal. In the canton of Zürich, a special appeal may be filed against the bankruptcy adjudication. Zürich appellate proceedings allow for an unlimited introduction of new facts. The debtor may, therefore, as a last resort, pay the debt and raise, in the appeal brief, the defence of payment. It is a prerequisite of this mechanism that the payment has been made prior to lodging the appeal and that the appeal brief is accompanied by documentary evidence of such payment.

Apparently, this mechanism was abused by debtors that were in fact insolvent. In a case in which the debtor was adjudicated bankrupt in September, October and December of the same year and each time paid the debt prosecuted in the last moment in order to have the bankruptcy adjudication set aside in the appeal proceedings, the Zürich Superior Court held that if it was obvious that the debtor was insolvent, payment of the prosecuted debt would no longer prevent a bankruptcy adjudication.[132]

Enforcement of foreign judgments

Legal basis

The recognition and enforcement of foreign judgments in general are governed by the fifth chapter of the PILA.[133]

Article 1 para. 2 of the PILA, however, gives a prerogative to treaties, which may govern the issue differently from the PILA. As already mentioned, Switzerland is a party to the Lugano Convention. Further, Switzerland has entered into a number of bilateral treaties relating to enforcement that are still in force.

The Lugano Convention was, as of March 1994, in force in Finland, France, Great Britain, Italy, Luxembourg, The Netherlands, Norway, Portugal, Sweden, and Switzerland.

Enforcement based on the PILA

A foreign judgment will be recognised (and, if necessary, enforced) in Switzerland if the following three prerequisites are met:

132. ZR 87/1988, Number 30.
133. PILA, Articles 25–32.

(1) The foreign court that issued the decision was competent;
(2) No ordinary remedy can be filed against the decision or the decision is final; and
(3) The decision does not violate public policy.

Switzerland accepts the competence of foreign courts if the PILA itself provides for it; or if the defendant, at the time the proceedings were commenced, lived in the country issuing the decision; in monetary disputes if the parties have entered into a jurisdiction clause which is valid under the PILA and which provided for the competence of the issuing court; if the defendant has unconditionally appeared before the foreign court; or if in case of a counterclaim, the issuing court was competent for the main claim and there is a sufficient connection between the main claim and counterclaim.

According to Article 27 of the PILA a foreign judgment cannot be recognised if the recognition would be incompatible with Swiss public policy (*ordre public*).

Further, the so-called formal public policy is violated and leads to non-recognition of a foreign judgment if the defendant sufficiently demonstrates that it was not properly served, which defence is not available if the defendant unconditionally appeared in court; the decision was rendered in violation of fundamental rules of Swiss procedural law, especially if the defendant was not granted his day in court; or a court action between the same parties and in the same matter was first pending or decided in Switzerland or was first decided in a third country, provided that the judgment rendered in such third country would be recognised in Switzerland.

Article 27, para. 3 of the PILA explicitly provides that otherwise the foreign judgment may not be revisited on the merits.

Under the PILA, the request for recognition or enforcement must be filed with the court competent according to the relevant cantonal CCP. In Zürich, this is the summary judge at the district court of the district in which the defendant resides.

If the question of recognition of a foreign judgment is a preliminary question in another proceeding, then no request to the summary judge is required. The court handling the proceeding may itself decide on the recognition.[134]

In the proceedings, the defending party must be granted the right to be heard.

According to Article 29, para. 1 of the PILA, the request for recognition and/or enforcement must be accompanied by the following documents:

134. PILA, Article 29, para. 3.

(1) A complete and legalised copy of the judgment;
(2) A confirmation of the issuing court that no ordinary remedy is available against the judgment or that the judgment is final; and
(3) In case of a default judgment only: an official document evidencing that the defendant was properly summoned and had an opportunity to defend the case.

Settlements that have been entered into between the parties before a court may be recognised or enforced in Switzerland in the same manner as judgments, if in the issuing country the court settlement has equal legal quality as a court decision.

Recognition and enforcement under the Lugano Convention

The bilateral treaties quite often do not differ substantially from the PILA, which was enacted in 1989 and attempted to grant foreign judgments from a non-treaty country a position equal to that originating in a country with which Switzerland has a treaty. Further, with the area of application of the Lugano Convention rapidly growing, bilateral treaties are becoming less and less important.

The Lugano Convention, which is a treaty parallel to the European Union Convention on Jurisdiction and the Enforcement of Judgments in Civil and Commercial Matters of 27 September 1968, substantially improves the position of foreign judgments.

Recognition and enforcement of foreign judgments are governed in Articles 25–49 of the Lugano Convention.

The basic rule is recognition and enforcement of state court judgments in civil and commercial matters.[135]

Article 27 of the Lugano Convention lists the grounds on which a judgment rendered in one of the treaty countries may be denied recognition and enforcement. The main grounds are:

(1) Recognition would contradict public policy of the enforcing country;
(2) The defendant who did not unconditionally appear has not properly received the summons or an equal document or has not received that document timely enough to be able to properly defend the case; or
(3) The judgment is incompatible with a judgment between the same parties which was rendered in the country that now should recognise the foreign judgment.

135. Lugano Convention, Article 26.

Certainly the most important improvement for the holder of a foreign judgment is Article 28, para. 4 of the Lugano Convention, which provides that the decision of the foreign court affirming its own competence may not be revisited and that the competence of the court is not part of public policy. A defendant in recognition proceedings may, therefore, not raise as a defence the fact that the foreign court violated public policy by affirming its own jurisdiction. Unlike under domestic law, i.e., the PILA, the Lugano Convention, therefore, prohibits the enforcing court to revisit the issue of competence except in those limited cases where competence is based on Articles 7–16 of the Lugano Convention.

Another major difference to the traditional enforcement legislation exists with respect to the quality of recognisable and enforceable judgments. According to Article 31 of the Lugano Convention, a foreign judgment must be enforced if it is enforceable in the issuing country. The defendant may, therefore, be prosecuted even prior to the judgment having become final. The enforcement proceedings may be stayed, however, if the foreign judgment has been appealed or if an appeal is still possible.[136]

Finally, there is a major change in traditional enforcement proceedings and certainly a major deviation from the procedure as provided for by the PILA because according to Article 34 of the Lugano Convention, the enforcement proceedings of the first instance are *ex parte* proceedings. The defendant may not be heard. This procedure disrupts the existing Swiss system of enforcement, especially with respect to the enforcement of money judgments.

Foreign money judgments are enforced in the same procedure as Swiss money judgments, that is, by way of debt collection proceedings. Traditionally, the issue of enforceability of foreign money judgments is part of the setting aside of objection. In proceedings to set aside an objection, the defendant doubtlessly has a right to be heard. The question, therefore, has come up whether, if a foreign judgment coming from a Convention country must be enforced, enforcement proceedings must be separate from debt collection proceedings or whether they nevertheless may be joined and, if so, what the defendant's rights are under such circumstances.

The canton of Zürich has chosen the following solution: Because the Lugano Convention[137] explicitly provides that the judge competent for enforcement of foreign judgments is the same judge competent for requests to set aside objections, both requests may be issued jointly. The defendant under Swiss debt collection and bankruptcy law has a right to be heard in the procedure to set aside opposition; this right must be respected. Should the defendant in these proceedings raise defences

136. Lugano Convention, Article 38.
137. Lugano Convention, Article 32.

against the enforceability, the first instance judge must ignore these defences and advise the defendant that he must bring them before the Zürich Superior Court.

With respect to appellate remedies, the debtor's situation is improved: To the extent the debtor wishes to raise defences against the judgment recognising enforceability, he may lodge a special appeal with the Zürich Superior Court during one month.[138] Should enforceability be denied, however, the Lugano Convention does not grant special delays or remedies. Accordingly, the creditor must file the special appeal within the delay granted by the cantonal CCP, which in Zürich is 10 days,[139] and which also applies if a creditor holding a Swiss or non-Convention country judgment prevails.

To the extent mere debt collection issues are concerned and the enforceability is not disputed, only the plea of nullity is available, which also must be lodged within 10 days.[140]

The claimant may choose, however, to separate the issue of enforceability from debt collection proceedings. This may be advantageous, because then the defendant indeed is not heard at all in the first instance. The claimant may then request that security measures as provided for in Article 39 of the Lugano Convention be put in place prior to the debtor being heard for the first time. The nature of this security measure has not yet been decided in Switzerland. Most likely the judgment creditor will be granted a right to attach assets of the debtor as provided for in Articles 271 *et seq*. of the Debt Collection Act, preventing the debtor to further dispose of these assets. Such attachment would be available not only to the holder of a Lugano judgment, but to any holder of a final and enforceable judgment.

APPEAL

Introduction

Judgments from the courts of first instance and, subject to various restrictions, from superior cantonal courts may be appealed in the case of procedural faults, or for alleged errors in the application of substantive law. As the grounds for appealing a judgment vary, so do the types of appellate remedies available and the appropriate jurisdictions.

Jurisdiction for appellate review generally lies with one of two authorities: the Swiss Confederation and the cantons. Typically, judgments rendered by lower cantonal courts can be appealed to one or more

---

138. Lugano Convention, Article 36.
139. Zürich CCP, Section 276.
140. Zürich CCP, Section 287, para. 2.

superior courts of the particular canton. However, if the court of first
instance was either the commercial court (in the case of the cantons of
Aargau, Berne, St. Gall and Zürich) or the superior cantonal court, the
available cantonal appellate remedies are very limited. The Federal Supreme Court generally has jurisdiction to finally review judgments or
appellate decisions handed down by the highest cantonal courts or superior courts. However, as will be discussed below, several restrictions exist
on appeals to the Federal Supreme Court.

Characterisation of the Swiss system of appellate remedies

Notwithstanding the differences between the civil procedural laws of the
26 cantons and the federal civil procedural rules, the Swiss system of
appellate remedies and procedures is characterised by the categorisation
of two main classes of appellate remedies: the ordinary and extraordinary
appellate remedies (*ordentliche und ausserordentliche Rechtsmittel*). The
difference lies in the interaction between the qualification of a judgment
as final or not.

If an ordinary appellate remedy is available, the judgment is not
deemed to be final. Conversely, a judgment that, by virtue of the non-
availability of ordinary appellate remedies, is deemed to be final may still
be attacked by way of an extraordinary appellate remedy, but as a rule
only for a limited number of grounds. A further difference lies in the fact
that ordinary appellate remedies usually entail a suspension of the effectiveness of the relevant judgment, whereas extraordinary appellate
remedies typically do not entail such suspension, unless the appellate
court so orders.

Whether an ordinary appellate remedy is available against a judgment,
that is, whether a judgment is deemed to be "final" in a procedural sense,
depends primarily on the amount in dispute. Except for the canton of
Vaud, all cantonal procedural laws do provide for a threshold exceeding
which an ordinary appellate remedy is available against judgments rendered by the lower cantonal court. This threshold ranges from SFR 5,000
(canton of Valais) up to SFR 12,000 (canton of Zürich). Judgments
rendered by a superior cantonal court may be appealed with the Federal
Supreme Court if the sum in dispute exceeds SFR 8,000.[141] Claims that
cannot be expressed in a monetary value may always be appealed with the
Federal Supreme Court, provided certain other criteria are met.

Extraordinary appellate remedies are generally subsidiary to ordinary
appellate remedies. Consequently, for so long as a judgment may still be
challenged with an ordinary appellate remedy, no extraordinary appellate
remedies will be available. However, in certain instances a party may

---

141. Federal Organisation Act, Article 46.

challenge a judgment rendered by a superior cantonal court with an ordinary and an extraordinary appellate remedy at the same time if the cantonal procedure laws so allow (which is, for instance, the case in the canton of Zürich), a judgment may be appealed against with a federal appeal (an ordinary appellate remedy) to be lodged with the Federal Supreme Court and, but only for alleged violation of cantonal civil procedural rules or gross errors in applying substantive law, with an extraordinary cantonal appellate remedy to be lodged with a respective cantonal court.

The time limit to lodge an appeal varies from canton to canton. Depending on the type of appellate remedy it extends from 10–30 days from the date of the valid formal announcement of the judgment. For federal appellate remedies the period is always 30 days.

Types of appellate remedies

Both cantonal and federal civil procedural laws do provide for several different types of appellate remedies. Taking into account the two different classes of appellate remedies as well as the two venue jurisdictions for appellate review, four sub-classes of appellate remedies may be distinguished:

Ordinary cantonal appellate remedies

All cantons do grant at least one ordinary appellate remedy against judgments rendered by a lower cantonal court: The regular appeal (*Berufung*). This appellate remedy usually allows an unlimited review of a judgment or jurisdictional decision by a cantonal appellate court. Consequently, an appellate court may consider all questions of fact and/or law on the taking of a regular appeal.

Whereas in several cantons the parties do have an unlimited right to submit to the appellate court new evidence and new factual allegations, most cantonal procedural laws do restrict this right in various different forms. Furthermore, in those five cantons where law suits which are subject to a federal appeal are decided only by the superior cantonal court (the cantons of Berne, Vaud, Valais, Neuchatel and Jura), as well as in those instances where a commercial court decides as the sole cantonal instance, no regular cantonal appeal is available against judgments rendered by such superior cantonal courts.

In most cantons of the German-speaking part of Switzerland (but not in the French-speaking part), the cantonal procedural laws do provide also for a special appeal (*Rekurs*) which allows for the (usually unlimited) review of certain types of procedural decisions or judgments. In those cantons where both regular and special appeals are available, the decision of whether a regular or special appeal is available depends largely on the substantive nature of the judgment or jurisdictional decision that will be challenged. Otherwise, almost no differences exist between the appeal and the special appeal. Also, in both cases, an appellate court may render a completely new decision substituting the decision of the lower court.

Extraordinary cantonal appellate remedies

All cantonal procedural laws do provide for some kind of an extraordinary appellate remedy by which a judgment may be challenged for procedural deficiencies or gross errors in applying the substantive law. The most common type of extraordinary appellate remedies is the petition for nullity (*Nichtigkeitsbeschwerde*, *recours en nullité* or *recours en cassation*). This type of remedy is usually available against final decisions rendered by lower cantonal courts against decisions of superior cantonal courts. Only a number of cantons do allow the filing of a petition for nullity (for example, the cantons of Zürich, Berne, Lucerne and Vaud). Since the petition for nullity is, as a rule, available only to remedy procedural faults, no new evidence relating to the underlying dispute may be submitted by the parties and no pleadings in respect of the merits of the case take place.

In addition, all cantons provide a remedy by which the setting aside of a final and binding judgment may be demanded from the court that originally rendered the judgment. However, this remedy (*Revision*) does usually allow the setting aside of a judgment only if one or both of the following grounds are present:

(1) The rendering of a judgment has been influenced by a criminal act to the detriment of one party;
(2) New substantive facts or evidence have been discovered subsequent to the rendering of the judgment.

If either is the case, the judgment is set aside and the proceedings start anew.

Appeal to the Federal Supreme Court

Once a superior cantonal court has rendered a decision or judgment which is, pursuant to the cantonal civil procedural law, final, then a party to such litigation may take an appeal to the Federal Supreme Court (*Berufung*). The Federal Organisation Act, however, provides for an appeal to the Federal Supreme Court to be permissible if either the sum in dispute exceeds SFR 8,000 or that the issue in dispute has no monetary value. Other than in the case of a regular appeal pursuant to cantonal procedural law, only a violation of federal substantive private law may be alleged with a federal appeal. The Federal Supreme Court may not reconsider or second-guess statements of cantonal courts relating to the facts nor may it consider new factual allegations.

On an appeal, the Federal Supreme Court may either directly rule on the merits of a case or remand the matter back to the antecedent cantonal court. If it issues a new judgment on the merits, this decision becomes final and is not subject to further appeal.

Extraordinary federal appellate remedies

As in all cantons, federal procedural law also provides for a petition for nullity against judgments rendered by cantonal courts (*Nichtigkeitsbeschwerde*) which may be lodged with the Federal Supreme Court. However, with a federal petition for nullity only three specific errors may be claimed:

(1) The violation of provisions of federal law relating to jurisdiction;
(2) The violation of provisions of the Federal Private International Law Act (PILA) and other federal conflict of laws rules; and
(3) That federal law instead of cantonal law or *vice versa* has been applied.

Furthermore, the federal petition for nullity is subsidiary to the federal appeal, that is, it is only available in cases where a federal appeal is impossible.

In addition, federal procedural law also provides for a very special remedy granting the right to have any kind of jurisdictional decision or judgment reviewed on constitutional grounds by the Federal Supreme Court (*Staatsrechtliche Beschwerde*). A petition to the Federal Supreme Court for examination of constitutionality typically may only be filed when a "final" cantonal judgment has been rendered. Exceptions from this prevailing principle are only allowed if violations of international treaties and of the constitutional guarantees relating to ordinary and constitutional organisation of courts, to the place of jurisdiction and to inter-cantonal enforcement procedures[142] are being alleged.

Furthermore, the Petition for the Examination of Constitutionality is exclusively permissible for allegations of violations of constitutional rights (or provisions of international treaties, such as, for instance, the Lugano Convention) that occurred either during the procedures or by virtue of the judgment handed down by a cantonal court. As in the case

142. Federal Constitution, Articles 58, 59 and 61.

of the federal petition for nullity, also the Petition for the Examination of Constitutionality is subsidiary to the appeal and, moreover, also to the federal petition for nullity.

Both extraordinary appellate remedies do not entail a stay of the judgment appealed but, if granted, result in a remand of the matter to the antecedent cantonal court.

Finally, federal procedural law or also contemplates the *Revision* by which the setting aside of a final and binding judgment rendered by the Federal Supreme Court may be demanded. However, the same Federal Supreme Court, through a different chamber, will rule anew on the case so set aside by it.

Common principles

All cantonal procedural laws do provide for the right of the adverse party to either join a regular appeal lodged by the other party, but with different motions, or to file an outstanding, independent appeal. If a party only joins an appeal with opposing motions, such an appeal is dependent on the outcome of the original appeal. Consequently, if the party lodging the appeal withdraws from the appeal, the joining appeal becomes moot. Not so in the case of an "own-standing", that is, independent appeal; it remains in full force and effect irrespective of the outcome of the other party's appeal.

Except for the regular appeal to the Federal Supreme Court, cantonal procedural laws do usually provide that a cantonal superior court concerned with a regular (or special) appeal is authorised to (but must not) order new or supplementary evidence taking proceedings instead of remanding the matter to the inferior court. In its review of the judgment of the inferior court, however, the appellate court is, bound by the particular motions submitted to it by one or both of the parties. Even if it finds other errors in the judgment which if so reviewed would influence its judgment, it has no authority to consider those errors if the effects thereof would not be covered by the parties' motions. The appellate court may also not modify the challenged judgment to the detriment of the party who has lodged the appeal.

Finally, the principle that a losing party will pay the court fees and indemnify the winning party for the latter's attorney's fees applies also for appellate proceedings.

CONCLUSIVENESS OF JUDGMENT

Res judicata

Swiss procedural law differentiates between formal and material *res judicata*. Formal *res judicata* exists from the moment no ordinary remedy is available anymore against a judgment, be it that the remedies have been exhausted, or that the delay granted to file a remedy has lapsed.

The term *res judicata* in a material sense denotes the validity of a judgment for future legal proceedings between the persons affected by the first judgment.[143] This means that a second court is bound by the first court's ruling or must decline to hear the case if either identical question between identical parties is litigated or if, in a second lawsuit between the same parties, the issue solved in the first ruling is a preliminary question.

In principle, *res judicata* is limited to the ruling itself and does not extend to the grounds leading to such ruling given by the court. It is obvious, however that in many cases the grounds must be taken into consideration because otherwise it does not become clear what the issue of the judgment was. This is especially true if the claimant was turned down or if the defendant was ordered to pay a certain sum of money.

Law of the case

In Switzerland, a court case of a higher court is not legally binding on lower courts having to deal with identical issues.[144] It is normal, however that lower courts follow the rulings of higher courts, which generally is in the interest of the parties seeking a judgment. Nevertheless, quite often the changes in the practice of the law have been introduced by the lower courts refusing to follow case law.

Accordingly, publication of court cases is less wide-spread than in Common Law countries. Not all cantons have publications containing their case law. Even where there are, such as in the cantons of Basel (*Basler Juristische Mitteilungen*), Zürich (*Blätter für Zürcherische Rechtsprechung*) and Geneva (*Journal des Tribunaux*), these publications contain a selection of cantonal case law, mostly a selection of more important upper level court cases.

Also, the Federal Supreme Court selects the material to be published, which appears in two publications: the *Entscheidungen des schweizerischen Bundesgerichtes* and the *Praxis des schweizerischen Bundesgerichts*. Naturally, all these publications are widely followed by the legal practitioners in their daily work.

143. Guldener, *Schweizerisches Zivilprozessrecht*, 3rd ed., Zürich 1979, p. 364.
144. Guldener, *Schweizerisches Zivilprozessrecht*, 3rd ed., Zürich 1979, p. 4.

CHAPTER 16

UNITED STATES

Frank S. Towner, Jr.
Robins, Kaplan, Miller & Ciresi
San Francisco, California

INTRODUCTION

The purpose of this chapter is to provide a summary overview of the procedural rules governing civil matters that might be of particular significance to persons who are not familiar with United States civil procedure, but who may find themselves in need of basic information about the system for judicially settling civil disputes there. Because of the prominence of the federal model in the civil procedural rules of the court systems for the 50 states of the United States, this chapter will focus on the guidelines provided by the Federal Rules of Civil Procedure (FRCP).

While the United States' legal system is Common-Law based, the procedural systems of all 50 states and the United States are largely statutory. To the extent that procedural statutes and rules are interpreted by Common Law, certain principles, such as fairness, justice and economy, generally prevail. It is not possible, within the confines of a single chapter, to fully explore the nuances of the American civil procedural system, or to provide a practice manual. When specific procedural issues arise in a case, the FRCP or the applicable state code of civil procedure[1] and local court rules should be consulted.[2] In addition, there

---

1. For the federal rules of civil procedure and accompanying case law annotations and discussion, see *Federal Rules of Civil Procedure, 28 United States Code Annotated* (USCA) (West Publishing Co., St. Paul, MN); annotated codes and treatises are also available that describe the rules of civil procedure for each of the states. For example, see West's Annotated California Code of Civil Procedure (West Publishing Co., St. Paul, MN). Virtually all United States district courts and state trial courts have adopted local rules supplementing the applicable Rules of Civil Procedure. For example, the United States district courts are now in various stages of implementing a civil justice expense-and-delay-reduction program (28 USC, Section 471). To the extent that a district court has adopted rules implementing a cost-and-delay-reduction program, such rules will be reflected in that court's local rules.

2. FRCP, Rule 83 permits each district court to adopt local rules governing their practice, not inconsistent with the Federal Rules.

are well-recognised treatises containing in-depth discussions of federal and state civil procedure that may also be consulted.[3]

United states civil court system

The court structure in the United States includes two independent, but at times parallel systems: a national or federal court system and the separate court systems of each of the 50 states of the United States. The principal difference between the two systems is in the nature of the substantive matters over which jurisdiction is vested in the federal courts and/or the state courts by the United States Constitution and as provided by Congress.[4] This division of jurisdiction flows from the principle that each of the 50 states of the United States is a sovereign political entity, with exclusive sovereignty over persons and property within its own territory, except as expressly reserved to the federal courts by Article III of the Constitution.

Federal court system

The federal court system includes 91 trial-level United States district courts,[5] a court of appeal system consisting of thirteen judicial circuits,[6] and a court of final review, the United States Supreme Court.[7] For instance, in California, the federal civil court system includes the Northern, Central, Eastern and Southern United States District Courts. The intermediate appellate court is the Court of Appeal for the Ninth Circuit, which may review decisions from all United States District Courts in Alaska, Arizona, California, Hawaii, Idaho, Montana, Nevada, Oregon, Utah and Washington. The United States Supreme Court is the court of final review for each of the 13 circuits of the courts of appeal. The Supreme Court may also review, by writ of *certiorari*, final judgments of the highest courts of a state involving the validity of a treaty or statute of the United States or where a statute of any state is questioned on the ground of its violation of the Constitution, treaties, or laws of the United States, or where any title, right, privilege, or immunity is claimed under

3. Two frequently referenced treatises on federal civil procedure are *Moore's Federal Practice and Procedure*, 1993 ed., Matthew Bender & Co., Inc., New York, and Wright & Miller, *Federal Practice and Procedure, Civil*, 2d ed., West Publishing Co., St. Paul, MN. Similar treatises are available for many state court systems; for example, Witkin, *California Procedure*, 3d ed. 1985 and Supp. 1993).

4. 28 United States Code (USC), Section 1251.

5. 28 USC, Sections 81–131.

6. 28 USC, Section 41.

7. 28 USC, Section 1.

the Constitution, treaties, or statutes of, or any commission held or authority exercised under, the United States.[8]

In 1938, pursuant to the Rules Enabling Act[9] authorising the Supreme Court to prescribe rules applicable to civil procedure, evidence and appellate procedure for all United States district courts, the Court adopted the FRCP. On 22 April 1993, the Court authorised Chief Justice Rehnquist to transmit to Congress proposed amendments effecting sweeping changes to the FRCP, particularly regarding the rules governing discovery.[10] Following intense public debate over the proposed changes and failed efforts to amend the proposed Rules in Congress, the revised FRCP became effective 1 December 1993, without modification.

State court system

The court system in each of the 50 states is composed of trial-level courts, intermediary appellate courts and a State Supreme Court, which is the court of final review for each state. Although the procedures controlling civil matters in the state courts are governed by the rules adopted by each of the 50 states, most have adopted rules which are either identical to or closely parallel the FRCP.[11]

Federal Rules of Civil Procedure

A review of the procedural rules applicable to civil cases in federal district courts generally reveals the impact of two interrelated concepts that have historically shaped the evolution of civil procedure in the United States. The first concept is that all parties residing or situated in the United States are entitled to equal access to the civil justice system, which is impartial and competent to hear the matter before it. This is reflected in the constitutional and statutory extensions and limitations on the power of the federal and state courts to hear cases and to exercise their power over the parties. The second concept is that all parties are entitled to an expeditious, economic and fair resolution of their claims and disputes. Thus, the Federal Rules provide for early voluntary exchange of relevant information, and vest in the courts broad powers to manage their cases as efficiently and effectively as possible.

8. 28 USC, Section 1257.

9. 28 USC, Section 2072.

10. 146 Federal Rules Decisions (FRD) 404.

11. See Oakley and Coon, "The Federal Rules in State Courts: A Survey of State Court Systems of Civil Procedure", Wash. L Rev. 61 : 1367, 1986.

SUBJECT MATTER JURISDICTION

If party A files a lawsuit against party B in a United States district court, the first jurisdictional issue raised is whether that court is authorised to decide the kind of case before it, or whether the case ought properly to be heard in a state court. The authority of district courts to hear cases is limited by the judicial power of the United States as specified by Article III of the Constitution and as granted by Congress. By contrast, state trial courts are courts of general jurisdiction and may hear all types of cases, except where the power to hear cases involving certain subjects has been reserved exclusively to the federal courts.[12]

Obtaining subject matter jurisdiction

The subject matter over which district courts may preside is defined by statute, subject to judicial interpretation. Subject matter jurisdiction may be obtained on the basis of the existence of a federal question,[13] which is an essential element of the plaintiff's case, or where there exists complete diversity of citizenship between the parties.[14]

Subject matter jurisdiction based on the existence of a federal question

28 USC, Section 1331 provides: "The district courts shall have original jurisdiction of all civil actions, arising under the Constitution, laws, or treaties of the United States."

If party A files his complaint against party B in a district court, or having filed his complaint in state court, party B removes the case to a district court,[15] the party seeking to obtain federal-question jurisdiction

12. In a number of instances, Congress has conferred exclusive jurisdiction to district courts over certain subjects, including: 28 USC, Section 1333, cases of admiralty or maritime jurisdiction; 28 USC, Section 1334, bankruptcy; 28 USC, Section 1338, patent and copyright law; 28 USC, Section 1351, actions against consuls, vice-consuls, and members of diplomatic missions of foreign countries as a defendant; 28 USC, Section 1355, suits to recover fines, penalties or a forfeiture under an Act of Congress; and, 28 USC, Section 1350, an action by an alien for a tort only, committed in violation of the law of nations or a treaty of the United States. In most instances, Congress has expressly or implicitly provided concurrent jurisdiction to states. Absent a specific Congressional intent to give exclusive jurisdiction to district courts, it is presumed that the state courts have concurrent jurisdiction. *Yellow Freight Sys. Inc.* v. *Donnelly*, 494 United States 820, 110 S Ct. 1566, 108 L Ed. 2d 834 (1990).

13. 28 USC, Section 1331.

14. 28 USC, Section 1332.

15. See discussion regarding removal of cases from state court pursuant to 28 USC, Section 1441 below.

must establish that the right that is the essential basis of party A's claim is supported by one interpretation of the Constitution, treaties or laws of the United States and defeated by a contrary interpretation. The existence of a federal question must appear from the allegations contained in party A's complaint; it may not be created by allegations in party B's answer. Nor may party A create jurisdiction by framing its complaint in anticipation of a federal defence.[16] Moreover, where party A's complaint properly pleads a federal question, party B may not defeat jurisdiction by not contesting the federal question or by pleading a defence available under state law.[17]

Where party A's complaint alleges a right or cause of action expressly created by federal statute, e.g., based on the patent, copyright or trade mark statutes, or the civil rights or antitrust statutes, the existence of a federal question is generally clear.[18] However, the issue becomes significantly more complex where the involved statute simply regulates or affects the activities giving rise to the cause of action alleged.

The Supreme Court, in *Cort* v. *Ash*,[19] set out four criteria which may determine if a federal question exists:

(1) Whether the plaintiff is a member of the class for whose benefit the statute was enacted;
(2) Whether there is evidence of legislative intent to create or deny the remedy sought;
(3) Whether it is consistent with the legislative scheme to imply the remedy sought; and
(4) Whether the claim alleged is one traditionally governed by state law, so that it would be inappropriate to imply its creation under federal law.

Subject matter jurisdiction based on complete diversity of the parties

28 USC, Section 1332 states in part:

The district courts shall have the original jurisdiction of all civil actions where the matter in controversy exceeds the sum or value of $50,000, exclusive of interest and costs, and is between:

(1) Citizens of different states;
(2) Citizens of a state and citizens or subjects of a foreign state;

16. See *United Jersey Banks* v. *Parell*, 783 F2d 360 (3d Cir.), cert. denied, 476 United States 1170, 106 S Ct. 2892, 90 LEd. 2d 979 (1986).
17. See The *Fair* v. *Kohler Die & Specialty Co.*, 228 United States 22, 33 S Ct. 410, 57 LEd. 716 (1913).
18. See *Cherokee Express, Inc.* v. *Cherokee Express, Inc.*, 924 F2d 603 (6th Cir. 1991).
19. 22 United States 66, 95 S Ct. 2080, 45 LEd.2d 26 (1975)

(3) Citizens of different states and in which citizens or subjects of a foreign state are additional parties; and

(4) A foreign state, defined in Section 1603(a) of this title, as plaintiff and citizens of a state or of different states.

The rationale often cited for diversity jurisdiction is that access to a United States district court by a foreign state party is required to protect against the risk of state court prejudice favouring its own citizens.[20] As will be discussed, where an action otherwise falling within the original jurisdiction of the federal courts is filed in a state court, a defendant may remove the case to a United States district court pursuant to 28 USC, Section 1441 and the requirements stated therein.[21]

A party's citizenship for diversity purposes is a question of federal substantive law rather than state law and is made at the time the complaint is filed.[22] A change in a party's citizenship after the action is filed will not create or defeat diversity jurisdiction.[23] While the statute does not define an individual's state of citizenship, courts have held that an individual is a citizen of the state in which he is domiciled.[24] An alien with permanent residency status in the United States will be deemed a citizen of the state in which he permanently resides.[25]

For purposes of determining citizenship, a corporation is deemed a citizen of any state where it is incorporated and of the state where it has its principal place of business.[26] While a corporation may have duel citizenship for diversity purposes, it can only have one principal place of business, regardless of whether it operates in multiple states.[27] A domestic corporation, with a foreign principal place of business, will not be deemed a citizen of a foreign state for diversity purposes, so as to defeat diversity jurisdiction.[28] However, a foreign corporation will be deemed a

20. See *Moore's Manual, Federal Practice and Procedure*, 1993, Section 5.06[1] at 5–22.

21. See Removal of state action to federal court below.

22. See *Field* v. *Volkswagenwerk AG*, 626 F2d 293 (3d Cir. 1980), wherein the court stated that jurisdiction is to be resolved based on the facts existing at the time the suit is filed, and held that diversity jurisdiction did not exist because the plaintiff and defendant were both aliens at the time the action was commenced.

23. *Hawes* v. *Club Ecuestre El Comandante*, 598 F2d 698 (1st Cir. 1979).

24. See *Galva Foundry Co.* v. *Heiden*, 924 F2d 729 (7th Cir. 1991), where the court dismissed the plaintiff's case for lack of complete diversity on the basis that the plaintiff and defendant were both citizens of Illinois, since the defendant had lived his entire life in Illinois and had no intent to permanently move to Florida, even though he also maintained a residence in Florida.

25. See 28 USC, Section 1332(a).

26. 28 USC, Section 1332(c)(1).

27. *Celanese Corp. of America* v. *Vandalia Warehouse Corp.*, 424 F2d 1176 (7th Cir. 1970).

28. *Cabalceta* v. *Standard Fruit Co.*, 883 F2d 1553 (11th Cir. 1989).

foreign citizen for diversity purposes even if it has its principal place of business within one of the states of the United States.[29]

The issue of a corporation's principal place of business is a question of law to be determined based on a factual analysis of the corporation's business activities.[30] Courts have applied various tests in deciding the location of a corporation's principal place of business, including the place from which the corporation's activities are directed or controlled, referred to as the "nerve center test", the location of the corporation's actual operations, and the centre of day-to-day corporate activity and management.

In direct actions against an insurance company, where the insured is not joined as a party defendant, the insurer is deemed to be a citizen of the state of which the insured is a citizen, in addition to any state where the insurer is incorporated or has its principal place of business.[31]

Federal amount in controversy requirement

With few exceptions, in order to obtain diversity subject matter jurisdiction, Section 1332[32] requires that the amount in controversy exceed $50,000, exclusive of interest and costs.[33] In that regard, the amount in controversy should be expressly pled and will generally be determined based on the amount of damages claimed in good faith by the plaintiff.[34] The good faith basis of the amount claimed is determined from the face of the pleadings.[35] Where it is apparent to a legal certainty

29. *Rouhi* v. *Harza Engineering Co.*, 785 FSupp. 1290 (ND Ill. 1992).

30. *Kelly* v. *United States Steel Corp.*, 284 F2d 850 (3d Cir. 1960).

31. 28 USC, Section 1332(c)(1).

32. In 1976, Congress excepted actions against the United States, its agencies or officers or employees sued in their official capacity, from the amount in controversy requirement. Also, in 1980, Congress eliminated the minimum-amount-in-controversy requirement to obtain federal question jurisdiction.

33. Under the Federal Interpleader Act, 28 USC, Section 1335, the party seeking to file an interpleader action must plead its custody or possession of money or property valued at $500 or more, or having issued a note, policy of insurance or other instrument of value or amount of $500 or more.

34. Where a single plaintiff pleads multiple claims against a single defendant, all amounts claimed may be aggregated to meet the jurisdictional minimum. Where a plaintiff asserts separate claims against multiple defendants, aggregation is permitted as to claims asserted against those defendants who are jointly liable. However, aggregation will not be permitted by multiple plaintiffs asserting separate claims against a single defendant, unless based on an integrated or undivided right. *Gibbs* v. *Buck*, 307 United States 66, 59 S Ct. 725, 83 LEd. 1111 (1939).

35. Significantly, where a plaintiff is ultimately adjudged to be entitled to recover less than $50,000, the court may deny costs to the plaintiff as part of its recovery or may order the plaintiff to pay costs, unless otherwise specifically provided for by United States statute (See 28 USC, Section 1332(b)).

from the facts pled that the plaintiff can have no reasonable expectation of recovery of an amount in excess of the jurisdictional minimum, the complaint will be dismissed for lack of subject matter jurisdiction.[36]

Where monetary damages are not claimed, as may be the case in a suit for declaratory judgment, an action for injunctive relief, or a suit to recover possession of property, the amount in controversy is generally determined based on the value of the property, contract, right or obligation at issue, from the plaintiff's point of view.[37]

Subject matter jurisdiction pleading requirements

The party invoking subject matter jurisdiction must plead all facts required to demonstrate its existence.[38] In the absence of sufficient facts pled or evidence establishing a basis for subject matter jurisdiction, the court will presume that it lacks subject matter jurisdiction and the case will be dismissed,[39] or if the case was removed from a state court to federal court,[40] the case will be remanded back to the state court from which it was removed.

Significantly, subject matter jurisdiction is a constitutional and statutory requirement founded on notions of federal versus state sovereignty.[41] Subject matter jurisdiction cannot be conferred on a court by the parties to the lawsuit by any means where it otherwise does not exist, nor can the lack of subject matter jurisdiction be waived. Moreover, jurisdiction may be challenged at any time, by responsive pleading or by motion,[42] even after trial.[43] Indeed, whenever it appears to the court that it lacks subject matter jurisdiction, the court must dismiss the case.[44]

36. *St. Paul Mercury Indemnity Co.* v. *Red Cab Co.*, 303 United States 283, 58 S Ct. 586, 82 LEd 845 (1938).

37. However, recent court decisions have determined the amount in controversy from the viewpoint of either the plaintiff or the defendant. *Mas* v. *Perry*, 489 F2d. 1396 (5th Cir. 1974), cert., denied, 419 United States 842, 95 S Ct. 74, 42 LEd.2d 70 (1970); *AFA Tours, Inc.* v. *Whitchurch*, 937 F2d. 82 (2d Cir. 1991); *McCarty* v. *Amoco Pipeline Co.*, 595 F2d. 389 (7th Cir. 1979).

38. FRCP 8(a)(1); *Hudson Insurance Company* v. *American Electric Corp.*, 957 F2d. 826 (11th Cir. 1992), cert. denied 113 S Ct. 411, 121 LEd.2d 336.

39. See *Boelens* v. *Redman Homes, Inc.*, 748 F2d. 1058 (5th Cir. 1984), rehearing. denied 759 F2d. 504 (5th Cir. 1985).

40. See discussion of removal of state court actions to federal court, pursuant to 28 USC, Section 1441 below.

41. See *Insurance Corp. of Ireland, Ltd.* v. *Compagnie des Bauxites de Guinee*, 456 United States 694, 102 S Ct. 2099, 72 LEd. 2d 492 (1982) and cases cited therein at 456 United States at 701–702.

42. 28 USC, FRCP Rule 12(b)(1) provides that a party may, at its option, assert a defence of lack of subject matter jurisdiction in a responsive pleading or by motion.

43. *American Fire & Casualty Co.* v. *Finn*, 341 United States 671 S Ct. 534, 95 LEd. 702 (1951).

44. 28 USC, FRCP Rule 12(h)(3).

Supplemental subject matter jurisdiction

Where a complaint states multiple claims, some of which meet federal jurisdiction requirements and others which do not, or where a defendant asserts state law claims against the plaintiff in the form of counterclaims, or cross-claims against a co-party, or third-party claims against parties not named in the original action, or where plaintiff amends its complaint to allege claims against a third-party defendant, the federal courts have developed common-law theories of ancillary and pendent jurisdiction as a basis for jurisdiction over the related claims and parties.

Under the doctrine of ancillary jurisdiction, a court has discretion to accept claims not independently supported by a basis of federal jurisdiction when in the interest of judicial economy, convenience and fairness to the parties, and where such claims and those for which jurisdiction does lie arise out of a common nucleus of operative facts.[45] The doctrine of pendent jurisdiction provides similar discretionary authority for jurisdiction over state law claims related to claims over which the court has original jurisdiction, where both claims are brought by a single plaintiff against a single defendant.[46]

By statute,[47] Congress codified Common Law ancillary and pendent jurisdiction under the label "supplemental jurisdiction". Section 1367(a) gives a district court discretion to exercise "supplemental jurisdiction" over all other claims that are so related to the claims for which jurisdiction exists that they form part of the same case or controversy. Where jurisdiction is based on diversity grounds, the court may not exercise supplementary jurisdiction over claims raised against or by a third party seeking to intervene, where the exercise of such jurisdiction would be inconsistent with the requirements for diversity jurisdiction.

Moreover, under Section 1367(c), a district court may deny supplementary jurisdiction if the related claim: involves unique or complex issues of state law; "substantially predominates" over the claim of which the court has jurisdiction; where the court has dismissed all other claims over which it has jurisdiction; or where exceptional circumstances dictate that jurisdiction be denied. Importantly, Section 1367(d) tolls the period of limitations as to supplemental claims presented under Section 1367(a) which are dismissed, and any other claims voluntarily dismissed at the same time or after the supplementary claim is dismissed,[48]

45. See *Cam-Ful Industries, Inc.* v. *Fidelity & Deposit Co.*, 922 F2d. 156 (2d Cir. 1991).

46. See *United Mine Workers* v. *Gibbs*, 383 United States 715, 86 S Ct. 1130, 16 LEd. 2d 218 (1966).

47. 28 USC, Section 1367.

48. 28 USC, Section 1367(d).

during their pendency and for 30 days after they are dismissed, unless state law provides a longer tolling period.

PERSONAL JURISDICTION AND SERVICE OF PROCESS

The power of a court to compel a party to appear and respond to a plaintiff's complaint, to submit to its authority to order discovery, decide the case and enforce its judgment, is determined by the court's jurisdiction over that party, or over the involved property, if the subject of the action is real or personal property. The method by which a district court establishes jurisdiction over a party is by its power to issue service of process. Such power is restricted by the geographical limits specified by federal statute or by the FRCP, by the affiliating contacts requirement of the Fifth Amendment to the Constitution, and by the Due Process Clause of the 14th Amendment to the Constitution.

FRCP Rule 4(k) sets forth the territorial limits of a district court's power to effectuate service of process. Under FRCP Rule 4(k)(1), service of a summons or the filing of a waiver of service will establish the court's jurisdiction over a defendant:

(1) Who could be subject to jurisdiction under the law of the state where the district court is located;
(2) Who is a party joined by a defendant as a third party under FRCP Rule 14 or as an indispensable party pursuant to FRCP Rule 19, and is served within a judicial district and not more than 100 miles from the location of the court issuing the summons;
(3) Who is subject to federal interpleader jurisdiction;[49] or
(4) When authorised by federal statute.[50]

Furthermore, FRCP Rule 4(k)(2) provides that in cases over which the court has federal-question jurisdiction, if the exercise of personal jurisdiction is consistent with the Constitution and laws of the United States, the service of summons or filing of a waiver will establish personal jurisdiction over any defendant who is not subject to the jurisdiction of any state court. The fundamental purpose of service of process is to provide the party against whom service is sought with adequate notice of the action and a reasonable opportunity to be heard by the court in which the action has been filed.

49. 28 USC, Section 1335.

50. See, for example, 28 USC, Sections 1335, 1397 and 2361, actions under the Federal Interpleader Act; 28 USC, Section 1655, actions involving liens against property where the defendant cannot be served within the state or will not voluntarily appear.

Obtaining jurisdiction over parties located within the state where the district court is located

Where a defendant located within the United States refuses to waive service of summons, FRCP Rule 4(e) permits service in any district of the United States, unless otherwise provided by federal law,[51] pursuant to the law of the state in which the district court is located, or of the state in which service is effected.

Service on individuals located within the state

Service on an individual is perfected by delivering a copy of the summons and complaint to the individual personally, or by leaving copies at the individual's residence with a person of suitable age and discretion who lives at the residence, or by delivering a copy to the individual's agent authorised by appointment or by law to receive service of process.

Service on corporations and associations located within the state

Where a domestic or foreign corporation, partnership or unincorporated association fails to waive service, service within the judicial district must be made in accordance with the manner prescribed by FRCP Rule 4(e)(1) for individuals or by delivering a copy of the summons and complaint on an officer, a managing or general agent, or to any other agent authorised by appointment or by law to receive service of process, and mailing a copy to the defendant.

Obtaining jurisdiction over parties located outside of the state where the district court is located

Personal jurisdiction is usually assured where party B is located in the same state as party A and party A complies with the procedural requirements of FRCP Rule 4.[52] However, where party B resides or is located outside of

---

51. A number of federal statutes expressly identify where a defendant may be served. For example, 28 USC, Section 1694 (patent infringement action) requires that where the defendant is not a resident in the district where the action is commenced but has a regular and established business, service may be made on the defendant's agent or agents conducting such business. In a stockholder's derivative action, 28 USC, Section 1695 requires service on the corporation in the district where it is organised or licensed to do business or is doing business.

52. See *Burnham v. Superior Court of California*, 495 United States 604, 110 S Ct. 2105, 109 LEd.2d 631 (1990), wherein the Court held that the defendant's mere presence within the state, even if unrelated to the action, at the time he was served with process was a proper basis for the court's exercise of personal jurisdiction.

the state in which the district court is held, or is a foreign resident, the limitations on the court's exercise of its power may become at issue and, as will be discussed below, the procedural requirements for effective service may be considerably more complex.

Where authority for personal jurisdiction over a non-resident party, served with process outside of the forum state, is based on a valid state long-arm statute, pursuant to FRCP Rules 4(k)(1)(A) and 4(e), 4(f), 4(g) or 4(h), it must first be determined whether the language of the long-arm statute provides for jurisdiction under the facts of the case. Second, the exercise of jurisdiction must not violate the due process requirements of the 14th Amendment of the United States Constitution.[53] The majority of state long-arm statutes permit the exercise of jurisdiction to the fullest extent allowed by the United States Constitution.[54] Importantly, where federal subject matter jurisdiction is based on diversity of the parties, state law will be applied in determining whether a non-resident has sufficient minimum contacts to satisfy the requirements of the state long-arm statute.[55] The United States Supreme Court, in *International Shoe* and its progeny, has defined the due-process requirement by application of a two-part test.

First, the party over whom jurisdiction is sought must, by virtue of an affirmative, purposeful act, have some minimum contact, tie or relation with the forum state from which the plaintiff's claim either arises or is related.[56] While it is difficult to state a clear litmus test for the sufficiency of the defendant's contacts, courts have found sufficient minimum contacts to be present where the defendant has purposefully availed itself of the privilege of conducting activities in the forum state such that the possibility of even a meritless lawsuit in that state is foreseeable by the defendant.[57] However, where the sale of a product in a particular state is not simply an isolated event, but is due to the efforts of the manufacturer or distributor to serve, directly or indirectly, the market for its product in

53. *International Shoe Co.* v. *Washington*, 326 United States 310, 66 S Ct. 154, 90 LEd. 95 (1945).

54. See, e.g., California Code of Civil Procedure Section 410.10, providing for jurisdiction on any basis not inconsistent with the Constitutions of the state or of the United States.

55. See *Arrowsmith* v. *United Press International*, 320 F2d. 219 (2nd Cir. 1963).

56. *International Shoe Co.* v. *Washington; Hanson* v. *Denckla*, 357 United States 235, 78 S Ct 1228, 2 LEd. 2d 1283 (1958).

57. See *Asahi Metal Industry Co.* v. *Superior Court*, 480 United States 102, 107 S Ct. 1026, 94 LEd. 2d 92 (1987); *Hanson* v. *Denckla* at 235; but see *World-Wide Volkswagen Corp.* v. *Woodson*, 444 United States 286, 100 S Ct. 559, 62 LEd. 2d 490 (1980), wherein the court after finding that the defendant's only contact with the forum state, Oklahoma, was that an automobile sold to the plaintiff in New York, while the plaintiff was a resident of New York, happened to be involved in an accident in Oklahoma, held that the defendant lacked sufficient minimum contacts to justify personal jurisdiction by an Oklahoma state court over the defendant.

that state, courts will likely find that such efforts constitute sufficient minimum contact to justify jurisdiction by the courts of that state over the manufacturer or distributor in lawsuits arising out of claims involving the product.[58]

In addition to minimum contact with the forum state, a second due process requirement is that maintenance of the suit "not offend traditional notions of fair play and substantial justice."[59] This requirement has been described in the context of whether the forum state has some special interest in applying its law to the controversy,[60] and whether the relative convenience of the parties supports maintenance of the lawsuit in the forum state.[61]

The decision in *Command-Aire Corp.* is instructive in this regard. The case involved a suit filed in the federal district court in Texas by a Texas plaintiff against a Canadian defendant who had purchased certain equipment from the plaintiff, but refused to pay because the equipment was defective. The defendant's agents went to Texas to discuss engineering specifications and contract terms with plaintiff and to take delivery of the equipment. The contract was finalised by telephone and in writing, and provided that Texas law would govern the sale and any disputes arising therefrom. The district court denied defendant's motion to dismiss for lack of personal jurisdiction.

The court of appeal affirmed, finding that the Texas long-arm statute permitted jurisdiction to the full extent allowed by the Constitution and that the due process requirements were met. After finding that the plaintiff's claim arose out of the defendant's contacts with Texas, the court held that the exercise of jurisdiction over the defendant did not offend traditional notions of fair play and substantial justice. The court was persuaded by the facts that the Canadian party freely contracted to litigate any disputes in Texas, its representatives traveled there, and Texas had a legitimate interest in providing an effective means by which its citizen could recover the defendant's debt.

Service on persons in a foreign country

Where a defendant located in a foreign country refuses to waive service, FRCP Rules 4(f)(1) and 4(f)(2) provide that service on an individual in a

---

58. *World-Wide Volkswagen Corp.* v. *Woodson* at 297–298.

59. *Burger King Corp.* v. *Rudzewicz,* 471 United States 462, 105 S Ct. 2174, 85 LEd.2d 528 (1985); *World-Wide Volkswagen Corp.* v. *Woodson* at 291–292; *International Shoe Co.* v. *Washington* at 316.

60. See *Keeton* v. *Hustler Magazine, Inc.,* 465 United States 770, 104 S Ct. 1473, 79 LEd. 2d 790 (1984).

61. See *Command-Aire Corp.* v. *Ontario Mechanical Sales & Service, Inc.,* 963 F2d. 90, 95 (5th Cir. 1992).

foreign country may be made by any internationally agreed means reasonably calculated to give notice, "such as those means authorised by the Hague Convention on the Service Abroad of Judicial and Extrajudicial Documents", or by other means not prohibited by international agreement. Absent an international agreement, or where the applicable agreement permits other means of service, service may be made in accordance with the laws of the foreign country, provided that service is reasonably calculated to give notice. Unless prohibited by the laws of the foreign country, personal service or service by mail, requiring a signed receipt to be dispatched by the clerk of the court to the party to be served, is also proper.

Service on a foreign corporation, association or partnership in a foreign country

Service outside the United States on a foreign corporation, which refuses to waive service of summons, must be made as prescribed by FRCP Rule 4(f), for individuals, other than personal delivery.[62] Formerly, FRCP Rule 4(i) limited service on foreign defendants to cases where extraterritorial service was authorised by federal or state law. FRCP Rule 4(f) eliminates that restriction and expressly makes the provisions of international Conventions for the service of process, such as the Hague Service Convention, mandatory for service on a foreign corporation, association or partnership that refuses to waive service of summons in federal court actions.[63] FRCP Rule 4(f)(3) does permit a court to authorise alternative methods of service not otherwise prohibited by the Convention or by the laws of the foreign state.

Proof of service under FRCP Rule 4(g), if service is not waived, must be filed with the court by the person making service as an affidavit. Where service is made outside the United States, proof of service must conform to the applicable treaty or Convention, if service is effected

62. Significantly, the revised Rules do not inflict any penalty on a foreign corporation or an individual declining to waive service of process.

63. However, with respect to a state court action, the Hague Service Convention may not necessarily be the exclusive means for service of process. See *Volkswagenwerk Aktiengesellschaft* v. *Schlunk*, 486 United States 694, 108 S Ct. 2104, 100 LEd.2d 722 (1988), wherein the Supreme Court refused to reverse an Illinois state court's denial of a defendant foreign corporation's motion to dismiss the plaintiff's lawsuit. The defendant contended that the plaintiff's service of summons on its wholly owned United States subsidiary failed to comply with the requirements of The Hague Service Convention. The court held that the Convention does not apply where state law authorises substitute service on a foreign corporation, so long as the manner of service complies with the Constitutional Due Process Clause. The Supreme Court found that the Illinois state long-arm statute permits service on a foreign corporation by substitute service on a domestic subsidiary without sending documents to the foreign corporation. The court reasoned that the Convention only applies where the law of the forum state requires service of documents abroad.

thereunder, or where service is otherwise, by including a receipt signed by the addressee or by other evidence of delivery satisfactory to the court.

Service under The Hague Service Convention

The Hague Service Convention is a multilateral treaty, which has been ratified or acceded to by 32 countries, including the United States. By its terms, the Convention applies to all civil or commercial matters where there is occasion to transmit a judicial or extrajudicial document for service abroad.[64] A central purpose of the Convention is to facilitate the service of documents. The Convention provides that a document may always be served by delivery to an addressee who voluntarily accepts it, unless violative of the receiving state's law.

Where service cannot be made voluntarily, Articles 2 through 6 require each member state to establish a "central authority" to assist other states with service of process when requested. The United States has designated the United States Department of Justice as its central authority. Once a request for service of a document is received in the proper form,[65] the central authority for the receiving state must serve the documents in accordance with its own laws, or by other means sought by the requesting party and compatible with its laws. If the document is to be served pursuant to the laws of the receiving state, the central authority can require that the document be translated into an official language of the receiving state and the part of the request, in the official form, which summarises the document to be served must be served with the document. The central authority must then provide a Certificate of Service, which conforms to the model form annexed to the Convention. The certificate must state that the document has been served and by what method, or if the document has not been served, the reasons that have precluded service must be stated. Under Articles 8–11 and 19, a member state may agree to methods for service of documents within its borders other than by a request to its Central Authority.[66]

---

64. See Article 1, Hague Convention on the Service Abroad of Judicial And Extrajudicial Documents In Civil or Commercial Matters, 28 USC, FRCP Rule 4 (Supplement 1993).

65. The requests must conform to the form of request annexed to the Convention.

66. Article 8 permits service of certain judicial documents directly through the requesting state's diplomatic or consular agents. A member state may oppose this method, unless the document is to be served on a national of the requesting state. Article 9 permits a state to use consular channels to send documents to another state's authorities designated for that purpose. Article 10 permits service by mail, by judicial officials of one state through the judicial officials of another state, and by any person interested in a judicial proceeding through the judicial officials or other competent persons in the state of destination, unless the state of destination objects. Article 11 permits two or more states to agree to alternative procedures for service of judicial documents.

Finally, Articles 15 and 16 limit the circumstances under which a default judgment may be entered against a defendant who must be served abroad but who fails to appear, and prescribes means for relief in the event a default judgment is entered in the forum court.

Waiver of personal jurisdiction

Whereas subject matter jurisdiction is a requirement intended to limit the power of federal courts as a matter of sovereignty, the requirement of personal jurisdiction is intended to protect individual liberty interests pursuant to the Due Process Clause. As with all individual rights it can be waived.[67] A party who elects to assert the court's lack of personal jurisdiction must do so in a responsive pleading or by motion.[68] The method by which a court obtains such jurisdiction is through service of process pursuant to the provisions of FRCP Rule 4.

Manner and method of obtaining service of summons

FRCP Rule 4(a) requires that the summons be signed by the court clerk, bear the court seal, identify the court and the name and address of the plaintiff's attorney, and state the time within which the defendant must appear and defend. The summons must notify the defendant that failure to do so will result in a default judgment for the relief demanded in the complaint. A summons is obtained under FRCP Rule 4(b) by filing the complaint and presenting a summons to the court clerk for signature and seal. A separate summons is required for each defendant.

Personal service

FRCP Rule 4(c)(1) requires that the summons be served with a copy of the complaint. FRCP Rule 4(c)(2) permits service of the summons and complaint by any person not a party to the action, who is at least 18 years

---

67. See Justice White's discussion in *Insurance Corp. of Ireland, Ltd.* v. *Compagnie des Bauxites de Guinee*, 456 United States at 696, 102 S Ct. at 2100, of the legal arrangements and actions by a defendant which may constitute an express or implied consent to the personal jurisdiction of the court, such as a contractual provision between the parties specifying personal jurisdiction in a particular court, a stipulation between the parties, or a defendant's use of certain state procedures. See also Rule 12(h) which provides "[a] defence of lack of jurisdiction over the person is waived" if not timely raised in the answer or a responsive pleading.

68. FRCP Rule 12(b)(2).

of age, or if requested, by a United States marshal or other person appointed by the court for that purpose.

Waiver of service of summons service by mail

The newly revised FRCP Rule 4(d) text is substantially derived from the former language of FRCP Rule 4(c)(C)(ii) pertaining to service by mail, now under the heading of "Waiver of Service; Duty to Save Costs of Service; Request to Waive".[69] FRCP Rule 4(d)(2) requires a court to impose on a defendant [70] the cost of perfecting service of summons where a defendant who is subject to service under the rules and who receives notice of an action in the manner provided by the rules[71] fails to waive service of a summons without good cause. FRCP Rule 4(3) provides that a defendant who timely returns a waiver is not required to answer the complaint until 60 days after the date the notice was sent, or 90 days if the defendant was addressed outside any judicial district of the United States. Such a waiver does not effect a waiver of objections to venue or to the court's personal jurisdiction.[72] If the defendant waives service, the plaintiff need not file a proof of service with the court,[73] and service is deemed effective as of the time the waiver is filed with the court.[74]

Time limitations for service of summons

Importantly, under FRCP Rule 4(m) if service is not made within 120 days after the complaint is filed, the court must dismiss the complaint without

---

69. The earlier language of FRCP Rule 4(c)(C)(ii) required that the party served return an Acknowledgement of Service, in order to effect service by mail. As such, service by mail under the former rule still required the co-operation of the party served. Absent a showing of good cause, FRCP Rule 4(c)(D) required the court to impose the costs of perfecting personal service on the party refusing to return the Acknowledgement of Service.

70. The language of FRCP Rule 4(2) specifically limits such penalties to cases where both the plaintiff and the defendant are located within the United States.

71. FRCP Rule 4(d)(2)(A) provides that a plaintiff may avoid the costs of service of summons by notifying the defendant of the commencement of the action and requesting that the defendant waive service of a summons. Among other requirements, the notice must be in writing, addressed to the defendant, if an individual, or if a corporation or association, to an officer or managing or general agent or other agent authorised to receive service of process, and sent by United States first-class mail or other reliable means. The notice must also include a copy of the complaint and a prepaid means of compliance and must allow the defendant at least 30 days to respond from the date on which the notice was sent, or 60 days if the defendant is addressed outside of any judicial district of the United States.

72. FRCP Rule 4(d)(1).

73. FRCP Rule 4(4).

74. FRCP Rule 4(d)(4).

prejudice, unless the plaintiff can show good cause for failure to do so. This rule does not apply to service within a foreign country pursuant to FRCP Rule 4(I).

Jurisdiction in rem and quasi in rem actions

In our hypothetical lawsuit, if plaintiff A asserts claims against defendant B who although not present within the forum state, owns real or personal property there, the question arises as to whether the federal or state court in the forum state may properly exercise jurisdiction over the property of defendant B.[75]

Historically, statutory law in all 50 states has provided various mechanisms by which a party can bring an action against an absent defendant by attaching property in the state belonging to the absent defendant and obtaining *quasi in rem* jurisdiction over the defendant by substituted service. The Supreme Court, in *Pennoyer* v. *Neff*,[76] held that such jurisdiction complied with Constitutional due process requirements, simply by virtue of the presence of the property in the forum state, irrespective of the relationship of the property to the claims asserted by the plaintiff and regardless of the nature or extent of the defendant's contacts with the forum state. However, in 1977, the Supreme Court, in *Shaffer* v. *Heitner*,[77] extended the minimum-contacts requirement of *International Shoe* v. *Washington* to all actions where service is sought on an out-of-state resident. In most *in rem* actions where the plaintiff asserts claims against personal or real property itself, such as one to establish exclusive ownership, the minimum-contacts test is likely to be satisfied. In writing the opinion for the Court, Justice Marshall discussed this issue specifically. He suggested that in such cases, the defendant's claim to property located in the state would normally indicate that he expected to benefit from the state's protection of his interest. The state's strong interests in assuring the marketability of property within its borders and in providing a procedure for the peaceful resolution of disputes about possession of that property would also support jurisdiction, as would the likelihood that important records and witnesses will be found in the state.

Moreover, in a federal court action to enforce a lien, or to remove an incumbrance or lien or cloud on the title to real or personal property within the state where the district court sits, the court may order an

---

75. An action requiring a judgment affecting the interests of all persons in the property is referred to as an *in rem* action. An action that affects only the interest of certain persons in the property is referred to as a *quasi in rem* action. See *Hanson* v. *Denckla*.

76. 95 United States 714, 24 LEd. 565 (1878).

77. 433 United States 186, 97 S Ct. 2569, 53 LEd. 2d 683 (1977).

absent property owner who cannot be served within the state or who does not voluntarily appear, to appear or plead by a date certain.[78] The court order to appear by a date certain must be served personally on the absent defendant if practicable, "wherever found", and also on the person(s) in possession or charge of the property. Where personal service is not practicable, service may be made by publication as the court may direct, but not less than once per week for six consecutive weeks. Failure of the non-resident party to appear will permit the court to proceed as if the party had appeared. Judgment may only be made against the subject property. Moreover, a defendant who has not been personally served and fails to appear has one year from the date of entry of judgment to appear and contest judgment, in which event the court must set aside its judgment.

However, if plaintiff A's suit against defendant B asserts claims involving rights other than to the property itself, such as a claim for injuries suffered on the land, or damages caused by defendant B's breach of contract, the court's power to exercise jurisdiction over the property, and hence over the absent defendant's rights in that property, becomes less certain. The existence of jurisdiction will depend on whether the defendant has the requisite minimum contacts with the forum state. For example, the Supreme Court has held that a court cannot exercise jurisdiction over a defendant having no contacts with the forum state by attaching the insurance obligation of an insurer to defend and indemnify the defendant in connection to the lawsuit, simply because the insurer was licensed to do business in that state, since the defendant had no control over the insurance company's decision to do business in that state.[79]

Even where minimum contacts are present so that the court's exercise of jurisdiction over the property is proper, unless the court can obtain personal jurisdiction over the absent defendant, any judgment will be limited to the value of the property. Moreover, due process requirements mandate that the property be brought within the jurisdiction of the court prior to judgment and that any manner of substituted service provided for in the statute be reasonably calculated to give the defendant actual notice and an opportunity to be heard.

REMOVAL TO FEDERAL DISTRICT COURT

Where plaintiff A has filed its lawsuit against defendant B in a state court, and the action is one for which the federal district court would have original jurisdiction, pursuant to the requirements of 28 USC, Section 1441,

78. 28 USC, Section 1655.

79. See *Rush* v. *Savchuk*, 444 United States 320, 100 S Ct. 571, 62 LEd. 2d 516 (1980).

defendant B may remove the case to a federal district court for the district where the case is pending, except as otherwise provided by Congress.[80]

Actions which may be removed

Section 1441(b) permits removal of any claim or cause of action of which the district court has federal question jurisdiction. Any other claim or cause of action that could have been brought in federal district court based on diversity jurisdiction may also be removed so long as none of the parties in interest properly joined is a citizen of the state in which the action is brought. All defendants must join in the notice of removal. Under Section 1441(c), where an independent claim for which federal question jurisdiction lies[81] is joined by the plaintiff with unrelated state claims, the entire case may be removed and the district court at its discretion may decide all issues or remand to state court all matters in which state law predominates.[82] In that instance, only the defendants to the separate, independent federal question claim or cause of action need join in the Notice of Removal.[83]

In addition, where any of the defendants is a foreign government, Section 1441(d) permits the defendant foreign government to remove the entire case to a federal district court, even if none of the claims asserted would otherwise invoke federal question or diversity jurisdiction, and even if none of the other defendants join in the removal.[84]

Procedure for removal

The procedures for removal of a state court civil action are described by 28 USC, Section 1446. Generally, all defendants who have been properly

80. 28 USC, Section 1445 identifies those actions for which Congress has prohibited removal. These include civil actions against a railroad arising under Title 45, Sections 51–60; civil actions against a common carrier for damages for delay, loss, or injury of shipments arising under Title 49, Section 11707, unless the amount in controversy exceeds $10,000; and civil actions arising under the state workers' compensation laws.

81. 28 USC, Section 1331.

82. See *Shamrock Oil & Gas Corp.* v. *Sheets,* 313 United States 100, 61 S Ct. 868, 85 LEd. 1214 (1941), wherein the Court strictly construed Section 1441, holding that a plaintiff does not become a defendant for removal purposes as a result of defending a cross action or counterclaim by a defendant separate and independent from the plaintiff's claim against the defendant and which otherwise would be removable on diversity grounds.

83. See *Lang* v. *American Electric Power Co.*, 785 FSupp. 1331 (ND Ind. 1992); Samuel Langham, 780 FSupp. 424 (ND Tex. 1992).

84. See *Verlinden BV* v. *Central Bank of Nigeria*, 461 United States 480, 103 S Ct. 1962, 76 LEd.2d 81 (1983); *Chuidian* v. *Philippine National Bank*, 912 F2d. 1095 (9th Cir. 1990).

joined in the lawsuit and served must join in a notice of removal,[85] signed pursuant to FRCP Rule 11. The notice of removal must contain in a short and plain statement all grounds for removal, together with a copy of all process, pleadings and orders served on the defendant in the action.[86]

The notice of removal must be filed with the federal district court within 30 days after the defendant receives a copy of the initial pleading filed in the state court, or of the summons, or if the initial action was not removable, the amended complaint, or motion or other paper from which it may first be determined that the matter is removable, except that a case may not be removed on the basis of diversity jurisdiction more than one year after the action is initially commenced.[87] Section 1446(d) requires written notice of the removal to all adverse parties promptly after filing of the notice of removal with the district court. A copy must also be filed with the state court where the action is pending, which effects the removal and precludes the state court from proceeding further with the action. The defendant's failure to file the notice of removal within the 30-day period will be deemed a waiver of the right of removal, as will any other action of the defendant evidencing a "clear and unequivocal intent" to waive the right of removal within the 30-day period.[88]

Procedures after removal

Assuming that defendant B has successfully removed the state court action to federal district court, if plaintiff A wishes to challenge the validity of the removal, it must file a noticed motion for remand with the district court within 30 days after the defendant's notice of removal is filed.[89] Moreover, failure to timely move for remand will constitute a waiver of any objections to the remand procedure.[90] However, if at any time before final judgment is entered it appears to the district court that subject matter jurisdiction is lacking, the court must remand the case to state court.[91] Significantly, in a removed action, the defendant who has not yet answered must answer or present its objections within 20 days after receipt of the complaint or service of process, or within five days after filing the petition

85. See *Getty Oil Corp.* v. *Insurance Co. of North America*, 841 F2d. 1254, 1262 (5th Cir. 1988); *Millstead Supply Co.* v. *Superior Court*, 797 FSupp. 569, 571–574 (WD Tex. 1992).

86. 28 USC, Section 1446(a).

87. 28 USC, Section 1446(b).

88. See *California Republican Party* v. *Mercier*, 652 F Supp. 928 (CD Cal. 1986).

89. 28 USC, Section 1447(c).

90. See *Mackay* v. *Vinta Development Co.*, 229 United States 173, 33 S Ct. 638, 57 LEd. 1138 (1913).

91. 28 USC, Section 1447(c).

for removal, whichever period is longer.[92] Moreover, where all pleadings have been served before removal, unless the party prior to removal has made a jury demand in accordance with state law, a party entitled to a jury trial must demand a jury trial within 10 days after the notice of removal is filed, if the party is the petitioner, or within 10 days after receipt of the notice of removal, if the party is the respondent.[93] Failure to demand a jury as required will result in waiver of the right to a jury trial.

Finally, 28 USC, Section 1447(d) provides that an order of remand to state court may generally not be appealed, except that a case remanded for reasons other than provided for by Section 1441 may be appealed.[94] However, the converse is not true. Failure to remand a case is subject to appellate review.

VENUE AND FORUM NON-CONVENIENS ISSUES

Even where a particular court has both subject-matter jurisdiction over the action and personal jurisdiction over the defendant, that court may still not be the proper location for the lawsuit. The concept of venue is intended to protect a defendant from being forced to appear in an unfair or inconvenient place of trial.[95] Thus, while plaintiff A may have a choice of several districts where the court would have jurisdiction, the concept of venue places a limitation on the location where plaintiff A may file its suit against defendant B.

Statutorily-mandated venue in diversity cases

In cases where federal jurisdiction is based solely on diversity, 28 USC, Section 1391(a) permits the lawsuit to be filed only in a district court where:

(1) Any defendant resides;
(2) A substantial part of the events or omissions giving rise to the claim occurred, or the subject property is situated; or
(3) If and only if venue cannot be founded on the first two options, the defendants are subject to personal jurisdiction at the time

92. FRCP Rule 81(c).
93. FRCP Rule 81(c).
94. See *Thermton Products, Inc.* v. *Hermansdorfer,* 423 United States 336, 96 S Ct. 584, 46 LEd.2d 542 (1976).
95. See *Leroy* v. *Great Western United Corp.*, 443 United States 173, 99 S Ct. 2710, 61 LEd. 2d 464 (1979).

the action is commenced, if there is no district in which the action may otherwise be brought.

Where defendant is a foreign state or its agency or instrumentality, venue is proper in any district where:

(1) A substantial part of the events or omissions giving rise to the claim occurred, or the subject property is situated;
(2) The vessel or cargo is situated if the claim is asserted under Section 1605;[96]
(3) The agency or instrumentality is licensed to do business; or
(4) In the District Court for the District of Columbia, if the action is brought against a foreign state or political subdivision.[97]

Statutorily-mandated venue in non-diversity cases

In all actions where jurisdiction is not based solely on diversity, unless otherwise provided by law, Section 1391(b) permits the action to be filed only in the district where:

(1) Any defendant resides if all defendants reside in the same state; or
(2) A substantial part of the events or omissions giving rise to the claim occurred, or the subject property is situated; or
(3) Any defendant may be found, if the first two options are not available. The qualification "unless otherwise provided by law" is a reference to specific kinds of federal action for which venue is especially mandated by statute.[98]

For venue purposes, generally the residence of a natural person is deemed to be the judicial district where the person has a regular home or domicile.[99] Section 1391(c) provides that for venue purposes a corporation is deemed to reside in any judicial district in which it is subject to personal jurisdiction at the time the action is commenced. Pursuant to Section 1391(d) an alien may be sued in any district.

96. 28 USC, Section 1605, general exceptions to the jurisdictional immunity of a foreign state.

97. 28 USC, Section 1391(f).

98. See, e.g., 28 USC, Sections 1396, actions for the collection of internal revenue taxes; 1397 actions of interpleader; and 1400, actions for patents infringement or relating to copyrights.

99. See First Pullen Commodity Services, Inc. v. AG Becker-Kipnis & Co., 507 FSupp. 770 (SD Fl. 1981).

Because venue pertains to the convenience of the parties and not the jurisdiction of the court over the action, the parties may stipulate to the appropriate venue, and may specify a particular venue by contract; the defendant may waive any objection to improper venue by failing to contest venue in a responsive pleading or by motion.[100]

Change of venue and forum non conveniens

The subject of *forum non conveniens* concerns whether, due to the location of plaintiff A and defendant B, the events giving rise to the lawsuit, the location of witnesses and the availability of an adequate remedy, a lawsuit ought to be heard by a court in one location versus another, even where the district court has subject-matter and personal jurisdiction, and venue has been properly placed.

Transfer of venue between districts

The ability to change venue between judicial districts is governed by 28 USC, Section 1404. This Section authorises a district court, at its discretion on motion for transfer by any party, by consent or stipulation of all parties, or *sua sponte*, to transfer any civil action to any other federal district court where the action might have been brought, for the convenience of parties and witnesses, in the interest of justice. The Supreme Court has held that the statutory reference to "all civil actions" enables a court to transfer any civil case to another district even where the lawsuit involves a statute that proscribes the venue.[101]

Dismissal based on forum non conveniens

Where a district court determines that a state court or a foreign court is a more convenient forum, Section 1404 provides no option to transfer the case to that court. The court can either retain or dismiss the case on a motion to dismiss for *forum non conveniens*.[102] This possibility can be particularly significant where either party or potential party is a foreign resident, or where some or all of the events giving rise to the dispute between the parties occurred, or some or all witnesses are located, in a foreign country.

100. 28 USC, FRCP Rules 12(b)(3) and 12(h)(1).
101. *Ex parte Collett*, 337 United States 55, 69 S Ct. 944, 93 LEd. 1207 (1949).
102. See *Piper Aircraft Co. v. Reyno*, 454 United States 235, 102 S Ct. 252, 70 LEd.2d 419 (1981), (rehearing denied 25 January 1982).

In *Piper Aircraft Co. v. Reyno*, the plaintiff represented the estates of several Scottish citizens killed in an air crash in Scotland in a wrongful death action against Piper Aircraft and Hartzell Propeller in the United States District Court for the Middle District of Pennsylvania. The petitioners[103] moved to dismiss the case on *forum non conveniens* grounds, which was granted by the district court on the basis that a more convenient forum was available in Scotland.[104] The plaintiff appealed and the Court of Appeal for the Third Circuit reversed the district court on the basis that dismissal was barred because the law of Scotland was less favourable to the plaintiff than the law of Pennsylvania.[105] On appeal to the Supreme Court, the Court affirmed the district court decision, holding that the possibility of a change in law should not, by itself, bar dismissal, and the district court had not abused its discretion. Citing its earlier decisions in *Gulf Oil Corporation v. Gilbert*[106] and its companion case, *Koster v. Lumberman's Mutual Casualty Co.*,[107] the Court reaffirmed the judicial policy that:

"[A] plaintiff's choice of forum should rarely be disturbed. However, when an alternative forum has jurisdiction to hear the case, and when trial in the chosen forum would 'establish oppressiveness and vexation to a defendant, out of all proportion to plaintiff's convenience', or when the 'chosen forum [is] inappropriate because of considerations affecting the court's own administrative and legal problems', the court may, in the exercise of sound discretion, dismiss the case."[108]

In evaluating the district court's application of *forum non conveniens* principles, the Court, recognising that the central focus of the *forum non conveniens* inquiry is convenience, divided the factors to be considered into two categories. First, factors relating to the private interest of the parties to the suit must be considered, including: the relative ease of access to sources of proof; the availability of compulsory process for the attendance of unwilling, and the cost of obtaining attendance of willing, witnesses; the possibility of view of the premises, if appropriate; and all other practical problems that make trial of the case easy, expeditious and inexpensive.[109]

103. When a case is appealed to the Supreme Court, the party requesting or petitioning the Court to review the decision of the lower court is the petitioner, while the party responding is the respondent. Here, Piper Aircraft and Hartzell petitioned the Court to reverse the Court of Appeal's decision to reverse the district court's dismissal of the plaintiff's action, and the plaintiff or respondent urged the Court to affirm the Court of Appeal's decision.

104. *Reyno v. Piper Aircraft Co.*, 479 FSupp. 727 (1979).

105. *Reyno v. Piper Aircraft Co.*, 630 F2d. 149 (3d Cir. 1980).

106. 330 United States 501, 67 S Ct. 839, 91 LEd. 1055 (1947).

107. 330 United States 518, 67 S Ct. 828, 91 LEd. 1067 (1947).

108. *Piper Aircraft Co. v. Reyno* below.

109. See also *Dowling v. Hyland Therapeutics Division, Travenol Laboratories, Inc.*, 767 FSupp. 57, 58 (SDNY 1991).

Second, public interest factors bearing on a *forum non conveniens* determination include: administrative difficulties resulting from court congestion; the local interest in having local controversies decided at home; the interest in having the trial of a diversity case in a forum that is at home with the applicable law; the avoidance of unnecessary problems in conflict of laws, or in the application of foreign law; and the unfairness of burdening citizens in an unrelated forum from jury duty.

In its analysis of the Court of Appeal's reliance on the argument that Scottish law was less favourable to the plaintiff than Pennsylvania law, the Court held that a *forum non conveniens* analysis "should ordinarily not give conclusive or even substantial weight" to the possible change in law.[110] The Court's reasoning was essentially that if the possibility of an unfavourable change in law were the determinative factor, even where trial in the chosen forum was clearly inconvenient, dismissal might be barred.[111] The Court emphasised that the *forum non conveniens* analysis must turn on the facts of the particular case and no single factor should be emphasised in that analysis, lest the flexibility that makes the *forum non conveniens* doctrine so valuable would be lost. Moreover, the Court cautioned that its holding did not mean that the possibility of an unfavourable change in law should never be considered; if the alternative forum provides a remedy which is so inadequate that it is no remedy at all, the unfavourable change in law may be given substantial weight and the court may conclude that dismissal would not be in the interest of justice.[112]

As with all matters that are left to the discretion of the court, a *forum non conveniens* determination will not be over-turned on appeal unless there has been a clear abuse of discretion by the court. Where the court has considered all relevant public and private interest factors, and there

110. *Piper Aircraft Co. v. Reyno*, 454 United States below.

111. *Piper Aircraft Co. v. Reyno* below.

112. See also *R Maganlal & Co. v. MG Chemical Co.*, 942 F2d. 164 (2nd Cir. 1991), wherein the Court of Appeal reversed the district court's dismissal of plaintiff, an Indian export trading company's breach of contract suit against a United States supplier for defective goods, on the basis that the court would be required to interpret and apply Indian law to decide the case. The Court of Appeal reversed, finding that issues involving Indian law were secondary to the principal issue in the case, whether the goods shipped by the seller conformed to the buyer's contract, and that the balance of public and private interest factors favoured venue in the United States. The Court acknowledged that a foreign plaintiff's choice of forum is entitled to less weight, but relied on the rule that this reduced weight "is not an invitation to accord a foreign plaintiff's selection of an American forum no deference since dismissal for forum non conveniens is the exception rather than the rule." A defendant must still show that the balance of convenience sufficiently favours trial in the foreign forum to overcome the presumption in favour of the plaintiff's choice. 942 F2d. at 167–168 (citing *Lacey v. Cessna Aircraft Co.*, 862 F2d. 38, 45–46 (3d Cir. 1988).

has been a reasonable balancing of these factors by the court, the district court's decision will be given substantial deference on appeal.[113]

In *Piper Aircraft Co.*, the district court, weighing the private interest of the parties, noted that while the plaintiff would have easier access to certain evidence in the district court, the defendants had established that fewer evidentiary problems would be posed by venuing the case in Scotland as a substantial amount of evidence was also located in Scotland. Significantly, the Court concurred with the district court's holding that trial in Scotland was supported by the defendants' inability to otherwise implead third-party defendants located in Scotland, such as the pilot, the owner of the aircraft or the company which chartered the aircraft, since their liability could act to relieve the defendants of all liability. While defendants could sue the third parties in Scotland for indemnity if they were found liable after trial in the United States, the Court concurred with the district court's conclusion that it would be far more convenient to resolve all claims in one trial and force the defendants to seek indemnity or contribution against the third parties in Scotland. The Court concluded that a finding that trial in the plaintiff's chosen forum would be burdensome is sufficient to support dismissal on *forum non conveniens* grounds.

In weighing public interest factors, the Court concurred with the district court's finding that applying Pennsylvania law and Scottish law in a trial in the district court would be confusing to the jury, and the district court itself, being unfamiliar with Scottish law, would have to rely on experts in Scottish law. The Court also noted that Scotland had a strong interest in the litigation since the accident occurred in its airspace, all decedents were Scottish and, except for the petitioning defendants, all other potential plaintiffs and defendants were either Scottish or English.

ASCERTAINING THE APPLICABLE LAW

Assuming that plaintiff A wishes to file suit in a United States district court against defendant B and the court has jurisdiction over both the subject matter of the action and over party B, an issue which may arise concerns whether United States law, state law or the law of a foreign state must be applied.

Substantive/procedural law to be applied

Generally, in cases predominantly involving issues arising under the Constitution, treaties and statutes of the United States, federal law

---

113. See *Piper Aircraft Co.* at 257, citing *Gulf Oil Corp.* v. *Gilbert*, 330 United States 501, 67 S Ct. 839, 91 LEd. 1055 (1947).

controls.[114] The possibility of a conflict of law problem more frequently arises in the context of a federal diversity case, since the subject matter of the lawsuit typically arises under state law. In that instance, the Supreme Court in *Erie R R* v. *Tompkins*,[115] held that "[e]xcept in matters governed by the Federal Constitution or by acts of Congress, the law to be applied in any case is the law of the state." Moreover, the Rules of Decision Act, 28 USC, Section 1652, as amended in 1948, provides:

"The laws of the several states, except where the Constitution or treaties of the United States or Acts of Congress otherwise require or provide, shall be regarded as rules of decision in civil actions in the courts of the United States, in cases where they apply."

However, it is important to note that in all cases in a federal district court, federal law governs the procedure applied. In other words, the FRCP apply to all such cases, even where the substantive law to be applied is state law.[116]

Which state law applies and conflict of law principles

Where the events, occurrences, transactions or contracts giving rise to the lawsuit involve multi-state contacts, resolution of the issue of which state substantive law must be applied depends on the law of the state where the action is filed. In the event a case is transferred from the venue of one state to another, the conflict-of-laws rule that would have been applied by the original court must be applied by the new court.

The determination of a particular state's choice of law rules is to be derived from the Common Law and statutory law of that state. Generally, most states apply a variation of the governmental-interest test in resolving conflicts-of-law questions. For example, the California Supreme Court adopted an interest analysis in *Reich* v. *Purcell*[117] and, in *Bernhard* v. *Harrah's Club*,[118] incorporated a second element into the analysis, the Comparative Impairment Analysis. The Governmental Interest-Comparative Impairment Analysis is now applied by California courts to most conflict-of-law issues.

114. However, there may be occasions where the choice of law is not clear, such as where the validity of an action under state law is at issue, or where there is a question of the existence of federal Common Law involving federal legislation relating to situations not expressly provided for by any federal statute.

115. 304 United States 64, 58 S Ct. 817, 82 LEd. 1188 (1938).

116. See *Hanna* v. *Plumer*, 380 United States 460, 85 S Ct. 1136, 14 LEd. 2d 8 (1965).

117. 67 Cal.2d 551 (1967).

118. 16 Cal.3d 313 (1976), cert. denied, *Harrah's Club* v. *Bernhard*, 429 United States 859, 97 S Ct. 159, 50 LEd. 2d 136 (1976).

The essential elements to be examined in the governmental interest analysis are the respective interests of the states involved and a determination of the law that most appropriately applies. Such facts as the principal place of performance of a contract; the place where the contract is made; or the location of the tort or events giving rise to the claim are considered in this analysis.

Many states specify by statute which law is to be applied in certain instances. For example, California requires a contract to be interpreted according to the usage of the place of performance or place where the contract was made, or as otherwise specified by the parties to the contract.[119]

PLEADING COMMENCING THE ACTION

FRCP Rule 7 permits only certain pleadings to be filed in a federal district court. They include: a complaint[120] and an answer; a reply to a counter-claim, an answer to a cross-claim, if the answer contains a cross-claim; a third-party complaint, if a person who was not an original party is summoned under the provisions of FRCP Rule 14; and a third-party answer, if a third-party complaint is served.

One objective of civil procedural rules in all United States jurisdictions is to provide for the speedy disclosure of the true nature of the dispute between the parties. A further objective of the rules is to promote the disposition of claims and defences based on their merits. FRCP Rule 84 references the Appendix of Forms to the FRCP, which complies with the FRCP, and is "intended to indicate the simplicity and brevity of statement which the rules contemplate." The Appendix of Forms gives a number of examples of various pleadings forms for illustrative purposes.

The complaint

As discussed earlier, a complaint to be filed in a United States District Court must state facts showing that that court has jurisdiction to decide the subject matter of the case. All complaints, whether filed in

119. California Civil Code Sections 1646 and 1646.5.

120. Whether in state or federal court, a plaintiff commences an action by filing a complaint. However, nearly all states and the federal jurisdiction require by statute that before an action based on tort can be commenced against a government entity, written notice of the claim must have been provided to the entity and rejected, subject to the time deadlines specified in the statute. See, e.g., 28 USC, Section 2675.

state or federal court, must also allege facts establishing compliance with statutory venue requirements. In most other respects, the FRCP and the rules of the majority of states simply require that a claim be sufficiently stated to provide fair notice of the nature of the claim and the factual basis for the claim. Rule 8(a) of the FRCP requires that a pleading which states a claim for relief[121] must contain the following:

(1) A short and plain statement of the grounds on which the court's jurisdiction depends;
(2) A short and plain statement of the claim showing that the pleader is entitled to relief; and
(3) A demand for judgment for the relief the pleader seeks.

While a complaint must allege the *prima facie* elements of the claim asserted, the elements of most claims may be alleged generally.[122] Thus, a claim based on the negligent[123] manufacture of a product might be stated as follows:

(1) At all times material herein, the defendant manufactured product X for sale to the public, and as such owed the plaintiff and others similarly situated a duty to exercise reasonable care in the manufacture of the product;
(2) Defendant breached its duty of due care by negligently manufacturing the product; and
(3) As a direct and proximate result of such negligence, the plaintiff was damaged in the amount of $100,000.

---

121. Such pleadings include a complaint, a counterclaim, cross-claim, or third-party complaint.

122. In all jurisdictions, certain claims such as fraud and deceit, or where the condition of the defendant's state of mind is an element, such as a claim for punitive damages, must be stated with particularity, e.g., specific facts of how, where, and when it occurred. See FRCP Rule 9(b). Because of the seriousness of the charge of fraud and deceit, fair notice requires that the complaint provide the fullest details of the claims so that the defendant can prepare a defence; and the court will be able to determine whether the alleged fraud, misrepresentation or concealment is material and actionable as a matter of law. See *Committee on Children's Television, Inc.* v. *General Foods, Corp.*, 35 Cal. 3d, 197, 216–217, 197 Cal. Rptr. 783 (1983); *Roberts* v. *Ball, Hunt, Hart, Brown and Baerwitz*, 57 Cal.App.3d 104, 109, 128 Cal.Rptr. 901 (1976).

123. The required elements of the tort claim for negligence are: (1) existence of a duty owing by the defendant to the plaintiff; (2) breach of that duty; (3) damages proximately caused by the breach; and (4) damages.

Likewise, a claim based on breach of contract[124] could be alleged as follows:

(1) Plaintiff entered into a written contract with the defendant, a true and correct copy of which is attached hereto as Exhibit "A";

(2) By the terms of contract, in consideration of the plaintiff's payment to defendant of $X, the defendant promised to deliver a product which was to comply with certain specifications provided by the plaintiff;

(3) Plaintiff fully performed its obligations under the contract by providing the specifications and making payment to the defendant of $X;

(4) The defendant breached the contract by failing to provide the product as specified;

(5) As a direct and proximate result of the defendant's breach, the plaintiff has been damaged in the amount of $100,000.

Moreover, FRCP Rule 8(e)(2) permits a party to state alternative theories of liability in one or separate counts. A party may also state as many separate claims as the party has regardless of whether they are inconsistent and whether based on legal, equitable or maritime grounds. Hence, a plaintiff may allege in a products liability negligence count that defendant A and/or defendant B wilfully or negligently manufactured the defective product.

Answer or other responsive pleadings

Unless otherwise provided by statute, a party served with a complaint is required by FRCP Rule 12 to respond within 20 days of receipt of service. Where a party elects to answer the complaint, FRCP Rule 8(b) specifies its contents: "[a] party shall state in short and plain terms the party's defences to each claim and shall admit or deny the averments on which the adverse party relies".

Denials

If the answering party is without knowledge or information sufficient to form a belief as to the truth of a fact contention, the party must so state in its answer. This has the effect of a denial.

124. The elements of a cause of action for breach of contract are: (1) a contract (the when, where, who and how the contract was formed must be plead and its terms alleged verbatim, or attached to the complaint, if in writing); (2) the plaintiff's performance or excuse for non- performance; (3) the defendant's breach; (4) damages caused by the breach; and (5) damages.

Significantly, FRCP Rule 8(b) requires the answering party to admit all material allegations or portions thereof which in good faith the party cannot deny. However, where the answering party intends in good faith to deny all allegations, including those on which jurisdiction is based, the party may do so by means of a general denial subject to the requirements of FRCP Rule 11.[125]

Affirmative defences

The FRCP and most state jurisdictions require certain defences to be stated in the answer as affirmative defences. FRCP Rule 8(c) requires a responding party to affirmatively plead a number of defences specified therein, including accord and satisfaction,[126] arbitration and award,[127] assumption of risk release,[128] statute of limitations,[129] and any other matter constituting an avoidance or affirmative defence.

Other responsive pleadings

Ordinarily, pleadings are liberally construed, consistent with substantial justice.[130] However, where a claim, whether made in a complaint, counterclaim or third-party complaint, violates the FRCP Rule 8(e)(1) requirement that each claim be stated simply, concisely and directly, the complaint may be subject to FRCP Rule 12(e) motion to strike. Moreover, failure to plead each of the requisite elements of the claim may subject the complaint to FRCP Rule 12(b)(6) motion to dismiss for failure to state a claim on which relief can be granted.

125. FRCP Rule 11 requires that all pleadings or other papers filed with the court be signed by an attorney of record certifying that to the best of the attorney's knowledge, information, and belief, formed after a reasonable inquiry under the circumstances, the filing is not being presented for any improper purpose; the contents are warranted by existing law, or by a non-frivolous argument for the modification of the law; and all fact contentions have evidentiary support, or are likely to have evidentiary support after a reasonable opportunity for further investigation or discovery. Violations may result, on the motion of any party or the court's own motion, in sanctions the court deems necessary to deter repetition of such conduct.

126. This defence arises when the plaintiff has accepted payment from the defendant in full satisfaction of all of the plaintiff's claims.

127. Where the plaintiff and defendant have previously arbitrated their claims and an award has been made and satisfied.

128. This is a defence to a negligence claim in some but not all states, and exists where the plaintiff had sufficient knowledge of the risk of using a certain product to avoid the risks, but elected to use the product anyway.

129. All state jurisdictions have rules that proscribe time limitations within which a claim must be asserted or forever barred.

130. FRCP Rule 8(F).

Counterclaims and crossclaims

Any party having claims against an opposing party, whether in equity or law, may assert them against that party as a counterclaim pursuant to FRCP Rule 13, even if the claim does not arise out of the same transaction or occurrence that is the subject matter of the opposing party's claim. However, any claim arising out of the same transaction or occurrence must be stated as a counterclaim or it will be barred. Thus, an answering defendant must state all compulsory counterclaims in its answer. Moreover, a defendant having compulsory claims against a co-defendant must assert them against that party as a cross-claim.

Failure of a party to plead compulsory counterclaims caused by mistake, oversight or excusable neglect may be added by supplemental pleading on obtaining permission from the court by noticed motion.

Amending or supplementing pleadings

The objective in resolving disputes based on their merits, as opposed to dismissing claims or defences based on a technical insufficiency, is furthered by FRCP Rule 15(a), which permits a party to amend its pleading once, as a matter of right, before a responsive pleading is served. Thereafter, the party may amend its pleading only on noticed motion requesting permission from the court to amend the pleading, or on written consent from the opposing party. Normally, unless prejudice to the other party will result, leave to amend is freely given by the court when in the interest of justice.

In addition to amendments to correct technical deficiencies, a pleading may be amended at any time to add additional claims or defences, or to drop or add parties, subject to limitations. The decision of the court whether to permit an amendment is discretionary and may only be overturned on appeal based on an abuse of discretion. Generally, amendments are permitted unless the amendment would unduly prejudice the other party, are made for some improper purpose such as delay of the proceedings, or where the party has already had a sufficient opportunity to state a claim or add the party.

Significantly, FRCP Rule 15(c) generally provides that an amended pleading will relate back in time to the filing of the original pleading, where the claim is not otherwise barred by an applicable statute of limitations,[131] or the claim or defence asserted in the amendment arises

---

131. The Statute of Limitations is that time period in which a particular claim must be filed or it will be forever barred. In federal-question cases, the court will look to the limitations period contained in the federal statute or law creating the federal right. Of course, in diversity cases the court must look to the applicable state statutory-limitations period.

out of the same conduct, transaction or occurrence alleged in the original pleading. Amendments adding a party will also relate back if the claim is related to the original claim plead and the new party will not be prejudiced in defending the action.[132] However, a defect in subject matter jurisdiction cannot be cured by amendment.

Joinder of parties

It should be noted that a complaint that fails to name an indispensable party as defined in FRCP Rule 19(b) must be dismissed. An indispensable party is one in whose absence the court cannot proceed in equity and good conscience with the existing parties because complete relief cannot be granted, or the absent party claims an interest in the subject matter of the action and is so situated that:

(1) Disposition of the action in the party's absence may as a practical matter impair the party's ability to protect its interest; or
(2) It will leave the other parties to the action subject to multiple or inconsistent obligations.

In addition, a new party may be joined pursuant to the permissive-joinder provisions of FRCP Rule 20(a). Generally, all parties must have the same claim arising out of the same transaction or occurrence and involving common questions of fact or law. Conversely, all parties against whom such claims are asserted may be joined as defendants.

Class actions

The method by which an action may be brought on behalf of or against a class of unnamed persons is controlled under the federal rules by FRCP Rule 23. In order to sue on behalf of or against one or more members of a class as representative parties, the party initiating the suit must establish that the members of the class are too numerous to be practically joined individually; there are questions of law and fact common to all class members; the claims or defences of the representative parties are representative of the claims or defences of the class; and the interests of the class will be fairly and adequately protected by the representative parties.

If these prerequisites are met, FRCP Rule 23 permits a class action where a single action for or against a class is preferable over separate

---

132. See the notice requirements set out in FRCP Rule 15(c)(3).

lawsuits, which would risk inconsistent results and potential prejudice to non-party class members. A class action is also permitted when injunctive or declaratory relief,[133] as respects the whole class, is appropriate because the party opposing the class has acted or refused to act for reasons generally applicable to the class. Alternatively, a class action will be permitted where the court determines that common questions of law or fact predominate over any questions affecting individual members, and where it is found that a class action is the best available method to fairly and efficiently adjudicate the controversy.

In addition, Rule 23 of the FRCP requires — as soon as practicable after the action is started — that the court determine whether the class action will be permitted.[134] This determination is made without concern for the underlying merits of the lawsuit. Rule 23 of the FRCP specifies notice requirements to class members regarding their right to request exclusion from the class action. Moreover, the Rule authorises the court to issue a wide variety of orders when necessary to promote efficiency and fairness in the conduct of the proceedings.

Interpleader

Where a party may be exposed to multiple liability, as a result of persons having claims against the party, such persons may be joined and required to interplead their claims. For example, an insurer who is liable on an insurance claim to multiple parties each of whom dispute the other's right to the proceeds may, pursuant to FRCP Rule 22, pay the amount

133. The method by which a party may obtain a court order that an adverse party do or refrain from doing some act prior to adjudication of the underlying lawsuit is by a noticed application for a preliminary injunction pursuant to Rule 65. The requesting party must establish irreparable harm in the absence of such relief that it has no alternative adequate remedy at law, and that there is a strong likelihood the party will prevail on the merits. FRCP Rule 65(b) allows a court, prior to deciding a request for a preliminary injunction, to temporarily restrain an adverse party from acting or refraining from acting, without notice, if the requesting party can clearly show by affidavit or verified complaint that the party will suffer immediate irreparable injury. Declaratory relief is the means by which a party may obtain a court order declaring the rights and obligations of parties to a contract. 28 USC, Section 2201 creates a specific declaratory judgment remedy applicable to cases of actual controversy within the court's jurisdiction, or in any civil action involving an antidumping or countervailing duty proceeding regarding a class of merchandise of a free trade area country.

134. The class action order may be conditional and subject to change (FRCP Rule 23(a)(1)). For example, the court may permit the class action to go forward only as to specified issues or the court may divide the class into subclasses.

owing into court and file an interpleader action requesting the court to determine the contesting parties' respective rights to the proceeds.

Intervention

On motion filed with the court, a party claiming an interest involving the property or transaction which is the subject matter of an action, or where a federal statute confers an unconditional right to intervene, FRCP Rule 24(a) requires the court to permit that party to join in the action. FRCP Rule 24(b) also permits joinder where the requesting party's claim or defence shares common questions of fact or law with the main action, or where a federal statute provides a conditional right to intervene. Joinder is permitted under these circumstances and the court's decision to permit intervention will depend on whether intervention will unduly delay the proceedings or prejudice the rights of the original parties.

OBTAINING EVIDENCE PRIOR TO TRIAL

One of the unique aspects of United States civil procedure is the very broad pre-trial discovery of evidence permitted by the federal rules. Indeed, FRCP Rule 26 permits the parties to obtain discovery regarding any matter, not privileged, which is relevant to the subject matter of the lawsuit and reasonably calculated to lead to the discovery of evidence admissible at trial.

Methods of discovery

The United States' Common-Law tradition of very broad evidence-gathering contrasts starkly with the discovery methods generally available in the rest of the world.[135] A principle, which is evident throughout the United States' discovery system, is that all parties have equal access to relevant evidence.

135. For example, in Civil Law countries and other Common Law countries, including the United Kingdom, discovery is conducted primarily by the courts. Evidence is gathered for trial not in the United States' manner of private lawyers conducting interrogatories and depositions, but by judges who choose which witnesses to interview and what questions to ask. The judge then prepares a summary record of the evidence, rather than a verbatim transcript. United States discovery methods are frequently described by other countries as a "fishing expedition". Report of the United States Delegation to the Eleventh Session of the Hague Conference on Private International Law, 8 ILM 785, 808 (1969).

The amended FRCP now establish two principal means by which parties may obtain discovery of relevant evidence.[136] The first is the new voluntary disclosure requirement. The second is the more traditional means of obtaining discovery from parties and from non-party witnesses.[137] These methods include: depositions by oral examination or written questions; written interrogatories; production of documents or things or permission to enter on land or other property for inspection or other purposes; physical and mental examinations; and requests for admissions.

New FRCP rule 26 voluntary disclosure requirements

GENERAL

The most significant 1 December 1994 change to the FRCP was the nearly wholesale revision of the rules governing the conduct of discovery. In particular, FRCP Rule 26(a) now requires voluntary disclosure of certain basic information between the parties before discovery can begin. The disclosure must include:

(1) The identity of persons likely to have discoverable information relevant to disputed facts alleged with particularity in the pleadings;

(2) A copy or description of all documents, or tangible things relevant to disputed facts alleged with particularity in the pleadings;

(3) A computation of any category of damages claimed and access to the evidence in support thereof; and

(4) Any applicable insurance policies.

The voluntary disclosure must be made within 10 days after the FRCP Rule 26(f) meeting between the parties.

136. For discovery purposes, "relevancy" is given a very broad scope by FRCP Rule 26 (b): "Any matter, not privileged, which is relevant to the subject matter involved in the pending action, whether it relates to the claim or defence of the party seeking the discovery or to the claim or defence of any other party, including the existence, description, nature, custody, condition, and location of any books, documents, or other tangible things and the identity and location of persons having knowledge of any discoverable matter. The information need not be discoverable at trial if the information sought appears reasonably calculated to lead to admissible evidence."

137. FRCP Rule 45 establishes the method by which a party may obtain discovery from non-party witnesses, by use of the court's subpoena power to command persons to provide deposition testimony, or produce documents and things or to permit inspection of premises.

FRCP RULE 26(F) MEETING OF COUNSEL

The parties or their counsel are now required by FRCP Rule 26(f) to meet as soon as practical or 14 days before the FRCP Rule 16(b) scheduling conference is held or scheduling order is due.[138] The essential purpose of the meeting is to prepare a discovery plan for the case. Thus, FRCP Rule 26(f) requires the parties to discuss the nature and bases of their respective claims and defences, the possibility of an early resolution of the case, and to make arrangements for the voluntary exchange of information required under FRCP Rule 26(a)(1). The parties must also file a joint discovery plan, stating each party's views and proposals concerning discovery in the case. Formal discovery may not be taken from any source prior to this meeting, unless permitted by the FRCP, by local rule, or agreement of the parties.

DISCLOSURE OF EXPERTS

When expert opinion testimony will be offered at trial, FRCP Rule 26(a)(2) requires the parties to disclose their experts. The disclosure must include a written report stating all opinions to be expressed by the expert: the supporting reasons or bases; all information considered by the expert; any exhibits to be used in support of the opinions; the expert's qualifications, the expert's compensation, and all other cases in which the expert has testified during the previous four years. The disclosure must be made no later than 90 days before trial. The deadline is extended by 30 days for rebuttal experts. Failure to disclose experts may result in the expert's being barred from testifying at trial.[139]

DUTY TO SUPPLEMENT AND PRE-TRIAL DISCLOSURE

A party is required to make its disclosures based on the information then reasonably available, and the fact that it may not have completed its investigation is no excuse. FRCP Rule 26 also imposes a duty on the parties to supplement or correct their disclosure responses with information later acquired. Amended FRCP Rule 26(a)(3) requires the pre-trial disclosure, at least 30 days before trial, of the identity of

138. FRCP Rule 16 permits the court to direct the parties to appear for conferences before trial for virtually any purpose which might assist in the court's management and control of the lawsuit, including the issuance of scheduling orders for the amendment of pleadings, filing of motions, and completion of discovery.

139. See FRCP Rule 37(c), providing that a party which, without substantial justification, fails to comply with the disclosure requirements of FRCP Rules 26(a) or 26(e)(1) shall not be permitted to use the information or witness as evidence in any motion, at a hearing or at trial, unless the failure was harmless.

witnesses and documents or other exhibits to be used at trial. A party who objects to the use of evidence disclosed must serve and file its objections and the bases thereof within 14 days after the disclosure. Failure to object may result in a waiver of the right to object to the evidence.

POWER OF THE COURT TO CONTROL DISCOVERY

The FRCP grants federal courts broad powers to manage the discovery process by controlling the frequency and extent of the various discovery methods provided for under the rules.[140] Hence, FRCP Rule 26(b)(2) expressly authorises the court to alter the number of depositions and interrogatories allowed under the Rules, as well as the length of depositions under FRCP Rule 30 and the number of requests for admissions under FRCP Rule 36(b) Depositions.

GENERAL

Fundamentally, a deposition is sworn court testimony, taken on examination out-of-court, before a person authorised to administer oaths or affirmations. The revised FRCP permits any party to take depositions of any person,[141] or party at any time after compliance with the FRCP Rule 26(f) meeting requirement. FRCP Rule 30(2)(A) limits each group to 10 depositions each. Additional depositions may be taken only after leave of court has been obtained by a noticed motion.

SPECIFIC REQUIREMENTS

Reasonable notice must be given in writing to all parties, stating the time and place of the deposition, the name of the person to be deposed and the method of recording. Documents to be produced at the deposition by a party or, in the case of a non-party witness, by *Subpoena Duces Tecum* served on the witness, must also be described in the notice.

140. The court may exercise its power on its own initiative after reasonable notice to the parties, or on a noticed motion by a party under FRCP Rule 26(c). FRCP Rule 26(c) allows a party or non-party from whom discovery is sought to obtain a protective order from the court avoiding or limiting the discovery, for good cause shown. However, the moving party must first have conferred or attempted to confer with the other affected parties to resolve the dispute without court intervention.

141. Non-party witnesses may be compelled by subpoena to appear for their deposition pursuant to FRCP Rule 45.

The revised FRCP Rule 30(b)(2) permits the deposition to be recorded by sound, video, or by stenography, without first obtaining court permission. Any other party may utilise another method of recording, so long as prior notice is given to the deponent and the other parties. Moreover, on written stipulation by the parties or order of the court, the FRCP permits depositions by telephone or other remote electronic means.

The officer taking the deposition must certify that the deponent was properly sworn and that the transcription or recording is a true record of the testimony given by the deponent. On a request either by the deponent or a party, FRCP Rule 30 permits the deponent to have 30 days in which to review the deposition transcript or recording and if there are any changes in form or substance, to sign a statement identifying the changes and the reasons therefore. The officer must state in the certificate whether a review was requested and must append any changes made in the transcript or recording, within the time allowed for making such changes. Finally, FRCP Rule 5(d) permits courts on motion by a party or on its own initiative to order that discovery not be filed with the court.[142]

CONDUCT OF THE DEPOSITION

The conduct of the examination and any cross-examination is governed by the Federal Rules of Evidence, just as if the testimony were being given during a trial. All objections must be noted by the officer recording the deposition in the record. All objections, except as to the form[143] of the question, are preserved. To reduce the frustration of discovery, which frequently results from speeches by attorneys made as an "objection" in order to suggest an answer to the witness, FRCP Rule 30(d) requires all objections to be stated concisely and in a non-argumentative and non-suggestive manner. Moreover, an attorney may not instruct a witness not to answer a question, except: to preserve a privilege to enforce a limitation on the evidence directed by the court or to present a motion under FRCP Rule 30(d)(3) for court sanctions.[144]

142. Pursuant to most state and federal district local court rules, discovery is not filed with the court.

143. Where the question posed is ambiguous, unintelligible or compound an objection as to the form of the question may be raised. Non-form objections based on the competency of the witness, or the relevancy of the testimony are not waived by failure to object at the time of the deposition, unless the objection could readily have been cured at the time. See FRCP Rule 32(d)(3)(A).

144. This provision permits a party to request that the court suspend or otherwise limit the manner and scope of the deposition, on a showing that the examination is being conducted in bad faith, or in such a manner as to unreasonably annoy, embarrasses or oppress the deponent. The court may order the party and/or its attorney, whose conduct wrongfully necessitated the motion, to pay the moving party's resulting costs and legal fees.

DEPOSITIONS IN FOREIGN COUNTRIES

The amended FRCP now encourages effective use of the Hague Convention on the Taking of Evidence Abroad in Civil or Commercial Matters.[145] FRCP Rule 28(b) permits depositions in a foreign country: in compliance with any applicable treaty or convention; by a letter of request; before a person authorised to administer oaths by the law of the foreign jurisdiction or by the United States; or by any person commissioned by the court. A letter of request[146] or commission is obtained from the court by application and will be issued on such terms as are "just and appropriate".

USE OF DEPOSITIONS AT TRIAL OR OTHER COURT PROCEEDINGS

The use of deposition testimony as evidence during a trial or other court proceeding is controlled by FRCP Rule 32 and the Federal Rules of Evidence.[147] Deposition testimony, so far as is admissible under the Rules of Evidence, may be used against any party who was present or represented at the deposition, or who had reasonable notice of the deposition, as permitted by FRCP Rule 32. Thus, deposition testimony may be used to impeach or contradict in-court testimony of a deponent, or for any other purpose permitted by the Rules of Evidence.[148] Deposition testimony may also be introduced by any party for any purpose where the deponent is an adverse party, or someone who at the time of the deposition was an officer, director, managing agent or other person authorised to testify on behalf of the adverse party.[149] Moreover, the deposition of a non-party witness may be used for any purpose, where the witness cannot be compelled to appear at the proceeding, such as where the witness is dead or resides outside the subpoena power of the court.[150] Deposition testimony is subject to the same objections as would exist if the testimony were being offered by a live witness.[151]

145. Convention on the Taking of Evidence Abroad in Civil or Commercial Matters, opened for signature 18 March 1970, 23 UST 2555, TIAS No. 7444, 847 UNTS 231, reprinted at 28 USCA Section 1781 (West. Supp. 1994). This treaty is also frequently referred to as "the Convention" or the "Hague Convention".

146. See 28 USC, Section 1781.

147. For the Federal Rules of Evidence and the accompanying case law annotations, see 28 USCA Federal Rules of Evidence (West Publishing Co., St. Paul, MN).

148. FRCP Rule 32(a)(1).

149. FRCP Rule 32(a)(2).

150. FRCP Rule 32(a)(3).

151. FRCP Rule 32(b).

Written interrogatories

GENERAL

Interrogatories are written questions served by one party on another party. The most significant revision to FRCP Rule 33 is the imposition of a limit on the number of interrogatories that can be asked to 25, including all discrete subparts. The limit may only be increased by leave of court, or on stipulation of the parties. FRCP Rule 33 also prohibits service of interrogatories before the FRCP Rule 26(f) meeting of the parties, without leave of court or stipulation of the parties.

SPECIFIC REQUIREMENTS

FRCP Rule 33, which controls this form of discovery, requires each interrogatory to be answered separately and fully in writing by the person served. Where the party served is a corporation, partnership or association, interrogatories must be answered by an officer or agent, who must provide as much information as is available to the party. The answers must be signed under oath by the person making them.

An objection may be stated in lieu of an answer, except that the responding party must answer as much of the interrogatory as is not objectionable. All objections to any interrogatory must be stated specifically or they will be waived, unless excused by the court for good cause. All objections must be signed by the attorney. All responses must be served within 30 days after receipt of service of the interrogatories. The time may be extended by written agreement of the parties, subject to the FRCP Rule 29 prohibition against undue delay.

USE OF INTERROGATORY ANSWERS AT TRIAL OR OTHER PROCEEDING

Interrogatory answers may be used at trial or in other court proceedings as permitted by the Rules of Evidence.[152] Moreover, while an interrogatory which involves an opinion or contention that relates to a fact or application of law to fact is proper, the court may extend the time to respond to the interrogatory until after certain specified discovery has been completed, or until after the pre-trial conference has been held.

152. FRCP Rule 33(c).

Requests for production of documents or things and entry on land for inspection

GENERAL

This form of discovery is governed by FRCP Rule 34 which allows any party to serve on any other party a request to produce documents for inspection and copying, or to inspect or copy, test, or sample any tangible things, within the scope of FRCP Rule 26(b) and in the responding party's possession, custody or control.[153] It is important to note that the term "documents" is very broadly defined by FRCP Rule 34 to include:

". . . writings, drawings, graphs, charts, photographs, phonorecords, and other data compilations from which information can be obtained, translated, if necessary, by the respondent through detection devices into reasonable usable form."

In addition to documents and things, a request may be made to permit entry on designated land or other property in order to inspect, measure, survey, photograph, test, or sample the property or any specified object or operation located on the land, within the scope of FRCP Rule 26(b).

SPECIFIC REQUIREMENTS

The requests must describe each document or thing, or category of documents or things, with "reasonable particularity". A reasonable time, place and manner of the inspection or related acts must be stated. Absent leave of court or written stipulation by the parties, requests under FRCP Rule 34 may not be served before the parties have met, pursuant to FRCP Rule 26(f).

The party receiving an FRCP-Rule 34 request must respond, in writing, within 30 days after service of the request, although the parties may extend the time to respond by written agreement, subject to FRCP Rule 29. A responding party may also request the court to extend the time to respond, for good cause. The response must state, as to each request, that inspection and related activities will be permitted, unless objected to, in which case the reasons for the objection must be stated. If an objection is made to only part of a request, that portion of the request objected to must be identified and inspection permitted of the remaining part. Any documents produced for inspection must be produced as they are kept "in the usual course of business" or shall be organised to "correspond with the categories in the request".

---

153. Non-parties may be compelled to produce documents and things or to submit to an inspection by subpoena, pursuant to FRCP Rule 45.

Requests for admissions

GENERAL

FRCP Rule 36(a) permits a party to serve on any other party, for purposes of the pending action, written requests for admission of the truth of any matters, separately stated that relate to statements or opinions of fact, or of the application of law to fact, or of the genuineness of any document described in the requests.

SPECIFIC REQUIREMENTS

The scope of requests for admission is limited by FRCP Rule 26(b)(1). As with all other formal discovery, without leave of court or a stipulation of all parties, requests for admissions may not be served prior to the FRCP Rule 26(f) meeting.

Each matter for which an admission is sought will be deemed admitted unless the party served answers or objects to the request within 30 days after receipt of service of the requests. The time to respond may be shortened or lengthened by order of the court or on written agreement of the parties, subject to FRCP Rule 29. The answer must admit or specifically deny the matter requested, or set forth the reasons why the responding party cannot truthfully admit or deny the matter. FRCP Rule 36 also requires a denial to "fairly meet the substance of the request". Where good faith requires that only part of a request be denied or that the answer be qualified, the responding party must admit the part of the matter that is true and deny or qualify the remainder. As with all other forms of discovery, the responses must be signed by the party or by the party's attorney.

Obtaining foreign discovery under the FRCP and The Hague Convention on the taking of evidence abroad

In the context of a civil action venued in a United States court involving non-United States parties, the parties must inevitably decide whether to conduct discovery pursuant to the FRCP, the Hague Convention on the Taking of Evidence Abroad, or other relevant treaty.[154] This decision will be influenced by the venue of the action, citizenship of the parties, and the resulting need to pursue discovery abroad balanced against the expense and inconvenience, and the strategy of the foreign party in

154. E.g., Inter-American Convention on Letters Rogatory (entered into force on 27 August 1988) (OAS, Treaty Series, No. 43, reprinted in ILM 339 (1976)); Consular Convention, 1 June 1964, *Martindale-Hubbell Law Digest,* United SSR–13 (1994).

responding to discovery. Attempts have been made to simplify the procedures to obtain foreign discovery through legislation,[155] international treaties,[156] case law and amendments to the FRCP.[157]

Aerospatiale: United States Supreme Court's balancing the FRCP with foreign sovereignty concerns

In 1987, the United States Supreme Court was asked to decide whether the Convention provides the exclusive and mandatory procedures for obtaining documents and information located within the territory of a foreign nation that has signed the Convention.[158] In *Aerospatiale*, the Court ruled unanimously that this was not the case. The Court split on the issue of whether the Convention should be the discovery procedure of first resort. Although the *Aerospatiale* minority suggested that first resort to the Convention is appropriate, the majority held that the discovering party must weigh "the particular facts, sovereign interests, and likelihood that resort to [Convention] procedures will prove effective". The United States Supreme Court concluded that the United States' signature to the Convention did not supplant the discovery provisions of the FRCP when citizens of signatory nations are subject to the jurisdiction of a United States court.

Significantly, the majority opinion did not address the issue of who bears the burden of proof on the decision whether to resort to Convention procedures. Lower courts that have implemented the *Aerospatiale* analysis of the relevant facts, relative sovereign interests, and the effectiveness of Convention procedures have, with few exceptions, placed the burden of proving the effectiveness of the Convention on the party advocating the use of the Convention.[159]

155. Legislation has been proposed in the United States Congress in 1951 and in two subsequent sessions that would require foreign companies with United States branches and United States companies with foreign holdings to produce documents related to their business. HR Res. 7339, 82d Cong., 1st Sess. (1951) (amending the Clayton Act, 15 USC, Sections 12–13, 14–21, 22–17, 44 (1976) (as amended); HR Res. 642, 84th Cong., 1st Sess. (1955); HR Res. 391, 83d Cong., 1st Sess. (1953).

156. The United States is party to several bilateral and multilateral treaties and agreements that address the issue of foreign discovery.

157. See FRCP Rule 28(b) and accompanying text.

158. *Societe Nationale Industrielle Aerospatiale* v. *United States Dist. Court for Southern District*, 482 United States 522, 107 S Ct. 2542, 96 LEd.2d 461 (1987).

159. Unlike the United States lower courts, the Convention signatory states believe "the burden of proof should be on the party wishing to resist application of the Convention." Hague Conference on Private International Law: Special Commission Report on the Operation of The Hague Service Convention and The Hague Evidence Convention, 28 ILM 1556, 1566 (1989). Furthermore, in the signatory nations other than the United States the Hague Evidence Convention takes precedence over any conflicting rules of civil procedure. See, e.g., LG München I, ZZP 1982, 363 (translated in A Heck, "Federal Republic of Germany and the EEC", 18 Int'l Law. 793, 796 (Fall 1984)).

Lower court response to Aerospatiale

UNITED STATES DISTRICT COURTS

In *Aerospatiale*, the Supreme Court indicated that lower courts should:

". . . take care to demonstrate due respect for any special problem confronted by the foreign litigant on account of its nationality or the location of its operations, and for any sovereign interest expressed by a foreign state."[160]

Presumably, the Supreme Court thus accommodated one of the essential purposes of the Convention, the prevention of conflicts between different judicial systems with overlapping sovereignties.[161] Decisions by the lower courts do not reflect the Supreme Court's comity concerns. The lower federal courts have almost unanimously ruled that the burden and expense to United States litigants of utilising Convention procedures outweigh the sovereignty concerns expressed by foreign parties. Accordingly, most lower federal courts have placed the burden of proof in the *Aerospatiale* analysis on the party that wishes to utilise Convention discovery procedures.[162] In every case subsequent to *Aerospatiale*, the party carrying the burden of proof in the *Aerospatiale* analysis has lost.[163]

In *Haynes* v. *Kleinwefers*, the New York court found that the West German defendant failed to offer any persuasive reasons to resort to the Convention procedures instead of the FRCP The court balanced the interest of the West German defendant in having discovery proceed under the Convention with the perceived inconvenience and delay of executing letters of request. The court concluded that the FRCP would result in a speedier completion of discovery and success in discovering requested documents.

In *Benton Graphics* v. *Uddeholm Corp.*, the defendant urged that the Convention would serve important Swedish interests, which included:

(1) Serving as an effective mechanism for co-operation between different legal systems;
(2) Minimising conflicts between the legal systems of Sweden and the United States; and
(3) Enabling Swedish courts to limit discovery in sensitive and protected areas of Swedish law such as trade secrets and national security.

160. *Aerospatiale*, 482 United States at 546, 107 S Ct. at 2557.

161. See Report of United States Delegation to Eleventh Session of Hague Conference on Private International Law, 8 ILM at 806–807.

162. See, e.g., *Haynes* v. *Kleinwefers*, 119 FRD 335 (EDNY 1988); *Rich* v. *KIS California, Inc.*, 121 FRD 254 (MDNC 1988); *In re Bedford Computer Corp.*, 114 Bankr. 2 (Bankr. DNH 1990).

163. *Kleinwefers*, 119 FRD at 337.

The court concluded that because the defendant failed to show a specific interest in specific evidence requests, the further delay of forcing discovery to proceed under the Convention was not warranted.

The North Carolina court in *Rich* v. *Kis California, Inc.* held that the United States plaintiff could conduct limited discovery into a French defendant's contacts with the United States to determine whether the court had personal jurisdiction over the defendant.[164] The court concluded that such discovery was not intrusive (although it arguably conflicted with the French blocking statute), and that the "efficiency" of the FRCP was preferred over the presumably less-efficient Convention procedures. Similarly, the bankruptcy court in *In re Bedford Computer Corp.* held that the FRCP applied to the discovery of personal jurisdiction issues rather than the Convention because there was no showing of any prejudice to sovereign interests.[165] However, the court did reduce the amount of discovery to ensure it was "unintrusive" and "pertinent".

In one federal case subsequent to *Aerospatiale*, a New York district court held it was appropriate to make a first resort to the Convention. The New York district court in *Hudson* v. *Hermann Pfanter GmbH & Co.* followed Justice Blackmun's minority analysis in *Aerospatiale* more closely than the majority analysis.[166] In deferring to Convention procedures, the court held that the FRCP are necessarily more offensive to the sovereign interests of Civil Law countries and that the plaintiffs failed to establish that the use of the Convention would frustrate their discovery efforts.

STATE COURTS

State courts have mirrored the federal decisions. A Texas court in *Sandsend Financial Consultants, Ltd.* v. *Wood* did not discuss the factors it balanced in deciding that discovery should proceed under the FRCP. The court concluded that "there are obviously reasons the Court can feel that discovery needs to be expeditious . . . and there might not be viable discovery from the other procedures."[167] Similarly, a New York court held in *Scarminach* v. *Goldwell GmbH* that the corporation-defendant in a personal injury action failed to meet its burden of requiring the plaintiff to use the Convention procedures.[168] The court acknowledged that *Aerospatiale's* majority decision was not entirely clear about which party

164. 121 FRD 254 (MDNC 1988).
165. 114 Bankr. 2 (Bankr. DNH 1990).
166. 117 FRD 33 (NDNY 1987).
167. 743 SW.2d 364, 366 (Tex. App. 1st Dist. 1988).
168. 531 NYS2d 188, 140 Misc.2d 103 (NYSup.Ct. 1988).

bears the burden of proof and thus looked to the subsequent federal decisions. The court chose to place the burden of proof on the Convention advocate, and held that the defendant failed to identify any special problems attributable to the defendant's nationality in responding to the interrogatories, failed to show how the discovery sought by the plaintiff implicated any specific sovereign interest, and failed to show how the Convention procedures would be more effective.

On the other hand, in *Orlich v. Helm Bros., Inc.*, an action that involved negligence, strict liability and contract claims, a New York court held that any discovery requests with respect to documents in the possession of a West German manufacturer had to proceed under the Convention.[169] The court held that if discovery is sought from a non-party in a foreign jurisdiction, application of the Convention is "virtually compulsory" in light of international comity. The court noted that since fact gathering is a judicial process in Civil Law nations, the non-judicial taking of evidence within West German territory would be an "affront to their sovereignty", especially since the respondent was not a party.

The response of the lower federal and state courts to the *Aerospatiale* decision suggests that the comity analysis proposed by the United States Supreme Court has failed to provide a coherent solution to the conflict inherent in foreign discovery in United States litigation. Most lower courts have balanced the United States party's interest in proceeding efficiently under the FRCP against the sovereignty interests of other nations, and held that "efficiency" won. Thus, in certain jurisdictions, United States litigants may successfully argue that forcing resort to Convention procedures after time is consumed by fighting to defend the application of FRCP procedures is not warranted. Foreign parties responding to a discovery request under the FRCP should recognise that in many jurisdictions they may need to produce all evidence they would likely produce under Convention procedures and challenge FRCP discovery only where they can present a specific challenge to specific discovery requests.

United States courts are authorised to compel production of evidence from a party over whom they have personal jurisdiction, even if the defending party asserts that a blocking statute prohibits production.[170] Failure to produce evidence pursuant to court order is grounds for sanctions.[171] Such sanctions may include money, injunctions, a finding of

---

169. 560 NYS2d. 10, 160 AD2d. 135 (1 Dept. 1990).

170. 28 USCA Sections 1783, 1784; see *United States* v. *Mann*, 829 F2d. 849 (9th Cir. 1987) (court enforced order to disclose banking information located in Cayman Islands, in contravention of blocking statute); *Societe Internationale Pour Participations Industrielles et Commerciales, SA* v. *Rogers*, 357 United States 197 (1958) (court enforced discovery order in contravention of Swiss blocking statute).

171. See Wright & Miller, *Federal Practice and Procedure*, Sections 2284–2289.

fact against the non-complying party, or issuance of a judgment against the non-complying party, resulting in dismissal of the case.[172] United States courts impose a comity-related balancing test for the application of sanctions where compliance with a court order is refused on the basis of a blocking statute.[173] Under this test, the issue is not whether blocking statutes are valid, but rather, conceding their validity, whether they excuse defendants from complying with a production order.[174] United States courts do not recognise blocking statutes as a defence to a discovery order, but only as a mitigating factor in the choice of sanctions imposed for failure to produce evidence.[175]

Obtaining and responding to foreign discovery under the Convention

The Convention establishes three basic methods to obtain evidence from signatory nations: letters of request,[176] use of diplomatic or consular officials,[177] and use of designated private commissioners.[178] When determining whether to invoke the Convention procedures to depose a witness, the initiating and responding parties should first consider whether the desired witness is subject to subpoena in the United States, or would appear voluntarily. In either case, it may be preferable to proceed with discovery in the normal course under the FRCP.[179] Where, however, an initiating United States party faces determined opposition

172. Unlike the sanctions available to a United States court, the authority of a German court over a party that refuses to comply with its orders or has violated a rule of civil procedure is limited to an admission-of-fact sanction. A Heck, "Federal Republic of Germany and the EEC", 18 Int'l. Law, 793, 798 (Fall 1984).

173. This balancing test was first adopted in American Law Institute Restatement (Second) of the Foreign Relations Law of the United States Section 40, and is broadly recognised by the courts. See, e.g., Note, "Foreign Nondisclosure Laws and Domestic Discovery Orders in Antitrust Litigation", 88 Yale LJ 612, 619–21 (1979).

174. See *In re Uranium Antitrust Litigation*, 480 FSupp. 1138, 1149 (ND Ill. 1979).

175. See, e.g., *Société Internationale Pour Participations Industrielles et Commerciales, SA* v. *Rogers*, 357 United States 197 (1958) (although liability under a foreign non-disclosure law does not automatically excuse compliance with a valid discovery order, dismissal or similarly harsh sanctions should not be used when a party makes a good faith effort to comply but is unable because of a foreign blocking statute).

176. Hague Evidence Convention, Articles 1–14.

177. Hague Evidence Convention, Articles 15, 16, 18–22.

178. Hague Evidence Convention, Articles 17–22.

179. The Convention has been available to litigants in United States courts for over 20 years, but there is relatively little evidence of its use. Consequently, there are few significant United States judicial decisions that guide United States and foreign parties in conducting discovery outside the United States. The *Aerospatiale* decision, as interpreted by several lower courts, discourages the use of the Convention in most contexts. See discussion notes 18–43 and accompanying text.

from the foreign responding party, proceeding under the FRCP may be a long, expensive and difficult process, and ultimately less successful in discovering important evidence than the Convention would be.

For the initiating party that decides to pursue discovery of documents under the Convention, it is advisable to have proceeded far enough with discovery within the United States to have accumulated the facts necessary to make specific requests for documents.[180] Most states that have signed the Convention have reserved their right to refuse to execute letters of request issued to obtain pre-trial discovery of documents under Article 23.[181] Certain countries have executed a blanket refusal to produce documents.[182] There is some evidence that this categorical refusal to execute document requests will be utilised primarily to limit such discovery to documents that are specifically identified and which are relevant and necessary to the lawsuit.[183]

LETTERS OF REQUEST

Letters of request under the Convention may be used to conduct examinations of persons, address specific questions to witnesses, and inspect documents and personal or real property. The requesting party must make a motion in the United States court in which litigation is proceeding for a letter of request in accordance with local court rules. Any "judicial authority" in the requesting state may issue a letter of request.[184] The information required in the letter of request pursuant to the Convention is straight forward:

180. For example, Britain has adopted a limited Article 23 declaration that provides that letters of request for the production of documents will only be executed if it specifies documents appearing to the requested court to be, or likely to be, in his possession, custody or control. See Int'l. Law Digest, *Martindale-Hubbell Law Directory*, pt. VI, at 22 (1991).

181. Hague Evidence Convention, Article 23; the Declarations and Reservations made by the nations that have signed the Convention are reprinted, with the text of the Convention at 38 USCA Section 1781, and in the Int'l Law Digest, *Martindale-Hubbell Law Directory*, pt. VI, at 14 (1991).

182. But see *Aerospatiale*, 482 United States at 564 n.22 (France modified its blanket Article 23 declaration to allow discovery of documents that are limitatively enumerated in the letter of request and have a direct and clear nexus with the subject matter of the litigation. Germany and several other nations have unqualified Article 23 declarations, but the German government has drafted new regulations that would permit pre-trial production of specified and relevant documents in response to letters of request).

183. For example, in *Rio Tinto Zinc Corp.* v. *Westinghouse Electric Corp.* (1978) AC 574; 610 (House of Lords, United Kingdom), an English court indicated that a master who finds a United States document request to be too broad may narrow the request without referring it back to the United States Court.

184. Hague Evidence Convention, Article 1.

(1) Identify the authority requesting the information and the authority requested to obtain it;
(2) The names and addresses of the parties to the proceedings and their representatives;
(3) The names and addresses of the parties to be examined;
(4) A description of the nature of the action; and
(5) A list of the questions to be put to the witness or a statement of the subject matter of the examination and/or a specification of documents sought.[185]

The description of the action should emphasise:

(1) That the proceeding involves commercial matters (the Convention only applies to judicial proceedings involving commercial matters);[186] and
(2) That the case is in litigation and the evidence sought is needed for trial.[187] Convention participants distinguish between evidence that will constitute proof at trial, which is discoverable, and evidence that may merely lead to evidence admissible at trial, which is not discoverable.[188] Therefore, United States requesting parties should only request evidence that can be specifically identified as necessary for trial, or the court of the responding state will not give effect to the request.

Foreign counsel can save a United States party time and money by advising on the form of letters of request for depositions and document requests. Where appropriate, a United States party should retain foreign counsel to review the form of the letter of request before it is submitted to the United States court to determine that it conforms to the practices of the foreign jurisdiction.

185. Hague Evidence Convention, Article 3.

186. The term "civil or commercial matters" is not defined in the Convention. (See Report of United States Delegation to Eleventh Session of Hague Conference of Private International Law, 8 ILM at 808.)

187. The Convention only applies to actual judicial proceedings involving commercial matters. Hague Evidence Convention, Article 1.

188. See, e.g., notes to Rules of the Supreme Court (Britain), Order 70: The English Court will refuse to make an order in aid of a foreign request for evidence if it appears or to the extent to which it appears that evidence is required, not for the purpose of proof at the foreign trial, where it is admissible and relevant to the issues in those proceedings, but for the purpose of discovery, something in the nature of a roving enquiry in which a party is seeking to "fish out" some material which might lead to obtaining admissible evidence at the trial, even though the procedure of the foreign court permits such a practice, as does, for example, Rule 26 of the United States Federal Rules of Civil Procedure.

Once issued by the requesting court, the letter is transmitted either through the Department of Justice or directly to the designated "central authority" in the state from which evidence is sought, and forwarded to the judicial authority competent to execute it. The procedures the judicial authority will use to execute the letter of request vary greatly from country to country, so it is important to involve foreign counsel at all stages of the proceedings. Foreign counsel may be able to save time by shepherding the request through the bureaucracy.

Normally, the receiving state's laws and procedures govern the execution of letters of request. However, Articles 9 and 10 of the Convention provide that the receiving state is bound to comply with requests to use a special method or procedure in the gathering of evidence, unless such request is either incompatible with the receiving state's internal laws or impossible to perform. Thus, the Convention permits the requesting party to specify that a verbatim transcript, or in some cases a videotape, be made of a deposition, and that a deponent be sworn in the same manner as a United States deponent. The requesting party may also request permission to be present and to ask questions at the deposition.[189]

It may be appropriate for the foreign party to challenge the issuance of the letter of request in the United States court, rather than waiting until the request is presented to the foreign court. Relevant considerations at this point include whether the request describes United States privileges available to a foreign deponent or to a party asked to produce documents. Article 11 of the Convention permits a witness to assert a privilege under the law of either the state of origin or the receiving state if the relevant privileges of the requesting state are denoted in the request. Consequently, counsel for the responding party should insist that relevant United States privileges are specified in the text of the request. The responding party should also review any requested "special procedures" under Article 9 of the Convention to insure they conform to appropriate United States and foreign procedures.

A receiving state will compel production of evidence pursuant to a foreign letter of request as it would an order by its own authorities in an internal proceeding. As discussed above in the Section on blocking statutes, the level of "compulsion" abroad may be less significant than that available in the United States under the FRCP. Presumably, if discovery under the Convention is not successful due to the failure of the responding party to co-operate, the requesting party may then proceed under the FRCP and avail itself of United States sanctions. A foreign party responding to United States discovery may derive some benefit from dragging out discovery in this manner, but may face severe sanctions by the United States court for doing so.

189. Hague Evidence Convention, Articles 7 and 9.

DIPLOMATIC OR CONSULAR OFFICIALS AND COMMISSIONERS

Articles 15–22 of the Convention set forth the procedures to take evidence outside the United States using diplomatic or consular officials and commissioners. Using these procedures, United States diplomatic or consular personnel serving in a country that has signed the Convention may take evidence from a United States citizen living in that country to be used in a United States court proceeding. Alternatively, a United States party may request that a Convention participant appoint a commissioner to take evidence in that state. Because evidence obtained under these procedures is not conducted by the foreign judiciary, the person taking the evidence has no power to compel the giving of evidence.[190] Nevertheless, these voluntary discovery procedures are used more frequently in practice than are the compulsory procedures pursuant to letters of request.[191]

The procedure to obtain evidence by diplomatic or consular officials and commissioners is similar to the procedure to obtain a letter of request. The party that wishes to have a diplomatic or consular officer take evidence must make a motion for an order to that effect in the United States court in which the action is pending. On issuance of the order, oral examination of United States parties or witnesses may proceed before the officer or commissioner at the United States Embassy. The responding party should entertain the same considerations in safeguarding the witness' interests as are discussed above in the section on letters of request.

DISMISSAL WITHOUT FULL TRIAL

The FRCP and the civil procedural rules of all state court jurisdictions permit courts to summarily decide cases in most jurisdictions, or specific issues within cases where there is nothing for the trier of fact to decide. In addition, under certain circumstances courts have the power to dismiss cases without trial and without any determination made on the merits of the case.

Summary judgment and summary adjudication of issues

When there is no genuine issue as to any material fact to be decided by the trier of fact, FRCP Rule 56 permits the court to decide the case or to

190. Hague Evidence Convention, Articles 15, 17.

191. See *Aerospatiale*, 482 United States at 560 n.16, 107 S Ct. at 2564. According to the French Government, the overwhelming majority of discovery requests by American litigants are "satisfied willingly before consular officials and, occasionally, commissioners, and without the need for involvement by a French court or use of its coercive powers." (citing Brief for Republic of France as *Amicus Curiae* 24.)

adjudicate specified issues in the case, without a trial. The intent of the Rule, of course, is to eliminate the delay and expense of a trial where no purpose would be served in having a trial and the moving party is entitled to judgment as a matter of law. In furtherance of this goal, FRCP Rule 56 allows a party to obtain summary judgment when facts are set out in detail by affidavits,[192] depositions, answers to interrogatories, and/or admissions on file when, viewed in the light most favourable to the opposing party, there are no genuine issues of material fact in dispute.

Where it appears from the face of the complaint, cross-complaint or third-party complaint and any responsive pleadings, again, viewed in the light most favourable to the opposing party that there are no genuine issues of material fact to be decided, then a motion for judgment on the pleadings, pursuant to FRCP Rule 12(c), may be appropriate. For example, on 20 August 1994, party A files a complaint asserting a claim for breach of a written contract. The complaint alleges the breach occurred in May 1988. Party B answers and in an affirmative defence alleges that the claim is barred by a six-year statute of limitations. Party A's complaint alleges no facts excusing his late filing. Because the pleadings themselves establish conclusively that there is no dispute when the breach, if there was one, occurred, party B may move for judgment on the pleadings on the basis that the breach of contract claim is barred by the statute of limitations. However, where the court must review matters outside the pleadings, then a motion for summary judgment is the proper means for deciding the matter.

Judgment for the claimant

FRCP Rule 56(a) allows the claimant, at any time after the expiration of 20 days from the start of the action, or after service of a motion for summary judgment by the adverse party, to "move with or without supporting affidavits, for summary judgment in the party's favour on all or any part thereof".

Let us assume that the pleadings in the above example show that the time of the breach was in dispute, such that a motion for judgment on the pleadings would be improper. However, discovery produces uncontroverted evidence, which when viewed in the light most favourable to the

192. An affidavit is essentially a written statement of facts made by a competent witness under oath. The form and substance of an affidavit is governed by Rule 56(e). Hence, affidavits presented in support or in opposition to a motion for summary judgment must be made on personal knowledge and shall state facts that would be admissible in evidence. The affidavit must state affirmatively that the person making the affidavit is competent to attest to the facts stated therein. Moreover, sworn or certified copies of any papers referred to in the affidavit must be attached or served with the affidavit.

defendant establishes that the breach occurred less than six years prior to the filing of the complaint. Party A may move for summary adjudication in its favour as to party B's six-year statute of limitations affirmative defence, on the basis that discovery shows conclusively that the breach occurred less than six years before the complaint was filed, and party A is entitled to judgment as a matter of law on the issue of the statute-of-limitations defence.

Judgment for the defending party

Significantly, under FRCP Rule 26(b), while the claimant must wait 20 days after the action is commenced before moving for summary judgment, the responding party may seek summary judgment with or without supporting affidavits, at any time, even before a responsive pleading is filed.

If, in the example given above, discovery produced evidence which conclusively established that the breach occurred more than six years prior to the filing of the complaint, party B could move for summary judgment on the basis that the evidence, when viewed in the light most favourable to party A, shows conclusively that the breach occurred more than six years before the complaint was filed, and party B is entitled to judgment as a matter of law.

In addition, the FRCP requires that all motions for summary judgment be served at least 10 days before the date set for hearing [note that local rules of federal courts may require service as many as 28 days before hearing]. The opposing party may serve opposing affidavits at any time before the hearing. Importantly, where the pleadings and the evidence show that genuine issues exist as to some but not all material facts, FRCP Rule 56(d) permits the court to order that certain facts are without substantial controversy and order that trial proceed only on the remaining material facts which are actually and in good faith controverted.

Default judgments

A default judgment may be entered against a party from whom affirmative relief is sought if that party fails to plead or otherwise defend, as provided by FRCP Rule 55(a).[193] Where the claim against the defendant

---

193. However, the decision to enter a default judgment is within the broad discretionary power of the court. See *Eitel* v. *McCool*, 782 F2d. 1470 (9th Cir. 1986) (although the defendant had not filed an answer held default not proper where the defendant had entered an appearance and was heavily engaged in settlement negotiations).

is for an amount certain, the clerk of the court may enter judgment on request by the plaintiff, with a proper showing made by affidavit of the amount due. In all other cases, the plaintiff must apply to the court for entry of judgment. If the defendant has made an appearance in the action, notice must be provided to the defendant at least three days before the hearing on the application. In such cases the court may order such hearings or other procedures as it finds necessary to properly determine any issues, including the amount of damages to be awarded in order to enter judgment.

However, FRCP Rule 55(c) provides that even after judgment has been entered, the court, for good cause, may set aside the entry of default or judgment in accordance with FRCP Rule 60(b). FRCP Rule 60(b) is a safety valve against injustice where on motion and "on such terms as may be just" the court may relieve a party from a final judgment, order or proceeding for reason of mistake, inadvertence or excusable neglect.[194] The decision to grant a motion pursuant to FRCP Rule 60(b) for relief from a default judgment is discretionary. Generally the moving party must show that it has a defence and that plaintiff will not be prejudiced under the circumstances. FRCP Rule 60(b) also permits the court to issue such relief where supported by a showing of newly discovered evidence, which by due diligence could not have been discovered in time to request a new trial under FRCP Rule 50(b), or fraud, misrepresentation or other-misconduct by an adverse party.

Dismissal for failure to prosecute

The effective corollary to a default judgment by the party seeking affirmative relief where the opposing party fails to defend is an FRCP Rule 41(b) involuntary dismissal. As provided by the Rule, a defendant may move the court to dismiss an action or claim against the defendant where the plaintiff has failed to prosecute or to comply with the rules or an order of the court. Moreover, unless the court specifies otherwise in its order of dismissal, the dismissal operates as an adjudication on the merits of the case. As a practical matter, such motions are generally granted only in very clear cases of extraordinary lack of diligent prosecution or for flagrant and repeated failures to comply with the rules or court orders by the plaintiff. The decision to dismiss

194. See *United States on behalf of Time Equipment Rental & Sales, Inc.* v. *Harre*, 983 F2d. 128 (8th Cir. 1993) ("entry of a default judgment for a marginal failure to comply with time requirements — in this case, being twelve days late — should be distinguished from dismissals or other sanctions imposed for wilful violations of court rules"); default judgment reversed.

by the court is discretionary as balanced against the strong judicial policy of deciding cases based on their merits.[195]

PRE-TRIAL AND ALTERNATIVE DISPUTE RESOLUTION

The dramatic increase in cases filed in both federal and state courts, frequently resulting in lengthy delays in commencement of trial and increased expense involved in civil litigation to all parties, has placed unprecedented pressure on federal and state courts to more efficiently and effectively manage the progress of lawsuits towards speedy resolution. In response, all jurisdictions have implemented judicial programme intended to give courts broad powers to manage cases by focusing on the real issues in dispute, by limiting discovery to that which is essential, and by encouraging creative mechanisms for early resolution.

Pre-trial conferences and judicially-assisted settlement

In general

Never has the policy of encouraging more efficient resolution of cases been more forcefully implemented than by the recent amendments to the FRCP. In particular, FRCP Rule 16(a) allows a court to order the attorneys to appear for pre-trial conferences to: expedite disposition of the case; establish early and continued control to avoid protracting the case due to lack of management; discourage wasteful pre-trial activity; improve the quality of trial through more thorough preparation; and facilitate settlement.

PRE-TRIAL CONFERENCES AND FRCP RULE 26

After receiving the FRCP Rule 26(f) report from the parties or after consulting with counsel, the court is required by FRCP Rule 16(b) to issue a scheduling order, limiting the time in which the parties may join additional parties or amend pleadings, file motions, and complete discovery. The relationship to FRCP Rule 26 is significant, because the voluntary disclosure provisions of FRCP Rule 26 provides a means for the parties, their counsel and the court to learn, before formal discovery begins, the true nature, scope and basis of the dispute. The court, working with counsel and the parties as provided for by FRCP Rule 16, can then more effectively focus discovery and work towards a prompt resolution.

195. See *Little* v. *Yeutter*, 984 F2d. 160 (6th Cir. 1993).

In that regard, FRCP Rule 16(c) lists a number of subjects the court may consider during a pre-trial conference and on which it may take action, in the interest of effective management of the case. The subjects range from formulation and simplification of the issues, the avoidance of unnecessary proof and of cumulative evidence to the appropriateness and timing of summary adjudication under FRCP Rule 56, and settlement and the use of special procedures to assist in resolving the dispute.

Final pre-trial conference

As required by FRCP Rule 16(d), any final pre-trial conference must be held as close to the date set for trial as reasonable under the circumstances. The purpose of the final pre-trial conference is to formulate a plan for the trial, including a method to facilitate the introduction of evidence. At least one attorney who will conduct the trial on behalf of each party must attend. Moreover, most local court rules require the submission of a pre-trial conference statement, which must identify the witnesses who will testify, as well as any documents that will be introduced during the trial.

Alternative dispute resolution procedures

The now commonly heard phrase "Alternative Dispute Resolution" (ADR) includes a wide range of methods used to resolve disputes short of trial. This includes, in addition to the court-assisted settlement mechanisms discussed above, an increasing number of private, voluntary ADR companies that specialise in facilitating settlement or adjudication when settlement cannot be reached. Most importantly, the various methods and combinations of ADR procedures can be custom-designed to fit the particular facts, issues or circumstances of virtually any manner of dispute.

Private ADR methods

The most frequently used ADR procedures are negotiation, arbitration, and mediation. Other ADR methods can include mediation-arbitration, mini-trials, moderated settlement conferences, neutral fact-finding, private judging, or some combination of each of the methods. Private dispute resolution procedures, which may be initiated at any time, can provide convenient and speedy results, substantial savings in time, costs and attorneys' fees, and can remain confidential and private.

These procedures are usually less formal than court litigation and avoid the strict application of rules.

Negotiation and mediation

Direct negotiation between the parties and/or their counsel is the most widely practiced form of dispute resolution and is generally conducted without the intervention of a neutral third party. Mediation involves a neutral third party who attempts to facilitate settlement negotiations between the disputing parties. Participants in a mediation include the parties, their attorneys or representatives, and the mediator. A mediator can clarify what the parties want and why, focus on their needs and interests, remain a source of trust and confidence for the parties, diffuse hostilities, reduce the adverse impact of emotions, and suggest alternative and creative ways to reach a resolution.

Arbitration

Arbitration involves the submission of a dispute to a neutral arbitrator who makes a decision following a hearing. There are generally three routes to arbitration: through a pre-dispute agreement, a post-dispute agreement, or state-court-mandated arbitration. In pre-dispute arbitrations, the parties agree in a contract to submit future disputes to arbitration. In post-dispute arbitration, the parties submit an existing dispute to arbitration. In court-mandated arbitrations, a judge orders the parties to arbitrate the dispute at some point during litigation. Arbitrations can involve hearings, with the parties presenting evidence through witnesses and/or documents. Moreover, arbitrators are generally not required to follow strict rules of procedure or evidence. An arbitrator usually decides a case by issuing a written arbitration award following the hearing. The award is the final decision in binding arbitration from which there is usually no appeal. Arbitration awards are legally binding and enforceable in all 50 states and in the federal courts. All states and the FRCP allow a party to "confirm" an arbitration award into an enforceable judgment.

Mediation-arbitration

In mediation-arbitration proceedings the parties attempt to mediate the dispute first and, if mediation fails, they then move into arbitration. The neutral who mediates the dispute with the parties may also be the arbitrator, or different individuals can split the roles. The mediation process may resolve the entire dispute, or only part of the dispute, with arbitration resolving the remaining issues.

Mini-trials

A mini-trial is an elaborate form of mediation for large-scale disputes between commercial entities. As an ADR procedure, a mini-trial is a private, consensual proceeding where each party makes a presentation before a panel of representatives selected by the parties. Lawyers present evidence and summary testimony in documentary form, making their best arguments. The intent of this procedure is to involve the parties' decision-makers at an early stage of a lawsuit in an attempt to forge settlements based on practical business considerations.

Moderated settlement conference

A moderated settlement conference is a forum for case evaluation and structured settlement negotiations between the parties and their attorneys. The trial attorneys present their cases before a panel of impartial third parties, usually lawyers, who evaluate the case and render an advisory, non-binding opinion for use by the parties in settlement negotiations.

Neutral fact-finding

Neutral fact finding should be considered whenever a *bona fide* dispute over a matter requiring expert opinion constitutes a significant barrier to settlement. It is particularly helpful when the dispute involves complex technical, scientific or economic issues and the parties hold widely divergent views as to how these issues will be decided at trial. Neutral fact finding may be invoked separately or in conjunction with another ADR procedure.

Private judging

The parties may also submit their dispute to a private judge who makes a decision after a trial. Some states have enacted statutes that allow the decision by the private judge, usually a former or retired court judge, to be enforced as if it were a judgment. One advantage of arranging a private judge is that the parties can select a judge with special experience in resolving the involved dispute. Perhaps most importantly, a private judge offers the parties the ability to select a date certain for the trial.

Private dispute resolution organisations

Many private dispute resolution organisations now exist which specialise in customised programme for parties involved in specific disputes. The advantage of these programme is that a system can be created and implemented to meet the precise needs of the parties. Examples of such organisations include the International Arbitration Association, the American Arbitration Association and the Judicial Arbitration and Mediation Service. Each of these organisations has its own rules, which describe what forms must be used, which documents are to be filed with the organisation, and what notice must be given to the other parties.

TRIAL PROCEDURE

Trial

A unique aspect of the United States' civil court system is the method by which trials are conducted. In the case of a jury trial, whether in a state or federal court, the trial commences with *voir dire* examination of jurors.[196] The attorneys, beginning with counsel for the plaintiff, make opening statements, describing for the trier of fact what their case is about and what the evidence will show. Counsel then presents the plaintiff's case through direct examination of witnesses.[197] The defence counsel is permitted to cross-examine the plaintiff's witnesses and to introduce evidence explaining or contradicting the plaintiff's witnesses through rebuttal witnesses. After completion of the plaintiff's case, counsel presents the defendant's case, also by direct examination of witnesses. The plaintiff's counsel may cross-examine the defence witnesses and introduce rebuttal witness testimony. After the defence case has been presented, the plaintiff's counsel and then defence counsel make closing arguments, wherein they are permitted to argue what the evidence has proven. Finally, the trier of fact, weighing all of the

196. FRCP Rule 47(a) permits the court to allow the parties or their counsel to examine potential jurors for prejudice and otherwise to insure their qualification to hear the case, or the court may conduct the examination. Where the court conducts the *voir dire*, the parties or their counsel must be permitted to supplement the examination as it deems proper. By local rule, many courts only permit parties or their counsel to submit written *voir dire* questions to be presented to the jurors by the court. Rule 47(b) permits each party or group of parties similarly situated three peremptory challenges or exclusions of jurors without cause, pursuant to 28 USC, Section 1870. However, FRCP Rule 47(c) permits a party unlimited challenges to jurors for good cause. Good cause may be established where it can be shown that a prospective juror is biased or is unable to render an impartial verdict based on the evidence to be presented during the trial.

197. FRCP Rule 43(a) requires that in all trials, testimony must be taken orally in open court, unless otherwise provided by an Act of Congress or by the rules, the Federal Rules of Evidence, or other rules adopted by the Supreme Court.

evidence, decides the disputed fact issues presented and, applying the law to the facts,[198] renders a decision, either by special verdict[199] or general verdict, accompanied by answers to specific interrogatories.[200]

Setting the case for trial and local court rules

FRCP Rule 40 provides that all district courts prescribe local rules for the placepent of actions on the trial calendar, either without the request of the parties, or on requests of a party with notice to all other parties, or by such other manner as the court finds expedient. In most cases, the court will order a status conference for the purpose of setting pre-trial conference dates, a discovery cut-off date, a mandatory settlement conference date and the trial date.

Nearly all state and federal trial courts have adopted local rules governing such issues as the content and submission of trial briefs,[201] jury instructions,[202] motions *in limine*,[203] and even the duration of opening

198. In the case of a jury trial, FRCP Rule 51 permits the judge to instruct the jury on the law to be applied at the close of the presentation of the evidence before or after closing argument, or both. In addition, FRCP Rule 51 permits any party to submit proposed jury instructions to the court and the court is required to advise counsel of its action on the instructions before closing argument. Any failure by the judge to an instruction or failure to give an instruction is waived unless made before the jury retires to consider its verdict.

199. FRCP Rule 49(a) permits the court to require a jury to return a special verdict in the form of a special finding on each issue of fact. If in instructing the jury concerning the matters thus submitted, the court omits an issue of fact raised by the pleadings or the evidence, each party waives its right to a jury trial of that issue, unless before the jury retires, the party demands its submission to the jury. If the judge fails to then decide the omitted issue, the issue will be deemed to have been decided in conformance with the judgment on the special verdict.

200. FRCP Rule 49(b) permits the court to instruct the jury to return a general verdict, e.g., the plaintiff is liable to the defendant for breach of contract in a given amount. The court may also submit to the jury written interrogatories to answer. If the general verdict rendered by the jury is consistent with its answers to the written interrogatories judgment may be entered pursuant to Rule 58. Where the answers are consistent with each other, but one or more is inconsistent with the general verdict, the court may enter judgment pursuant to FRCP Rule 58, as indicated by the answers, or send the jury back for further deliberations, or order a new trial.

201. A trial brief is essentially a summary of the case submitted to the judge by the parties explaining each party's case. Generally a trial brief will summarise the facts to be presented and the law to be applied.

202. Each party submits jury instructions, for approval by the court, instructing the jury on the law to be applied in deciding its verdict.

203. A motion *in limine* is a request that the court exclude specific evidence from the trial. Usually such motions are made to exclude evidence that is deemed to be prejudicial or irrelevant and which the party anticipates an opposing party may attempt to introduce into evidence. The motion is most often made before trial is commenced to avoid the risk that the evidence will be heard by the jury before counsel can object to its introduction.

statements and closing arguments by the parties. As such, counsel should consult the local court rules for the court where the trial will be held when preparing for trial.

Jury or court trial

The United States civil procedure system is generally unique in its preservation of the right to trial by jury in civil cases. FRCP Rule 38(a) declares:

The right of trial by jury as declared by the Seventh Amendment to the Constitution or as given by statute of the United States shall be preserved to the parties inviolate.

The Seventh Amendment to the Constitution guarantees the right to a jury trial in all suits at Common Law, where the amount in controversy exceeds US $20. Although the right does not attach to equitable claims,[204] because both equitable and legal issues most often appear in the same action, as a practical matter nearly all civil actions will give rise to a right to trial by jury.

Since the Constitutional or statutory right to a jury trial is not jurisdictional, it is waived by failure to timely demand it.[205] Once made, a demand for a jury trial cannot be withdrawn without the consent of the parties. Rule 48 of the FRCP requires a civil jury to be comprised of not less than six nor more than 12 jurors.[206] Moreover, unless the parties stipulate otherwise, the verdict must be by unanimous vote of the jurors. Because failure of a jury to arrive at a unanimous vote will result in mistrial and the need for another trial, parties are often well advised to stipulate to a verdict by a majority vote, as is permitted by Rule 48 of the FRCP .

Notwithstanding a timely demand for a jury trial, the parties may agree to trial of the case by the court. This may be appropriate in highly complex cases or in short trial matters where trial by jury would unduly lengthen the time of trial.

---

204. All other actions, e.g., those based on equity are triable to the court. Thus, action for injunctive relief, rescission and cancellation, reformation and specific performance of a contract do not accord a right to trial by jury.

205. FRCP Rule 38(b) permits "any party to demand a trial by jury of any issue triable of right by jury by (1) serving on the other parties a demand therefor in writing at any time after commencement of the action, and not later than 10 days after service of the last pleading directed to such issue, and (2) filing the demand as required by FRCP Rule 5 (d). The demand may be endorsed on a pleading by the party".

206. The Local Rules for the United States District Court for the Northern District of California provide that a civil jury shall consist of six jurors.

Consolidation or separation of trials

When multiple actions having common questions of law or fact are before the court, FRCP Rule 42(a) permits the court to order a joint hearing or trial on all matters at issue in the actions, or it may order that the actions be consolidated, when in the interest of judicial economy. Likewise, FRCP Rule 42(b) permits a court to order separate trials of matters, such as claims, counterclaims or third-party claims, in order to avoid prejudice or in the furtherance of judicial economy or convenience.

In addition, when civil actions involving one or more common questions of fact are pending in different districts, 28 USC, Section 1407(a) authorises the transfer of all such actions to any district court for co-ordination or consolidated pre-trial proceedings. Transfers are made by the Judicial Panel on Multidistrict Litigation established by this Section when it is determined "that transfers for such proceedings will be for the convenience of the parties and witnesses and will promote the just and efficient conduct of such actions." Furthermore, Section 1407(c) provides that such actions may be transferred on the judicial panel's own initiative, or on motion filed with the panel by a party to any action in which transfer is appropriate. Such a motion must also be filed in the district in which the party's action is pending.

Evidence

The method by which parties present their case to the trier of fact is through the introduction of evidence of relevant facts and/or opinions, by the testimony of parties, non-party lay witnesses, expert witnesses and/or the introduction of documents. In United States courts, the Federal Rules of Evidence (FRE) govern the character and form of evidence presented in all proceedings.[207] The purpose of the FRE is stated by Rule 102 as follows:

"These rules shall be construed to secure fairness in administration, elimination of unjustifiable expense and delay, and promotion of growth and the development of the law of evidence to the end that the truth may be ascertained and proceedings justly determined."

An overriding objective of the FRE is to insure that proceedings are determined based exclusively on relevant evidence that is reliable, probative

207. See 28 USCA Federal Rules of Evidence (West Publishing Co., St. Paul, MN). Annotated rules of evidence are also available for state courts. For example, see the California Code of Evidence (West publishing Co., St. Paul, MN). There are also a number of well-respected treatises on evidence, such as Weinstein and Berger, *Weinstein's Evidence*, Matthew Bender & Co., New York (1994), and McLaughlin, *Federal Evidence Practice Guide*, Matthew Bender & Co., New York (1994).

of a fact issue material to the proceedings and not unduly prejudicial. In that regard, FRE Rule 401 defines "relevant evidence" as "evidence having a tendency to make the existence of any fact that is of consequence to the determination of the action more probable or less probable than it would be without the evidence."

Generally, relevant evidence is admissible and irrelevant evidence is not admissible.[208] However, even where relevant, evidence may be excluded if its probative value is substantially outweighed by the risks of unfair prejudice, confusion of issues, misleading the jury, or by considerations of undue delay, or unnecessary presentation of cumulative evidence.[209]

Moreover, certain kinds of evidence, although highly relevant, are excluded by rule. Thus, evidence of character to prove conduct,[210] subsequent remedial measures,[211] settlements and offers to settle,[212] payment of medical expenses,[213] and liability insurance[214] are not admissible to prove liability.

Witness testimony

During trial, each party presents its case through witness testimony. The court is required to control the order and mode of the witness interrogation and presentation in order to encourage the determination of truth, to avoid unnecessary time, and to protect the witness from harassment or undue embarrassment.[215] Cross-examination is limited by rule to the scope of the subject matter of the direct examination, and to the credibility of the witness, except that the court may, in its discretion, permit questions into other matters as if on direct examination.[216] Ordinarily, leading questions, e.g., "On 5 May 1994, is it true that you learned that the valve failed under pressure?" are not permitted during direct examination. Such questions are permissible during

---

208. See FRE Rule 402.

209. See FRE Rule 403.

210. See FRE Rule 404. Evidence of character may be introduced for a purpose other than to prove conduct, e.g., truthfulness of a party or witness.

211. See FRE Rule 407. This exclusionary rule is most often at issue in negligence or product liability cases involving an allegedly defectively-designed product where design improvements have been incorporated in subsequent product models that eliminate the alleged defect. However, such evidence is admissible for a purpose other than to show that the product is defective, e.g., to prove ownership, control, or feasibility of eliminating the defect, if controverted, or for impeachment.

212. See FRE Rule 408.

213. See FRE Rule 409.

214. See FRE Rule 411.

215. See FRE Rule 611(a).

216. See FRE Rule 611(b).

cross-examination or during the examination of an adverse party, a witness identified with an adverse party, or a hostile witness.

LAY WITNESS TESTIMONY

The general rule of competency, as described in Rule 501, is that "every person is competent to be a witness, except as otherwise provided in these rules." The exceptions provided in the rules preclude testimony from a witness to a matter unless evidence is presented sufficient to establish that the witness has personal knowledge of the matter.[217] Nor may a witness offer testimony in the form of opinions or inferences unless the opinion or inference is rationally based on the perception of the witness, and is helpful to a clear understanding of the witness's testimony or the determination of a fact.[218] Every witness must first declare that he or she will testify truthfully, by oath or affirmation.[219] When an interpreter is required, the interpreter is subject to the same rules relating to expert witness's qualification as any other expert,[220] and must declare by oath or affirmation that he or she will make a true translation.

EXPERT TESTIMONY

When scientific or other specialised knowledge will help the trier of fact understand the evidence, opinion testimony is admissible if made by a witness qualified by knowledge, skill, experience, training or education.[221] The factual basis for the expert's opinion may be that which has been perceived by the expert at or before the hearing. The facts need not be admissible if they are of the type reasonably relied on by other experts in the same field.

IMPEACHMENT

A testifying witness's credibility may be attacked by any party.[222] Methods of attacking or impeaching the credibility of a witness may include opinion and reputation evidence of the untruthfulness of the witness,[223]

217. See FRE Rule 602.

218. See FRE Rule 701. Lay opinions relating to the weather, e.g., it was cold or hot, or to time and distance are common examples of permissible lay opinion testimony.

219. See FRE Rule 603.

220. See FRE Rule 702.

221. See FRE Rule 702.

222. See FRE Rule 607.

223. See FRE Rule 608. However, evidence of truthful character may only be admitted after evidence of the untruthful character of the witness has been presented.

or evidence of prior conviction of a felony, or some lessor crime if the crime involved dishonesty or false statement.[224] A witness may also be impeached by confronting the witness with evidence of prior inconsistent oral or written statements.[225]

HEARSAY OBJECTIONS TO EVIDENCE

Consistent with the principle that evidence must be reliable to be considered by the trier of fact, the "hearsay rule" is defined by FRE Rule 801(c) as:

". . . a statement [oral, written, or non-verbal conduct intended by the person as an assertion], other than one made by the declarant while testifying at the trial, or hearing, offered in evidence to prove the truth of the matter asserted."

The rules provide that certain statements are not hearsay.[226] A prior statement by a witness at trial, which is inconsistent with the witness' testimony, is admissible to prove the truth of the matter asserted in the statement, if it was made under oath in a court proceeding or deposition. A prior consistent statement may only be offered to rebut a claim that the witness' testimony was fabricated or due to improper influence or motive.[227] An out-of-court statement may also be offered against a party if it was made by the party, by one authorised to make the statement, or by an agent or employee acting within the scope of the agency or employment.[228]

EXCEPTIONS TO THE HEARSAY RULE

There are numerous exceptions to the hearsay rule. Most are founded on the idea that there are certain circumstances that insure that the offered evidence is sufficiently reliable to be considered by the trier of fact. There are two groups of hearsay exceptions: those for which a witness's availability is immaterial,[229] and those for which a witness must be unavailable.[230]

224. See FRE Rule 609.
225. See FRE Rule 613. Frequently, an attorney will attempt to impeach a witness by presentation of an inconsistent statement made while under oath during a deposition.
226. See FRE Rule 801(d).
227. See FRE Rule 801(d)(1).
228. See FRE Rule 801(d)(2).
229. FRE Rule 803 excepts certain types of statements from the hearsay rule, even when the declarant who made the statement is available as a witness.
230. FRE Rule 804 only excepts certain types of statements from the hearsay rule, when the declarant who made the statement is not available as a witness.

The first group of exceptions applies to certain hearsay statements, regardless of whether the declarant who made the statement is available to testify.[231] An out-of-court statement of a present sense impression, describing an event or condition, made while the witness was perceiving the event or condition or shortly thereafter, is excepted from the hearsay rule.[232] The underlying rationale is that the statement and the event or condition are sufficiently close in time to negate the risk of misrepresentation. This rationale also supports the exception for out-of-court statements by a declarant of his or her then-existing state of mind, emotion, sensation, or physical condition.[233]

The FRE also creates an exception for out-of-court statements, in the form of certain types of records, because the circumstances of their creation insure reliability. Thus, a record may be offered to supplement a forgetful witness's testimony on a matter about which the witness once had knowledge, if the record was made when the witness's knowledge of the matter was fresh, and to reflect that matter accurately.[234] Likewise, statements in public records, ancient documents, and market reports or commercial publications generally used and relied on by the public or persons in a specific profession, are excepted from the hearsay rule.

The second group of exceptions applies only when the declarant who made the out-of-court statement is unavailable to testify.[235] Former testimony of a witness in another hearing or deposition, if the party against whom the testimony is offered had an opportunity and similar motive to develop the testimony through examination, is excepted from the hearsay rule because it does not rely on special circumstances to replace the oath and cross-examination.[236]

Trustworthiness is also assured for statements made by a declarant against his or her own pecuniary or proprietary interest.[237] Moreover, the FRE gives the court discretion to exclude from the hearsay rule statements that the court determines are more probative on the matter than any other evidence that can reasonably be obtained by the party offering the statement, and the general purpose of the FRE[238] and the interest of justice will best be served by admission of the statement into evidence.[239]

231. These exceptions are described in FRE Rule 803.
232. See FRE Rule 803(1).
233. See FRE Rule 803(3).
234. See FRE Rule 803, which specifically sets out each exception to the hearsay rule.
235. See FRE Rule 804.
236. See FRE Rule 804(1).
237. See FRE Rule 804(3).
238. See FRE Rule 102.
239. See FRE Rule 804(5).

Documentary evidence

To be admitted into evidence at trial, a document must not only be probative of a material fact, but the fundamental principle of reliability must also be satisfied. The document must be shown, by proper authentication or identification evidence that it is what its proponent claims it to be.[240] FRE Rule 901(b) gives examples of proper authentication or identification: testimony of a witness with knowledge that the matter is what it is claimed to be;[241] opinions of the genuineness of handwriting by non-experts, based on familiarity not acquired for purposes of litigation;[242] public records, e.g., evidence that a writing is authorised by law to be recorded or filed in a public office and in fact was recorded or filed in a public office, or evidence that a purported public record, in any form, is from the public office where such records are kept;[243] and an ancient document, in any form, which is in a condition that creates no suspicion about its authenticity, was in a place where authentic documents of such type would normally be, and has been in existence for at least 20 years.[244]

In addition, under the FRE, certain documents are self- authenticating, i.e., no evidence of authenticity is required;[245] because of the circumstances of their creation, their authenticity cannot be reasonably questioned. Examples are: domestic public documents bearing an official seal and signature attesting that the document is official;[246] foreign public documents attested in an official capacity by one authorised by the foreign state to do so, and accompanied by a final certification of the genuineness of the signature and official position of the attesting person; [247] certified copies of public records;[248] and commercial paper and related documents to the extent provided by commercial law.[249]

---

240. See FRE Rule 901(a), which sets out the requirement of authentication or identification of documents.

241. See FRE Rule 901(b)(1).

242. See FRE Rule 901(b)(2).

243. See FRE Rule 901(b)(7).

244. See FRE Rule 901(b)(8).

245. See FRE Rule 902.

246. See FRE Rule 902(1).

247. See FRE Rule 902(3). A final certificate may be made by a United States consular official, or by a diplomat or consular official of a foreign country assigned to the United States. Final certification is not required where the parties have had reasonable opportunity to investigate the authenticity and accuracy of the document, and the court finds good cause to treat the document as presumptively authentic.

248. See FRE Rule 902(4).

249. See FRE Rule 902(9). Examples of applicable commercial law are found in the Uniform Commercial Code Sections 1–202, 3–307, and 3–510 concerning third-party documents, signatures on negotiable instruments, protests, and statements of dishonour.

Commonly referred to as the "best evidence rule", FRE Rule 1002 requires that the content of a writing, recording or photograph be proven by an original writing, recording or photograph.[250] However, all jurisdictions in the United States now permit use of duplicate copies in place of the original, unless there is a genuine question about the authenticity of the original, or the court finds that it would be unfair to admit a copy in place of the original.[251] Moreover, when there is a good reason that the original cannot be produced at the trial or hearing, FRE Rule 1004 permits proof of the contents of the writing, recording or photograph by evidence, other than the original.[252]

Privileges

The existence and scope of privileges available to a witness, person, government, state, or political subdivision are governed by Common Law under the federal rules.[253] The common and statutory laws of virtually all states recognise privileges against disclosure of communications arising out of certain relationships. These commonly include: attorney-client, trade secrets, secrets of state, husband-wife, priest-penitent, doctor-patient, etc.

A strong public policy underlies each of these privileges. For example, without the protection afforded by the attorney-client privilege, an attorney and his or her clients would be unable to fully and freely consult for fear their communication might be subject to discovery. Free discovery of trade secrets would serve as a disincentive for investment into research and development of new products, procedures or technologies, if investors were fearful that their investment return could be readily lost to competitors.

JUDGMENT

Entry of judgment

When a general verdict has been reached, or where the court has determined that a party shall recover a sum certain or costs or that all relief shall be denied, the clerk, unless the court orders otherwise, shall "forthwith prepare, sign, and enter the judgment without waiting any direction by the court."[254] Where the court has decided to grant other relief, or

250. See FRE Rule 1002.
251. See FRE Rule 1003.
252. See FRE Rule 1004.
253. See FRE Rule 501.
254. See FRCP Rule 58.

where a jury has rendered a special verdict or general verdict with answers to interrogatories, the court must promptly approve the form of the judgment, which shall then be entered by the clerk.

In non-jury trials, FRCP Rule 52 provides that the court must find that the facts specially and separately state the conclusions of law based thereon. Judgment must then be entered in accordance with FRCP Rule 58. No later than 10 days after entry of judgment, a party may move the court to amend its findings or make additional findings and amend its judgment as may be appropriate.

Judgments as matter of law

In actions tried to a jury, if a party has presented its case to the jury and, based on all of the evidence presented, no reasonable jury could find for the party, the court may determine the issue(s) against the party and grant a motion for judgment as a matter of law pursuant to FRCP Rule 50 against that party on all claims or defences that cannot be maintained without a favourable finding on the issue(s). As with an FRCP Rule 56 motion for summary judgment, the court must review the facts in the light most favourable to the opposing party. If no reasonable jury could reach a contrary conclusion, then judgment as a matter of law must be granted.[255] Such motions may be made at any time before the case is submitted to the jury. In cases tried without a jury, FRCP Rule 52(c) similarly permits the court, at any time during the trial, to enter judgment against any party, fully heard on an issue, based on a finding against the party on that issue.

Costs and attorney's fees

Ordinarily, following judgment, FRCP Rule 54 permits the prevailing party to be awarded costs, other than attorney's fees, unless the court directs otherwise. The clerk may tax such costs on one day's notice. On motion served five days thereafter, the cost award may be reviewed by the court.[256]

255. See *Garrett* v. *Barnes*, 961 F2d. 629 (7th Cir. 1992), wherein plaintiff sued the mayor and the city claiming that his employment had been terminated for political reasons. At trial, the court granted the defendants' motion for judgment as a matter of law, directing a verdict in favour of the defendants and plaintiff appealed. The Court of Appeal found that plaintiff had produced virtually no evidence to support his contention on which a jury could find for the plaintiff and affirmed the directed verdict.

256. See FRCP Rule 54(d)(1). Attorney's fees are not normally recoverable unless provided by statute or pursuant to a contractual right.

POST-TRIAL MOTIONS, JUDGMENT AND NEW TRIALS

Following the trial and entry of judgment, any party who unsuccessfully moved for a judgment as a matter of law, prior to submission of the case to the jury, may renew its motion for judgment as a matter of law, within 10 days after entry of judgment, pursuant to FRCP Rule 50. The moving party may also attach a motion for new trial under FRCP Rule 59.

Judgment as a matter of law after verdict

When a judge harbours doubt as to the merit of a motion for judgment as a matter of law, the judge may deny the motion and allow the case to be decided by the jury. The judge may then reconsider the motion after the jury returns its verdict. If the judge then grants the motion and is reversed on appeal, the judge can simply reinstate the jury verdict and avoid the need for a new trial. However, failure of a party to move for judgment as a matter of law prior to submission of the case to the jury results in a waiver of any right to bring a motion after the verdict is returned. Nor may the party challenge the adequacy of the evidence supporting the verdict on appeal.

Motion for new trial or to amend judgment

Within 10 days after entry of judgment following a trial, FRCP Rule 59 permits a party to move the court for a new trial to all or any of the parties and as to all or some of the issues. The court on its own motion, after giving the parties notice and an opportunity to be heard, may order a new trial for any reason on which it might have granted a new trial on motion of a party.[257]

A motion for new trial is addressed to the "sound discretion of the court."[258] In most cases, the court will specify the grounds for its granting or denying a motion for new trial in its order, and it is required to do so when acting on its own motion.[259] The grounds most frequently cited as the basis for a motion for new trial include: errors in admitting or failing to admit evidence during the trial, errors in instructing or failing to instruct the jury, excessive or inadequate damages, or improper conduct by court personnel or by an attorney.

257. FRCP Rule 59(d).

258. See *Montgomery Ward & Co.* v. *Duncan,* 311 United States 243, 61 S Ct. 189, 85 LEd. 147 (1940).

259. FRCP Rule 59(d).

Moreover, within the 10-day time limitation any party may move the court for an order amending the judgment under FRCP Rule 59(e). Such motions are often made to amend the damages award to comply with a statutory limitation of damages, or to add statutory interest to the judgment, to correct clerical mistakes in the judgment, or to vacate the judgment. FRCP Rule 60 permits the court on its own motion or that of a party to correct clerical mistakes in the judgment. However, the court may also relieve a party, so moving, from a final judgment for, among other reasons cited in FRCP Rule 60: mistake, inadvertence, or excusable neglect; discovery of new evidence, which with due diligence could not reasonably have been discovered in time to move for a new trial under FRCP Rule 59; or fraud, misrepresentation or other misconduct by an adverse party.[260] Generally, motions for new trial, or for relief from judgment, will be denied when the court in its discretion finds that the error, in virtually whatever form, cited as the basis for the motion did not adversely effect the substantive rights of the parties.[261]

ENFORCEMENT AND EXECUTION OF JUDGMENTS

Writ of execution

The method for enforcement of judgments for the payment of money provided by the FRCP is by writ of execution, unless the court directs otherwise. FRCP Rule 69(a) provides that the procedure in all proceedings supplementary to and in aid of the execution, is controlled, either by an applicable federal statute, or in conformity with state law. To assist in the execution of a judgment for money, FRCP Rule 69(a) permits a judgment creditor to obtain discovery from any person, including the judgment debtor, under state or federal discovery practice. The purpose is to permit the judgment creditor to obtain evidence of the extent and nature of all assets on which the money judgment against the judgment debtor can be executed.

Specific performance and sequestration of property

When a judgment requires a party to convey land or deliver deeds or other instruments, or to perform any other specific act, and the party fails to do so, the court may, pursuant to FRCP Rule 70, direct the act to be done by another person appointed by the court, at the disobeying party's costs. Alternatively, when real or personal property is within the district, the

260. FRCP Rule 60(b).
261. See FRCP Rule 61.

court may enter judgment divesting the title of any party in the property
and vesting it in others. Furthermore, a party entitled to performance may
apply to the court to have the court issue a writ of attachment or
sequestration against the property of the disobedient party to compel
compliance with the judgment.

Registration of judgments

Where judgment has been entered in one district, but because of the location
of real or personal property, the judgment can only be executed in another
district. 28 USC, Section 1963 permits a final judgment for recovery of money
or property to be registered in the other district. Specifically, a final
judgment entered in a district court or the Court of International Trade
may be registered by filing a certified copy of the judgment in any other
district, or in the case of the Court of International trade, in any other
judicial district. A registered judgment is treated, in all respects, as though
it had been issued by the district court where the judgment is registered.

Recognition and enforcement of foreign judgments

The recognition and enforcement of foreign judgments are not addressed
directly by the FRCP. Rather, actions to recognise and enforce foreign
judgments, in cases founded on diversity subject matter jurisdiction, are
matters of state law.[262]

Uniform foreign money judgments recognition act

In 1962, the National Conference of Commissioners on Uniform State
Laws and the American Bar Association adopted the "Uniform Foreign
Money Judgments Recognition Act", codifying state rules applied by a
majority of courts in the United States. The Uniform Act has been
adopted by most state courts.[263]

Pursuant to the Uniform Act, foreign judgments either granting or
denying a money judgment are generally deemed conclusive and are
enforceable in the same manner as the judgment of a sister state, which is
entitled to full faith and credit, subject to exceptions enumerated in the

262. See *Turner Entertainment Co.* v. *Degeto Film GmbH*, 25 F3d. 1512 (11th Cir. 1994).

263. See, e.g., California Uniform Foreign Money Judgments Recognition Act,
California Code of Civil Procedure Sections 1713–13.08 (West 1994), New York
Uniform Foreign Money Judgments Recognition Act, New York Civil Practice Law &
Rules, Sections 5301–09 (McKinney 1978).

Act.[264] Specifically, the Uniform Act does not recognise the conclusiveness of foreign judgments rendered under a system that does not provide impartial tribunals or procedures compatible with the requirements of due process of law, or where the foreign court does not have personal jurisdiction over the defendant or jurisdiction over the subject matter.

Moreover, a court may deny recognition of a foreign judgment if: the defendant did not receive notice of the proceedings in sufficient time to defend the claim; where the judgment was obtained by fraud; where the claim or defence on which the judgment was based violates public policy; where the judgment conflicts with another final and conclusive judgment; where the foreign proceedings conflict with an agreement of the parties to dispose of dispute other than by proceeding in the foreign court; or, in a case of jurisdiction based on personal service, if the foreign tribunal was a seriously inconvenient forum for trial of the action.

However, lack of personal jurisdiction shall not be grounds for refusal to recognise a foreign judgment if the defendant was personally served or voluntarily submitted to or agreed to submit to the jurisdiction of the foreign court. The same is true in other cases where the defendant had certain contacts with the foreign state, such as a principal place of business, place of incorporation, or a business office, and the claim arose out of such contacts.[265]

Generally, enforcement of a foreign judgment may be obtained by filing a complaint, counterclaim, cross-claim, or by affirmative defence. In addition, relief may be sought by expedited procedure, such as by an FRCP Rule 56 Motion for Summary Judgment.

Recognition and enforcement of foreign arbitral agreements and awards

The enforcement of foreign arbitral agreements and awards is the subject of the "Convention on the Recognition and Enforcement of Foreign Arbitral Awards of 10 June 1958", signed by the United States in 1970.[266] 9 USC, Section 202 defines arbitration agreements or awards falling within the Convention to include those which arise out of a commercial relationship. Agreements or awards arising out of a relationship exclusively between citizens of the United States do not fall within the Convention, unless involving property located abroad, or where the parties intended performance or enforcement abroad, or when there is a reasonable relationship to the foreign state.

264. See, e.g., California Code of Civil Procedure Section 1713.4.

265. See, e.g., California Code of Civil Procedure Section 1713.5.

266. Chapter 2 of 9 USC, See also the enabling statute, 9 United States Code Annotated Sections 201–08, vesting district courts with the authority to confirm foreign arbitral awards. Section 201 provides: "The Convention on the Recognition and Enforcement of Foreign Arbitral Awards of 10 June 1958, shall be enforced in the United States courts in accordance with this chapter."

The procedure for applying for enforcement of an arbitration award is found in 9 USC, Section 207, which permits any party to apply, within three years after an arbitral award is granted, to any court having jurisdiction, for an order confirming the award against any party to the arbitration. Where the parties have previously agreed that the judgment of a particular court shall be entered on the award, Section 209 permits any party to apply to that court for an order confirming the award, within one year of the award.[267]

APPEAL

Issues subject to review

The courts of appeal were created by Congress in 1891 and have only such jurisdiction as conferred by statute. 28 USC, Section 1291 provides that "final" decisions are appealable to the court of appeals. The determination of whether the decision of a lower federal court is final is governed by federal law.[268] In general, dismissals for failure to state a claim, orders granting judgments on the pleadings (FRCP Rule 12(c)), default judgments, orders granting removal, and summary judgment (FRCP Rule 56) as well as judgments after trial constitute final judgments.

With few exceptions, an appeal taken from a decision that is not final is beyond the appellate court's jurisdiction (e.g., granting or denying motions to transfer venue, or order staying proceedings). Abstentions that dismiss an action are final. Rulings relating to discovery matters, pre-trial conference orders, or other orders that do not terminate the action (e.g., orders granting or denying amendments of the pleadings or sanctions short of dismissal) do not constitute final decisions subject to appeal. However, the court of appeals may issue extraordinary writs (e.g., *mandamus*) which direct the lower court to alter a prior ruling. Moreover, under 28 USC, Section 1292, courts of appeal may review interlocutory orders such as preliminary injunctive relief.

Scope of review

Although an appeal regarding particular claims may be governed by other standards of review,[269] district court decisions are ordinarily reviewed by

267. See *Daihatsu Motor Co.* v. *Terrain Vehicles, Inc.*, 13 F3d. 196, 198 (7th Cir. 1993).

268. [*Budinich* v. *Becton Dickinson & Co.* (1988) 486 United States 196, 108 S Ct. 1717].

269. For example, orders granting judgments on the pleadings are subject to "strict scrutiny" *Sutter Home Winery, Inc.* v. *Vintage Selections, Inc.*, 971 F2d. 401, 405 (9th Cir. 1992).

the court of appeals on an abuse of discretion standard.[270] Such abuse includes the lower court's applying incorrect legal standards or if it relied on facts that are clearly erroneous. Moreover, the evidence must be viewed by the appellate court in a light most favourable to the appellee, and if there is evidence of a probative value or a reasonable inference therefrom which supports the lower court's judgment or if the evidence conflicts such that reasonable minds draw different conclusions, the decision will be affirmed.

There are two types of appeals: as of right and permissive. The latter category includes the consideration of federal questions asserted in a case, as well as review of state statutes, to determine whether they are invalid under the United States Constitution. Appeals as of right from a district court final judgment must be filed within 60 days after entry of judgment. Failure to timely file a proper notice of appeal eliminates the jurisdiction of the court of appeal. In multi-party litigation, however, the timing of when an appeal may be made may be determined at the district court's discretion.

Lastly, appeals that are patently frivolous are sanctionable under the Federal Rules of Appellate Procedure, Rule 38, as well as 28 USC, Sections 1912 and 1927.

RES JUDICATA AND COLLATERAL ESTOPPEL CONCEPTS

The effects of *res judicata* should be considered in terms of claim preclusion and issue preclusion. The doctrine is applied to prohibit any litigation concerning matters that were not raised but should have been raised during prior litigation,[271] as well as prohibiting relitigation of matters that have previously been adjudicated. Under general principles of comity, federal courts ordinarily honour the decisions of state courts and *vice versa*.

The underlying rationales behind application of the doctrine include protecting parties from the burden of relitigation, and promoting judicial economy.[272] The doctrine also avoids the consequences of inconsistent results.[273] More importantly, application of the doctrine provides a final resolution to parties' disputes. Both issue and claim preclusion may be raised during a second action by the party seeking the doctrine's protection. The doctrines have also been applied independently by both the district and appellate courts.

270. This standard will apply to such rulings as whether amendments to pleadings, motions for continuances, and the awarding of costs are allowed.

271. For many years, the term "collateral estoppel" was utilised to describe this phenomena.

272. *Parklane Hosiery Co. v. Shore*, 439 United States 322, 326, 99 S Ct. 645, 649 (1979).

273. *Montana v. United States*, 440 United States 147, 154, 99 S Ct. 970, 974 (1979).

For claim preclusion to be applied, there must be a prior decision by a court with proper jurisdiction, a final judgment on the merits and no fraud or similar conduct on the part of party asserting the doctrine. Moreover, claim preclusion only operates against parties to the previous action or parties closely related to the prior lawsuit. More importantly, the subsequent litigation must involve the same transaction. What constitutes the same transaction is a matter often in dispute, but includes whether the underlying facts are related in time, space, origin, or motivation.[274]

Regarding issue preclusion applications, the courts will consider whether there is substantial overlap between the evidence and contentions, and whether the discovery will cover the same matters, as well as the similarity of claims in both proceedings.

---

274. See Restatement Second of Judgments, 1981 Section 24.

CHAPTER 17

INSTITUTIONS OF THE EUROPEAN UNION

Thieffry & Associés
Paris, France and Brussels, Belgium

INTRODUCTION

The three Treaties instituting the European Communities (European Coal and Steel Community, European Atomic Energy Community, and the European Economic Community) established institutions which are empowered to make decisions that are binding on their Member States, natural persons and legal persons: a Council of Ministers, a Parliament, an executive body referred to as the Commission, and a European Court of Justice. While only the first three institutions participate in the legislative process, it should be stressed at the outset that the decisions of the European Court of Justice have had an enormous impact on the construction of a "United Europe".

Although the rules concerning procedure before the Court of Justice that are contained in the three Treaties have much in common, this study will be limited to actions in the context of the European Economic Community, recently renamed the European Community (EC) by the Treaty on the European Union, which entered into force on 1 November 1993.

The European Court of Justice's overriding mission is to ensure consistency in the interpretation and application of the European Community Treaty.[1] The Treaty itself includes a number of provisions on the various types of procedures before the Court. Other rules bearing on the Court's organisation and procedure are found in the Protocol and Statute of the Court of Justice (Protocol, annexed to the European Community Treaty), and in the Rules of Procedure established by the Court of Justice itself.[2]

On 1 September 1989, a Court of First Instance (CFI) was created in order to alleviate the heavy caseload that had hampered the efficient adjudication of Community law matters before the Court of Justice. The Court of First Instance was initially entrusted with limited types of disputes, particularly in the competition area. Since 1 August 1993, it has jurisdiction over all direct actions brought against regulations and decisions of Community institutions.

1. European Community Treaty, Article 164.
2. OJ Eur. Comm. (No. L 176) 7 (1991).

With regard to actions for anti-dumping or anti-subsidies levies, or for safeguard measures, the date for the transfer of jurisdiction from the Court to the Court of First Instance has not yet been determined, however, and the Court of Justice retains jurisdiction.[3] The result of this change is that, with respect to certain direct actions, such as appeals for annulment and appeals against failure to act, or actions for damages resulting from an act or failure to act of a Community institution, the Court of Justice will no longer decide questions of fact but rather will sit as an appellate court charged solely with the determination of questions of law appealed from Court of First Instance decisions. It was found that lengthy and complex factual determinations were extending the time necessary to fully dispose of cases, and that the creation of a court with initial jurisdiction had therefore become necessary.

Unlike the European Court of Justice or the Court of First Instance, the European Commission is not a court but rather a quasi-executive body charged with the smooth functioning of the Common Market. The Commission possesses the right of initiative in the European Community law-making process. From both a legal and practical standpoint, it is the Commission which is best situated to move Member States and other Community organs toward supranational integration. For example, when a Member State fails to comply with the treaty or other European Community provisions, an administrative procedure before the Commission must precede the commencement of an action before the Court of Justice.

Importantly, the Commission also has wide powers against private and public companies in competition matters. In order to enforce these powers, the Commission may impose significant fines and daily penalties. However, the decisions are themselves appealable to the Court of First Instance. The Commission's broad powers are provided for in Council Regulations, and in particular, Regulation 17/62 of 6 February 1962.[4]

This chapter will deal with the procedure before the European Court of Justice, the Court of First Instance and the Commission, although *vis-à-vis* the latter, its focus will be on competition matters, specifically, the cartel provisions set forth in the European Community Treaty.[5]

ESTABLISHING JURISDICTION

An action may be brought before the European Court of Justice if it involves the interpretation of a Community law provision, or a breach

3. Council Decision 93/350 of 8 June 1993, 36 OJ Eur. Comm. (No. L 144) 21 (1993).

4. OJ Eur. Com. Number 13/204 of 21 February 1962.

5. European Community Treaty, Articles 85 and 86.

thereof by a Member State or a Community institution. By contrast, the Court of First Instance hears only those actions brought directly against Community institutions, including actions for damages stemming from their activities.

It should also be noted at the outset that access to the European Community Courts is much more limited for individuals and companies than for Member States or Community institutions. For example, a question of interpretation of Community law may be raised before the European Court of Justice by a national court in cases that involve the compatibility of a national law with a European Community rule of law.

International jurisdiction

The Commission has jurisdiction over competition matters for all agreements, concerted practices, abuses of dominant positions, mergers or subsidies that have actual or potential effects within the European Community even if the companies concerned do not maintain their headquarters or a branch in the Community.[6] As a general rule, however, European Community competition rules are applicable only where trade between at least two Member States is affected. If this is not the case, national competition authorities maintain exclusive jurisdiction.

For this reason, a *de minimis* rule has arisen.[7] In practice, agreements on the production or distribution of goods or on the provision of services are considered not to fall within the scope of European Community competition rules if the firms involved hold no more than 5 per cent of the relevant market of such goods or services and if the aggregate annual turnover of the participating firms does not exceed 200-million ECU.[8]

Types of jurisdiction

There are six basic actions that may be brought in the European Community Courts:

(1) Review of legality;
(2) Failure to act;

6. Joint cases 89, 104, 114, 166, 117, 125–129/85, *Ahlströhm e.o.* v. *Commission* (1988) European Court Reports (ECR) 5193.

7. Case 5/69, *Völk* v. *Verbaecke* (1969) European Court Reports 295.

8. Commission Notice on Agreements of minor importance, 29 OJ Eur. Comm. (No. C 231) 2 (1986); note that the turnover of all companies within the group are considered.

(3) Damages;

(4) Request for preliminary ruling;

(5) Infringement of community law; and

(6) Infringement of competition rules.

Review of legality

The Court of First Instance provides a forum to challenge arbitrary or abusive actions of European Community institutions. Any person may challenge before the Court of First Instance a Community decision or judgment rendered against it, as well as a regulation or a decision rendered against or affecting another person where that regulation or decision is of direct and individual concern to the challenging party.[9]

Acts that affect all persons indiscriminately cannot be challenged by private persons unless they suffer some unique injury by reason of certain attributes that are peculiar to them.[10] It is, for example, insufficient that a party is affected by a Community act because he belongs to a category designated abstractly and as a whole.[11]

Most annulment proceedings are initiated by private parties challenging decisions rendered directly against them, such as those prohibiting concerted practices or imposing fines in competition matters. Such proceedings must be initiated within two months of publication of the challenged act, or within two months of its notification to the challenging party, or, in the absence thereof, within two months of the day on which the party obtains actual notice, as the case may be.[12]

There are four grounds for annulment of a Community act, all of which have their origins in French administrative procedure:

(1) Lack of jurisdiction;

(2) Infringement of an essential procedural requirement;

(3) Infringement of the Treaty or of any rule of law adopted on the basis of the Treaty; and

(4) Misuse of power.

While these grounds are normally to be invoked before the Court of First Instance and, then in appeals only before the European Court of Justice,

9. European Community Treaty, Article 173, Section 2.

10. Case 25/62, *Plauman v. Commission* (1963) European Court Reports 95, and its progeny.

11. By way of contrast, the European Coal and Steel Community Treaty is more lenient than the European Community Treaty with regard to the right of private parties to bring annulment proceedings. ECS Treaty, Article 33.

12. European Community Treaty, Article 173(3).

matters of commercial policy such as anti-dumping remain within the sole jurisdiction of the European Court of Justice, for the time-being.

A European Community institution whose act has been declared void is required to take the necessary action to comply with the judg-ment.[13] It may be required to provide compensation for damages suffered as a result of an act that has been annulled, but such compensation would be granted on the basis of Articles 178 and 215 European Community Treaty.

Failure to act

Where European Community institutions are required to issue rulings and clearances to parties requesting guidance as to the propriety of engaging in certain types of activities, a person may bring an action before the Court of First Instance or the European Court of Justice, claiming that a Community institution has failed to fulfill such obliga-tions. In competition matters, for example, a plaintiff can make use of this possibility in order to compel the Commission to proceed with an inquiry on anti-competitive behaviour or practices against which it has filed a complaint.[14] However, where the ruling requested from an institu-tion is a non-binding recommendation or opinion, persons affected are not entitled to compel action through the courts.[15]

An action may be brought only if the institution concerned (usually the Commission) has been first called on to act by demand of the complaining party. If within two months of such demand the Community institution has still not defined its position, an action to compel may be brought within a further period of two months.[16] The fact that the action taken by the institution following the formal request to act is different from that requested by the applicant is immaterial, in that an institution may define its position informally without actually issuing a ruling that can be challenged through an annulment proceeding. An administrative letter issued at the request of a party by a high official of the Commis-sion and announcing a finding of no infringement of competition provisions constitutes an "act" defining the Commission's position.[17] Furthermore, the fact that the Commission does not initiate an action

13. European Community Treaty, Article 176, Section 1.
14. Case T–28/90, *Asia Motor France* v. *Commission* (1992) European Court Reports II 2285.
15. European Community Treaty, Article 175(3).
16. European Community Treaty, Article 175(2).
17. Case 125/78, *Gema* v. *Commission* (1979) European Court Reports 3190.

against a Member State alleged by a claimant to have violated European Community law is not considered a failure to act.[18]

An institution whose failure to act has been declared contrary to the European Community Treaty shall be required to comply with the judgment. Again, compensation for damages may be possible, but separate action shall be necessary.

Damages

The European Community must compensate any and all damages caused by its institutions or servants in the performance of their duties.[19]

Actions for annulment or for failure to act, on the one hand, and claims for damages on the other, are separate and autonomous proceedings that must fulfill different specific requirements.[20] However, compensation is difficult to obtain for persons where legislative action involving measures of economic policy is concerned.

A Community institution will incur tort liability only where the defendant institution has committed a flagrant violation of a superior rule of law, for example, the violation of a Treaty provision or general principle of law.[21] In legislative matters, where institutions enjoy wide discretion in the implementation of a Community policy, liability will be found only where the institution concerned has manifestly and strongly disregarded the limits of its powers.

Moreover, actions will be dismissed in cases in which the application for compensation is actually directed against measures adopted by Member State authorities for the purpose of applying Community law. Such actions should be brought before national courts. The same is true for claims seeking restitution of sums paid to a national authority under European Community law.[22]

The statute of limitations in proceedings against Community institutions based on tortious conduct is five years from the occurrence of the event giving rise to the cause of action.[23]

18. Case 247/87, *Star Fruit Company* v. *Commission* (1989) European Court Reports 291.

19. European Community Treaty, Article 215.

20. Cases 5,7 and 13–24/66, *Firma Kampffmeyer* v. *Commission* (1967) European Court Reports 317.

21. Cases 83 and 94/76 and 4,15 and 40/77 *Bayerische HNL Vermehrungsbetriebe GmbH* v. *Commission and Council* (1978) European Court Reports 1209.

22. Case 20/88, *Roquette* v. *Commission* (1989), European Court Reports 1553; case C–106 and 317/90 and C–129/91, *Emerald Meats Ltd.* v. *Commission* (1993), not yet published.

23. Protocol, Article 43.

Request for preliminary ruling

The European Court of Justice has exclusive jurisdiction to issue a preliminary ruling on the interpretation of the European Community Treaty as well as on the validity and interpretation of an act of a Community institution.[24] Such a ruling is issued in response to a request from a national court for clarification of issues of European Community law essential to the resolution of a case pending before it.

The purpose of such preliminary rulings is to ensure the uniform interpretation of European Community law as determined by the European Court of Justice. Where a question is raised in a case pending before a national court from whose decisions there is no further appeal available (for example, the French "Cour de Cassation" France's supreme court for civil matters), such court must bring the matter before the European Court of Justice.[25] All inferior courts of a Member State may decide at their own discretion to ask a ruling of the European Court of Justice.[26] They also determine whether questions are ripe for adjudication notwithstanding the stage of the national procedure.[27]

An arbitral tribunal is not considered to be a court for the purposes of Article 177 and, as a consequence, it may not request the European Court of Justice for a preliminary ruling.[28] However, an appellate committee set up by a professional body, the decisions of which may affect the exercise of rights granted by European Community law, is considered a court for such purpose.[29]

The European Court of Justice may not directly pass judgment on questions brought by national courts.[30] The European Court of Justice will generally provide the national court with an interpretation of European Community law that will allow the case to be resolved by the national court.[31] Furthermore, the Court is not empowered to issue advisory

24. European Community Treaty, Article 177.

25. European Community Treaty, Article 177, Section 3.

26. Case C–231/89, *Krystyna Gmurzynska-Bscher* v. *Oberfinanzdirektion Köln* (1990) European Court Reports I–4003.

27. Case 72/83, *Campus Oil Ltd.* v. *Minister for Industry and Energie* (1984) European Court Reports 2727.

28. Case 102/81 *Nordsee GmbH* v. *Reederei Mond a.o.* (1982) European Court Reports 1095.

29. Case 246/80 *Broekmeulen* v. *Huisarts Registratie Commissie* (1981) European Court Reports 2311.

30. Case C–188/91, *Deutsche Shell AG* v. *Hauptzollamt Hamburg-Harbrug* (1993) not yet published.

31. Case C–196/89, *Enzo Nespoli* v. *Giuseppe Crippa* (1990) European Court Reports I–3647.

opinions, as it only has jurisdiction to render a ruling where there is a genuine dispute before the national court.[32]

Through the use of its power to issue preliminary rulings, the Court has done much to develop and specify European Community law. The ability to seek a preliminary ruling has proved to be the best means available for citizens to challenge actions of Member States and European Community institutions that violate European Community law. The European Court of Justice ruling must be respected by the national court, which must then apply the ruling to the circumstances of the case pending before it. It must be noted, however that preliminary rulings of the Court are applicable to all persons within the Community, not just named parties. This is particularly clear for European Community actions that are held to be invalid.[33]

It is a corollary of the national court's duty to respect preliminary rulings that those rulings be applied in a way that adheres to the Court's interpretation of the legal issue.[34] However, a national court may always request a new preliminary ruling as to a question on which the European Court of Justice has already spoken.[35]

In exceptional circumstances, the European Court of Justice may decide that its interpretation of a Community rule will only have effect from the date that it specifies in the judgment.[36] Of course, the financial consequences of such a decision may be harsh for the party for whom the interpretation is unfavourable.

Infringement of community law

Persons who suffer harm from a Member State's violation of European Community law may file a complaint with the Commission.[37] Such persons may not go directly before the Court of First Instance or the European Court of Justice. There are no specific requirements for such complaints, and the Commission decides at its own discretion whether to process the complaint. Where the Commission refuses to take action,

32. Case 104/79 *Foglia* v. *Novello* (1980) European Court Reports 745; Case C–83/91 *Wienland Meilicke* v. *ADV/ORGA FA Meyer AG* (1992) European Court Reports I–4871.

33. Case 66/80, *ICI* v. *Administrazione delle finanze dello Stato* (1981) European Court Reports 1191.

34. Cases 66, 127 and 128/79, *Administrazione delle Finanze* v. *Meridionale Industria Salumi* (1980) European Court Reports 1237.

35. Cases 28–30/62, *Da Costa en Schaake* v. *Administration fiscale néerlandaise* (1963) European Court Reports 74.

36. Case C–163/90, *Administration des douanes et droits indirects* v. *Léopold Legros* (1992) European Court Reports I–4625.

37. European Community Treaty, Article 169.

no legal remedy exists and it is not possible to institute proceedings against the Commission for failure to act.

An administrative stage precedes the judicial procedure itself. If the Commission determines that a Member State has failed to fulfil an obligation under the Treaty, it grants the Member State the opportunity to present arguments in defence of the suspect action. After due consideration of all factors before it, the Commission then issues a written opinion.[38] It is only if, in response to the Commission's opinion, the Member State fails to comply within the appropriate time period that the Commission may bring the matter before the European Court of Justice.[39] A high proportion of cases is resolved without recourse to such judicial proceedings.[40]

Member States also have the ability to bring proceedings against other Member States that have allegedly infringed Community law.[41] In view of the political ramifications of challenging another Member State, however, such actions are in practice very rare.

If the European Court of Justice finds that a Member State has failed to abide by its obligations under the Treaty, the said Member State shall be required to comply with such ruling.[42] A Member State is liable for violations of European Community law committed by its public agencies or regional authorities, even where such agencies or authorities are legally or constitutionally independent of the Member State.[43]

Member States have put forth a number of justifications for their non-compliance with European Community law. These arguments are generally rejected by the Court. A frequent violation is the untimely incorporation of European Community directives into the Member States' national laws in a foot dragging pattern that delays the completion of the European internal market; the European Court of Justice is constant in its condemnation of such behaviour.

In the original European Community Treaty, there was no formal mechanism by which the European Court of Justice could compel Member State compliance with judgments rendered against them. The Treaty on the European Union, which has entered into force on 1 November 1993, provides for the imposition of fines against Member States in the case of such infringements.[44]

38. European Community Treaty, Article 169(1).

39. European Community Treaty, Article 169(2).

40. Tenth Annual Report on the Control of the Application of Community Law 1992, COM (92) 320 final.

41. European Community Treaty, Article 170.

42. European Community Treaty, Article 171.

43. See, for example, Case C–2/90, *Commission v. Belgium* (1992) European Court Reports I–4431, where Belgium was held in violation of European Community law for the actions of its Walloon region.

44. European Community Treaty, Article 171.

Infringement of competition rules

Any victim of an agreement or practice that is contrary to the competition rules provided for in Articles 85 and 86 of the European Community Treaty may file a claim with the Commission, the authority charged with administering antitrust disputes. The Commission may also proceed *sua sponte* against suspicious agreements or practices.

If the Commission fails to issue a ruling within a reasonable period of time following the receipt of a complaint, the plaintiff may institute proceedings to compel a decision pursuant to Article 175 of the European Community Treaty.[45] A complaint may only be dismissed by means of a reasoned opinion, and the complainant then has two months from the time the unfavourable ruling was issued to commence an annulment proceeding before the Court of First Instance.[46]

The Commission may choose to forego the initiation of proceedings where the matter does not present a sufficient "Community interest." Before the Commission decides to do so, however, it will verify that the plaintiff's interests can be adequately protected before the national courts. The Commission recently published a notice in which it sets forth its policy with regard to complaints in European Community antitrust matters.[47]

In this Notice, the Commission announced that it will only concern itself with the most important and complex antitrust cases. Where case law is well established, national courts are able and required to apply European Community law directly. Member States' courts may decide to void an agreement or practice and award damages to the plaintiff. By contrast, the Commission merely imposes fines and enjoins the termination of violating practices.

ASCERTAINING THE APPLICABLE LAW

Jurisdictional issues are closely linked with the specific nature of European Community law, most of which must be implemented into the Member States' national laws. Nevertheless, citizens have been granted private rights of action against public authorities where European Community law has been violated or conflicts with national law. The supremacy and direct effect of European Community law

45. Case T–28/90, *Asia Motor France* v. *Commission* (1992) European Court Reports, II–2285.

46. Case T–24/90, *Automec* v. *Commission* (1992) European Court Reports, II–2223.

47. Commission Notice Regarding the Co-operation Between National Jurisdictions for the Application of Articles 85 and 86 of the Treaty of Rome, OJ Eur. Comm. (No. C 39) 6 (1993); see also Van Doorn, "La protection juridique du plaignant en droit communautaire de la concurrence" DPCI, 1992, T 18, Number 4, p. 618–632.

vis-à-vis Member State's national laws were affirmed in some of the European Court of Justice's earliest rulings.[48]

Given the relationship between European Community and Member State's laws, the above-discussed preliminary ruling procedure takes on great importance. National courts are required to set aside domestic laws that are found to be in conflict with European Community law. Furthermore, they are not obligated to wait for their respective national legislatures to modify or abolish the offending national provisions, as they are empowered to immediately implement the European Court of Justice's decision.[49]

There are a number of sources of European Community law.

Treaty provisions

The European Community Treaty is an organic law that functions as the constitution of the Community. The original European Community Treaty endowed the institutions it created with legislative, administrative, and judicial powers that were previously held by the individual Member States. Moreover, it sets forth common economic and social policies to be implemented by these institutions via "secondary Community legislation" that is based on Treaty provisions.

The European Community Treaty was supplemented with a second organic law, enacted in 1987 and which came into force on 1 January 1993, the Single European Act (SEA). The SEA extended the powers of the Community in economic matters.

As of 1 November 1993, a third organic law, the Treaty on the European Union, aims at further reinforcing Community integration through, *inter alia*, the implementation of a common monetary policy, and enlarge Community jurisdiction in non-economic fields.

Secondary community legislation

The most frequently employed European Community legislative instrument is that of Regulations. Regulations are proposed by the Commission to the Council, and adopted by the Council after consultation with the Parliament. A Regulation generally applies throughout the Community is binding in its entirety, and is directly applicable in all Member States.[50]

48. Case 26/62 *Van Gend en Loos* v. *Nederlandse Administratie der Belastingen* (1963) European Court Reports 1; case 6/64 *Costa* v. *Enel* (1964) European Court Reports 585.

49. Case 106/77 *Administrazione delle Finanze dello Stato* v. *Simmenthal* (1978) European Court Reports 629.

50. European Community Treaty, Article 189(2).

Another European Community legal instrument, Directives serve to harmonise the Member States' disparate national laws.[51] The right to initiate such Directives, as with Regulations, rests with the Commission. Although the Council is still charged with the ultimate approval of Directives, the European Parliament is becoming more and more involved in the legislative process since the Single European Act and the Treaty on the European Union. Once adopted by the Council, Directives must be implemented by the Member States within a specified deadline. Implementation is accomplished through the passage of national legislation by the Member States. While said legislation must ensure respect of the material provisions of the Directive, Member States are free to choose whatever form or method of implementation they desire.[52]

Another important category of secondary Community legislation is that of simple Decisions. Decisions are not universally applied throughout the Community, but rather impact solely on the Member State or private parties to whom they are addressed.

Community legislation touches most of the European Community's economic activity and trade. It is therefore not surprising that lobbying of Community institutions has increased significantly in the wake of the single market reforms of 1992.[53]

International agreements

In order to put into place a common commercial policy, the Community enters into binding international Treaties with non-Community countries. Negotiations are conducted by the Commission with all decisions subject to final approval of the Council, the latter having sought the advice of the European Parliament prior to granting its approval.[54]

Prior to the signature of a Treaty, the Council, the Commission, or a Member State may seek an opinion of the European Court of Justice as to whether the agreement contemplated is compatible with the provisions of the European Community Treaty.[55] Where the Court has found incompatibility, the Treaty will not be binding unless the European Community Treaty itself is amended.

One circumstance in which compatibility opinions are sought from the European Court of Justice is where there are disagreements over the

51. European Community Treaty, Articles 100 and 100 A.

52. European Community Treaty, Article 189(2).

53. See, for example, Thieffry and Van Doorn, "Lobbying in Brussels and Strasbourg" in *European Community Law After 1992, A Practical Guide For Lawyers Outside The Common Market*, Kluwer 1993, p. 77.

54. European Community Treaty, Articles 113 and 228.

55. European Community Treaty, Article 228(2).

extent of European Community jurisdiction in international affairs. Member States have indeed contested the full transfer of Treaty-making power to the Community, and require at least their national Parliaments' approval together with the approval of the Council of Ministers.[56]

Importantly, the European Court of Justice has held that, under certain conditions, Treaties concluded by the Community, have a direct effect. As a consequence, there are private rights of action before the Court of First Instance against Community acts which conflict with the terms of such Treaties. The European Court of Justice has also held that Treaties may be enforced in national courts against conflicting national laws.[57]

General principles of law

General principles of law are a very important source of Community law. The European Court of Justice refers to them for guidance in the interpretation of Treaty provisions or secondary legislation. They are also used to fill gaps in European Community law where the existence of such a gap would lead to a denial of justice.[58]

An example of such general principles, fundamental rights,[59] include the right to a fair hearing (particularly important in competition proceedings), equality of treatment in identical or comparable situations, proportionality, and legal certainty.

These general principles are frequently invoked before the Court of First Instance or European Court of Justice against unfavourable Commission decisions in competition law matters.

COMMENCING THE ACTION

Application or complaint

Actions before the court of first instance and the european court of justice

A claim for damages, for review of legality, or for failure to act shall be brought before the Court of First Instance or a claim involving commercial

56. For the most recent example: Opinion 2/91 of the European Court of Justice of 19 March 1993 OJ Eur. Comm. (No. C 109) 1 (1993), concerning the conclusion of an ILO agreement.

57. BEBR, *Agreements concluded by the Community and their possible direct effect*, CMLR 1983, p. 35.

58. Vaughan, Law of the European Communities, Volume I, p. 358 (2)–291.

59. Case 11/70 *Internationale Handelsgezellschaft* v. *Einfuhr-und Vorratstelle für Getreide und Futtermittel* (1970) ECR 1125; Case 4/73 *Nold* v. *Commission* (1974) ECR 491.

policy before the European Court of Justice, via written application
addressed to the Registrar of the Court. The application must contain:

". . . the applicant's name and permanent address, a description of the signatory, the
name of the party against whom the complaint is made, the subject matter of the dispute,
the submissions, and a brief statement of the grounds on which the application is based."[60]

It must also include an address for service of process in Luxembourg,
and the name of a person who is authorised and has expressed willingness
to accept service.[61] In addition, counsel of record must file with evidence
that he is admitted to practise before the courts of a Member State.[62]

An application made by a legal entity governed by private law, for
example, a corporation or a partnership, must be accompanied by proof
of its existence in law. In addition, such entity must provide proof that
the authority vested in its lawyer to bring legal action on its behalf has
been granted by a person possessing the requisite authority.[63]

While requests for preliminary rulings made by national courts are
reviewed by the European Court of Justice, the national court suspends
its proceedings.

An action against a Member State for infringement of European Community law can be brought by private or public parties before the
Commission. The latter maintains the power to commence judicial proceedings before the European Court of Justice after first conducting an
administrative proceeding. The complainant has no right to appear
before the Court in such cases. Notice of the particulars of the case is
given in the *Official Journal of the European Communities* (Series C),
including the date of registration of the complaint, and includes the
names and addresses of the parties, the subject matter of the proceedings,
the type of order sought by the applicant, and a summary of the pleadings
and main supporting agreements.[64]

Competition matters before the Commission

Complaints for infringement of European Community competition
laws are brought before the Commission by a simple application, which
need not be in any particular form, but must allege that the challenged

60. Protocol, Article 19, Section 1.

61. Rules of Procedure of the European Court of Justice Article 38(2), and of the
Court of First Instance, Article 44(2).

62. Rules of Procedure of the Court of Justice, Article 38(3), and of the Court of
First Instance, Article 44(3).

63. Rules of Procedure of the Court of Justice, Article 38(5), and of the Court of
First Instance, Article 44(5).

64. Rules of Procedure of the Court of Justice, Article 16(6), and of the Court of
First Instance, Article 24(6).

behaviour affects intra Community trade. Evidence should accompany the Complaint, if possible, as well as a power of attorney.

Agreements and mergers which fall within the scope of European Community law may, and in some cases must, be notified to the Commission on specific forms which require detailed information about the parties and market conditions.[65]

Defence

As for proceedings involving a review of legality for failure of an institution to act an application is served on the defendant institution, which then has one month to file a response. This time-limit may be extended by the President of the Court for just cause.[66]

Unlike the above-mentioned proceedings, a proceeding brought pursuant to Article 177 of the European Community Treaty for a preliminary ruling is not adversarial in the sense of involving an applicant who prosecutes a claim against a defendant. However, if it is a Council action which forms the basis for the question certified to the European Court of Justice, the parties, the Member States, the Commission, and the Council itself will be informed of the request and entitled to file *amicus* briefs within two months of the notification.[67]

As for complaints for infringement of European Community competition law filed with the Commission, it may not render a decision against a defendant before having granted him the opportunity to be heard on the merits.[68] The Commission notifies parties in writing of the objections raised against them, and fixes a time within which they may respond.[69]

Defending parties may set forth any matters relevant to their defence, and include any relevant documents in support of those defences.[70] In rendering a decision, the Commission shall address only those issues that

65. See, for example, for co-operation agreements: Commission Regulation Number 27/62 of 3 May 1962, implementing Council Regulation Number 17/62, last amended by Regulation Number 2526/85 of 5 August 1985, OJ Eur. Comm. (No. L 240) 11 (1985); for mergers: Commission Regulation Number 2367/90 on the Notifications, Time limits and Hearings of Council Regulation Number 4064/89 on the Control of Concentrations between Undertakings, OJ Eur. Comm. (No. L 219) 5 of (1990); see for example, Thieffry, Van Doorn, and Nahmias, "The Notification of Mergers Under the New European Community Merger Control Regulation" 25 *The International Lawyer*, 615, (1991).

66. Court of First Instance Rules of Procedure, Article 46; Rules of Procedure of the Court of Justice, Article 40.

67. Protocol, Article 20.

68. Regulation 17/62, Article 19(1).

69. Regulation 99/63, Article 2.

70. Regulation 99/63, Article 3.

have been argued on the merits.[71] Any transgression of this principle subjects the decision to annulment by the Court of First Instance. The same applies when the Commission examines a notified agreement. The Merger Control Regulation sets forth similar rules.[72]

Reply

In proceedings for the review of legality for failure to act, or for damages, the application initiating the proceedings and the defendant's Answer may be supplemented by a Reply from the applicant and by a rejoinder from the defendant. The President of the Court fixes the time within which these pleadings are to be filed, but he must justify the delay.[73]

In proceedings before the Commission in competition cases, a complainant's right of reply to defendant's answer is not statutory.

Supplemental pleadings

No further pleading may be introduced in the course of proceedings unless it is based on matters of law or fact which came to light during the course of the proceedings in the European Court of Justice and the Court of First Instance. Where a party has been permitted to file supplemental pleadings, the President of the Court may, even after the filing date has passed, allow the other party time to respond to the new pleading.

Intervention

Member States and European Community institutions may intervene in cases pending before the European Court of Justice or the Court of First Instance, as may any other person who can establish an interest in the outcome of the proceedings. This right does not exist, however, in matters between Member States, between Community institutions, or between Member States and institutions. Pleadings on an application to intervene are limited to supporting the pleadings already submitted by one of the parties.[74]

71. Regulation 99/63, Article 4.
72. Commission Regulation Number 2367/90, Articles 11 *et seq.*
73. Rules of Procedure of the Court of Justice, Article 42(1) Rules of Procedure of the Court of First Instance, Article 48(1).
74. Protocol, Article 37.

An application to intervene must be made within three months of the date of publication of the notice of the proceeding in the *Official Journal of the European Communities*. The application to intervene must contain descriptions of the case, of the parties, the name and address of the intervening party, its address for service of process, the claim for relief in support of which the intervening party moves, and a statement of the intervenor's interest in the outcome of the case.[75]

The application to intervene is served on all parties. The President of the Court allows the parties the opportunity to submit both written and oral arguments on the merits prior to ruling on the application.[76] If the President permits intervention, the intervening party receives a copy of every document served on the other parties. Again, confidential documents may be omitted on the request by one of the parties.[77]

The intervening party must accept the case as it finds it at the time of intervention.[78] Within a time limit set by the President, the intervenor may submit a "statement in intervention" detailing the form of order sought by the intervenor in support of or opposing the relief sought by the parties, the pleas in law and arguments relied on by the intervenor, and, where appropriate, the nature of any evidence to be offered.[79]

After the statement in intervention has been filed, the President sets a time limit within which the parties may respond if necessary.[80]

In competition law matters pending before the Commission, third parties may solicit to be heard where a sufficient interest in the outcome of the proceedings is demonstrated.[81] Where the Commission intends to grant a negative clearance pursuant to Article 2 of Regulation 17/62 or grant an individual exemption in application of Article 85 of the European Community Treaty, it must publish a summary of the application or notification, and invite all interested third parties to submit their observations within a time limit of not less than one month.[82]

75. Rules of Procedure of the European Court of Justice, Article 93(1); Rules of Procedure of the Court of First Instance, Article 115(1).

76. Rules of Procedure of the Court of Justice, Article 93(2); Court of First Instance Rules of Procedure, Article 116(1).

77. Rules of Procedure, Court of Justice, Article 93(3); Court of First Instance Rules of Procedure, Article 116(2).

78. Rules of Procedure of the European Court of Justice, Article 93(4); Rules of Procedure of the Court of First Instance, Article 116(3).

79. Rules of Procedure of the European Court of Justice, Article 93(5); Rules of Procedure of the Court of First Instance, Article 116(4).

80. Rules of Procedure of the European Court of Justice, Article 93 Section 6; Rules of Procedure of the Court of First Instance, Article 116(5).

81. Regulation 17/62, Article 19, Section 2, and Regulation 99/63, Article 5.

82. Regulation 17/62, Article 19, Section 3.

Appointment of judge-rapporteur

Immediately after a case filed with the Court of First Instance or the European Court of Justice has been registered, the President designates a Judge-Rapporteur. After the answer, if any, has been filed, the President fixes a date by which the Judge-Rapporteur is to present his preliminary report to the Court. Such report shall recommend whether a preparatory inquiry or any other measure should be undertaken, and whether the case should be referred to a plenary session or to a chamber composed of a different number of judges.

The regulations governing competition proceedings before the Commission do not provide specific rules on this subject. In practice, however, an official will be appointed to function as a reporter. This person does the basic inquiry, determines whether the Commission is in possession of all relevant information, and drafts an initial report, which is transmitted to the person charged with rendering a decision.

OBTAINING INFORMATION PRIOR TO HEARING

European court of justice or court of first instance

After hearing the Advocaté-General and soliciting arguments from the parties, the European Court of Justice or the Court of First Instance issues an order setting forth the facts to be proved[83] and requiring all or some of the following:

(1) The personal appearance of the parties;
(2) A request for information and production of documents;
(3) Oral testimony;
(4) The commissioning of an expert's report; and
(5) An inspection of the place or thing in question.[84]

These proofs may be taken by the Court itself, by a specially appointed Chamber, or by the Judge-Rapporteur.[85] The parties may be present when measures of inquiry are taken.[86]

83. Rules of Procedure of the European Court of Justice, Article 45(1); Court of First Instance Rules of Procedure, Article 66(1).

84. Rules of Procedure of the European Court of Justice, Article 45(2); Court of First Instance Rules of Procedure, Article 65.

85. Rules of Procedure of the European Court of Justice, Articles 45(3), and 46(1); Court of First Instance Rules of Procedure, Article 67(1).

86. Rules of Procedure of the European Court of Justice, Article 46(3); Court of First Instance Rules of Procedure, Article 67(2).

Obtaining information in matters pending in the commission

As for Commission proceedings, one must distinguish between measures of inquiry in proceedings that feature violations of Community law by a Member State — Article 169 Proceedings — and measures of inquiry in competition proceedings involving individuals and/or companies as parties.

Actions against Member States

Secondary community legislation will very frequently obligate Member States to inform the Commission of their implementation progress. The failure to communicate such information is itself a serious violation of the requirement of co-operation between Community institutions and the Member States,[87] and will be sanctioned by the Court.[88]

The Commission may not sue a Member State before it has had the opportunity to reply to a reasoned opinion. Such reasoned opinion is prepared by the Commission on the basis of information obtained from the plaintiff, from contacts with national authorities, and from various other sources, for example, members of the European Parliament. If the Member State in question can demonstrate that its national law had been brought into conformity with European Community law prior to the initiation of court proceedings, it will be terminated. However, if the Member State complies after the commencement of judicial proceedings, the Commission may pursue the case and the Court will find that infringement occurred until the date of compliance.[89]

Competition matters

In investigating competition matters, the Commission gathers evidence via "requests for information" and "inspections".

REQUESTS FOR INFORMATION

The Commission may first issue requests for information.[90] A request must state the legal basis for the Commission's investigation and the purpose of the request, as well as the penalties for supplying incorrect

87. Article 5 of the Treaty.
88. Case C–293/91 *Commission* v. *France* (1993), European Court Reports I–1.
89. Case C–243/89 *Commission* v. *Denmark* (1993), not yet published.
90. Regulation 17/62, Article 11.

information. When a company or association of companies supplies incomplete information or fails altogether to supply the information requested within the deadline fixed by the Commission, the Commission issues a decision pursuant to which production of the required information is compelled. The decision specifies what information is required, fixes a deadline within which the information must be supplied, states the penalties that may be levied where full compliance is not forthcoming, and informs the company of its right to have the decision reviewed by the Court of Justice.[91]

This two-stage procedure has been approved by the European Court of Justice.[92] As for the aforementioned sanctions, they consist of fines of up to 5,000 ECU and/or daily penalty payments of up to 1,000 ECU.[93]

The Commission often solicits information from competitors and customers of parties to a challenged agreement or concerted practice. As for requests made to companies against which the inquiry is brought, the questions should be formulated in such a way that they do not force the companies to incriminate themselves.[94]

INSPECTIONS

The power of the Commission to investigate companies in antitrust matters[95] has given rise to an abundance of case law. Commission officials are authorised to examine corporate books and other business records, to make copies of or extracts of corporate books and business records, and to enter any company premises or properties. The Commission may even conduct surprise interrogations of officers and employees on company premises.[96]

Despite these broad powers, Commission officials must provide the party being investigated with written proof that the investigation has been authorised by the Commission and specifying the subject matter and purpose of the investigation. The Commission must also inform the party being investigated of penalties that may be imposed for failure to co-operate with an investigation.[97] Companies may refuse to grant access to their premises.

91. Regulation 17/62, Article 11(5).
92. Case 136/79 *National Panasonic United Kingdom Ltd.* v. *Commission* (1980) European Court Reports 2033.
93. Regulation 17/62, Article 15(1)(b), and Article 16.
94. 374/87 *Orkem* v. *Commission* (1989) European Court Reports 3283; 27/88 *Solvay* v. *Commission* (1989) European Court Reports 3355.
95. Regulation 17/62, Article 14.
96. Thieffry, Van Doorn and Arnold, "Les pouvoirs d'enquête de la Commission CEE en droit de la concurrence" *Gazette du Palais*, 8/9 June 1990, p. 7–11.
97. Regulation 17/62, Article 14(2).

In most cases, the Commission will then issue a decision,[98] compliance with which is mandatory. Failure to comply may result in the imposition of a fine and/or periodic penalty payments (the amounts of such fines and payments are the same as for unsatisfactory replies to requests for information). A company may challenge the decision before the Court of First Instance. It is doubtful whether an appeal would prevent an inspection from taking place, but where the appeal is ultimately successful, the Court might prohibit the Commission from making use of the information.[99]

If a company continues to refuse to comply with the Commission's order (some companies prefer to bar the investigation and treat penalty payments as a business expense), Commission officials may ask the concerned Member State's authorities to assist in compelling compliance.[100]

The Commission has similar fact-finding powers in merger control proceedings.[101]

INTERIM PROTECTION

When challenging legality of Community acts before the Court of First Instance, a party may seek provisional remedies that prevent the act in question from being enforced. The Court may also prescribe interim measures. In addition, the Commission is empowered to order interim measures in competition law matters.

Temporary injunction of Community act

If the Court determines that circumstances so require, it may order that the challenged act be suspended.[102] In addition, the President of the Court may, by way of summary procedure, rule on applications to suspend the execution of a Community act.[103]

An application to suspend a measure adopted by a Community institution will only be heard if the applicant also seeks a permanent remedy from that measure in proceedings pending before the Court.[104]

As for the contents of the application, it must include a statement of the subject matter of the dispute, the circumstances justifying an immediate

98. Regulation 17/62, Article 14(3).
 99. Kerse, *EEC Antitrust Procedure*, London, 1988, p. 99 at 3.29.
100. Regulation 17/62, Article 14(6).
101. See Notification of Mergers Under the New EEC Merger Control Regulation.
102. European Community Treaty, Article 185.
103. Protocol, Article 36.
104. Court of Justice Rules of Procedure, Article 83, Section 1; Court of First Instance Rules of Procedure, Article 104, Section 1.

remedy, and the pleas of fact and law required to establish a *prima facie* case for the suspension sought.[105] The President of the Court may then prescribe a short period within which the opposite party may submit a written or oral response. The right to respond is not absolute, however, and the President may grant the application before a response is even submitted. The Court is free to modify or revoke its decision on its own motion.[106]

In response to an application, the Court must issue a reasoned order. Generally, the order lapses when final judgment is rendered, such an order having only an interim effect and being without prejudice to a final judgment of the Court.[107]

Finally, a party may move to have the order modified or revoked on account of a change in circumstances.[108]

Interim relief in other instance

A distinction must be made between interim relief ordered by the Court and those ordered by the Commission.

Interim relief ordered by the Court

The European Court of Justice and the Court of First Instance may in any matter pending before them prescribe any interim measure they deem necessary.[109]

Again, the President may act via summary procedure. The same provisions apply as those that are applicable to the suspension of challenged community acts. It is therefore indispensable for the moving party to establish the necessity of the interim measure it seeks. The Court must be convinced of the urgency of the matter, and that a *prima facie* violation of a superior rule of law is present.

Competition matters pending before the Commission

Although there is no express statutory or administrative provision that confers on the Commission the power to grant interim relief, the Court

105. Court of Justice Rules of Procedure, Article 83, Section 2; Court of First Instance Rules of Procedure, Article 104, Section 2.

106. Court of Justice Rules of Procedure, Article 84; Court of First Instance Rules of Procedure, Article 105.

107. Court of Justice Rules of Procedure, Article 86; Court of First Instance Rules of Procedure, Article 107.

108. Court of Justice Rules of Procedure, Article 87; Court of First Instance Rules of Procedure, Article 108.

109. European Community Treaty, Article 186.

of Justice has held that such a power exists by virtue of Regulation 17/62.[110] Although the Camera Care decision has given Regulation 17/62 great practical effect, the Court laid down strict guidelines (most concerning abusive practices of dominant companies) which must be complied with before the Commission may grant interim relief. The most well known case is that of *ECS*, a small English company that sought and obtained interim protection against AKZO Chemie, the Community's largest producer of organic peroxide. The Commission found that AKZO was engaged in predatory pricing, in that it was selling its products at a loss to ECS' own clients that such practices would drive ECS from the market, and enjoined AKZO from selling its products below a set price.[111]

The Commission can only grant interim relief after having examined the legitimate interests of the parties and companies concerned. In practice, the following conditions must be fulfilled:

(1) A *prima facie* violation of Articles 85 or 86;
(2) A danger of serious and irreparable injury to the public interest;
(3) The measures adopted will be of a temporary nature and must be limited in view of their provisional character;
(4) The rights of defence must be respected; and
(5) The measure must be adopted in such a form that it may be challenged by any party injured by it.[112]

The Commission may not refuse to grant interim relief on the grounds that it did not find a clear and serious violation of European Community competition rules at the time it first reviewed the matter. If it were to do so, the Court would be engaging in an erroneous interpretation of the above-mentioned conditions.[113]

Note that the Merger Control Regulation empowers the Commission to enjoin mergers. Such action is justified by the fact that very strict time limits are imposed on the Commission's inquiry.[114]

DEFAULT JUDGMENTS

A default judgment is rendered against a party who, after having been duly summoned, fails to file an answer. To set aside a default judgment,

---

110. Case 792/79 R *Camera Care* v. *Commission* [1980], European Courts 119.

111. *ECS/AKZO* [1983] OJ EUR. COM. (L 252) 13.

112. Piroche, *Les mesures provisoires de la Commission des Communautés européennes dans le domaine de la concurrence*, RTDE 1989, p. 439–470, at p. 450 and recently Case T–23/90, *Peugeot* v. *Commission* [1991] European Community Reports II–653.

113. Case T–44/90, *La Cinq* v. *Commission* [1992] European Courts II–1.

114. Regulation 4064/89, Article 7.

the defaulted party may lodge an objection against the judgment within one month of it being notified. The objection does not have the effect of staying enforcement of the default judgment, unless the Court decides otherwise.[115]

In competition matters, the Commission is obliged to "give the undertakings or associations of undertakings concerned the opportunity of being heard on the matters to which the Commission has taken objection" before it may decide matters involving the application of Articles 85 or 86 EEC or the imposition of sanctions.[116] The same rule applies with regard to the Merger Control Regulation.[117] If the company concerned does not avail itself of this right, the Commission may decide the matter *ex parte*.

HEARING

Hearings before the European Court of Justice consist of:

(1) The presentation of a report by a judge acting as Rapporteur;
(2) Oral arguments as presented by agents, advisers, and/or lawyers;
(3) The presentation of the Advocate-General; and
(4) The taking of testimony from witnesses and experts.[118]

A party may address the Court only through its agent, adviser, or lawyer.[119] The proceedings are public unless the Court, on its own initiative or on the request of the parties, decides otherwise for just cause.[120] In principle, the time during which oral arguments may be heard cannot exceed 30 minutes. In some cases, oral arguments may be dispensed with, but this requires the express consent of the parties. The President, the other judges, and the Advocate-General usually ask questions to counsel during the course of the hearing.[121]

The Advocate-General delivers his opinion orally at the end of the hearing.[122] The intervention of an Advocate-General in proceedings

---

115. Protocol, Article 38, Court of Justice Rules of Procedure, Article 94; Court of First Instance Rules of Procedure, Article 122.

116. Regulation 17/62, Article 19.

117. Regulation 4064/89, Article 18.

118. Protocol, Article 18, Section 4.

119. Court of Justice Rules of Procedure, Article 58; Court of First Instance Rules of Procedure, Article 59.

120. Protocol, Article 28.

121. Court of Justice Rules of Procedure, Article 57; Court of First Instance Rules of Procedure, Article 58.

122. Court of Justice Rules of Procedure, Article 59.

before the Court of First Instance is rather exceptional. The President declares the proceedings closed at the end of the hearing.[123]

Minutes are made of each hearing and are signed by the President and the Registrar.[124] They are the official record of the proceedings, and parties may inspect the minutes at the Registry and obtain copies at their own expense.[125]

In competition law proceedings before the Commission, the right to a hearing is expressly provided for in most types of proceedings, including proceedings for the formal rejection of complaints.[126] In practice, the right to be "heard" consists of the opportunity to file written arguments, as the Commission's procedure is written in nature.[127] The Commission has issued a specific regulation on hearings.[128] Pursuant to this Regulation, the Commission must inform parties in writing of the objections brought against them. The subject companies may then respond within a fixed time limit,[129] and in their answer, may request a hearing. The request for a hearing will be granted where the requesting company has demonstrated a sufficient need, or, where the Commission seeks to impose fines or periodic penalty payments.[130]

It is the Hearing Officer's duty to ensure that the rights of defence — i.e., due process — are respected. On completion of the oral stage of the hearing, the Officer ensures that the statements made by each person are duly recorded in the minutes.[131] The Officer conducts the hearing, but does not act as a judge. A failure to communicate the Officer's report to the defendant(s) does not constitute a violation of the rights of defence.[132]

Where a non-party can demonstrate a material interest in the proceedings, it may submit an *amicus* brief[133] or present oral arguments.[134]

In rendering its decisions, the Commission may only address those issues that the defendants have been afforded the opportunity to contest on the merits.[135] Likewise, the Commission may not base its decision on evidence that was not presented to the defendant or which the defendant

123. Court of First Instance Rules of Procedure, Article 60.

124. Protocol, Article 30.

125. Court of Justice Rules of Procedure, Article 62; Court of First Instance Rules of Procedure; Article 63.

126. Regulation 17/62, Article 19.

127. Kerse, EEC Antitrust Procedure, London, 1988, p. 124 at 4.13.

128. Commission Regulation No. 99/63, OJ EUR. COM. (NO. L 127) 2263 (1962).

129. Regulation 99/63, Article 2.

130. Regulation 99/63, Article 7.

131. Commission's annual report on Competition policy (1982), No. 36.

132. Case T–15/89, *Chemie Linz* v. *Commission* [1992] European Courts, II–1275.

133. Regulation 99/63, Article 5.

134. Regulation 99/63, Article 7, Section 2.

135. Regulation 99/63, Article 4.

was not permitted to challenge.[136] However, the Commission's final decision should not be a "copy" of the statement of objections that were at issue during the proceedings.[137]

The Merger Control Regulation specifies that the Commission may base its decision only on those objections that the parties have been able to contest on the merits. Furthermore, the rights of defence must be respected and full access to the file guaranteed, at least with respect to the parties directly involved (yet subject to their legitimate interest of protecting confidential business secrets).[138] Other persons that may be granted the opportunity to be heard include non-parties that can demonstrate a legitimate interest in the proceedings, and officers or employees of the companies concerned.[139]

JUDGMENT AND KINDS OF RELIEF

Final judgment

A judgment of the European Court of Justice states the reasons on which the Court's decision is based and is signed by both the President and the Registrar. It is read in open court,[140] and is binding from the date it is issued.[141]

In the area of competition law, not all proceedings before the Commission lead to a formal decision. As is shown in the Commission's annual reports on Competition policy, most cases are in fact dealt with informally whereby the Commission attempts to work with companies to modify agreements or practices that are suspected of being restrictive of competition. Only very important cases or cases that pose novel legal questions will pass through all procedural stages to a final, formal decision. In practice, the resolution of a case from the initial filing of an application through the handing down of a final judgment is very long: procedural safeguards put in place to guarantee the defendant's rights must be respected, fact finding must be completed, appropriate review and approval of various stages of the proceedings must be obtained from various hierarchical levels within the Commission, representatives of the

136. Case T–9/89, *Hüls v. Commission* [1992] European Community Reports II–499; case T–10/89, *Hoechst v. Commission* [1992] European Community Reports II–629.

137. Case T–66/89, *Publishers Association v. Commission* [1992] European Courts II–1995.

138. Regulation 4064/89, Article 18 Section 3.

139. Regulation 4064/89, Article 18, Section 4.

140. Protocol, Article 34.

141. Court of Justice Rules of Procedure, Article 65; Court of First Instance Rules of Procedure, Article 83.

Member States must be consulted, and translated versions of the final decision must be produced in each of the Community's nine official languages.

In a recent annual report, the Commission announced the adoption of internal measures that were designed to expedite the treatment of notified co-operative agreements where the subject parties have agreed to accept a so-called "comfort letter".[142] A comfort letter expresses the "approval"of the agreement by the services of the Commission, but does not possess the legal effect of a formal decision. The fact that the Commission publishes notice of its approval in the *Official Journal*, pursuant to which the comments of all interested parties are solicited, does not alter the legal effect of a comfort letter.[143]

As for mergers review, only those decisions that impose conditions and/or obligations on the parties or which prohibit illegal concentrations are published in full in the *Official Journal*.[144] For the vast majority of cases, only two small notices are published, a first notice indicating that a concentration has been notified to the Commission, and, one month later, another indicating very briefly the final disposition of the matter, i.e., compliance of the operation with the Merger Control Regulation or non-application of the Regulation).

Kinds of relief

With regard to the various legal actions available before the Community Courts, the following kinds of relief can be had.

Annulment of challenged act

If a claim for review of legality is well founded, the Court of First Instance or the European Court of Justice must declare the subject act null and void.[145]

The institution whose act has been annulled is required to take all necessary steps to comply with the judgment.[146] Damages may be had where a party has been injured as a result of an act that has been annulled. Ordinarily, however, an action for damages should be introduced on the basis of Articles 178 and 215 of the EEC Treaty.

142. Commission's annual report on Competition policy (1992), No. 123.

143. Joint cases 253/78 and 1–3/79 *Guerlain, Rochas, Lanvin* and *Nina Ricci* [1980] European Courts 2327; case 31/80, *L'Oréal* [1980] European Courts 3771.

144. Regulation 4064/89, Article 20.

145. European Community Treaty, Article 174, Section 1.

146. European Community Treaty, Article 176, Section 1.

Requirement to act

The European Community Treaty mandates that a Community institution that has "failed to act" or has acted in contravention of the Treaty will be required to take all necessary steps to comply with a judgment.[147] Here, again, compensation for damages may be possible, but a separate action, brought on the basis of Articles 178 and 215, will be necessary.

Compensation for damage

Cases in which the complainant succeeds in its claim for compensation are rare, and the European Court of Justice does not generally award a specific amount of damages. Rather, the Court renders an interlocutory judgment, which establishes the Community's liability, and sets forth the criteria according to which the applicant must be compensated. It is then up to the parties concerned to agree on a figure for damages. Only where the parties fail to reach an agreement will the Court intervene and order that a specific sum be paid.[148]

Preliminary ruling

The European Court of Justice's interpretation of Community law is binding on national courts, who must then apply the Court's ruling to the specific case pending before them. In practice, however, preliminary decisions of the Court apply to all persons and entities within the Community regardless of national court action. This is particularly true where Community acts have been invalidated by the Court[149] or where the Court has issued an interpretation concerning how a Community act should be applied.[150] However, a national court may always request a new preliminary ruling on a question to which the Court has already addressed itself.[151]

In exceptional circumstances, the European Court of Justice may rule that its interpretation of a Community law provision will have effect only

---

147. European Community Treaty, Article 176, Section 1.

148. Vaughan, *Law of the European Communities*, Volume I, page 231, at 2.92.

149. Case 66/80, *ICI* v. *Administrazione delle finanze dello Stato* [1981] European Courts 1191.

150. Cases 66, 127 and 128/79, *Administrazione delle Finanze* v. *Meridionale Industria Salumi* [1980] European Courts 1237.

151. Cases 28–30/62, *Da Costa en Schaake* v. *Administration fiscale néerlandaise* [1963] European Courts 74.

from a date specified in the judgment forward.[152] While such a ruling is issued for reasons of legal security, the financial consequences of the ruling may indeed be very onerous for the affected party(s).

Requirement for Member State compliance with judgment

If the Court of Justice finds that a Member State has failed to fulfil an obligation under Community law, the Member State is required to take all necessary measures to comply with the Court's judgment.[153]

Competition law

When the Commission finds that a company has infringed Articles 85 or 86, it may enjoin the subject behaviour.[154] Even where the infringement has ceased prior to the Commission's ruling, the Commission may declare that the contested agreement or behaviour constitutes a violation of Community law. The purpose of such declaratory rulings is to clarify the Commission's position in order that similar violations may be avoided in the future.

A finding of violation will normally not be accompanied by fines where there was no case law in existence governing such violations before the violation was challenged.[155] In other cases, the Commission is empowered to impose fines of 1,000 to 1-million ECU or a sum in excess thereof. In any event, the sum may not exceed 10 per cent of the turnover in the preceding business year of each of the undertakings participating in the infringement where, either intentionally or negligently, the undertakings infringe Article 85, Section 1, or Article 86 of the Treaty, or, where they commit a breach of any obligation imposed pursuant to an individual exemption. In fixing the amount of the fine, the Commission considers both the gravity and duration of the infringement.[156] For example, Tetra Pak was ordered to pay — then the highest fine ever imposed by the Commission — 75-million ECU for having abused its dominant, virtually monopolistic, position on the so-called, aseptic markets in machines and cartons intended for the packaging of liquid foodstuffs.[157] At the end of 1994, a fine in excess of ECU 240-million was imposed on a cement cartel.

152. Case C–163/90, *Administration des douanes et droits indirects* v. *Léopold Legros* [1992] European Community Reports I–4625.
153. EEC Treaty, Article 171.
154. Regulation 17/62, Article 3.
155. See, for example, *Decca Navigator System* [1989] OJ EUR. COM. (No. L 43) 27.
156. Regulation 17/62, Article 15, Section 2.
157. Decision *Tetra Pak*, OJ EUR. COM. (No. L 72) 1 (1992).

The Merger Control Regulation also empowers the Commission to levy fines of up to 10 per cent of the aggregate turnover of the companies concerned where they:

(1) Fail to comply with the terms of a decision;
(2) Proceed with a merger prior to obtaining the requisite approval of the Commission; or
(3) Proceed with the merger subsequent to a Commission ruling that the combination in question is incompatible with the common market.[158]

POST-TRIAL MOTIONS

Third-party proceedings

Member States, Community institutions and any business entity or person may, under certain conditions, institute third-party proceedings to challenge a judgment rendered by the European Court of Justice or the Court of First Instance. Such proceedings must be initiated via the filing of an application that must satisfy the normal requirements for applications. In addition, the applicant must explain why it was unable to take part in the original proceeding and prove that the judgment is prejudicial to its rights.[159] These conditions are applied very strictly by the Court.[160]

Where the judgment has been published in the *Official Journal* of the European Communities, the third-party application must be filed within two months of its publication.[161]

In exceptional circumstances, the Court may stay execution of the judgment. Where an argument(s) of the third party is deemed dispositive, the Court will modify the contested judgment accordingly.[162]

Revision

The circumstances in which a judgment may be revised are extremely limited. An application for revision of a judgment may be filed with the

158. Regulation 4064/89 Article 14, Section 2.

159. Protocol, Article 39; Court of Justice Rules of Procedure, Article 97, Section 1; Court of First Instance Rules of Procedure, Article 123, Section 1.

160. For example case T–35/89 TOI, *Ascasibar Zubizarreta* v. *Albani* [1992] European Courts II–1599.

161. Court of Justice Rules of Procedure, Article 97, Section 1, in fine; Court of First Instance Rules of Procedure, Article 123, Section 1 in fine.

162. Court of Justice Rules of Procedure, Article 97, Section 3; Court of First Instance Rules of Procedure, Article 123, Section 3.

Court only on discovery of a fact which is of such a nature as to be a "decisive" factor, and which, at the time the judgment was rendered, was unknown to the Court and to the party moving for revision.[163] Revision is not considered to be an appeal, and the above conditions are very strictly applied.[164]

An application for revision must be made within ten years of the date of the judgment.[165] In addition, it must be made within three months of the date on which the new facts on which the application is based became known to the applicant.[166]

Interpretation of judgment

If the meaning or scope of a judgment is unclear, the Court will render an explanatory opinion at the request of any party or institution of the Community that can establish an interest in the proceedings.[167] The explanatory opinion is itself a judgment, and is issued after the parties and the Advocate-General have had an opportunity to be heard.[168]

An interpreting judgment is binding on all of the parties to the main judgment. Third, parties establishing an interest in the proceedings may be permitted to intervene.[169]

ENFORCEMENT AND EXECUTION

There are no established means by which the European Court of Justice or the Court of First Instance may enforce their judgments against Member States. In a number of circumstances, the Commission is therefore obliged to bring another proceeding before the court before pursuant to Article 171 of the European Community Treaty. In addition, Article 171 was revised by the Treaty on the European Union so as to provide a mechanism whereby Member States may be compelled to pay fines where they have failed to comply with a judgment. In all other cases,

163. Protocol, Article 41 Section 1.

164. Cases T–4/89 REV BASF v. Commission [1992] European Courts II–1591 and T–8/89 REV, DSM v. Commission [1992] European Courts II–2399.

165. Protocol, Article 41, Section 3.

166. Court of Justice Rules of Procedure, Article 98; Court of First Instance Rules of Procedure, Article 125.

167. Protocol, Article 40.

168. Court of Justice Rules of Procedure, Article 102, Section 2; Court of First Instance Rules of Procedure, Article 129, Section 3.

169. Joined cases 41, 43, 44/73, Suiker Unie v. Commission [1977] European Courts 445.

judgments[170] and decisions of the Commission, the latter imposing a pecuniary obligation on persons other than States,[171] are enforceable.

Actual enforcement is governed by the civil procedure rules of the Member State where the judgment is to be executed. The order seeking enforcement must be appended to the judgment or the decision by the national authority designated for this purpose by the governments of each Member State.[172] When these formalities have been completed, the party concerned may obtain enforcement from the relevant Member State authority.

Enforcement may be suspended only by a decision of the Court. However, the courts of the Member State concerned have jurisdiction over complaints that enforcement is being carried out in an irregular manner.[173]

APPEAL

There is no appeal possible from judgments rendered by the European Court of Justice. As a consequence, this sub-chapter will deal with appeals from decisions of the Commission and from judgments of the Court of First Instance.

Conditions for appeal

Against judgments of the Court of First Instance

Decisions of the Court of First Instance may be appealed to the European Court of Justice on questions of law only,[174] and may be brought in the following three circumstances:

(1) Lack of jurisdiction of the Court of First Instance;
(2) A breach of procedure adversely affected the interests of the appellant; or
(3) The Court of First Instance acted in violation of Community law.[175]

An appeal may not be brought on the basis of jurisdiction if the decision does not dispose of all substantive issues. The appeal must be filed within

170. European Community Treaty, Article 187.
171. European Community Treaty, Article 192, Section 1.
172. European Community Treaty, Article 192, Section 2.
173. European Community Treaty, Article 192, Section 4.
174. European Community Treaty, Article 168(a).
175. Protocol, Article 51.

two months from the date when the decision was notified,[176] and may be brought by any party that has been unsuccessful, in whole or in part. However, an intervenor other than a Member State or Community institution may appeal only where the decision of the Court of First Instance directly affects it.[177]

Any person whose application to intervene has been dismissed by the Court of First Instance may appeal that decision to the European Court of Justice within two weeks of the decision's notification.[178]

Against decisions of the Commission

The same conditions apply as those already set forth above for actions against decisions of the Commission.

Appellate procedure

Procedures before the Court of First Instance against a Commission decision mirror those that are applicable in matters before the European Court of Justice as described above.

Where an appeal is brought from a judgment of the Court of First Instance, the procedure before the European Court of Justice has both a written and oral stage. With the agreement of the Advocate-General and the parties, the European Court of Justice may dispense with the oral procedure.[179]

When the appeal is clearly inadmissible or unfounded, the European Court of Justice may at any time, acting on a report from the Judge-Rapporteur and after hearing the Advocate-General, dismiss the appeal in whole or in part via reasoned order.[180]

Stay

An appeal does not generally have the effect of staying the proceedings.[181] A separate application to enjoin the operation of a measure adopted by an institution may be made.

176. Protocol, Article 49, Section 1.
177. Protocol, Article 49, Section 2.
178. Protocol, Article 50, Section 1.
179. Protocol, Article 52, and Court of Justice Rules of Procedure, Article 120.
180. Court of Justice Rules of Procedure, Article 119.
181. Protocol, Article 53, Section 1.

A judgment of the Court of First Instance that voids a general decision takes effect two months after notification of the principal judgment, or, where an appeal has been brought within that period, from the date of dismissal of the appeal.[182]

Consequences

As for judgments issued by the Court of First Instance, the consequences are those already discussed above.

When the European Court of Justice overturns a decision of the Court of First Instance, it may remand the case back to the Court of First Instance for judgment or may itself render final judgment in certain circumstances.[183] Where a case is remanded to the Court of First Instance, the Court of First Instance is bound by the decisions of the European Court of Justice on questions of law.[184]

182. Protocol, Article 53, Section 2.
183. Protocol, Article 54, Section 1.
184. Protocol, Article 54, Section 2.

INDEX